W9-AHJ-995

Personal Financial Planning

Personal Financial Planning

G. Victor Hallman, Ph.D, J.D.

Member of the Pennsylvania Bar
and Lecturer, Wharton School,
University of Pennsylvania

Jerry S. Rosenbloom, Ph.D.

Professor, Department of Insurance and
Risk Management, Wharton School,
University of Pennsylvania
and Academic Director of the Certified
Employee Benefit Specialist Program

Seventh Edition

McGraw-Hill
New York Chicago San Francisco Lisbon London
Madrid Mexico City Milan New Delhi San Juan
Seoul Singapore Sydney Toronto

The *McGraw·Hill* Companies

Copyright © 2003 by The McGraw-Hill Companies, Inc. All rights reserved. Printed in the United States of America. Except as permitted under the United States Copyright Act of 1976, no part of this publication may be reproduced or distributed in any form or by any means, or stored in a database or retrieval system, without the prior written permission of the publisher.

4 5 6 7 8 9 0 DOC/DOC 0 9 8 7 6 5

ISBN 0-07-141944-6

This publication is designed to provide accurate and authoritative information in regard to the subject matter covered. It is sold with the understanding that neither the author nor the publisher is engaged in rendering legal, accounting, or other professional service. If legal advice or other expert assistance is required, the services of a competent professional person should be sought.

> —*From a Declaration of Principles jointly adopted by a Committee*
> *of the American Bar Association and a Committee of Publishers*

McGraw-Hill books are available at special quantity discounts to use as premiums and sales promotions, or for use in corporate training programs. For more information, please write to the Director of Special Sales, McGraw-Hill, 2 Penn Plaza, New York, NY 10121-2298. Or contact your local bookstore.

Library of Congress Cataloging-in-Publication Data

Hallman, G. Victor.
   Personal financial planning / by G. Victor Hallman and Jerry S. Rosenbloom.—7th ed.
      p. cm.
Includes bibliographical references and index.
   ISBN 0-07-141944-6 (alk. paper)
   1. Finance, Personal. I. Rosenbloom, Jerry S. II. Title.
   HG179.H24 2003
   332.024—dc21

                                          2003004188

 This book is printed on recycled, acid-free paper containing a minimum of 50% recycled de-inked fiber.

Contents

9. Common Stocks   150

10. Other Equity Investments   174

11. Fixed-Income Investments   189

Preface

In the preface to the first edition of this book, written in 1975, we noted that consumerism has been a rising tide and that personal financial planning really is consumerism applied to an individual's or a family's personal financial affairs. We also noted that since the end of World War II, our economy has developed an almost unheard-of level of affluence that has made financial planning important for larger and larger numbers of people. We further observed that the increasing role of women in the work force, particularly at the executive and professional levels, and the rapid growth of multi-income-earner families in the United States are placing more and more persons in a position in which they need to apply sophisticated financial planning techniques to their personal and family affairs. In recent years this also has been referred to as private wealth management, particularly for higher net worth people.

It is surprising how well those statements apply today, even more than they did then. The impact of all these forces simply has become stronger in recent years. In particular, given the uncertainty of the equity markets following the market adjustment that began in 2000 and continues today, such planning is especially important. As the seventh edition goes to press, there is real concern about a possible "double-dip" recession or possibly even worse for the economy. At a minimum, people wonder when the stock markets will begin to show signs of real growth again and in what people should be investing their money. Throughout the book, a guiding principle for dealing with such concerns is diversification and how to achieve it. The book is designed to deal with private wealth management in the good times we all hope for, as well as the bad, or "for all seasons." Thus, it is clear that an environment exists in which personal financial planning is necessary to preserve wealth and meet the financial objectives of both wealthy and middle-income persons.

Financial institutions have recognized this and have developed many products and services to serve the financial planning or wealth management needs of the public. In addition, there is an ever-increasing number of professional financial planners who are applying the concepts of sound financial planning to meet the needs of the public.

In this edition of the book, as in the previous editions, we consider personal financial planning as the process of determining an individual's or a family's total financial objectives, considering alternative plans or methods for meeting those objectives, selecting the plans and methods that are best suited for the person's circumstances, implementing those plans, and then periodically reviewing the decisions made and making necessary adjustments. In this process, a person's or family's overall financial affairs—investments, savings programs, insurance and annuities, retirement plans, other employee benefits, income tax planning, estate planning, and so forth—should be considered as a coordinated whole, rather than on a piecemeal basis. This means that individual financial instruments, such as stocks, bonds, life insurance, annuities, mutual funds, real estate, trusts, and various kinds of employee benefits and compensation arrangements should be considered in terms of a person's overall financial objectives and plans rather than in isolation. It also means that the professional financial planners who are rendering financial planning services to the public should be knowledgeable in a variety of disciplines. It is an objective of this book to help achieve these results.

The development of appropriate, unbiased, and efficient methods for meeting the public's need for personal financial planning and wealth management is an issue. Many financial institutions and a large number of professionals now are addressing this issue. The Internet has also become an important medium to communicate such information, and nearly all financial services firms now have large and sophisticated Web sites for interacting with customers.

Since the publication of the sixth edition of this book, there have been many changes affecting financial planning. Foremost among them has been the Economic Growth and Tax Relief Reconciliation Act (EGTRRA) passed in 2001. EGTRRA has made very significant changes in income taxation, employee benefits and their taxation, and federal estate taxation. Due to its "sunset provision" and deferred implementation, it has also brought considerable uncertainty to the planning process. The seventh edition has been updated to take into account all these changes.

A number of areas have been added or expanded in this edition. These include

- coverage of the Economic Growth and Tax Relief Reconciliation Act and its impact on planning, as just noted
- an entirely new chapter on financing education expenses, including the popular Section 529 plans

- increased coverage of mutual funds, including exchange-traded funds (EFTs)
- increased attention to asset allocation and diversification in investment planning
- increased coverage of planning for retirement plan distributions
- increased attention to planning for employee stock plans and stock arrangements
- increased coverage of IRAs and particularly the revised education savings accounts (education IRAs)
- increased coverage of fixed-income investing
- coverage of grantor retained annuity trusts (GRATs) and the concept of zeroed-out GRATs (Walton GRATs)
- increased coverage of sales and loans within the family for wealth transfer purposes

Thus, the seventh edition has not only been updated, but it also has been expanded in these and other areas.

G. Victor Hallman
Jerry S. Rosenbloom

PART

1

Coordinated
Financial Planning

1

Personal Financial Planning–The Process

Most people are in great need of personal financial planning. They have certain basic financial goals they want to attain. To help meet their goals, a bewildering array of investments, insurance coverages, savings plans, tax-saving devices, retirement plans, trusts, charitable giving arrangements, and the like is constantly being offered to the public, but these financial instruments and plans often are presented in a piecemeal fashion. Furthermore, the very affluence of our society, coupled with rising educational levels, creates a situation in which more and more people can benefit from financial planning techniques.

What Is Personal Financial Planning?

Personal financial planning is the development and implementation of total, coordinated plans for achieving one's overall financial objectives. The term *private wealth management* also is increasingly being applied to this process, particularly when it involves larger investment portfolios and estates.

Most people use a variety of financial instruments to achieve their objectives. Thus, such basic financial tools as common stocks, bonds, mutual funds, insurance, fixed and variable annuities, money market accounts, certificates of deposit, savings accounts, individual retirement accounts, qualified retirement plans and other employee benefits, personal trusts, and real estate may be elements of soundly conceived financial plans.

Also involved in the planning process is the development of *personal financial policies* to help guide a person's financial operations. An example of such policies in investments would be deciding what percentage of an investment portfolio is to go into bonds (or other fixed-dollar securities) and what percentage into common stocks (or other equity-type investments). Another example, involving life insurance, is that a consumer may want to purchase mainly cash-value life insurance or decide to buy mostly term life insurance and place the savings dollars elsewhere. Unfortunately, many people do not follow consistent policies in making these decisions.

In financial planning, people consciously or unconsciously make assumptions about the current economic climate and what they think the economy holds for the future. A commonly held view, for example, has been that the U.S. economy generally will experience real long-term growth, accompanied by at least some price inflation, for the indefinite future. On the other hand, others may fear that economic conditions will change at some point and they may plan their financial affairs accordingly.

Focus on Objectives

Each person's financial objectives may differ in terms of individual circumstances, goals, attitudes, and needs. However, the objectives of most people can be classified as follows:

1. Protection against the personal risks of
   a. Premature death
   b. Disability losses
   c. Medical care expenses
   d. Custodial care expenses (or long-term care expenses)
   e. Property and liability losses
   f. Unemployment

2. Capital accumulation for
   a. Emergency fund purposes
   b. Family purposes
   c. Educational needs
   d. General investment portfolio

3. Provision for retirement income

4. Reduction of the tax burden
   a. During lifetime
   b. At death

5. Planning for one's heirs (estate planning)

6. Investment and property management (including planning for property management in the event of disability or incapacity)

Need for Personal Financial Planning

Who Should Plan?

Most people find themselves in need of financial planning to some degree. Some of the more sophisticated wealth management techniques tend to be used mainly by those with high incomes and large property or business interests, but partly this is so because less wealthy persons may lack information about financial planning. If they knew of the techniques, they would use them more. Interestingly, our economic growth, the tax structure, the fact that two-income-earner families are now the norm, and other social and economic changes have tremendously increased the need for and the complexity of financial planning.

Why Planning May Be Neglected

People fail to plan for a host of reasons. They often feel that they do not have sufficient assets or income to need planning or that their affairs are already in good order. Both these assumptions are frequently wrong. There is also the natural human tendency for busy people to procrastinate with respect to planning. Finally, some people may be deterred by what they think will be the high cost of planning services. Actually, however, high-quality planning services usually are well worth the cost. Also, knowledgeable consumers can secure some valuable planning services without additional cost. For example, stockbrokers, trust officers, insurance agents and brokers, and others stand ready to give advice in the areas of their specialties without extra cost to consumers beyond that already built into the cost of their products or services. Of course, consumers must evaluate the advice they receive in light of the advisor's experience, knowledge of the field, and objectivity.

Fees charged for some planning services may be deductible for federal income tax purposes. The tax law permits the deduction of expenses incurred for the management, conservation, or maintenance of property held for the production of income, except to the extent incurred in earning tax-exempt interest or income.[1] An income tax deduction also may be taken for expenses incurred in connection with the determination, collection, or refund of any tax. However, such investment expenses, tax preparation expenses, and other miscellaneous itemized deductions, as well as most employee business expenses, are considered together as a single category of itemized deductions and are deductible only to the extent that, combined, they exceed 2 percent of the taxpayer's adjusted gross income.

[1] Except to the extent that such expenses relate to rents and royalties, they are deductible only from adjusted gross income to arrive at taxable income. Expenses incurred to earn rents and royalties are deductible from gross income to arrive at adjusted gross income.

Costs of Failure to Plan

While there may be understandable human reasons why people neglect to plan, the costs of failing to do so can be high indeed. A family may be unprotected or inadequately protected in the event of personal catastrophes such as death, disability, serious illness, an automobile accident, prolonged unemployment, incapacity to manage one's property, confinement in a custodial care facility, or similar risks of life. There may not be enough money set aside for education and retirement. Failure to properly diversify an investment portfolio can result in substantial losses. And failure to plan can result in higher-than-necessary income, estate, gift, and perhaps generation-skipping transfer taxation.

When there is a closely held business interest in the family, failure to plan for the future disposition or retention of this interest can result in severe problems in the event of the death, disability, or retirement of one of the owners. In the same vein, failure to engage in proper estate planning not only can result in higher-than-necessary taxation and estate settlement costs but, perhaps more important, also can cause disputes and harsh discord within the family, resulting in unhappiness for the very persons the estate owner wishes to benefit.

Finally, a person's own objectives in life may not be realized. These may include the ability to change jobs, pursue educational opportunities, travel, retire early, and so forth.

Steps in the Planning Process

The financial planning process involves the translation of personal objectives into specific plans and finally into financial arrangements to implement those plans. To this end, the following is a brief overview of the logical steps in the process.

Gathering Information and Preparing Personal Financial Statements

The first step is getting together useful information about the person's financial and personal situation. The kinds of information needed vary with the situation, but they usually include information about the person's or family's *investments; life, health, long-term care, and property and liability insurance policies; retirement and other employee benefits; tax situation*—income, estate, and gift taxes; *wills, trusts, and other estate planning documents; powers of attorney* and related instruments; and similar financial documents and information.

In summarizing a person's present financial position, it is helpful to prepare some simplified personal financial statements, much like those that businesses use. These can include a *personal balance sheet,* a *personal income statement,* and other financial statements that would be helpful. A sample family balance sheet (Table 1.1) and a sample family income statement (Table 1.2) are given at the end of this chapter. Of course, these samples can be modified as individuals or their advisors wish for their own needs and purposes.

As an illustration of how these statements can be used, a sample balance sheet and income statement are filled out for a hypothetical family. In this example, the assets, liabilities, incomes, and expenses of the husband and the wife are combined in the statements. On the other hand, a separate income statement and balance sheet can be prepared for each family member, if desired. In addition, many financial concerns and practitioners have or use forms and reports that consumers or their advisors may find useful, particularly in the areas of their specialties.

Identifying Objectives

The next step is the identification and setting of objectives, as outlined previously in this chapter. This is such an important step that Chapter 2 is devoted to it.

Analyzing Present Position and Considering Alternatives

The third step is an analysis of the person's present position in relation to his or her objectives and then consideration of alternative ways of remedying any deficiencies found.

Developing and Implementing the Plan

Given the facts of the case, the person's objectives, an analysis of his or her present financial position, and consideration of alternatives, recommendations can be made for a financial plan to meet the indicated objectives.

Periodic Review and Revision

No plan should be considered "cast in bronze." Circumstances change. There are births, marriages, divorces, deaths, job changes, different economic conditions, and a host of other factors that may make revisions in financial plans desirable or necessary.

Use of Financial Planning Statements

The financial statements shown here are not meant to be exhaustive. Other statements often are used in the planning process. Two of these are the *person-*

al budget and a personal *cash flow statement.* A budget is an advance plan for anticipated expenditures and income. It is very helpful in keeping a person's or family's expenditures under control and within their income. A cash flow statement shows the sources and timing of a person's or family's cash receipts and of cash outlays.

However, the two basic statements shown here normally are good starting points in the planning process. They can be modified for many purposes, as can be seen throughout the book. The illustrative dollar figures shown in these tables are expressed in even thousands for the sake of convenience.

Table 1.1. Family balance sheet (as of present date)

Assets

Liquid assets (in own name[s]):

Cash and checking account(s)	$5,000	
Savings account(s)	0	
Money market funds	40,000	
U.S. savings bonds	0	
Brokerage account cash balances	0	
Other	0	
Total liquid assets		$45,000

Directly owned marketable investments (in own name[s]):

Common stocks	160,000	
Corporate bonds	0	
Municipal bonds	0	
U.S. Treasury bonds	0	
Certificates of deposit	0	
Other	0	

Directly owned mutual funds (in own name[s]):

Common stock funds	100,000	
Corporate bond funds	0	
Municipal bond funds	40,000	
U.S. Treasury bond funds	0	
Balanced funds	20,000	
Other funds	0	
Total directly owned marketable investments and mutual funds		320,000

Life insurance and annuity cash values:

Life insurance cash values	25,000	
Annuity accumulations	0	
Total life insurance and annuity cash values		25,000

Table 1.1. (*Continued*) Family balance sheet (as of present date)

Directly owned "nonmarketable" investments and business interests (in own name[s]):		
Active business interests (proprietorships, partnership interests, and stock in closely held corporations)	0	
Investment real estate	0	
Other tax-sheltered investments	0	
Interests in limited partnerships	0	
Total directly owned "nonmarketable" investments and business interests		0
Assets held in trust:		
Revocable living trusts	0	
Other trusts and similar arrangements	0	
Total assets held in trust		0
Retirement plan accounts:		
Pension accounts	0	
Savings plan accounts [Section 401(k) Plans]	300,000	
Profit-sharing accounts	0	
IRA accounts	100,000	
Other plans	0	
Total retirement plan accounts		400,000
Employee stock plans:		
Stock options (ISOs and nonqualified options valued at intrinsic value for vested options)	50,000	
Balance in employee stock purchase plan	15,000	
Other plans	0	
Total employee stock plans		65,000
Personal real estate:		
Residence	250,000	
Vacation home	100,000	
Total personal real estate		350,000
Other personal assets:		
Auto(s)	20,000	
Boat(s)	3,000	
Furs and jewelry	16,000	
Collections, hobbies, etc.	4,000	
Furniture and household accessories	25,000	
Other personal property	2,000	

Table 1.1. (*Continued*) Family balance sheet (as of present date)

Total other personal assets		70,000
Total assets		**$1,275,000**
Liabilities and Net Worth		
Current liabilities:		
Charge accounts, credit card charges and other bills payable	$20,000	
Installment credit and other short-term loans	0	
Unusual tax liabilities	0	
Total current liabilities		$20,000
Long-term liabilities:		
Mortgage notes on personal real estate	100,000	
Mortgage notes on investment real estate	0	
Home equity loans	0	
Bank loans	0	
Margin loans and other investment loans	40,000	
Life insurance policy loans	0	
Other liabilities	0	
Total long-term liabilities		140,000
Total liabilities		$160,000
Family net worth		$1,115,000
Total liabilities and family net worth		**$1,275,000**

Table 1.2. Family income statement (for the most recent year)

Income		
Salary(ies) and fees (after before-tax contributions to employee retirement plans):		
The individual	$75,000	
His or her spouse	70,000	
Others	0	
Total salaries		$145,000
Investment income:		
Interest (taxable)	3,000	
Interest (nontaxable)	2,000	
Dividends (common stock and mutual funds)	8,000	
Real estate	0	
Realized capital gains (on sales of assets and from mutual fund distributions)	7,000	
Other investment income	0	
Total investment income		20,000

Table 1.2. (*Continued*) Family income statement (for the most recent year)

Bonuses, profit-sharing payments, etc.		0
Other income		0
Total income		$165,000
Expenses and fixed obligations:		
Ordinary living expenses	$46,000	
Interest expenses:		
Consumer loans	1,000	
Bank loans	0	
Margin and other investment interest	3,000	
Mortgage notes	7,000	
Home equity loans	0	
Insurance policy loans	0	
Other interest	0	
Total interest expenses	11,000	
Debt amortization (mortgage notes consumer debt, etc.):	6,000	
Insurance premiums:		
Life insurance	3,000	
Health insurance	2,000	
Long-term care insurance	0	
Property and liability insurance	3,000	
Total insurance premiums	8,000	
Charitable contributions	4,000	
Tuition and educational expenses	18,000	
Payments for support of aged parents or other dependents	6,000	
Taxes:		
Federal income tax	32,000	
State and local income taxes	6,000	
Social Security tax(es)	11,000	
Local property taxes	7,000	
Other taxes	0	
Total taxes	56,000	
Total expenses and fixed obligations	$155,000	
Balance available for discretionary investment		**$10,000**

2

Setting Financial
Planning Objectives

In this chapter we shall analyze the financial objectives common to most people and outline briefly the sources available to help meet these objectives. These sources will be explained in greater detail in subsequent chapters of the book.

Importance of Setting Objectives

As a general principle, it is desirable to formulate and then state one's objectives as explicitly as possible. However, once established, a person's financial objectives do not remain static, but rather change over the person's life cycle and with changed circumstances.

Organizing Objectives

While the emphasis on particular objectives will change during a family's life cycle, the following classification provides a systematic way for identifying objectives and needs.

Protection Against Personal Risks

Premature Death. A major objective of most people is to protect their family or others from the financial consequences of their deaths. Some people also are concerned with the impact of their deaths on their business affairs or their estate's liquidity and conservation picture. The following are various financial losses that may result from a person's death.

Loss of the Deceased's Future Earning Power That Would Have Been Available for the Benefit of His or Her Surviving Family or Others. Most families live on the earned income of one or both of the spouses. The death of an income earner results in the loss of that person's future earnings from the date of death until he or she would have retired or otherwise left the labor force.

Costs and Other Obligations Arising at Death. Certain obligations are created at a person's death, such as funeral expenses, costs of estate settlement, and federal estate and state death taxes. In addition, there often are obligations that may come due at death, such as credit cards, mortgage notes, and other personal debts that his or her estate either must pay or chooses to pay.

Increased Expenses for the Family. The death of a family member may result in increased expenses for the family to replace the economic functions performed by that person as a homemaker.

Loss of Business Values. When an owner of a closely-held business dies, the business may die financially with the deceased or suffer considerable loss in value. Also, many businesses have key employees, whether owners or not, whose premature death can cause considerable financial loss to the business.

Estate Shrinkage at Death. Larger estates often suffer considerable reduction in value due to federal and state death taxes. This tax burden may substantially reduce the wealth passing to the estate owner's heirs if steps are not taken to reduce the shrinkage or to make up for it.

Sources of Protection Against Premature Death. While each of these sources is described in greater detail in later chapters, they are shown here in outline form to give an overview of possible sources.

1. Life insurance
   a. Individual life insurance
   b. Group life insurance
      (1) Through the insured's employer or business
      (2) Through an association group plan
   c. Credit life insurance payable to a creditor of the insured
2. Social Security survivors' benefits
3. Other government benefits
4. Death or survivors' benefits under private pension plans
5. Death benefits under deferred profit-sharing plans
6. Death benefits under savings (Section 401[k]) plans
7. Death benefits under tax-sheltered annuity (TSA) plans, plans for the self-employed (HR-10 plans), individual retirement account or annuity (IRA) plans, nonqualified deferred-compensation plans, personal annuity contracts, and the like

8. Informal employer death benefits or salary-continuation plans
9. All other assets and income available to the family after a person's death

Disability Income Losses. Loss of earned income due to the disability of the income earner can be referred to as the *disability income exposure*. Such an exposure, particularly total and permanent disability, is a serious risk.[1] Virtually all experts agree that consumers should give greatest attention to protecting themselves against long-term disability rather than being unduly concerned with disabilities that last only a few weeks.

Sources of Protection Against Disability Income Losses. These sources are outlined as follows and are described in greater detail in Chapter 5.
1. Health insurance
   a. Individual disability income insurance
   b. Group disability income insurance
      (1) Through the insured's employer or business
      (2) Through an association group plan
   c. Credit disability income insurance payable to a creditor of the insured
2. Disability benefits under life insurance policies
   a. Waiver-of-premium benefits
   b. Disability benefits under group life insurance
3. Social Security disability benefits
4. Workers' compensation disability benefits
5. Other government benefits
6. Disability benefits under private pension, profit-sharing, and nonqualified deferred-compensation plans
7. Noninsured employer salary-continuation (sick-pay) plans
8. All other income, investment or otherwise, available to the family

Property Management in Case of Physical or Mental Incapacity. The incapacity of someone who owns property may give rise to special problems because the incapacitated person might be unable to handle his or her own affairs effectively.

Sources of Meeting Property Management Problems in the Event of Physical or Mental Incapacity. While this exposure becomes more important as people reach advanced ages, incapacity can strike people of any age. The following outlines some ways to meet this problem. Planning for this exposure is described in greater detail in Chapter 28.

---

1 Actually, the probability that someone will suffer a reasonably long-term disability (90 days or more) prior to age 65 is considerably greater than the probability of death at those ages. For example, the probability of such a long-term disability at age 32 is about 6½ times the probability of death at that age.

1. Powers of attorney
   a. Existing durable general powers of attorney
   b. Springing durable general powers of attorney
   c. Health care powers of attorney
2. Revocable living trusts
   a. Funded revocable living trusts
   b. Revocable living trusts in conjunction with durable powers of attorney

Medical Care Expenses. There is little need to convince most people of the need to protect themselves and their families against medical care costs. For planning purposes, we can divide medical costs into three categories.

Normal or Budgetable Expenses. These are expenses the family can pay out of its regular monthly budget. Traditional thinking holds that, as a general principle, the larger the amount of annual expenses a family can afford to assume, the lower will be its overall costs.

On the other hand, one of the features of health maintenance organizations (HMOs) is coverage of most kinds of medical expenses, including routine expenses, on a comprehensive basis with little cost sharing by the covered person. Thus, if the individual or family has HMO coverage, this category of medical expenses generally will be covered automatically.

Larger-than-Normal Expenses. These are medical expenses that exceed those that are expected or budgetable. To meet such expenses, most people need insurance or other coverage.

Catastrophic Medical Expenses. These are expenses so large as to cause severe financial strain on an individual or family. They are important to plan for because they are potentially so damaging. In many cases this division is dealt with for the individual because his or her employer provides medical expense benefits. However, employees increasingly may choose among several medical expense options offered by their employers. Also, when both husband and wife are employed outside the home, one of them often can elect to *waive or limit coverage* under his or her employer's medical plan and thus save or reduce the employee's contribution to the plan. The traditional approach for protecting against catastrophic expenses is coverage under major medical plans. But HMOs and other managed care arrangements also provide comprehensive and catastrophic coverage.

Sources of Protection Against Medical Care Expenses.
1. Health insurance and benefits
   a. Employer-provided medical expense coverages
   b. Individual medical expense coverages
2. Social Security medical benefits (Medicare)

3. Medical payments under liability and auto insurance policies
4. Workers' compensation medical benefits
5. Other government benefits
6. Other employer medical reimbursement benefits
7. Other assets available to the family
8. Medical savings accounts to the extent available

Custodial Care Expenses (Long-Term Care Expenses). These generally are expenses incurred to maintain persons when they are unable to perform at least several of the normal activities of daily living. Thus, these expenses are for *custodial care* for persons who are no longer able to care for themselves, rather than for the treatment and potentially the cure of *acute medical conditions* as discussed in the preceding section. Custodial care can take a variety of forms, such as skilled nursing home care, intermediate institutional care, adult day care, and home health care.

Sources of Protection Against Custodial Care Expenses.
1. Long-term care (LTC) insurance
    a. Individual LTC insurance purchased by the covered person, his or her family, or others
    b. Group LTC insurance
        (1) Through the insured's employer or business (usually paid for by the employee)
        (2) Through an association group plan
    c. LTC insurance as riders to life insurance policies
2. Accelerated death benefit provisions in life insurance contracts
3. Medicaid
4. Other income and assets available to the family

Property and Liability Losses
Property Losses. Ownership of property brings with it the risk of loss to the property itself (*direct losses*) and the risk of indirect losses arising out of loss or damage to the property (*indirect or consequential losses*). A planning decision in this area is how much property exposure should be assumed and how much should be insured.

Liability Losses. By virtue of almost everything a person may do, he or she is exposed to possible liability claims made by others. Such liability can arise out of the person's own negligent acts, the negligent acts of others for which the person may be legally responsible, liability he or she may have assumed under contract (such as a lease), and liability imposed by statute (such as workers' compensation laws). Since a large liability claim potentially can be financially devastating, planning for adequate liability insurance is critical.

Sources of Protection Against Property and Liability Losses. For most persons, the main source of protection is adequate insurance.

Capital Accumulation

Many people and families do not spend all their disposable income and thus have an investable surplus, many also have various semiautomatic plans that help them build capital, and some receive gifts or inheritances. There are a number of reasons people want to accumulate capital.

Emergency Fund. An emergency fund may be needed to meet unexpected expenses; to pay for deliberately retained disability losses, medical expenses, and property losses; and to provide a financial cushion against the risks of life, such as unemployment.

The size of the emergency fund varies greatly and depends on such factors as family income, number of income earners, stability of employment, assets, debts, insurance deductibles and uncovered health and property exposures, and the family's general attitudes toward risk. The size of the emergency fund often is expressed as so many months of family income—such as three to six months. By its very nature, the emergency fund should be invested conservatively.

Education Needs. The cost of higher education has increased dramatically, particularly at private colleges and universities. For example, it may cost $38,000 or more per year in tuition, fees, and room and board alone for a student to attend some private colleges.

The size of an education fund depends on the number of children, their ages, their educational plans, any available financial aid, and the size of the family's available assets and income. It also depends on the attitudes of the family toward education. The issue of financing education costs, along with some special tax-favored plans for doing so, has become so important that it is covered in a separate chapter—Chapter 29.

Retirement Needs. This is an important objective. Because of its importance and unique characteristics, it is dealt with as a separate objective later in this chapter.

General Investment Fund. People often accumulate capital for general investment purposes. They may want a better standard of living in the future, a second income in addition to their earnings, greater financial security, the ability to retire early, or a capital fund to pass on to their children or grandchildren, or they may simply enjoy the investment process.

How Capital Can Grow. The size of a person's investment fund depends on how much capital there originally was to invest, how much the person can save each year, any other sources of capital, and how successful the person or his or her advisors are at the investment process.

There are a number of ways people can accumulate capital and many possible investment policies they might follow. However, in terms of the objective of capital accumulation, an individual basically has the following factors to consider:

- an estimate of how much capital will be needed at various times in the future (perhaps including an estimate for future inflation) amount of funds currently available (and possibly available in the future) for investment
- an estimate of how much will be saved each year in the future
- the amount of time left to meet the person's objectives
- the general investment constraints under which the person must operate in terms of security of principal, stability of income, stability of principal, tax status, and the like
- the average annual compound rates of total return that are expected on various kinds of investments
- the adoption of an investment program that will give the best chance of achieving as many of the person's financial objectives as possible.

As illustrations of how capital can grow, Tables 2.1 and 2.2 give some growth rates for capital at assumed rates of return over various time periods.

Table 2.1 shows the amount to which an investment of $1000 will grow. This is known as the *future value of a sum*. For example, suppose a person is age 35 and has $10,000 to invest. If the *net* rate of return (*after* investment expenses and income taxes) is only 4 percent, the person can accumulate $14,800 by age 45, $21,910 by age 55, and $32,430 at age 65. But if this *net* rate of return can be increased to 6 percent, the person can accumulate $17,910 by age 45, $32,070 by age 55, and $57,440 by age 65. And with an increase of this *net* return to 10 percent, the comparable figures would be $25,940 by 45, $67,727 by 55, and $174,490 by 65.

We can approach this calculation somewhat differently. If, say, a mother age 35 with a $10,000 investment fund feels she needs approximately $20,000 in 12 years for her children's education, she can see from Table 2.1 that she will have to earn a net rate of return of about 6 percent on the money to achieve her goal ($10,000 at 6 percent per year for 12 years = $20,120). (It should be noted that the same result can be determined more accurately by using calculators or computers.)

It may also be desirable to know how much a certain amount saved each year will accumulate in a specified period, known as the *future value of an annuity*. This can be determined from Table 2.2, which shows how much $100 per year will grow at certain assumed rates of return for the number of years

Table 2.1. Values of a $1000 investment fund invested for specified numbers of years at various rates of return (future value of a sum)

Percent annual net rate of return (compounded)	Number of years the $1000 is invested							
	5	8	10	12	15	20	25	30
3%	1,159	1,267	1,344	1,426	1,558	1,806	2,094	2,427
4%	1,217	1,369	1,480	1,601	1,801	2,191	2,666	3,243
5%	1,276	1,478	1,629	1,796	2,079	2,653	3,386	4,322
6%	1,338	1,594	1,791	2,012	2,397	3,207	4,292	5,744
8%	1,469	1,851	2,159	2,518	3,172	4,661	6,848	10,064
10%	1,611	2,144	2,594	3,138	4,177	6,727	10,835	17,449
15%	2,011	3,059	4,046	5,350	8,137	16,367	32,919	66,212

indicated. Assume that a person age 35 can save $1200 per year (about $100 per month). If the person receives a *net* rate of return of 8 percent on the money, he or she can accumulate $17,388 by age 45 ($1449 × 12), $54,912 by age 55, and $135,936 by age 65.

Again, we can approach this calculation in a different way. A person may want to know how much he or she must invest (save) each year in order to reach a desired amount in a given number of years, assuming a certain net annual rate of return. Suppose, for example, that a father wants to know how much he needs to invest by the end of each year to produce $80,000 for his children's education in 12 years. If he assumes a net rate of return of 6 percent, he can see from Table 2.2 that he will need approximately $4,740 by the end of each year to produce the $80,000 in 12 years [($80,000 ÷ $1687) × 100].

Investment Instruments for Capital Accumulation. A wide variety of investment instruments can be used, as are described in Part 3.

Table 2.2. Values of a periodic investment of $100 per year at the end of specified numbers of years at various rates of return (future value of an annuity)

Percent annual net rate of return (compounded)	Number of years the $100 is invested							
	5	8	10	12	15	20	25	30
3%	531	889	1,146	1,419	1,860	2,687	3,646	4,758
4%	542	921	1,201	1,503	2,002	2,978	4,165	5,608
5%	553	955	1,258	1,592	2,158	3,307	4,773	6,644
6%	564	990	1,318	1,687	2,328	3,679	5,486	7,906
8%	587	1,064	1,449	1,898	2,715	4,576	7,311	11,328
10%	611	1,144	1,594	2,138	3,177	5,728	9,835	16,449
15%	674	1,373	2,030	2,900	4,758	10,244	21,279	43,474

Provision for Retirement Income

This objective has become increasingly important because today most people can anticipate living to enjoy their retirement years. There are a number of ways to plan for retirement. Many involve tax-favored retirement plans; some do not. Following is a brief outline of these sources. They are covered in more detail in Part 5.

1. Social Security retirement benefits and other government benefits
2. Private pension plans
   a. Employer-provided pension plans
   b. Retirement plans for the self-employed (HR-10 plans)
3. Savings plans (including plans with a Section 401[k] option)
4. Deferred profit-sharing plans (including HR-10 plans)
5. Individual retirement accounts or annuities (IRA plans, various types)
6. Simplified employee pension (SEP) plans
7. Savings incentive match plan for employees (SIMPLE) plans
8. Tax-sheltered annuity (TSA) plans
9. Nonqualified deferred-compensation plans
10. Individually purchased annuities
11. Life insurance cash values
12. Investments and other assets owned by the individual

Reducing the Tax Burden

Most people have the legitimate objective of reducing their tax burden as much as legally possible. People may be subject to many different taxes. These include sales taxes, real estate taxes, Social Security taxes, federal income taxes, federal alternative minimum tax, state and local income taxes, federal estate tax, state death taxes, federal (and sometimes state) gift taxes, and the federal tax on generation-skipping transfers (GSTs). The relative importance of these taxes varies considerably among families.

A variety of tax-saving plans are being used today. In general, they fall under one or more of the following *basic tax-saving techniques:*

- eliminating or reducing taxes
- shifting the tax burden to others who are in lower brackets
- allowing wealth to accumulate without current taxation and thus postponing taxation
- taking returns as capital gains rather than as ordinary income
- avoiding taxation of capital gains entirely.

These techniques are covered in Parts 3, 4, and 5 of this book.

Planning for One's Heirs

This is commonly called *estate planning*. An *estate plan* has been defined as "an arrangement for the devolution of one's wealth." For many people, such an arrangement can be relatively simple. But for larger estates or estates with special problems, estate plans can become quite complex. Estate planning often involves diverse areas of knowledge, such as wills, trusts, tax law, insurance, investments, and accounting. Thus, it frequently is desirable to bring together several professionals or specialists into an estate planning team to develop a well-rounded plan. Estate planning is discussed in Part 6.

Investment and Property Management

Need for Management in General. The need and desire to obtain outside investment or property management vary greatly among individuals and families. However, the increasing complexity of dealing with investments, tax problems, and the like generally has increased this need.

Sources of Aid for Investment and Property Management. There are many such sources now available. They include the following:

Use of Financial Intermediaries. Broadly speaking, a financial intermediary is a financial institution that invests people's money and pays them a return on that money. Such institutions serve as conduits for savings into appropriate investments. They may include:

- Investment companies (mutual funds, closed-end investment companies, and unit investment trusts)
- Commercial banks (offering certificates of deposit, bank money market accounts, and various types of savings accounts)[2]
- Life insurance companies
- Savings institutions

Trusts. One of the basic reasons for establishing trusts is to provide experienced and knowledgeable investment and property management services for the beneficiaries of the trust.

Investment Advisory Firms. There are many investment advisory firms, ranging in size and types of services provided, that offer their clients professional investment advice on a fee basis. Many commercial banks and securities firms also offer investment advisory services.

In terms of investment decision-making authority, investment advisors may

---

[2] Commercial banks also provide trust and investment advisory services that are covered later in this chapter.

operate in one of three ways: (1) on a strictly discretionary basis, under which the advisor actually makes investment decisions and buys and sells securities for the client without prior consultation with the client, (2) under an arrangement whereby the advisor basically makes investment decisions but consults with the client to inform him or her of the reasons for the decisions before taking action, and (3) under an arrangement by which the advisor and clients consult extensively before investment decisions are made, but clients reserve the actual decision making for themselves.

Annual fees charged by investment advisors vary, depending on such factors as the size of the client's portfolio, the extent of the services rendered, whether the account is discretionary or nondiscretionary, and the kinds of securities (or property) in the portfolio. For example, an annual fee might start at, say, 1 percent of principal with a minimum annual fee of, say, $3000 or more. Unfortunately, use of investment advisors by smaller investors frequently is made impractical by the minimum annual fees charged.

Securities Firms. Investors, small and large, also can obtain valuable investment and research advice from account executives and others with stock brokerage firms. It must be pointed out, however, that the relationship between stockbrokers and their customers is not the same as that between investment advisors or trust departments and their clients. Brokers often are paid commissions based on the transactions in their customers' accounts, while advisors and trustees are paid on an annual-fee basis. However, professional-minded brokers recognize that long-term success ultimately depends on the investment success of their customers and act accordingly. Also, other compensation arrangements for brokers now are being used.

Other Advisors. There are other important sources from which individuals can secure aid in managing their affairs. Attorneys provide legal and other advice. The old adage, "The person who acts as his or her own lawyer has a fool for a client," still holds true. Accountants provide many people with advice concerning their financial affairs, particularly in the tax area. Mutual fund representatives and persons offering tax-sheltered and other investments can provide advice on how they can be used in financial planning. Life insurance agents and brokers can offer valuable advice concerning life insurance, annuities, health insurance, and pensions, as well as other financial products and services. Similarly, property and liability insurance agents and brokers provide advice on personal risk management, property and liability insurance, and other financial products and services.

The concept of total financial services also has fostered the development of a new kind of financial planning or wealth management organization. These organizations typically provide coordinated planning for their client in such areas as investments, insurance, pensions and other employee benefits, and tax and estate planning. Their goal is to deal with the client's total picture. Independent financial planners, banks, securities firms, and other wealth management organizations may offer this kind of service.

Planning for Investment and Property Management in the Event of Disability or Incapacity. This is an entirely different issue that has already been noted in the section entitled "Property Management Problems in Case of Physical or Mental Incapacity."

Adjusting Objectives for Inflation and Possible Deflation (Recession or Depression)

Inflation has been a persistent worldwide economic problem for many years. Also, prudent and careful people really should not rule out deflation (recession or even depression) as an economic phenomenon to be considered in their planning.

Adjusting for Inflation

Objectives for future financial needs can be adjusted for assumed rates of inflation. For example, if Mr. Jones, age 50, estimates that he and his wife will need a retirement income of about $3000 (after income taxes) per month by the time he reaches age 65, or in 15 years, and that the price level in the economy will remain stable over this period, then Mr. Jones and his wife need to plan to have retirement income of only $3000 per month at age 65. If, however, this assumption is not realistic in view of past inflationary trends and if an inflation rate of 3 percent is assumed for the next 15 years, then their retirement income objective (expressed in dollars at retirement age 65), to be realistic, should be adjusted for the expected inflation. Assuming a 3 percent compound annual diminution in the value of the dollar, $1 today will be worth only 64.19 cents in 15 years. This is also the present value of $1 due at the end of 15 years at 3 percent compound interest.

Therefore, to convert a retirement income objective of $3000 per month in current dollars to a corresponding dollar amount of equal purchasing power 15 years hence at an inflation rate of 3 percent per year for the 15-year period, we should divide the $3000 per month by the present value of $1 due at the end of 15 years at 3 percent compound interest (or 0.6419). The result is an adjusted retirement income objective of $4674 ($3000 ÷ 0.6419).

Considering Recession or Even Depression

Planning for a recession or even a depression is more difficult. There has been more or less persistent inflation since the end of World War II and there has not been a depression in the United States since the 1930s. However, some think severe recession or even depression is still possible.

During a severe recession or depression, the general price level tends to fall; the values of certain assets, such as most common stocks, real estate, business interests, and other kinds of equity-type assets, generally drop sharply; and interest rates normally decline. Various kinds of incomes, such as from wages, businesses, rents, and dividends from many common stocks, generally also fall, and sometimes severely. Thus, the fundamental problem during deflation is not maintaining the purchasing power of a given income stream (which actually will rise due to generally falling prices in the economy), but rather maintaining, as much as possible, the person's or family's income stream and the values of assets and investments. The modifications of objectives for deflation, then, generally involve attempting to secure conservative, guaranteed sources of income and to hold assets that will maintain, or perhaps even increase, their values during severe recession or depression.

Unfortunately, the secure, guaranteed kinds of assets (and sources of income) that likely will maintain their values during deflationary times, which might be termed *deflation hedges,* are often not the ones that will grow in value (or provide increased income) during prosperity. The effect of this dilemma is that there is a conflict of objectives in such planning areas as asset allocation strategy for one's investment portfolio and other assets. While some may resolve this conflict by assuming that only one set of economic conditions will occur (such as continued prosperity with low inflation), perhaps the better approach for many people is to set objectives as if either economic scenario could occur and then to use the principle of *diversification* to try to protect themselves to some degree either way. The latter is the approach generally followed in this book.

Adjusting Objectives to Changing Tax Laws

The tax laws are an important force affecting all aspects of financial planning and they are constantly changing. For example, many important changes were made by the Economic Growth and Tax Relief Reconciliation Act of 2001 (EGTRRA).

Economic Growth and Tax Relief Reconciliation Act (EGTRRA)

EGTRRA is an unusual, uncertain, and confusing piece of tax legislation. This is so because many of its provisions are not effective until years in the future and it contains a "sunset provision" that provides that all of its terms and provisions will no longer apply after December 31, 2010. In summary, the main changes (among many others) made by EGTRRA are as follows:

- Reductions in individual income tax rates from 2001 through 2006 and thereafter
- Marriage penalty relief starting in 2005 through 2008 and thereafter
- Greatly improved education planning opportunities mainly through qualified tuition programs (Section 529 plans) and education savings accounts (education IRAs) generally starting in 2002 and thereafter
- Substantially increased contribution and deduction limits for qualified retirement plans, IRAs, and other plans, with varying effective dates from 2002 through 2007 and thereafter
- The ability of all 401(k) participants to make all or part of their Section 401(k) elective contributions as after-tax Roth contributions if the plan allows such contributions, but only effective for 2006 and thereafter
- Increases in the federal estate tax and generation-skipping transfer (GST) tax applicable exclusion amounts in stages from 2002 ($1,000,000 and $1,060,000) through 2009 (each $3,500,000), repeal of the federal estate tax and GST tax entirely in 2010, and then reinstatement of these taxes as they were in 2001 for 2011 and thereafter
- Repeal of the step-up in income tax basis at death rule and adoption of a modified carry-over basis at death rule for 2010 only with reinstatement of the step-up in basis rule for 2011 and thereafter.

Sunset Provision of EGTRRA

In order to conform to the so-called "Byrd Amendment,"[3] Congress provided that all provisions of EGTRRA will expire on December 31, 2010. At that time, the tax law as it existed in 2001 would again become the law of the land.

This "sunset provision" obviously creates uncertainty in planning. There are several possibilities that may occur, depending largely on what Congress and the White House do prior to 2011. They could do nothing and allow the "sunset provision" to take effect. Most commentators do not believe this will happen. Or, sometime before 2011, they could repeal the "sunset provision" and make EGTRRA permanent or adopt an entirely new tax law. Finally, sometime before 2011, tax legislation could be enacted that will freeze EGTRRA's provisions as of a certain date and make the law permanent. However, no one knows what will happen.

[3] The Congressional Budget Act of 1974, as amended.

For general planning purposes, most people are taking full advantage of the favorable provisions of EGTRRA. In estate planning, where the federal estate and GST taxes may or may not finally be repealed, probably most commentators are recommending planning as usual for now with some modifications. In most cases, flexibility in planning will be desirable in light of this tax uncertainty.

Using Insurance Effectively

3

Personal Insurance Principles and Selecting Insurers

Insurance provides an important means of meeting the financial objectives of most people.

Personal Risk Management

The term *risk management* normally means consideration of all alternative methods for dealing with risk. Business firms commonly use this approach in managing their exposures to risk. It can also be used by individuals in managing their personal exposures, in which case it sometimes is called *personal risk management*. It should be noted, however, that most people are less able than larger business firms to use techniques other than insurance.

The logical start of any risk management program is the recognition of one's exposures. This may not be as easy as it seems at first glance. For example, if a person hires a domestic worker in his or her home, what liability for workers' compensation or employment practices may exist? If the person serves on the board of directors or trustees of a corporation or local organization, could he or she be personally liable for actions taken by the organization, under directors' and officers' liability? What about a person's potential liability for libel, slander, invasion of privacy, and other "intentional" torts? Also, what about any business or professional liability exposure? These and other personal risk exposures should be identified and evaluated in personal financial planning.

The basic risk management techniques are avoidance of risk, loss prevention and reduction (loss control), retention (planned assumption) of risk, and transfer of risk. *Insurance* is the most important transfer device. For the remainder of this chapter, we shall concentrate on property and liability insurance for individuals.

The Insurance Principle

Not all risks are insurable. However, there are many potentially serious events that can be insured against. In essence, insurance is a means of eliminating or reducing the financial burden of such events by dividing the losses they produce among many individuals or firms exposed to the events. This is the concept of *pooling*, which lies at the heart of insurance.

Insurance Purchase Decisions

People make decisions concerning which risks should be insured and which risks should be handled in other ways. To help do this, a convenient measure that shows the types of risks that can wipe out an individual or family financially is contained in the following simple formula:

$$\text{relative value of a risk} = \frac{\text{total amount at stake or potential liability}}{\text{total wealth}}$$

The greater the result of this formula, the less able an individual is to assume any given risk and the more he or she needs to insure the risk.

Thus the first principle of insurance buying is to place primary emphasis on those risks that potentially could wipe out or substantially deplete the person's or family's net worth. This sometimes is called the *large-loss principle*. Note that the *severity* of a potential loss, not its *frequency*, should be the determining factor.

Use of Deductibles and Other Cost-Sharing Devices

Whenever feasible, use of deductibles should be considered in insurance planning. A deductible requires the insured to pay the first portion, such as the first $500, of a covered loss before the insurance comes into play. Use of deductibles often benefits the insured because they normally make insurance considerably *less expensive*. Deductibles eliminate small losses and hence the disproportionately high administrative expenses of settling such claims.

Considerations in Choosing an Insurer

Selection of insurers is one of the practical problems faced in buying insurance. In some cases, this problem may be resolved either by selecting an agent or broker, who then determines the insurer to be used, or by using insurance-buying facilities (such as the Internet). However, customers may take an interest in the actual choice of insurers.

It should be noted at the outset that *no generalization should be made con-*

cerning choice of a particular insurer solely on the basis of its legal form of organization—that is, whether the insurer is, for example, a stock company (owned by stockholders and operated for profit), a mutual company (technically owned by its policyholders and operated on a nonprofit basis), or a reciprocal (operated through an attorney-in-fact). Instead, an insurer should be evaluated on such grounds as its *financial soundness,* the extent and quality of the *service* it renders, the *types of coverage and policies* the insurer offers, and the *price* it charges for a particular coverage.

Financial Soundness

General Considerations. The financial soundness of an insurer is of paramount importance to potential insureds. Unfortunately, it may be difficult for the average person to assess the financial status of an insurer.

Buyers of insurance may receive some assurance about the strength and stability of insurers through the regulatory procedures of the various states. While the financial requirements that insurers must meet vary among the states, there may be some indication that an insurer is stable and financially sound if it is authorized to sell insurance in states with effective insurance regulation. People often cite New York as an example in this regard.

Financial Ratings of Insurers. Perhaps the measure of financial soundness or claims-paying ability of insurance companies that is most widely used and readily available to consumers is the *financial ratings* given to many insurance companies, particularly the larger ones, by independent insurance rating services. Three of the most widely followed services are *A. M. Best, Moody's,* and *Standard & Poor's.* Two other frequently mentioned services are *Fitch* and *Weiss Research.* Each of these services differs at least to some degree from the others and their rating grades and standards are not uniform. This has created a situation in which a given insurer may have several ratings from different rating services.

Nevertheless, as a practical matter, the services' ratings are probably the main, or perhaps the only, measures that most consumers will have of the financial soundness or claims-paying ability of particular insurance companies. Before purchasing insurance from an insurer, consumers should check into whether the company has been rated by one or more of the rating services and, if so, what its financial strength ratings are from each of the services that rated the insurer. Consumers also should inquire into whether any of the services have recently downgraded the company's ratings and, if so, why.

While the rating systems of the services do not exactly correspond to each other, it will be helpful at least to list here the hierarchy of insurance company financial strength ratings for the three most widely followed rating services. (The ratings of these services, listed from highest to lowest, are not necessarily

Moody's	Standard & Poor's	A. M. Best
Aaa	AAA	A++
Aa1	AA+	A+
Aa2	AA	A
Aa3	AA–	A–
A1	A+	
A2	A	B++
A3	A–	B+
Baa1	BBB+	
Baa2	BBB	B
Baa3	BBB–	B–
Ba1	BB+	
Ba2	BB	C++
Ba3	BB–	C+
B1	B+	
B2	B	C
B3	B–	C–
Caa	CCC	D
Ca	CC	E
C	R	F

consistent with each other just because they are placed parallel in this listing.)

State Insurance Guaranty Funds. Some protection is provided to consumers by state guaranty funds, which may reimburse insureds and claimants for certain losses they may suffer due to the insolvency of insurance companies in the state. All states now have such guaranty funds that separately cover life insurance companies and property and liability insurance companies.

While these funds offer valuable protection to policyholders and claimants in the event of insurer insolvencies, there are limits to the amount of protection they provide to individual claimants and the funds may not be available to cover all losses or in all circumstances. Therefore, it does not seem prudent for buyers of insurance to place primary reliance on state guaranty funds to protect them against insurer insolvencies.

General Observations on Insurer Financial Soundness. Unfortunately, there are no hard-and-fast rules to guide consumers only to financially secure insurers. All that really can be offered are some general observations that may prove helpful to buyers of insurance.

- It is very helpful for the insurer to have ratings from *at least two* of the independent rating services and that the ratings be consistent, stable, and on the high side of the hierarchy. What would be the minimum acceptable ratings? That is very difficult to say, but an example might be that an insurer should be at least within the top four grades of at least two rating services, unless there is an adequate explanation of why it is not.
- It is also helpful for the insurer to do business in and be subject to the regulation of one or more states with capable, effective insurance regulation, such as New York.
- Consumers should watch the general financial press for any unfavorable or positive news items about the insurer.
- If the insurer's products or rates seem too good to be true, they probably are, for a sound insurer. Thus, if an insurer's product terms, prices, or rates of return are way out of line with those of comparable products generally available from other insurance companies, watch out!
- From the viewpoint of financial strength, there may be advantages in dealing with insurers with proven track records of financial soundness and stability over a reasonably long period of time. However, it must be stated that this comment has not held true in a few cases of well-established, formerly highly regarded insurers that ran into financial problems unexpectedly (at least from the perspective of their policyholders).
- If an insurer weakens financially, the policy owner should evaluate whether (in the case of property and liability insurance) to secure other coverage and then cancel the coverage with the weakened insurer or (in the case of life insurance or annuities) to exchange a life insurance policy or an annuity contract with the weaker insurer for a comparable contract with a stronger insurer (which would be a tax-free exchange under Section 1035 of the Internal Revenue Code, provided the tax law requirements for such exchanges are met).

Service

There are many facets to the service an insurer might be expected to offer its customers. Naturally, *claims service*—the expeditiousness and fairness with which claims are settled—is a major consideration. Other services may also be important. For example, *life and health insurance needs analyses and other estate analysis* services in life insurance and *risk analysis and insurance surveys for property and liability insurance* may be of considerable importance.

Types of Coverage

The types of contracts an insurer offers are a consideration. Some insurers have a broader portfolio of policies than others. Also, some insurers may offer more attractive policies (in terms of coverage or price or both) in some areas, while other insurers may have better contracts in other areas.

Price

It is self-evident that the price charged for insurance is of significance to buyers. However, price considerations should never be placed above financial safety, since protection from an unstable organization is a questionable buy at any price. Also, if a particular policy is available at a lower cost because the insurer provides less service, customers should evaluate how important service is to them.

Considerations in Choosing an Agent or Broker

General Considerations

How do individuals go about finding good insurance agents or brokers? Here are some pertinent questions to ask. What experience do they possess in terms of years and extent of practice? Are they noted specialists in any certain line? Do they do business mostly with individual households, with business firms, or generally across the board? Do they engage in survey selling, estate analysis, or perhaps financial planning generally? Do they present a unified program of coverage based on a careful analysis of exposures or needs? Do they represent sound companies? Do they hold professional designations in insurance or financial planning, as explained in the next section?

Information About Advisors

Obtaining information about agents, brokers, and other sales representatives is more difficult than investigating insurers. One positive indication of a financial planner's or an insurance representative's knowledge and basic professional commitment to his or her career is whether he or she has earned designations as Certified Financial Planner (CFP), Chartered Life Underwriter (CLU) or Chartered Financial Consultant (ChFC), Certified Employee Benefit Specialist (CEBS), Chartered Property Casualty Underwriter (CPCU), and other corresponding professional degrees or designations.

Depending on the particular program, to obtain these designations a practitioner must have passed a series of examinations covering such diverse fields as insurance and risk management, law, economics, social legislation, finance, investments, accounting, taxation, estate planning, employee benefits, and management. Although it is true that many competent practitioners do not have these designations and that designations do not always indicate competence, the consumer should be aware of the existence and meaning of CFP, CLU, ChFC, CEBS, and CPCU.

4

Life Insurance and Social Security

This chapter deals with various forms of life insurance protection, social security survivors' benefits, and the decision factors involved in life insurance planning.

Sources of Life Insurance Protection

These sources can conveniently be broken down into three categories: individually purchased policies, employer-sponsored benefits, and government-sponsored coverages.

Individually Purchased Life Insurance

In this case the individual applies for and, if found insurable, is issued an individual contract of life insurance. The main ways in which individually purchased life insurance now is sold are as follows.

Ordinary Life Insurance. This category typically is sold through an agent or broker. A person can apply for any amount he or she wishes, as long as the insurer is willing to write it and the applicant can afford the coverage.[1] This is by far the most important category of individually purchased life insurance.

---

[1] There often is confusion concerning the term *ordinary* as it pertains to types of life insurance. The word *ordinary* can have two different meanings. *Ordinary life* can be used to mean that type of insurance in which a minimum amount of insurance is written on an annual premium basis. It is thus used to distinguish this type of insurance from group insurance and industrial insurance. This is how the term is used here. But *ordinary* also may be used to indicate the kind of policy whereby protection is furnished for the whole of life. In this regard, *ordinary* is used interchangeably with *whole life* and *straight life*.

Industrial Life Insurance (Home Service Life Insurance). This form is issued in small amounts, with premiums payable weekly or monthly, and with premiums generally collected at the home of the insured. It is a high-cost form of insurance and normally is not recommended for consumers.

Fraternal Life Insurance. This life insurance is available through membership in a lodge or fraternal order, religious group, or the like. Today, fraternal insurance generally is sold much like ordinary life insurance.

Association Group Life Insurance. A person may become eligible to buy this insurance by being a member of one or more associations, such as professional, fraternal, alumni, and community service groups. The insurance usually is sold through the mail, with limited individual selection, and with the insured person paying the entire cost. Only certain plans and amounts of coverage are normally available.

Employer-Sponsored Life Insurance

This coverage is provided through the employer-employee relationship. Most of it is group term life insurance under the employer's benefit plan.

Group Life Insurance. Group life insurance generally is available with part or all of the cost paid by the employer and generally is issued without individual evidence of insurability. The amount of insurance on individual employees normally is determined by some type of benefit formula.

Wholesale Life Insurance. This is a hybrid between individual and group life insurance and normally is used for groups too small to qualify for group coverage and for association group cases. An individual policy is issued to each covered person in the group and there is some individual underwriting.

Salary Savings Life Insurance. This plan involves selling regular forms of individual life insurance to employees under an arrangement for paying premiums through their employer. Individual evidence of insurability is required and there normally are little or no cost savings for the insured employees.

Group Universal Life Insurance. This is a group, employee-pay-all version of individual universal life (UL) or individual variable universal life (VUL) insurance.[2]

Federal Government Life Insurance Programs

Although not normally thought of as life insurance, social security provides survivorship benefits which, in essence, represent significant death benefits.

[2] Individual UL and VUL insurance are described in greater detail late in this chapter.

These survivorship benefits are described next. Also, at various times the federal government has issued or arranged for life insurance for persons serving in the armed forces.

Social Security

Before considering in more detail the private approaches to providing retirement income, death benefits, disability benefits, and health benefits, it will be helpful to describe briefly the very important social insurance system for providing such benefits in the United States—Social Security.

Overview of Social Security

While the bulk of Social Security benefits are paid as retirement benefits, the Social Security system (or old age, survivors, disability and health insurance system, OASDHI) actually provides four distinct categories of benefits: *old-age* (retirement) benefits for covered workers and their eligible dependents, *survivors'* (death) benefits for eligible surviving dependents of covered workers, *disability* benefits for covered workers and their eligible dependents, and *health insurance* benefits (Medicare) for covered persons age 65 or older and certain other beneficiaries.

Many people and their advisors regard Social Security as a significant base layer of income or protection that they can supplement with private insurance, private investments, retirement plans, employee benefits, and other sources. This is the role Social Security properly is intended to fulfill. Other persons, however, may be relying on Social Security as their primary or perhaps sole source of income or protection. This is undesirable and even dangerous. In most cases, Social Security alone will not be sufficient to provide adequate income for a person or his or her family.

Coverage and Benefit Eligibility

Almost everyone will be covered under the Social Security system and is paying or will pay Social Security taxes during their working years.

Covered Persons. All employees and self-employed persons working in the United States and certain possessions are covered, except for a few groups specifically excluded by law.

Insured Status. In addition to being a covered worker, a person's eligibility for benefits depends on having the appropriate insured status at the time of his or her retirement, disability, or death. There are three types of insured status requirements: fully insured, currently insured, and disability insured.

A worker attains *fully insured status* if he or she has 40 quarters of coverage. If not, he or she still may be fully insured by having a specified minimum of quarters, depending on the benefit involved, the year of a worker's death or disability, and the worker's date of birth, subject to some special provisions. A minimum of six quarters is required in any event.

A worker meets the requirements for *currently insured status* if he or she has at least six quarters of coverage during the 13 quarters ending with his or her death, eligibility for old-age benefits, or disability.

Disability-insured status has the strictest requirements of all. Workers who are age 31 or older when they become disabled must be fully insured and have at least 20 quarters of coverage during the 40-quarter period ending when their disability begins. There are somewhat more liberal requirements for workers age 30 or younger who become disabled and for workers disabled because of blindness.

Social Security Taxable Earnings Base (Covered Earnings) and Tax Rates. Covered earnings are those to which Social Security tax rates (FICA taxes) are applied and that also generally serve as a maximum in calculating a worker's average monthly earnings for purposes of determining his or her primary insurance amount (PIA). Social Security benefits are based on a worker's PIA.

For employees, all their compensation (up to the maximum, if any) from employment is subject to FICA tax. For self-employed persons, taxable compensation includes income from self-employment, which essentially means net earnings from operating an unincorporated trade or business as determined for federal income tax purposes.

The amount of the Social Security taxable earnings base (and benefit base) has constantly increased over the years, from a low of $3000 per year for 1937 through 1950 to $87,000 for 2003. For the hospital insurance (HI) tax under Medicare, all (unlimited) compensation is taxable.[3] This tax and benefit base will increase in the future in proportion to the increase in average annual wages in the United States.

The total FICA tax rate for employees was 7.65 percent for 2003. There is an equal tax rate on employers. For self-employed persons, the FICA tax rate is 15.30 percent for 2003; however, one-half of this FICA tax is allowed as an income tax deduction from gross income and self-employment income is

[3] Beginning in 1994, the hospital insurance (HI) tax rate of 1.45 percent for employees and 2.90 percent for self-employed persons (which is included in the 7.65 percent and 15.30 percent totals here) is applied to a person's total taxable earnings or self-employment income. Thus, this HI tax effectively becomes an additional income tax on personal earnings (or self-employment income) with no maximum limit. It also effectively requires the annual valuation of amounts deferred under nonqualified deferred-compensation plans for highly compensated executives.

reduced by 7.65 percent (without regard to the maximum earnings base) in determining taxable self-employment income.

Primary Insurance Amount and Family Maximum Benefit. Social Security benefits (other than Medicare) are based on the worker's *primary insurance amount* (PIA). In turn, the *family maximum benefit* (FMB), which is the total amount of benefits that may be paid to a worker and his or her eligible dependents, also is determined on the basis of the worker's PIA. A worker's PIA is calculated by applying a formula (which varies according to the year of eligibility for benefits) to the worker's average monthly earnings over a certain number of years.

Calculation of a person's or family's Social Security benefits is complicated. Fortunately, this complication is substantially diminished for planning purposes by personal earnings and benefit estimate statements available from the Social Security Administration. These forms can be secured from a local Social Security Administration office.

Social Security Survivorship (Death) Benefits

The focus of this chapter is on the benefits to certain survivors of deceased actively employed workers, disabled workers, or retired workers. These survivorship benefits are based on the covered worker's PIA and are paid in the form of monthly income to the eligible family member. In addition, there is a $255 lump-sum death benefit to a surviving spouse or, if there is no surviving spouse, to eligible children.

Surviving Spouse. The surviving spouse of a deceased worker who had fully insured status can receive a survivor's benefit, provided the surviving spouse is age 60 or older or is disabled and at least age 50. The amount of this benefit is 100 percent of the deceased worker's survivor PIA if the surviving spouse has reached the full-benefit retirement age (currently age 65). The benefit is reduced for widows or widowers between ages 60 and 64. Further, a surviving divorced spouse, who had been married to the deceased worker for at least 10 consecutive years or who has an eligible child in his or her care, may be eligible for a survivor's benefit in generally the same manner as a surviving spouse.

Other Dependents. *Unmarried children* (and, in certain circumstances, unmarried grandchildren) of a deceased worker (whether actively employed, disabled, or retired at the time of his or her death) are entitled to a child's monthly survivor's benefit. This benefit is equal to 75 percent of the deceased parent's PIA, provided the child is under age 18, under age 19 and an elementary or secondary school student, or 18 or older but disabled before age 22.

In addition, the surviving spouse of a deceased worker is eligible for a *moth-*

er's or father's survivor's benefit equal to 75 percent of the deceased worker's PIA as long as the surviving spouse is caring for an eligible child who is under age 16 or is older and disabled before reaching age 22. The surviving spouse is eligible for this benefit at any age. A surviving divorced spouse also may be eligible for this benefit. Further, a surviving *dependent parent* who is at least 62 years old may be entitled to a monthly survivor's benefit.

As is the case for other Social Security benefits, there is a family maximum benefit (FMB) that applies to the combined survivors' benefits from the PIA of a deceased worker.

Taxation of Social Security Benefits

The Social Security Amendments of 1983 introduced a previously unthinkable concept: the possibility of taxing Social Security benefits.

The first step is to determine whether any of a person's or couple's benefits will be subject to tax. This will occur if their so-called provisional income for this purpose exceeds certain base amounts. Provisional income is the sum of (1) 50 percent of the Social Security benefit payable, (2) the person's or couple's adjusted gross income (AGI) for federal income tax purposes (with certain additions), and (3) tax-exempt interest (from municipal bonds[4]). If this provisional income does not exceed $25,000 for a single taxpayer and $32,000 for a married couple filing a joint return, Social Security benefits remain tax-free.

In the second step, if provisional income exceeds the appropriate base amount but does not exceed $34,000 for a single taxpayer and $44,000 for married taxpayers filing a joint return, the amount of benefits includible in gross income is the smaller of one-half the Social Security benefits or one-half the excess of provisional income over the base amount.

Finally, in the third step, if provisional income exceeds $34,000 for a single taxpayer and $44,000 for married taxpayers filing a joint return, the amount includible in gross income is the smaller of 85 percent of Social Security benefits or the sum of (1) the smaller of the amount calculated in the second step or $4500 for a single taxpayer or $6000 for married taxpayers filing a joint return and (2) 85 percent of the amount by which provisional income exceeds $34,000 for a single taxpayer or $44,000 for married taxpayers filing a joint return.[5] Thus, higher income taxpayers could be taxed on as much as 85 percent of their Social Security benefits. Fortunately, the IRS Forms and

[4] The sum of a person's or couple's regular adjusted gross income, with certain additions, and their tax-exempt interest is referred to as their *modified adjusted gross income* (or modified AGI) in this calculation.

[5] For married taxpayers filing separate returns, gross income includes the smaller of 85 percent of the Social Security benefit or 85 percent of the taxpayer's provisional income.

Instructions booklet contains a worksheet to help taxpayers determine the taxable amount, if any, of their Social Security benefits.

Types of Individual Life Insurance Contracts

In the past, there were three traditional types of individual life insurance contracts: term, whole life, and endowment. However, in recent years a number of newer types have been developed.

Strategies for Purchasing Individual Life Insurance

Assuming a person needs individual life insurance, one of the fundamental issues that must be decided is what type or types of contracts to purchase and from which insurance company or companies. However, in making this choice the consumer really has to make decisions on several underlying issues.

The first is whether to rely largely or entirely on term life insurance for his or her insurance needs. If so, then presumably the person will look to non-life-insurance investment media for his or her investment or savings needs and will not purchase much, if any, life insurance that accumulates a cash value.

On the other hand, if the person is interested in developing a cash value (in effect, an investment element) as part of the life insurance contract, then he or she should consider one or more of the various types of cash-value or permanent life insurance for part or all of his or her insurance portfolio.

This is the longstanding term or cash-value debate. Actually, many people resolve this issue by using both term and cash-value contracts to meet their life insurance needs.

Assuming at least some cash-value life insurance is to be purchased, the next question is to determine who is to make the investment decisions and bear the investment risks with regard to the cash value. One choice would be to buy a policy for which the insurance company guarantees the cash value and a minimum rate of return (which might be termed *guaranteed-dollar* or *fixed-dollar* policies) and for which the investment decisions and investment risks fall on the insurance company. The other choice would be life insurance for which the policy owner decides upon the investment of the cash value from among the sub-accounts (investment funds) available under the policy (*variable* life insurance), and so the investment decisions and the investment risks inherent in the accounts fall on the policy owner. Thus, this issue is whether the buyer wants *guaranteed-dollar life insurance* or *variable life insurance*.

Again assuming cash-value life insurance is to be purchased, another issue is whether the premium should be fixed or flexible. In *fixed-premium contracts,* the periodic premiums are set in advance by the insurer based on the insured's age and sex, on whether the insured is a smoker or nonsmoker, and possibly on the insured's preferred risk status. Under *flexible-premium* contracts, the policy owner can decide, within limits, what, if any, premium to pay in any given year, provided enough is paid to keep the policy from lapsing.

Thus, from the viewpoint of selecting the type or types of individual life insurance to buy, the consumer is faced with the following choices.

1. Term insurance
2. Cash-value or permanent life insurance
   a. Guaranteed-dollar policies
      (1) Traditional (fixed-premium) cash-value life insurance
      (2) Flexible-premium policies (universal life [UL] insurance)
   b. Variable policies
      (1) Variable life insurance (VL)
      (2) Variable universal life insurance (VUL)

Term Insurance

Term life insurance provides protection for a specified period. If the insured dies during the period, the face amount of the policy is paid; if the insured survives the period, there is no payment. Term policies generally have no cash or loan values. Since term insurance provides only a death benefit without also building up a cash value, as of a given age at purchase it will have a lower premium per $1000 of insurance than comparable whole life policies.

Considerations in Buying Term Insurance. While term insurance is rather simple in concept, there are a number of contracts on the market that the consumer might consider. Also, the prices charged for term insurance can vary considerably among life insurance companies, so some shopping by the consumer (on the Internet, for example) or by an agent or broker representing the consumer may produce premium savings.

Annually Renewable Term (ART). For this term product, which is also called *yearly renewable term* (YRT), the premium charged per $1000 of insurance increases for each successive year as the insured ages. As a result, the cost of a level amount of term insurance will continually rise year by year. It will be quite low when the insured is younger (say, under age 40), but it will increase dramatically as the insured gets older.

Level Term. Here the premium remains fixed or level for a stated period of coverage, such as 10, 15, or even 20 or 30 years, after which the premium increases according to the age of the insured. Many level term policies allow renewal for additional similar level term periods, but usually at greatly higher premium rates.

Reentry Term. This type of policy provides that, after a certain number of years of coverage, often 10 years, insureds who pass a new physical examination are permitted to continue their coverage at a given set of increased rates (usually the same rates as a new buyer of term insurance at the same age would pay), but if the insured does not submit to the examination or fails to pass it, the renewal rates will be substantially higher. Because of this repricing feature, reentry term may carry a lower premium rate per $1000 of insurance than other term products, but because a physical is required, it also carries greater risks for the policy owner.

Decreasing Term. This form provides a declining amount of insurance over the period of the contract. A good example is mortgage protection insurance designed to cover for an amount that will pay off a home mortgage. Sometimes it also may be used to meet the current protection needs for a family when it is perceived that the need for life insurance will decrease over time as children become self-supporting or as a separate investment fund may grow.

Renewable and Convertible Term. Many term policies are *renewable* for successive periods of time at the policy owner's option, without any requirement of evidence of insurability at renewal. The age to which such policies may be renewed often is limited. Term policies also generally are *convertible*. This means the policy owner has the right during the conversion period to change the term policy into a whole life or other permanent policy of a like or lesser amount of insurance without any requirement of evidence of insurability at the time of conversion. Again, the age up to which a term policy may be converted usually is limited. The renewable and convertible features of term policies can be particularly valuable for insureds who later become uninsurable or insurable only on a substandard basis.

Term Premium Structures. Term policies may have guaranteed rate structures or may be indeterminate-premium policies.

When there is a *guaranteed rate structure,* the premium rates for each age are set when the policy is issued and cannot be increased in the future. Naturally, as the insured grows older, the premium rate applied will increase; however, the whole rate schedule by age is guaranteed once the policy is issued. *Indeterminate-premium policies,* on the other hand, have a lower *current* rate structure, which can be increased (or decreased) by the insurance company according to its actuarial experience, but cannot be increased beyond a higher maximum *guaranteed* level of rates. Some term policies are participating (i.e., they pay policy dividends), while others are not.

Preferred Term. A policy generally is called *preferred term* when potential insureds are subject to stricter underwriting standards (requirements for insurability) than for other term products. Preferred term insurance normally carries considerably lower rates than comparable term insurance that is not considered preferred.

Term with Whole Life Insurance. Insurance companies often can offer life insurance contracts that are combinations of term insurance and whole life insurance. These policies are sometimes called *hybrids*. They are intended to lower the initial premiums for the policy owner while still providing some cash value in the policy. Further, some policies that are nominally whole life policies are structured so that the cash value develops so slowly that they are essentially term policies. These are sometimes called *term-like* policies.

Cash-Value or Permanent Life Insurance

This broad classification embraces those policies that are designed to develop a cash value inside the life insurance contract. Traditionally, this cash value developed because of the level-premium approach to paying for this kind of life insurance, in contrast with the increasing premiums for term insurance. Periodic growth in the cash values of life insurance contracts is often referred to as the *inside buildup* in permanent life insurance policies.

Guaranteed-Dollar Cash-Value Policies

There are a variety of policies in the guaranteed dollar category. Because the cash values of these policies are invested by the insurance company and thus constitute part of its overall assets or general portfolio, these policies are sometimes called *portfolio products*. Because the cash values of these policies are included in the general assets of the insurance company, they are subject to the claims of creditors in the event that the insurer becomes insolvent.

Traditional (Fixed-Premium) Cash-Value Life Insurance

These policies have a *fixed premium* that is determined primarily by the insured's age at issue, sex, and whether the insured is a smoker or a nonsmoker.[6] Premiums per $1000 of life insurance may also be lower for policies with larger face amounts of insurance.

---

[6] The premium for any life insurance policy also may be affected by the insured's health and other individual underwriting factors. Thus, so-called substandard policies that do not meet the insurer's underwriting requirements for standard policies normally are rated in that they have a higher premium per $1000 of insurance than do comparable policies issued at standard rates. Also, as noted, so-called preferred policies may have lower rates than non-preferred standard policies.

These traditional forms can be *participating* (paying policy dividends based on the actuarial experience of the insurer) or *nonparticipating* (paying no policy dividends). If they are participating, it is the gross premium (before dividends) that is fixed; the final cost and financial results of the policy often will be substantially affected by the policy dividends (which are *not* guaranteed) that are declared on the policy in the future by the insurance company. These future and uncertain policy dividends on participating life insurance are a major reason it is so difficult to compare policies.

Gross premiums for these policies are set when the policy is issued and their guaranteed cash values increase according to a schedule contained in the policy. Thus, the cost elements (mortality cost for death claims, charges for expenses, and the interest rate credited by the insurer on policy values) are not shown to the policy owner separately; hence, these policies may be referred to as *bundled* contracts.[7]

Also, these policies in effect are front-end-loaded for expenses. This is because, for the first several years a policy is in force, normally either there is no cash value or the cash value is significantly less than the premiums paid. While there is no separately stated expense charge for traditional cash-value policies, the reason for this reduced cash-value pattern is to reflect the expenses of the insurance company in writing the policy. Therefore, the owner of such a policy will lose money if he or she surrenders the policy after it has been in force for only a few years.

The following are various kinds of traditional, fixed-premium life insurance contracts. By far the most common is whole life insurance.

Whole Life Insurance. This policy provides protection for the whole of life. Premiums may be paid throughout the insured's lifetime or over a limited period, such as 10, 20, or 30 years, or to a specified age. The premium also may be paid in one lump sum at the inception of the policy, in which case the policy is referred to as a *single-premium whole life* (SPWL) policy. When the insured is to pay premiums throughout his or her lifetime, the policy is commonly referred to as *ordinary life* or *straight life*. When the insured is to pay premiums over a specified period, it is referred to as *limited-payment life*.

Endowment Insurance. Endowment life insurance offers insurance protection against death for a specified period of time, such as 10, 20, or 30 years, to age 65, and so forth; then, if the insured lives to the end of the period, the contract pays the face amount. Endowment insurance is of minor significance in the United States today.

---

[7] This is in contrast to policies that are *unbundled*, such as universal life, as discussed later in this section.

Modified Life Insurance. Here the premiums normally are lower for the first few years than for the remainder of the contract.

Graded-Premium Whole Life. These contracts are somewhat similar in concept to modified life, except that the initially lower premiums increase annually for a longer period of time (such as from 5 to 40 years) until they level off. During this annually increasing premium period, there are no or low cash values in these policies.

Family Income-Type Riders or Policies. Under this type of contract, if the insured dies during a specified family income period, income payments (which might be $10, $15, or even $20 per month for each $1000 of face amount) are paid to the beneficiary until the end of the family income period, at which time the face amount of insurance is paid.

Family Maintenance-Type Riders or Policies. This is similar to the family income policy or rider, except that the income period is for a stated number of years after the insured's death.

Family Policy. This policy includes coverage on all family members in one contract. Most family policies provide whole life insurance on the breadwinner, designated as the insured, while term insurance is provided on the spouse and children.

Adjustable Life Insurance. These are whole life policies that allow the policy owner to make changes in the face amount, cash value, or premiums in case of certain events in the person's life cycle, such as children entering school, retirement, or unemployment. This approach once attracted some interest, but has declined in use.

Current Assumption or Interest-Sensitive Whole Life

This is basically a cross between the traditional whole life policy and universal life insurance, to be discussed next. The policy normally has an *initial premium* that can be *redetermined* (recalculated by the insurance company) periodically, based on new actuarial assumptions and the level of the policy's current accumulation account. The company provides some guarantees as to minimum interest rates and perhaps maximum mortality and expense charges in setting any new actuarial assumptions.

The policy's current *accumulation account* (cash value) is determined by using the current experience of the insurance company. From the periodic premium as currently set by the insurer, an expense charge may be deducted and the net amount added to the previous year's accumulation account. Then, interest is credited at the current rate being assumed and a mortality charge calculated on the pure life insurance protection (the policy face less the accumulation account) is deducted. The balance is the policy's accumulation account at the end of the year.

Universal Life

General Features. The keynotes of universal life (UL) insurance are flexibility for the policy owner and identifiable cost elements. The policy cash value is set up as a cash-value fund (or accumulation fund) to which is credited any net premium payments by the policy owner and a current interest rate and from which is taken the cost of term insurance (as a mortality charge) at the insured's attained age and any annual expense charges. This separation of the cash value from the death benefit has been referred to as *unbundling* the traditional life insurance product or as an *open architect* product.

Premium Payments. For UL these are at the discretion of the policy owner, except that there must be a minimum initial premium to start coverage and then there must be at least enough cash value in the policy each month to cover the mortality and any expense charges so the policy will not lapse. Insurers also set maximum premium payments.

Death Benefits. There are two general types of death benefit systems under UL: option A and option B. Under option A, there is a level death benefit, so if the cash value increases, the net amount of pure (or term) death protection (also called the *net amount at risk*) declines. Under option B, the death benefit is equal to a specified face amount selected by the policy owner when the policy is purchased plus the policy's current cash value; thus, the death benefit will increase if the cash value increases. Which of these options the policy owner should purchase depends on how much insurance protection is desired relative to the investment element in the policy. Option B provides more death protection relative to cash value than option A. Finally, insurers often allow policy owners to increase or decrease their death benefits as they desire, except that if the death benefit is increased, individual evidence of insurability normally must be shown by the insured.

Interest Credits. The cash value under UL is credited with an interest rate (usually monthly). There is a guaranteed minimum interest rate specified in the policy, and then the insurer may pay a higher current crediting rate. The interest rates paid by an insurer on its UL policies may be determined in several ways.

One is a *portfolio rate,* which is one rate set by the insurer and generally based on the investment performance of the insurer's whole investment portfolio. This is the most common approach. A potential second is a *new money approach,* in which the insurer sets more than one rate, depending on when the policy premiums were paid. Third, some UL policies credit interest rates that are *indexed* to some outside interest rate measure, such as a percentage of average long-term corporate bond rates. This is known as *interest-indexed life insurance*. Finally, a few policies have been sold that base the current return on some outside equity index, such as the Standard and Poor's (S&P) 500 stock index. This is called *equity-indexed universal life* (EIUL)

UL policies often are sold based on certain assumptions (projections) of the interest rates that will be paid on cash values far into the future. The same is done for other kinds of life insurance policies. The consumer should beware of these long-term projections because no one can know what interest rates (or the other cost elements of life insurance) will be 10, 20, 30 or more years from now. Instead, the consumer should note the current interest rate on any policy being considered, the history of the insurer with regard to interest rates paid, and the minimum guaranteed rate in the policy. Naturally, the financial strength and general reputation of the insurer are of paramount importance.

Mortality Costs. A *mortality charge* is deducted each month from the cash value based on the insured's attained age and the policy's current net amount at risk. The net amount at risk is the policy's death benefit minus its cash value. UL policies typically have a schedule of guaranteed maximum mortality charges, but the insurer often charges less than the guaranteed maximum as the current charge. However, the insurer can increase (up to the maximum) or decrease the current mortality charges.

Expense Charges. Insurers also may levy expense charges against premiums or cash values. Some UL policies have *front-end loads:* an expense charge is made for the first policy year and then often lower charges in subsequent years. Other policies have *back-end loads:* charges are levied on the surrender or exchange of the policy. Such back-end loads normally diminish year by year as the policy remains in force, reaching zero at a certain point (say, after 10 to 15 years). Some policies have both front-end and back-end loads.

UL policies may not charge any front-end load but rather credit the full first-year premium directly to the policy's cash value. In this case, however, insurers normally recover the costs of writing the policy (mostly sales costs) from the spread between what the insurer earns on its investment portfolio and the interest rate credited to the policy. This is one of the things that make it difficult to compare UL policies with traditional whole life policies. Traditional whole life policies charge initial costs to the first few premiums (in effect, having a front-end load) and hence have no or reduced early cash values. However, once there is a cash value, they may credit it with higher interest rates. UL policies, on the other hand, may have no front-end load and hence no or little reduction in cash values, but they may credit lower interest rates.

Cash Withdrawals. Since UL policies are unbundled, they normally allow the policy owner to make cash withdrawals (partial surrenders) from the cash value while the policy is in force. This can be an attractive feature. However, any such withdrawals reduce the policy's death benefit dollar for dollar. UL policies also have policy loan provisions like other permanent life insurance policies.

Target Premiums. UL policies usually have target premium amounts that are *suggested* annual level premiums that will keep the policy in force, given certain actuarial and interest assumptions. These are not guaranteed or required premiums, but only projections based on assumed levels of credited interest. However, insurers do offer riders to UL policies that provide certain guarantees. One guarantees that the policy will not lapse and the face amount will be paid at death up to age 100 if specified premiums are paid. Another extends the life insurance benefit beyond age 100 with no further premiums.

The UL policies of different insurance companies can vary considerably. They can vary as to the current interest rate being credited, the guaranteed interest rate, the method used to credit interest, mortality charges, and the nature and amount of any expense charges. A consumer may want to consider all of these factors.

Variable Policies

General Features. In contrast with the guaranteed- or fixed-principal approach just discussed, variable policies allow the policy owner, within limits, to allocate his or her premium payments among investment sub-accounts (mutual funds) offered by the insurance company and also to shift cash values among the sub-accounts. The amount of the policy cash values and perhaps the death benefit depend on the values (investment performance) of the sub-accounts to which the policy owner has allocated the funds. Hence, the investment decisions and the corresponding investment risks fall on the policy owner rather than on the insurer.

Investment Accounts. The sub-accounts offered under variable life policies (and under variable annuities described in Chapter 21) really are mutual funds held by the insurance company in a separate account that is distinct from the insurer's general investment portfolio. Insurers may offer a significant number of sub-accounts with a wide range of investment objectives in their variable products. Policy owners also may be given the option of having their funds invested in the general investment portfolio of the insurance company (a fixed-principal account). These sub-accounts are much like a group (or *family*) of mutual funds and, in fact, in many cases the same investment management firms that manage groups of mutual funds also provide sub-accounts to insurers for their separate accounts.[8]

One important reason for the development of variable life insurance was to allow policy owners to invest their policy cash values in whole or in part in common stock funds or balanced funds that would be more competitive with other kinds of investment media (such as mutual funds generally) and that would maintain or improve the purchasing power of policy values in the face of inflation. However, the investment performance of sub-accounts can vary considerably among life insurance companies. Also (like other investment companies), an analysis of insurance company sub-account performance should be over a considerable period of time—such as 5, 10, 15, or even 20 years, if available—rather than for only one or a few good years. Policy owners may follow other investment strategies in these sub-accounts as well, such as in bond or other sub-accounts.

Changes in Asset Allocation. A significant investment/tax advantage of variable insurance products (either variable life insurance or variable annuities) lies in the ability of the policy owner to move the policy cash value among the sub-accounts inside the policy without any current income tax liability. This allows the policy owner to make changes in his or her asset allocation strategy within the policy without adverse tax consequences.

For example, assume Norman Wong purchased a variable universal life (VUL) insurance policy (described next) a number of years ago and has paid a total of $20,000 in premiums for the policy, which has a $300,000 face amount. He has elected to have the policy's cash value placed in a common stock sub-account, which is now worth $50,000. However, Mr. Wong has become concerned that he has too much of his overall investment portfolio in common stocks. Therefore, he has decided to change the VUL policy's $50,000 cash value from the policy's common stock account to its investment-grade bond account. This transfer is not deemed a sale or exchange of a capital asset for capital gains tax purposes.

Further, if he becomes dissatisfied with the investment management of the sub-accounts in his VUL policy, he can exchange his policy for another life insurance policy with a different insurer, without being liable for income taxes, under the provisions of Section 1035 of the tax code. Of course, any surrender charge (back-end load) applicable to his VUL policy would apply to such a tax-free exchange.

Thus, the policy owner can have considerable flexibility in changing the

---

[8] However, for tax reasons the sub-accounts under variable life insurance and variable annuities cannot be the same as the mutual funds offered by these firms to the public.

asset allocation under a variable life (or variable annuity) policy.[9]

Variable policies are of two general types: *variable life* insurance and *variable universal life* insurance.

Variable Life (VL) Insurance. This is a fixed-premium contract that is similar in some ways to traditional fixed-premium (not variable) whole life insurance. In VL, however, the cash values and death benefits vary with the investment experience of the sub-accounts to which premiums are allocated. However, VL policies have a guaranteed minimum death benefit.

Variable Universal Life (VUL) Insurance. This is the more common form of variable life insurance. It is universal life combined with the variable life concept. The policy owner can decide into which sub-accounts his or her flexible premiums will go. The cash value then will be determined by the investment experience of the sub-accounts chosen. The death benefit will depend on the UL option selected by the policy owner—option A (level death benefit) or option B (face amount plus cash value at death). Thus, under VUL the policy owner has the greatest flexibility of all—flexibility with regard to both investment of cash values and payment of premiums.

Expense Charges in VUL. There are *expense loadings* in VUL products, which can be significant. First, VUL policies often have initial sales charges (front-end loads). Further, they also may have back-end loads upon surrender—referred to as *surrender charges* or *contingent deferred sales charges*. Like UL policies, these back-end loads decline with policy duration and after 10 to 15 years usually reach zero.

Second, there are annual (or periodic) *investment management fees* levied against the net assets of the particular sub-accounts. The amounts of these fees vary depending on the nature of the sub-accounts. For example, an investment management fee might be 1.2 percent for a growth common stock account, 0.8 percent for a bond account, and 0.5 percent for a money market account.

---

[9] By way of comparison, if instead these investment funds had not been in sub-accounts under a variable life policy (or variable annuity), but rather had been mutual funds in a family of mutual funds (as explained in Chapter 12), then the exchange of one mutual fund (say, a common stock fund) for another mutual fund (say, an investment-grade bond fund), as in this illustration, would be considered an exchange of one capital asset for another for capital gains tax purposes and hence result in a currently taxable gain or a loss. In this illustration, there would be a currently recognized $30,000 capital gain ($50,000 value [amount realized] - $20,000 adjusted basis = $30,000 capital gain). There would, of course, have been the same gain if Mr. Wong had held the stocks and then the bonds directly rather than through a family of mutual funds. On the other hand, if there had been a capital loss on this transaction, it would have been better tax-wise to have held the assets in a mutual fund or directly, because then he could have taken the loss currently against any capital gains he might have had that year and then against ordinary income to the extent of $3000 per year. See Chapters 12, 14, and 15 for a more complete discussion of these tax concepts.

These fees are to cover the expenses of investing the sub-accounts and may be referred to as *fund-* or *account-level fees.*

Third, there also are annual (or periodic) *mortality and expense* (M&E) *risk charges* levied against the assets of each policy. M&E charges are to cover expenses and provide a margin for the insurer. M&E risk charges vary among insurers: they might range from 0.6 percent to 1.0 percent or more. They sometimes are referred to as *policy-* or *contract-level fees.*

Fourth, there may be annual or periodic *administrative charges.* These may be a fixed amount per policy or a percentage of premiums or values. There may be a further charge for premium taxes.

The total of these annual (or periodic) expense loadings vary considerably among insurers, but they may range from 1.5 percent to 2.5 percent or more per year of the assets standing behind a VUL policy.[10] Since these expense loadings can be significant, the consumer should compare them among VUL policies.

Mortality Costs in VUL. In addition to the expense loadings just described, VUL policies also charge for the *mortality cost* or *term cost* of the pure life insurance protection they are providing. This is a periodic mortality charge that varies with the insured's attained age and is applied to the net amount at risk under the policy, as was described earlier for UL policies.

Second-to-Die or Survivorship Life Insurance

All the previously discussed forms of life insurance cover only one person's life as the insured. Second-to-die life insurance (also called *survivorship* or *joint and last survivor* life insurance) normally insures *two lives* in the same policy and the policy proceeds are payable at the death of the *second* insured to die. The two lives insured are usually a husband and wife.

Premiums on second-to-die policies normally are considerably less than the premiums for comparable policies on single lives of the same ages, sex, and amount. This is because two lives are insured and the proceeds are not payable until the second death.

One thing to consider in purchasing second-to-die life insurance is whether the policy allows the owners to *split it* into two single life plans, one for each

[10] This percentage of assets is somewhat analogous to the expense ratio of mutual funds, which is discussed in Chapter 12. The comparison is not completely appropriate, however, because mutual funds themselves do not provide life insurance protection, and some of the periodic expense loadings of variable policies are for creating or administering the life insurance coverage (although not for the actual term cost). Although there are limitations on the comparison, the expense ratios of comparable mutual funds are generally lower than the expense loadings as a percentage of plan assets for variable life insurance.

life insured, in amounts on each equal to the second-to-die policy benefit or some other amount, or to change it into a single life plan on only one of the insureds. Most policies allow such a split. This right may be valuable for spouses in the event of divorce or other family discord, possible changes in the estate tax law, or changes in their estate situation or plans.

Joint Life Insurance

Under this form of insurance, *two or more lives* are insured in the same policy and the policy proceeds are payable to the beneficiary at the death of the *first* insured to die. The lives insured may be a husband and wife or others, such as the owners of a closely held business pursuant to a buy-sell agreement. For example, both spouses may be working outside the home and both their incomes may be needed to support their family, so insurance is needed when either of them dies. Or suppose there are three stockholders of a closely held corporation who have agreed to buy each other out in the event one of them dies (a buy-sell agreement). The agreement could be funded with a joint life policy insuring all three of them.

Joint life policies often allow the policy to be split into two or more single life plans. Since a joint life policy usually terminates after the first death, the policies may contain an option for a surviving insured to continue insurance under a separate single life policy or, if there is more than one survivor, under a new joint life policy.

Low-Load Life Insurance

A few life insurance companies sell their policies directly to consumers without using agents or brokers. These policies generally have no direct sales loads (commissions to an agent or broker), which normally constitute the main part of the costs of placing a new policy on the insurer's books. These companies usually sell their policies through the mail, by telephone, or over the Internet.

A Diversification Strategy in Purchasing Life Insurance

With the sometimes bewildering growth in different kinds of life insurance policies and the current emphasis on insurer financial soundness, insurance advisors may recommend that persons buying life insurance, particularly if the amounts are substantial, should diversify their purchases by kind of policy and also among insurance companies. This is simply transferring to insurance purchases the diversification concepts we routinely employ in the investment area.

As an illustration, assume that Jane Smith is the divorced mother of two young children. She earns a good salary and her future career prospects are bright, but she works for a smaller company that provides her with only $50,000 of noncontributory group term life insurance. To protect her children and provide for their educations if she should die prematurely, Ms. Smith feels she needs at least $800,000 of insurance on her life. To satisfy the need for an additional $750,000 of life insurance, she might use several policies. She might purchase $350,000 of preferred term (she is in excellent health) from one insurance company to get immediate, low-cost protection. This term should be renewable and convertible. She also might purchase $200,000 of traditional whole life insurance from another company to get guaranteed premiums and to start building a guaranteed cash value. Policy dividends (if the policy is participating) can be used to purchase paid-up additions to increase gradually her life insurance protection and cash values. Finally, she might purchase $200,000 of variable universal life insurance from a third company. She could allocate the cash value of this policy to one or more of its sub-accounts (including common stock accounts), but in making this decision she should consider her overall asset allocation strategy.

This example is only meant to illustrate the diversification concept. There is no correct diversification model for everyone. Different combinations of policies could be recommended depending on a person's or couple's needs, current premium-paying ability, tolerance for risk, relative desire for flexibility and guarantees, investment philosophy, and other factors.

It should also be noted that there are some downsides to diversification. The first is complexity. Second, sometimes life insurance is less expensive when purchased in larger policies. Finally, sometimes consumers have a single insurance-buying philosophy that they wish to follow. However, as in asset allocation generally, for people buying significant amounts of life insurance, diversification often seems the better strategy.

Definitions of Life Insurance for Income Tax Purposes

Tax Advantages of Life Insurance: An Overview

Life insurance contracts have a number of income tax advantages for the policy owner and beneficiary. First, life insurance proceeds paid when the insured dies normally go to the beneficiary free from income tax. Second, the periodic increase of policy cash values or changes in sub-accounts in variable products are not taxed currently as income. Third, loans secured by life insurance policies are treated for tax purposes as loans and not as potentially taxable distributions. Fourth, there is no 10 percent penalty tax on premature distributions (generally, distributions before age 59½) from life insurance policies. Fifth, partial surrenders (withdrawals), where permitted by the policy, are viewed as coming first tax-free from the policy owner's investment in the contract (income tax basis) and then, when that tax basis is recovered, from potentially taxable investment earnings inside the policy.[11] And finally, one life insurance policy can be exchanged tax free for another life insurance policy or for an annuity contract under Section 1035 of the Internal Revenue Code.

General Tax Definition of Life Insurance (IRC Section 7702)

However, in order to get these rather substantial tax advantages, a policy issued after December 31, 1984, must be a life insurance contract under state law and must meet one of two alternative tests under Section 7702 of the Internal Revenue Code: a cash-value accumulation test or a guideline premium and corridor test. As a practical matter, the policies sold by life insurance companies are designed to meet this tax law definition.

Modified Endowment Contracts

A modified endowment contract (MEC) is a policy that meets the general tax law definition of life insurance, was entered into on or after June 21, 1988, and does not meet a special seven-pay test given in the law. A policy will not meet this seven-pay test if the accumulated premiums at any time during the first seven years of the policy are more than what would have been the sum of the net level premiums for a paid-up policy at the end of seven years. In essence, this rather complicated definition means that if premiums are paid faster than those for a hypothetical seven-pay life policy, it is an MEC.

The significance of being an MEC is that such a policy loses some, but not all, of the income tax benefits from being a life insurance contract. Loans secured by an MEC are treated as taxable distributions, there is a 10 percent penalty tax on premature distributions, and distributions from MECs are viewed as first coming from the investment earnings inside the policy (and hence taxable) and then as a tax-free return of the policy owner's investment in the contract.[12]

A policy entered into before June 21, 1988 that otherwise would be an MEC generally is grandfathered: the regular tax rules applying to life insurance apply to it unless it is materially changed. Of course, life insurance contracts whose pre-

[11] The income tax status of life insurance policies is discussed further in Chapter 27. Also, as noted next, some of these tax advantages do not apply to modified endowment contracts.

[12] It may be noted that these income tax rules also apply to regular (nonqualified) annuity contracts as explained in Chapter 21. Thus, in effect, the tax writers applied some of the non-qualified annuity income tax rules to life insurance contracts *when they are MECs.*

mium-payment patterns meet the seven-pay test are not MECs regardless of when they were entered into. Most life insurance policies are not MECs.

Single-Premium Whole Life Insurance

This represents primarily an investment-type life insurance product. The policy owner pays a single premium and receives a fully paid-up life insurance contract. Single-premium policies also have been written as variable life, universal life, and variable universal life. As just explained, they now are taxed as MECs (unless grandfathered).

The Life Insurance Contract

There are a number of features of individual policies that may be useful in planning. They are explained next.

Some Important Policy Provisions

Assignment. Life insurance contracts are freely transferable (assignable) by the owner. There are two types of assignments. One is the *absolute assignment*, under which all ownership rights are transferred to another. An absolute assignment may be used, for example, when a policy is given to another person or to an irrevocable trust to avoid federal estate taxation (see Chapter 27). The second type is the *collateral assignment*, whereby only certain rights are transferred to another when the policy is to serve as security for a loan.

Grace Period. This is a period after the premium for a life insurance policy is due, commonly 31 days, during which the policy remains in full force even though the premium has not yet been paid.

Incontestability. This provision states that after a life insurance contract has been in force a certain length of time (called the *contestable period*), normally two years, the insurer agrees not to deny a claim because of any error, concealment, or misstatement by the applicant.

Suicide. Life insurance contracts contain a suicide provision stating that if the insured commits suicide during a certain period of time after the policy is issued, generally two years, the insurer is liable only to return the premiums paid. After the two-year period, suicide is a covered cause of death.

Reinstatement. This clause usually gives the insured the right to reinstate the policy within a specified period, usually three years, of any default in premium payment, subject to furnishing evidence of insurability and payment of back premiums.

Policy Loan Provision. This provision allows the policy owner to take a loan (technically an *advance,* because it does not have to be repaid) up to an amount that, with interest on the loan, will not exceed the cash (loan) value of the policy. The rate of interest may be stated in the contract or may vary periodically according to some standard. Loans on older policies may have a 5 or 6 percent guaranteed interest rate and on more recent policies an 8 percent guaranteed rate. Some policies allow for lower loan rates after the policy has been in force for a certain period of time and on loans below a certain percentage of the cash value. Loan rates may also be expressed on a net interest basis, such as 2 percent over the rate of return in the policy.

The policy loan provision enables the policy owner to draw on policy cash values to meet financial needs without surrendering the contract. It also enables the policy owner to take money out of his or her life insurance policy (except for an MEC) without any income tax liability.

On the other hand, an important disadvantage of policy loans is that death proceeds will be reduced by any policy loans outstanding at the death of the insured. Further, interest paid by individuals on policy loans generally is not deductible for federal income tax purposes. Finally, many insurance companies include in their policies a *direct recognition provision* under which policy dividends or credited interest rates are less for policies with policy loans against them than for comparable policies without such loans.

Automatic Premium Loan Provision. This provision operates when a policy owner fails to pay a premium when due. In this event, the premium is paid as a policy loan and the policy does not lapse, as long as there is enough loan value in the contract.

Beneficiary Designation. A life insurance contract allows the policy owner to select the person or persons who will receive the proceeds of the contract in the event of the insured's death. When the owner reserves the right to change the beneficiary, the beneficiary designation is called *revocable.* When the owner does not reserve this right, the designation is called *irrevocable.* An irrevocable beneficiary becomes, in effect, a joint owner of the policy rights. Revocable beneficiary designations are used in most cases. It also usually is advisable to name a second or contingent beneficiary to receive the proceeds in case the first (primary) beneficiary predeceases the insured.

Policy Ownership. Life insurance policies generally state on the front of the contract who owns the policy—the person, persons, or entity who legally owns the right to exercise all rights and powers under the contract, which are technically called *incidents of ownership.* The policy owner may be the same person as the one whose life is insured or it may be someone else or another entity (such as the trustee of a trust, a corporation, a partnership, or other business entity). Ownership of a life insurance contract may be transferred to another by gift or by sale during the insured's lifetime.

Cash Values and Nonforfeiture Options

Life insurance contracts are required to include certain nonforfeiture provisions (options). These options normally include a cash surrender value, reduced paid-up life insurance, or extended term life insurance.

Cash Surrender Value. Under state nonforfeiture laws, a cash value generally is required, at the latest, after premiums have been paid for three years and the policy produces a nonforfeiture value. Many traditional whole life policies today, however, provide for some cash value at the end of the second (or even first) year. Also, for universal life (UL), variable universal life (VUL), and interest-sensitive whole life there may be a cash value the first year.

When a policy owner elects the cash-value option, the policy is surrendered to the insurance company for cash, the life insurance protection ceases, and the insurer has no further obligation under the policy. Further, surrender of a life insurance contract will produce ordinary income for the policy owner to the extent the cash surrender value received exceeds the net premiums paid for the contract. Hence, in general, surrendering life insurance policies for cash may be a questionable financial and tax strategy. Some strategies for taking cash out of life insurance contracts without surrendering them are discussed in Chapter 27.

Reduced Paid-up Insurance. This option permits the policy owner to use the cash value to produce paid-up insurance of the same type as the original policy but for a reduced face amount. This option might be appropriate when a smaller amount of permanent insurance is satisfactory and it is desirable to discontinue premium payments. Further, if the policy is participating, policy dividends will continue to be paid.

Extended Term Insurance. This nonforfeiture option allows the policy owner to exchange the cash value for paid-up term insurance for the full face amount of the policy for a limited time period.

Uses of Policy Dividends

Policy owners who have participating life insurance contracts may use the policy dividends in various ways, called dividend options.

Types of Dividend Options. These options usually include the following: (1) take in cash; (2) apply toward payment of future premiums; (3) leave with the insurance company to accumulate at interest; (4) use to buy additional

amounts of paid-up insurance, called *paid-up additions;* and (5) use to purchase one-year term insurance.

Cash dividends frequently are taken when a policy is paid up. This may be
done, for example, during retirement under a paid-up policy or when the
reduced paid-up nonforfeiture option is elected to provide an additional
source of retirement income. The use of dividends toward the *payment of future
premiums* may be a convenient and simple way to handle dividends.

If dividends are left with the insurer to *accumulate at interest* (dividend accumulations), the interest earnings constitute current gross income for tax purposes to the policy owner. This is a disadvantage of this option.

A popular dividend option is *paid-up additions*. These paid-up additions
have cash values of their own and are themselves participating. Further, the
growth in the cash values of paid-up additions is not subject to current income
taxation. *One-year term insurance*, generally equal to the cash value of the policy, is offered by many insurance companies.

Vanishing Premium Insurance (Quick-Pay Plans). This idea for participating
life insurance policies is to use policy dividends and possibly cash values of surrendered paid-up additions to pay the current policy premiums. The concept
is that when a policy has been in force long enough, the premium can be paid
by the current year's policy dividend and, if that dividend is not sufficient to
pay the whole premium, by the cash value from the surrender of just enough
previously purchased paid-up additions to make up the difference. The policy
duration at which this can be done depends on the insurance company's dividend scale and *is not guaranteed.*

Thus, it must be emphasized that quick-pay is *not the same as paid-up life
insurance.* When a life insurance policy is paid up, it means that the accumulated values in the policy are equal to the net single premium for the face
amount of insurance, and so it is guaranteed that no further premiums are
required to keep the policy in force. Both participating and nonparticipating
policies can become paid up.

Settlement Options

Life insurance policies provide that when the proceeds become payable, the
insured or the beneficiary may elect to have such proceeds paid in some form
other than a lump sum. These forms are called *settlement options.* They include
the (1) interest option, (2) fixed-amount option, (3) fixed-period option, and
(4) life income options. One of the planning decisions a policy owner must
make is whether to have his or her life insurance payable on the insured's death
in a lump sum, under one or more policy settlement options, or to a trust. This
issue is discussed further in Chapter 27.

Interest Option. The proceeds of a life insurance policy may be left with the insurer at a guaranteed rate of interest, such as 3 or 4 percent. In addition, most life insurers pay an additional, not guaranteed rate of interest consistent with the earnings on their investments (called *excess interest*). Proceeds left under the interest option may carry a limited or unlimited right of withdrawal by the beneficiary. The beneficiary also may be given the right to change to another option or options.

Fixed-Amount Option. This option provides a stated amount of income each month until the proceeds are exhausted. Each payment is partly interest and partly a return of principal. Again, the insurer usually guarantees a minimum rate of interest but actually pays a rate closer to that being earned on its investments.

Fixed-Period Option. This option is similar to the fixed-amount option, except that the period of time over which payments are made is fixed and the amount of each monthly installment varies accordingly.

Life Income Option. Under this option, the insured or beneficiary elects to have the proceeds paid for the rest of his or her life or for the life of one or more beneficiaries. This amounts to using the proceeds to buy a life annuity or a life annuity with a survivorship feature.

Retained Asset Accounts (RAAs). While not strictly settlement options, these accounts are commonly used for lump-sum payments to beneficiaries, rather than simply sending the beneficiary a check. When the beneficiary desires, he or she can then write checks against the RAA or leave the funds in the RAA at interest. It is a convenience for beneficiaries.

Supplementary Benefits Added to Individual Life Insurance Contracts

Supplementary benefits or riders are a way of adding additional amounts and/or types of benefits to a basic life insurance contract.

Guaranteed Insurability. For an additional premium, this option permits the policy owner to purchase additional amounts of insurance at stated intervals without further proof of insurability.

Double Indemnity. This clause or rider, often referred to as an *accidental death benefit,* provides that double (or sometimes triple or more) the face amount of life insurance is payable if the insured's death is caused by accidental means. From an economic standpoint, there seems little justification for double indemnity.

Waiver of Premium. This benefit may be added for an extra premium or it may be included in the basic rates. It provides that, if the insured becomes totally disabled before a certain age, typically 60 or 65, premiums on the life insurance policy will be waived during the continuance of disability. The values in the policy continue just as if the disabled insured actually were paying the premiums.

Disability Income Riders. Some life insurance companies have allowed disability income benefits to be added to permanent life insurance policies for an extra premium. Disability insurance written in this fashion is not common today, but may exist under older policies.

Long-Term Care Riders. Life insurers may offer riders to individual life insurance contracts, for an additional premium, that provide long-term care (LTC) benefits for skilled or intermediate nursing home care, custodial care, and home health care. LTC coverage is described in greater detail in Chapter 6.

Accelerated Death Benefit Provisions. Many life insurance contracts provide that the discounted value of all or a portion of the policy death benefit will be paid to the policy owner if the insured contracts a dread disease, at the onset of a terminal illness, or perhaps in specified other events (such as permanent residence in a nursing home). Such accelerated benefits reduce the cash value and death benefits of the underlying policy. There may be no initial premium charged for this benefit.

Other Riders. There can be a variety of other riders or options on life insurance contracts. These might include options to provide additional amounts of life insurance and cash values through increased premiums, options to make one-time payments (dump-ins) into life policies, children's insurance riders, payor's benefit riders, term insurance riders, options to change premium patterns, and transfer-of-insureds riders.

Planning and Using Life Insurance
Life Insurance Premiums and Dividends

Preferred Life Insurance. If an insured can qualify, he or she may realize substantial premium savings by shopping for true preferred life insurance. Of course, consumers should beware of so-called preferred policies that do not really offer lower costs but are just marketing ploys.

Premiums Graded (Reduced) by Size of Policy. Most life insurers follow the practice of grading premium rates by the size of the policy issued. That is, the larger the face amount of the policy, the lower the premium rate per $1000 of insurance. As a practical matter, another way of doing this is by offering certain policies only in minimum face amounts. The practical effect of grading premium rates by size of policy is that it may be less expensive to buy one larger policy than several smaller ones.

Lower Cost for Women. Women have lower mortality rates than men. Life insurance companies have lower premium rates for women than for men, and sometimes the difference can be substantial.

Life Insurance Policy Dividends. One of the basic decisions in buying traditional whole life insurance is whether to buy participating or nonparticipating insurance. Unfortunately, there is no pat answer to this question, but the following information may be helpful in making this choice.

Participating life insurance refunds a portion of the gross premium to the policy owner in the form of policy dividends that are based on the insurer's actual mortality experience, investment earnings, and administrative expenses. Such policy dividends cannot be guaranteed by the insurer and depend on its actual experience. Policy dividends do not constitute gross income for the policy owner for income tax purposes, but they may reduce a policy's income tax basis.

Nonparticipating (nonpar) policies are sold at fixed premiums that do not provide for any dividends. Thus, the policy owner knows in advance what his or her cost will be under a nonpar policy.

For most plans of participating whole life insurance, a given dividend scale will produce dividends that generally increase with policy duration. However, an insurer may increase or decrease its whole dividend scale depending on its experience.

Beneficiary Designations

The right to name a beneficiary is vested in the policy owner. Most policy owners also reserve the right to change the beneficiary.

Consider this beneficiary designation: "Sue Smith, wife of the insured, if living at the death of the insured, otherwise equally to such of the lawful children of the insured as may be living at the death of the insured." Here Sue Smith is the primary beneficiary and the children are contingent beneficiaries. Also, second contingent beneficiaries may be designated in the event that none of the primary or contingent beneficiaries survive the insured. If a policy is owned by someone other than the insured (a trust, for example), the policy owner also should be named as beneficiary.

An insured, who is also the owner of the policy, may wish to have the death proceeds paid to a trustee as beneficiary, with the trust to be administered for his or her family, rather than to individual beneficiaries. Such a trust may be established under an agreement signed by the insured during his or her lifetime or under the insured's will. Sometimes insureds name an individual (e.g., wife or husband) as primary beneficiary and a trustee as contingent beneficiary. This is referred to as a *contingent life insurance trust.*

How Should Life Insurance Be Arranged in the Financial Plan?

The issues of how life insurance should be owned, who or what entity should be the beneficiary, how it should be arranged for tax purposes, how it can provide liquidity for an estate or business, and similar matters are important and can be complex. Therefore, they are considered in greater depth in Chapter 27.

Substandard Risks

Most applicants who cannot qualify for individual life insurance at standard rates can still obtain insurance on a so-called substandard (rated) basis. Life insurance underwriting has been refined and improved over the years so that increasing numbers of previously uninsurable applicants can now be afforded coverage on some reasonable basis.

Further, an insured who has been issued insurance on a substandard basis may subsequently learn that he or she is eligible for new insurance at standard rates or at least under better terms. In that case, the insured should appeal to the insurer for reconsideration of the original substandard rating. An insurer generally will consider a premium reduction for an insured who demonstrates an improved condition.

Also, if an applicant has been told he or she can get insurance only on a rated basis, the applicant or his or her advisors may want to check with other life companies to see what kind of offer of insurance coverage may be available from them. Reputable life companies can differ in their underwriting of certain conditions, so shopping around a little may secure a lower rating or perhaps even none at all.

Nonmedical Life Insurance

Nonmedical insurance typically refers to regular life insurance issued without requiring the applicant to submit to a medical examination. The amounts of insurance that will be issued on a nonmedical basis vary by age groups, with the largest amounts being permitted at younger ages. There may be an age limit beyond which nonmedical insurance is not available.

What Actions Can an Uninsurable Person Take?

First, a person considered uninsurable can see if it is possible to remove or reduce the reason for the uninsurability. Second, he or she should check with several insurers. Underwriting standards vary: a person considered uninsurable by one insurer may be regarded as insurable on a substandard basis by another company. Also, the life insurance industry has made considerable progress in making insurance available to people previously uninsurable.

Third, the person should look for sources of insurance that do not require the showing of individual evidence of insurability. Group insurance, for example, may be available through the place of employment. Also, the person should check other groups or associations to which he or she belongs to see if group insurance is available through them. However, association group coverage often requires at least some individual underwriting. Also, nonmedical insurance may be available on an individual basis. Remember, though, that nonmedical insurance involves individual underwriting. Finally, persons can sometimes qualify for life insurance on a so-called guaranteed-issue basis, where members of a group cannot be denied coverage by the insurer.

Group Life Insurance

Most people who are eligible for group life insurance obtain such coverage through their place of employment. This coverage normally is term insurance.

Group Term Life Insurance

This insurance provides covered employees with pure insurance protection (with no cash values) while they are working for the employer. If an employee leaves the employer, group term coverage normally terminates 31 days after employment ceases, subject to the right of the employee to convert the group insurance to an individual permanent life insurance contract. (This conversion privilege is discussed later.) Group term coverage may also continue during retirement in reduced amounts and in certain other situations.

Elective Group Coverages

Employers may make several group life plans available to their employees. Such arrangements may specify that an employee must sign up for a basic plan to be eligible to elect coverage under one or more other group plans. Such *elective plans* often include additional levels of group term insurance. Additional levels of group term insurance also usually are available under flexible-benefits (cafeteria compensation) plans.

Other Group Plans

Group Universal Life Plans (GULPs). These plans are made available to employees on a voluntary basis, with the employees being able to decide, within limits, how much life insurance they wish to purchase and how much premium they wish to contribute to the savings element of the plan. Participating employees may withdraw their cash values from the plan, take policy loans against them, and upon termination of employment continue the coverage by making premium payments directly to the insurance company.

The insured employees pay the full cost of a GULP from their after-tax pay (through salary withholding). The employer does not contribute to the GULP. However, there may be certain advantages to participating employees. They normally can secure certain amounts of life insurance on a guaranteed issue basis (i.e., with no individual underwriting). In addition, there may be periodic open enrollment times during which employees may later decide to enroll in the plan (again with no individual underwriting). Further, some of the rating factors may be somewhat more favorable under a GULP than for individual policies.

Survivor Income Plans. Another type of employer-employee group plan is designed to provide a monthly income that becomes payable to surviving dependents specified in the plan upon the death of an employee.

Conversion Rights

An insured employee has the right to convert up to the face amount of his or her group term life insurance to an individual policy of permanent insurance under certain conditions. Typically, the employee may convert, within 31 days after termination of employment, to one of the insurer's regular permanent forms at standard rates for his or her attained age *without evidence of insurability.* For employees who are in poor health or even uninsurable, this can be a valuable provision.

Coverage After Retirement

Nowadays, a number of group life plans continue at least some life insurance coverage after retirement.

How Much Life Insurance Is Needed?

This question often perplexes consumers. Unfortunately, there is no one answer. It obviously depends on the purpose or purposes for which the insurance is intended.

Estate Planning and Business Insurance Needs

For estate liquidity and conservation purposes, the amount of life insurance needed depends on the size of the estate or estates, the potential estate shrinkage, any other liquid assets or arrangements available, and the person's overall estate plan, as explained in Chapter 26. The person or couple also may have other estate planning goals involving life insurance, such as the possible establishment of a dynasty trust, replacement of family wealth going to charity under charitable remainder trusts, or other charitable giving needs. These possible needs will be covered throughout the book.

For business life insurance needs, it depends on the owners' goals for their business, on the business values involved, and on the particular business plans adopted, as explained in Chapter 30. Life insurance also is commonly used in business compensation planning. The amounts needed for this depend on compensation levels, the plans involved, and other factors.

Family Protection Needs

The traditional function of life insurance has been to protect a person's loved ones in the event of his or her death. For this purpose, most people with an earned income and family or personal responsibilities need life insurance protection. There are a number of approaches that are used or have been used to estimate the amount of life insurance needed for family protection.[13] The main ones are described next.

A Justification for Approximation. Before discussing specific approaches, it may be noted that in determining these amounts approximation is quite acceptable, for several reasons. First, family needs, available resources, and other factors are estimated far into the future and who knows what the future will bring? Second, with our mobile society, family structures and needs will change in many cases. Third, investment returns may be used in these calculations and those cannot be predicted with any accuracy and confidence. Fourth, inflation may also affect future needs and that is another imponderable. Finally, the cost of term life insurance, particularly for younger persons

---

[13] An excellent discussion of this subject can be found in *McGill's Life Insurance*, Appendix (pp. 873-894), Edward E. Graves, ed., The American College, Bryn Mawr, PA, 1994.

who normally have the greatest family protection needs, is quite low today and so it often doesn't cost too much to be a little conservative in estimating the amount of life insurance needed.

Just Buying an Arbitrary Amount of Insurance. Sometimes consumers are presented with proposals to buy a stated amount of insurance without really evaluating their needs. This is not a logical approach from a planning perspective. Of course, it probably is better than nothing if the coverage is needed.

A Multiple of Gross Earnings. This is a rough approximation of needs. The person is asked to buy, say, from six to 10 times his or her annual earnings. The multiple can be roughly estimated from the person's family situation and perceived needs. This approach is easy to use, but is only a general approximation of needs.

For Earnings Replacement and Cash Needs. This is a more complete but more complicated approach. The goal is to estimate the amount of capital needed to replace each spouse's or person's personal earnings if he or she were to die today.

This process starts with each person's gross annual earnings from his or her personal efforts.

Then, taking each person separately when they are both working outside the home, estimate *what percentage of gross earnings should be continued* to survivors if the person were to die. This percentage often is around 70 to 80 percent. The concept behind this is that some annual outlays will not continue after the person's death but others (like child care expenses) may increase.

The third step is to estimate what *existing sources of income* will be available after the person's death. These sources may include annual earnings of a surviving spouse, Social Security survivorship benefits, investment income, pension survivorship benefits, and other income sources.

The fourth step is to subtract the existing sources of income to the survivors from the gross income desired for the survivors to arrive at any *deficit in the amount of annual income desired.*

The fifth step is to convert this deficit into a *lump-sum amount of capital needed* to meet the earnings replacement need. This is a difficult step and advisors differ on the technique to be used. Some argue that only enough capital is needed to take care of the deficit until the youngest child finishes college or graduate school. Others argue that this capital fund should be used up (liquidated) over the surviving spouse's life expectancy or some other time period. However, the technique favored by the authors is a simple capitalization-of-income approach using a conservative interest rate that may reflect assumed inflation. This approach assumes the capital fund is to remain intact over the surviving spouse's lifetime and then be passed on to the children or others at the surviving spouse's death. This approach is more conservative and will produce a need for more life insurance, but it is defended on the grounds that the future is uncertain and unexpected needs may arise.

Next, consider the cash needs that will exist after the person's death. These may include an emergency fund, a mortgage and other debt liquidation fund, and an education fund, depending on the circumstances.

Finally, combine the lump sum personal earnings replacement need and the cash needs and then subtract the person's other assets and present life insurance coverage from the total need for coverage to determine the amount of new life insurance (if any) the person needs.

The same analysis should be repeated for each person involved. Each person should be considered separately because they will have different earnings, resources, and perhaps needs.

If one spouse works in the home while the other works outside the home, this analysis can be done for the spouse working outside the home. Then the need can be determined for a childcare fund and the other expenses that will be necessary in event of the death of the spouse working in the home. This will provide the basis for estimating the amount of life insurance needed on that spouse's life.

Fortunately, it normally is not necessary for consumers to perform these calculations for themselves. Life insurance agents, brokers, insurance companies, and other advisors often have computer programs that will use this approach (or one like it) or the programming approach described next to make recommendations to consumers as to how much life insurance they need.

Programming or Needs Approach. For many years this approach was the main method used in the marketplace for determining how much life insurance a person should have. It is more detailed than the method just described because it takes into consideration changes in the income stream for the family over the years.[14] However, in recent years the programming approach has not been used nearly as much.[15]

Human Life Value Approach. This approach attempts to measure the economic worth of an individual to his or her family. It was popularized many decades ago (1924) in the writings of Dr. Solomon S. Huebner, a pioneer in insurance education (*The Economics of Life Insurance*, 1927). However, it has not been used in practice for many years and so will not be described here.[16]

---

[14] For example, Social Security survivorship benefits will cease when the youngest child reaches age 18 or 19 and will not begin again until the surviving spouse reaches age 60 (or age 65 for full benefits). This is commonly called the Social Security *gap* or *blackout period.*

[15] For a very complete discussion of this and related methods, see Kenneth Black, Jr., and Harold D. Skipper, Jr., *Life and Health Insurance*, 13th edition, Chapter 14, Prentice-Hall, Upper Saddle River, NJ, 2000. Also see the fifth edition of this book, pp. 113–117.

[16] For an illustration of how this method was used, see Black and Skipper, *Life and Health Insurance*, 5th edition, pp. 111–113.

5

Health
Insurance

There are two traditional types of health losses against which people should protect themselves and their families: *disability income losses* and *medical care expenses*. They are covered in this chapter. Another type of related loss—*custodial care expenses*—is the subject of Chapter 6.

Sources of Health Insurance Protection

Social Insurance

The main social insurance programs that provide health benefits are the disability portion of the federal Social Security system, the Medicare portion of the federal Social Security system, state (and federal) workers' compensation laws, nonoccupational temporary disability benefits laws of some states, and the Medicaid program (although it is not social insurance as such).

Group Coverages

Group coverages are the predominant way of providing private health benefits in the United States. Group health coverage generally is a benefits arrangement made by an employer for its employees.

Individual Coverages

Individual health policies are contracts with an insurer made by individuals to cover themselves and perhaps members of their family.

Franchise and Association Group Insurance

Franchise health insurance is a mixture of the individual and group approaches. It involves issuance of individual policies to employees or members of other groups under an arrangement with the employer or other entity. Association group insurance is similar to franchise insurance, except that it is typically issued to members of professional or trade association groups.

Other Insurance Coverages

Health benefits also may be provided under a variety of other insurance coverages, as noted in Chapter 2.

Disability Income (Loss-of-Time) Coverages
Features Affecting Disability Income Coverage

Maximum Benefit Period. This is the maximum period of time during which disability benefits will be paid to a disabled person. It may be expressed in weeks or months or extending to a specified age or even for life. Generally speaking, the longer the maximum benefit period, the better the coverage for the insured.

Perils Insured Against. These perils normally are either *accident alone* or *accident and sickness.* Coverage of disability caused by accident only is limited in scope and normally should be avoided. Coverage generally should be purchased for both accident and sickness.

Waiting (Elimination) Period. This is the period of time that must elapse after a covered disability starts before disability income benefits begin. If, for example, a plan has a 30-day elimination period for accident and sickness and an insured person becomes disabled as defined by the plan, he or she must wait 30 days after the start of disability before beginning to collect benefits.

Definition of Disability. This important provision describes when a person is considered to be disabled for purposes of collecting benefits. Definitions can be structured in terms of the inability to perform occupational duties, in terms of loss of earned income, or both.

When the definition is structured in terms of the insured's inability to perform occupational duties, there are essentially three varieties of definitions of disability in use today—the "any occupation" type, the "own occupation" type, and the so-called split definition.

As it was originally conceived, the "any occupation" type defines disability as the complete inability of the covered person to engage in any occupation whatsoever. This is a very strict approach. So the modern tendency is to phrase an "any occupation" definition in a way that will consider total disability as the "complete inability of the insured to engage in any gainful occupation for which he or she is or becomes reasonably fitted by education, training, or experience," or some similar wording. The "any occupation" approach is the least liberal from the consumer's viewpoint.

The "own occupation" type defines disability as when the covered person is "prevented from performing any and every duty pertaining to the employee's (or insured's) occupation." In some policies this may be phrased as the insured's "inability to engage in the substantial and material duties of his or her regular occupation or specialty" or some similar broader wording. This "own occupation" (or "own occ") approach is the most liberal from the consumer's viewpoint.

The split definition is a combination of these two approaches. An example is as follows:

> "Total disability" means complete inability of the insured to engage in *any* [emphasis added] gainful occupation for which he (or she) is reasonably fitted by education, training, or experience; however, during the first 60 months of any period of disability, the Company (insurer) will deem the insured to be totally disabled if he (or she) is completely unable to engage in *his* (or *her*) [emphasis added] regular occupation and is not engaged in any form of gainful occupation.

This definition, in effect, applies an "own occ" definition for a specified period—five years in this example—and then applies an "any occupation for which the insured is reasonably fitted" definition for the remainder of the benefit period.

The other general method for defining disability is in terms of loss of a certain percentage of the insured's earned income due to accident or sickness. It may be used as the sole definition of disability or an occupational approach may be used for a policy's basic disability benefit and then a loss-of-income approach employed for the policy's residual disability benefit.

Social Security Disability Benefits

Benefits Provided. There are two basic kinds of Social Security disability benefits: cash disability income benefits and freezing of a disabled worker's wage position for purposes of determining his or her future retirement or survivorship benefits.

An eligible worker is considered disabled when he or she has a medically determinable physical or mental impairment that is so severe that the worker is unable to engage in any substantially gainful work or employment. This amounts to an "any occupation" definition of disability and is strict by health insurance standards. In addition, the disability must last five months before benefits can begin. After five months of disability, benefits are payable if the impairment can be expected to last for at least 12 months or to result in death or if it has actually lasted 12 months. This amounts to a five-month waiting (elimination) period.

The amount of monthly Social Security cash disability benefits payable to a disabled worker and his or her dependents is based on the worker's wages subject to Social Security taxes. Here is an example. Harry Smart is age 34 and makes about $35,000 per year. His wife, Alice, is age 30. They have three children—John, age 6, Susan, age 4, and Cindy, age 1. One day, Harry is involved in a serious automobile accident (not work connected) and, as a result, becomes totally disabled and unable to earn a living. After five months of disability, Harry and his family will be entitled to the disability benefits listed as follows, regardless of any private insurance benefits he also may have. For illustrative purposes, assume that Harry's basic Social Security disability benefit is $825 per month.

- Harry $825 per month, until he recovers, dies, or reaches age 65
- Alice $412 per month, until Cindy (the youngest) reaches age 16 (or for 15 years)
- John $412 per month, until he reaches age 18 (or for 12 years)
- Susan $412 per month, until she reaches age 18 (or for 14 years)
- Cindy $412 per month, until she reaches age 18 (or for 17 years)

Because of the maximum family benefit, however, this total is reduced to about $1237 per month. Thus, as long as Harry remains disabled, his family will receive $1237 per month for 17 years (by which time Alice, John, Susan, and Cindy will no longer be eligible) and then $825 per month for the next 14 years (by which time Harry will be 65 and Alice will be 61). When Harry reaches 65, his Social Security retirement benefits will begin.

Taxation of Benefits. As explained in Chapter 4, Social Security benefits may be subject to federal income tax. However, it is likely that Harry's disability benefits will not be taxable. Therefore, assuming Harry's taxes averaged about 15 percent of his earned income prior to his disability, the $1237 per month of tax-free disability benefits is equivalent to about $1455 per month of taxable income. But even this $17,464 of equivalent benefits is a far cry from the $35,000 per year Harry earned prior to his disability.

Workers' Compensation Disability Benefits

These laws are intended to provide benefits only for work injuries and diseases; they really cannot be relied upon in health insurance planning.

Employer-Provided Group Disability Income Benefits

Group coverages as part of employee benefit plans may provide two basic kinds of disability benefits: short-term benefits and long-term benefits.

Benefits Provided. *Short-term plans* are characterized by a schedule of weekly benefits based on earnings categories, but with relatively low maximum benefits, short elimination periods, and short maximum benefit periods (e.g., 13, 26, or 52 weeks).

Long-term plans (commonly called *LTD coverage*) are designed to take care of more serious, long-term disabilities. They are characterized by benefits stated as a percentage of earnings (such as 60 percent of base salary), a relatively high maximum monthly benefit ($3000, $5000, or more), a longer elimination period (such as 90 days or five months), a split definition of disability, and longer maximum benefit periods (such as five or 10 years or to a certain age, such as 65 or 70).

Coordination of Benefits. Most group LTD plans have *coordination-of-benefits* provisions that indicate how other disability income benefits will affect the benefits payable under the group plan. Such provisions are important in planning disability protection. They are not uniform, but a fairly typical provision might provide that the benefit otherwise payable will be reduced by any benefits paid or payable under (1) any workers' compensation or similar law, (2) the federal Social Security Act (based on the maximum family benefit),[1] (3) any disability or early-retirement benefits actually received under the employer's pension plan, (4) any state disability benefits law or similar legislation, (5) any other employer-sponsored disability plan, and (6) any salary payments by the employer. Thus, group plans normally do not reduce their benefits on account of individual disability income insurance that is not provided by the employer.

Let us see how a noncontributory group LTD plan that provides a benefit of 60 percent of salary up to $5000 per month up to age 65 after a five-month elimination period would operate in our hypothetical case of Harry Smart. Harry's base salary is $35,000 per year, or about $2917 per month. Sixty percent of $2917 is $1750 per month, which is less than the plan's maximum monthly benefit. Therefore, after the five-month elimination period, Harry could recover up to $1750 per month from the group plan. However, under the coordination-of-benefits provision cited here, the Social Security benefit of $1237 per month would be deducted from the benefit otherwise payable by the group plan. Thus, the group plan benefit would become $513 per month ($1750 - $1237) for the first 17 years of Harry's disability. Note that if Harry

---

[1] Sometimes only the disabled employee's basic Social Security benefit is taken as a deduction.

had a personally owned disability income policy, its benefits would not reduce his group benefit.

Termination of Coverage. A covered employee's group disability income coverage typically terminates when (1) the employee leaves his or her employment, (2) the employee retires, (3) the group policy is terminated by the employer, or (4) the employer fails to pay the premium for the employee. Also, in contrast with group life insurance, a terminating employee may not have the right to convert the group coverage to an individual disability income policy.

Taxation of Benefits. The tax code provides that amounts received through accident or health insurance for personal injuries or sickness are not considered gross income for federal income tax purposes, *except* for amounts received as an employee to the extent that such amounts are attributable to employer contributions that were not includible in the employee's gross income. Thus, disability benefits from personally purchased disability income insurance are not gross income, nor are benefits received as an employee from an employment-related plan to the extent that the employee contributed to the cost of the benefits. However, to the extent that disability income benefits for an employee are attributable to employer contributions that are not includible in the employee's gross income (as normally would be the situation for employer-provided disability income benefits), they constitute gross income to the disabled employee. Thus, in the hypothetical case of Harry Smart, the group LTD benefits would be gross income to Harry, since his employer paid the full cost of the plan.

Individual Disability Income Insurance

Need for Coverage. There are several reasons why people might need individual coverage despite the growth of group benefits. They may not be members of groups that provide such coverage or they may not yet be eligible to participate in a group plan. Group benefits may be inadequate, either in amount or duration. Some people may not want to rely entirely on their employer's group benefits. Finally, individual policies may be used where business health insurance is needed.

Benefits Provided. Individual policies provide monthly benefits for a specified period (maximum benefit period) during the continuance of the insured's total (and sometimes partial) disability. Individual disability income insurance should be analyzed mainly in terms of the *perils covered,* the *maximum benefit period,* the *definition of disability,* the *elimination period,* and the *amount of coverage.* Any individual health insurance should also be analyzed in terms of its *renewal or continuance provision.* Naturally, *cost* also is an important consideration. Premiums can vary among insurers.

Individual policies may cover disability either resulting from accidental bodily injury or resulting from accidental bodily injury or from sickness. As we said before, it is important to protect against both accident and sickness, as opposed to accident only.

Today, there usually is a wide choice of maximum benefit periods, ranging from six months to the time until the insured reaches age 65 or 70 or for life. The period selected should depend on the person's needs. However, assuming that permanent protection is needed, consider buying or recommending coverage with longer maximum benefit periods, such as to age 65 or 70, or for life, for both accident and sickness. To buy shorter benefit periods (usually to reduce the cost) may result in benefits running out before the person reaches retirement age and, presumably, starts receiving retirement benefits.

When insurers use a split definition of disability, in general the longer the "own occupation" period, the better for the consumer. Of course, an "own occupation" definition for the entire maximum benefit period is better yet for the consumer.

There normally is a fairly wide choice of elimination periods. They may range, for example, from none for accident and seven days for sickness to one year or more for accident and sickness. There are several factors that may be considered in choosing an appropriate elimination period.

1. *Coordination with other disability coverage.* Other disability benefits may be available during an initial period of a disability, such as an employer's noninsured salary-continuation (sick-pay) plan.
2. *Other resources.* For example, an emergency fund could be maintained to take care of short periods of disability, among other purposes.
3. *Cost saving.* A relatively small increase in the elimination period will normally reduce premiums considerably.

Amount of Coverage. Within limits, applicants can choose the amount of coverage for which they want to apply. This, of course, depends on the amount of benefits they need, want, and can afford to buy. It also may depend on the amount of insurance insurers are willing to write on a given individual.

In underwriting individual disability income insurance, insurers have issue and participation limits. An *issue limit* is the maximum amount of monthly benefit an insurer will write on any one individual. A *participation limit* is the maximum amount of monthly benefits from all sources in which an insurer will participate (i.e., write a portion of the coverage). In addition, to try to avoid overinsurance, insurers limit the amount of disability income insurance they will issue to a person, so that monthly benefits from all sources will not exceed a specified percentage of the person's earned income.

These underwriting rules may limit the amount of coverage available to a consumer. However, since rules vary among insurers, consumers or their advisors may be able to get the amount of coverage desired by shopping around a little.

Supplementary Benefits. Some of the more important supplementary benefits include the following.

- *Waiver of Premium.* This provision is included automatically in most individual policies and is comparable to the similar benefit in life insurance.
- *Residual Disability (Partial Disability) Benefit.* This benefit may be an integral part of the disability contract, but it is often written as an optional rider for an extra premium. The residual disability benefit normally pays a proportionate part of the total disability benefit when the insured suffers at least a specified percentage reduction (such as at least 20 percent) in his or her earned income. Loss of income often is the coverage trigger for this benefit. Many policies will pay this benefit only after a period of total disability.
- *Guaranteed Insurability.* This commonly provides that on stated policy anniversary dates the insured may purchase specified additional amounts of disability income benefits with no evidence of insurability.
- *Cost-of-Living Adjustment (COLA).* This benefit provides specified cost-of-living increases in disability benefits after a total disability has lasted a certain period, such as one year. COLA coverage also may be purchased that will apply to disability income benefit limits.
- *Social Security Supplement Coverage.* This coverage provides additional benefits when the insured is disabled and receives no Social Security benefits. This may be helpful because the Social Security definition of "disability" generally is considerably stricter than the definition in most individual policies, so benefits may be payable under an individual policy but not by Social Security.
- *Accidental Death or Accidental Death and Dismemberment (AD&D) Coverage.* This is similar to double indemnity in life insurance. As with life insurance, the logic of buying this kind of coverage is highly questionable.
- *Accident Medical Reimbursement, Hospital Income, or Other Medical Expense Benefits.* These medical expense-type benefits usually can be added to disability income policies.
- *Benefits That Increase the Amount of the Basic Disability Income Coverage.* One such benefit is a *family income-type benefit* that provides for a decreasing amount of disability income insurance. Another is a variable benefit that allows the amount of monthly income to vary during an initial period of disability, to coordinate with other disability benefits.

Coordination of Benefits. In general, individual disability income policies pay their benefits regardless of other disability benefits. However, insurers *may* place certain provisions relating to other insurance in their contracts, but they usually do not do so. Also, most individual policies are written on a "24-hour basis." This means they pay for both occupational and nonoccupational disabilities.

Termination of Coverage. As explained later, policies that are noncancelable or guaranteed renewable typically provide that coverage will continue, if the insured continues to pay the premiums, until a specified age, such as age 65. Some policies allow the insured to continue coverage beyond age 65 on a guaranteed renewable basis, on a conditionally renewable basis, or at the option of the insurer, usually provided the insured continues to be gainfully employed. Policies may have a terminal age, such as 70 or older, beyond which the coverage cannot be continued in any event.

Taxation of Benefits. As noted earlier, benefits paid from personally purchased disability income insurance are not gross income for federal income tax purposes.

Other Disability Benefits

Group Life Insurance Disability Benefits. Several types of disability provisions may be used in group term life insurance plans. However, the most common is a *waiver of premium* that provides for continuing a disabled employee's group term life coverage after termination of employment during continuation of disability.

Disability Benefits Under Pension Plans. Pension plans may contain some disability benefits, such as the following:

- A number of plans allow an employee who has become totally and permanently disabled to take early retirement under certain conditions.
- Some pension plans provide a separate disability benefit for a totally and permanently disabled employee who has met specified requirements.
- Many plans allow full vesting of an employee's pension benefits in the event of total and permanent disability.
- Some plans provide a disability benefit akin to waiver of premium or the disability freeze in the Social Security system. This benefit allows a disabled employee's pension credits to continue to accumulate during his or her disability.

Medical Expense Coverages

Managed Care Versus Fee-for-Service (Indemnity) Benefits

A basic choice for many people today is whether they will have their medical expense coverage under a traditional fee-for-service (FFS, also called an *indemnity*) plan or under a managed care plan. They also may have several choices within each category.

Fee-for-Service (Indemnity) Plans. These are primarily reimbursement mechanisms that pay for covered health care within the limits of the plan. They allow covered persons to decide when, from whom, and how much health care to use, and then they usually pay the "reasonable and customary" (or some similar term) fees or charges for that care, subject to the limits of the plan. They do not attempt to control access to care or utilization of care. Today, most fee-for-service plans are major medical plans, but there can be more limited plans as well.

Managed Care Plans. This term can embrace a number of health care arrangements. However, the basic idea is that the plan not only finances health care but also organizes the care and to some degree controls access to care. Thus, providers of care (doctors, hospitals, pharmacies, and so forth) have contracted with or are employed by the managed care plan and are, in varying degrees, controlled by the plan.

Types of Managed Care Plans. There is considerable diversity among managed care plans, but the main types are as follows.

Traditional Health Maintenance Organizations (HMOs). These are the original managed care plans. A covered person selects a primary care physician from among those participating in the HMO. This physician then manages the person's medical care and may refer the person to specialists, hospital care, and other medical services, again generally from among those participating in the HMO.

There are several types of HMOs, but they generally have the following characteristics: (1) comprehensive benefits, including emphasis on preventive care such as routine physical examinations, well baby care, and inoculations; (2) little or no cost sharing (deductibles and coinsurance) by covered persons; (3) few or no claim forms to fill out; (4) generally paying only for services rendered in network; (5) providing care in limited geographic areas; and (6) often being low-cost plans for the coverage provided.

Preferred Provider Organizations (PPOs). PPOs contract with certain providers to form a network of providers. The providers agree to render health care to persons covered by the PPO (such as employees) and to be paid according to a negotiated fee schedule, which is usually discounted from their regu-

on a reasonable and customary basis. In this situation, the policy would pay as shown below:

Total covered charges $25,000
Deductible   - 200
                           $24,800   (effect of deductible)
Coinsurance   × 0.80   (80 percent of covered charges payable)
                           $19,840   (effect of coinsurance)

Therefore, potential cost sharing by the covered person would be $5160 ($200 deductible and $4960 coinsurance). However, the stop loss provision limits this to $1500, so the recovery is $25,000 - $1500, or $23,500.

Excess Major Medical. Some insurance companies write excess major medical coverage on an association group basis or as an individual policy. Excess major medical applies after other medical expense coverage has paid its limits or the insured has satisfied a large deductible.

Medicare

Persons age 65 and over who are not currently employed may rely primarily on Medicare for their medical expense protection, although they may also have retiree health coverage from their former employer, use individual plans to supplement Medicare, or be covered by so-called Medicare HMOs. Private plans are generally coordinated with Medicare so their benefits will not overlap.[2]

The original Medicare program comprises two major plans: Part A—Hospital Insurance (HI) and Part B—Supplementary Medical Insurance (SMI). These original plans include the original Medicare program (HI and SMI) or the original Medicare program plus a supplemental private insurance policy, called a Medigap policy. These original plans are on a fee-for-service basis and are described in the next section.

However, the Balanced Budget Act of 1997 increased the options available to covered persons through a new Medicare Part C (called Medicare + Choice), as well as providing certain benefits and protections to covered persons. Medicare + Choice will be described after the original plans.

Hospital Insurance (HI). Nearly everyone age 65 or over is eligible for HI, which provides the following main benefits (as of 2003):

■ HI covers up to 90 days of inpatient care in any participating hospital for each benefit period. For the first 60 days, HI pays for all covered services

---

[2] Under federal law, for active workers and their spouses over age 65, their employers' health plans are primary over Medicare. For retired workers and their spouses, Medicare can be made primary, and usually is made so, by any employer's health plan for retirees.

except for an $840 deductible. For the 61st through the 90th days, it pays for all covered services except for a deductible of $210 per day.

- There is an additional lifetime reserve of 60 hospital days. For each of these days used, HI pays for all covered services except for a deductible of $420 per day.
- After hospital confinement, HI covers up to 100 days of care in a participating extended care facility (nursing home). It pays for all covered services for the first 20 days and all but a $105-per-day deductible for up to 80 additional days.[3]
- Further, HI covers unlimited home health visits by a participating home health agency (e.g., a participating visiting nurse service) on a part-time, intermittent basis.
- HI also covers certain hospice care services.

Supplementary Medical Insurance (SMI). This portion of Medicare is voluntary, although persons eligible for HI are covered automatically unless they decline SMI coverage. SMI is financed by individuals age 65 and over who participate and by contributions from the federal government. It generally pays 80 percent of the reasonable charges for covered medical services after a $100 deductible in each calendar year. The following are some of the major services covered by SMI:

- Physicians' and surgeons' services and supplies
- Home health services on an unlimited basis
- Other medical and health services, such as diagnostic tests
- Outpatient physical and occupational therapy services
- All outpatient services of participating hospitals

Expenses Not Covered by Medicare (Medicare Gaps). These noncovered expenses give rise to the planning issue of whether and how Medicare should be supplemented to cover these gaps. The following are some of the main gaps in Medicare coverage:

- Custodial care intended primarily to meet the daily living needs of persons who can no longer be self-sufficient
- Cost-sharing provisions under HI and SMI (e.g., deductibles and coinsurance)
- Periods of hospitalization and skilled nursing home services beyond the HI limits on numbers of days
- Prescription drugs outside the hospital or skilled nursing facility

[3] All these deductibles or cost-sharing provisions are adjusted periodically to reflect changes in hospital costs. Some of what we have called *deductibles* (because that is their effect) are technically called *coinsurance* by Social Security.

- Routine physical examinations and immunizations
- Eyeglasses and regular eye examinations
- Hearing aids and regular audiological examinations
- Cosmetic surgery (except where immediately required due to accidental injury)
- Routine foot care and orthopedic shoes
- Ordinary dentures and dental work
- Doctors' charges and other charges above what Medicare will pay as reasonable charges
- Private-duty nursing in a hospital or skilled nursing facility
- Private room in a hospital or skilled nursing facility (unless medically necessary)
- Medical care outside the United States

Medicare Supplements. People may seek to supplement Medicare with individual or association group policies.[4] The policies sold by insurance companies to supplement Medicare—called *Medicare supplement policies* or *Medigap policies*—essentially are standardized. There now are 10 approved Medigap policies that can be sold to the public. In effect, if insurers are in the Medicare supplement market, these are the plans (with some exceptions) they can offer.

All these standard plans contain a basic core of benefits, which include the 20 percent SMI coinsurance, the HI daily copayment for the 61st through the 90th days of hospitalization, coverage for 365 additional days of hospitalization beyond the 90 days provided by HI, and coverage of the patient's charges for the first three pints of blood each year. One standard plan provides only these core benefits. The other nine plans provide these core benefits and one or more additional optional benefits.

In addition to the standard policy requirements just described, persons enrolling in Medicare Part B (SMI) after November 1, 1991, are given a *six-month open enrollment period* during which insurers may not deny the person a Medigap policy or discriminate against him or her in pricing such coverage due to the person's health status, claims experience, or medical condition. This open-window enrollment period can provide protection for Medicare enrollees who are in poor health and desire Medigap coverage.

---

[4] An employer may provide continuing medical expense coverage for its retired, former employees and often their spouses (retiree health coverage). When the retired, former employees and their spouses (if covered) are age 65 or over and hence are covered by Medicare, this retiree health coverage is secondary to Medicare and thus supplements Medicare. Whether a retired, former employee and his or her spouse with reasonable retiree health coverage needs to supplement Medicare further with individual coverage is questionable, depending as always on the circumstances.

Medicare HMOs. Some HMOs have contractual arrangements with Medicare (the Centers for Medicare and Medicaid Services) under which eligible HMO subscribers receive their Medicare benefits through the HMO and the HMO also may provide additional services that supplement Medicare.

Medicare pays the HMO directly for the Medicare benefits it provides, and the subscriber may pay the HMO an additional premium for any supplementary benefits. However, some HMOs do not charge any additional premium.

Medicare Premiums Charged to Covered Persons. Social Security beneficiaries do not pay any additional premium for Part A (HI). They do, however, pay a monthly premium for Part B (SMI), which has increased rather dramatically over the years. Nevertheless, eligible persons generally should enroll in Part B because the coverage is well worth the cost.

The relatively few persons who are age 65 and over but who are not otherwise eligible for Medicare can enroll voluntarily in Part A (HI) and part B (SMI) and pay a rather substantial monthly cost for both or enroll only in Part B and pay a lesser monthly cost.

Medicare + Choice. The Balanced Budget Act of 1997 created *Medicare Part C* (Medicare + Choice), effective January 1, 1999. Under this program, each year Medicare beneficiaries have the opportunity to choose the Medicare plan in which they wish to participate. First, Medicare beneficiaries who are already enrolled in the original Medicare plan (HI and SMI), the original plan with supplemental insurance, or a Medicare HMO may remain with their plan if they wish. However, Medicare beneficiaries who are entitled to Part A and enrolled in Part B and those newly eligible for Parts A and B may choose to enroll in a new Medicare + Choice option under Part C, rather than in Parts A and B.

There are two options under Medicare + Choice. One is termed *coordinated care plans* (or *Medicare managed care plans*) and is a managed care option. The plans available under this option include traditional HMOs, provider-sponsored organizations (PSOs) (which are like HMOs but organized by health care providers), HMOs with point-of-service options, and PPOs. These plans may provide additional benefits, but some may also charge an additional premium.

A second option is private fee-for-service (PFFS) plans. Under this option, beneficiaries can choose their own providers of care, but providers may charge beneficiaries more than the amount allowed for their services by the plan (up to a limit). In this case, the beneficiary must pay the difference to the provider. This is referred to as *balance billing*. Balance billing is not permitted under the original Medicare plan if the provider accepts assignment of Medicare benefits. Even if a provider does not accept assignment, there still generally is a limit on the amount doctors and other providers can charge over the Medicare approved amount (called the *limiting charge*). If the PFFS option is chosen, Medicare pays the PFFS plan a premium and the PFFS plan provides all Medicare benefits and perhaps additional benefits to the beneficiary. The beneficiary also may have to pay an additional premium.

Planning Issues Under Medicare + Choice. Some of the factors involved in making selections between the original Medicare plan and Medicare + Choice (and, if Medicare + Choice, which option) include:

1. Control over access to care (choice of providers)
2. Services covered and availability of extra benefits, such as outpatient prescription drugs, vision care, hearing aids, and routine physical exams
3. Cost sharing by beneficiaries
4. Ability of providers to bill beneficiaries for more than plan benefits (balance billing)
5. Additional premium for beneficiaries
6. Geographical limitations on coverage

Workers' Compensation

Workers' compensation laws provide unlimited medical benefits to employees injured on the job. Other plans normally exclude expenses for which a covered person is entitled to workers' compensation benefits.

Employer-Provided Medical Expense Benefits (Group Benefits)

The lion's share of private medical expense benefits in the United States is provided under group coverages established by employers for their employees. Therefore, the beginning point in medical expense coverage planning is to determine what, if any, group protection applies.

Who Is Covered? Group plans cover employees and their dependents. The definition of *dependents* is important and perhaps will indicate some dependents for whom other arrangements may need to be made.

Plans may allow employees to waive coverage for certain dependents (such as spouses working outside the home), provided they have other coverage. They also may offer employees financial incentives to do so. This may be something for employees to consider (when applicable) as a cost-saving measure.

Benefits Provided. Group plans can provide any of the benefits previously described. The group technique generally makes possible the provision of broader benefits at lower cost than can be provided under individual policies.

Coordination of Benefits. Most group plans include a coordination-of-benefits (COB) provision, which has the effect of setting a priority of payment among plans and limiting the total amount recoverable from group plans (and certain other coverages) in effect for a person to 100 percent or some other percentage (such as 80 percent) of the expenses covered under any of the plans. This serves to avoid duplication of benefits when a person is covered under more than one group plan. In most cases, however, group plans do not coordinate with individual policies.

Termination of Coverage. Since group coverage often is the backbone of a family's medical expense protection, it is important to consider the alternatives in case this coverage is terminated. An employee's group coverage may terminate when the employee terminates his or her employment. Dependents' coverage may terminate when the employee's coverage terminates or when their dependency status changes.

COBRA Continuation Rights. The *Consolidated Omnibus Budget Reconciliation Act of 1985* (popularly called *COBRA*) requires most employers to provide continued coverage under group health plans to covered employees and other qualified beneficiaries (spouse and dependent children) in case of certain qualifying events, such as termination of employment or reduction of hours, death of the employee, divorce or legal separation, and a child's reaching the maximum age for coverage, without requiring the qualified beneficiary to show any evidence of insurability.

The continued coverage is the same as under the group health plan and must be available for 18 or 36 months, depending on the nature of the qualifying event. The eligible person must elect this continuation and a premium may be charged for it up to 102 percent of the cost of the coverage to the plan. Such continuation generally is not available when there is coverage under another group plan or Medicare. When a qualified beneficiary's continuation coverage expires, the beneficiary must be given the option of enrolling in the conversion health plan that otherwise is available under the group plan.

Health Insurance Portability. Another federal measure broadening the rights of employees and their dependents under group health plans is the *Health Insurance Portability and Accountability Act of 1996* (HIPAA). For most group health plans, this law regulates the terms of any preexisting-conditions exclusion and requires group plans to give credit for prior coverage under a wide variety of other health plans in meeting the requirements of any preexisting-conditions exclusion.

Suppose, for example, that Maria Hernandez has been covered for five years as an employee under the group health plan of the ABC Corporation and that her 12-year-old son is covered as a dependent. Unfortunately, her son has a congenital heart condition that is treated regularly. Maria has just received a very attractive job offer from XYZ Corporation. XYZ also has a group health plan, but it has a 12-month preexisting condition exclusion. Maria is worried that, if she changes jobs, her son will lose health coverage for 12 months under her new employer's plan. She need not worry! HIPAA requires XYZ's plan to count her prior coverage under ABC's plan toward its 12-month exclusion period, so there will be no preexisting condition exclusion applying to her son under XYZ's plan.

HIPAA also does not permit group health plans to discriminate as to eligibility or premiums for coverage based solely on health status, medical condition, claims experience, medical history, genetic information, evidence of insurability, and certain other factors. Thus, XYZ's plan could not impose stricter eligibility requirements or higher premiums on Maria's son because of his health impairment.

Retiree Health Coverage. Employers may continue medical expense coverage for their retirees and often the retirees' dependents. When these benefits are provided, there normally are some age and/or service requirements to qualify. Thus, one factor employees should consider in deciding on when to retire or whether to accept an early retirement offer is how the decision will affect their eligibility for retiree benefits.

Once retired, former employees and their spouses age 65 and over are eligible for Medicare. Retiree health coverage is coordinated with Medicare so there is not duplicate coverage, with Medicare being the primary coverage. In effect, these plans supplement Medicare.

One point for retirees and employees to consider is whether an employer that now has retiree health coverage may at some time in the future attempt to modify or terminate those benefits. Employers normally reserve the right to modify or terminate retiree health coverage (as well as other employee benefits, for that matter) for the future. However, many employers, particularly larger employers, have maintained rather generous retiree health coverage for many years and apparently plan to continue to do so for the foreseeable future.

Strategies in Planning for Terminated Coverage. There are several possibilities for a person whose group coverage has terminated.

1. The person may be eligible immediately for other group insurance.
2. The person may be eligible for Medicare upon reaching age 65. In this case, the person (and possibly his or her spouse) may be fortunate enough to have retiree health coverage.
3. The person may elect continuation of group coverage under COBRA. In this case, he or she also will have conversion rights at the end of the COBRA period.

4. The person (and covered dependents) may have the right to convert the terminating group insurance to an individual policy without evidence of insurability. As just noted, conversion rights must also be made available at the end of a COBRA continuation period (through election during the preceding 180 days).
5. The person may purchase new individual insurance to replace terminated group coverage. HIPAA requires insurers to offer such coverage without individual evidence of insurability under certain conditions.

Employer-Provided Cafeteria Compensation or Flexible Benefits Programs.
A number of employers have organized their employee benefit plans so that employees can choose at least part of their benefit package from among several types and levels of benefits. This is referred to as *cafeteria compensation* or *flexible benefits.*[5]

Employees frequently are given a set number of dollar credits that they can spend on a menu of benefit choices. These choices may include one or more medical expense plans, group term life insurance, dependent group life insurance, and disability income benefits. If an employee spends more than his or her allotted credits, his or her salary is reduced *before tax* to pay for the extra cost. On the other hand, if the employee spends less, his or her salary may be increased by the difference or it may be placed in certain retirement plans. When employees are offered a wide choice of benefits, such as just described, it is sometimes referred to as *full flex.* Employers may offer more limited forms of flexible benefits plans as well.

Another more limited kind of flexible benefits program is the health care *flexible spending account* (FSA). An employee may elect to have his or her salary reduced by a certain amount (up to a limit specified in the plan) and this amount then is placed *before tax* in a separate account from which medical expenses that are not otherwise covered by the employer's plan can be paid. However, employees should take care not to place more in an FSA than will be covered by it in a given year. If the amount in an FSA at the end of a year exceeds the benefits paid from it during the year, the employee will forfeit the balance. This is referred to as the "use it or lose it" rule. The attraction of FSAs is that otherwise uncovered medical expenses can be paid on a *before-tax basis.* There also may be FSAs for dependent care expenses. FSAs may be part of a full flex program or may stand alone.

---

[5] Since these plans are permitted by Section 125 of the Internal Revenue Code, they also are called Section 125 plans.

Individual Health Insurance

A great many individual and family medical expense policies are available to the public from many insurers. These policies may offer consumers broad coverage, but some provide only limited coverage. Therefore, such policies should be evaluated carefully.

Who Is Covered? Individual medical expense insurance can be written to cover the insured person, the insured's spouse, and other dependents.

Benefits Provided. The same kinds of medical expense benefits can be provided under individual policies as under group coverages, except that individual policies often offer somewhat less liberal benefits.

Coordination of Benefits. Since people are free to buy individual medical expense policies from a number of insurers, may have group coverage, and may also be covered by other medical expense benefits, they may find themselves with several sources of recovery for medical expenses. This is not necessarily bad, but it is an area that can be analyzed to see if premium dollars can be saved by dropping any unnecessary coverage. Individual policies usually do not contain provisions that would coordinate or prorate their benefits with other coverage. Insurers generally try to avoid overinsurance by their underwriting requirements.

Termination of Coverage. Individual policies may terminate the insured's or spouse's coverage when he or she reaches age 65 or first becomes eligible for Medicare. Of course, Medicare supplement policies are not so terminated.

Individual Health Insurance Policy Provisions

Several kinds of policy provisions may be important in making policy purchase decisions.

Renewal or Continuance Provisions

Renewal or continuance provisions relate to the insured's rights to continue his or her individual coverage from one policy period to another. They generally can be classified as follows.

Policies have been issued that were *renewable at the option of the insurer* (or optionally renewable). This approach generally is not used today. Another approach that sometimes is used is that policies may be *conditionally renewable* (or nonrenewable for stated reasons only), in that there are restrictions on the insurer's right of nonrenewal. An example is in franchise or association group coverages, where the insurer may not be able to refuse renewal unless the insured ceases to be a member of the association, the insured ceases to be actively engaged in the occupation, or the insurer refuses to renew all policies issued to members of the particular group.

A common approach is for individual policies to be *guaranteed* renewable. In this case, the policy provides that the insured has the right to renew coverage for a specified period of time, such as to age 65 or, in some cases, for life. Also, during this period, the insurer cannot by itself make any change in the policy, *except that the insurer retains the right to make changes in premium rates for whole classes of policies.* This means the insurer cannot change the premium or classification for an individual policy, but may change the rates for whole rating classifications.

For policies issued after June 30, 1997, HIPAA requires most individual medical expense contracts to be guaranteed renewable at the option of the policyholder. It would seem desirable for policyholders to make this election, even if the cost is somewhat higher. Nonrenewal is allowed only in limited circumstances. Insurers also may write disability income coverages on a guaranteed renewable basis.

The final category is the *noncancelable and guaranteed renewable* (or noncancelable) type. When the term *noncancelable,* or *noncan,* is used alone to describe a renewal provision, it means the noncancelable and guaranteed renewable type. This provision gives the insured the right to continue the policy in force by the timely payment of premiums *as specified in the policy,* usually for a specified period of time, such as to age 65. The insurer retains no right by itself to make *any* change in *any* policy provision during this period. The distinction between this and a guaranteed renewable policy is that the insurer guarantees the premium rates for noncancelable contracts, but reserves the right to change premiums for whole classes of insureds under guaranteed renewable contracts.

Not surprisingly, the greater the renewal guarantees contained in a policy, the higher the premium will tend to be. Thus, assuming the consumer has a choice among renewal provisions, the question becomes: How much is he or she willing to pay for renewal protection? In general, it probably is better to try to purchase noncancelable coverage if it is available; otherwise, he or she should purchase guaranteed renewable coverage.

Preexisting Conditions

Individual health insurance policies normally limit coverage for conditions existing prior to the effective date of coverage. Group health plans, on the other hand, may cover preexisting conditions on the same basis as other conditions or may use a preexisting-conditions exclusion that meets the requirements of HIPAA.

However, a section of the "time limit on certain defenses" provision, which is a required provision in individual health insurance policies, in effect provides that after a policy has been in force for two (or three) years, coverage cannot be denied by the insurer on the grounds that a loss was caused by a preexisting condition, unless the condition is specifically excluded in the policy. Also, many states have further restricted the application of preexisting-conditions exclusions.

General Provisions

Time Limit on Certain Defenses. In addition to the part of this provision dealing with preexisting conditions, this provision specifies that after a policy has been in force for two (or three) years, no misstatements, except fraudulent misstatements, made by the applicant in securing the policy can be used to void the policy or to deny liability for a loss commencing after the two- (or three-) year period. It is similar in concept to the incontestable clause used in life insurance.

Grace Period. Like life insurance policies, individual health contracts allow a grace period for the payment of premiums.

Notice and Proof Requirements. The policy indicates certain time limits for the insured to give written notice of a claim and furnish the insurer with completed proofs of loss.

Medical Savings Accounts

The concept behind medical savings accounts (now called Archer MSAs) is for persons (or employers on behalf of their employees) to be able to set aside annual contributions on a tax-favored basis to an MSA from which medical expenses can be paid. In addition, the persons would have a high-deductible health plan to take care of catastrophic medical expenses. Archer MSAs are similar in concept to IRAs, except for health care. It has been a controversial idea. A test program for MSAs was launched by HIPAA in 1996.[6] *Eligible persons* under this pilot program are self-employed persons and employees of small employers (having 50 or fewer employees).

The tax treatment of MSAs is quite favorable. Contributions (within certain limits) are deductible from the person's gross income and, if made by the individual's employer, are excluded from his or her gross income. Investment earnings on the assets in an MSA are not currently taxable income to the individual

---

[6] There was also a test program for Medicare MSAs as part of Medicare + Choice.

owner. Distributions from an MSA to pay qualified medical expenses for the individual, his or her spouse, or his or her dependents are excluded from the individual's gross income. Distributions for any other purpose are taxable.

The future for MSAs is unclear at this point. Archer MSAs have a cut-off year after which they will no longer be available, unless the cut-off year is extended or the program is made permanent. However, even after the cut-off year, active Archer MSA participants will be able to continue them.

Health Reimbursement Arrangements (HRAs)

This is a newer plan provided and financed entirely by employers to reimburse out-of-pocket medical expenses and health coverage premiums incurred by employees and their dependents. HRAs are defined contribution plans in that contributions are made by employers to HRA accounts for employees. However, they differ from flexible spending accounts (FSAs) in that there is no employee salary reduction and unused HRA balances can be carried forward to future years. HRAs cover only expenses not covered by other health plans and may be established by employers independently or in combination with other health plans.

6

Long-Term Care Insurance and Medicaid Planning

The nature of the long-term care or custodial care exposure was outlined in Chapter 1. It has attracted increasing attention and concern over the years.

Nature of Exposure

Long-term care can be financially devastating. If, for example, a loved one requires skilled nursing facility care, an average cost might be around $150 (or more) per day, or $54,750 per year, for nursing home care alone. This amount normally will be deductible for federal income tax purposes by the person paying the cost as an itemized medical expense.[1] However, even with a tax deduction this level of expense can be a financial disaster for most families. Of course, different levels of care may cost less, but it still will be significant.

The persons who may be at financial risk for such care include, of course, the person who needs the care and his or her spouse. However, they also may include children, grandchildren, other family members, and their spouses who may be faced with parents, grandparents, or other loved ones who need custodial or long-term care.

---

[1] Medical and dental expenses paid by a taxpayer for himself or herself, his or her spouse, or his or her dependents are deductible as an itemized deduction (i.e., from adjusted gross income to arrive at taxable income, if the taxpayer itemizes his or her deductions) to the extent that the expenses exceed 7.5 percent of the taxpayer's adjusted gross income for the year.

Under the Health Insurance Portability and Accountability Act (HIPAA) of 1996, unreimbursed expenses for qualified long-term care services are considered to be for medical care and are deductible under the medical expense provision of the Internal Revenue Code. Qualified long-term care services generally are services or care given to provide assistance to a chronically ill or disabled individual. They are explained further in this chapter.

There are several possible levels of long-term care services that may be utilized, depending on the situation and the desires of the parties. These include the following, listed from the highest level of care to the lowest.

- *Skilled nursing care facilities,* which have the staff and equipment necessary to provide skilled nursing or rehabilitative services on a daily basis.
- *Intermediate-care facilities,* which provide primarily custodial care but also have skilled nursing and rehabilitative services available if needed.
- *Custodial care facilities,* which are residential facilities designed to provide primarily custodial care and are not equipped to provide skilled nursing services.
- *Adult day care,* on a nonresidential basis.
- *Home health care,* which may cover services provided by a qualified home health care agency or others.

Basic Planning Approaches

The following planning approaches are being used to meet this exposure.

- Purchase of long-term care (LTC) insurance. This involves advance planning and funding for this expense.
- Planning to become eligible for government benefits, essentially Medicaid.
- Other estate planning decisions made with long-term care needs in mind.

Long-Term Care Insurance and Other Arrangements

Long-term care (LTC) insurance is the main source of advance insurance funding for the long-term care exposure.

Sources of LTC Insurance

- Individual LTC insurance purchased by consumers
- LTC insurance purchased by individuals through association group plans
- LTC riders and accelerated death benefits added to life insurance contracts
- Group LTC insurance purchased by employees through their employers
- Coverage available through continuing care retirement community (CCRC) plans

General Nature of Coverage

LTC insurance customarily provides a specified reimbursement or an indemnity benefit per day (a per diem benefit) for covered care, after an initial waiting period of a stated number of days, up to certain maximum benefits. Under present contracts, there usually are multiple definitions of when coverage begins, but benefits generally are payable when the insured person becomes unable to perform a certain number (usually two or three) of a list of *activities of daily living* (ADLs) that are stated in the policy. Examples of ADLs are eating, bathing, dressing, taking medication, toileting, and transferring and walking.

Insured persons normally can select from a range of elimination (waiting) periods, maximum daily benefits, and maximum lifetime benefits. LTC policies often provide optional inflation protection, guaranteed insurability, and other optional benefits. They usually have waiver-of-premium provisions. When LTC benefits are offered on a group basis as an employee benefit, coverage normally is voluntary and employees generally must pay the full cost. When LTC coverage is purchased as a rider to a life insurance contract, the benefits may or may not be a function of the face amount of life insurance.

Covered Services (Levels of Care)

The kinds of services that may be covered under LTC policies include skilled nursing facility care, intermediate nursing facility care, custodial nursing facility care, other custodial facility care, home health care, home care, adult day care, respite care, and hospice care. Many commentators have suggested that consumers are better protected by purchasing coverage with a relatively broad range of covered services that include not only nursing home care but also custodial facility care, home health care, and probably adult day care. This is because many people will want to receive custodial care other than in an institutional format, when possible.

Benefit Amounts Provided

LTC policies provide a specified dollar amount per day for the covered levels of care. The insured often has a choice from a range of daily benefit amounts (such as from $50 to $300 or more per day), with the premium naturally increasing as the daily benefit increases.

The daily benefit may vary with the level of care used. On the other hand, many LTC policies today provide the same daily benefit for all covered levels of care. This is preferable for the consumer.

In choosing the benefit amount, the consumer must balance adequate protection against premium cost. Of course, other resources (such as an investment fund) may affect this decision. However, many people prefer not to deplete their other resources unduly, especially since they do not know how long they might need custodial care in the future. They often want to preserve their estates for their spouses, children, or other heirs.

There are two ways the daily benefit amount can be structured. The first is to pay actual charges incurred, up to the policy's daily benefit amount. This is referred to as an *expense reimbursement policy.* The other is to pay the policy's daily benefit regardless of the actual charges incurred. This is called a *per diem policy.* The tax treatment of an LTC policy depends on which form is involved.

Maximum Benefits

LTC plans normally have maximum lifetime benefit limits. This is the maximum aggregate *time period* (number of days or months) or *dollar amount* of benefits the insurer will pay during the lifetime of an insured. In addition, some plans impose a maximum limit for each period of confinement, period of care or each illness. This is less desirable for the insured. A few policies have an unlimited benefit period.

The insured often is given a choice among several maximum limits. In general, it seems better to select the longest (or largest) maximum benefit available, even though the cost will be greater. The insured has no way of knowing how long he or she may need long-term care in the future.

Elimination Period (Waiting Period)

The waiting period is the number of days of continuous confinement or care that must be incurred before LTC benefits will commence. Most LTC insurance has a waiting period, ranging from 15 to 20 days to 100 days or more. LTC policies often give the purchaser a choice of several waiting periods, with premium reductions for longer waiting periods. One way to reduce cost is to purchase coverage with a longer waiting period. On the other hand, the consumer needs to consider whether the premium savings are really worth the potential loss of benefits.

Coverage (or Benefit) Triggers

Modern LTC policies commonly have several definitions of when a covered person can qualify for benefits. These are called *definitions of disability* or *coverage triggers.* The following are possible alternative coverage triggers.

- The covered person is unable to perform a specified number (usually two or three) of a list of activities of daily living (ADLs).
- The covered person has a *cognitive impairment,* which generally means the deterioration in or loss of intellectual capacity that can be measured by clin-

ical evidence and standardized tests. Examples would be the organic brain disorders of Alzheimer's disease and Parkinson's disease.[2]

■ A physician certifies that the covered person needs long-term care services as a *medical necessity.* This alternative definition may be liberal for the insured, since his or her own physician may be able to certify the need for benefits.

Most policies allow coverage if one of the first two benefit triggers exist, but some use all three. All three would be more liberal for the insured.

Continuance (or Renewal) Provisions

The consumer should seek to buy individual LTC coverage that is at least guaranteed renewable, as was explained in Chapter 5. LTC insurance normally is not available on a noncancelable basis. When LTC insurance is purchased as association group coverage, check to see what rights, if any, the insured person has to continue the coverage directly with the insurance company in the event the group policy is terminated.

Issue Ages

Insurance companies often limit the persons to whom they will sell LTC coverage to certain age ranges, commonly ages 50 to 80. Once issued, LTC policies usually can be continued for life.

Extent of Individual Underwriting

Individual and association group plans almost always require some measure of individual underwriting for each applicant for insurance. Larger group plans may allow coverage on a guaranteed issue basis without individual selection.

Premiums and Nonforfeiture Values

The premiums for LTC insurance normally depend on such factors as the insured's age, sex, maximum benefit period, waiting period, daily benefit amount, any inflation protection or other optional benefits, and perhaps the state where the policy is issued. Premium rates normally are level, based on the insured's age when the policy was originally issued. That is, the premium (as of the original issue age) remains level as the insured gets older, except for pos-

[2] The National Association of Insurance Commissioners (NAIC), in its Model Act on LTC insurance, requires that LTC policies cover Alzheimer's disease, Parkinson's disease, and other organic brain disorders that occur after the LTC policy has been issued. Individual state insurance laws (which are controlling) may or may not follow this Model Act.

sible rate increases applied to whole classes of insureds under guaranteed renewable policies. Obtaining lower, level premiums for the rest of the insured's life is one advantage of buying LTC coverage early. In addition, the person may become uninsurable for LTC coverage as he or she gets older.

LTC policies may contain nonforfeiture benefits, which provide continuing benefits for the policy owner if he or she should stop paying premiums after the policy has been in force for a reasonable period of time. The nonforfeiture benefit may take the form of a paid-up policy for a reduced daily benefit or extended term coverage for the same daily benefit for a given period of time. LTC policies normally do not provide cash values.

Benefits Under Life Insurance Policies

Life insurance benefits may include *long-term care (LTC) riders* that can provide essentially the same kinds of benefits as the LTC policies just discussed and *accelerated death benefit provisions*. Both of these benefits were described in Chapter 4.

Tax Treatment of LTC and Accelerated Death Benefits

Accelerated death benefits paid under life insurance contracts (described in Chapter 4) are excluded from gross income for federal income tax purposes if the insured is *terminally ill*. For this purpose, a terminally ill person has an illness or physical condition that has been certified to be reasonably expected to result in death within 24 months. Also excluded from gross income are life insurance accelerated death benefits on insureds who are *chronically ill*, as defined in the next paragraph.[3]

Federal income tax law treats qualified LTC insurance contracts as accident and health insurance for tax purposes. *Qualified long-term care insurance contracts* are insurance contracts (either LTC riders on life insurance policies or other LTC policies) that provide only coverage for "qualified long-term care services" and meet certain other requirements.[4] *Qualified long-term care services* include necessary diagnostic, preventive, therapeutic, curing, treating, mitigating, rehabilitative, maintenance, and personal care services for a

---

[3] Such qualified amounts received from viatical settlement providers, if a life insurance contract is assigned or sold to such providers, as explained later in this chapter, also are excluded from gross income.

[4] For example, the contract must be guaranteed renewable, not have a cash surrender value, not duplicate Medicare benefits, and satisfy various consumer protection provisions of the long-term care insurance Model Act and regulations promulgated by the National Association of Insurance Commissioners (NAIC).

"chronically ill individual" that are provided pursuant to a plan of care prescribed by a licensed health care practitioner. A *chronically ill individual* is a person who is unable to perform at least two activities of daily living[5] due to loss of functional capacity or a similar level of disability or who requires substantial supervision because of severe cognitive impairment. In essence, then, a qualified LTC insurance contract for tax purposes provides benefits for personal care and services to maintain and care for a chronically ill individual defined in terms of the inability to perform at least two activities of daily living or a severe cognitive impairment.[6]

The tax benefits from being a qualified LTC insurance contract are as follows:

1. Benefits received are excluded (or partially excluded) from gross income for federal income tax purposes. Periodic payments (e.g., daily benefits) that do not exceed the actual costs incurred are entirely tax-free. When benefits do exceed the actual costs incurred (as they might, for example, under a per diem-type LTC contract), they are excluded from gross income only up to a maximum of $220 per day in 2003.[7]

   Suppose, for example, that Mary Donnelly is insured under a per diem-type qualified LTC contract providing a daily benefit of $250. Further assume that she becomes unable to perform two out of six ADLs (a benefit trigger under her policy) and is confined in a covered nursing home where she incurs actual costs of $200 per day for qualified LTC services. In this case, $220 (in 2003) of the $250 per day she receives will be excluded from Mary's gross income for federal tax purposes and the other $30 will be gross income to her. Thus, benefits from per diem-type qualified LTC contracts will be income tax free to the extent just described. On the other hand, benefits received from expense reimbursement–type qualified LTC contracts will be entirely tax-free since they are payable only to the extent of actual costs incurred.

2. Premiums paid by employers for employer-provided qualified LTC insurance generally are excluded from covered employees' gross income.

3. Premiums for qualified LTC insurance are included in the income tax deduction available to self-employed individuals for their health insurance expenses.

---

[5] The activities of daily living included are eating, toileting, transferring, bathing, dressing, and continence. At least five of these activities must be used in the contract before it will be treated as a qualified long-term care insurance contract.

[6] Note that for tax purposes a terminally ill individual is not considered chronically ill.

[7] This excluded amount is indexed for inflation based on changes in the medical care component of the consumer price index in $10 multiples.

4. Finally, as cited in note 1 of this chapter, unreimbursed amounts paid for qualified long-term care services provided to a taxpayer or the taxpayer's spouse or dependents may be deductible as medical care for individuals. In addition, premiums paid for qualified LTC insurance, up to specified limits based on the insured's attained age,[8] similarly may be deductible as medical expenses. It must be remembered, however, that medical expenses (including LTC expenses and premiums) are deductible only if the taxpayer itemizes his or her deductions and only to the extent that total medical expenses in a year exceed 7.5 percent of the taxpayer's adjusted gross income (AGI).

Viatical Arrangements

These arrangements allow terminally ill and other life insurance policy owners to sell their policies to viatical settlement companies for a percentage (such as from 50 percent to 80 percent) of the policy's face amount. Viatical companies may be willing to purchase a policy when the insured has been diagnosed with a terminal illness (or is chronically ill), the policy has been in force beyond the contestable period, and the insurer is creditworthy. Such purchases are called *viatical transactions*. They also may purchase policies when the insured is not terminal but is elderly. In this case the purchases are called *life settlement transactions*. The policyholder must apply for a viatical settlement and the company normally will review the applicant's medical history and condition. Viatical settlements may be controversial and are increasingly being regulated by the various states. As in the case of accelerated death benefits, a terminally ill insured can exclude amounts received from the sale of a life insurance contract to a viatical settlement provider from gross income.

Medicaid Planning for Long-Term (Custodial) Care

Assuming a person has not made adequate advance preparation for the long-term care exposure through LTC insurance, another strategy is to seek coverage for this exposure through government programs—mainly the Medicaid program. There are various techniques and possible pitfalls involved in this approach, which will be explored in this section.

---

[8] These annual dollar limits range from $250 for persons not more than 40 years old to $3,130 for persons over age 70 as of 2003.

Medicare and Private Health Insurance and the Long-Term Care Exposure

Medicare and private health insurance (other than LTC insurance) really cannot be counted on to meet the long-term care exposure. The Medicare benefits most likely to respond to the long-term care exposure—coverage of skilled nursing home care and home health care—are limited. For example, *Medicare nursing home coverage* applies only to skilled nursing care or skilled rehabilitative care, after medically necessary hospitalization for at least three consecutive days, and to admission to the skilled nursing facility within 30 days after the hospital discharge, only after a physician certifies the need for skilled care. Many custodial care facilities and levels of care would be precluded by these requirements. Further, Medicare covers only a maximum of 100 days of skilled nursing facility care, with a copayment for days 21 through 100. *Medicare home health care coverage* applies only to part-time or intermittent care to housebound patients under a physician's care who certifies the need for care.

In general, Medicare is designed to provide coverage for acute medical conditions rather than custodial care. However, limited coverage still may be available from Medicare, and it certainly should be investigated when faced with an actual need.

Private health insurance, aside from LTC insurance, normally specifically excludes expenses incurred for custodial care. This includes Medigap policies, which only fill the gaps in Medicare, rather than broadening that coverage to include LTC benefits. However, as in the case of Medicare, all forms of available private health insurance should be used to the extent feasible.

Medicaid

Medicaid is a federal-state public assistance (welfare) program aimed at providing broad medical expense benefits to certain categories of the needy. The overall standards for the program are established by the federal government, but the specific eligibility requirements and benefits provided vary among the states. Therefore, the specific requirements of a person's own state must be consulted in Medicaid planning.

Eligibility Requirements in General. To be eligible for Medicaid, persons must be in an eligible category and also must meet certain financial requirements of need. These financial requirements include resource (asset) limits and income limits. Some states place limits on both the assets a person may have and the income he or she may receive; other states limit only assets. However, even in states with no eligibility cap on income, a Medicaid recipient will be required to pay (spend down) virtually all of his or her privately available income for any nursing home care received before Medicaid will pay for the remaining cost.[9] Federal regulations define such income broadly as "… anything you receive in cash or in kind that you can use to meet your needs for food, clothing or shelter." The resource limit varies by state but generally is from $2000 to $3000 in nonexempt assets.

Benefits Provided. The services covered by Medicaid are very broad and, with a few exceptions, do not require any copayments, deductibles, or coinsurance by eligible recipients. They embrace not only comprehensive coverage for acute care but also substantial coverage for long-term care, such as unlimited nursing home care and home health care services.

What Assets and Income Are Considered in Determining Medicaid Eligibility?

Both Spouses Considered. The nonexempt assets of both spouses are considered in determining the eligibility of one spouse (or both spouses) for Medicaid. One spouse, for example, may be entering a nursing home for custodial care while the other still may be living independently in the outside community. The spouse in the nursing home may be referred to as the *institutionalized spouse* (who may be seeking eligibility for Medicaid), while the other, who is still living independently in the general community, may be referred to as the *community spouse* (or *healthy spouse*). In such a case, the nonexempt assets of both spouses will be counted in determining whether the resource limitation has been exceeded at the time that the institutionalized spouse applies for Medicaid.

There are, however, several exceptions to this general statement that may offer planning opportunities. First, this counting of the community spouse's assets is made only once, when the institutionalized spouse applies for Medicaid. It is like a snapshot picture of the community spouse's assets at that time. Therefore, nonexempt assets the community spouse may acquire after that date do not count toward the resource limit of the institutionalized spouse.

Second, the community spouse is allowed to keep the greater of a minimum amount or one-half the couple's total nonexempt assets up to a maximum dollar amount, without it being considered a resource. Further, states can increase this minimum up to the maximum amount.[10] Thus, the community spouse does not have to be completely impoverished in order for the institutionalized spouse to be eligible for Medicaid.

[9] Depending on state law, a Medicaid recipient may keep from $30 to $60 per month of his or her own income while in a nursing home.

[10] The minimum and maximum that the community spouse can keep in his or her own name without disqualifying the other spouse for Medicaid are indexed for inflation. The healthy spouse also may be able to keep additional assets, depending on the couple's income and expenses.

Third, the community spouse can keep all of his or her *own income* without affecting the other spouse's eligibility. Thus, it may be desirable to shift income to the community spouse, such as through the purchase of an annuity (subject to certain conditions).

Finally, the community spouse may be able to keep a portion of the *Medicaid recipient's income,* depending on the community spouse's expenses and the federal poverty rate of income for a two-person household.

Trust Assets or Income as a Resource of a Trust Beneficiary. With regard to *living (inter vivos) trusts*[11] created by anyone other than the Medicaid applicant or the applicant's spouse, and with regard to *testamentary trusts*[12] created by anyone, any trust assets or income that are required to be paid to a beneficiary or any trust assets or income that a beneficiary has the power to withdraw will be counted as a resource or as income for purposes of the beneficiary's eligibility for Medicaid. Hence, a planning technique may be to use discretionary trusts created by someone other than a potential Medicaid applicant or his or her spouse or discretionary testamentary trusts.

With regard to *living trusts* created by a Medicaid applicant or the applicant's spouse (as grantor) for the benefit of either of them, any trust assets or income that the trustee *may* pay out to the Medicaid applicant or the applicant's spouse, assuming full use of the trustee's discretion in favor of the Medicaid applicant or his or her spouse, will be counted as a resource or as income for purposes of determining the grantor-beneficiary's (or grantor-spouse's beneficiary's) eligibility for Medicaid. Under this rule, the applicable trust assets or income are deemed available to the applicant or his or her spouse whether they are actually paid to them by the trustee or not. These are referred to as *Medicaid qualifying trusts* (MQTs); such trusts cannot be used to facilitate eligibility for Medicaid. However, *testamentary trusts* created by anyone and *supplementary needs trusts* created by others are not MQTs and will not cause their assets or income to be counted as resources or income for a beneficiary's Medicaid eligibility.

Qualified Retirement Plans and IRAs as Available Resources. Qualified retirement plans, such as Section 401(k) plans, often are not counted as available resources for Medicaid eligibility and often are not required to be liquidated by a Medicaid applicant even when he or she is able to do so. On the other hand, IRAs and retirement plans for the self-employed (HR-10 plans) may be considered available resources and hence must be liquidated and spent down

---

[11] These are trusts created while the grantor or creator of the trust is alive. They are normally created by a deed of trust.

[12] These are trusts created after the grantor's or creator's death under the terms of the grantor's or creator's will.

before their owners can seek Medicaid nursing home coverage. Therefore, as a planning matter, it may not be desirable for someone who is likely to become a Medicaid applicant to roll over his or her qualified retirement plan balance into an IRA if it can be kept in a former employer's qualified retirement plan.

Exempt Assets. There are various assets a Medicaid applicant (or his or her spouse) can own that will not be counted in determining Medicaid eligibility. For example, an exempt asset may be an applicant's principal residence, subject to certain conditions and the possibility that the government may place a lien on the home to recover nursing home costs, which lien generally is exercisable at death or on the sale of the home. There are other exempt assets as well. Owning exempt assets and possibly converting nonexempt assets into exempt assets can present Medicaid planning possibilities.

Transferred Assets. Certain gratuitous transfers of assets (gifts) by the applicant or the applicant's spouse will cause the value of those assets to be considered resources of the applicant and may result in the applicant's being ineligible for Medicaid for a period of time. Thus, transfers of assets to family members or others (other than the applicant's spouse, since their assets are considered together) to get below the resource limit for Medicaid eligibility must be done within certain rules for proper planning. These rules are discussed separately in the next section.

Asset Transfers and Medicaid Eligibility

Persons who are faced with the need for long-term nursing home care (or their families) may want to transfer as much of their assets as possible to family members and then qualify for Medicaid. The alternative (assuming there is no LTC insurance) would be for the person to exhaust (spend down) almost all his or her nonexempt assets in paying for the care before he or she could reach the resource limit to qualify for Medicaid. In this case, there probably would be little left after the person's death. However, the government has placed rules and possibly roadblocks in the way of such planning.

The Lookback Rule and Planning Techniques. Transfers of assets for less than fair market value (gifts) by a potential Medicaid applicant or his or her spouse within the so-called lookback period will be attributed back to the applicant as available resources and may cause the applicant to be temporarily ineligible. The lookback period is 36 months (or 60 months for transfers to certain trusts) prior to the date of application for Medicaid. The period of ineligibility for Medicaid that results from transfers of nonexempt assets within the lookback period (other than exempt transfers, described next) is the period in months measured by the value of the gratuitous transfer divided by the particular state's average monthly cost for private-pay nursing home care. Any such period of ineligibility begins to run from the date of the transfer within the lookback period.

Medicaid planning involving asset transfers may be used when there are enough assets (or insurance) so that application for Medicaid can be delayed until after the 36-month lookback period has ended. Suppose, for example, that John Smith, who is age 72 and divorced, owns $500,000 of nonexempt assets in his own name and needs to enter a nursing home for custodial care. The nursing home cost is $130 per day, or about $4000 per month. At the urging of his children, John transfers about $356,000 of his nonexempt assets to his children (or others) and retains around $144,000 to pay (spend down) for nursing home care for the 36-month lookback period ($4000 per month x 36 months = $144,000). At the end of the lookback period (perhaps even allowing a little longer for safety's sake), John would apply for Medicaid. The transfer to his children would not be counted as a resource because it was made before the lookback period began (36 months before applying for Medicaid). He would have virtually no nonexempt assets, because he had already spent them down for nursing home care and other expenses over the past 36 months. Thus, he would at that point be eligible for Medicaid, which would pay for nursing home care from then on.[13]

Exempt Transfers. Certain transfers are excluded from the previously described rules. These exempt transfers sometimes can present planning opportunities.

Cautions in Transferring Assets to Attain Medicaid Eligibility

There are downsides as well as advantages in transferring assets to attain Medicaid eligibility. To qualify for Medicaid, an applicant must virtually impoverish himself or herself, with the exception of exempt assets and other techniques discussed here. This has several implications.

It may cause intergenerational conflicts. The aged parent who seeks nursing home care may resist giving away virtually all of his or her life's savings, while the children may want to preserve at least some of those assets for themselves or future generations. Further, if the institutionalized person's condition should improve sufficiently to return to the community, what then? Some have suggested that there may be less favorable treatment in nursing homes for Medicaid patients than for private-paying patients. Such discrimination against Medicaid

---

[13] If John had income during this period, he might have to spend down the income before Medicaid would pay or, depending on state law, he might be ineligible for Medicaid. Also, if John had had a noninstitutionalized (community) spouse at the time he applied for Medicaid, her nonexempt assets (over the allowance discussed previously) would also be considered as available resources in determining John's eligibility.

patients is illegal, but the perception still may be that it exists. Finally, the coverage for persons on Medicaid, while broad, does have some limits.

Further, to the extent that lifetime giving is employed to attain Medicaid eligibility, the general cautions about making lifetime gifts (discussed more fully in Chapter 25) apply here. Particularly, if an aged person gives away assets with a low income tax basis (say, to children) and then dies, the assets do not get a stepped-up income tax basis in the hands of the children as they would if the children had inherited them at death. On the other hand, the general advantages of lifetime giving apply. Much depends on the facts of the particular situation.

Finally, it is clear that government policy does not favor transfers of resources to qualify for Medicaid. The Health Insurance Portability and Accountability Act (HIPAA) of 1996 introduced the bizarre concept of criminalizing transfers of assets that result in a period of ineligibility for Medicaid. In this statute, criminal penalties (a $10,000 fine and up to one year in prison) could be imposed on both persons transferring the assets and anyone knowingly advising them to do so, if disposing of the assets resulted in a period of ineligibility for Medicaid.[14] This provision of HIPAA was highly controversial, to say the least. In fact, it was amended just one year later (in the Balanced Budget Act of 1997) to make anyone potentially liable for criminal penalties only if they, for a fee, knowingly counsel or assist an individual to transfer assets to qualify for Medicaid, if such transfer results in a period of ineligibility. While this highly questionable law may be changed again, repealed, or declared unconstitutional in the future, the point is that the government clearly is attempting to discourage transfers to qualify for Medicaid. Who knows what rules may be in place in the future?

Thus, for persons or families who are in a position to make advance preparation for the custodial care exposure, such as through the purchase of adequate LTC insurance, these cautioning factors should be carefully considered. It may be better to insure against the LTC exposure. Of course, if a person is already advanced in years or is uninsurable and is in need of nursing home care, Medicaid planning may be the only viable alternative.

Overview of Medicaid Planning Techniques

We have seen that there can be a number of techniques that will aid in becoming eligible for Medicaid and conserving assets for the family. One possibility is to *convert nonexempt assets into exempt assets* to the extent feasible. For exam-

---

[14] As a matter of interest, see Patricia L. Harrison, "Granny's in the Clink—And Her Lawyer's There Too," *Probate & Property*, May/June 1997, pp. 7-11.

ple, cash and liquid assets (e.g., securities) could be used to pay off a mortgage on a residence or even to purchase a residence. Other exempt assets could also be purchased. Also, *nonexempt assets could be transferred to a community spouse* (an exempt transfer) so that the community spouse can have the maximum amount of assets allowed by law without having those assets considered in determining the institutionalized spouse's eligibility.

Another technique might be *to transfer a residence* (or other exempt assets) *to a community spouse* before the other spouse applies for Medicaid. Once the institutionalized spouse has qualified for Medicaid, the community spouse will be free to sell the residence or other exempt assets without disqualifying the institutionalized spouse.

Further, *income can be provided for a community spouse* because that spouse's income is not counted in determining Medicaid eligibility of the institutionalized spouse. One way to do this is for the community spouse to purchase an annuity contract with the income payments not to extend beyond the life expectancy of the community spouse. Such an annuity may not be considered a resource for Medicaid eligibility purposes, but rather as a source of income for the community spouse. A potential Medicaid applicant may also use *exempt transfers* of his or her nonexempt assets to the extent possible to shift these assets to other eligible family members.

As explained earlier, a common planning technique is to *transfer* part of a potential Medicaid applicant's *nonexempt assets to family members* (other than the applicant's spouse) before the lookback period begins (36 months or 60 months for certain trusts).

Finally, in their estate planning, others may consider the Medicaid eligibility status of family members. For example, suppose a potential community spouse has assets that he or she would like to leave at death for the benefit of a spouse who may be institutionalized. Instead of leaving the assets outright to the spouse (which might later disqualify that spouse for Medicaid), the propertied spouse might leave the assets under a testamentary trust, with the other spouse being a discretionary beneficiary only. Other family members also may use trusts that give broad discretionary powers to the trustee for the benefit of persons who may need to qualify for government assistance benefits.

7

Property and Liability Insurance

Buying appropriate property and liability insurance is important in planning for personal financial security. This is particularly true for liability insurance, because people in general have become so litigious and claims-conscious.

Property Insurance

There are two basic approaches to insuring property: specified perils coverage and all risks coverage (or all causes of physical loss coverage).

1. *Specified perils coverage* protects against the specific perils (causes of loss) named in the policy. Some common examples include homeowners policies 1, 2, and 4 (for personal property), 6 and 8, and certain dwelling forms (such as DP-1 and DP-2).
2. *All risks (or all causes of loss) coverage* protects against all the risks or perils that may cause loss to the covered property, *except* those specifically excluded in the policy. Thus, the exclusions are important in determining the real extent of all risks-type coverage. All risks coverage frequently is broader than specified perils coverage, but it also usually costs more. Some common examples of all risks coverage are homeowners policy 3, personal articles floater coverage (e.g., on furs, jewels, fine arts, stamp collections, and cameras), and automobile comprehensive physical damage insurance.

Which Coverage and in What Amount?

The question then becomes, which policies or coverages should be purchased? This often can be decided through an insurance survey of needs conducted by a qualified insurance professional.

Once decisions have been made about types of coverage, the amounts of insurance must be determined. Insureds normally want policy limits (including sublimits) that are adequate to cover losses likely to occur from covered damage to the various kinds of property at risk, including adequate limits to meet any replacement cost provisions in homeowners policies.

Personal Liability

A potentially greater risk is the loss of assets or earnings through the judicial process as a result of one's negligence or other legal liability. Large liability judgments and settlements are commonplace today. When consumers look at their personal liability exposures, the following general *categories of exposures* come to mind:

1. Ownership, rental, and/or use of automobiles
2. Ownership and/or rental of premises
3. Professional or business activities
4. Directorships or officerships in corporations, credit unions, school boards, and other organizations
5. Employment of others
6. Ownership, rental, or use of watercraft or aircraft
7. Other personal activities

These exposures can be covered by a variety of liability insurance coverages. We shall consider first the *comprehensive personal liability coverage,* which can be purchased separately but usually is bought as a part of a homeowners policy.

Comprehensive Personal Liability Coverage

Daily nonbusiness activities entail a host of exposures to loss through legal liability. A person's dog bites a neighbor, a visitor trips and falls on the front walk, or a tee shot on the eighth hole slices and hits another golfer—all these accidents could result in liability losses.

Comprehensive personal liability (CPL) insurance (using the Liability Coverages—Section II of the homeowners policy for illustrative purposes) agrees to pay on behalf of an insured[1] all sums up to the policy limit that the insured becomes legally obligated to pay as damages because of bodily injury and property damage. The insurance company also agrees to defend the insured in any suit that would be covered by the policy, even if the suit is groundless, false, or fraudulent. However, the insurer's duty to defend ends

---

[1] The word "insured" includes the named insured and, if residents of his or her household, his or her relatives and any other person under the age of 21 in the care of an insured.

when the amount the insurer pays for damages resulting from an occurrence equals the policy's limit of liability. This is an important reason to carry adequate limits of liability.

The above stated insuring agreement is limited by certain important exclusions.

Coverage does not apply to the following, for example:

1. Business or professional pursuits. (Separate liability insurance is available for such exposures and some insurers endorse limited coverage on their homeowners forms.)
2. Ownership, maintenance, or use of automobiles, larger watercraft, and aircraft. (Separate policies are used to cover each of these exposures.)
3. Injury or damage caused intentionally by the insured. (Some forms of intentional torts can be covered by personal injury coverage that can be purchased through umbrella liability policies discussed elsewhere in this chapter.)
4. Benefits payable under any workers' compensation law.
5. Liability assumed by the insured under any unwritten contract or agreement or under any business contract or agreement.
6. Damage to property rented to, used by, or in the care of the insured (except for property damage caused by fire, smoke, or explosion) or property owned by an insured or bodily injury to an insured.
7. Bodily injury or property damage arising from controlled substances, criminal activities, communicable diseases, and certain other activities of insureds.

In addition to basic liability coverage, CPL insurance also covers medical payments and damage to property of others. Medical payments coverage agrees to pay reasonable expenses incurred by persons other than insureds within three years from the date of an accident for necessary medical, surgical, dental, and similar services for each person who sustains bodily injury caused by an accident while on the insured's premises with permission, and elsewhere, if the accident is caused by an insured, a resident employee, or an animal owned by the insured. Note that this provision is not based on the insured's legal liability. Damage to property of others promises to pay under certain conditions for loss of property belonging to others caused by an insured up to a policy limit, again without regard to the legal liability of the insured.

Limits of Liability

CPL insurance provides bodily injury liability and property damage liability coverage on a single-limit basis—which means that one limit of liability, such as $100,000 or $300,000 or more, applies to each occurrence regardless of the number of persons injured or the amount of separate property damage. Medical payments coverage is written subject to a per-person limit for each accident.

Homeowners Insurance

When basic property coverages and CPL coverage are added to some other coverages (such as personal theft insurance) or, in some cases, written on an all risks basis, the resulting package is called a *homeowners policy.*

Types of Policies

There are basically six variations of homeowners policies, as follows:

Policy Type	Description
Homeowners 1 (HO-1) (basic)	Provides limited property coverage. Not commonly used today.
Homeowners 2 (HO-2) (broad form)	Provides broader specified perils property coverage.
Homeowners 3 (HO-3)	All risks on buildings and broad form on personal property.
Homeowners 4 (HO-4)	Personal property coverage only (broad form); for tenants.
Homeowners 6 (HO-6)	Personal property and loss-of-use coverage (broad form), and certain dwelling coverage within the unit and for which the unit owner may have insurance responsibility under an association agreement, for condominium and cooperative unit owners.
Homeowners 8 (HO-8)	Coverage on buildings and personal property somewhat more limited than HO-1; used to provide coverage on homes that may not meet the insurer's underwriting requirements for other homeowners forms.

Homeowners policies contain a set of standard coverages that may be altered by endorsements that increase the amount of insurance, broaden the coverage, or modify conditions or restrictions. The table shows an example of coverages and limits under an HO-3.[2]

Section I Property Coverages		
Coverage A	Dwelling	$150,000 (selected by the insured or recommended by the insurer)
Coverage B	Other structures	$15,000 (10% of dwelling amount, but may be increased)
Coverage C	Personal property (unscheduled[3]) that is anywhere in the world	$75,000 (50% of dwelling amount, but may be increased, or reduced to 40%)
	Personal property, usually at a residence of an insured other than the residence premises described in the policy	$7500 (10% of the Coverage C limit, but not less than $1000)
Coverage D	Loss of use (including additional living expenses)	$30,000 (20% of dwelling amount)

Section II Liability Coverages		
Coverage E	Personal liability	$300,000 each occurrence
Coverage F	Medical payments to others	$1000 each person

Replacement Cost Provision

The replacement cost provision that applies to coverages A and B (the dwelling and other structures) is advantageous to the insured because, if the proper amount of insurance is maintained, the insured can recover any loss to the

[2] Homeowners policies generally follow this basic pattern, but variations exist in certain states and under the forms used by some insurers.

[3] *Unscheduled* means property that is not specifically named or listed in a schedule in the policy. As we shall see later, a policyholder sometimes needs to list certain luable property in a separate schedule for full coverage.

dwelling and private structures (but not personal property, unless additional coverage is purchased to provide replacement cost coverage on replaceable personal contents) on the basis of the full cost to repair or replace the damaged property *without any deduction for depreciation.* Without such a provision, the homeowners policy would pay only the actual cash value at the time of the loss of lost or damaged property. Actual cash value (ACV) normally means replacement cost new minus the amount the property has physically depreciated since it was built or was new. Note that property physically depreciates even though its market value may be rising or falling.

But the insured must carry enough insurance relative to the value of the dwelling to get the benefit of this replacement cost provision. Specifically, the homeowners policy provides that if the insured carries insurance on a building equal to at least 80 percent of its replacement cost new, any covered loss to the building will be paid to the extent of the full cost to repair or replace the damage without deducting depreciation, up to the policy limit. The policy provides for a lesser recovery if the insurance is less than 80 percent of replacement cost. Therefore, it is important to maintain enough insurance to meet the 80 percent requirement.

Instead of this standard replacement cost provision, however, some homeowners policies may have added to them a replacement or repair cost protection endorsement under which, if the insured allows the insurance company to adjust the coverage A dwelling limit (and the premium) in accordance with a property evaluation by the insurer, the limit of liability on the dwelling will automatically increase to its current replacement cost if there is a loss that exceeds the limit stated in the policy. (There are also corresponding proportionate increases in the limits for coverages B, C, and D.) In addition, if the insured conforms to the terms of the endorsement, losses to the dwelling and other structures will be paid on a replacement cost basis. This endorsement is valuable since it relieves the insured of the problem of estimating the right amount of insurance to meet the requirements of the standard replacement cost condition.

Further, in most states the insured can buy an *inflation guard endorsement* on homeowners policies that automatically increases coverage limits periodically by small percentage amounts. Finally, it may be possible to purchase for an additional premium a personal property replacement cost endorsement that extends replacement cost coverage to personal property (coverage C) under certain conditions.

Internal Limits (Sublimits)

Another thing to consider in property and liability insurance planning is the smaller internal limits (called *sublimits*) that apply to certain kinds of property under homeowners policies. Following are some of the more important of these sublimits.

1. $200 aggregate limit on money, bank notes, bullion, gold other than goldware, silver other than silverware, platinum, coins, and medals
2. $1000 aggregate limit on securities, accounts, deeds, and similar property, or stamps, including philatelic property (stamp collections)
3. $1000 aggregate limit on watercraft, including their trailers, furnishings, equipment, and outboard motors
4. $1000 aggregate limit on trailers not used with watercraft
5. $1000 aggregate limit for loss by theft of jewelry, watches, precious and semiprecious stones, and furs
6. $2000 aggregate limit for loss by theft of firearms
7. $2500 aggregate limit for loss by theft of silverware, silver-plated ware, goldware, gold-plated ware, and pewterware
8. $2500 aggregate limit on property on the residence premises used at any time for any business purpose

The effect of these internal limits may be to make it necessary to schedule specifically additional amounts of insurance on certain property items. This can be done under a *scheduled personal property endorsement* added to the homeowners policy or under a separate *personal articles floater.* Kinds of property that often are separately scheduled and insured include jewelry, furs, cameras, musical instruments, silverware, golf equipment, guns, fine arts, stamps, and coins.

Liability Exclusions

Proper planning for personal liability requires analysis of the liability exclusions under homeowners policies and making sure that there are no uncovered exposures. The following are some potential liability exposures that should be reviewed and evaluated:

1. Watercraft owned by an insured with inboard or inboard-outdrive motor power, or rented to an insured if it has inboard-outdrive motor power of more than 50 horsepower, or a sailing vessel of 26 feet or more in length owned by an insured, or if it is powered by outboard motor(s) of more than 25 horsepower and owned by any insured under certain conditions. For excluded watercraft, boat or yacht insurance may be needed.
2. Aircraft or aircraft exposures.
3. Rendering or failing to render professional services.
4. Most business pursuits of an insured.
5. Any premises, other than an insured premises, owned by or rented to any insured.

6. Cases where the insured is liable to provide workers' compensation benefits or does provide such benefits.
7. Bodily injury or property damage that is expected or intended by the insured.

Eligibility

To be eligible for homeowners coverage, a dwelling must be occupied by the owner. Seasonal dwellings not rented to others are considered to be owner-occupied.

Cost

Homeowners premiums reflect many factors and can vary among insurers. The policies usually have a deductible applying to losses under property damage coverages, which can be increased for a reduced premium.

Automobile Insurance
Coverages Provided

Personal auto policies typically may provide the coverages shown in the table.

Part A	Liability coverage (including bodily injury and property damage liability)
Part B	Medical payments coverage
Part C	Uninsured motorists coverage (or uninsured/ underinsured motorists coverage)
Part D	Damage to covered autos (including comprehensive, collision, towing and labor, and transportation expenses)

About half the states have enacted some form of no-fault auto insurance that may remove at least some auto accidents from the realm of negligence liability. Auto policies issued to residents of these states contain the appropriate no-fault endorsement or coverage for that state. These no-fault benefits may be called *personal injury protection* (PIP), *basic reparations benefits,* or by other names. They basically are payable to injured, covered persons by their own insurance company without their having to show that anyone was negligent in causing their injuries. Depending on state law, the injured persons then may or may not have restrictions placed on their right to sue the negligent motorists who caused their injuries. Some states have adopted what are called *choice* no-fault plans. Under these plans, insured persons can voluntarily relinquish a part of their right to sue in return for reduced auto insurance premiums. This is something to consider as a cost-saving measure.

The insuring agreement of the automobile liability policy covers the insured's liability arising out of the ownership, maintenance, or use of owned and nonowned automobiles. Commonly used policies, such as the *personal auto policy* (PAP), have a single limit of liability that applies to all covered liability arising out of an accident, regardless of the number of persons injured or the amount of separate property damage.

Liability (bodily injury and property damage)	$300,000 each occurrence
Medical payments	$5000 each person in any one accident
Uninsured motorists	$30,000 each occurrence
Collision and/or other than collision (subject to a $100 deductible)	Actual cash value
Statutory	Personal injury protection per endorsement

For example, some sample limits for a PAP might be as follows:

Uninsured motorist coverage generally provides a minimum limit for bodily injury from uninsured and hit-and-run motorists. An insured may also purchase underinsured motorists coverage, which covers in the event another motorist has valid liability insurance but the limits are insufficient to pay the full amount of the insured's legally recoverable damages against the other motorist.

The next coverages are property insurance (technically called *physical damage* coverage) on the insured's own car. *Other than collision* (or comprehensive) provides broad all risks coverage except for collision. Recovery is made on an actual cash-value basis. *Collision* also is written on an actual cash-value basis. A deductible(s) normally applies to both collision and comprehensive coverages. Finally, in the illustrative limits cited here, the policy contains a mandatory state no-fault endorsement. This would not be so in states that do not have automobile no-fault laws (although they might provide out-of-state no-fault coverage).

Persons Insured

Under the PAP, the following are considered to be a "covered person" in terms of liability coverage:

1. The "named insured" (i.e., the person named in the policy declarations), his or her spouse if a resident of the same household, and any family member (i.e., a person related to the named insured or spouse by blood, marriage, or adoption and a resident of the insured's household) with respect to the ownership, maintenance, or use of any auto or trailer
2. Any person using the insured's covered auto
3. Any other person or organization with regard to the insured's covered auto, but only for legal responsibility for the acts or omissions of a person for whom coverage otherwise is provided under the liability part of the policy
4. Any other person or organization with regard to any auto other than the insured's covered auto, but only for legal responsibility for the acts or omissions of the named insured, his or her spouse, and any family member covered under the liability part of the policy

This can be generally summed up by saying that the auto insurance follows the insured and a covered auto.

As always, exclusions are important in defining the coverage of an insurance contract. The following are some of the important liability exclusions of the PAP.

1. Damage to property owned or being transported by a covered person.
2. Damage to property rented to, used by, or in the care of a covered person.
3. Bodily injury to an employee of a covered person during the course of employment; however, this exclusion does not apply to a *domestic employee* unless workers' compensation benefits are required for or made available for that employee.
4. Liability arising out of the ownership or operation of a vehicle while it is being used to carry persons or property for a fee; however, this exclusion does not apply to normal share-the-expense car pools.
5. The ownership, maintenance, or use of a motorcycle or other self-propelled vehicle having fewer than four wheels. (Additional liability coverage is needed for this kind of exposure.)
6. The ownership, maintenance, or use of any vehicle, other than the insured's covered autos, that is owned by or furnished or available for the regular use of the named insured or his or her spouse.
7. The ownership, maintenance, or use of any vehicle, other than the

insured's covered autos, that is owned by or furnished or available for the regular use of any family member; however, this exclusion does not apply to the named insured or his or her spouse.

8. Any person using a vehicle without a reasonable belief that the person is entitled to do so.

Cost

The rating of automobile liability insurance generally is based on four factors: (1) age and perhaps sex of drivers, (2) use of the auto, (3) territory where the car is garaged, and (4) the operators' driving records. Auto physical damage rates generally are affected by such factors as the cost (new) of the car and its age. As the years go by, the actual cash value of a car diminishes through depreciation and thus the physical damage premium also declines. However, at some point in the life of a car, it normally is economical for the insured to consider dropping his or her collision (and perhaps comprehensive) coverage. The value left to insure simply is not worth even a reduced premium.

It generally costs relatively little to increase auto liability limits to a more adequate level. There is no simple formula to determine the "correct" limit of liability an insured should carry. The problem, however, generally is best solved by paying the small cost difference for the higher limits. Of course, the problem also can be solved by carrying an adequate excess or umbrella liability policy, described later in this chapter.

The cost of automobile insurance can vary considerably among insurance companies. Thus, consumers or their advisors may secure significant savings by shopping around for their automobile insurance. Of course, as explained in Chapter 3, cost is not the only factor that should be considered. In the area of physical damage insurance, one major cost-cutting technique that often is not utilized fully is the use of higher deductibles.

Variations in Policies

Up to this point, we have been talking about the personal auto policy (PAP). Many individuals and families are covered by the PAP. However, some insurers (including some large ones) use their own forms of automobile insurance policies.

In addition, there are other kinds of automobile policies used, each serving its own purpose. A *basic automobile form* is used to insure commercial vehicles as well as some private passenger automobiles. A *comprehensive automobile policy* also may be used by businesses or individuals.

Other Property and Liability Policies to Consider

Personal Excess (Umbrella) Liability

The desire of individuals for higher liability limits and broader protection inspired the creation of the personal excess liability, catastrophe liability, or umbrella contract. It is "excess" insurance and so there are required underlying liability policies, such as automobile and homeowners policies. Many personal umbrella policies are issued with a minimum limit of $1 million, but higher limits are available. In fact, some insurers are willing to write very high limits for high-net-worth persons. Personal umbrella policies are issued by many insurers, but they are not standardized. The umbrella policy is designed to pay and defend liability claims after the limits of underlying liability policies are exhausted.

For example, suppose John Doe is involved in an auto accident and, as the result of his negligence, Richard Roe is seriously injured. A jury finds John liable to Richard for damages of $500,000. John's automobile policy, written with a single limit of $300,000, which John thought was "more than adequate," pays its limit of $300,000. Unfortunately for him, John remains personally liable for the remaining $200,000. However, if John had purchased a personal umbrella policy with, say, a $1 million limit, this excess policy would have paid the $200,000 on his behalf.

In addition, personal umbrella policies are written on a broad coverage basis. This results in some important extensions of coverage, such as:

- Property damage liability for loss to property of others in the insured's care, custody, or control
- Worldwide coverage (no territorial restriction)
- Coverage of specified personal injury claims, which might include libel, slander, false arrest, wrongful entry, invasion of privacy, malicious prosecution, and the like.

Such extensions, which are not covered by the underlying liability policies, are subject to a deductible (called a *self-insured retention* or SIR) that might be $250 or more.

Most people, whether they think of themselves as well off or not, should consider buying personal umbrella liability insurance. While the likelihood of a jumbo or catastrophic liability loss is small, such a loss would destroy the person financially. That is not a risk people can afford to take. Furthermore, the premium is not burdensome. Also, a personal umbrella policy may require underlying liability insurance with lower limits than the insured now is carrying. Thus, the insured may be able to reduce some present liability limits and save some premium there.

Directors and Officers Liability

A trend by the courts of imposing liability on officers and directors of corporations (and other organizations) in connection with the performance of their duties therein has increased the need for insurance to meet this risk. The directors and officers liability (D&O) policy covers any "wrongful act," which generally is defined as a breach of duty, neglect, error, misstatement, misleading statement, or omission.

For persons serving on various kinds of boards of directors or otherwise subject to this exposure, there is the potential for catastrophic financial loss. This has been particularly true in recent years, with the increased concern over corporate governance. Thus, persons so exposed or invited to serve on boards should inquire into what protection they are afforded by the corporations or organizations in question. Sometimes the organization agrees to indemnify its directors and then carries D&O coverage to protect itself, while other times the organization carries D&O coverage that directly covers its directors.

Professional Liability

Many professionals and businesspeople need liability coverage to protect themselves against claims and suits arising out of possible or alleged negligence or errors or omissions in the practice of their professions or business pursuits. Such claims and suits are not covered under other personal liability coverages.

Specialized professional liability forms are needed to cover this exposure. Such professional liability policies often are written on a *claims-made* basis. This normally means the event or incident covered must occur after a retroactive date stated in the policy and a claim arising out of the event or incident must be made and reported to the insurance company during the policy period.

The other kinds of liability insurance policies discussed in this chapter are *occurrence* forms. This means the covered injury or event must occur during the policy period, but claim can be made for it and reported to the insurance company during the policy period or after the policy period ends. Occurrence forms generally are more favorable from the insured's viewpoint than claims-made forms.

Coverage Under Business Liability Policies

Sometimes executive officers or employees can be sued personally for their activities on behalf of their employer (say, a corporation). It may be alleged that they caused bodily injury, property damage, or personal injury to others. Business liability policies (such as the commercial general liability form) normally broadly define who is insured so as to include executive officers and employees so long as they are acting within the limits of their employment or duties with the employer. If a person feels that he or she may have a business liability exposure, the person or his or her advisors may want to check into the employer's liability coverage.

Workers' Compensation and Other Employment Liability

The states, the District of Columbia, and the federal government have workers' compensation laws that set forth the benefits payable to employees who suffer on-the-job injuries and occupational diseases. This risk may seem somewhat remote in the context of personal risk management, but certain states include domestic and/or casual employees under their workers' compensation acts. Therefore, depending on the particular state law, a person may need or voluntarily carry workers' compensation insurance for such employees.

Another area of liability that some individuals, particularly those with high net worth, could face is employment practices liability. This would involve claims by their employees that they suffered various forms of employment discrimination. Some insurers include employment practices liability coverage in the personal umbrella forms for some insureds.

Investment Properties

Investment properties a person may own or manage present risks of loss similar to those discussed previously. Because homeowners policies are limited to owner-occupants, commercial policies may be used to provide the necessary property and liability protection.

Flood Exposure

Homeowners policies exclude property damage caused by flood or mudslide. In some areas, these can be important exposures. In most cases, the only source of flood and mudslide coverage for individuals is through the National Flood Insurance Program (NFIP). This is a federal program, but the insurance is sold through private insurance agents, brokers, and some insurance companies.

Insurance Companies and Premiums

As in other lines of insurance, the final cost of property and liability insurance to the consumer can vary considerably among insurers. Therefore, consumers or their advisors often can save money by shopping for coverage. The Internet can be a resource in this respect.

Insurer Selection

Security, service, and cost are the three yardsticks against which insurers should be measured. These criteria were discussed in Chapter 3.

Types of Property and Liability Insurers

Property and liability insurers sell their products in different ways; these approaches may have cost implications. In this sense insurers are (1) independent agency companies (distribution through independent insurance agents who represent several insurance companies), (2) exclusive agency companies (which distribute their products through agents representing only the one company), and (3) direct writers (distribution through company-employed salespeople or the mails). Additionally, insurers can be classified on the basis of their organizational form as stock insurers, mutual insurers, reciprocal exchanges, and so forth.

Investments and Investment Planning

8

Basic Investment Principles

A financial objective of many people is to accumulate capital. However, once a person has acquired capital, he or she needs to consider how to invest the capital and make it grow. Perhaps the most widely followed technique for accomplishing this is *asset allocation*, which is discussed in Chapter 13

The Basic Investment Objective

The basic investment objective of most people is to *earn the maximum possible total, after-tax rate of return* on the funds available for investment, *consistent with the person's investment objectives and the investment limitations or constraints under which he or she must operate.* This statement does not mean that rate of return is the only investment consideration. There are a number of other factors to be considered. However, after all these factors are taken into account, most people want the highest total, after-tax rate of return they can get, given the choices open to them.

Investment Directly or Through Financial Intermediaries

People can invest by buying and holding assets directly in their own names or jointly with their spouse or someone else. Then, the responsibility for investment selection, management, and performance falls on the persons themselves, but they do not have to pay any direct or indirect investment management fees and administrative charges.

On the other hand, people can invest through financial intermediaries that will perform investment selection and management functions and render certain administrative services. For performing these functions, the intermediary levies a fee or charge in some fashion, either directly or indirectly. Some important financial intermediaries and the way in which they charge for their services are listed below.[1]

Financial intermediary	Way of charging for investment management and other services
Investment companies (e.g., mutual funds)	Annual percentage charge against the assets in the fund (called the *expense ratio*)
Variable annuities	Annual percentage charges against the assets in the account (referred to as the *account level charge*) and against the assets in the various subaccounts selected (referred to as the *fund level charge*)
Variable life insurance	Annual percentage charges against the assets in the account (referred to as the *account level charge*) and against the assets in the various subaccounts selected (referred to as the *fund level charge*)
Revocable trusts (through banks or trust companies, either as separately administered trusts or through common trust funds)	Annual trustees' fees, usually expressed as an annual percentage charge against trust assets and perhaps trust income (usually with a minimum annual fee that is higher for separately administered trusts than for trusts invested in the bank's mutual funds or common trust funds)
Investment management accounts	Annual management fees, often expressed as an annual percentage charge against assets under management (usually with a *minimum annual fee)*

There are, of course, other financial intermediaries that provide guaranteed

---

[1] There may be other costs for some of these financial intermediaries, such as sales costs (marketing loads or costs), other administrative charges, and insurance-type fees. These also must be evaluated when considering a particular intermediary in terms of the value provided to consumers. It also may be argued that investment options under some kinds of employee-benefit plans, such as qualified savings plans, can be considered like financial intermediaries.

principal products for the public, including CDs from banks and thrift institutions, traditional or universal (nonvariable) life insurance from life insurance companies, fixed (nonvariable) annuities from life insurance companies, and others. These investment media, however, do not provide separate investment management to the public for a fee. The cost of their services really is reflected in the interest rates they pay.

The classical arguments for investing through financial intermediaries include professional management, diversification, relief from the burdens of investment decision-making, and convenience for investments of small amounts. Balanced against these advantages is the cost of financial intermediaries. Thus, the real questions for the consumer in deciding whether to invest directly or through one or more financial intermediaries are two: Are these advantages worth the cost? and Does the consumer feel able to do on his or her own about as well as through the intermediary or perhaps even better? There also are income tax implications in investing directly or through various intermediaries. Of course, investors can diversify their decisions in this area and invest some of their assets directly and others through one or more intermediaries.

Investment and Speculation

At one time it was common to draw a rather sharp distinction between *investment* and *speculation*. For example, high-grade bonds were considered investments, while common stocks were viewed as speculative. Now, however, such distinctions are blurred. Good-grade *blue-chip* common stocks generally are looked upon today as investment-grade securities, while below-investment-grade *junk bonds* may not be. Also, many people today invest for capital gains as well as for dividends or interest income.

In general, however, the term *speculation* probably can be used to mean the purchase of securities or other assets in the hope that their fluctuations in value will produce relatively large profits in a comparatively short time. In other words, the *speculator* takes risks in the hope of immediate and sizeable gains.

Are prudent investors to avoid speculation, as we have just defined it? The answer seems to be that it depends on such things as how much of the total investment portfolio the investor wants to risk in speculation, what other kinds of assets are available for the family, how good the investor or his or her advisors are at speculating, and whether the investor has the temperament to take speculative losses as well as speculative gains. Although speculation is not necessarily bad, it seems reasonable to say that most people are not really prepared to speculate successfully. They generally are better off investing more conservatively for the long pull.

Factors in the Choice of Investments

A number of factors or investment characteristics may be considered in choosing among categories of investments or individual investments. The following commonly are included:

- Security of principal and income
- Rate of return (yield)
- Marketability and liquidity
- Diversification
- Tax status
- Size of investment units or denominations
- Use as collateral for loans
- Protection against creditor's claims
- Callability
- Freedom from care

No single kind of investment is superior to all others in every one of these characteristics. For example, to earn a higher rate of return, it is usually necessary to sacrifice security of principal and income. Stated in a different way, higher investment returns normally are associated with higher investment risks. Thus, when any investment is considered in relation to these factors, investors should do so in terms of *their needs and objectives,* the *characteristics of alternative investments,* and *the degree of overall investment risk* (in terms of variability of asset values and incomes) the investor is willing to assume in his or her overall (total) portfolio.

Security of Principal and Income

For many investors, security of principal and income is of paramount importance. They want to be able to get their money back or not lose money on their investments. This is perfectly natural and may be referred to as being *risk-averse.*

But when this factor is analyzed more closely, other fundamental questions arise, such as what kinds of "security" we mean and over what investment time frame. Thus, investors or their advisors really need to keep in mind five different types of risks to investment values: financial risk, market risk, interest rate risk to values of existing investments, interest rate risk to income from investments, and purchasing power risk. They also should consider how these risks are correlated with each other in a total investment portfolio.

Financial (or Credit) Risk

This risk arises because the issuers of investments may run into financial difficulties and not be able to live up to their promises or expectations. For example, a person who buys a corporate bond runs the financial risk that the issuing corporation will default on the interest payments and/or the principal amount at maturity. The buyer of common stock runs the financial risk that the corporation will reduce or eliminate its dividend payments or go bankrupt, so that its stock becomes worthless.

Market Risk

This is the risk arising out of price fluctuations for a whole securities market, for an industrial group, or for an individual security, regardless of the financial ability of particular issuers to pay promised investment returns or stay solvent. Thus, even if an investor selects a high-quality stock that has prospects for good earnings growth and low financial risk, the stock still may experience price declines if the investor's market timing is bad or if market expectations are temporarily out of line with reality.

Interest Rate Risk to Values of Existing Investments

This risk is a little complex: it involves price changes of *existing* investments because of changes in the general level of interest rates in the capital markets. In general, a *rise* in general market interest rates tends to cause a *decline* in market prices for existing securities and, conversely, a *decline* in interest rates tends to cause a *rise* in market prices for existing securities. Thus, market prices for existing securities tend to move *inversely* with changes in the general level of interest rates.

Example. It is not difficult to see why this is true. Assume, for example, that 10 years ago an investor purchased a newly issued, high grade corporate bond with a 7 percent interest rate for $1000 (at par). The bond was to come due (mature) in 30 years. Therefore, the investor receives interest of $70 per year from the bond. At the time the investor bought the bond (10 years ago), the prevailing level of interest rates in the capital markets for bonds of this type, grade, and duration was around 7 percent; otherwise this bond issue could not have been sold successfully to the public. But in the meantime the general level of interest rates in the capital markets for bonds of this type, grade, and remaining duration has risen, and now (10 years later) the prevailing interest rate for comparable bonds with a 20-year duration is about 9 percent.

What effect does this have on the existing bond? First of all, the 7 percent interest rate (coupon rate) on the bond does not change, because this was set by the terms of the bond indenture when it was originally issued. So the investor still will get interest of $70 per year until the bond matures 20 years from now. Also, when the bond matures in 20 years, the investor will get the full $1000 maturity value from the issuing corporation. Unfortunately, however, the current market price of the bond in the bond markets will have declined to somewhere in the vicinity of $816.[2] Why is this so if it is a $1000 bond? Because at about this price the yield to maturity (in 20 years) of this bond would be 9 percent and this is the prevailing market interest rate. Therefore, since we assume investors can buy newly issued bonds at around 9 percent, the prices of existing bonds carrying lower interest rates must decline in the market to the point where they will offer generally comparable yields to maturity for a buyer. When the market price of bonds declines in this manner below their maturity value, they are said to be selling *at a discount* and are called *market discount bonds.*[3]

Now, what will happen if interest rates in the capital markets should decline? Assume, for example, that five years pass and during that time the prevailing interest rate for comparable bonds moves from 9 to 6 percent. This would mean that the current market price of the existing 7 percent bond would rise to somewhere around $1,098 (or to a premium). Again, why? Because at about this price the yield to maturity (in 15 years) of this bond would be 6 percent, and this is now the prevailing market interest rate.

Applications. We have illustrated this interest rate risk in terms of a 30-year corporate bond. Does it also apply to other types of securities? Yes! Changes in the general level of interest rates have some influence on the prices of all securities. For example, when interest rates generally rise, bonds may become more attractive than common stocks for some investors, thus exerting a downward pressure on the stock market. Of course, the reverse is true when general market interest rates fall.

In general, prices of securities that are of high quality because of their low financial risk tend to be the *most* affected by changes in interest rates. This is so because the financial risk factor has relatively little impact on their market prices. *High-grade bonds* fall into this category. However, prices of other securities, such as *high-quality preferred stocks* and *certain types of common stocks* (such as *high-grade utility, insurance,* and *bank stocks*), also may be significantly influenced by changes in interest rates.

Further, the longer the maturity of bonds, the more influenced their prices will be by changes in market interest rates. This is because, once a bond

---

[2] A bond calculator (or table) shows that a 20-year bond with a 7 percent coupon rate will yield 9 percent to maturity if it is priced at 81.60 ($816).

[3] Bonds also may be originally issued at a discount from their ultimate maturity value, so that some or all of their annual interest return comes from the gradually accruing increase in their value as the bond approaches maturity. These are called original-issue discount (OID) bonds and are of a different nature than the point being made in this section.

matures, it will be paid off by the issuer at par (its maturity value), regardless of the prevailing level of interest rates. Thus, for example, a 30-year U.S. Treasury bond will be much more affected by this interest rate risk than will, say, a five-year U.S. Treasury note.

Analysis of Possible "Rate Shocks." Investment portfolios containing a significant percentage (asset allocation) of high-grade bonds may be particularly subject to this interest rate risk. Portfolio managers and other investment professionals may attempt to evaluate the impact of possibly rising interest rates on their bond portfolios by using so-called "rate shock tests." Such tests show the hypothetical effect of assumed interest rate increases on the prices of particular high-quality bonds. Here is an example of a "rate shock table."

Maturity Existing Bond[1]	5-Year		10-Year		30-Year	
Market Interest Rate Increase	1% Point Increase	2% Points Increase	1% Point Increase	2% Points Increase	1% Point Increase	2% Points Increase
Price Change in Existing Bond[2]	−4.03%	−7.40%	−7.50%	−13.93%	−13.56%	−24.46%

1. These figures are based on U.S. Treasury notes and bonds of these maturities as of October 2002.
2. These price changes assume a decrease in bond prices over one year.

Individual investors may use such data to evaluate this interest rate risk to their bond portfolios (including bond mutual funds). For example, suppose John O'Malley has $300,000 of U.S. Treasury notes and bonds in his portfolio as follows: $100,000 of five-year Treasury notes, $100,000 of 10-year Treasury notes, and $100,000 of 30-year Treasury bonds. If market interest rates were to rise by 2 percentage points (200 basis points) in a year, the value of his bond portfolio would decline about 15.27 percent or $45,800 [($100,000 × .074) + ($100,000 × .139) + ($100,000 × .245) = $45,8000], according to the above rate shock table. Of course, directly owned bonds ultimately will be paid at face value at maturity and the prices and values of directly owned bonds and bond mutual funds will rise if market rates rise.

Interest Rate Risk to Income from Investments

From the viewpoint of maintaining the income from an investment portfolio, however, changes in interest rates may present a different kind of investment risk—that of declining interest (or dividend) income from bonds and preferred stocks that are *called* (redeemed) by their issuers prior to maturity and securities that mature when interest rates are lower than when they were issued or purchased.

Redemption or Call Risk. With respect to the *call risk,* the issuers of callable bonds and preferred stocks may redeem them when comparable market interest rates fall significantly below the coupon rates being paid on the securities. Thus, when securities are callable, the issuers can pay them off (redeem them) before maturity under certain conditions. This is disadvantageous for the holder of the called security, because he or she now must reinvest the principal at the present lower market yields.

For example, suppose Tina Rinaldi invested $100,000 in investment-grade, 30-year municipal bonds that paid 8 percent interest (coupon rate). Thus, her interest income from the bonds was $8,000 per year. Assume further that the bonds are callable at par (i.e., they can be redeemed by the municipality for the $1,000 face amount of each bond) any time after 10 years from time of issue. Suppose now that 10 years after these bonds were issued, interest rates for comparable bonds (i.e., 20-year, investment-grade, callable municipal bonds) have fallen to 5 percent. Under these conditions, it is almost certain that the municipality will call these bonds. Now Tina has her $100,000 back, but if she wants to invest in similar bonds, she can secure only 5 percent interest, which means an income of $5,000 per year, rather than the $8,000 per year she enjoyed for 10 years.

It can be seen that this call risk is important when investors would like to lock in current interest rates or yields for a reasonably long period of time, such as during their retirement years or in saving for a child's education. How to secure protection against the call risk is discussed later in this chapter under "Callability."

Short-Maturity Risk. This interest rate risk is from securities and other investments that mature when interest rates are lower than when they were purchased. The investor then must reinvest the proceeds at lower yields. This *reinvestment risk* really arises from investing in or holding short-term securities and other investments. For example, suppose that George and Martha Wilson place $75,000 of their retirement savings in three-year insured CDs (certificates of deposit) that then pay 6 percent interest. Thus, their annual income from these CDs is $4,500. However, at the end of the three-year period, when the CDs come due and the Wilsons are ready to roll them over into new CDs, assume the economy is in recession, the Federal Reserve has pushed shorter-term interest rates down to try to stimulate a recovery, and the interest rates currently being paid on comparable CDs and other similarly secure investments are around 3 percent. Now if the Wilsons place their $75,000 into comparable new CDs, their annual interest income will drop from $4,500 to $2,250, or a 50 percent decline. Of course, if shorter-term interest rates should rise, the reverse would be true and the Wilsons would be better off with their shorter-term investments.

A protection from reinvestment risk is to buy longer-term bonds or other securities with full or at least partial call protection, so as to lock in current interest rates for a reasonable period of time. Also, if market rates should fall, the market prices of long-term bonds would rise. But the downside of this strategy is that if market interest rates rise, the market prices of the long-term bonds would fall and the investor would lose his or her opportunity to invest at the higher current rates until the long-term investments matured or were sold, possibly at a loss.

There is no perfect answer to these interest rate risk dilemmas. If one expects market interest rates to rise, it is better to be in shorter-term bonds and other investments (i.e., to shorten maturities). On the other hand, if one expects market interest rates to fall, it is better to be in longer-term bonds and other investments with adequate call protection (i.e., to lengthen maturities). The problem is, of course, that no one can foretell which way interest rates will go in the future and what the relationship between short-term and long-term rates will be (i.e., what the yield curve will look like).

Laddered Diversification to Deal with Interest Rate Risks

In view of the uncertainties concerning interest rates just noted, one possible approach for the risk-averse investor is to diversify the bond or bond and CD portion (the fixed-income portion) of the overall portfolio according to the maturity of the instruments in the portfolio. This is referred to as *laddering* a bond portfolio.

Thus, just as an example, the bond and CD portion of an investor's overall portfolio might be laddered as shown in the table.

Maturity Range	Percentages of bond and CD portion of the overall fixed-income portfolio
1-5 years (short-term bonds or CDs)	33 1/3%
5-15 years (intermediate-term bonds)	33 1/3%
15-30 years (long-term bonds)	33 1/3%

With this kind of allocation, there would be some protection for the investor no matter which way interest rates went. If market rates declined, the investor would benefit at the long end of the portfolio and be harmed only at the short end. The portion of the portfolio with longer maturities could provide a locked-in interest income stream. On the other hand, if interest rates rose, the investor would not be greatly harmed at the short end of the portfolio and would be significantly harmed in terms of price only at the long end, although there would be at least some bond price declines at all maturity levels. The values of any bank-distributed CDs would not change except for possible interest penalties for early redemption. Further, at the short end of the portfolio, there would be some bonds or CDs maturing each year whose maturity values then could be reinvested at the current higher rates.

The allocation of maturities in a portfolio could be periodically reviewed in light of the investor's expectations for future interest rates. If rates are expected to rise, relatively greater weight can be given to shorter maturities; the strategy can be reversed if rates are expected to decline. Or the investor can simply stick with a more balanced and longer-term allocation, as shown in the example, and not try to outguess the economy.

Purchasing Power Risk

This is uncertainty over the future purchasing power of the income and principal from an investment. Purchasing power depends on changes in the general price level in the economy. When prices rise, purchasing power declines; and when prices decline, purchasing power rises. Since around 1940, the United States has experienced a rather steady inflationary trend, given some periods of general price stability, with a consequent generally consistent decline in the purchasing power of the dollar. This has led many investors to seek investments whose principal and income they hope will increase during an inflationary period, so that the purchasing power of their investment dollars at least will not decline. Such investments are often called *inflation hedges*.

The purchasing power risk to investment values is a real one, but the concept of some investments being good hedges against inflation must be considered with care. First, no investment generally available in the United States can be counted on to fluctuate at all times so that its purchasing power will be maintained.[4] Second, while some types of investments, such as common stocks, *may* increase in value at the same time that the general price level is rising, there is no assurance that this will be true for an individual stock, several stocks, the stocks of a whole industry group, or the stock market as a whole. The only thing that can be said is that economic studies have shown that over long periods of years broad indexes of common stock prices have *tended* to move in the same general direction as consumer prices. There have been a number of times, however, during which common stock prices and consumer prices did *not* move together. Finally, *an investor's goal is not really to hedge against inflation, but rather*

---

[4] Exceptions to this statement include the inflation-indexed U.S. Treasury securities that were first issued by the government in 1997 and the Series I U.S. savings bonds. They are described further in Chapter 11. Some foreign governments have also issued inflation-indexed bonds.

to obtain the best after-tax total investment returns possible, consistent with other objectives. Common stocks as a group generally have done that over substantial periods of time. On the other hand, fixed-dollar investments—such as bonds, CDs, savings accounts, nonvariable life insurance cash values, and nonvariable annuity cash values—normally will not increase in value during an inflationary period. But in investment decision making, investors are probably better off to consider how a given investment is expected to perform in the future, its potential price variability over time (risk), asset allocation principles, and what the investors' needs are, rather than worrying about whether the investment is called a hedge against inflation or not.

Also, it should be remembered that, although consumer prices generally have been rising (inflation), there have been periods during which prices were stable and even declined, and that it is possible for them to decline in the future (deflation or depression). Fixed-dollar assets will *lose* purchasing power during an *inflationary* period, but they will *gain* purchasing power during a *deflationary* period.

Other Risks

There may also be other risks to an investment's principal or income. For example, in investing in international securities that are issued in foreign currencies, there would be the *currency risk*. This is the risk that the value of the foreign currency in which the investment is denominated will fall relative to the value of the dollar.

Rates of Return

The primary purpose of investing is to earn a return on one's capital. Investors normally want to maximize their *total after-tax returns* (investment income and capital gains combined). But to increase expected total investment return at any given time, an investor normally must take greater investment risks. Thus, yield and degree of investment risk are directly related—*the higher the yield, the greater the risk.*

Annual Rates of Return from Income (Yield)

There are several ways of measuring annual rates of return represented by the periodic income from an investment. They include the *nominal yield*, the *current yield*, and the *yield to maturity.*

Nominal Yield. This is the annual amount of interest or dividends paid compared with a security's par or face value, shown as follows:

$$\text{Nominal yield} = \frac{\text{annual interest or dividends}}{\text{investment's par or face value}}$$

The nominal yield is often called the *coupon rate* when applied to bonds and the *dividend rate* when applied to preferred stocks with a par value. For example, a bond with a maturity value (face amount) of $1000 that pays interest of $70 per year has a nominal yield (coupon rate) of 7 percent. Nominal yield really has no meaning for common stocks and other forms of investment.

Current Yield. This measure normally is more significant than nominal yield. The *current yield* is expressed as the annual amount of income received from an investment compared with its current market price or value. It normally is used for common and preferred stocks and frequently for bonds as well. It can be calculated as follows:

$$\text{Current yield} = \frac{\text{annual investment income}}{\text{investment's current price or value}}$$

An investment's current yield normally will change over time because its market price will fluctuate and its annual investment income may change.

As examples of current yield, a common stock selling at $50 per share with an annual dividend rate of $1.00 has a current yield of 2 percent and a 5 percent bond (coupon rate) that is selling for $800 has a current yield of about 6.25 percent.[5]

Yield to Maturity. Another measure of yield commonly applied to bonds is the yield to maturity. Bonds have a definite maturity date when their par or face amount is to be paid by the issuer. However, investors can purchase bonds for less than their maturity value (at a discount) or for more than their maturity value (at a premium). Thus, the concept of yield to maturity for a bond can be illustrated by taking the bond's annual interest income and either adding the annual gain (discount) or deducting the annual loss (premium) that will be realized if the bond is held to maturity. The result is divided by the average investment in the bond. To illustrate the principle involved, *approximate* formulas for calculating yield to maturity can be shown as follows.

For a bond selling at a discount:

$$\text{Yield to maturity} = \frac{\text{annual coupon interest} + (\text{discount} \div \text{number of years to maturity})}{(\text{current market price of bond} + \text{par value}) \div 2}$$

For a bond selling at a premium:

$$\text{Yield to maturity} = \frac{\text{annual coupon interest} - (\text{premium} \div \text{number of years to maturity})}{(\text{current market price of bond} + \text{par value}) \div 2}$$

[5] Annual bond interest of $50 ($1000 maturity value × 5%) divided by $800 equals 00.0625, or 6.25%.

Thus, for bonds selling at a discount, the yield to maturity is greater than either the current yield or the coupon rate, while for bonds selling at a premium, the opposite is true. When a bond is selling at or near par, the coupon rate, current yield, and yield to maturity will be essentially the same. In most cases, when an investor plans to hold a bond until maturity, the yield to maturity is considered the most accurate measure of annual investment return.

The current yields for stocks and bonds are often shown in newspapers and similar sources. Bond yields to maturity for different coupon rates, bond prices, and remaining periods to maturity are available from *bond yield tables.*

Capital Gains and Total Rates of Return

People often invest for capital gains as well as regular annual income. Capital gains generally result from the appreciation in the value of assets. Of course, there can be capital losses too.

Advantages of Taking Returns as Capital Gains.

1. Capital gains are not taxed until actually realized and recognized for tax purposes, such as by a sale. Therefore, an investor generally can determine when, if ever, the gain is to be taxed.
2. If an investor does not sell and realize a gain, but instead holds appreciated property until his or her death, the estate or heirs will get a stepped-up income tax basis in the property equal to its value for estate tax purposes (generally the date of death value) and the capital gain prior to death will forever escape taxation. Note, however, that under the Economic Growth and Tax Relief Reconciliation Act there will be a modified carryover basis at death system in 2010.[6] But even under this system, if it ever actually takes effect, the carryover basis at death can be increased by $1,300,000 generally and by an additional $3,000,000 for qualifying transfers to a spouse.
3. If an investor needs current income from investments (or cash for other purposes), he or she can periodically sell (at capital gains tax rates) a portion of his or her appreciated property to produce the same result as a stream of interest or dividend income. In fact, the investor in this situation can select the best investment assets to sell for both investment and tax considerations.
4. The income tax rates are lower on capital gains than on ordinary income. The top tax rates on long-term capital gains may be 18 or 20 percent, depending on how long the taxpayer has held the capital asset and when

[6] The federal income tax system, including how capital gains are taxed, is described more fully in Chapter. 14.

it was acquired. In contrast, the top rate on ordinary income ranges from 38.6 percent in 2003 to 35 percent by 2006 and thereafter.

5. There are numerous planning techniques aimed at avoiding capital gains taxation entirely, deferring taxation, or stretching out any gain over a period of years. These techniques are discussed in Chapter 15.

Limitations on Taking Returns as Capital Gains. On the other hand, capital gains as a form of investment return can have disadvantages.

1. Capital gains are inherently uncertain. There is no assurance an investment will appreciate in price or value. Thus, capital gains generally involve a higher degree of investment risk (in terms of uncertainty or *variability* of outcomes) than other forms of investment returns, such as interest and dividends.

2. Once a person has achieved unrealized capital gains and holds highly appreciated assets in his or her investment portfolio, a dilemma may result. The person may hesitate to sell, for fear of capital gains taxation. This may be referred to as the *capital gains lock-in problem*, which is discussed further in Chapter 15.

3. It can be argued that investing for capital gains places greater emphasis on investment skill, since these returns are less certain.

Measuring Capital Gains and Total Returns. Rates of return from capital gains are difficult to measure. First, no one can know what, if any, capital gain there may be on a given investment. An investor really can reason only from *experience* with the particular investment or similar investments and possibly from *estimates* of the expected capital gains. Second, even measuring past rates of return can be difficult—and there is no assurance that past results will be repeated in the future. Finally, most investors suffer some capital losses as well as realize capital gains. Despite these problems, however, it is important to measure capital gains rates of return, because capital gains constitute an important part of the total returns from some important categories of investment media—particularly common stocks and real estate.

One fairly simple approach for doing this is to estimate the *average annual compound rate of gain* from the change in the price of an asset or assets (without reinvestment of cash flows—dividends and rents) for the time period being considered.[7] Thus, if one knows the time period involved, the initial value of the asset at the beginning of this period, and the ending value of the asset at the end of the period, one can calculate the average annual compound rate of gain over the period.

[7] This change in price technically is known as an asset price index, which shows the appreciation or depreciation in the price of an asset or group of assets over a time period without any reinvestment of cash flows.

For example, let us say an investor bought XYZ Company common stock 10 years ago at $20 per share and now it is worth $40 per share. If we use a calculator, a computer, or a compound interest table, we can see that he or she has had about a 7 percent average annual compound rate of capital gain from this stock over the 10 years. The so-called *Rule of 72* can also be used to estimate an average annual rate of gain.[8]

However, we have not yet considered any periodic cash flows from the asset or assets. An investment's *total return* for a given year is the change in its price or value (up or down) in that year plus any cash flow (dividends, interest, or rents) for the year. For example, if a common stock's price is $40 per share at the beginning of the year and $44 at the end of the year, and if the stock paid $1.20 in dividends during the year, its *total return for the year* is $5.20 per share or 13 percent (10 percent capital gain plus 3 percent dividend income) on the initial share price. This same approach can be used for calculating total returns on other assets, like bonds.

But we often want to measure total returns over a period of years, not just for one year. The most accurate measure of total investment returns over time is generally considered to be the *average annual compound* (or *geometric*) *rate of total return* for the asset or group of assets.[9] This is the annual rate at which an initial investment will accumulate to equal the final value of the investment at the end of the period considered, assuming reinvestment of the cash flows received during the period and the capital gains. To calculate this annual rate, one needs the initial value of the asset or assets, any annual cash flows (e.g., dividends, rents, etc.) during the time period involved, and the final value of the asset or assets at the end of the time period. This approach is often used to compare the long-term historical returns from different categories of investment media, which is important in asset allocation decisions today (see Chapters 9 and 13).

---

[8] This is done by dividing the number of years it takes an investment to double in value into 72. The result is approximately the average annual rate of return over those years. In this situation, for example, $72 \div 10 = 7.2$ percent per year. Using a calculator, the average annual compound rate of gain in this illustration is 7.18 percent.

[9] Note that this measure involves total returns—capital gains (or losses) and cash flows from the asset or assets. Note also that it is a geometric average, which involves the process of compounding returns. There could be an average annual arithmetic rate of return, which would be just the arithmetic average of a series of yearly total returns. This does not involve the compounding of returns. Unless the yearly total returns are exactly the same, the geometric average annual rate of return will be less than the arithmetic average annual rate of return. As noted in the text, the geometric average is the proper way to measure long-term investment returns. However, the arithmetic approach is seen in investment materials and reports.

These rates of return may also be adjusted for estimated taxes (giving an after-tax average annual rate of return), for inflation (giving a real average annual rate of return), or possibly for both.

The concept of an average annual compound (geometric) rate of return may also be used for other investment values over time. For example, one corporation recently reported that the annual dividend rate on its common stock over a 15-year period had grown from $0.59 per share to $1.68 per share or at a 7.2 percent annual compound rate.

After-Tax Yields

Up to this point, we have not considered the effect of income taxes on investment returns. As a practical matter, however, investors want to know what their investment returns are after taxes. This is what they get to keep. However, this further complicates comparing investment yields, because different kinds of investments are taxed in different ways, investments may be placed in tax-deferred (advantaged) vehicles (like Section 401[k] plans or IRAs) that have their own tax rules, there are multiple tax brackets, and tax rates and rules often change.

For purposes of estimating after-tax yields, we shall view the returns from investments as (1) income that is taxable currently as ordinary income, (2) income that is entirely tax-exempt, and (3) returns that are taxable when realized (and recognized), if ever, as capital gains.[10] The taxation of returns in and distributions from various tax-deferred (advantaged) plans are discussed in Chapters 17 to 21.

Taxable Income. Investment income that is fully taxable as ordinary income, such as interest on certificates of deposit, taxable money market funds or accounts, corporate bonds, U.S. Treasury bonds, and dividends from common stocks, is easy to express on an after-tax basis. The *after-tax yield* can be determined by multiplying the current yield by 1 minus the investor's highest marginal income tax rate. Thus, if a married taxpayer's highest tax bracket were 27 percent, a CD paying 4 percent interest would provide the following after-tax yield.

After-tax yield = current yield (1 - tax rate)
$$= 0.04 (1 - 0.27)$$
$$= 0.04 (0.73)$$
$$= 0.0292 \text{ or } 2.92\%$$

---

[10] This is intentionally a somewhat simplified classification. Some forms of investment income, for example, are entirely tax-exempt for regular income tax purposes but are a tax preference item for alternative minimum tax (AMT) purposes. See Chapters 13 and 14 for discussion of the income taxation of different kinds of investments.

Tax-Exempt Income. The after-tax yield for a fully tax-exempt investment equals the current yield. Thus, the after-tax yield for a 4½ percent municipal bond is 4½ percent. It is common practice also to express what a fully taxable security would have to earn to equal the yield from a tax-free security at different income tax rates. For example, a 4½ percent tax-free yield received by a married investor in a 35 percent tax bracket is worth 6.92 percent to him or her on a fully taxable basis.[11] This is often referred to as a *taxable equivalent yield.*

After-Tax Total Returns. It becomes more complicated to determine after-tax yields when investment returns are in the form of capital gains (or losses) or are partly ordinary income and partly capital gains (or losses).

Tax Impact on Capital Gains. Net short-term capital gains (net gains realized and recognized on capital assets held for 12 months or less) are taxed at the same rates as ordinary income. Therefore, they present no special tax advantage. Net long-term capital gains (technically, these are *net capital gains* as defined in Chapter 14), which are net gains realized and recognized[12] on capital assets held for more than 12 months, generally are taxed at a top rate of 18 or 20 percent, depending on how long the capital asset has been held and when it was acquired. However, the actual impact of income taxes on capital gains depends on whether a gain is ever realized and recognized for tax purposes, on how long an asset has been held before the gain is realized and recognized, on the applicable capital gains tax rate, and other factors. Thus, after-tax total returns depend on the circumstances.

Here is an example to illustrate these principles. Assume that Mary Kim owns a $300,000 portfolio of common stocks directly (i.e., not through a mutual fund or a tax-advantaged vehicle). Also assume the portfolio has an estimated total annual return of 10 percent (3 percent from dividend income and 7 percent average annual compound rate of capital gain). Assume further that Mary is in the 35 percent top income tax bracket for ordinary income, all capital gains are long-term, and the tax rate on all capital gains is 20 percent.

---

[11] Any similar equivalent yields can be calculated by dividing the tax-free yield by 1 minus the investor's highest marginal income tax rate. In this case, 4½% ÷ (1 - 0.35 or 0.65) = 6.92%. The highest marginal income tax rate used also can include state and local top marginal income tax rates if the income from the security also is exempt from those taxes as well as from the federal income tax.

[12] The term realized and recognized is technical but important in tax terminology. A gain is realized when there is an actual sale or exchange of a capital asset at a gain. The gain also is recognized for tax purposes unless there is a specific nonrecognition provision in the tax code that delays recognition of the gain. The taxation of capital gains and losses is treated more fully in Chapter 14.

Income and Capital Gains Taxed Each Year. First, let us assume that Mary is taxed on her dividend income each year as ordinary income (which would be the case) and also is taxed on *all* her estimated capital gains each year (which is unlikely). In this case, her *annual after-tax total return* would be 7.55 percent, determined as shown in the table below.

	Before-tax returns	After-tax returns[13]
Dividends	3%	1.95%
Capital gains	7%	5.60%
Total return	10%	7.55%

Income Taxed Each Year but Capital Gains Taxation Deferred. Now let us change the assumptions and suppose that Mary is taxed on the dividend income each year (and does not reinvest it), but holds the common stocks for a period of time before selling them and realizing the long-term capital gains. This is a more likely assumption.

When taking capital gains is deferred, the after-tax returns are increased, and the longer the period of deferral, the greater the after-tax returns. This is because the unrealized capital gains are compounding tax-free. The same principle applies to any tax-deferred investment gains.

For example, if Mary holds her stocks for 10 years[14] before selling them, her annual after-tax total return would be as shown in the table below.

	Before-tax returns	After-tax return[15]
Dividends	3%	1.95%
Capital gains (on assets for 10 years)	7%	5.90%
Total return	10%	7.85%

Income Taxed Each Year but Capital Gains Never Taxed. This happy assumption of course produces the best after-tax total return, as shown in the table at the top of the next page.

---

[13] These returns were calculated for dividends as 3% × 0.65 (1 - 0.35) = 1.95% and for capital gains as 7% × 0.80 (1 - 0.20) = 5.60%.

[14] This is just an assumption for the purpose of this illustration. In practice, people hold assets for varying periods of time and they even may not dispose of them at all during their lifetimes. They may also have capital losses as well as gains. It is also assumed for the purpose of this illustration that Mary (or Mary and her husband) own(s) these stocks directly and not in tax-advantaged plans—(like 401[k] plans or IRAs)—or in mutual funds, to which different tax principles would apply.

	Before-tax returns	After-tax returns
Dividends	3%	1.95%[16]
Capital gains (which are never taxed)	7%	7.0%
Total return	10%	8.95%

A logical question is how capital gains can escape income taxation in this way. The answer lies in provisions of the tax code that allow taxpayers or their estates and heirs to avoid potential capital gains taxation entirely and other provisions that permit assets to be disposed of or arranged without current capital gains taxation and perhaps ultimately with no capital gains taxation at all. These planning techniques are described in Chapters 14, 15, and 16.

Combination of Circumstances. For most investors, the situation regarding taxation of capital gains will be a mixed bag. Some assets will be bought and sold in a fairly short time period; others will be bought and held for the long-term and then sold; while still others will be bought and held until death, or capital gains will be avoided in some other fashion.

Planning Considerations Regarding After-Tax Yields. From this discussion, some general planning issues emerge:

■ It generally is better to take investment returns as long-term capital gains than as ordinary income.
■ It generally is better taxwise to allow capital gains to accumulate over time before taking them.
■ When consistent with other goals, it is desirable to avoid capital gains taxation entirely.
■ An analysis should be made of the relative attractiveness of tax-free investment income (e.g., interest on most municipal bonds) as compared with taxable investment income for the particular investor. This depends on the investor's marginal income tax rates (federal, state, and local), the current

---

[15] For dividends, the return is calculated as 3% × 0.65 (1 - 0.35) = 1.95%. For capital gains, if we assume an investor starts with $1000, has an average annual compound rate of capital gain of 7%, and sells the investment at the end of 10 years, the investor would have $1967, of which $1000 would be return of the original investment and $967 would be long-term capital gain subject to a 20% tax rate. The after-tax amount would then be $1774 [$1000 + (0.8 × $967)]. The average annual compound rate of return needed for $1000 to grow to $1774 in 10 years is 5.90%.

[16] For dividends, the return is calculated as 3% × 0.65 (1 - 0.35) = 1.95%. No tax is imposed on capital gains.

yield (or yield to maturity) on tax-free bonds, and the total after-tax yield on alternative investments.

Of course, these general planning considerations should always be taken within the context of the investor's overall objectives, investment strategies, and general financial constraints.

Yields on Mutual Funds. The principles just discussed also generally apply to assets held in mutual funds. However, there are some special tax rules applying to mutual funds, which are explained in Chapter 12.

Assets Held in Tax-Advantaged Plans. Some of the principles just described also apply to assets held in income tax-deferred plans like qualified savings plans (usually with a Section 401[k] option), regular IRAs, Roth IRAs, and investment annuities. However, different tax rules apply to these plans, which will affect their after-tax returns. These plans and the tax rules applying to them are discussed in Chapters 17, 18, 19, and 21.

Marketability and Liquidity

Sometimes the terms *marketability* and *liquidity* are used to mean almost the same thing, but they do have a difference in meaning. *Marketability* means the ability of an investor to find a ready market should he or she wish to sell an investment. *Liquidity* means an investment is not only marketable but also highly stable in price. In other words, an asset is liquid when an investor feels reasonably sure he or she can dispose of it quickly and also can receive approximately the amount as put into it. Investors normally desire to keep some percentage (or amount) of their overall portfolio in liquid assets (also called *cash equivalents*).

Diversification

The basic purpose of diversification is to reduce or minimize an investor's risk of loss (variability of overall returns and values). It is primarily a defensive policy.

Forms of Diversification

One form is to *diversify among various types of investment media*—such as common stocks, bonds, CDs, money market funds and other liquid assets, life insurance and annuities, real estate, and perhaps other tax shelters. The prices or values of all types of investment media do not go up or down at the same time or in the same magnitude (i.e., they are uncorrelated; see Chapter 13), and so investors can protect themselves against economic fluctuations this way.

An example is that prices of common stocks and high-grade bonds may move in opposite directions over a business cycle. During periods of prosperity, the stock market generally rises because of higher corporate profits and dividends. However, the prices of high-grade bonds may decline, because interest rates may rise as the result of increasing demands for capital. During recession or depression, the opposite occurs: stock prices fall because of declining business, but high-grade bond prices tend to rise due to falling interest rates, because the demand for capital diminishes and the monetary authorities follow a low interest rate policy to try to stimulate the economy. This traditionally has been known as the *countercyclical price movement of high-grade bonds.*

Another form is *diversification within a particular class or type of investment media.* For example, the investor may own common stocks of several companies and in several industries, may buy some growth-type stocks and some stocks primarily for income, may purchase some speculative issues but generally invest in more stable stocks, and so on. Also, use of financial intermediaries for this form of diversification can be quite effective.

A third form is *diversification of investments according to maturity or time of purchase.* For securities with a fixed maturity date (such as bonds or CDs), this form of diversification was discussed and illustrated earlier under "Laddered Diversification to Deal with Interest Rate Risks." Investors may also want to buy other securities, such as common stocks, from time to time, rather than all at once, so that the market risk can be spread over both good and bad markets. This may be achieved through dollar cost averaging, as explained in the next chapter.

Another aspect of diversification is to reduce the overall risk level of inherently risky investments. Examples might include certain tax-sheltered investments (such as oil and gas limited partnerships) and high-yield (junk) bonds. The idea behind investing in these inherently risky types of assets is that the losses on some of them will be more than offset by the higher returns on others, with the result that the overall return will be quite satisfactory relative to other investment categories. But to do this, there must be a broad enough spread or number of these investments so that the good will have a chance to outweigh the bad. Thus, regardless of any other merits or demerits of investing in these categories of assets, there must be a broad enough spread of risk (diversification) to give it a chance to work.

Methods of Diversification

1. Investments can be made through financial institutions (intermediaries) that diversify their investments. Such institutions include:
   a. Investment companies (including mutual funds)

    b. Life insurance companies

    c. Real estate investment trusts (REITs)

2. The investor can purchase one or more securities or units periodically over a long period of time (such as dollar cost averaging in buying common stocks or mutual funds, as discussed in Chapter 9).

3. The investor can deliberately follow a diversification strategy in buying, selling, or holding assets in several investment categories (stocks, bonds, real estate, cash, and so forth) and with a reasonable number of individual investments in each category. The idea is not to have the portfolio over-weighted (too dependent) on any one asset or asset class.

Tax Status

An investment's tax status can have an important bearing on its attractiveness. This is discussed more fully in Chapters 13, 14, and 15.

Size of Investment Units (or Denominations)

In some cases, an investment can be made only in certain minimum amounts. For example, municipal bonds frequently are sold in lots of $5000 or more. Also, direct investments in real estate require a down payment and payment of closing costs, as well as adequate mortgage financing.

Use as Collateral for Loans

Many forms of property can be used as collateral for loans. However, some kinds serve better than others. For example, good-quality securities (other than municipal bonds), life insurance policies, and improved real estate may operate well in this regard. In contrast, some types of property are unattractive. For example, tax-free municipal bonds involve tax pitfalls when used as collateral or even when they are owned and other property is used as collateral for loans, as discussed in Chapter 15.

Callability

Nature of Callable Securities

As discussed earlier under "Interest Rate Risk to Income from Investments," callability (or redeemability) can be an important factor when investing in bonds and preferred stocks. Many issuers of corporate and municipal bonds have reserved the right to call or redeem the bonds before maturity, usually subject to certain conditions. Most issues of preferred stock also are callable. On the other hand, most U.S. government bonds and some municipal and corporate bonds are not callable prior to maturity.

Callable bonds and preferred stocks are usually redeemed when market interest rates are below their coupon rates. *Other things being equal, securities that are not callable or that have limited callability are more attractive to investors than callable securities.* But, as is so often true, other things may not be equal, because callable bonds and preferreds normally carry higher yields than comparable noncallable securities. Thus, it really may be a trade-off between call protection and higher yield.

Ways for Investors to Protect Against Callability

- They can buy noncallable securities (such as U.S. Treasury notes and bonds). However, when municipal and corporate bonds are issued on a noncallable basis, they may be for relatively shorter maturities.
- They can buy securities with *call protection*.[17]
- They can buy bonds or preferreds selling at a *deep discount* (market discount) from their maturity or par value. (See Chapter 11 for a discussion of deep discount bonds.) However, sometimes such deep discount securities are scarce in the bond markets, and the investor normally must accept a lower yield on them than for comparable securities selling around par.
- They may be able to diversify their purchases over time so that only a small portion of the portfolio will be called at any one time.
- They may purchase high-quality, higher-yielding common stocks, which, of course, have no maturity date and are not callable. However, dividends on common stocks could be cut or eliminated by the corporation during "hard" economic times.

Freedom from Care

This may include freedom from the time and work involved in managing investments and freedom from worry and concern over investment results. These freedoms are quite important to some people but of little concern to others.

---

[17] The types of call protection used in bonds and preferred stock are covered in Chapter 11.

9

Common
Stocks

Characteristics of Common Stocks

Common stock may be defined as the residual ownership of a corporation that is entitled to all assets and earnings after other claims have been paid and that generally has voting control. In short, common stock is the fundamental ownership equity.

In modern asset allocation planning (see Chapter 12), it is recognized that common stocks as a group historically have provided superior total returns over reasonably long time periods as compared with certain other investment media (e.g., bonds and Treasury bills) and so generally should be included in a diversified investment program. Therefore, people should either learn to select common stocks themselves or place that function in the hands of a financial intermediary or an investment advisor.

Some Measures of Value for Common Stocks

Several basic calculations may serve as convenient preliminary indicators of the worth of a common stock: earnings per share, price earnings ratio, book value per share, liquidating value per share, and yield.

Earnings per Share

The traditional way to compute earnings per share (EPS) is to divide the income available to common shareholders (net corporate profits after taxes less any preferred dividends) by the average number of common shares actually outstanding. This may be illustrated as follows.

Over the most recent 12 months in which it reported earnings, the XYZ Company had a profit of $2,300,000 after deduction of expenses, interest, and taxes. Preferred dividend requirements for the year were $200,000. The remaining $2,100,000 amounted to $3 per share on the average 700,000 shares actually outstanding for the year ($2,100,000 ÷ 700,000 = $3). These are the company's *basic earnings per share*. Earnings per share are computed in the same way for quarterly or semiannual periods. Nonrecurring items contained in current income may or may not be excluded when computing earnings per share.

The example just given is based on what are called *trailing earnings* because the earnings figure is for the most recent past actual earnings. However, sometimes analysts will *estimate* future earnings and base their calculations in whole or in part on these estimated earnings.

Corporations also report *diluted earnings per share*. Diluted earnings per share are computed by dividing the income available to common shareholders by the average common shares actually outstanding *plus* the potential common shares that would be outstanding if the dilutive effect of employee stock options and other stock awards outstanding, convertible securities, and warrants were considered. Thus, the potential effect of these plans and securities (called *dilutive potential common shares*) on average outstanding common shares is taken into account by this adjustment. This can be significant, depending on the corporation.

Still another adjustment to earnings per share that can be found in the reported earnings of some companies or in a footnote in the annual reports of other companies is the effect on earnings and earnings per share if the company used a fair value at vesting approach to valuing stock-based compensation plans (e.g., employee stock options) in determining their cost to the corporation.[1] Thus, in the footnote (if options are not expensed in reporting earnings) the company shows what the *pro forma net income* and *pro forma earnings per share* would have been if the company had used the fair value method (usually based on a recognized option-pricing model) in valuing options and stock-based compensation vesting that year instead of the intrinsic value method (which usually produces a zero cost for options when they are granted).

---

[1] At this writing, some companies have decided to expense options granted under employee stock option plans and use a fair value or market value approach (which may be based on an option-pricing model, like Black-Scholes) to value options in determining their reported earnings. Other companies, however, have opted not to expense employee stock options and value them at their intrinsic value at grant (which normally would be zero). However, under the present rules of the Financial Accounting Standards Board of the American Institute of Certified Public Accountants, if a firm does not use a fair value approach in determining reported earnings, the firm must show the effect of the fair value method on earnings in a footnote in its annual report. This may be referred to as a pro forma statement of earnings or earnings per share.

For example, one large corporation that does not expense options reported the following earnings per share in its annual report for a recent year:

Basic reported earnings per share: $7.71
Diluted reported earnings per share: $7.17

Then, in a footnote to its consolidated financial statements in its annual report, the corporation further indicated:[2]

Pro forma basic earnings per share: $7.46
Pro forma diluted earnings per share: $6.94

The impact of this option valuation issue on reported earnings (when stock options are *expensed*) or on pro forma earnings in a footnote (when they are *not expensed*) depends on the extent to which a firm uses stock-based compensation plans. This issue is complex and controversial. As of this writing, new accounting rules may soon be forthcoming.

In discussing corporate earnings per share, analysts may refer to *basic earnings per share* or *diluted earnings per share*, but they often use diluted earnings per share.

Investors and analysts generally place great emphasis on earnings per share and particularly on the trend of earnings per share in evaluating common stocks. It can be argued that a going business's value lies mainly in its potential earning power and that any present and future dividends depend on earnings. Thus, a stock's market price ultimately tends to keep pace with the growth or decline of its earnings per share.

Analysts also sometimes calculate a figure called *cash flow per share*. This is derived by adding back depreciation expense and possibly other noncash expenses to net profit less preferred dividends and then dividing by the average number of common shares. The idea is to be able to better compare companies with varying depreciation policies. Other figures that some may use include *earnings before interest and taxes* (EBIT) (to adjust for differences in capital structures) and *earnings before interest, taxes, depreciation, and amortization* (EBITDA) (to adjust for differences in capital structures and depreciation and amortization policies).

A number of other per-share figures may also be found in analyses of common stocks. They may include sales per share, dividends per share, capital spending per share, research and development (R&D) costs per share, working capital per share, and cash per share.

[2] As just stated, these pro forma figures assume valuation of stock-based compensation awards granted during the year on a fair value basis. For this purpose, this company used a modified Black-Scholes option-pricing model. It used the intrinsic value method for valuing options granted in calculating reported earnings and reported earnings per share. Valuation of employee stock options is discussed in more detail in Chapter 22.

Price-Earnings Ratio

The price-earnings (P/E) ratio of a common stock is the market price of the stock divided by the current earnings per share of the corporation. Thus, if XYZ Company common stock sold for $63 per share at a time when its reported earnings over the latest 12 months amounted to $3 per share, its P/E ratio (on a "trailing earnings" basis) would be 21 ($63 ÷ $3). The price-earnings ratio is a commonly used measure of stock value, because it gives an indication of stock price measured against the earning power of the stock.

An investor may find a review of past price-earnings ratios of a stock helpful in estimating its current value relative to the past. Assume, for example, that over a 10-year period, XYZ Company common stock has shown consistent growth in earnings per share and market price and that its P/E ratios have ranged from around 18 on the low side to a high of 42 on the high side. Therefore, since this stock currently is selling for a price-earnings ratio of 21, that ratio is historically relatively low and thus the stock might be a good buy at this time. On the other hand, if XYZ common were selling for $120, its P/E ratio (40) would be on the high side historically.[3] Of course, investors must consider other factors about the stock in making a final decision. They also must evaluate the stock's P/E ratio in light of present economic and stock market conditions and what those conditions are expected to be in the future.

Net Asset Value (Book Value) per Share

The net asset value per share, commonly referred to as the *book value* per share, attempts to measure the amount of assets a corporation has working for each share of common stock. It is calculated by taking the *net balance sheet values* of corporate assets, subtracting the face value of creditors' and preferred stockholders' claims, and dividing the remainder by the average number of outstanding common shares.

For example, the XYZ Company at the end of its last fiscal year had total assets of $33 million and debts and preferred stock totaling $12 million. The remaining $21 million indicated a net asset value of $30 for each of its 700,000 common shares outstanding.

In most cases, book value per share is much less important than the ability of those assets to generate a stream of earnings. The market prices of common stocks of successful companies normally are many times book value per share. On the other hand, for declining firms, market price may be less than book

[3] Historical data on price-earning ratios for common stocks are readily available to investors. For example, the Standard & Poor's Corporation Standard Stock Reports give this information for many stocks.

value. On the whole, net asset value per share is not a very useful measure for evaluating the investment merits of a company's common stock. However, investors may measure the current market price level of a stock, an industry group, or the whole market in relation to past price levels by a measure often called *price to book* (market price divided by book value).

Liquidating Value per Share

This measure is determined by using the market or liquidating value of a corporation's assets rather than the balance sheet values (which generally are based on historical cost). Thus, this is the estimated amount that could be realized per share if the corporation's assets were sold off, its liabilities paid, and the balance distributed to the shareholders. It is not a going concern value, but rather a liquidation value.

Yields

As we saw in Chapter 8, the *current dividend yield for common stocks* refers to the percentage that the annual cash dividend bears to the current market price of the stock. In some cases, dividend yield can be an indicator of the reasonableness of a stock's market price.

However, there are several factors that may lessen the importance of current dividend yield in evaluating common stocks. One is that some companies have a history of increasing their dividends per share over a substantial period of time. This results in a constantly increasing dividend yield when measured against the original purchase price of the stock. On the other hand, dividends are not guaranteed and can be cut or even eliminated. Further, as we saw in Chapter 8, the most accurate measure of *total returns* on common stocks is the average annual compound rate of gain (or loss) over a set period of time, assuming reinvestment of dividends. This considers capital gains and losses as well as annual dividends. Finally, some companies whose common stocks have proved to be excellent investments have followed a policy of paying no dividends or very modest dividends. Their returns come entirely or almost entirely from capital gains.

Information About Common Stocks

There are many sources of information about common stocks. Only some are mentioned here. One source is the financial pages of newspapers. For example, the following is how the quotation for the common stock of a hypothetical firm called Typical Manufacturing Company might appear in the New York Stock Exchange tables of a newspaper:

52 weeks		Stock and div. in dollars	P/E	Sales in 100s	Open	High	Low	Close	Net Chg
High	Low								
32¼	20¾	Typ. Mfg. 1.20	13	29	25¼	26	25	25½	+½

There are a number of stock market barometers (market averages) that are useful. Among the best known probably are the Dow Jones Averages, Standard & Poor's 500 Stock Index, the New York Times Index, the New York Stock Exchange indexes, the NASDAQ over-the-counter indexes, the Value-Line index, the Russell 2000, and the Wilshire 5000. The Dow Jones Averages include four averages: 30 industrials, 20 transportations, 15 utilities, and a composite of the 65 stocks.

A number of financial newspapers and periodicals carry news of interest to investors. Some of these are *The Wall Street Journal, Barron's, Financial Daily, Commercial and Financial Chronicle, Standard & Poor's Outlook, Forbes,* and *The Magazine of Wall Street,* plus such business news magazines as *Fortune* and *BusinessWeek.* Another way of getting information on a specific company is in one of the major reference works of financial information, such as *Standard & Poor's, Moody's,* or *Value-Line.*

Still another source of information is stockbrokers. Depending on their research facilities, brokerage houses frequently have reports on companies and industries. Finally, investment information is available on the Internet.

The Investment Process

Successful investing in common stocks cannot be based on hunch, hope, or hearsay. It is founded on the study of particular companies and industries.

Consider the Industry

An important step is evaluating the industry or industries involved. The following are some questions to consider in doing so.

- Does the industry provide products or services for which demand is substantial and growing?
- Is the industry cyclical or relatively stable?
- Is the industry likely to be affected by new developments?
- Is the industry growing rapidly, growing at a more stable rate, or perhaps declining relative to other industries?
- Is the industry subject to rapid technological change or development?

Analyze the Company

The characteristics to look for depend largely on the investment philosophy being followed. Some investors are looking for short-term speculations. Others want turnaround situations or are following the depressed-industry approach. Still others may be investing primarily for income. Many investors, however, are looking for strong, high-quality companies with good growth prospects over a reasonably long period of time. They are generally following a buy-and-hold approach and are looking for *growth-type* stocks. Given this kind of philosophy, following are some characteristics that investors might consider in selecting common stocks.

- The company should have *good, stable management.*
- The company should provide *good products or services* that have strong competitive positions in their industry.
- The company should be *reasonably diversified* and not largely dependent on only one product or patent.
- The company should have had *consistent earnings growth* over a reasonable period of time, such as the last 10 years. This does not mean the company cannot have had declines in earnings for one or two years, but they should be exceptions and the trend should be decidedly upward.
- The previous characteristic can be quantified by saying there should be an *average annual compound rate of growth in earnings per share* over the time period being considered of at least a certain figure—such as ranging from 10 to 20 percent.
- As far as can be determined, the company should have *good prospects for growth of earnings* in the immediate future.
- The company should have a *good return on equity* over a period of years.
- The company should have a *strong financial position.*
- Depending on the industry, companies usually should be devoting *reasonable resources to research and development.*
- Investors who want current dividend income should consider the stock's *current dividend yield and past record of dividend increases.*
- Finally, the stock's *purchase price should be reasonable.* The "reasonableness" of a common stock's price is often measured in terms of its price-earnings (P/E) ratio.

In evaluating companies with these characteristics, the real question often is how investors know what is a reasonable P/E ratio. Normally, one would expect higher P/E ratios for high-quality, growth-oriented stocks than for the stock market as a whole. For particular stocks, P/E ratios can vary considerably over time. As noted earlier, an investor might evaluate a stock's current P/E ratio in terms of its past P/E ratios over a period of, say, 10 years. An investor might also evaluate a stock's P/E ratio in terms of the ratios of other stocks in its industry or of the stock market as a whole. However, conditions change and P/E ratios for the whole stock market historically have varied markedly. In reality, there probably is no sure way of knowing whether a stock currently has a reasonable P/E ratio. Judgment is called for—and perhaps some good luck. It is also true that common stocks that once met the criteria for being high-quality and growth-oriented may fall from grace and no longer fit that category. Knowing when to sell such stocks also is a matter of judgment.

As a practical matter, it is difficult, if not impossible, for most individual investors to research and analyze personally such factors as industry characteristics, competitive positions of companies, and the investment characteristics of a given company. However, various professional investment concerns, investment services, stockbrokers, and other investment advisors are in a position to do such research, and this type of investigation frequently is readily available to individual investors. Investors should make it a practice not to buy a stock unless they have determined its fundamental position from such sources or perhaps from their own personal research.

Diversifying a Common Stock Portfolio

Assuming an investor wants to hold stocks directly, investment diversification does not mean that if, for example, a person is investing $200,000, he or she should try to split it by arbitrarily buying stock in 40 companies. Investors normally should not own stock directly in more companies than they or their investment advisors can reasonably follow. It probably would be sensible to put the $200,000 into, say, 10 to 15 individually owned stocks. Of course, diversification can also be secured by investing through financial intermediaries.

Periodic Review

Investors or their advisors should reexamine the investment situation periodically and adjust commitments accordingly.

Decisions Concerning Selling Common Stocks

Although much of the emphasis concerning common stock investment has been on buying, the question of when to sell also is important. There may be many reasons for selling stocks. One is the need for cash. Another is to take a profit (or reduce a loss) when an investor thinks a stock (or the market as a whole) has reached an upper limit. Or, investors may sell if they believe other stocks will perform better or their money can earn a higher rate of return if invested elsewhere. Further, an important reason to sell may be that the investor's portfolio is too heavily concentrated in one or a few stocks.

It should be remembered, however, that there are transfer costs (i.e., broker-age commissions) and capital gains taxes on any profits when a stock is sold. This means the attractiveness of any alternative investment must, over time, outweigh the costs of selling.

Investment decisions should not be considered as irrevocable. Keep track of the current performance of stocks in the portfolio and change its composition as conditions and prices dictate. On the other hand, do not panic into selling without good reason. If investments have been made with care and for the long term, do not let every change in the price of stocks be a signal for gaiety or gloom. Remember that the nature of the stock market is one of fluctuation.

Dollar-Cost Averaging

One diversification technique for long-term common stock investing is dollar-cost averaging. This is the investment of a certain sum of money, at regular intervals, in the same stock or stocks or the same investment intermediary. The method normally results in a lower average cost per share than the average market price per share during the period in question, because the investor buys more shares with the fixed amount of money when the stock is low in price than when it is high. Then, when the stock rises again (if it does), the investor shows a profit on the greater number of shares purchased at the lower prices. Table 9.1 shows how the principle of dollar-cost averaging could work.

Dollar-cost averaging frequently works, unless the stock goes into a persist-ent decline. It takes a certain strength of conviction. The investor must be con-vinced that, whatever happens from time to time, the stock or investment intermediary is a good long-term investment. Thus, dollar-cost averaging may be particularly well suited for investors who generally do not want to try to forecast stock prices.

The Mechanics of Buying and Selling Common Stocks

Various kinds of buy and sell orders may be used in common stock trans-actions.

The most common type of order is the *market order,* an order to buy or sell securities at the best price obtainable in the market at the moment. It is

Table 9.1 Illustration of dollar-cost averaging

Date	Amount invested	Market price paid	Number of shares purchased
1st period	$500	$20	25
2nd period	500	12½	40
3rd period	500	10	50
4th period	500	12½	40
5th period	500	25	20
	$2500		175
Total amount invested over 5 periods			$2500
Number of shares purchased			175
Average market price per share			$16.00
Average cost per share ($2500 ÷ 175 shares)			$14.29

expressed to the broker as an order to buy or sell *at the market*. For many stock transactions, a market order is reasonable.

However, when market prices are uncertain or are fluctuating rapidly, it may be better for an investor to enter a *limit order* that specifies the maximum price the investor is willing to pay or, if selling, the minimum price the investor is willing to accept.

Most types of orders include a time reference. *Open orders* are good until canceled. Another type is the *day order*, which is good only for the day on which it is ordered.

Another common type of order is a *stop loss order*. It is generally used to sell a stock once its price reaches a certain point, usually below the current market price. As an example, suppose a stock's current price is 100 and the investor feels the stock market is so uncertain that the price of the stock could fluctuate markedly in either direction. To minimize potential loss from the 100 level, the investor might enter a stop order at, say, 90. If the market price declines, the stock will be sold if the market price reaches 90.

A stop loss order becomes a market order once the specified price is reached and the stock will be sold immediately at whatever price the broker can secure. Of course, if the market price goes up or never declines to the stop loss price, the investor would have lost nothing by placing the order.

An investor who wishes to use a stop order only at a specific price would enter a *stop limit order*. In the preceding illustration, this order would instruct the broker to sell at 90, and 90 only. If the transaction cannot be executed at 90, it will not be executed at all.

Margin Accounts

Investors may open *cash accounts* with their brokerage firms. As the name implies, all transactions are for the full amount of the trade in cash. That is, a $5000 trade requires a $5000 cash settlement within three full business days after the trade is made.

A *margin account* allows investors to put up some of their own money and borrow the remainder. Margin accounts for listed securities can be opened through either a brokerage house or a commercial bank. The minimum down payment, or *margin requirement,* is set by the board of governors of the Federal Reserve System.

Let us consider a specific example. Suppose the margin requirement is 50 percent and Mr. A buys 100 shares of ABC Corporation common stock at $70 per share. If this is a margin trade, he is required to come up with only $3500 in cash (or its equivalent in other securities). He then borrows the rest ($3500) from a bank or broker at the interest rate for this type of loan. Margin interest rates charged by different brokers can vary considerably; also, they often are less for larger loan balances. The entire $7000 worth of securities is then put up as collateral for the $3500 loan. Federal Reserve requirements specify only the *initial margin,* the minimum margin required at the time a loan is made.

But if the price of ABC common declines, so that Mr. A's equity in the account decreases, he may get a maintenance margin call. *Maintenance margin* is the minimum equity position investors can have in their accounts before they are asked to put up additional funds. In this illustration, for example, assuming maintenance margin is 30 percent, ABC common could fall to a price as low as 50 without a margin call.[4] It can be seen that by borrowing to buy securities, investors stand a chance of magnifying their losses, just as they do of magnifying their gains. Thus, it is a more risky (aggressive) investment strategy.

Selling Short

Selling short means selling securities that the investor either (1) does not possess, and therefore must borrow to settle the account; or (2) does possess, but does not wish to deliver.[5] The former is the typical short-sale when an investor expects the stock to decline in price. The latter is called *selling short against the box* and formerly was often used to lock in a profit on a stock and postpone

---

[4] Since Mr. A must maintain an equity position of 30 percent in his margin account, he can borrow up to 70 percent of the value of the securities. His present loan is $3500. Therefore, $3500 divided by 0.70 (70 percent) equals the minimum value of securities Mr. A can have in his margin account without having to add more margin (cash or securities). In this case, the amount is $5000 ($3500 ÷ 0.70), or $50 per share.

paying taxes on the capital gain. However, the Taxpayer Relief Act of 1997 generally eliminated the selling short-against-the-box technique for this purpose, except in very limited circumstances. (The planning techniques for deferring or avoiding capital gains are covered in Chapter 15.)

The reason for selling short is that the investor anticipates a declining market price for the security. A typical example would be selling today at 100 with the hope of *covering*, say, a month from now, at a lower price, say, 80 or less. Covering involves buying securities to replace the borrowed ones. Of course, the reverse may occur and the price of the stock may not decline—it may rise, thereby making it necessary to buy the stock later at a higher price than that at which it was sold. Selling short is normally considered an aggressive investment policy.

Securities Investor Protection Corporation

Following several sizable brokerage house failures, in 1970 the Securities Investor Protection Act was passed, which created the Securities Investor Protection Corporation (SIPC). The SIPC is intended to provide funds to protect customers of an SIPC member firm if the firm becomes insolvent and is liquidated under the provisions of the act. If a member firm is to be liquidated, a trustee is appointed to supervise the liquidation. The trustee attempts to return to customers the securities that can be "specifically identified" as theirs. (Generally, these are fully paid securities in cash accounts and excess margin securities in margin accounts that have been set aside as the property of customers.) SIPC pays any remaining claims of each customer up to $500,000, except that claims for cash are limited to $100,000.[6] In general, customers' securities and cash held by SIPC member firms are covered by the act. Other kinds of property, such as commodities accounts, are not covered. The SIPC, of course, is not intended to provide any protection to investors against losses resulting from everyday fluctuations in securities prices.

Investment Categories of Common Stocks

Securities firms and investment analysts use many different classification systems of the investment characteristics of common stocks. The basic system we shall follow is to classify stocks as (1) growth, (2) income, (3) growth (moder-

---

[5] In the common sequence of transactions, where investors buy a security that they hope eventually to sell at a higher price, they have assumed what is called a long position. When the order to sell these transactions is reversed—sell first and hope to cover the sale later by buying at a lower price—the investor has taken a short position.

[6] Many firms also provide private insurance protection for their customers up to higher limits.

ate) and income, (4) defensive, (5) cyclical, (6) blue chip, (7) speculative, (8) special situations, (9) small and medium-sized companies, and (10) foreign. It should be recognized that these categories are not mutually exclusive. The common stock of a particular company may fit into several of these categories.

Growth Stocks

The term *growth stock* is hard to define, but such a stock is usually considered to be of a company whose sales and earnings are expanding faster than the general economy and faster than those of most stocks. The company usually is well-managed, is research- or innovation-oriented, and plows back most or all of its earnings into the company for future expansion. For this reason, growth companies often pay no or relatively small dividends. Over time, however, investors hope that substantial capital gains will accrue from the appreciation of the value of their stock. The characteristics presented earlier in this chapter for high-quality, growth-type stocks generally are descriptive of this category.

The market price of growth stocks can be volatile, particularly over the short run. They often go up faster than other stocks, but at the first hint that the *rate of increase* in their earnings is not being sustained or that they will not meet the *expectations* of investors or analysts, their prices can come down rapidly.

Income Stocks

Sometimes people buy common stocks for current income. Stocks may be classified as *income stocks* when they pay a higher-than-average current yield. When general economic conditions become uncertain, investors often become more interested in current dividend income from stocks.

Growth (Moderate) and Income Stocks

This category really just represents a combination of the previous two groupings. These stocks pay reasonable dividends and offer reasonable growth potential.

Defensive Stocks

Some stocks are characterized as *defensive.* Such stocks are regarded as stable and comparatively safe, especially in periods of declining business activity. Their products tend to be staples and thus may suffer relatively little during recessions or depressions. The shares of utilities and food companies are examples of defensive issues.

Cyclical Stocks

Considerably different from defensive stocks are cyclical shares. A *cyclical company* is one whose earnings and share price tend to fluctuate sharply with the business cycle or with a cycle peculiar to its own industry. Automobile manufacturers, machine tool companies, and property and liability insurers have been examples of cyclical companies.

Blue-Chip Stocks

Blue-chip stocks generally are considered to be high-grade, investment-quality issues of major, well-established companies that have long records of earnings stability or growth and dividend payments in good times as well as bad. *Blue chip* is a rather vague term that is not very helpful in investment analysis.

Speculative Stocks

Speculative stocks generally are those presenting far greater risks for the investor than common stocks generally. Some high-flying glamour stocks are speculative. Likewise, some hot new issues and penny mining stocks are speculative. Other types can be identified from time to time as they come and go. Some are easy to identify; others are more difficult.

Also, there usually comes a point in a bull market when small, hitherto unknown companies go public or new small companies are formed. The public offering of their shares may find a fierce speculative demand and their prices often rise precipitously. Unfortunately, a day of reckoning usually follows.

Special Situations

There are stocks that may show rapid price appreciation due to some special and unique development that will affect the company positively. There might be a new process or invention, a natural resource discovery, a new product, a dramatic management change, a turnaround situation, and so forth. Companies normally in other categories can become a special situation in the face of such a development.

Small and Midsize Company Stocks

As the name indicates, small and midsize company stocks are stocks of smaller corporations—sometimes called *small-cap* (market capitalization) stocks. Some studies of stock returns over relatively long time periods have shown that, on average, the performance of small company stocks has been better than that of their larger counterparts but with greater volatility.

Foreign Stocks

Americans can buy the stocks of foreign companies through American Depositary Receipts (ADRs). An ADR is a negotiable U.S. certificate representing ownership of shares in a foreign corporation. ADRs are quoted and traded in U.S. dollars in markets in the U.S. and associated dividends are paid to investors in U.S. dollars. ADRs were created to make it easier for U.S. investors to buy, hold, and sell foreign stocks.

Some Theories of Common Stock Investment

There are many theories of how to invest in common stocks. They tend to rise and fall in popularity depending on market and economic conditions. Clearly, there is no agreement on any one theory. Some examples of such theories follow.

Growth Theory

The growth theory has been popular. The theory advocates analysis of corporate and industry data to select those quality issues that show continuing growth from one business cycle to another and a growth rate that well exceeds that of the overall economy. Implicit in this theory is that the investor is seeking returns primarily in the form of capital growth rather than dividend income.

If an investor can identify and purchase the stock of such companies in their early developmental and growth stages, and the companies go on to become leaders in a growing field, the investor probably will have spectacular results. However, the odds against selecting the right company or companies in this initial stage are considerable. Thus, in many cases the most likely course for the growth theory investor is to wait until a growth industry has passed through its initial, competitive stage, and then attempt to select several of the strongest companies that have emerged from the struggle.

Another approach for the growth theory investor is to purchase mutual funds (or accounts through other financial intermediaries) that specialize in certain industries the investor considers to be growth industries or in funds with growth or aggressive growth as investment objectives. This way the investor gets (and pays for) professional management in selecting growth stocks.

There are no pat answers with respect to growth stocks. Properly selected, they can produce substantial profits over the long run. But they are no investment panacea: investors who purchase growth stocks when they are most popular and high-priced may not be psychologically prepared for any substantial declines in their market prices. While such declines may be only temporary, some investors do not have the patience to hold securities under such circumstances. And, of course, the decline (or lack of growth) may not be temporary. However, if an investor analyzes the facts carefully, uses common sense, invests for the long term, and is patient, many believe the growth stock approach will yield handsome results over the years.

Value Investing

The value investing theory now generally calls for investing in the stocks of good-quality companies that have strong balance sheets and whose stocks appear to be temporarily undervalued by the stock market. This undervaluation often results from some temporary setback for the company or its industry. The value investor thus looks for good-quality stocks that are currently out of favor with the market in general. This theory requires careful security analysis and considerable patience. Value investors also argue that their theory involves lower market risk because the stocks they consider are already selling at low prices relative to other stocks.

The value investing approach was popularized by Benjamin Graham and David Dodd in their classic work, *Security Analysis: Principles and Techniques,* originally published in 1934. The financial criteria for stock selection originally advocated by Graham and Dodd were more rigorous than those generally used today, but the overall concept was the same. The Graham and Dodd book, with its subsequent editions, has influenced value theory investors to this day.

Moderately Growing Industries and Income Approach

Other investors prefer a policy of purchasing common stocks of good-quality companies that pay reasonable dividends and have prospects for at least some growth.

Depressed-Industry Approach

Almost the opposite of the growth stock theory is the depressed-industry approach, where the investor endeavors to select comeback industries and companies. The idea is that stocks in depressed industries may be selling at low prices that substantially overdiscount their troubles. Also, in applying this theory, investors probably are best advised to select the highest-grade, or at least one of the highest-grade, securities in a depressed industry.

Other Theories

This listing of theories is not meant to be exhaustive. Others could be given, but the ones mentioned here are followed today.

Common Stocks and Market Cycles

Investors in common stocks need to be aware of stock market cycles. When carried very far in either direction, stock market price movements often are recognized to have been irrational (or too exuberant) in retrospect, no matter how logical they may have appeared when they were taking place. Investor psychology toward common stocks in general can change and attitudes toward different companies and industries can follow a similar pattern. Thus, investors normally should maintain a reasonably balanced asset allocation strategy so as not to be completely dependent on any one investment medium (like common stocks).

The Case for Long-Term Investments in Common Stocks

To many people, *investment* has almost come to mean buying common stocks. There are several historical reasons for this. First is the long-term general decrease in the purchasing power of the dollar. Second, generally rising stock markets during much of the 1950s and 1960s, and particularly during the 1980s and 1990s, provided substantial (and sometimes spectacular) capital gains for many people who were in the market.

Studies of Historical Returns

The case for long-term investment in a diversified portfolio of common stocks as the best way to accumulate wealth is largely based on a number of studies comparing past total returns from common stocks with those from certain other investment media. These studies have found that the average annual compound rates of total return for large groups of common stocks were considerably higher than the corresponding rates of total return for long-term taxable U.S. Treasury bonds, U.S. Treasury bills, municipal bonds (after taxes were considered), and gold over various relatively long time periods.

Perhaps the best exposition of this thesis is contained in the excellent book, *Stocks for the Long Run* by Jeremy J. Siegel.[7] To illustrate the research involved here, Table 9.2 shows selected rates of return determined by Siegel for the time periods indicated for common stocks, long-term government bonds, and short-term government securities. (These returns are not adjusted for inflation, transaction costs, or taxes.) Table 9.2 illustrates only a small portion of the data Siegel developed. His book contains many valuable insights for investors, and it is recommended reading.

---

[7] Jeremy J. Siegel, *Stocks for the Long Run,* 3rd Edition (New York: McGraw-Hill, 2002).

Table 9.2. Comparative long-term returns* and risk** from common stocks, long-term U.S. government bonds, and short-term U.S. government bonds for various time periods

Period studied	Common Stocks			Degree of risk	Long-term bonds (total return)	Degree of risk	Short-term bonds (rate of return)	Rate of inflation (consumer prices)
	Dividend yield	Capital*** appreciation	Total*** return					
1871-2001	4.6%	4.2%	9.0%	18.5	4.4%	7.5	3.8%	2.0%
1926-2001	4.1%	5.8%	10.2%	20.3	5.3%	9.5	3.9%	3.1%
1946-2001	3.9%	7.5%	11.6%	16.8	5.5%	10.7	4.5%	4.1%
1966-1981	3.9%	2.6%	6.1%	17.2	2.5%	12.3	6.9%	7.0%
1982-2001	2.9%	-0.9%	14.1%	14.9	12.0%	13.8	6.1%	3.2%

*These returns are all nominal returns. That is, they are not adjusted for inflation. When they are so adjusted, they are referred to as real returns.

**Risk is determined by using the standard deviation of the arithmetic returns for the periods indicated. See the discussion of degree of investment risk and the standard deviation in this chapter. Also see Chapter 8 for the difference between arithmetic returns and geometric returns.

***These returns are geometric compound annual returns (average annual compound rates of return). See Chapter 8 for a discussion of this concept. Source: Jeremy J. Siegel, *Stocks for the Long Run*, 3rd Edition (New York: McGraw-Hill, 2002), pp. 10-16.

There have been a number of other studies that reached the same general conclusions. They include the 1964 study by Lawrence Fisher and James H. Lorie that contained rates of return on all common stocks listed on the New York Stock Exchange for 22 periods between January 1926 and December 1960.[8]

Another important study along the same lines was that of Roger G. Ibbotson and Rex A. Sinquefield in 1976.[9] The average annual rates of return and standard deviations for common stocks and other investment media, along with other statistical data, are updated annually by Ibbotson and Associates.[10] These data are widely used in the securities and mutual fund industries and by financial commentators generally. They are sometimes referred to as Ibbotson yields. There have been other studies as well.[11]

Degree of Risk

These studies that compare historical stock market average annual returns and the returns of other investment media are also concerned with the fluctuations or volatility of the yearly returns around the average return for a period of years. Such fluctuations or volatility represent the *degree of risk* for a particular investment or class of investments.

Perhaps the most commonly used statistical measure of volatility of annual returns (and hence of investment risk) is the *standard deviation*. The standard deviation measures the dispersion of individual yearly returns around the average return. Thus, it measures the risk that the actual annual returns will not correspond to the calculated average return for the period being studied. Therefore, *the larger the standard deviation,* the greater the volatility and *the greater the degree of investment risk.*

As an example, Table 9.2 shows that the average annual compound total return for common stocks from 1926 through 2001 was 10.2 percent. The standard deviation of the arithmetic returns was 20.3.[12] As a general principle, if the yearly returns follow a normal statistical distribution (a bell curve), then about 66 percent of the time the actual yearly returns will be within the range of one

[8] Lawrence Fisher and James H. Lorie, "Rates of Return on Investment in Common Stocks," *Journal of Business*, University of Chicago, January 1964.

[9] Roger G. Ibbotson and Rex A. Sinquefield, "Stocks, Bonds, Bills, and Inflation: Year-by-Year Historical Returns (1926-74)," *Journal of Business*, University of Chicago, January 1976.

[10] The source is *Stocks, Bonds, Bills, and Inflation Yearbook*, Ibbotson and Associates, Chicago.

[11] For a good discussion of such research, see Siegel, pp. 73-79. Also, William Greenough did similar research, which provided the conceptual foundation for the College Retirement Equities Fund (CREF).

[12] Siegel, p. 13. This is the standard deviation of the arithmetic returns. The average annual total arithmetic return for this period was 12.2 percent. See Chapter 8 for the distinction between a geometric average and an arithmetic average.

standard deviation above or below the average return, and about 95 percent of the time the actual yearly returns will be within the range of two standard deviations above or below the average return. Thus, using the data just given for 1926 through 2001 and assuming a normal distribution, we can say with 95 percent confidence that the actual yearly total returns on common stocks for this period will fall within a range from a loss of 28.4 percent [12.2% - (2 × 20.3)] to a gain of 52.8 percent [12.2% + (2 × 20.3)], using the 12.2 percent average annual total arithmetic return as the benchmark average return for this period.

There are other measures of investment risk. For example, the *alpha* is the measure of an investment's return that is not associated with overall market changes. The *beta* measures an investment's return (price movement) relative to the overall market or a market index. When a stock increases or decreases in the same proportion (percentage) as the overall market or index, its beta will be 1. If a stock's price moves in the direction opposite the market direction (e.g., the stock's price falls while the market is rising), it will have a negative beta. If a stock's price increases or decreases less rapidly (by a lower percentage) than the market as a whole, its beta will be positive but less than 1. On the other hand, if a stock's price increases or decreases more rapidly (by a higher percentage) than the market as a whole, its beta will be positive and more than 1. In general, the higher a stock's beta, the more volatile its price relative to that of the overall market or index. Another possible measure is the *variance,* which determines how much of the performance of an investment (or a mutual fund) is associated with that of a market index.

Some Conclusions Regarding the Studies

These studies have shown that average annual total rates of return and standard deviations have varied among types of investment media (stocks, bonds, U.S. Treasury bills, gold, and so forth) and varied over different time periods. But what they also universally show is that over relatively long time periods diversified portfolios of common stocks have performed significantly better than the other investment media studied (mainly U.S. Treasury bonds and U.S. Treasury bills).

As an example, this conclusion can be seen from Table 9.2 for the period 1926 through 2001. This (or perhaps a period with a somewhat earlier starting year) is a widely cited period because it is of long duration, covers all kinds of economic conditions (prosperity, depression, and recession), and includes long periods of peace but also several times of war. During this period, the average annual compound total return for common stocks was 10.2 percent while the comparable return for long-term government bonds was 5.3 percent. The yield on stocks was almost twice that of bonds. Other studies have produced very similar results for this period. However, the risk factor (volatility) for common stocks for this period, as measured by the standard deviation of yearly returns, was also significantly higher for common stocks than for bonds. The standard deviation for stocks was 20.3, while for bonds it was 9.5.

This means that although a diversified portfolio of common stocks can be expected to perform much better over a relatively long period of time than a portfolio of investment-grade bonds, the price of this better return is greater volatility of results from year to year—higher risk. (Note that these conclusions are based on data that have not been adjusted for inflation.)

An interesting insight on the return-risk analysis just presented comes from the research of Siegel. He determined that when one observes average annual *real returns*—returns adjusted for inflation—there is a remarkable stability over time in the real total returns of stocks as compared with those of long-term bonds and Treasury bills. The real returns on stocks have also been substantially higher than for bonds in most periods.[13]

These studies of historical returns have had a profound impact on investment thinking. They have helped make common stocks the preferred investment medium for many investors and their advisors. While the studies are based on historical data and there is no guarantee that the results shown will be repeated over long periods in the future, the consistency of the studies' results, the careful research that has gone into them, and the characteristics and variety of the long periods covered by the studies make them quite persuasive. It is hard to argue with the facts. After all, as the quote goes, "Those who do not learn from the lessons [mistakes] of history are doomed to repeat them."

These studies, which we shall refer to as the *historical yield approach,* relate particularly to asset allocation decisions. They may encourage investors to allocate as large a percentage of their investable assets as possible (given their time frames, tolerance for risk [volatility], and other considerations) to common stocks for the long term. This is discussed further in Chapter 13. Our tax system also tends to favor common stock investment over the long run.

Some Caveats

While the case just presented for a diversified portfolio (or index) of common stocks for superior long-term returns is persuasive, there always are caveats applying to any planning strategy. The first—that there is *no guarantee history will repeat itself*—has already been discussed.

---

[13] Siegel, pp. 12-15.

Need for Diversified Long-Term Approach

The second is that the studies have been done using large numbers of stocks (e.g., all the stocks listed on the New York Exchange, the S&P 500, and so forth) and therefore would seem to be valid only if an investor has a *reasonably diversified portfolio* of common stocks. A portfolio heavily weighted in only one or a few stocks may not perform like the general averages. Mutual funds may provide such diversification. Index funds (described in Chapter 12) are designed to duplicate the averages. Or an investor can diversify his or her directly owned stock portfolio.

Third, the studies' results are obtained only for relatively long holding periods. Thus, an investor should be prepared to hold a *fairly consistent* stock position over a *relatively long time*, which may include bad times as well as good. However, this historical yield approach does *not* seem to imply that a reasonably diversified portfolio cannot be actively managed by selling some stocks and buying others.

Need to Be Aware of Bear Markets

Fourth, it must be recognized that over the time periods being analyzed there have been *significant bear markets* for common stocks. A *bear market* may be defined as a reasonably long period of time during which common stocks in general consistently decline by a significant amount. What amount is "significant" can be a matter of opinion, but many consider it a bear market when the decline is 20 percent or more over a period of six months or longer.[14]

We noted earlier the concept of degree of risk based on the standard deviation of yearly returns over a period of time. However, since we are looking at history, there also have been a number of bear markets in stocks that have lasted longer than a year. Investors must deal with actual, possibly sustained stock market declines, rather than just with statistical yearly deviations from the average.

Therefore, it will be fruitful in evaluating the possibility and extent of declines in a stock portfolio to look at some past bear markets in common stocks. Table 9.3 presents selected actual bear markets based on the Dow Jones Industrial Average, except where indicated. It starts with the famous (or infamous) Great Depression of the 1930s and then moves to post-World War II bear markets. Finally, it takes a look at the recent decline in the Japanese stock market (the Nikkei 200), just for some international perspective.

---

[14] Another term sometimes used in this respect is a market correction. In general, a market correction is not as severe as a bear market and is a sudden, sharp decline in stock prices that lasts a shorter time (such as a few days or weeks). The other side of the coin to a bear market is, of course, a bull market.

Table 9.3. Some significant stock market declines* —bear markets

Date of Market Decline	Length of Market Decline (Bear Market Duration)	Percentage Decline	Recovery Period (to Previous High)**
Sept. 1929-July 1932	35 months	89	25 years (to Nov. 23, 1954)
Post-World War II U.S. Stock Market Declines*			
April 1956-Oct. 1957	19 months	19	11 months
Dec. 1961-June 1962	7 months	27	14 months
Feb. 1966-Oct. 1966	8 months	25	73 months
Dec. 1968-May 1970	18 months	36	29 months
Jan. 1973-Dec. 1974	23 months	45	95 months
Sept. 1976-Feb. 1978	17 months	27	37 months
April 1981-Aug. 1982	16 months	24	3 months
Aug. 1987-Oct. 1987	2 months	36	22 months
July 1990-Oct. 1990	3 months	21	6 months
Jan. 2000-Present	38 months (to date)	29	Unknown
Nikkei Average			
1990-Present	12 years (to date)	76	Unknown

*These data are based on the Dow Jones Industrial Average except where indicated.

**These recovery periods are based on stock prices only. They would be shorter if dividends paid on common stocks were considered. Dividends were not considered because interest or other income could have been earned on the funds had they not been placed in stocks.

These data may be useful to the investor in helping to estimate how large a potential stock market decline to be prepared for in investment planning. The long-term stock investor should expect such bear markets and be prepared to stay the course.

It would be splendid, of course, if one could forecast when bear markets were coming and what the bottom is going to be, and then sell high and buy low. Unfortunately, like the weather, everyone talks about bear markets but no one does anything about them. No one really knows when bear markets will occur and how severe they will be. However, it seems only prudent to assume they will occur periodically as they have in the past.

So the difficult question is how large a stock market decline should an investor plan for. As just admitted, no one really knows. However, as history has helped us estimate long-term stock market returns, it can give us some clues here, too. We saw from Table 9.2 that, based on the lengthy period of 1926 through 2001, we have 95 percent confidence that common stocks will not decline more than about 30 percent (28.4 percent) in any one year.

However, we also have seen from Table 9.3 that bear markets often have lasted longer than one year. Considering only post-World War II U.S. stock market declines, the most severe percentage decline was about 45 percent during the 23 months between January 1973 and December 1974. Therefore, to take a worst-case post-World War II kind of scenario for the U.S. market, we might assume just for planning purposes that common stocks could fall somewhere between 40 and 50 percent during a given bear market. Since we prefer to err on the financially conservative side, we shall assume a potential decline of as much as 50 percent.[15] This is the percentage we shall use in our asset allocation discussions in Chapter 13.

Before ending the discussion of bear markets, it should be noted that there also have been bear markets in investment media other than common stocks. This has been true of bonds (particularly during the late 1970s and the 1980s) and real estate (particularly in the late 1980s and early 1990s). Some data for bonds are presented in Chapter 11.

Will the Stock Market Universe Change?

A final caveat is the nagging concern that stock market conditions may not be the same today as they were during many of the periods often studied (such as 1926 to 2001, for example). In particular, a great many investors today are convinced that common stocks are where they should place as much of their investable assets as possible. They believe common stocks will produce far superior results in the future because they have done so in the past.

But a question is whether this very faith in common stocks will cause stock prices to be bid up so high that the superior results of the past cannot be duplicated in the future. During considerable periods of time between 1926 and 2001, for example, common stocks were not held in nearly the same kind of investment favor as they are at this writing.

No one knows the answer to this question. Thus, the prudent course for most investors may be to heed the lessons of the past with respect to the long-term superior performance of common stocks, but also to structure their asset allocation strategies so that they are not wholly dependent on common stock performance. We shall explore this further in Chapter 13.

---

[15] It may be noted that this assumption rather ignores the catastrophic 89 percent decline at the beginning of the Great Depression. We think conditions are sufficiently different today that such a drastic rout of stock values is unlikely now. However, this is a matter of judgment; no one knows for sure.

10

Other Equity Investments

Real Estate

Historically, real estate has been a widely used investment medium for income and capital gains. A great many people have an investment in real estate, in a sense, in that they own their house, condominium, or cooperative apartment. Many people also own a second or vacation home. Others own income-producing properties or REITs as an investment. A few have larger real estate interests of various kinds.

Advantages of Real Estate as an Investment

Attractive Total Returns on Equity. It is possible to earn a higher-than-average total after-tax return on well-selected real estate investments. This may result from the inherent advantages of owning well-selected real estate, the use of financial leverage, and tax advantages. One difficulty in comparing the yields on real estate with those of other investments is that there are specialized concepts for measuring real estate returns, and some of them are quite complex. They are beyond the scope of this book. However, to give a point of reference, here is a simple formula used in real estate as a rough rule of thumb for comparing the operating yields on different investment properties:

$$\text{Operating rate of return} = \frac{\text{net operating income from property before interest and depreciation}}{\text{purchase price for property}}$$

To illustrate, suppose an investor purchased a small apartment house for $800,000. To finance the property, the investor paid $120,000 down (in cash) and took a $680,000 25-year, 7½ percent mortgage on the property. Considering the local real estate market, the investor expects net operating income (NOI) and the market price for the real estate to increase at about 2 percent per year. Thus, if current annual NOI—annual revenue (rents) less property taxes and other expenses of operation, but before interest, depreciation, and income taxes are deducted—is $64,000, the operating rate of return is as follows:

$$\text{Operating rate of return} = \frac{\$64,000}{\$800,000} = 0.08 \text{ or } 8.0\%$$

The taxable income for federal income tax purposes for the first year of operation would be as follows:

NOI	$64,000
Less:	
Depreciation	-$24,400
Interest paid	-$51,000
Taxable income (loss)	($11,400)

The depreciation in this example assumes that about $672,000 of the $800,000 purchase price (84 percent) is allocated to the building and its improvements (the depreciable portion of the property). Land cannot be depreciated. Depreciation is taken on a straight-line basis over a 27.5-year useful life. Note that depreciation is a noncash expense that serves to reduce current taxable income. This is the main *tax-shelter* aspect of real estate as an investment.

It can be seen that this real estate investment will produce a loss for federal income tax purposes in its first year. An important issue is whether the investor will be able to deduct this loss against other taxable income (i.e., use it to shelter other income). This issue is explored later in this chapter with respect to the *passive activity loss* (PAL) rules. However, unless the investor is essentially a real estate professional or the individual taxpayer exception applies, this loss would be a PAL and deductible currently only against passive activity income.

The taxable income (loss) from this property will change over time. The NOI may rise or fall depending on real estate market conditions and operating expenses. The interest paid will decline as the amortizing mortgage is paid off.

Availability of Substantial Financial Leverage. *Leverage* is simply the use of borrowed funds to try to increase the rate of return that can be earned on the investor's own funds invested in a project. In general, when the cost of borrowing is less than what can be earned on the investment, it is considered *favorable leverage* (or a *positive carry*), but when the reverse is true, it is called *unfavorable leverage* (or a *negative carry*).[1] The example just given has favor-

[1] Leverage can also be viewed as the use of borrowed funds with the hope that the value of the real estate will increase at a faster rate than the cost of borrowing the funds. This is a more risky view of leverage.

able leverage because the operating rate of return on the property is greater than the interest rate being paid on the mortgage.

Real estate investors typically employ substantial financial leverage—often from 60 to 90 percent of a property's value. They may also use leverage to *pyramid* their real estate holdings through leverage on acquisitions, refinancing of appreciated properties, reinvestment, and tax-free exchanges (covered later in this chapter). In the simple illustration used here, 85 percent of the initial purchase price was financed through a mortgage loan, while the investor's initial equity in the property was $120,000 ($800,000 value less $680,000 mortgage).

Favorable Cash Flow. Good-quality income property normally will produce a *favorable cash flow.* This is because it should produce a reasonable NOI and because depreciation is a noncash expense that will diminish taxable income but not cash flow. *Cash flow* for the first year of our example can be calculated as follows:

NOI (first year)	$64,000
Less:	
Annual debt service (principal and interest on mortgage loan)	-53,900
Cash flow before tax	$10,100
Less:	
Income tax payable	-(3,990)[2]
Cash flow after tax	$14,090

If, however, the investor cannot take the $11,400 loss against other income because of the PAL rules and has no passive activity income to reduce, then the first year's cash flow will be the same as the before-tax figure. Even in this case, however, the investor can reduce other taxable income through the accumulated, suspended PALs by selling the real estate in a fully taxable transaction.

Hedge Against Inflation. Real estate, like other equity investments, is considered a good hedge against inflation. This is because property values and rents tend to rise during inflationary periods.

Tax Advantages. First, as just noted, improved real estate allows the investor to take depreciation as a noncash income tax deduction. However, if the real estate is later sold in a taxable transaction, the depreciation previously deducted will reduce the property's income tax basis and result in a correspondingly higher capital gain (or lower capital loss). Thus, in the case of a subsequent

---

[2] The income tax payable figure here is negative because it represents the reduction in the tax otherwise payable by the investor due to the $11,400 loss for tax purposes. It assumes the investor is in the 35 percent marginal income tax bracket ($11,400 × 0.35 = $3,990).

sale, the depreciation deduction really defers the tax and converts gain from ordinary income to capital gain.

Second, the costs to operate and maintain property, such as property taxes, management fees, insurance, and repairs, are deductible. Third, real estate can be traded or exchanged for like-kind property on a tax-free basis under Section 1031 of the Internal Revenue Code (IRC).

Fourth, on the sale of investment real estate, any gain normally is a capital gain.[3] In addition, an installment sale can be arranged so any capital gain will be spread over the installment period. Finally, since borrowing against real estate is not considered a sale or exchange for capital gains tax purposes, refinancing real estate traditionally has been a way for taking value out of the real estate without incurring capital gains taxation.

Control and Pride of Ownership. Direct real estate ownership may give investors the opportunity to select, manage, and control their investments.

Disadvantages of Real Estate as an Investment

Lack of Marketability. There is usually relatively slow marketability in real estate. It can take substantial time to buy or sell real estate. Further, the expenses of buying and selling are relatively high.

Need for Large Initial Investment. A relatively large initial investment often is required. In the illustration used previously, for example, the investor would need $120,000 (equity) to purchase the apartment house.

Real Estate Cycles and Leverage. It may be difficult to determine the proper value for real estate, particularly for the uninitiated. Real estate is not uniform and there are definite cycles in the real estate market. Also, during the down phase of the cycle, the very financial leverage that was so attractive when real estate prices (and rents) were rising works against the investor.

High Risk Level. Real estate is considered by many to be an inherently risky form of investment. It is basically fixed in location and character. Also, real estate values will fall during a period of economic recession as rapidly as, or perhaps even more rapidly than, other kinds of equity investments.

How Investments in Real Estate Can Be Made

Individual and Joint Ownership. First of all, investors can simply buy property in their own names or as joint tenants or tenants in common with someone

---

[3] However, for certain depreciable real property (such as residential real property), net capital gain attributable to allowable depreciation on the property will be taxed at a maximum rate of 25 percent rather than the normal 20 percent maximum rate on net capital gains.

else. This is the traditional way of holding real estate, but it limits the size of the investment that can be made to the amount of capital the investor and perhaps a few others can raise.

Partnerships. Many individuals invest in real estate by buying units in limited partnerships (LPs) that hold real estate. The LP has been a common vehicle for real estate investment, with investors as the limited partners and a promoter, builder, or developer as the general partner. In this way, the limited partners can invest their capital with only limited liability for partnership debts and the earnings (or losses) from the real estate can be passed through the partnership organization to the individual limited partners without being taxed to the partnership. The earnings (or losses) are taxable to (or, to the extent permitted by the tax law, deductible by) the individual partners.

The general partners manage the real estate investment. But note the importance of the character, ability, and experience of the general partners, because they are in control. Also, real estate LP interests generally have very limited marketability and liquidity. There are some secondary markets for these interests, but investors who dispose of their LP interests before the partnership itself terminates usually must accept large price discounts. Real estate could also be owned through limited liability companies (LLCs) and possibly corporations.

Real Estate Investment Trusts (REITs). A real estate investment trust (REIT) is similar in concept to a closed-end investment company. (See Chapter 12 for a description of closed-end funds.) It is a corporation or business trust that meets the tax law requirements to be a REIT and invests primarily in real estate. A REIT can give investors the advantages of centralized management, limited liability, continuity of interests, and transferability of ownership (marketability). Further, a REIT can avoid the corporate income tax by distributing most of its earnings to its shareholders. The distribution is then taxed to the shareholders as ordinary income or capital gains. However, unlike partnerships, REITs are not allowed for tax purposes to pass losses through to their shareholders.

REITs vary considerably in size, origin, and types of real estate investments made. Therefore, investors should consider the investment objective of any REIT being considered. Also, the management of a REIT is critical. Shares of many REITs are traded on organized stock exchanges.

There are three general types of REITs, based on one's investment approach. *Equity REITs* derive their revenues primarily from rental income and capital gains from properties they own. *Mortgage REITs* receive their revenues mainly from interest income from mortgage loans they make. *Hybrid REITs* are combinations of the equity and mortgage approaches. REITs may also specialize in particular kinds of real estate or mortgage loans.

An aspect of equity REITs is the *umbrella partnership REIT (UPREIT)*. An UPREIT is a limited partnership with a REIT as the general partner that manages the partnership affairs and with persons or partnerships that contribute their existing properties or partnership interests to the limited partnership in exchange for limited partnership interests. This exchange will not cause taxation on any appreciation in the existing properties or real estate partnership interests contributed, because the contribution of appreciated property to a partnership in exchange for a partnership interest is a tax-free exchange.[4] Thus, contributors can diversify their real estate interests without recognizing capital gains. Also, after a period of time, UPREITs usually allow limited partners to exchange some or all of their limited partnership interests for cash or REIT shares. This, however, will result in capital gains taxation on any appreciation involved.

Sub-Accounts in Tax-Advantaged Plans. Some qualified retirement plans, variable annuities, and possibly variable life insurance have sub-accounts invested in real estate that participants or owners can select. However, since the investment income of these plans is not taxable currently anyway and all distributions from them are taxed as ordinary income, the tax advantages of direct real estate investments essentially are lost when real estate is held through these plans.

Kinds of Real Estate Investments

In terms of investment and tax considerations, real estate can be classified as follows:

- Unimproved land (bare land)
- Improved real estate (held for rental), including:
  - New and used residential property (apartment houses and the like)
  - Low-income housing
  - Old buildings and certified historic structures[5]
  - Other income-producing real estate (such as office buildings, shopping centers, warehouses, hotels and motels, and various industrial and commercial properties)
- Mortgages
- Vacation and second homes

---

[4] See Chapter 14 for a listing of nonrecognition provisions in the tax law for capital gains tax purposes. This is one of the important nonrecognition provisions.

[5] Certain special tax incentives may apply to these types of real estate investments.

Disposition of Investment Real Estate

At some point, real estate investors may wish to dispose of properties. Depending on the circumstances and the owner's objectives, there are several approaches to doing so.

Cash Sale. In this case, the investor sells the property and gets the purchase price within one year. Using the previous illustration, suppose our investor holds the apartment house for 10 years and then sells it for cash. Assuming the market price increases by 2 percent per year, the sale price would be approximately $975,000. The outstanding mortgage has declined to about $600,000 and the investor's income tax basis in the property now is $556,000 (which is the original basis of $800,000 reduced by annual depreciation of $24,400 for 10 years, or $244,000).[6]

Given these facts, the *tax status* of this sale would be as follows:

Sale price	$975,000
Less:	
Transaction costs (at 7%)	-$68,250
Adjusted basis ($800,000 less	
accumulated depreciation of $244,000)	$556,000
Long-term capital gain	$350,750
Amount of gain attributable	
to depreciation taxed at 25%	
($244,000 × 25% = $61,000)[7]	$61,000
Remainder of net capital gain	
taxed at 20% ($106,750 × 20% = $21,350)	$21,350
Total tax payable	$82,350

In addition, if the investor has suspended passive activity losses (PALs) from the past 10 years,[8] he or she can use them against passive and nonpassive income in the year the entire interest in a passive activity (the apartment house in this case) is disposed of. The suspended PALs are used first against the income or gain from the passive activity disposed of, then against passive income from any other passive activities, and finally against nonpassive income or gain (e.g., salary, interest, or dividends).

The *after-tax equity position* of the investor then would be as follows:

Sale price	$975,000

---

[6] This assumes there have been no other changes in basis (such as improvements to the property that would increase basis).

[7] See footnote 3.

[8] See the discussion of the PAL rules later in this chapter.

Less:

Transaction costs (at 7%)	-$68,250
Mortgage loan balance	-$600,000
Capital gains tax payable	-$82,350[9]
Net after-tax equity position	$224,400

As a result, the investor would have this cash for other investments or other purposes. However, the investor would realize and recognize capital gain in the year of the sale.

Installment Sale or Sale for a Private Annuity. An *installment sale* occurs when payment for an asset is made over more than one taxable year. Any taxes due are payable pro rata as each installment payment is made. Real estate is often sold on an installment basis. However, when property is sold in this fashion, the seller still retains some risk that the buyer will not make the payments.

A sale for a *private annuity* is much less common and normally is done as part of family estate planning. Private annuities are described in Chapter 25.

Like-Kind Exchanges. These are tax-deferred exchanges of similar (*like-kind*) property under Section 1031 of the IRC. These transactions are often called *like-kind exchanges* or *Section 1031 exchanges*. They are important in real estate because they allow a property owner to exchange property for other real estate without recognizing capital gain on the property exchanged. Thus, the investor can change holdings with no or limited tax consequences. The tax rules for like-kind exchanges are complex and must be carefully followed to secure non-recognition treatment. The income tax basis of an owner in the property being exchanged carries over to the new property received.

Like-kind exchanges may involve the receipt of *boot* in addition to the exchanged properties. Boot is cash or personal property (*unlike property*) received in addition to the like-kind exchanged real estate. Boot may be necessary to even out the values in an exchange. The receipt of boot will result in current taxation to the extent of the boot. The remainder of the gain will not be recognized.

Refinancing of Properties. While not technically a *disposition* of real estate, refinancing allows owners of appreciated real estate to get cash out of their properties without taxation. However, it also means they will increase their leverage (debt) with the resulting risks or benefits.

If, for example, after 10 years the investor in our previous illustration decided to refinance the apartment house with a mortgage at 85 percent of its current appraised value ($975,000), instead of selling or exchanging it, the following would be the result (ignoring the expenses of refinancing):

---

[9] This would be reduced by any tax savings from suspended PALs, as just explained.

New mortgage loan (85% of $975,000) $828,750
    Current mortgage loan balance   -$600,000
    Cash available from refinancing $228,750

The investor could use this cash as equity for the purchase of additional real estate (and thus pyramid his or her real estate portfolio), invest it elsewhere, or use it for other purposes.

Gifting of Property Interests. Real estate, like other property, can be given away to family members as part of an estate-planning gifting program. The advantages and disadvantages of lifetime giving are explored in Chapter 25.

Oil and Gas (Natural Resource) Ventures

Oil and gas ventures can be risky investments, but they can yield handsome returns if successful. They tend to be specialized investments and their economic characteristics are beyond the scope of this book.

Some basic tax incentives exist for oil and gas investments.

- The deduction from income of intangible drilling costs (IDCs), which could be up to 80 or 90 percent of the initial cost of a productive well. The tax law permits persons with a *working interest* in oil and gas drilling operations (i.e., persons who generally have unlimited liability for their own share of the costs) to deduct their losses from these operations against other taxable income. However, a limited partnership interest is not such a working interest; losses of limited partners normally would be passive activity losses (PALs).
- A percentage depletion allowance, which taxpayers may deduct from their gross incomes from oil and gas investments.

People can, of course, invest directly in oil and gas operations. However, oil and gas limited partnerships are offered to the public as a way of investing in oil and gas.

Other Tax Shelters

Other kinds of tax-sheltered investments include cattle feeding and other farming enterprises, horse and cattle breeding, timber, minerals and mining operations, equipment leasing, movies, and research and development ventures, among others. Space does not permit a discussion of each of them in this book.

Impact of Passive Activity Loss Rules

The kinds of investments just described traditionally have been called *tax-sheltered investments* because losses (even though they may not have been real economic losses) were used to reduce an investor's other taxable income.[10] Such tax losses might arise, for example, from depreciation in real estate investments and intangible drilling costs and percentage depletion in oil and gas ventures.

The Issue

The result was that many high-income persons invested in tax shelters with the aim of reducing their taxable income. Naturally, it was hoped the tax-sheltered investments would show a profit at some point, but then the investor could sell them and take the gains at least partially as capital gains. Investors could also continually make new tax-sheltered investments and get new losses.

As a result of alleged abuses in tax-sheltered investments, the Tax Reform Act of 1986 adopted the passive activity loss (PAL) rules. The main concept of the PAL rules is to prohibit taxpayers (with some exceptions) from using what are defined as *passive activity losses* to offset or *shelter* other kinds of taxable income.

What Constitutes a Passive Activity

For purposes of these rules, a passive activity is (1) a trade or business in which the taxpayer does not *materially participate* on a regular, continuous, and substantial basis[11]; or (2) an activity primarily involving the rental of property, whether the taxpayer materially participates or not. Thus, rental activities (including rental real estate) generally are passive, regardless of material participation by the owners. There is an exception to this rule for real estate in the case of *real estate professionals* who materially participate in the rental activity. The law defines such persons rather closely. There is also an individual real estate investor exception, as explained shortly.

---

[10] While the term *tax-sheltered investments* traditionally has been used as just described, it may also be loosely used to describe many other tax-favored arrangements.

[11] There also are objective tests in the income tax regulations as to what the statutory term materially participates means. For example, a taxpayer is considered to materially participate in an activity if he or she participates more than 500 hours during the year, or if he or she participates more than 100 hours and no one else had greater participation, or if his or her participation during the year constituted substantially all the participation of anyone, among other tests.

Who Is Affected

Taxpayers affected by these rules include any individual acting as an individual, a partner in a partnership, a member of an LLC, or a stockholder in an S corporation; estates; trusts; and certain closely held C corporations. When there is a passive activity, the tax law provides that expense deductions in excess of income (i.e., passive activity losses) generally may be used only to offset passive activity income from other passive activities. Thus, PALs may not be used currently to offset income from other sources, such as salary or personal earnings (called *personal service income*), taxable interest and dividends (referred to as *portfolio income*), and taxable income from *active business pursuits* (i.e., a trade or business in which the taxpayer does materially participate).

However, unused PALs are not lost entirely, but are merely suspended until the taxpayer can use them against passive activity income in the future (if any) or until the taxpayer sells the passive activity in a fully taxable transaction (at which time they can be taken against other income as previously described) or to a certain extent at the death of the taxpayer.

Individual Real Estate Investor Exemption

There is a special exemption from these rules that allows an individual taxpayer who "actively participates" in a rental activity to deduct up to $25,000 of losses from rental real estate each year from his or her taxable income from other sources, provided the taxpayer's adjusted gross income (AGI) is less than $100,000. For taxpayers with AGIs over $100,000, this $25,000 exemption is phased out by reducing it by 50 percent of the amount the taxpayer's AGI exceeds $100,000.[12]

Put and Call Options

Trading in options to buy or sell common stocks (*calls* or *puts*) on organized exchanges is a technique used by some investors. A *call* is an option allowing the buyer *to purchase* from someone a certain stock or other asset at a set price (called the *exercise* or *strike price*) at any time within a specified period. A *put* is an option allowing the buyer *to sell* to someone a certain stock or other asset at a set price at any time within a specified period. Options normally are for round lots (100 shares) of common stock. The expiration date is the last day on which the holder of an option can exercise it. Listed options have standardized quarterly expiration dates.

---

[12] Thus, the phaseout occurs with AGIs between $100,000 and $150,000.

Buying Options

People may buy options when they want to speculate on whether a stock is going up or down or is going to fluctuate beyond certain limits or for other reasons. The price paid for the option is called the *premium*.

For example, suppose a person thinks XYZ Common is too low and the price soon will go up. In this case, he or she might buy a call option for XYZ Common. Further suppose that on June 1, XYZ Common is selling at $62 a share and that a listed XYZ Common October 60 call option is purchased for a premium of $7 per share, or $700 for the 100-share option. This means that for $700 (exclusive of commissions, for the sake of simplicity) the person has purchased a standardized contract allowing him or her to buy (call) 100 shares of XYZ Common stock at $60 per share (the exercise price) at any time prior to the end of October (the expiration date). Now if XYZ Common climbs to $72 a share by September 1, the October 60 call will become more valuable in the listed options market and, let us say, the premium for this option is $13 per share on September 1. If the person decides to close out the option position on September 1, he or she would sell the call option for $13 per share. In this case, the profit (exclusive of commissions) would be as follows:

June 1—Purchased call option for	$700
September 1—Sold call option for	$1300
Profit on the three-month transaction	$600

It can be seen that this profit is 85 percent of the $700 premium for the option, while the price of the underlying stock rose only 16 percent (from $62 to $72 per share). But if the price of XYZ Common stays around $62 or declines during the five-month period, the option buyer will lose the $700 premium and suffer a 100 percent loss. However, the option buyer's risk of loss will be limited to the premium paid for the option.

While leveraged speculation is the main reason for buying calls, there are other possible reasons, such as to sell some existing investments to release cash while still maintaining a short-term market position, to protect against short-term market uncertainty, and to have a hedge against short sales.

On the other hand, if the person thinks XYZ Common is overpriced and soon will fall substantially, he or she might buy a put option. It would work basically the same way as a call, except in the opposite direction.

Another reason for buying puts may be to protect an investment position from the risk of a declining market. As explained in Chapter 15, buying put options can be part of investment *collar transactions* designed to protect the value of highly appreciated stocks from market declines without actually selling the stocks and realizing capital gains.

More sophisticated traders can engage in a variety of option techniques.

One is the *straddle,* in which a put and a call on the same stock are purchased with the same exercise price and expiration month. Here the speculator will profit if the underlying stock's price moves far enough in either direction to more than offset the premiums on both options.

Selling (Writing) Options

The motivation for selling options normally is entirely different from the motivation for buying them. The option writer normally wants to secure an attractive yield on an existing investment. This increased yield comes from the premiums received by the option writer on the options granted to buyers. The option writer, however, gives up the opportunity for capital appreciation on stock he or she owns that is called away. But if the price of the stock declines, the option writer bears this risk (except that the writer still has the premium for the call).

But writing so-called *naked* call options is highly speculative. These are options where the writer does not own the underlying security. Generally, calls should be sold only on securities in the option writer's portfolio or on securities purchased for this purpose. Also, puts should be sold only against cash and only on stock the writer would otherwise want in his or her portfolio.

Selling call options is the other part of investment collar transactions noted previously and described in Chapter 15.

New Issues or Initial Public Offerings (IPOs)

Stocks and bonds offered by corporations for the first time are called *new issues* or *initial public offerings* (IPOs). Some have been offered by corporate giants, but most new issues are made by smaller, less known, or newly formed corporations. Many of them do not have an established track record of operations and earnings. Hence, they are often speculative. Some investors, however, like to buy such new issues as speculations. Those that prove successful offer phenomenal gains for their original buyers. There also *may be* rapid, initial run-ups in price immediately after an IPO. But many such issues do not prove successful in the long run.

Commodity Futures Trading

Persons usually engage in commodity futures trading in hopes of profiting from price changes in one or more basic commodities, including wheat, corn, oats, soybeans, potatoes, platinum, copper, silver, orange juice, cocoa, eggs, frozen pork bellies, lumber, and iced broilers. One can speculate on price changes in these commodities by buying and selling futures contracts.

A *futures contract* is an agreement to buy or sell a commodity at a price stated in the agreement on a specified future date. While futures contracts call for the delivery of the commodity (unless the contract is liquidated before it matures), this is rarely done. Speculators in commodity futures almost always close out their positions before the contracts mature. This way the commodity itself never actually changes hands among speculators. On the other hand, contracts to buy or sell the physical commodities are made in the cash (or *spot*) market.

As an illustration, suppose a person thinks the price of corn is going up. He or she might enter into a futures contract to buy 5000 bushels of corn (a full contract in corn) for delivery in December at a price of $3 per bushel, which would be the market price for December corn at the time the buy order was executed (assuming it was a market order). This is referred to as being *long* in the commodity. Now suppose the person is correct and in a month the price of December corn futures rises 20 cents per bushel to $3.20. The speculator now might decide to close out the transaction by selling 5000 bushels of December corn and taking a profit of 20 cents per bushel, or a total of $1000 (5000 × 0.20 = $1000), exclusive of commissions and other costs. However, the speculator could have magnified this profit through the leverage of trading on margin. Margin requirements in commodities are relatively low—usually 5 to 10 percent of the value of the commodity traded. If the margin requirement in this example had been 10 percent, the speculator would have had to deposit with the broker only $1500 as security for the futures contract that had a value of $15,000. Thus, such leverage can magnify a speculator's potential profits (and losses) in terms of the amount the speculator actually puts up. Of course, if the price of December corn futures had declined and the speculator had closed out the transaction, he or she would have suffered similar speculative, leveraged losses.

Suppose, instead, that the speculator thinks the price of corn is too high and is going down. In this case he or she would sell short and might, for example, enter into a futures contract to sell 5000 bushels of corn for delivery in December at a price of $3 per bushel. Here the speculator hopes to close out the transaction (cover the short position) when the price of December corn has fallen below $3 per bushel. Of course, if the price of December corn futures rises and the speculator covers the short position, he or she will lose on the transaction. There are many other techniques for dealing in commodity futures that are not discussed here.

A word of caution is in order. While the opportunities for speculative profits in commodity futures trading can be enormous and quick, the risks are equally so. Trading in commodity futures is inherently speculative and risky.

Art, Antiques, Coins, Stamps, Gold, and Other Precious Metals

Some people are interested in investing in more unusual items. In the past, properly selected items in some areas have shown substantial increases in price.

Some of these items are unique and specialized, so buying them successfully requires a knowledge of what one is doing. Also, they produce no investment income—only possible price appreciation. Of course, many people have a collector's interest in such property anyway, so it may be quite logical for them to acquire these items.

11

Fixed-Income Investments

The previous two chapters have dealt with various equity-type investments. Yet, for most individuals, equity investments should form only part of their overall asset allocation strategy. One or more types of *fixed-income* securities generally should also be included. Simply stated, fixed-income investments generally promise the investor a stated amount of income periodically and in most cases also promise to pay the face amount at its maturity date.

Types of Fixed-Income Investments

Fixed-income securities and investments include the following:

- Corporate bonds
- Municipal bonds
- Marketable U.S. government obligations
- U.S. savings bonds
- U.S. government agency securities
- Zero-coupon bonds (corporate, municipal, and U.S. government)
- Certificates of deposit (CDs)
- Guaranteed investment contracts (GICs)
- Liquid assets (cash equivalents)
- Preferred stocks

Ways of Taking Returns from Bonds

Before beginning to discuss the various types of bonds, it will be helpful to note the ways in which investors can purchase marketable bonds and take returns from them. This discussion will help explain the income tax status of various bonds. Further, as with common stocks, the *total return* from a bond over a given period is the market price at the end of the period less the market price at the beginning of the period (capital gain or loss) plus interest paid during the period.

Bonds Purchased at Par

When the purchase price of a bond is equal to its value at maturity (par value or face amount), it is purchased at par. The investor receives the interest payments (coupon rate) until maturity, at which time the investor receives the face amount. If the investor sells or redeems the bond prior to maturity, the investor will realize a capital gain (or loss) if the sale price is more (or less) than his or her tax basis (cost) in the bond.

Market Discount Bonds

These are bonds purchased in the open market after issuance at a price less than the face amount of the bond (assuming the bond was originally issued at par). For example, an investor might purchase a 4½ percent $1000 face amount bond due to mature in 2013 for $937. In this case, the investor receives the interest payments (coupon rate of 4½ percent times $1000 or $45 per year) until maturity, at which time the investor will receive the $1000 face amount, which includes $63 of market discount.

If the investor sells or redeems the bond prior to maturity, he or she will realize a gain (or loss) if the sale price is more (or less) than his or her adjusted tax basis in the bond. A gain may be partially a recovery of market discount and partially a capital gain. A loss will be a capital loss.

Original Issue Discount (OID) Bonds

Here the bonds are originally issued at a price less than the face amount of the bond. When these bonds pay no current interest (they have a coupon rate of 0), they are called *zero-coupon bonds* or *zeros*. For example, an investor might purchase a $1000 bond with a 0 percent coupon rate due to mature in 2024 for a price of $255. In this case, he or she receives no current interest payments but at maturity receives the $1000 face amount, which includes $745 of original issue discount. If the investor sells the bond prior to maturity, he or she will realize a gain (or loss) if the sale price is more (or less) than his or her adjusted tax basis in the bond.

Bonds Purchased at a Premium

These are bonds purchased in the open market after issuance at a price greater than the face amount (assuming the bond was originally issued at par). For example, an investor might purchase a 6¼ percent $1000 face amount bond due to mature in 2031 for a price of $1091. In this case, the investor receives the interest payments (coupon rate of 6.25 percent times $1,000 or $62.50 per year) until maturity, at which time he or she receives the $1000 face amount, but in effect loses the $91 premium. If the investor sells or redeems the bond prior to maturity, he or she will realize a capital gain (or capital loss) if the sale price is more (or less) than his or her adjusted tax basis in the bond.

Bonds Held by Intermediaries

When bonds are held in mutual funds, variable life insurance and variable annuity products, or in qualified retirement plans, their returns are treated like returns generally in these funds or accounts.

Corporate Bonds

These are bonds issued by private corporations that usually are based on the creditworthiness of the issuing corporation. They are viewed as less secure than U.S. Treasury issues (the most secure) and also less secure than most municipal bonds.

Security for Corporate Bonds

Some bonds, such as equipment trust certificates and mortgage bonds, are secured by a lien on all or a portion of the property of the company. Many bonds, however, are *debentures*—bonds backed by the full credit of the issuing corporation but with no special lien on the corporation's property. Debentures generally have first claim on all assets not specifically pledged under other bond indentures. *Subordinated debentures* have a claim on assets after the claims of senior debt. Bond issues may have sinking-fund provisions designed to retire a substantial portion of the bonds before maturity.

Call Provisions

Many corporate bonds can be redeemed or *called* before maturity. However, many corporations now issue securities that offer investors protection against call for a specified period. Investors are willing to accept lower yields in exchange for some call protection or for bonds that are not callable at all. Call protection in bonds tends to vary with economic conditions. Unfortunately, no one really knows how interest rates will move in the future.

Tax Status of Corporate Bonds

As a general principle, the investment income from corporate bonds is fully taxable for federal income tax purposes. It also is generally fully taxable for state income tax purposes. (Some states do not have income taxes.) The *current interest paid* (coupon rate) is taxable as ordinary interest income. *Market discount* also is generally taxed as ordinary income. *Original issue discount* (OID) is taxed as ordinary income.

If a corporate bond is purchased *at a premium,* the investor may elect to amortize the premium over the remaining life of the bond (or sometimes until an earlier call date). Depending on when the bond was purchased, the investor may use the amount amortized each year to reduce the otherwise taxable interest on the bond or as an itemized deduction. Either way, the amount amortized serves to reduce otherwise taxable ordinary income. The amount amortized also reduces the investor's tax basis in the bond. If the investor does not elect to amortize the premium, it is added to basis and either reduces capital gain on disposition of the bond for more than basis or produces a capital loss on disposition for less than basis.

If a corporate bond is sold or redeemed prior to maturity, amounts received in excess of basis generally are taxable as capital gains. However, in the case of market discount bonds or OID bonds, part or all of any gain may be taxed as ordinary interest income.

Municipal Bonds (Munis)
Tax-Free Versus Taxable Returns

An important feature of municipal bonds is interest that is exempt from federal income tax and from state and local income taxes in the states in which the bonds are issued. Municipals are particularly attractive to persons whose income tax brackets enable them to realize greater after-tax return from tax-free interest than from interest that is fully taxable. Columns 2, 3, and 4 of Table 11.1 illustrate the relationship between the effective after-tax returns on municipal bonds and those of certain other fixed-income investments. Column 5 shows the equivalent taxable yields to a 5½ percent tax-free yield at various marginal federal income tax rates applicable in 2003.

For example, a husband and wife who file a joint return and are in a 30 percent federal income tax bracket would keep on an after-tax basis all the income

Table 11.1. After-tax returns on fixed-income investments[*]

1	2	3	4	5[**]
Federal tax bracket	After-tax return from a municipal bond paying a tax-free yield of 5½%	After-tax return from a bank paying 5% taxable	After-tax return from a corporate bond paying 7% taxable	For the investor to keep 5½% (tax-free) from a taxable investment, it would have to pay an equivalent taxable yield of
15	5.5	4.25	5.96	6.47
27	5.5	3.65	5.11	7.53
30	5.5	3.50	4.90	7.86
35	5.5	3.25	4.55	8.46
38.6	5.5	3.07	4.30	8.96

*All values are in terms of percentages. These yields do not consider the possible effects of state or local government income taxation, which can very considerably among the states.
**This equivalent taxable yield is calculated by dividing the tax-free yield (5½% here) by 1 minus the top marginal federal income tax rate.

from a tax-free municipal bond (or 5½ percent as shown in Table 11.1). But this same couple could keep only 3.50 percent from a CD paying 5 percent (taxable) and 4.90 percent from a 7 percent corporate bond (taxable). Based on these figures, this couple probably should consider municipals. Note that while yields will change over time, it is the *investor's top marginal tax rate* combined with *the relationship* between municipal bond yields and generally comparable taxable yields that are the basic points for the investor to consider.

If state and local taxes are considered, the after-tax yields on municipals that are free from federal, state, and local taxes are even more attractive.[1] To determine the *combined effective federal and state top marginal income tax rate*, assuming an investor itemizes federal income tax deductions, it is necessary to adjust the top marginal state tax rate to reflect the fact that state and local income taxes are deductible in arriving at federal taxable income.[2] This adjustment involves multiplying the state rate by 1 minus the marginal federal rate to determine the effective state rate.

[1] These are sometimes called *triple-tax-free* municipal bonds. They are free of federal income tax and states and municipalities generally do not tax the interest (and sometimes the capital gains) on municipal bonds issued in the state.

[2] A complication here is that until 2006 and thereafter up to 80 percent of certain itemized deductions (including the deduction for state and local taxes) is phased out for taxpayers with an adjusted gross income (AGI) over a certain amount. Thus, high-income investors may not have to worry much about this adjustment. Also, under the Economic Growth and Tax Relief Reconciliation Act of 2001, this limitation on itemized deductions will be phased out starting in 2006.

If we assume the married couple in our example has a top marginal state and local tax rate of 6 percent and itemizes federal deductions, their effective state rate is 6 percent × (1 - 0.30) or 4.20 percent. Their combined effective federal and state rate then is 34.20 percent (30 percent federal rate + 4.20 percent effective state rate). In this event, the after-tax (federal, state, and local) return from the 7 percent corporate bond from Table 11.1 would be 4.61 percent and the equivalent taxable yield for a 5½ percent municipal would be 8.36 percent.

If an investor does not itemize deductions for federal tax purposes (or if deductions are mostly phased out)—and, hence, state and local income taxes are not deductible or mostly not deductible—the combined effective federal and state rate can simply be stated as the top federal rate plus the top state rate (or 30 + 6 = 36 percent in the previous illustration). Note that this analysis does not apply to U.S. Treasury securities or other direct U.S. government obligations, because their interest is exempt from state and local income taxation.

Call Provisions

Like corporate bonds, municipals are often callable. However, they may be callable only after a certain date and/or have other call protection. Also, some municipals are not callable at all.

Kinds of Municipal Bonds

General-Obligation Bonds. This is an important category of municipal bonds; they are secured by the full faith, credit, and taxing power of the issuing state or municipality. General-obligation bonds are normally considered to offer a high level of security for the investor, consistent, of course, with the credit rating of the issuer.

Special Tax Bonds. These bonds are payable only from the proceeds of a single tax, a series of taxes, or some other specific source of revenue.

Revenue Bonds. Revenue bonds are issued to finance various kinds of projects, such as water, sewage, gas, and electrical facilities; hospitals; dormitories; hydroelectric power projects; and bridges, tunnels, turnpikes, and expressways. The principal and interest on such bonds are payable solely from the revenues produced by the project.

Housing Authority Bonds. These bonds are issued by local authorities to finance the construction of low-rent housing projects and are secured by the pledge of unconditional, annual contributions by the Housing Assistance Administration, a federal agency. Housing authority bonds are considered top-quality investments.

Industrial Development Bonds (IDBs). These bonds are issued by a municipality or other authority but are secured by lease payments made by industrial corporations that occupy or use the facilities financed by the bond issue.

Insured Municipal Bonds. Many municipal bonds carry insurance to protect investors against the risk of default on the bonds. Such insurance enhances the creditworthiness of the bonds and normally gives them the highest quality rating. Three large insurers of municipal bonds are the Financial Guaranty Insurance Company (FGIC), Municipal Bond Investors Assurance (MBIA), and the American Municipal Bond Assurance Corporation (AMBAC). It is the financial strength of these private insurers that stands behind their insurance of municipal bond issues.

Municipal Bond Ratings

Quality ratings on municipal bonds are provided by Moody's and Standard & Poor's, the financial services that also rate corporate bonds. (See the section in this chapter, "Bond Ratings and Investment Quality.") In general, high-grade municipals rank second in quality only to securities issued by the U.S. government and government agencies.

Tax Status of Municipal Bonds

Interest on all municipal bonds issued prior to August 8, 1986, generally is exempt from all federal income taxation. However, for municipal bonds issued after August 7, 1986 (or other applicable dates), there is a three-tiered system of federal income taxation, as follows: (1) interest on public-purpose municipals remains free from all federal income taxation; (2) interest on tax-exempt private-activity municipals (*qualified bonds* or *AMT bonds*) is exempt from regular federal income taxation, but generally is a preference item for alternative minimum tax (AMT) purposes; and (3) interest on taxable private activity municipals is fully taxable for federal income tax purposes. To date, relatively few fully taxable municipals have been issued.

Since the interest on AMT bonds (private activity bonds used to finance such projects as airports, stadiums, and student loan programs) is a preference item for AMT purposes, it will cause AMT at either a 26 or a 28 percent rate for those subject to the AMT system.[3] For those investors, AMT bonds are not attractive. However, since AMT bonds normally have higher yields than comparable public-purpose bonds, they may be attractive for investors who are not subject to the AMT.

[3] The AMT system is described in Chapter 14.

For municipal bonds purchased after April 30, 1993, accrued *market discount* generally is taxed as ordinary income upon sale, redemption, or maturity of the bond. For bonds purchased before May 1, 1993, market discount is treated as capital gain.

Original issue discount (OID) in municipal bonds is not taxable, but for municipal bonds both issued after September 3, 1982, and acquired after March 1, 1984, the owner's tax basis is increased by accrued tax-exempt OID.

If a fully tax-exempt coupon-paying municipal bond is *purchased at a premium,* the owner must amortize the premium over the remaining life of the bond (or sometimes until an earlier call date). However, the amount amortized each year is not deductible nor does it reduce otherwise taxable interest. Instead, it simply reduces the tax-free interest received. Also, the owner must reduce his or her basis in the bond by the amount amortized each year.

If a municipal bond is *sold or redeemed* prior to maturity, amounts received in excess of basis generally are taxable as capital gains. However, for market discount bonds, part or all of any gain may be interest income.

U.S. Government Obligations

Treasury Bills

Treasury bills are issued on a discount basis and are redeemed at face value at maturity. They generally have maturity periods of 13 weeks, 26 weeks, and 52 weeks and are considered highly liquid, secure, short-term securities (cash equivalents).

Treasury Notes

Treasury notes have maturities from one to 10 years. They are issued at or near par and their interest is paid semiannually.

Treasury Bonds

Treasury bonds mature in more than 10 years. The so-called long bond has been a 30-year bond. Treasury bonds also are issued at or near par, and their interest is paid semiannually.

Call Provisions

In general, Treasury notes and bonds are not callable. Some long-term bonds are callable at par five years before maturity, but otherwise they are not callable. This lack of call risk and their highest credit standing can be important factors in planning a bond portfolio. They may lead investors to use long-term Treasuries for the longest-maturity rung in laddering a bond portfolio (see Chapter 8). This way, the investor can get call protection and the highest credit rating at the long end of the portfolio, and then use tax-free municipals or possibly corporates (both of which callable) for the intermediate and shorter maturities.

Tax Status of Treasury Notes and Bonds

The interest income from U.S. Treasury notes and bonds is taxable for federal income tax purposes. However, it is exempt from state and local income taxation. This somewhat increases the after-tax yields from Treasuries, depending on the level of state and local taxation (if any) where the investor resides.

The *current interest paid* (coupon rate) is taxable as ordinary interest income. *Market discount* also is generally taxed as ordinary income. In addition, *OID* is taxed as ordinary income. If Treasury notes or bonds are *purchased at a premium,* the investor may elect to amortize the premium over the remaining life of the bond. This operates in the same way as for corporate bonds. The *sale* of Treasury notes and bonds also produces the same general federal tax results as for corporate bonds.

Inflation-Indexed Treasury Notes and Bonds

The Treasury has issued Treasury Inflation-Protection Securities (TIPS). These are Treasury notes or bonds with a fixed interest rate that is applied to a principal amount that is adjusted periodically for inflation or deflation based on an adjusted Consumer Price Index for urban consumers (CPI-U). They pay semi-annual interest and then the principal amount (including any inflation or deflation adjustments) at maturity. However, there can be a minimum guarantee payment at maturity if the principal at that time is less than the principal at issuance.

As an example, suppose the Treasury issued a $1000 10-year inflation-indexed note with a fixed interest rate of 3½ percent. Further, assume that during the first year inflation was at 3 percent. At the end of the year, the note's principal amount would be adjusted to $1030 and the 3½ percent interest would be paid on that amount ($36.05 per year). The principal amount would be adjusted regularly over its duration and paid to the bondholder at maturity. For tax purposes the investor has gross income each year equal to the current interest paid plus any adjustment to principal for inflation (or less any deflation adjustment), even though the adjusted principal is not paid until maturity. Thus, an investor can have tax liability on an inflation adjustment without current cash from the note or bond with which to pay the tax. Thus, TIPS may be best suited for tax-advantaged vehicles (like IRAs).

Savings Bonds

U.S. savings bonds are registered, noncallable, and nontransferable (i.e., non-marketable) securities. Two kinds of savings bonds being issued are Series EE (or E), now called Patriot Bonds, and Series I, which are inflation-indexed. There are also Series HH bonds.

Series EE bonds are sold in face-value denominations of $50 to $10,000, with the purchase price being 50 percent of the face amount. EE bonds pay no current interest; instead, they are issued at a discount and are redeemable at face value on the maturity date. The interest rate on EE bonds is 90 percent of the average return on marketable five-year Treasury notes. This is referred to as a *market-based rate* and is set by the Treasury every six months. EE bonds are redeemable at any time starting six months after issue, but redemption within the first five years reduces the effective yield.

Series I bonds are sold at face amount and accrue earnings until they are redeemed or mature (in 30 years). They accrue annual earnings at a composite rate consisting of a fixed rate for the bond's duration and a semiannual inflation rate (or deflation rate). When investors redeem EE and I bonds or when they mature, they normally are taxed on the difference between the purchase price and the redemption value as ordinary interest income. However, investors can elect to be taxed annually as bond interest accrues, but few do so. In addition, interest on EE bonds used for tuition and fees at colleges, universities, and qualified technical schools can be excluded from the bond-owner's income under certain conditions. Also, savings bond interest is exempt from state and local income taxes.

Series HH bonds are interest-paying savings bonds that pay interest every six months. They can be secured at par in exchange for EE and similar bonds. HH bonds may be redeemed six months after issue, but they may be held to earn interest for as long as 20 years. If EE bonds are exchanged for HH bonds not more than one year after the EE bonds mature, the accrued interest on the EE bonds will not be taxed until the HH bonds are redeemed or mature. This can result in a long period of tax deferral for such accrued interest. However, the current semiannual interest on the HH bonds is taxed when paid.

Other U.S. Government and Agency Securities

U.S. Government Agency Securities. These securities are not issued directly by the federal government, but some have government guarantees. They typically carry somewhat higher yields than comparable U.S. government securities. Some of the governmental agencies that issue these securities are the federal home loan banks, the Federal National Mortgage Association (Fanny Mae), the Government National Mortgage Association (Ginnie Mae), and the International Bank for Reconstruction and Development (World Bank).

Flower Bonds. These were U.S. government bonds that the federal government formerly accepted at par in payment of federal estate taxes. However, they are no longer being issued and the last issue outstanding matured in 1998. Therefore, they now are of historical interest only.

Pass-Through (Participation) Securities. This is a participation in a pool of assets (e.g., federally insured mortgages) by which the investor receives a certificate evidencing his or her interest in the underlying assets. Probably the most important are those issued by the Government National Mortgage Association—the Ginnie Mae pass-throughs. These certificates permit investors to earn high mortgage yields with principal and interest guaranteed by the federal government.

A special feature of these securities is that part of the principal is returned with the interest each month as the underlying mortgages in the pool are amortized by the borrowers. Thus they provide a higher level of secure income. On the other hand, there is an interest rate risk inherent in pass-throughs in that, if market interest rates decline significantly, mortgage borrowers will tend to pay off and refinance their loans at the lower rates. This will cause higher principal payments to the pass-through investors, who then must reinvest these payments at the current, lower interest rates.

In this general area, there are several categories of securities. *Mortgage-backed securities* are participations in pools of mortgages; *asset-backed securities* are similar participations in pools of consumer loans; and *collateralized mortgage obligations* (CMOs) are a form of mortgage-backed security but that may consist of portions with different investment characteristics.

Market Discount Bonds
General Characteristics

As noted previously, market discount bonds sell in the market for less than their face amount (par value). Investors may like such bonds for several reasons. First, in effect, they provide automatic call protection because their coupon rates are relatively low compared with current market interest rates. Also, their issuers normally must pay at least par value on redemption, which increases the cost of a call. In addition, they provide built-in income (or gain) upon maturity. Any kind of bond—corporate, municipal, or U.S. government—may sell at a discount in the open market. The availability of such bonds and the extent of the discounts depend on movements of interest rates. Rising interest rates—and hence declining bond prices—tend to produce market discount bonds.

Tax Status of Market Discount Bonds

For taxable bonds *issued* after July 18, 1984, or bonds issued on or before July 18, 1984, and *purchased* on the open market after April 30, 1993, any gain on sale, redemption, or maturity to the extent of accrued market discount will be taxed as ordinary interest income, rather than capital gain.[4] Any gain in excess of this amount will be taxed as capital gain and any loss will be treated as capital loss. (For other taxable bonds, accrued market discount on sale, redemption, or maturity will be taxed as capital gain.)

However, cash-basis bondholders may elect to include accrued market discount each year in their gross income and have it taxed then, rather than deferring taxation until sale, redemption, or maturity of the bond. Most bondholders will not make this election; however, it might be made if the bondholder has unused interest expense to carry investments that can only be deducted against investment income (taxable interest or dividends) or in certain other situations.

For tax-exempt obligations (munis) *purchased* after April 30, 1993, any gain on sale, redemption, or maturity to the extent of accrued market discount will be taxed as ordinary interest income, rather than capital gain.

Zero-Coupon Bonds (Zeros)
General Characteristics

These are original issue discount (OID) bonds sold without any stated coupon rate; hence they pay no current interest income. They are sold originally at usually substantial discounts from par, and their return to the investor is measured by their yield to maturity. Zeros may be U.S. government bonds (taxable), corporate bonds (taxable), or municipal bonds (tax-exempt). The main advantage of zeros for investors is to lock in current interest rates for the duration of the bond.

---

[4] There is a de minimis rule that ignores any market discount of less than one-quarter of 1 percent of the stated value at maturity times the number of years until maturity.

Tax Status of Zero-Coupon Bonds

For *taxable bonds* (issued after July 1, 1982) an annual amount of accrued original issue discount (calculated by applying the bond's yield to maturity to an adjusted issue price) is currently taxable to the owner as ordinary interest income, even though the investor currently receives no cash income from the bonds.[5] This treatment of *taxable zeros* has caused them to be used almost entirely in tax-protected vehicles like IRAs, qualified retirement plans, variable annuities, and variable life insurance, because in these vehicles, otherwise taxable income is not taxed currently.

For *tax-exempt zeros* (municipal bonds), accrued OID is not included in gross income. It is tax-exempt like interest on other tax-free munis. This treatment of *tax-exempt zeros* results in investors holding them directly, since the accrued OID is not taxable.

Planning Considerations

Zero-coupon bonds in general can be attractive for investors who wish to accumulate a fixed amount by a specified maturity date and lock in a current interest rate until maturity with no risk of call in normal circumstances, but who do not need current income until maturity. They also can be used for the long-maturity end of a laddered bond portfolio, since they normally are not callable.

Preferred Stocks

Preferred stocks (or *preferreds*) represent equity capital of a corporation. The claim that preferred stockholders have against the assets of the corporation follows the claim of bondholders but precedes that of common stockholders. In almost all cases, a company must pay dividends on its preferred stock before paying anything on its common. But a corporation can pass (omit) its preferred dividends without becoming insolvent. Thus, it is less risky for a corporation to issue preferred stock than bonds or some other debt instrument. On the other hand, the corporation cannot deduct preferred dividends for corporate income tax purposes, although it can deduct interest on bonds or other true indebtedness.

The dividend rate on preferred stock is usually fixed. When dividends are *cumulative,* any arrears of preferred dividends must be paid before dividends can be paid on the common stock. On the other hand, when dividends are

---

[5] There is a de minimis rule here, too, like that indicated in note 4. Also, for OID bonds issued before July 2, 1982 (and after December 31, 1954), OID is included in gross income when the bond is sold, is redeemed, or matures.

noncumulative, common dividends can be paid even though preferred dividends have been omitted in the past and remain unpaid. Although preferreds typically do not have fixed maturities, they may be subject to call. Preferred stockholders normally do not have voting rights, but they may have them in some cases or under certain conditions. Some preferreds are convertible into common stock. Preferred dividends constitute ordinary dividend income for federal income tax purposes when paid to the owners.

Guaranteed Principal Fixed-Income Investments

The types of fixed-income investments we have discussed so far provide guaranteed investment income and/or a promised value at maturity, but during the term of the investment (e.g., until a bond matures), the market price of the security can fluctuate depending on market interest rates and other economic conditions.

The fixed-income investments we are now considering have both a guaranteed principal value throughout their term and certain guaranteed investment income. Such investments do not have any market risk or interest rate risk to their principal value. They may, however, have some financial risk in that their security (in the absence of government insurance) depends on the ability of the issuer to meet its financial commitments.

Certificates of Deposit (CDs)

Traditional Fixed-Dollar CDs. These are interest-bearing, redeemable evidences of time deposits issued and sold through banks and savings institutions. They are sold in varying amounts and with maturities ranging from a few months to 10 years or more. The interest rate usually is fixed and guaranteed for the duration of the CD, with the rate normally being higher the longer the maturity. There is an interest penalty for early withdrawal if these CDs are redeemed prior to maturity, but any penalty is deductible by the investor from gross income to arrive at adjusted gross income. In most cases, CDs are insured up to $100,000 per eligible account through the Federal Deposit Insurance Corporation (FDIC). Also, an investor may purchase insured CDs up to $100,000 each from multiple banks and still be fully insured. Interest payable on CDs is fully taxable for federal and state purposes as ordinary interest income.

Negotiable CDs. These are CDs that are not redeemable by the issuer before maturity but can be traded in a secondary market prior to maturity. If they are sold before maturity, the value received may be less (if market interest rates rise) or more (if market rates fall) then the face amount (purchase price). However, the full face amount is payable at maturity. In this sense they are much like bonds. Negotiable CDs are issued by banks but usually sold through investment firms.

Market-Linked CDs. Some banks issue CDs whose principal (original investment) is guaranteed by the issuer and often is insured up to $100,000 by the FDIC but whose investment return is based on some equity index (like the S&P 500 stock index), provided the purchaser holds the CD until maturity. In other words, if the market goes up, the investor receives his or her original principal plus an investment return based on the appreciation of the applicable market index. If the market goes down, the investor is guaranteed to receive at least his or her original investment back. However, these CDs, which are often called *market-linked deposits* (MLDs), may not pay 100 percent of the original investment or any investment income if an investor withdraws from them prior to maturity.

A difficulty with MLDs is that the depositor does not receive any investment returns until maturity, but those gains are taxed currently as ordinary income. For this reason, MLDs are often considered for tax-protected accounts.

Guaranteed-Dollar Life Insurance Cash Values

As noted in Chapter 4, the cash values of guaranteed-dollar life insurance contracts (traditional whole life, universal life, or interest sensitive whole life) can be viewed as a guaranteed principal fixed-income investment.

Guaranteed-Dollar Annuity Cash Values

Guaranteed-dollar (or fixed-dollar) annuity cash values also can be considered guaranteed principal fixed-income investments. The characteristics of investment annuities are discussed in Chapter 21.

Guaranteed Investment Contracts (GICs)

These are investment options for employees under certain kinds of qualified retirement plans provided under a contract with a life insurance company. The insurer guarantees the principal and interest of the GIC for the specified period of time. Employees should remember, however, that the security behind a GIC is the financial soundness of the insurance company providing it.

Liquid Assets

Liquid assets (cash equivalents) should be *highly liquid* (convertible into cash immediately with no loss of principal) and *financially secure* (low or no financial risk). On the other hand, these assets are *short term* and tend to offer a *lower yield* than other fixed-income securities.[6] Investors may want liquid assets for possible emergencies, for flexibility to be able to take advantage of investment opportunities, as an investment strategy if interest rates are expected to rise significantly, or as a repository for cash while deciding on an investment or other large expenditure. The types of liquid assets that may be held in a portfolio were noted in Chapter 2 and Chapter 8.

Conversion Privileges in Fixed-Income Securities

Investors may consider whether to buy *convertible bonds* or *convertible preferred stocks,* which provide the security of a bond or a preferred, but also provide an opportunity for capital appreciation through anticipated appreciation of the underlying common stock. Convertible bonds and preferreds give the holder the right to convert the security into a certain number of shares of common stock at a predetermined price for the common.

But this opportunity is not free. The price effectively is the difference between the yield on a convertible bond or preferred and the yield on an otherwise comparable nonconvertible security. Convertible securities generally are callable.

Bond Ratings and Investment Quality

Bonds issued or guaranteed by the U.S. government are considered the safest of investments. Other bonds have varying quality ratings in terms of financial risk.

Bond Rating Systems

To help investors assess the investment quality of many corporate and municipal bonds, bond ratings are published, periodically reviewed, and revised when needed by independent rating agencies. The two main rating agencies

---

[6] This statement reflects the general principle that for a given quality of fixed-income investment, the yield will rise with duration. This may be referred to as the yield curve for fixed income securities. However, under certain economic conditions, this yield curve can be quite flat (with little or no difference in yields between shorter-term and longer-term securities of the same type) or even inverted (with shorter-term yields higher than longer-term yields). A flat or inverted yield curve may occur, for example, when investors generally believe that interest rates will fall significantly in the future and thus are seeking to lock in the present rates by buying (and hence bidding up the prices of) longer-term securities with adequate call protection (such as longer-term Treasuries).

Table 11.2. Bond rating systems

Quality	Standard & Poor's†	Moody's†
Investment grade:		
Highest quality*	AAA	Aaa
High quality	AA	Aa
Upper medium grade	A	A
Medium grade	BBB	Baa
Below investment grade:		
Moderately speculative*	BB	Ba
Speculative	B	B
Highly speculative	CCC	Caa
Lowest quality (including in default)	C, D	C

*These are abbreviated terms used to describe these rating systems and are not the complete descriptions used by the rating agencies themselves to describe their ratings.

†There may be subclasses within these letter ratings, designated as 2 or 3 by Moody's and + or – by Standard & Poor's.

are Moody's and Standard & Poor's.[7] The corporate and municipal debt rating systems of these two agencies are outlined in Table 11.2. These ratings are of the creditworthiness or financial ability to meet the specific obligations of the issuer of the particular bonds involved. Bonds with one of the top four ratings from one or both agencies are often considered to be *investment grade*.[8] Bonds with lower ratings are considered by the rating agencies as having varying degrees of *speculative elements*.

High-Yield Bonds

High-yield or *junk bonds* generally are considered those with ratings below investment grade. As can be seen from Table 11.2, however, this can embrace a fairly wide range of financial risk. Therefore, in evaluating high-yield bonds, the investor should consider the relative degrees of financial risk involved. In other words, some bonds are "junkier" than others. Also, of course, the spread between the yields on investment-grade bonds and high-risk bonds should be evaluated to see if the extra financial risk is worth it.

[7] These agencies also rate many insurance companies for financial soundness or claims-paying ability, as described in Chapter 3. They also rate commercial paper.

[8] Moody's judges bonds in its top two ratings to be of high quality.

Bond Ratings and Yield

General Considerations. A major question in high-yield investing is whether the higher yields on lower-quality bonds at least make up for the higher default rates on such bonds. Part of this question, of course, is what the real, long-term, average annual default rates are on bonds of lower quality. While a review of the research on this issue is beyond the scope of this book, it appears at this writing that no one really knows.

Diversification Issues. Diversification seems to be the key idea in this area. First, to be a successful investor in high-risk bonds, it seems necessary to be reasonably diversified over a number of issues and perhaps maturities. The investor really has no way of knowing which particular bond or bonds may default. For investors with relatively small amounts of these bonds, mutual funds may be a logical answer to their diversification needs. It may also be desirable to invest only a small percentage of one's overall portfolio in high-risk bonds.

Application of Modern Portfolio Theory

Modern portfolio theory suggests that a basic element in diversification of risk (with *risk* defined as the variation of actual returns around an expected return) is allocating the assets in an investment portfolio among categories of investments whose statistical performance correlations to each other are relatively low (or even that have no correlations or negative correlations). *Statistical correlations* measure the extent to which the performance of an asset class tends to move in the same direction as that of other asset classes (either up or down). A statistical correlation of 0 means there is no relationship between the performances of two asset classes—they are independent of each other. A positive correlation means they tend to move in the same direction. A high positive correlation indicates they tend to move together more closely (to a higher degree), while a lower positive correlation means they tend to move together but to a lesser extent. A negative correlation indicates they tend to move in opposite directions. The statistical correlations are calculated from historical data on the performance (variability) of asset categories. Therefore, as with other historical statistical studies, the historical period used can be significant.

The essential idea is to manage or control portfolio risk (i.e., the variability of returns of the whole portfolio) by allocating the portfolio among uncorrelated asset classes or among asset classes with low correlations. That way, if one asset class declines, another asset class may not decline, may not decline to nearly the same degree, or may actually rise, depending on how correlated the classes are.

Thus, according to modern theory, the addition of a higher-return asset class, like high-yield bonds, to a portfolio that consists, say, mainly of U.S.

common stocks and high-grade U.S. bonds will not necessarily increase over-all portfolio risk if there is a low correlation between high-yield bonds and the other asset classes. This can be a rationale for adding some high-yield bonds to a portfolio.

Bond Insurance

As noted earlier, many municipal bonds and a few corporate bonds are insured against default. Insurance normally earns a bond the highest rating—triple A—from one or more of the rating agencies.

Strategies for Investing in Fixed-Income Securities

As the discussion in this chapter has unfolded, it can be seen that there are several areas where investors need to develop strategies with respect to the fixed-income portions of their overall asset allocations.

Investment Duration Considerations

One approach to duration issues would be to adjust maturities, at least to some degree, with regard to expected changes in interest rates. As a general rule, maturities should be lengthened when interest rates are expected to decline and should be shortened when interest rates are expected to rise. In this way, investors will have committed their funds at the present high rates when future rates are expected to be lower and will have funds available to commit later at the expected higher rates when it is anticipated that interest rates will be higher. Of course, no one really knows which way interest rates will move in the future. On the other hand, investors can follow a *diversified approach* toward the maturity structure. Such a strategy (laddering) was illustrated in Chapter 8.

Taxable Versus Nontaxable Considerations

Investors need to evaluate the relative after-tax attractiveness of taxable as compared to tax-exempt securities. This should be done considering federal, state, and local income taxes, particularly in states with high income taxes. The factors involved in this analysis were discussed earlier in this chapter.

Strategies for Call Protection and Interest Rate Risk

Investors also need to evaluate their exposure to the two kinds of interest rate risk. Some strategies for doing this were discussed in Chapter 8 (e.g., laddering).

Investment-Quality Considerations

We have already discussed the relationship between yield and bond ratings and have noted that there do not seem to be any pat answers. Much depends on an investor's personal circumstances, investment objectives, and tolerance for risk. On the other hand, modern portfolio theory tells us that if lower-quality bonds have low correlations with other asset categories in a portfolio, overall portfolio risk may not be increased (and may even be decreased) by the addition of high-return, high-financial-risk, but low-correlation bonds.

There can be a variety of strategies regarding investment quality. Very risk-averse investors may decide to purchase only bonds rated in the top two or three grades according to Moody's or Standard & Poor's and U.S. Treasuries or U.S. government-guaranteed or -backed bonds or to invest only in mutual funds or other financial intermediaries that have these investment objectives. In contrast, other investors may decide to allocate the bulk of their bond portfolio—say, 75 to 80 percent—only to such investment-grade securities, while allowing the balance to be in below-investment-grade bonds if market conditions and yield spreads seem propitious. At the other end of the scale, more aggressive investors may be willing to allocate a larger portion of the fixed-income portion of their portfolio to higher-yield bonds when they think market conditions and yield spreads warrant it.

Diversification Strategies

Investors should decide when and how they wish to diversify their fixed-income investments. This might include diversification by maturities (laddering), by high-quality and high-yield issues, and by investing in a number of different issues.

12

Mutual Funds and Other Investment Companies

Mutual funds are registered investment companies that offer investors (shareholders) an interest in a portfolio of investment assets.

Kinds of Investment Companies

In popular usage, the term *mutual fund* often is used to refer to any kind of investment company. Actually, however, there are three basic kinds of investment companies: those that sell face-amount certificates (the issuer promises to pay the investor a stated amount at maturity or a surrender value if tendered early), unit investment trusts (the fund invests in a fixed portfolio of securities), and so-called management companies. The most important of these are the management companies, which, in turn, can be classified as closed-end funds and open-end or *mutual funds*. The open-end or mutual fund is by far the most important variety.

Why Invest in Mutual Funds?

A number of *advantages* are given for investing in mutual funds. First, by pooling their investable capital, smaller investors are able to enjoy a degree of *diversification* they could never achieve on their own. Second, mutual funds may offer experienced *professional management* to select and manage the securities in which the funds' resources will be invested. And, third, mutual funds offer *convenience* and *ready marketability* through the funds' obligation to redeem their shares. Further, funds provide investors with *reasonable investment unit size* so that many persons can invest through them. In addition, fund distributions normally can be reinvested systematically and investors' holdings can usually be liquidated systematically.

Disadvantages of Mutual Funds

As with any financial intermediary, there are *costs* associated with investing through mutual funds. Expenses vary among funds, as discussed later in this chapter. Second, investors still must find those funds whose investment objectives are consistent with their own and whose performance and costs are satisfactory. Thus, the investor still has a *selection issue,* even though the choice of individual investments is transferred to the fund's management. Further, for investors who want to *concentrate* their investments in one or only a few issues, the risk-averse diversification strategy inherent in mutual funds may not be for them. Also, investors who want to *make their own investment selections* for part or all of their portfolios would not use investment intermediaries for their personal selections.

Types of Funds—Some Planning Considerations

Investment companies can be classified in several ways. One of the major distinctions is between open-end and closed-end funds. Another important choice is between load and no-load mutual funds. Unit investment trusts also can be used.

Open-End Funds

A mutual fund is, by definition, an open-end investment company. They are called *open-end* because the number of outstanding shares is not fixed. Instead, the number of shares is continually changing as investors purchase or redeem shares. When people buy shares in an open-end fund, they buy them from the fund itself. And when they want to redeem shares, the fund must stand ready to buy them back. The price for purchase or redemption is based on the most recent net asset value (NAV) of the shares. NAV per share is the total value of all securities and other assets held by the fund, less any fund liabilities, divided by the number of outstanding shares. It is calculated daily.

Closed-End Funds

A closed-end investment company is similar in many respects to a typical corporation. It issues a fixed number of shares, which does not fluctuate except as new stock may be issued. It can issue bonds and preferred stock to leverage the position of the common shareholders. The closed-end fund uses its capital and other resources primarily to invest in the securities of other corporations.

The shares of closed-end funds are bought and sold in the market just like the stock of other corporations. The price for closed-end shares is determined by supply and demand in the market and is not tied directly to a fund's NAV per share. When the market price of a fund's shares exceeds its NAV, the fund is said to sell *at a premium.* On the other hand, when the stock price is less than a fund's NAV, it is said to sell *at a discount.* At any given time, some closed-end funds may sell at a *premium* while others sell at a *discount.*

Open-End Versus Closed-End Funds

This is a debatable question; there are no pat answers. But here are some things to consider.

First, both types provide professional investment management, diversification, and periodic distributions of investment income and capital gains to investors. They both also are readily marketable, but in different ways—an open-end fund through redemption of its shares by the fund itself and a closed-end fund by sale of its shares on the open market. There are many more open-end funds than closed-end funds from which to choose, and they often are sold by sales representatives or brokers who handle mutual funds.

When an investor buys or sells a closed-end fund, he or she pays stock market commissions and other costs. The sales charge paid for mutual fund shares depends on whether it is a *load* or *no-load* fund, as described next. What fund shares are worth at any given time is determined differently. In the case of a mutual fund, it is the NAV of the fund shares at that time; for a closed-end fund, it is the price on the stock market at that time. Investors cannot buy a mutual fund for less than its NAV per share, but they frequently can buy a closed-end fund at a discount or at a premium.

Load and No-Load Mutual Funds

Open-end funds are sold on either a load or a no-load basis. A *load* generally refers to the sales charge levied on an investor by a fund for executing a transaction.

The most common arrangement is where the investor pays the charge when purchasing shares but then pays no charge when redeeming them. This is referred to as a *front-end load.* Front-end loads might range from 4 to 8½ percent of the offering price.[1] Thus, when a load fund is purchased, the investor pays the net asset value plus the load. No-load funds traditionally do not charge a sales commission (load) when the shares are purchased or redeemed. Thus, both transactions occur at the fund's NAV per share.

Investors also should note that some funds levy what are called *12 b-1 fees* (named after the 1980 SEC rule that first permitted them). These are annual sales fees taken against fund assets to reimburse the fund for distribution costs.

Funds may also charge a contingent-deferred sales fee (called a *back-end load*) if shares are redeemed within a few years of their purchase or at any time. These fees may decline over time or they may not.

Finally, some funds are known as *low-load* funds since they charge relatively lower loads at purchase.

Open-end fund values and prices are given daily in the financial pages of most newspapers. Prices are quoted on a NAV basis and an offering price (offer) basis. Any spread between the NAV and the offering price is the load. For a no-load fund, the quoted NAV and the offering price would be the same.

For load funds, the percentage load is normally reduced as an investor makes larger dollar purchases. The amounts at which the percentage sales charge declines are called *discounts* or *breakpoints*. Also, an investor may be entitled to an *accumulation discount* or *right of accumulation* on the basis of previous fund purchases. Thus, all fund shares held at the time an additional purchase is made may be taken into account in determining the sales load.

In addition to the sales loads of load funds and any annual 12 b-1 sales fees, both load and no-load funds charge investment management fees and other expenses annually against the fund's net assets. These annual fees are expressed as a percentage of the fund's average net assets; this is referred to as a fund's *expense ratio.*

Assuming an investor has decided to invest in mutual funds, he or she should consider whether to buy a load fund or a no-load fund. This is a controversial question; again there are no pat answers. The greater part of the load paid by investors is received as a commission by the sales representative or broker. No-load funds frequently are not sold through sales representatives. Their shares normally are purchased and redeemed directly through the fund itself.[2] Thus, no-load funds avoid the sales representative's commission. On the other hand, the mutual fund purchaser loses the advice and sales efforts of the representative.

---

1 Note that this results in a slightly higher percentage load based on the net amount actually invested (i.e., the offering price less the sales load, or the NAV per share). An 8.5 percent load, for example, is equal to 9.3 percent of the amount actually invested. The Investment Company Act of 1940 limits the loads mutual funds can charge. The limit on single-payment and completed contractual plans (described later in this chapter) is 9 percent of the total amount invested.

2 Brokerage houses through which load funds channel their business are generally willing to handle transactions for affiliated no-load funds.

Unit Investment Trusts

Unit investment trusts (UITs) are registered investment companies that generally buy and hold a relatively fixed portfolio of stocks, bonds, or other securities until termination of the UIT. Thus, a UIT does not actively manage the investment portfolio over its lifetime. UITs also have a stated date for termination, which is not usually the case for other investment companies. UITs can have a number of different types of investments, such as corporate bonds, equities, mortgage-backed securities, municipal bonds generally, state-specific municipal bonds, U.S. government securities, and others. Investors may redeem their UIT units from the trust at any time for their NAV.

UITs may or may not charge a sales load. Their annual expenses (expense ratios) generally are low. Since they have a relatively fixed portfolio, there are no investment management fees. Also, their transaction (buying and selling of securities) costs are low and, since there is virtually no turnover of investments in their portfolios, investors' taxes also are kept low. Thus, for investors who want diversification and initial portfolio selection, but who do not want continuing active portfolio management, UITs may be attractive mainly because of their lower costs. Most UITs have been municipal bond funds.

Regulation of Investment Companies

Investment companies are mainly regulated under the federal securities laws. Sales of shares or units are regulated under the Securities Act of 1933 and the Securities Exchange Act of 1934. A prospectus must be delivered to investors who purchase shares or units. The companies' day-by-day operations and structures are regulated under the Investment Company Act of 1940. Further, fund investment managers are governed by the Investment Advisors Act of 1940. The U.S. Securities and Exchange Commission (SEC) administers these federal laws. There may also be state securities regulations.

How to Invest in Mutual Funds

There are a number of ways to invest in mutual funds, including outright purchase, voluntary accumulation plans, contractual periodic payment plans (so-called *contractual* plans), single-payment plans, and the reinvestment of dividends and realized capital gains payable from the fund.

Acquisition plans are available for investors who want to make purchases on a regular, periodic basis. For example, under a *voluntary accumulation* plan, investors indicate, without any binding commitment, that they will periodically invest in the fund. Any sales charge is level for each purchase made and investors can terminate the plan at any time without penalty. Another kind of periodic investment approach is the *contractual* plan, whereby the investor agrees to invest a certain amount in periodic payments over a specified period of time. Despite the term *contractual*, the investor is under no legal obligation to make the regular payments or to complete the plan.

Contractual plans have been subject to criticism. The bulk of this has been directed at the practice of deducting the total sales charges that would be assessed if the plan were completed from the periodic payments in the first few years of the plan. Up to 50 percent of the payments made during the first year of a contractual plan may be deducted as sales charges.[3] This practice exacts a particularly heavy burden on those investors who, for whatever reason, are unable to complete the plan. A *single-payment plan* is essentially an outright purchase under a contractual-type arrangement. The shares are held by a bank as custodian.

Mutual funds (and some closed-end investment companies) have *automatic reinvestment plans* whereby investors can reinvest dividends and capital gains distributions from the fund in additional fund shares.

Distributions from and Exchanges of Mutual Funds

Mutual funds may offer *systematic withdrawal plans* to investors. An investor, for example, might establish a plan to pay a periodic amount to him or her, such as $2000 per month, as long as there are fund shares to do so. Remember, however, that such a systematic withdrawal plan is not the same as a life annuity. The periodic payments are not guaranteed for the investor's or a spouse's lifetime. Also, if an investor cashes in fund shares (either for periodic payments under a withdrawal plan or otherwise), he or she may have a capital gain or loss for income tax purposes, depending on whether the fund shares have appreciated or depreciated in value.

Management companies that handle several mutual funds (a *family* of funds) often permit investors to *exchange* all or part of their shares in one fund for those in another fund or funds they manage at net asset value. Thus, an investor who may have purchased shares in a growth stock fund during his or her working years might exchange them for shares in an income fund at retirement. Such an exchange, however, will be considered a sale or exchange of a capital asset for income tax purposes and hence normally will result in the

---

[3] The portion of the first 12 monthly payments that can be deducted as a sales load is legally limited by the Investment Company Act of 1940 to a maximum of 50 percent.

investor's realizing and recognizing a capital gain or loss at that time. Further, load funds usually require the investor to pay any difference (increase) in the sales loads between the fund the investor had and the one into which he or she is exchanging shares. There may also be exchange fees for making such exchanges. Finally, funds often place restrictions on this exchange privilege to avoid excessive trading by investors in fund's shares.

Mutual Funds and Their Investment Objectives

There are mutual funds to meet just about any investment goal. A fund's investment objective and policies are described in its prospectus.

Equity Funds

Equity funds invest their assets in common stocks (and corresponding assets). They may include the following categories.

Growth Funds. The primary objective of these funds is capital appreciation rather than current dividend income. Growth funds hold the common stocks of more established, larger growth-type companies.

Aggressive Growth Funds. Again, the primary investment objective is capital appreciation. However, the investment policies tend to be more aggressive and riskier than for growth funds. These funds may hold common stocks in start-up companies, newer industries, and turnaround situations, as well as regular growth-type stocks. They also may use other investment techniques, such as option writing.

Growth and Income Funds. These funds are in the category referred to as *total return funds*. They invest in common stocks of well-established companies that are expected to show reasonable growth of principal and income and that also pay reasonable current dividends. Their risk level is moderate.

Income-Equity Funds. These are another type of *total return fund*. They tend to invest in common stocks of companies with stable and good dividend returns. The emphasis is on secure and reasonable dividend yields and not on capital appreciation. Risk tends to be relatively low.

Option-Income Funds. These funds also invest in dividend-paying common stocks, but they seek to maximize current return by writing call options on the stock they hold.

International Equity Funds. These funds invest mainly in the stocks of foreign companies.

Global Equity Funds. These funds invest in the common stocks of both foreign and U.S. companies.

Small-Stock (Small-Cap) Funds. As the name implies, the objective of these funds is to invest in common stocks of smaller, lesser-known companies. Some argue that over the years small-cap stocks have generally performed better than their larger-cap brethren but are more volatile. This has been shown in the historical yield studies described in Chapter 9. Mutual funds seem to be a particularly appropriate vehicle for investing in smaller stocks, because most investors probably do not have the time, knowledge, or resources to evaluate a large number of lesser-known companies.

Precious Metals Funds. The investment objective here is to invest primarily in the common stocks of gold-mining companies and companies that produce other precious metals. These stocks can be viewed as surrogates for holding gold or other precious metals directly, since the prices of these stocks tend to move with the market prices of the precious metals they produce rather than with the stock market in general. Thus, these funds can be used by investors for any gold or precious metals component of their asset allocation, if they desire such a component.

Sector Funds. These funds invest in common stocks of companies in particular fields or industries, such as financial services, health care, science and technology, natural resources, utilities, and so forth. They give investors an opportunity to concentrate their holdings in fields they view as attractive.

Hybrid Funds

These funds maintain a diversified portfolio in terms of kinds of investment media.

Asset Allocation Funds. Funds of this type are required to maintain a fixed weighting (asset allocation) of stocks, bonds, and perhaps money market instruments. Thus, they may enable investors to implement an asset allocation strategy largely through the purchase of one mutual fund, rather than several funds or other assets. One mutual fund group, for example, maintains four separate asset allocation funds, ranging from one with a growth orientation (80 percent stocks and 20 percent bonds) to one designed mainly for income (20 percent stocks, 60 percent bonds, and 20 percent cash reserves).

Balanced Funds. The investment approach of these funds is to have a diversified portfolio of common stocks, preferred stocks, and bonds. The asset allocation of these investment media will be indicated in the fund's prospectus or elsewhere and may change depending on the investment policies of the fund's management. The objectives of these funds are to conserve principal, pay reasonable current income, and achieve long-term growth in principal and income consistent with the prior two objectives. They differ from asset allocation funds in that they do not maintain a fixed weighting of asset classes.

Flexible Portfolio Funds. These funds differ from balanced funds mainly in that they may change their asset allocation more rapidly and may hold up to 100 percent of their assets in only one type of asset at any given time.

Income-Mixed Funds. The investment objective of these funds is high current income. This is achieved by investing in good dividend-paying common stocks and also corporate and government bonds.

Taxable Bond Funds

These funds invest primarily in taxable bonds of various kinds, depending on the investment objective of the particular fund. It may be noted that when an investor invests in bonds through a mutual fund or other pooled intermediaries, rather than owning the bonds directly, there is no fixed maturity date for the mutual fund shareholder. The NAV of the bond fund shares fluctuates with the current market prices of the bonds in its portfolio.

U.S. Treasury Bond Funds. These funds invest primarily in U.S. Treasury bonds. They are therefore viewed as completely safe in terms of financial risk, while their interest rate risk depends on their average duration. As noted earlier, U.S. Treasuries normally are not callable prior to maturity. In terms of duration, U.S. Treasury bond funds can have varying maturities, such as short-term, intermediate-term, and long-term. Such funds can be used to diversify a bond portfolio by duration and to provide call protection.

U.S. Government Income Funds. These funds seek a somewhat higher yield by investing in a variety of U.S. Treasury bonds, federally guaranteed securities, and other government securities.

Ginnie Mae (Government National Mortgage Association) Funds. As the name implies, these funds are invested mainly in government-backed, mortgage-backed securities.

Corporate Bond Funds. The objective of some corporate bond funds is to invest in a diversified portfolio of high-quality bonds. In this case, the fund's financial risk is low and its interest rate risks depend on the bonds' maturities and call protection. Maturities can be short-term, intermediate-term, and long-term.

High-Yield (High-Risk or Junk) Bond Funds. The objective of these funds is to secure higher yield by accepting the greater financial risk of buying lower-quality bonds. However, not all high-yield bond funds are equally risky. They vary in the average quality of the bonds in their portfolios and the levels of their cash reserves.

Income-Bond Funds. These funds invest in a combination of corporate bonds and government bonds for greater yield.

International Bond Funds. These funds invest in the bonds of foreign companies, foreign governments, or both. The market prices of the bonds are expressed in the currencies of the foreign countries whose bonds are held by the fund. Thus, as the value of these countries' currencies changes in relation to the dollar, so will the share value of these funds expressed in dollars. As a result, there can be three kinds of investment risks in these funds: financial risk, interest rate risk, and currency risk. Thus, purchase of these funds enables investors to take an indirect position in foreign currencies and diversify their portfolios in terms of currencies. (Of course, an investor could buy directly one or more foreign currencies or purchase some mutual funds that invest in foreign currencies.) This currency exposure is also present in international stock funds and in varying degrees in global equity funds and global bond funds. Some international bond funds seek to hedge against this currency risk in various ways. In this case, investors may not have full exposure to currency fluctuations.

Global Bond Funds. These funds invest in bonds of foreign companies and countries as well as bonds originating in the United States.

Municipal Bond Funds

National Municipal Bond Funds. These funds invest in the bonds and other securities issued by states, cities, and other municipalities throughout the nation. In terms of duration, there are long-term, intermediate-term, and short-term funds. There are also funds that invest only in investment-grade municipal securities, while others may buy lower-quality (junk) municipals.

State Municipal Bond Funds. These are municipal bond funds that invest only in the securities of a particular state. This enables the residents of that state to buy a fund for their state only and thus have tax-free interest income from the fund for both federal and state and local income tax purposes.

Money Market Mutual Funds

General Considerations. These funds are highly secure, liquid investments that frequently are used by investors for the cash portion of their portfolios. They are generally viewed as cash equivalents because the mutual fund management companies selling their shares expect and intend to be able to redeem them at all times at a fixed value, normally $1 per share. Many money market funds also offer investors check-writing privileges. Thus, these funds are intended to be safe, liquid, and convenient. They also generally provide higher yields than bank money market accounts.

However, there is no guarantee that the shares of money market mutual funds will be redeemed at the fixed value or par. It is possible that a fund's expense ratio or poor investments could result in its not redeeming its shares at par. Thus, investors should pay attention to the expense ratios and the nature and quality of the underlying short-term assets of money market mutual funds. Bank money market accounts, on the other hand, technically are accounts in the bank that normally are insured up to $100,000 per eligible account by the FDIC.

Taxable Money Market Funds. The dividends paid by these funds are gross income to shareholders for federal income tax purposes and perhaps for state and local income taxes as well. Some taxable funds invest only in direct *U.S. Treasury obligations*. These would be the safest in terms of financial risk. Others invest in *U.S. Treasury obligations and other obligations guaranteed by the U.S. government or its agencies*. Still others invest in a *variety of money market investments*, such as CDs, commercial paper, and bankers' acceptances.

Tax-Exempt Money Market Funds. The dividends paid by these funds generally are excluded from shareholders' gross income for federal income tax purposes and may also be excluded for state and local income tax purposes. These funds may be *national tax-exempt money market funds* or *state tax-exempt money market funds*.

Index Funds

Active Versus Passive Investment Management. The mutual funds we have considered thus far are *actively managed funds*. That is, fund managers attempt to select investments that will show superior results and will outperform the overall market.

However, a newer concept in mutual funds is for a fund's portfolio to duplicate or track a specific group or index of securities. These are *index funds*. They are considered to be *passively managed* because the fund manager does not attempt to pick individual securities but only to track the outside index.

General Considerations. Index funds can invest in common stocks, bonds, and other securities, but they generally have been common stock funds. They can be based on a variety of indexes, such as the Standard & Poor's (S&P) 500 (consisting of large company stocks), the Wilshire 5000 (generally all stocks traded in the U.S. stock markets), the Wilshire 4500 (the Wilshire 5000 minus the S&P 500), the Russell 2000 (small-cap stocks traded in the U.S. stock markets), and various international indexes, such as the EAFE (stocks from Europe, Australia, and the Far East).

Rationale for Index Funds. There are several *arguments advanced in favor of* index funds.

Cost. Index funds tend to have significantly lower expense ratios than actively managed funds. Since they are passively managed, their investment management and research expenses are much lower. Further, since they have a low turnover of securities, their transaction costs are low.

Alleged Difficulty in Beating the Market. It has been suggested by commentators that, as a practical matter, it is difficult for a managed fund (or for other investors either) consistently to outperform the overall market for any sustained period of time. Also, actively managed funds in some cases may not even perform as well as the overall market. Therefore, the argument goes, one might just as well invest with the overall market or a part of it and reap the advantage of lower costs of index funds.

Tax Considerations. Since index funds have low turnover, there are relatively few sales of stocks by the fund and hence relatively low capital gains being passed through to shareholders. This tax advantage really applies to any fund with low turnover.

Limitations of Index Funds. There naturally are also *arguments against* index funds.

Alleged Superior Investment Performance of Actively Managed Funds. Proponents of actively managed funds argue that their particular fund will outperform the overall market, as some in fact have. Thus, the counterargument goes, their superior performance will more than justify any increased costs. This is really the crux of the argument. An investor can evaluate this argument by analyzing past comparable performance over a substantial period of time for the particular actively managed fund or funds and the index fund or funds being considered. Of course, as with any analysis of past performance, investors must recognize that it may not be repeated in the future.

Loss of Investor Selection. Some investors like to select among actively managed mutual funds to try to identify the better performers. Also, investors may want to buy some actively managed sector funds in areas or industries they view as particularly attractive.

Market Risks. By their nature, stock index funds are fully invested in equities at all times because they simply mirror a stock index. During bull markets, this will result in good returns. However, during market declines or bear markets, the reverse may be true, since the index fund will remain in the market. Actively managed funds, on the other hand, may hold varying proportions of their assets in cash or other securities, depending on their view of market conditions. Thus, they may be in a better position to face market declines.

Tax-Managed Funds

Another newer concept is the tax-managed mutual fund. These are funds that operate with the objective of minimizing the impact of income taxes on the investment returns to their shareholders. Dividends and interest received and capital gains realized by mutual funds each year are passed through and taxable to the shareholders. The mutual fund itself pays no income taxes. Tax-managed funds follow investment policies intended to minimize this tax impact on shareholders. Such policies might include the following:

- Minimizing the realization and distribution of capital gains. This essentially involves a buy-and-hold approach that minimizes portfolio turnover.
- Emphasizing lower-current-yielding securities. Current dividends are taxable each year to shareholders. Hence they are de-emphasized. This tends to favor a long-term growth-type approach.
- Adopting a tax-efficient selling selection policy. When these funds sell appreciated securities for investment reasons, they seek to sell particular lots of securities that will produce long-term capital gains (as opposed to short-term gains) and that have the highest income tax bases (thereby reducing the long-term gains). They also seek to offset gains by realizing capital losses on other securities in the same year, when feasible.[4]
- Meeting shareholder redemptions by distributing appreciated securities in kind. Some funds may follow this policy.

Other Types of Funds

One specialized type of fund is the dual fund. A *dual fund* is organized as a closed-end investment company and is really two funds in one. Dual funds are based on the premise that some investors are interested exclusively in capital gains while others are interested only in income. Thus, half of a dual fund's shares are sold as capital shares and the other half as income shares. The capital shares benefit from any capital appreciation of the entire fund, while the income shares receive all the income. Capital gains are not distributed annual-

---

[4] It is noteworthy that these policies can be employed just as effectively by individual investors in managing their own investment portfolios tax-efficiently. See Chapter 15 on basic tax-saving techniques.

ly. Rather, the fund is organized for a specific period of time, typically 10 to 15 years, after which the income shares are retired at a fixed price. All capital growth then goes to the capital shareholders.

At one time, there were tax-free exchange mutual funds, but because of adverse taxation no new offerings of these funds have been made since 1967. However, the concept of exchange funds as a way of deferring recognition of capital gains on appreciated securities still exists. The present exchange funds are usually organized as limited partnerships and are discussed in Chapter 15.

Getting Information About Mutual Funds

A commonly used source of information is the prospectus prepared by the mutual fund. The prospectus gives information, for example, on the fund's investment objectives and program; how to purchase, redeem, and transfer shares; minimum initial and periodic investments; periodic purchase and systematic withdrawal plans; the officers and directors of the fund; recent purchases and sales of securities; the current composition of the fund's portfolio; the fund's financial statements; and so on. Funds also prepare less comprehensive quarterly reports for shareholders.

Closed-end funds prepare annual reports similar to those of other publicly held corporations. Moody's and Standard & Poor's financial manuals also provide comprehensive information on closed-end funds.

Forbes magazine, *Money* magazine, and *Barron's* publish periodic reviews of the performance of many funds. In addition, publications like *The Wall Street Journal, Investor's Daily,* and *Business Week* contain reviews or other helpful information on funds.

Among mutual fund services, *Thomson Financial, Morningstar Mutual Funds, Value Line Mutual Fund Survey, Lipper Analytical Services,* and others are widely used.

Mutual Fund Performance

Several areas of performance should be of interest to investors.

Administrative Performance

One area is the investment management fees and other administrative costs to the investor. This is generally evaluated by expressing total operating expenses as a percentage of a fund's net assets (the *expense ratio*) or as a percentage of fund income (the *income ratio*).

Investment Performance

A commonly used measure of investment performance is to analyze the *total return* (annual income dividends paid, realized capital gain distributions, and price fluctuations of the fund's shares) over a period of time. For example, assume a fund's purchase price at the beginning of a period—say a year—is $40 and at the end of the year is $42. Also assume the fund paid $1.00 in annual income dividends and had $1.80 in realized capital gain distributions for the year. In this case, the fund's total return for the year would be $4.80. Assuming the investor did not redeem the shares at the end of the year, $1.00 of this total return would be taxable to the shareholder as ordinary income and $1.80 would be taxable as either short-term or long-term capital gains (depending on how long the *fund* held the securities sold).[5]

Thus, in this example, the *before-tax total return* for the year, based on the original purchase price, would be 12 percent ($4.80 ÷ $40 = 0.12 or 12 percent).

Assuming the shares were directly held (i.e., not in a tax-protected vehicle) and the shareholder was in a 35 percent income tax bracket, the *after-tax total return* would be 10.2 percent ($0.65 after-tax income dividend + $1.44 after-tax long-term capital gain distribution + $2.00 increase in share price = $4.09 after-tax total return ÷ $40 = 0.102 or 10.2 percent).[6]

Funds usually show total return performance data over several time periods, such as one year, three years, five years, and 10 years. Longer time periods probably are more meaningful for comparison purposes, since one- or even three-year periods may include unusual years, either up or down.

One way in which funds show total return performance is *cumulative total return* (as a percentage of initial share value) over a given time period. This is the total change in the value of the fund's shares over the time period, assuming reinvestment of income dividends and capital gain distributions.

Another common way is *average annual compound rate of total return* (usually called *average annual total return*) over the time period. This is the same rate of total return concept explained in Chapter 8. It is the compound level rate of return required each year to cause the initial share value to equal the

[5] The change in the fund's share price would not be subject to income taxation until the shareholder actually redeemed the shares. At that time, the total change would be a short-term or long-term capital gain or a short-term or long-term capital loss, depending on how long the shareholder held the fund shares redeemed and whether there was a gain or a loss at redemption. Of course, if the fund shares were held in a tax-protected vehicle, like an IRA or Section 401(k) plan, there would be no income taxation until distributions are taken from the tax-protected plan.

[6] Note that, for the sake of simplicity, it is not assumed that income dividends and capital gain distributions are reinvested in this illustrative example.

share value at the end of the period, assuming reinvestment of income dividends and capital gain distributions.

These figures for cumulative total percentage return and average annual compound rate of total return for a particular fund often are compared with similar data for other indexes and averages. In the case of load funds, these performance measures can be *load-adjusted* to reflect the fund's sales charges. Such an adjustment can substantially reduce one-year returns, but it tends to diminish in importance over longer time periods.

To illustrate these concepts, Table 12.1 shows performance data from the prospectus of a load growth mutual fund for various periods.

Table 12.1. Performance data from the prospectus of a load growth mutual fund

Average annual total returns (%)	Over the past 1 year	5 years	10 years
This fund	9.11%	14.92%	13.79%
This fund (load-adjusted)*	5.84	14.22	13.44
Lipper Growth Funds (average)	11.76	13.09	11.33
S&P 500 Stock Index	19.82	16.42	13.37
Cumulative total returns (%)			
This fund	9.11%	100.45%	263.91%
This fund (load-adjusted)*	5.84	94.44	252.99
Lipper Growth Funds (average)	11.76	87.43	203.06
S&P 500 Stock Index	19.82	113.93	251.11
*This fund has a 3 percent front-end load.			

It can be seen from this illustration that when a longer time horizon is used (such as 10 years), differences among the performances being compared narrow considerably. This also is true for mutual funds generally.

Tax-managed funds and other funds may show average annual total returns on a before-tax and an after-tax basis.[7] For example, one tax-managed growth mutual fund showed the following comparison for a 10-year period.

Average annual total returns (before shareholder taxes)

This tax-managed growth fund:	14.9%
Average of 190 growth funds:	13.5%

---

[7] Such comparisons, of course, require assumptions concerning taxes and tax rates. In this example, the highest historical individual federal income tax rates were assumed. State and local income taxes and any taxes due on redemption of shares were ignored.

Average annual total returns (after assumed shareholder taxes)

This tax-managed growth fund:	14.2%
Average of 190 growth funds:	10.9%

Volatility

Various measures of volatility of mutual fund share prices are used. These include the beta, R-squared, alpha, and standard deviation. They are described in Chapter 8.

Considerations in Evaluating Investment Performance

Mutual fund investment performance data should be evaluated before investing in a fund. However, certain cautions are in order in making such evaluations. First, comparisons should be made based on a number of years of performance, such as five, 10, or even 20 years. Be careful, too, about evaluating performance only during good times. Second, it is important to consider the investment objectives of a fund. For example, a balanced fund should do better than a growth fund in a declining market, while the opposite should be true in a sharply advancing market. Also consider the risks of market volatility involved.

Mutual Fund Expenses

Fund expenses are required to be summarized and illustrated at the beginning of each fund's prospectus. The following summary of expenses for a load growth stock fund is given only as an illustration.

Summary of Fund Expenses

A. *Shareholder transaction expenses:*

Sales charge on purchases (the front-end load for a load mutual fund):	3.00%
Sales charge on reinvested distributions:	None
Deferred sales charge on redemptions (the back-end load used by some funds):	None
Exchange fee (imposed by some funds for the privilege of exchanging one fund for another within a family of mutual funds):	None

B. *Annual fund operating expenses (as a percentage of average net assets):*

Management fee (investment management fees generally charged by mutual funds):	0.45%

12 b-1 fee (sales and marketing fees charged
   by some mutual funds in addition to
   any sales load):   None
Other expenses (such as administrative
   or servicing fees):   0.21%

Total fund operating expenses: 0.66%

The *expense ratio* of the fund illustrated is 0.66 percent. Expenses vary considerably among funds. They should be evaluated in conjunction with a fund's
overall investment performance over a significant period of time.

Factors Involved in Selecting Mutual Funds

Here are some ideas that may be helpful in this important choice.

- Determine whether the fund's *objectives, investment style,* and *investment policies* generally coincide with the investor's objectives and asset allocation strategy.
- Decide whether the investor wants an *actively managed fund* or a *passively managed index fund.*
- Consider the fund's *past performance* in light of its objectives.
- Ascertain the *qualifications and experience of the people managing the fund's portfolio.* The *tenure of the portfolio manager* (how long the manager has been managing the fund) also is significant.
- Briefly look over the *securities in the fund's portfolio* to see how well selected they seem to be.
- If it is a load fund, *consider its sales charges* to see how they compare with those of similar funds.
- Consider the fund's *annual operating expenses (expense ratio)* in comparison to those of similar funds and in light of fund performance.
- Consider the *shareholder services* the fund will make available to investors, including the right of accumulation, available investment plans, systematic withdrawal plans, and any exchange privilege.
- Remember that *funds normally are considered long-term investments.* Therefore, do not be too concerned with strictly short-term changes in fund values.
- Consider the fund's *turnover rate* for its portfolio. The turnover rate is cal-culated by dividing the smaller of the fund's total purchases or total sales of securities by its average monthly assets. A turnover rate of 60 percent, for example, means the fund has sold and replaced 60 percent in value of its assets during the year. A high turnover rate may mean the fund will have large capital gain distributions, and hence tax liabilities, for its shareholders.

It also may increase transaction costs for the fund. And finally, it implies a very active investment management style.

■ Look out for *style slippage* in fund investment policies. Style slippage exists when a significant difference develops between the investment style or policies proclaimed by a fund and those actually followed. As a practical matter, this may be difficult for an investor to detect.

■ Consider *how long the fund has been in existence.* Recent funds have not had much time to develop a track record for investors to consider.

■ Consider any *minimum investment amounts* required by the fund.

Planning Considerations for Mutual Funds

Investors often use mutual funds for at least part of their asset allocation or in various tax-advantage accounts, such as IRAs. The mutual fund advantages of professional management and/or diversification may be particularly important in certain areas, such as high-yield bonds, small-cap stocks, international bonds or stocks, and sector funds. Further, an investor may want to diversify his or her mutual fund holdings among several funds.

Tax Aspects of Mutual Funds

Mutual funds are taxed as regulated investment companies. Thus, funds pay out investment income to shareholders as various kinds of dividends and the shareholders report those dividends on their own tax returns as taxable or nontaxable, depending on the nature of the dividends. The fund itself pays no tax and operates essentially on a pass-through basis.

Types of Distributions for Tax Purposes

There are three kinds of such dividends: ordinary income dividends from the fund's net investment income (interest and dividends), tax-exempt-interest dividends (provided at least 50 percent of the fund's assets are in tax-exempt securities), and capital gains dividends (as long-term or short-term capital gains to the fund, regardless of how long the shareholder owned the fund's shares). Ordinary income dividends are taxed as dividend income to shareholders; tax-exempt-interest dividends are not included in shareholders' gross income (except for alternative minimum tax [AMT] purposes in the case of certain private activity municipal bonds); and capital gains dividends are taxed as capital gains of shareholders in the year they are received.

Dividends that are automatically reinvested in additional fund shares are treated as constructively received by the shareholder and are taxed currently to the shareholder. However, if mutual fund shares are used as the investment medium for a plan that itself is tax-sheltered (e.g., an IRA), then the net investment income and capital gains dividends are not taxable until paid out from the tax-sheltered plan. The same, of course, would be true for any investments used in such plans.

Redemptions and Exchanges of Mutual Fund Shares

The preceding discussion dealt with taxation of distributions to shareholders of the investment income of funds. However, a mutual fund shareholder may have a taxable capital gain or a capital loss in the event he or she sells, exchanges, or redeems his or her mutual fund shares.

To illustrate, suppose Harry Wilson invested $10,000 in a growth stock mutual fund 15 years ago and all dividends were automatically reinvested. The shares are now worth $55,000; Harry's income tax basis in them (the initial $10,000 purchase price plus the dollar amount of the reinvested dividends) is $17,000. Harry is planning to retire and would now like to pursue a more conservative asset allocation approach. Therefore, he is planning to exchange his growth stock fund for shares in a growth and income fund maintained in the same family of funds. The fund permits such exchanges without another sales load and with no exchange fees. However, this exchange of one fund for another is a *sale or exchange* of a capital asset for capital gains tax purposes and results in a long-term capital gain in this case. Therefore, Harry has an amount realized of $55,000 and an adjusted income tax basis of $17,000, which results in a long-term capital gain realized and recognized in the year of the exchange of $38,000 ($55,000 - $17,000 = $38,000). The result would be the same had Harry exchanged his growth fund for any other mutual fund or had redeemed his shares from the fund. But if the growth stock fund were inside a plan that is tax-sheltered—say, an HR-10 plan or a rollover IRA—then the exchange (or a redemption) would not result in any capital gains tax. Instead, the assets would be taxable as ordinary income when they are finally distributed from the tax-sheltered plan.

Income Tax Basis of Fund Shares

When a mutual fund shareholder sells, redeems, or exchanges all the shares he or she owns, the total income tax basis of the shares is used to calculate any capital gain or loss as just illustrated. Also, if a shareholder acquired all his or her shares at the same time and with the same basis, the sale, redemption, or exchange of only part of the shares owned will be at the shareholder's basis and holding period for that part of the shares.

However, if the mutual fund shares were acquired over a period of time and for different prices, as in an automatic dividend reinvestment plan, for example, the taxpayer has some flexibility in determining the income tax basis in the case of a sale, redemption, or exchange of only part of the shares owned. If the shareholder can adequately identify the group from which the shares sold, redeemed, or exchanged came, that basis and holding period can be used (as is true of securities in general, as noted in Chapter 15). If the shareholder cannot identify the group adequately or elects not to use this *specific identification method,* he or she has three other choices in determining the basis and holding period for the shares disposed of. The shareholder may assume that the earliest acquired shares were those sold. This is a *first-in, first-out (FIFO) concept.* Or, the shareholder may elect to use either one of two *average cost methods* for determining basis and holding period. The two alternative averaging methods are a *double-category method* and a *single-category method.* The shareholder qualifies to elect one of these averaging methods if the shares are held in a custodial account maintained for the acquisition or redemption of fund shares and the shareholder purchased or acquired the shares at different bases.

Once a shareholder elects to use one of these four methods for the shares of a particular fund, he or she is not permitted to switch to another method for that fund. However, an investor may employ different methods for different funds.

Closed-End Companies

If a closed-end company elects to be taxed as a regulated investment company, its shareholders will be taxed as described previously for mutual fund shareholders.

Look Out for Buying a Dividend

The situation referred to as *buying a dividend* occurs when a purchaser of fund shares buys them shortly before the *ex-dividend date* (or *record date*) of a distribution from the fund. This normally is not tax-efficient, because the value of the shares usually will fall by about the amount of the dividend payable, but the dividend will be taxable to the purchasing shareholder. Thus, the purchaser's total position (shares plus after-tax dividend) will be reduced by the amount of the income tax on the dividend, as compared with the purchaser's total position (shares ex-dividend) if he or she had waited until after the ex-dividend date to buy the fund shares. Mutual funds often will provide the dates and estimated amounts of future distributions so investors can plan accordingly. This same general principle also applies to purchases of common stocks.

Exchange-Traded Funds

Unlike mutual funds, exchange-traded funds (ETFs) are traded on an organized exchange, bought and sold through brokerage firms that charge brokerage commissions, and their market prices may be more or less than the NAV of the securities in the ETF. The market prices of ETF shares are determined by the values of the securities in the fund and supply and demand conditions in the stock market for fund shares. Their market prices should be reasonably close to underlying fund values, but there is no assurance of that. ETFs are not redeemable from the funds, as are mutual funds. The arguments made for ETFs are that they have continual pricing, can be traded through limit orders, can be sold short, and can be bought on margin. They also may have lower operating costs. ETFs generally are index funds.

Hedge Funds

Hedge funds differ from mutual funds in several respects. First, while mutual funds are registered investment companies whose operations are regulated under the Investment Company Act of 1940, domestic hedge funds are normally organized as *investment limited partnerships,* with the investors being limited partners and the investment manager a general partner who runs the partnership's affairs. Hedge funds are largely unregulated. Second, while hedge funds charge management fees that are a percentage of assets under management, they also commonly charge *incentive fees,* which are a percentage (such as 20 percent) of the realized and unrealized gains of the fund. In addition, for tax reasons, hedge funds can accept only a *limited number of investors* (limited partners) and those investors must be *qualified purchasers.* This normally means investors must have a minimum liquid net worth.

Hedge funds have traditionally been characterized by their *investment strategies.* The classical concept is that hedge funds have an advantageous risk-return situation because they may take opposite investment positions at the same time and thus profit from their hoped-for superior investment selection models and techniques whether an overall market goes up or down. They hope to have very low or no correlations in investment risks and returns among the investment positions they take. As an example, hedge funds may purchase (be long in) common stocks they believe will outperform the market and at the same time sell stocks short (be short in) other stocks they believe will underperform the market. If the overall stock market rises, investors hope that the good long positions will rise more than any losses in unfavorable short positions (which may even be profitable if well selected) and thus investors will make money. Correspondingly, if the overall market declines, it is hoped the good short positions (the favorable ones in this scenario) will fall more than the now unfavorable long positions (which may even hold their value or rise if well selected) and thus again the fund investors will make money. Thus, hedge fund investors hope for superior and stable returns.

In addition to short sales, hedge funds may make extensive use of financial leverage to magnify their positions. They also may use arbitrage, options, futures, and other derivatives to enhance returns and help control risk. There are many different kinds of hedge funds that may use a variety of financial techniques and invest globally.

Some hedge funds are structured to invest in other hedge funds. They are called "funds of funds." In recent years, some securities firms have established funds of funds with smaller required initial investment amounts.

13

Asset Allocation
Strategies and Models

Fundamentals of Asset Allocation

Asset allocation is a system for determining what percentages of an investment portfolio should be in different asset classes and subclasses. The system is based on the expected after-tax total returns on various asset classes, the investor's financial situation, the time horizon, personal factors and investment constraints, the investor's investment objectives and policies, and the investor's ability to tolerate risk.

A Planned Approach

Asset allocation involves comprehensive and coordinated planning of an entire investment portfolio. It means looking at all the kinds of investment assets held, whether they are held directly, in tax-advantaged vehicles, in trusts, or elsewhere. Finally, the analysis should include potential rights to assets, like employee stock options.

A Long-Term Approach

Asset allocation takes a long-term view of investment planning. Thus, it operates best when an investor has a reasonably long time horizon for which to plan. However, people should be prepared for short-term fluctuations and problems. That also is part of asset allocation planning.

Generally a Risk-Averse Strategy

Asset allocation normally is a risk-averse strategy because it involves dividing a

232

portfolio among several asset classes, which often have different risk characteristics (i.e., asset classes that have low or no risk correlations) and it involves an analysis of the investor's tolerance for risk. On the other hand, some investors prefer an asset concentration strategy. This obviously does not involve diversification among asset classes and may not be as risk-averse.[1] However, it can be viewed as an asset allocation strategy so long as the investor plans for such a strategy and considers its risk characteristics.

Steps in the Asset Allocation Process

The following are possible steps in this process.

1. Consider the investor's personal situation—including investment constraints, time horizon, financial position, and tax status.
2. Consider the investor's investment objectives.
3. Review the investor's present asset allocation.
4. Consider and select the asset classes to be included in the particular investor's allocation.
5. Estimate, to the extent possible, the long-term return-risk features of the asset classes selected. Logically this step might be done concurrently with the preceding one, since long-term return-risk characteristics are important in deciding which asset classes to include in a portfolio.
6. Decide on the percentage allocations of the selected asset classes in the portfolio. This, of course, is the critical step.
7. Decide on strategy and allocations within each asset class selected.
8. Consider, to the extent possible, how the various asset classes should be held (i.e., directly owned, through financial intermediaries, or in tax-advantaged accounts or plans).
9. Implement the plan.
10. Periodically review and reevaluate the plan.

Personal Factors and Asset Allocation
Overall Financial Situation and Tax Status

As for most forms of financial planning, one's personal or family financial sit-

---

[1] However, some well-regarded commentators might argue that, over a long period of time (a long investment horizon) and in real dollar terms, a policy of concentration in a diversified portfolio of common stocks involves less risk, or not much more, than, say, investment in bonds. See Jeremy J. Siegel, *Stocks for the Long Run*, 3rd Edition (New York: McGraw-Hill, 2002), pp 36-39.

uation—personal balance sheet and income statement—is a valuable starting point. Also, tax status is important, since the after-tax returns from investments will be considered.

Time Horizon

The longer the time horizon, the more discretion and flexibility there can be in asset allocation. There are several reasons for this. First, the long-term total return and variability data for common stocks, bonds, and cash equivalents (from such studies as those discussed in Chapter 9), which are so important in modern asset allocation thinking, are based on long-term historical studies of returns and variability for those asset classes. Hence, they need a long investment horizon in which to work out. Second, since no one can be sure when short-term economic declines or personal problems may arise, it seems prudent to be ready for them today. Therefore, if an investor has only a short time (such as up to five years) to prepare for an economic need, such as college expenses, a more conservative asset allocation strategy may be in order, at least until he or she meets the short-term need.

Investment Constraints, Investor Attitudes, and Other Factors

Here are some investment constraints and other factors that might be considered.

1. The investor's *ability to risk loss of investment income and principal.* This in turn is influenced by a number of factors, such as:
   a. Personal earnings and the nature and stability of his or her employment, as well as the personal earnings, if any, of his or her spouse.
   b. Other sources of income.
   c. Age, health, family responsibilities, and other obligations.
   d. Ownership of closely held business interests.
   e. Any likely (or possible) inheritances.
   f. Plans to use investment principal for particular purposes, such as education expenses, retirement, or other large expenditures.
   g. The extent to which current investment income is needed for living expenses.
2. The *degree of liquidity and marketability* needed in the portfolio.
3. How well the investor is *able to weather the ups and particularly the downs in the securities markets.*
4. The *quality of available investment management services.*
5. The investor's *attitudes and emotional tolerance for risk.*

Investment Objectives

Making investment decisions without defining the person's objectives is like trying to steer a ship without a rudder. Investment objectives are shaped by a person's overall financial position, investment constraints, and many personal factors. Further, a person's investment objectives normally change over his or her life cycle and as circumstances change. Finally, a person often has a combination of objectives at the same time. The following can be listed as typical investment objectives.

Maximum Current Income

This objective emphasizes current yield over other factors. It is typical of people who must rely on investment income for part or all of their livelihood.

Preservation of Capital

This is a common objective. In its purest form, it means that the dollar value of the portfolio should not fall. This is a rather rigorous form of this objective. However, in a more flexible form, it means investing so that the potential for declines in the overall value of the portfolio is within tolerable limits. In this form, it is a common and quite logical objective.

Reasonable Current Income with Moderate Capital Growth

This modifies the first objective in that current investment income is not the only aim. While current income is important, capital gains also are sought.

Long-Term Capital Growth

This objective aims primarily at capital gains over a relatively long period of time. It may be typical of investors who do not need current investment income to meet their living expenses. It implies a greater degree of risk in the portfolio.

Aggressive Capital Growth

This objective seeks maximum capital growth and implies making riskier investments with considerable investment analysis and management.

Tax-Advantaged Investments

A person's top marginal income tax bracket may make tax-free or tax-sheltered investments attractive.

As previously noted, these objectives are not mutually exclusive; in fact, an investor often will have some combination of them. What is important, however, is for investors to decide what their objectives are and to follow them.

Investment Policies

Investors should establish policies to meet their objectives within the framework of their investment constraints. In setting investment policies, the following kinds of issues might be considered.

Aggressive Versus Defensive Policies

Aggressive policies seek to maximize profits and, thus, accept above-average risks. On the other hand, *defensive policies* seek to minimize investment risks and, perhaps, accept correspondingly lower profits.

In general, aggressive and defensive policies can be distinguished as follows. To maximize returns, an aggressive portfolio includes securities of greater financial risk than would be true of a defensive portfolio. Again, to earn maximum returns, an aggressive investor tries to make profits by timing purchases and sales of securities according to his or her views on how the market will go. A defensive investor, on the other hand, tends to follow a buy-and-hold philosophy or use dollar-cost averaging or other such plans and usually does not try to outguess the market. An aggressive investor may use many techniques and investment media, such as stock warrants, puts and calls, initial public offerings (IPOs), and short sales, that often are not used in more defensive portfolios. An aggressive policy may involve borrowing to increase profit potential, while a defensive policy generally does not use credit in this way. Finally, an aggressive policy may concentrate purchases in a relatively small number of securities to maximize the investor's (or advisor's) skill at selection.

Probably few people consistently follow only aggressive policies or only defensive policies in all respects. However, many investors probably tend more toward defensive-type policies in general.

Liquidity and Marketability

Setting the proper degree of liquidity in a portfolio is largely a matter of judgment. It can be done by deciding to hold a certain number of dollars, say $20,000, in liquid assets; or to hold a certain percentage of assets, say 10 percent, in liquid form; or to hold some combination of the two. In asset allocation models, liquid assets are often stated as a percentage of the overall portfolio.

Diversification Versus Concentration

As just stated, diversification is basically a defensive policy. The opposite of diversification is concentration. A portfolio may be concentrated in only one asset class (like common stocks or real estate) or even in just one or a few issues within an asset class. Sometimes events cause investment concentration without any conscious policy. This may occur, for example, when a corporate executive's portfolio becomes overweighted in his or her company's stock. The problem then becomes how to diversify in an efficient manner.

Possible Asset Classes to Be Considered

Each investor needs to select those asset classes he or she wants to include in his or her asset allocation decision making. The following are some possible asset classes.

- Domestic common stocks
- Foreign common stocks
- Domestic bonds (investment grade)
- Foreign bonds
- High-yield (junk) bonds
- Cash-type assets (cash equivalents)
- Longer-term fixed-dollar (guaranteed principal) assets
- Investment real estate
- Other tax-sheltered investments
- Convertible securities
- Gold and precious metals
- Other assets

Investment Vehicles to Be Considered

These asset classes can be found in a number of different investment vehicles. Each of them needs to be considered in asset allocation planning, because a person is exposed to an asset class no matter how it is held.

Directly Owned Assets

These are assets owned by a person in his or her own name or jointly with another. They may be titled to the person or held in brokerage or other accounts in the person's name.

Assets Held Through Financial Intermediaries

Here the person owns shares or interests in a financial intermediary that owns and manages the investment assets. Mutual funds and real estate investment trusts (REITs) are common examples.

Assets Held in Qualified Retirement Plans

Many employer-provided qualified retirement plans are *defined contribution* or *individual account plans* where specific accounts are allocated to individual employees.[2] Participating employees may or may not have control over how these account balances are invested. However, either way participants usually can identify the asset classes in which their account balances are invested.

IRAs

IRA owners can invest their account balances in mutual funds, self-directed brokerage accounts, and annuities.

Life Insurance Cash Values

Traditional fixed-dollar policies and universal life (UL) policies have fixed-dollar (portfolio product) cash values. They are guaranteed principal assets. On the other hand, the asset classifications of variable life (VL) and variable universal life (VUL) policies depend on the sub-accounts into which their cash values are placed.

Investment Annuity Cash Values

Traditional fixed-dollar annuities have fixed-dollar (portfolio product) cash values and thus are guaranteed principal assets. Variable annuities (VAs) have cash values the annuity owner can elect to place in one or more sub-accounts. The sub-accounts chosen determine the asset class.

Employee Stock Options and Stock Plans

Many employees have been granted stock options or are eligible for other stock plans (e.g., restricted stock, employee stock purchase plans, stock appreciation

---

[2] The other major category of qualified retirement plan is the defined benefit plan. For these plans, the specific assets that may be behind the employer's promise to pay retirement benefits cannot be identified for individual employees. Hence, they cannot be counted in asset allocation decision making. However, they may provide important retirement security for employees to consider in making those decisions. These plans are described in Chapter 17.

rights, and so forth). Such options and plans clearly represent an investment interest in the employer's stock, but they may be difficult to value. (These plans and their valuation are discussed in Chapter 22.)

For our present purposes, we shall value unexercised stock options by subtracting the grant price (option price) from the current market price of the stock and multiplying by the number of shares for which the option can be exercised. This is referred to as the *intrinsic value* of the option.[3]

For example, assume that two years ago John Herrera was granted a nonqualified stock option (NQSO) with a duration of 10 years to purchase 1000 shares of his employer's stock at a price of $20 per share (grant price) and the market price of the stock is now $45 per share. The option's present intrinsic value is $25,000 ($45 - $20 = $25 × 1000 shares). Of course, if an option already has been exercised (or stock has been acquired under some other plan), the stock is simply counted as directly owned common stock.

Trust Assets

Some people are beneficiaries of trusts. This can involve many different arrangements. Some people have set up funded revocable living trusts. The assets in these trusts (which can be terminated or amended by the creator at any time) should be counted in the creator-beneficiary's asset allocation because, for all practical purposes, he or she still owns them. Other times a person may be a beneficiary of an irrevocable trust established by someone else. These trust assets may or may not be counted for asset allocation purposes, depending on what kinds of rights the beneficiary has in the trust's property. This is a judgment call.

Return-Risk Considerations

An important objective in asset allocation is to maximize after-tax total returns at an acceptable level of risk. In this sense, *risk* is defined as the variability of actual returns around expected returns. Since people do not mind making more money than they expected, it is really downside deviations from expected returns with which we are concerned. In other words, we are worried about the risk of investment losses. People want to have some idea about how much a given portfolio might decline in the face of economic problems—such as a severe recession (or even depression) that might last two or three years or

---

[3] As noted in Chapters 9 and 22, another approach to valuing options is to use an option-pricing model to calculate an economic value for the option. While this may be economically more accurate, we prefer to use intrinsic value for asset allocation purposes.

longer. Since no one can know the future, estimates about likely percentage declines for various asset classes can be based only on experience, should probably be made using conservative assumptions, and should be recognized as only general estimates.

Some General Return-Risk Estimates

Table 13.1 gives some return-risk estimates for several commonly used asset classes. The specific numbers shown here can change with economic conditions and are based in part on the judgment of the analyst or planner. The important thing is to consider return and risk relationships in making asset allocation decisions.

Column 2 of Table 13.1 shows estimated average annual total long-term returns for the asset classes. The returns for common stocks were derived from the data in Table 9.2 and the general historical studies discussed in Chapter 9. It is also assumed that growth stocks will show a somewhat different yield pat-

Table 13.1. Return-risk estimates for certain asset classes

(1)	(2)		(3)		(4)
Asset class or subclass	Expected average annual total long-term returns (before tax)		Expected average annual total long-term returns (after tax)*		Maximum likely decline during a severe recession or other bear market
Growth common stocks	Dividends	1.0%	Dividends	0.6%	
	Capital gains	11.0%	Capital gains	8.8%	
	Total return	12.0%	Total return	9.4%	50%
Diversified common stocks	Dividends	3.0%	Dividends	1.8%	
	Capital gains	7.0%	Capital gains	5.6%	
	Total return	10.0%	Total return	7.4%	40%
Long-term U.S. Treasury bonds		5.7%		3.65%	20%
Long-term municipal bonds		5.0%		5.0%	20%
Money market funds (taxable)		2.0%		1.2%	0
Guaranteed principal assets (5-year CDs and GICs)		4.0%		2.4%	0

*This assumes a 35 percent top marginal federal income tax rate and a combined effective top marginal federal and state income tax rate of 40 percent. It also assumes a capital gains tax rate of 20 percent. It further assumes all assets are held directly. Finally, it assumes capital gains are taxed each year.

tern than a diversified portfolio of stocks that would include some defensive issues. The returns for long-term U.S. Treasury bonds (for the 30-year U.S. Treasury), long-term municipal bonds, taxable money market funds, and guaranteed principal assets were those in existence when the table was prepared. They, of course, will change over time.

Column 3 shows these estimated returns after certain assumed income tax rates. Other important assumptions are that these asset classes are held directly or through intermediaries like directly owned mutual funds and that capital gains are taxed each year. If the assets (other than municipal bonds) were held in tax-advantaged accounts or plans, their after-tax results would be different. (See the discussion of how investments should be held later in this chapter.)

Column 4 gives some estimates of maximum percentage declines for each asset class separately (i.e., not for the portfolio as a whole, so that the degree to which the asset classes are uncorrelated or have low correlations is not considered here) during a severe bear market.[4] These are the risk factors. The estimates for common stocks come from the analysis in Chapter 9. Greater variability (risk) was assumed for growth stocks because a diversified stock portfolio would contain some defensive issues.

Bonds also have bear markets, sometimes severe. When interest rates move sharply higher, bond prices fall dramatically. In the post-World War II period, for example, from December 1976 through March 1980 (a period of 40 months), bond prices (10-year maturity) fell more than 32 percent. Then, from June 1980 through September 1981 (a period of 15 months), bonds fell more than 29 percent. These were their steepest post-war bear markets. And in recent years, bonds have become increasingly volatile (see Table 9.2).

Table 9.2 shows that, for the period from 1926 to 2001, the historical standard deviation (degree of risk) for long-term U.S. government bonds was 9.5 and the expected total return was 5.3 percent. Therefore, based on these historical data and with a 95 percent confidence level, we can say that the annual total returns for these bonds will vary from -13.7 percent [5.3% - (2 × 9.5%)] to + 24.3 percent [5.3% + (2 × 9.5%)]. However, as for stocks, we believe most people are not just concerned about the risk of market declines for only one year but think in terms of bear markets that may last two years, three years, or longer. Therefore, using the data from Table 9.2 and considering the bear markets in bonds since World War II, we have chosen a likely maximum decline of 20 percent for long-term U.S. Treasury bonds and a similar one for long-term investment-grade municipals. (However, others may make different judgments. Obviously, this is a judgment call.) The money

---

[4] See the next section, "Modern Portfolio Theory and Asset Correlations," for a discussion of how estimates of asset correlations can be included in the analysis.

market funds and guaranteed principal assets by definition will maintain their dollar value in the face of adverse economic conditions.

Modern Portfolio Theory and Asset Correlations

In the previous section, we have only considered downward risk of individual asset classes. However, modern portfolio theory is concerned with controlling risk (risk management) for the whole portfolio by allocation among asset classes that may each be volatile (and correspondingly have higher returns), but whose returns are uncorrelated or have low correlations with each other. (See Chapter 11, "Application of Modern Portfolio Theory," for an explanation of asset correlations.) Simply put, risk is managed by investing in asset classes that are not expected to go down (or up) at the same time or to the same degree. In effect, this means that adding higher-return, more volatile asset classes to a portfolio will not necessarily increase the volatility (risk) of the portfolio as a whole, if the asset classes are uncorrelated or have low correlations.[5]

Modern portfolio theory employs mathematical models to analyze expected returns, volatility, and correlations of individual asset classes. Many sophisticated techniques and investment vehicles can be used to help manage investment risk within desired parameters and, hopefully, to enhance returns. These methods and techniques are beyond the scope of this book.

However, we suggest that most individual investors want to have some general idea of what the maximum downside risk might be in any portfolio or portfolios they are considering. For this purpose, the estimates in column 4 of Table 13.1 may be helpful. As stated before, in these estimates the correlation or lack of correlation of the asset classes (stocks and bonds in this case) was not considered. Hopefully, however, some asset classes will have low correlations, be uncorrelated, or even have a negative correlation, so risk may be reduced for the portfolio as a whole. In other words, if a portfolio contains, say, both common stocks and investment-grade bonds, we would hope that when stocks decline in a bear market for stocks, the bonds would decline proportionately less, not decline at all, or, most likely, rise in price.

At various times in the past during recessions or depressions, when common stock prices fell significantly, the prices of investment-grade bonds did rise. This was referred to earlier as the *countercyclical movement* of bond prices.

On the other hand, there have been times when the prices of stocks and bonds tended to move (e.g., decline) together. For example, from September

---

[5] These ideas were pioneered by Harry Markowitz, author of a seminal article, "Portfolio Selection" (1952), and others.

1976 through February 1978, stock prices declined almost 27 percent. Also, from December 1976 through March 1980, bond prices declined more than 32 percent.

Thus, estimates of the likely percentage of downside risk for different asset classes remain essentially a matter of individual judgment. The estimates in column 4 of Table 13.1 are meant only to be general starting points. What is important, however, is for investors to consider risk (downside potential) in their asset allocation decision making.

Allocations Within Asset Classes

There are also decisions to be made within each asset class included in a portfolio. Such decisions have already been discussed in earlier chapters.

How Investments (Asset Classes) Should Be Held

Basically, this issue is whether investments should be held directly or in tax-advantaged vehicles. How much planning can be done in this area depends largely on the circumstances. Some people have almost all their investable assets in tax-advantaged plans, so their choices are limited. Others have few tax-advantaged plans available to them. In still other cases, participants in tax-advantaged plans may have limited or no choice as to how their plan assets are to be invested. Finally, from a tax point of view, the choice is not always clear-cut. The tax-advantaged vehicles we are considering include qualified retirement plans, traditional IRAs, variable annuity contracts, and variable life insurance policies, among others.

Advantages of Directly Owned Assets

- Capital gains are not realized and recognized (taxable) until the asset is sold or exchanged in a taxable transaction.
- Long-term capital gains are taxed at favorable rates.
- Capital assets presently get a stepped-up income tax basis at death.
- Planning can be done to postpone or even totally avoid capital gains taxation.
- Capital losses can reduce or eliminate capital gains and then any remaining losses can reduce ordinary income up to $3000 per year. Unused capital losses can be carried forward.
- Investors have control over the investment of their assets.

Limitations of Directly Owned Assets

- Dividends and taxable interest are taxable each year as received.
- In order to change investments or an asset allocation, it will be necessary to realize and recognize capital gains (and pay capital gains taxes) if appreciated assets are sold or exchanged.
- Mutual funds and other investment companies may produce capital gains for shareholders through fund turnover.

Advantages of Holding Assets in Tax-Advantaged Plans

- All investment income (dividends, taxable interest, and capital gains) is not taxed *currently* to the participant. Taxation (as ordinary income) is deferred until distributions are actually made from the plan.
- Changes in investments or in asset allocation can be made tax-free as long as they are made within the tax-favored plan. Thus, if assets have gains, these plans may be a good place to make changes in asset allocation. On the other hand, if assets have losses, directly owned assets may be the better ones to sell, since the realized losses can offset other capital gains or up to $3000 per year of ordinary income.
- Distributions usually can be deferred a long time, resulting in long periods of tax-deferred earnings.

Limitations of Holding Assets in Tax-Advantaged Plans

- All investment income (dividends, taxable interest, and capital gains), as well as any taxable principal in these plans, will be taxed as ordinary income when distributed. (Roth IRAs and education IRAs are exceptions. Their distributions are tax-free.) Also, the balances in these plans must be distributed at some point. (The minimum distribution rules are covered in Chapter 20.) However, life insurance death proceeds are treated differently, as explained in Chapters 4 and 27.
- There is no step-up in basis at death for investments in these plans and lower capital gains rates do not apply even though investment returns in the plan may have come in the form of capital gains.
- Participants must abide by the terms of the particular plan; employers can change plan terms for the future.
- There may be penalty taxes for taking premature distributions (10 percent penalty tax) or for failing to take minimum required distributions (50 percent penalty tax).

Some Observations

While it can be seen from the preceding discussion that there are few hard and fast certainties in this area, the following are some general observations.

■ Tax-free municipal bonds should always be held directly, since their interest is tax-free.

■ Zero-coupon taxable bonds should be held in tax-advantaged accounts. Otherwise, their annual accrued interest will be taxed currently to the owners even though not yet received in cash.

■ An argument can be made that growth-type common stocks (with low or no current dividends) that are being held for the long term probably should be held directly. The investor then would get tax-deferred or tax-free compounding of capital gains, lower capital gains tax rates if he or she sells or exchanges before death, and at present a step-up in basis if the stock are held until death. (Investors also may engage in other techniques to delay or avoid capital gains taxation, as described in Chapter 15.)

■ An argument can be made that taxable bonds and guaranteed principal investments that pay current interest might be placed in tax-advantaged plans, to defer the tax on the current interest payments.

■ If changes are to be made in investments or in asset allocation and appreciated assets are involved, it may be better to try to make them in tax-advantaged plans, so as to not incur capital gains taxes. On the other hand, if assets with investment losses are involved, it is better to sell directly owned assets so capital losses can be realized to offset any capital gains or up to $3000 per year of ordinary income.

Illustrations of Asset Allocation Strategies

There can be wide differences of opinion concerning asset allocation strategies, even with a given factual situation. The two case situations given here are meant simply to illustrate general asset allocation techniques.

A Young Professional Couple

Harry and Susan Modern are married, they both have careers outside the home, and they have two children, ages 6 and 4. Harry, age 37, is a lawyer with his own practice (a sole proprietor). Susan, age 36, has an undergraduate degree in chemical engineering and an MBA. She is an executive with a large pharmaceutical company. They each earn approximately $110,000 per year. Harry has recently established a retirement plan for the self-employed (an HR-10 plan) and Susan has a qualified pension plan and a qualified savings plan from her employer with a Section 401(k) option (with five separate investment options among which she can select). Her savings plan account balance is one-half in her company's stock and one-half in a diversified stock fund.

Harry carries $500,000 face amount of life insurance on his life, with $100,000 from a VUL policy (having an $8000 cash value in its common stock account) and $400,000 as term insurance. Susan also carries $500,000 face amount of life insurance on her life, with $100,000 from a traditional fixed-premium whole life policy (with a $2000 cash value) and the remainder as group and individual term insurance.

Two years ago, Susan's employer granted her a nonqualified stock option (NQSO) to purchase 1000 shares of the company's stock at an option price of $50 per share. The market price of the stock is now $90 per share. The NQSO is vested, but Susan has not yet exercised it.

From an employee stock purchase plan with Susan's employer (different from the NQSO), a lump-sum distribution from Harry's former employer's profit-sharing plan when he left the firm, their personal savings, and a small inheritance from Harry's mother, they have accumulated other investable assets of $300,000. They own their home, now valued at $500,000, on which there is a $400,000 adjustable rate mortgage with interest currently at 5.12 percent. As of now, they have decided not to use their investable assets to pay off the mortgage.

Susan and Harry file a joint income tax return and are in the 35 percent federal and 40 percent combined federal, state, and local top marginal income tax brackets. They also have indicated that they wish to plan their asset allocations on a combined basis, rather than individually. (Of course, each spouse could plan his or her own asset allocations separately, if they desired.)

With respect to their investment objectives and policies, the Moderns would like to accumulate assets first to fund their children's educations so the children do not need to take out loans, then to prepare for their own comfortable retirement, which they hope will be no later than age 60, and finally to establish a general investment fund for their economic security. Since their older child is age 6 (with about 12 years before he begins college), all these goals have a reasonably long time horizon. Both Harry and Susan believe in the long-term growth and superior returns of the stock market. Harry wants to put all their available assets in common stocks, but Susan is concerned about the volatility of the market. Both agree that current dividend income is not important to them. Harry eventually would like to invest in and manage sound income-producing real estate, which he says he comes across from time to time in his law practice. Susan agrees with this idea, but they both agree that investment real estate is for the future.

As of now, they both agree that they might consider the following asset classes for their portfolio:

- Growth common stocks (including the stock of Susan's employer, Growth Drugs)
- Diversified common stocks (as a second choice to growth stocks)
- Investment-grade corporate bonds (if held in tax-advantaged plans or accounts)
- Investment-grade municipal bonds (held directly)
- Guaranteed principal assets (if held in tax-advantaged plans or accounts)
- Cash equivalents (liquid assets)
- Investment real estate (for the future)

Considering the return-risk estimates in Table 13.1 and their own situation and opinions, Harry and Susan have decided that for now they would like to plan for the following percentage allocations:

Growth and diversified common stocks (with mostly growth stocks)	70%
Corporate bonds (held in tax-advantaged accounts)	15%
Guaranteed principal assets (held in tax-advantaged accounts)	10%
Cash equivalents	5%

They also prefer not to have more than 20 percent of their portfolios in any one stock or security.

Given this desired asset allocation, Table 13.2 gives an analysis of the Moderns' return-risk situation, making the assumptions indicated in the table footnotes. Based on these estimates and assumptions, which hopefully are conservative, the Moderns can expect a greater than 7.52 percent after-tax long-term total return on their entire portfolio.[6] They should also be ready to take as much as a 38 percent decline in their overall portfolio in the event of a severe economic recession. (Note that this percentage estimate does not take into consideration any lack of correlation between the asset classes considered here—growth common stocks and investment-grade corporate bonds—as modern portfolio theory might.[7] This makes our estimate more conservative.)

The Moderns presently have an overall investment portfolio of about

[6] It is greater than 7.52 percent because of the compounding effect of long-term capital gains and the anticipated long period of tax deferral under the tax-advantaged vehicles (an HR-10 plan, a qualified savings plan, and a VUL policy in this case).

[7] In other words, in the face of a severe economic recession when the prices of common stocks are falling dramatically, the market prices of investment-grade corporate bonds probably would rise as interest rates decline.

Table 13.2. Analysis of return-risk relationships for desired asset allocation of the Moderns

(1)	(2)	(3)	(4)	(5)	(6)	(7)
Asset class or subclass	Expected average annual total long-term returns (before tax)*	Expected average annual total long-term returns (after tax)**	Maximum likely percentage decline during a bear market†	Percentage weight of asset classes in portfolio	Weighted after-tax total returns (col. 3 × col. 5)	Weighted maximum likely declines (col. 4 × col. 5)
Growth common stocks‡	12.0%	9.4%	50%	70%	6.58%	35%
Corporate bonds	6.9%	4.1%	20%	15%	0.62%	3%
Guaranteed principal assets	4.0%	2.4%	0	10%	0.24%	0
Money market funds (tax-free)	1.5%	1.5%	0	5%	0.075%	0
Total weighted portfolio					7.515%	38%

*Figures from Table 13.1 and from other sources for corporate bonds and tax-free money market funds.
**This assumes all returns (capital gains, dividends, and interest) are taxed each year at a combined 40 percent rate on ordinary income and a 20 percent rate on capital gains. This is done for the sake of simplicity, but it overstates the tax effect and understates the after-tax yields because capital gains will not be taken each year and the corporate bonds and guaranteed principal assets are in tax-advantaged vehicles for which taxation will be deferred for a long, long time in this case.
†Percentages from Table 13.1.
‡For the sake of simplicity, all common stocks are considered growth stocks since the Moderns want to invest mainly in that category.

$460,000. Almost all of this is in growth (or diversified) common stocks, as follows: $40,000 account balance under Harry's HR-10 plan; $70,000 account balance under Susan's Section 401(k) plan; $8,000 cash value of Harry's VUL policy; the $40,000 intrinsic value of Susan's stock option ($90 - $50 = $40 ×1000 shares = $40,000); and almost all of their $300,000 of directly owned assets (which include $95,000 of Growth Drugs stock purchased under Susan's employee stock purchase plan), growth-type stock mutual funds, and other growth-oriented common stocks. Only the $2000 cash value of Susan's traditional whole life policy is otherwise invested.

However, according to their asset allocation goals, they should have approximately $322,000 in growth (or perhaps diversified) common stocks, $69,000 in bonds, $46,000 in guaranteed principal assets, and $23,000 in cash equivalents. Further, they have a concentration problem with respect to Susan's Growth Drugs stock. They now have $170,000 in Growth Drugs stock— $35,000 under Susan's 401(k) plan, $95,000 held directly, and the $40,000 value of her stock option—which is almost 37 percent of their portfolios.

To implement their desired asset allocation strategy, Harry and Susan should add bonds, guaranteed principal assets, and cash equivalents to their portfolio. They should also reduce their stock holdings, particularly in Growth Drugs. Naturally, they want to incur as little in the way of capital gains taxes as possible. With these thoughts in mind, the following actions might be suggested to the Moderns.

- Harry might change the investments in his HR-10 plan and VUL policy from stocks to investment-grade corporate bonds or bond funds. This would not result in current taxation.
- Susan might change the allocation of her contributions to her 401(k) plan from stocks (particularly Growth Drugs stock) to the plan's GIC. To the extent the plan permits it, she might also change her present account balance to the GIC or the plan's corporate bond account. Again, this would not result in current taxation.
- When Susan exercises her NQSO, she might use Growth Drugs stock that they presently own as part of the purchase price (to the extent permitted by the plan). She also might sell part or all of the stock received after exercise, so as not to realize capital gains. These actions will reduce her exposure to Growth Drugs stock with lessened taxation. (See Chapter 22.)
- When Susan and Harry have savings available for investment, proceeds from sales of securities, or other funds available for investment, they might first place the funds in a tax-free money market account (cash equivalent) until it reaches the desired level and then acquire directly held investment-grade municipal bonds until the overall bond portion reaches the desired level.

- If Harry and Susan are making charitable gifts, they might consider giving the most appreciated Growth Drugs stock instead of cash. This will help reduce their investment exposure to Growth Drugs stock. (See Chapter 16.)
- Finally, Susan and Harry may have to just bite the bullet and sell some appreciated stock and pay any capital gains taxes due. They probably do not have enough assets and possibly are too early in their life cycle to consider more sophisticated techniques for deferring capital gains as discussed in Chapter 15.

A More Mature Retired Couple

Now let us consider an entirely different case. Assume that John and Martha Senior are married, their three children are out of their home and self-supporting, and they are retired. John is 67 and Martha is 64. John receives Social Security retirement benefits and a pension from his former employer for his and Martha's lifetimes (with a 50 percent survivor's benefit for Martha if he should predecease her). Martha has not yet begun to receive Social Security retirement benefits, but she will begin to do so when she reaches age 65. Martha receives a small pension of her own and is the income beneficiary for her lifetime of a modest trust established for her under her mother's will. John is covered by Medicare and Martha presently has COBRA continuation coverage under John's former employer's medical plan. Martha will be eligible for Medicare when she reaches age 65. John carries $100,000 face amount of traditional whole life insurance that has a cash value of $40,000.

When John retired, he rolled over all of his account balance under his former employer's qualified savings plan into a regular rollover IRA. He now has $300,000 in this rollover IRA, with $200,000 invested in two-year insured CDs and $100,000 in investment-grade corporate bonds. From their personal savings, John and Martha have another $200,000 in directly owned assets, of which $100,000 is in three-year insured CDs and $100,000 is in a diversified common stock mutual fund.

As investment objectives and policies, Martha and John would like to preserve their capital as much as possible, receive reasonable current income with moderate capital growth, protect their investment income against declines in interest rates as much as possible, maintain reasonable liquidity, and have reasonable diversification. They need a reasonable income from their investment portfolio to maintain a comfortable standard of living. They do not wish to consider the corpus of Martha's trust in their asset allocation planning.

The Seniors file a joint income tax return and are in the 27 percent federal and 32 percent combined federal, state, and local top marginal income tax brackets. They want to consider their asset allocation decisions together.

As of now, John and Martha agree that they would consider the following asset classes for their portfolio:

- Diversified income-producing common stocks or stock funds
- Investment-grade corporate bonds
- U.S. Treasury bonds
- Guaranteed principal assets
- Cash equivalents (liquid assets)

Considering the return-risk estimates in Table 13.1 and their own situation and opinions, the Seniors have decided that they would like to plan for the following percentage allocation of their portfolios.

Investment-grade corporate bonds (five- to 15-year maturities)	25%
U.S. Treasury bonds (20- to 30-year maturities)	25%
CDs (two- to three-year maturities)	20%
Diversified income-producing common stocks	20%
Other guaranteed principal assets (e.g., life insurance cash values)	5%
Cash equivalents	5%

In this allocation, they are planning to ladder their bond and other fixed-income portfolio to protect themselves against call risk as well as against interest rate risk to bond values. Hence, they plan to have about 25 percent of their assets in shorter-term securities (cash equivalents and two- to three-year CDs), 25 percent in intermediate-term bonds (five- to 15-year corporate bonds), and 25 percent in long-term bonds (20- to 30-year U.S. Treasuries). Their bonds could be held directly (outright or through mutual funds) or in the IRA.

Given this desired asset allocation, Table 13.3 presents an analysis of the Seniors' return-risk situation, making the assumptions indicated in the table notes. Based on these estimates and assumptions, which hopefully are conservative, the Seniors can expect almost a 3.9 percent after-tax long-term total return on their entire portfolio.[8] They also should be ready to take as much as a 15 percent decline in their overall portfolio in the event of a severe economic recession or other problem. (Again, note that lack of correlations among asset classes is not taken into consideration here.)

To implement their desired asset allocation strategy, Martha and John need to move some of their assets now in CDs into U.S. Treasury bonds, corporate bonds, and a money market account in the appropriate amounts. These assets can be held directly or in the IRA. These shifts probably can occur as the CDs

---

[8] It is greater than 3.9 percent for the same reasons previously stated in note 7. However, the deferral periods presumably will be shorter for the Seniors. Also, the Seniors (at ages 67 and 64) are much more likely to benefit (or their heirs will benefit) from the step-up in basis at death for capital assets.

Table 13.3. Analysis of return-risk relationships for desired asset allocation of the Seniors

(1) Asset class or subclass	(2) Expected average annual total long-term returns (before tax)*	(3) Expected average annual total long-term returns (after tax)**	(4) Maximum likely percentage decline during a bear market†	(5) Percentage weight of asset classes in portfolio	(6) Weighted after-tax total returns (col. 3 × col. 5)	(7) Weighted maximum likely declines (col. 4 × col. 5)
U.S. Treasury bonds (long term)	5.7%	4.2%	20%	25%	1.05%	5.0%
Investment-grade corporate bonds (intermediate terms)	5.0%	3.4%	10%	25%	0.85%	2.5%
CDs (2- to 3-year maturities)	3.0%	2.0%	0	20%	0.40%	0
Diversified income-producing common stocks	Dividends 3% Capital gains 7% Total return 10%	Dividends 2.0% Capital gains 5.6% Total return 7.6%	40%	20%	1.52%	8.0%
Money market funds (taxable)	2.0%	1.4%	0	5%	0.07%	0
Insurance cash values‡	N/A	N/A	0	5%	N/A	0
Total weighted returns and risks on whole portfolio					3.89%	15.5%

*Figures from Table 13.1 and from other sources.
**Same assumptions as in Table 13.2, except that tax rates are 27 percent federal and 32 percent combined for ordinary income and 20 percent for capital gains.
†Percentages from Table 13.1, except that the percentage is reduced for intermediate-term bonds.
‡This is difficult to present because no income is currently coming from these cash values, but it could if John so elects. See text discussion.

mature so no early withdrawal penalties need to be paid. There also should be no tax consequences.

John has more cash value in his traditional whole life policy than he would like: 5 percent of their $540,000 portfolio or $27,000). He has indicated that he wants to keep the insurance in force to protect Martha against a reduction in retirement income if he should predecease her. Generally, one tries not to take taxable amounts from life insurance contracts. With these factors in mind, John has several options with respect to this policy. They are discussed more fully in Chapter 27.

Finally, John and Martha already have about the desired amount of common stocks. These could be held directly or through mutual funds.

4

Income Tax Planning

14

Income Tax Fundamentals

Most people are concerned about saving on their income taxes. This chapter covers briefly the structure of the federal income tax system.

The Federal Income Tax on Individuals

Basic Tax Structure

The federal income tax law is detailed and complex. But the basic formula for determining an individual's tax can be shown briefly as follows.[1]

Gross income. This means all income from whatever source derived, unless specifically excluded by a provision of the tax code. (This approach is described as gross income being an "all-inclusive concept.")

Less: Deductions to arrive at adjusted gross income (referred to in tax parlance as "deductions above the line"), including:

- Trade or business expenses (not incurred as an employee).
- Expenses of producing rents and royalties.
- Losses from sale or exchange of nonpersonal property.
- Contributions to retirement plans for the self-employed (HR-10 or Keogh plans), SEP plans, and SIMPLE plans.
- Contributions to individual retirement accounts or annuities (IRAs) for eligible persons (i.e., contributions that are tax deductible, but not the non-tax-deductible contributions that may be permitted).

[1] The basic income tax structure presented here is not meant to be exhaustive. There are a number of excellent income tax publications that taxpayers can consult for more detailed information on deductions, exemptions, and so on.

- Alimony paid.
- Self-employment tax deduction (equal to one-half of any Social Security self-employment tax payable for the year).
- Interest penalty on early withdrawal from time savings accounts.
- An increasing percentage (with 100 percent deductible in the year 2003 and thereafter) of amounts incurred by self-employed persons for health insurance on themselves, their spouses, and their dependents as a trade or business expense.
- Moving expenses.
- Contributions to medical savings accounts (MSAs).
- Interest paid on "qualified education loans" with an annual limit and income limits.
- Qualified higher education expenses up to $3,000 per year with income limits.

Equals: Adjusted gross income (AGI).

Less: Itemized deductions,[2] which are referred to as "deductions below the line" (or the standard deduction at the option of the taxpayer), including (as itemized deductions):

- Medical and dental expenses (in excess of 7½ percent of AGI).
- Taxes (other than state and local sales taxes).
- Charitable contributions (subject to certain limitations described in Chapter 16).
- Certain interest expense. (Deductible interest for individuals includes "qualified residence interest," which is mortgage interest on a taxpayer's principal residence and a second residence up to either the "cost basis" (generally the purchase price plus the cost of any improvements) or the fair market value of the property, whichever is less. Mortgage interest still may be deducted on loan balances over this limit if the indebtedness is for medical or educational expenses. This limit also does not apply to interest on mortgage debts incurred on or before August 16, 1986. Effective as of 1988, there are additional dollar limitations on the deductibility of personal mortgage interest. First, when the interest is on *aggregate residence indebtedness,* which is indebtedness incurred in acquiring, constructing, or substantially improving a taxpayer's residence, it is deductible only to the extent that the indebtedness does not exceed $1,000,000. Second, when the interest is on *home equity indebtedness,* it is deductible only to the extent that the indebtedness does not exceed $100,000 or the taxpayer's equity in the residence

---

[2] The overall amount of certain itemized deductions is phased out for certain higher-income taxpayers. However, this phaseout is reduced in stages starting in 2006 and is repealed entirely in 2010 under the Economic Growth and Tax Relief Reconciliation Act.

whichever is less. The $1,000,000 limitation does not apply to interest on indebtedness incurred prior to October 14, 1987. However, *consumer interest expense* (other than qualifying residence interest just described) is not deductible. On the other hand, interest expense for loans on personal investments—*investment interest* or *portfolio interest*—is deductible to the extent of investment income (if the taxpayer itemizes).

■ Casualty losses (in excess of $100 for each loss and 10 percent of AGI for all losses).

■ Miscellaneous deductions (in excess of 2 percent of AGI with certain exceptions).

Less: Personal exemptions.[3]

Equals: Taxable income.

Federal income tax (determined by applying income tax rates to taxable income).

Less: Credits (i.e., amounts deducted from the tax itself), including:

■ Credit for the elderly or permanently and totally disabled.

■ Child care and care of disabled dependent or spouse credit.

■ Child tax credit and adoption credit.

■ Education credits (Hope credit and Lifetime Learning credit).

■ Earned income credit.

■ Credit for qualified retirement savings contributions.

Equals: Federal income tax payable.

Plus: Other taxes payable, including:

■ Alternative minimum tax (AMT) to the extent that it exceeds the regular income tax.

■ Self-employment tax (Social Security tax paid by the self-employed on their earnings subject to Social Security taxes).

Equals: Total federal taxes payable.

Federal Income Tax Rates

Scheduled Tax Rates. Under the Economic Growth and Tax Relief Reconciliation Act (EGTRRA) of 2001, the federal income tax rates for various filing statuses (see later discussion of filing status) are 10 percent, 15 percent, 27 percent, 30 percent, 35 percent, and 38.6 percent for 2002-2003. Thereafter

---

[3] As with certain itemized deductions, the overall amount of a taxpayer's personal and dependency exemptions are phased out for certain higher-income taxpayers. Again, under the Economic Growth and Tax Relief Reconciliation Act, this phaseout is reduced in stages starting in 2006 and is repealed entirely in 2010.

these tax rates will decline in stages until they become 10 percent, 15 percent, 25 percent, 28 percent, 33 percent, and 35 percent from 2006-2010.

Thus, the *top nominal marginal* individual federal income tax rate is 38.6 percent, declining in stages to 35 percent. The *average* income tax rate for a taxpayer is the total tax payable divided by the taxpayer's taxable income. For individuals and trusts and estates, the average rate will always be less than the marginal rate. It is the top marginal rate that normally is used for planning purposes. This assumes that the income or deductions being considered come at the top bracket or are the last items received or paid. This assumption may tend to overstate the effect of taxes on ordinary income, since the tax rates are quite progressive.

Indirect Rate Increases. The situation becomes more complex, however, when we consider certain indirect rate factors. Certain itemized deductions (i.e., deductible taxes, deductible interest other than investment interest, charitable contributions, job expenses and most other miscellaneous deductions, and other miscellaneous deductions other than gambling losses) are phased out (not allowed) for higher-income taxpayers. For taxpayers in the phaseout range (AGI over $139,500 for most taxpayers for 2003 taxes), the rate of reduction in these itemized deductions effectively is 3 percent. Therefore, the effective tax rate is the nominal rate increased by 3 percent. For example, for taxpayers subject to phaseout who are in the 35 percent bracket, the effective federal tax rate (considering only the itemized deduction phaseout) would be 36.05 percent [35% + (3% × 35% or 1.05%) = 36.05%]. Under EGTRRA, this phaseout of certain itemized deductions is reduced in stages starting in 2006 and is repealed entirely in 2010.

In addition, the Medicare tax rate, which is currently 1.45 percent (2.90 percent on earnings from self-employment), is now applied to all earned income without limit. Therefore, higher-income taxpayers effectively must pay an additional 1.45 percent (2.90 percent if self-employed) on *personal earnings* over the earnings cap.

Finally, personal and dependency exemptions are also phased out for higher-income taxpayers. This increases the actual tax rate for persons in the phaseout range. But under EGTRRA, this phaseout also is reduced and finally repealed.

Trust Tax Rates. Most irrevocable trusts are taxed as separate entities with their own tax rates.[4] Trust and estate tax brackets are very steeply progressive. For

---

[4] Depending on their terms, certain irrevocable trusts can be grantor trusts. These trusts are defined in the IRC. Grantor trusts are trusts whose assets (corpus) are deemed to be owned by the grantor or creator of the trust for federal income tax purposes only. Therefore, the income and deductions of grantor trusts are treated as income and deductions of the grantor and are taxable to or taken by him or her. Revocable trusts also are grantor trusts.

example, in 2003 trust taxable income reached the top tax bracket when it exceeded only $9,350. This rapid progression of trust tax rates has planning implications. It may not be desirable taxwise to accumulate sizeable amounts of taxable income in trusts. It may be better to have such income distributed currently to trust beneficiaries so it will be taxable to them at possibly lower brackets. Also, when trust income is to be accumulated (such as for a minor), it may be desirable to invest trust corpus so as to produce as little taxable income as possible (such as in municipal bonds, growth common stocks, or tax-deferred vehicles).

Filing Status

There are separate federal income tax rate schedules for five categories of individual taxpayers: married individuals filing joint returns (and also a qualified surviving spouse during the first two years after the death of the other spouse), heads of households, single individuals, married individuals who elect to file separate returns, and estates and trusts. This is referred to as the taxpayer's *filing status.* Determining the appropriate filing status is one aspect of income tax planning.

Indexing for Inflation

The tax law adjusts annually for the effects of inflation the individual tax brackets, standard deduction amounts, the amount of personal and dependency exemptions, the thresholds for phasing out certain itemized deductions and the personal and dependency exemptions, and certain other limits or features in the tax law. This is referred to as *indexing* the tax schedules and other amounts.

Phaseout of Personal and Dependency Exemptions and Certain Itemized Deductions

As noted earlier, there are phaseouts and limitations on deductions for personal and dependency exemptions and certain itemized deductions for higher-income taxpayers. Itemized deductions of individuals whose AGI exceeds a certain threshold amount (indexed for inflation) will be reduced according to the *smaller* of two limitations. The first is that deductions will be reduced by 3 percent of the amount by which the taxpayer's AGI exceeds the threshold amount. The second is that the reduction may not exceed 80 percent of the allowable itemized deductions.

However, itemized deductions for *medical expenses, investment interest, casualty losses,* and wagering losses to the extent of wagering gains are not counted in the phaseout process. Thus, for example, if a taxpayer pays interest on debt incurred to carry a portfolio of securities (e.g., margin interest), the investment interest would be fully deductible (but always limited to the extent of the investor's investment income). Again, however, under EGTRRA both of these phaseouts are reduced in stages starting in 2006 and repealed entirely in 2010.

Taxation of Children and the Unearned Income of Certain Minor Children (Kiddie Tax)

When children receive income, it normally is taxable to the child at the child's tax rate. This has made planning to shift taxable income from higher-bracket taxpayers to lower-bracket children (or to others in lower brackets) reasonably attractive. However, there are tax limitations on shifting income to lower-bracket children and grandchildren.[5] First, the tax law provides that an individual who is eligible to be claimed as a dependent on another taxpayer's return may not take a personal exemption on his or her own return.

Further, such a dependent's standard deduction may not exceed the larger of a specified amount that is indexed for inflation ($750 for 2003) or $250 (indexed for inflation) plus the dependent's earned income, subject to the regular standard deduction limits.

Finally, there is the so-called kiddie tax. This novel concept provides that the net unearned income of children under age 14 is taxed to the child but at the child's *parents'* top marginal federal income tax rate, assuming this rate is higher than the child's tax rate. But this special rule can apply only when a child has unearned income in excess of a specified amount ($1,500 for 2003), which is indexed for inflation. Therefore, there normally would be no income tax advantage in shifting unearned income that will be subject to this kiddie tax.[6]

However, despite these limitations, planning is still possible. For example, earned income can still be received by a child, taxed at the child's rate, and with the full standard deduction available. Also, shifting unearned income over the annual limit can be delayed until after a child reaches age 14. Further, income can be accumulated in a trust for the child (and hence be taxable to the trust rather than the child) until the child reaches age 14. In this case, however, the highly progressive tax rates applying to trusts must be considered. Planning may involve distributing just enough trust income to a child (or to a custodial account for the child) to avoid the kiddie tax while allowing the remainder to be accumulated and taxed to the trust. Finally, the investment of property transferred to minors under age 14 can be planned so as to produce as little

---

[5] The subject of gifts to minors as part of estate planning is covered in Chapter 25.

[6] Parents in some cases may elect to include their children's unearned income over $1,500 (indexed) in their own returns to avoid having to have the child file a return.

currently taxable unearned income as possible. Such investments might include growth common stocks, municipal bonds (such as zero-coupon municipals), and tax-deferred vehicles (such as life insurance).

But on the bright side, for each dependent child of a taxpayer under age 17, the tax law provides a tax credit of $600 per year from 2001-2004 and then increasing in stages to reach $1,000 for 2010 and thereafter. This credit is indexed for inflation and is partially refundable. However, it is phased out for higher-income taxpayers. The phaseout begins at an AGI of $110,000 for married persons filing a joint return and $75,000 for unmarried persons.

Income in Respect of a Decedent (IRD)

This is a concept commonly encountered but easily misunderstood. Income in respect of a decedent (IRD) will arise when a deceased person was entitled to items that would have been gross income for federal income tax purposes, but which were not includable in the decedent's gross income for the year of his or her death. IRD items generally are treated as gross income to whoever receives them after the decedent's death. They do *not* receive a step-up in basis following the decedent's death, as do capital assets at present.

There are numerous IRD items. Here are some common examples:

- Distributions after an employee's or former employee's death from *qualified retirement plans*. This is an important source of IRD in many cases.
- Distributions from a decedent's *individual retirement account* (IRA), other than a Roth IRA. This is another important source of IRD.
- Distributions after an employee's or former employee's death from *tax-sheltered annuity* (TSA or Section 403[b]) *plans.*
- Accrued and as yet untaxed interest on U.S. savings bonds as of the death of the owner.
- Death benefits under *nonqualified deferred compensation plans.*
- Distributions of as yet untaxed investment income from *investment annuity contracts* after the death of the annuitant.
- The taxable portion of payments made after death from sales made on the installment method.

An IRD item will not only produce gross income to the recipient of the item (e.g. a beneficiary or the decedent's estate or heirs), but also be included at full value in the decedent's gross estate for federal estate tax purposes (and counted for generation-skipping transfer [GST] tax purposes as well). Thus, IRD items are heavily taxed at death. Some relief is provided, however, by allowing the recipient to take an *itemized income tax deduction* on his or her federal income tax return for any *federal estate tax (or GST tax) attributable to the IRD item* in the decedent's estate. The amount of this itemized deduction is determined by calculating the federal estate tax (or GST tax) payable with the IRD item included in the decedent's estate and then calculating the estate tax (or GST tax) without the IRD item. The difference is the income tax deduction. Of course, if no federal estate tax (or GST tax) is payable, there will be no deduction.

Here is an illustration. Suppose that Joan Martin, who is divorced, is a participant in a qualified savings plan with a Section 401(k) option. She has a current account balance in the plan of $200,000 and her adult daughter, Amy, is named as beneficiary. Joan also has other property, so that the total value will place her in a 43 percent top marginal federal estate tax bracket. Suppose now that Joan dies. Amy, as plan beneficiary, will receive the $200,000 account balance, which is IRD to her. Further, the $200,000 is in Joan's gross estate for federal estate tax purposes. Thus, the $200,000 is gross income (ordinary income) to Amy in the year she receives it, but she will have an itemized deduction of $86,000 for the estate tax attributable to the account balance.[7] If Amy receives the account balance over more than one taxable year (such as over her life expectancy), she will receive gross income as it is paid out to her and also a proportional part of the itemized deduction each year.[8]

Actual and Constructive Receipt of Income

There are two generally accepted methods for recognizing income and expenses for income tax purposes—the *cash basis* and the *accrual basis*. Most individuals and many smaller businesses are cash-basis taxpayers.

For *cash-basis taxpayers,* items of income (or expenses) are considered received (or paid), and hence taxable for income tax purposes, in the year they are actually or constructively received. *Actual receipt* means a taxpayer actually possesses the income. *Constructive receipt* is when the income has been credited to the taxpayer or set apart so that he or she can actually receive it at any time without any substantial limitation or restriction on his or her right to do so.

For example, if Martha Jones is paid her salary this year and cashes her payroll check during the year, she is in actual receipt of the compensation this year

---

[7] This assumes the full $200,000 account balance falls into the 43 percent estate tax bracket in Joan's estate. There is no GST tax in this case because Amy is not a "skip person" with respect to Joan. (See Chapter 24 for an explanation of the GST tax and the definition of a skip person.) We are also assuming Joan has no income tax basis in her Section 401(k) plan and there is no state death tax credit available to her estate.

[8] In planning for distributions from qualified retirement plans, a common strategy is to defer the distributions and the income taxes on them for as long as possible under the circumstances. In this case, this would normally be for Amy's lifetime or her life expectancy. (See Chapter 20 for a discussion of planning for taking distributions from retirement plans.)

and will be taxed on it this year. If, instead, her employer places 10 percent of her salary this year in an investment account in her name from which she has the unrestricted right to withdraw the money at any time, Martha will be in constructive receipt of the 10 percent placed in this account even if she does not withdraw it this year.

This concept of constructive receipt can be important for planning purposes. Assume, for example, the same facts as just noted for Martha Jones except that Martha will be entitled to the 10 percent of her salary placed in the investment account (and the earnings on the account) only in the event of her termination of employment, disability, death, the passage of time, or other substantial limitation or restriction.[9] In this case, Martha would not be in constructive receipt this year of the 10 percent of her salary, because her right to receive it is subject to a substantial limitation or restriction. She will be taxed only when the funds are actually paid to her or made available to her without restriction, which normally would be many years in the future. This is the principle underlying nonqualified deferred compensation plans offered by many employers to certain of their employees. The doctrine of constructive receipt applies only to cash-basis taxpayers.

For *accrual-basis taxpayers,* items of income are includible in gross income for the year in which the right to receive the income becomes fixed and the amounts receivable become determinable with reasonable accuracy.

Assignment of Income

In general, income from property is taxable to the owner of the property. Thus, if one wishes to transfer the income from property to another, ownership of the property must be transferred (given or sold) to the intended recipient or to a trust for the recipient.

Merely assigning only the income from property, while retaining ownership, will not shift the tax liability on that income to the donee; the tax liability will remain with the property's owner. Similarly, income from personal services (personal earnings) is taxable to the person rendering the services. The tax liability on personal earnings cannot be transferred to another by assigning the right to receive the earnings to the other person.

To use the famous analogy of Justice Oliver Wendell Holmes, if one wishes to transfer the fruit from a tree (for tax purposes), one must transfer the whole tree.[10]

---

[9] In general, an amount is not constructively received if it is only conditionally credited to the taxpayer, is indefinite in amount, is subject to substantial limitation or restriction, or if the payer lacks funds.

[10] See *Lucas v. Earl,* 281 U.S. 111 (1930).

Capital Gains Taxation

General Considerations. Capital gains and losses are realized from the sale or exchange of capital assets. With some exceptions, capital assets include the property taxpayers own. Some examples are common stocks, bonds, preferred stocks, investment real estate, collectibles, partnership interests (generally), personal residences, and other personal assets. These gains and losses also are recognized in the year of the sale or exchange unless there is some specific nonrecognition provision in the Internal Revenue Code that defers recognition. The common nonrecognition provisions are outlined in the next section. The difference between the *amount realized* from the sale or exchange and the *adjusted basis* of the asset in the hands of the taxpayer is the amount of the *capital gain or loss.*

Amount Realized and Adjusted Basis. The *amount realized* generally is the value received from the sale or exchange of a capital asset. The *adjusted basis* depends on how the taxpayer acquired the property. In general, adjusted basis is determined in certain common situations as follows:

- If a taxpayer originally *purchased the property,* its adjusted basis is its cost plus any purchase commissions.
- If a taxpayer acquired the property as a *lifetime gift* from another, its adjusted basis is its basis in the hands of the donor (plus any gift tax on unrealized appreciation of the gift property).
- If a taxpayer *inherited the property* from a decedent, its adjusted basis at present is the property's fair market value at the date of death (or alternative valuation date for federal estate tax purposes). This is the important rule on step-up in income tax basis at death.
- If a taxpayer receives new stock or securities in a *tax-free reorganization or merger* (as one of those tax-free reorganizations defined in the Internal Revenue Code), the new basis of the stock or securities will be the former basis of the stock or securities the taxpayer exchanged for the new stock or securities (called a *carryover basis*).
- If a person acquires a partnership interest by a *contribution of property* (including money) to the partnership, the basis of the person's interest in the partnership generally is the money contributed plus the adjusted basis to the contributing partner of the property contributed (a carryover basis from the property contributed).
- Also, if a partner receives a *distribution of property in kind* from his or her *partnership,* the partner takes the partnership's basis in the property (a carryover basis) but not greater than the partner's basis in his or her partnership interest.
- If a person or persons *transfer property to a corporation solely in exchange for*

stock in such corporation and immediately after the exchange the person or persons have control of the corporation (at least 80 percent ownership), the basis of the person's stock in such corporation generally is the same as the basis of the property the person transferred to the corporation in exchange for its stock.

- If a person or entity owns an interest in a pass-through business entity (i.e., partnerships, S corporations, or limited liability companies [LLCs]), his or her basis in the interest will be adjusted to reflect the profits, losses, and other operations of the pass-through entity. (See Chapter 30 for a more complete description of these entities.)
- A taxpayer may increase his or her adjusted basis in property by the cost of any improvements and reduce it by any depreciation, depletion, or amortization.

These statements do not include all the situations or rules for determining basis. They are intended to be representative of fairly common situations. Other rules for determining basis are discussed elsewhere in this book. Finally, a taxpayer may increase his or her basis at sale or exchange by any expenses of sale (such as brokers' fees, commissions, transfer taxes, and the like), unless these expenses were taken from the amount realized as reported on the tax return.

Calculation of Capital Gains and Losses. *Net capital gains* are net long-term capital gains (long-term capital gains less long-term capital losses) less any net short-term capital losses (short-term capital losses less short-term capital gains). For this purpose, short-term capital gains and losses are those on capital assets held for one year or less and the taxpayer first determines any *net* short-term capital gain or loss for the year. Long-term capital gains and losses are those on capital assets held for more than one year and the taxpayer also determines any *net* long-term capital gain or loss for the year. Thus, under this system, capital losses offset capital gains and, to the extent of $3000 per year, other ordinary income of the taxpayer.

As an example, assume a taxpayer had the following gains and losses during a year:

$12,000 in long-term capital gains
$3000 in long-term capital losses
$1000 in short-term capital gains
$2500 in short-term capital losses

Thus, this taxpayer has *net long-term capital gains* of $9000 ($12,000 - $3000), *net short-term capital losses* of $1500 ($2500 - $1000), and *net capital gains* of $7500 ($9000 - $1500). The importance of this calculation is that the tax rate for individuals on net capital gains is 20 percent (or 10 percent for individual taxpayers in the 10 or15 percent brackets), while the rate on ordinary income and net short-term capital gains can be as high as 38.6 percent, declining in stages to 35 percent in 2006 and thereafter.

As just noted, capital losses are first used to offset capital gains of the same type and then any net capital loss (short-term or long-term) can be used to reduce the taxpayer's other ordinary income dollar for dollar, up to a maximum of $3000 in any one year. Any unused net capital losses may be carried forward by the taxpayer indefinitely and used in future years, first to offset any capital gains, and then to offset ordinary income up to $3000 per year.

Here is an illustration. Suppose Harry Baker had the following capital gains and losses on his stock and bond transactions this year.

> Long-term capital gains: $1000
> Short-term capital gains: $2000
> Short-term capital losses: $6500

In addition, Harry and his wife had other ordinary taxable income of $90,000. Harry first can offset his capital gains against his capital losses so that he has a net capital loss for the year of $3500. He then can use up to $3000 of this net capital loss to reduce the other ordinary taxable income to $87,000. Since Harry and his wife file a joint return and are in a 27 percent top marginal tax bracket, this would save them $810 in income taxes this year. Also, they can carry the remaining $500 of net capital loss forward to the next and subsequent tax years. Thus, a taxpayer with capital losses can use these losses to save on income taxes by realizing them at the proper time. This is sometimes called *tax loss selling*.

Tax Rates on Capital Gains. At present, the tax rate for individuals on net capital gains generally is 20 percent, except for taxpayers in the 10 or 15 percent brackets for ordinary income, for whom the rate is 10 percent. However, for tax years beginning after December 31, 2000, the tax rate for individuals on net capital gains on assets held for more than five years and for which the holding period begins after December 31, 2000 (i.e., for assets purchased in 2001 and thereafter) is 18 percent (or 8 percent for taxpayers in the 10 or 15 percent brackets, regardless of when the holding period began).

There are some exceptions to these capital gains tax rates. One is that net capital gains on collectibles (art, coins, stamps, etc.) are taxed at a maximum rate of 28 percent. Also, for sales or taxable exchanges of certain depreciable real estate (such as residential rental property), the portion of the net capital gain attributable to allowable depreciation is taxed at a maximum rate of 25 percent. Net short-term capital gains are taxed at the same rates as ordinary income.

Constructive Sales. Normally, a capital gain or loss is not realized and recognized for tax purposes until there has been a sale, exchange, or other taxable disposition of a capital asset. At this point, the difference between the amount realized and the adjusted basis of the asset is the capital gain or loss.

However, the Taxpayer Relief Act of 1997 introduced a new concept of constructive sales of appreciated financial positions. The idea behind this provision is generally to prohibit the use of certain hedging techniques that essentially had allowed holders of highly appreciated assets (mainly securities) to eliminate the risk of owning the securities without actually selling the securities and realizing a sizeable capital gain. Thus, realizing the gain could be deferred or perhaps even eliminated (through the step-up in basis at death rule or other techniques). Under the constructive sale rules, however, transactions that use these techniques are considered to be sales and are taxed at the time of sale.

For this purpose, an *appreciated financial position* is a position in any stock, debt instrument, or partnership interest (with certain exceptions) where there would be gain if the position were sold or otherwise terminated at its fair market value. A *constructive sale* of an appreciated financial position is considered to occur if the holder (or a related person) (1) enters into a *short sale* of the same or substantially identical property (in effect, selling short against the box), (2) enters into an *offsetting notional principal contract* (a *swap*) with respect to the same or substantially identical property, (3) enters into a *futures or forward contract* to deliver the same or substantially identical property, (4) has entered into one of the previous transactions and acquires the same property as the underlying property in the position, and (5) to the extent prescribed in regulations, enters into *other transactions having substantially the same effect* as the transactions previously named.

This provision has essentially eliminated several formerly popular techniques (particularly selling short against the box) for deferring and perhaps eliminating significant capital gains.[11] However, some other techniques still may be available. They are discussed in Chapter 15.

Nonrecognition Provisions

It was noted at the beginning of this discussion that capital gains are *realized* as a result of the sale or exchange of a capital asset and also are *recognized* for tax purposes in the year of the sale or exchange *unless* there is a specific provision in the tax code that defers recognition. Such provisions are called *nonrecognition provisions*. The effect of a nonrecognition provision is to defer income taxation on any gain to some future transaction or event when, depending on the prop-

[11] The law does provide that certain short-term hedges (that close before the end of 30 days after the tax year in which the transaction was entered into and where the taxpayer is at risk on the appreciated financial position for an additional 60 days) will not be considered constructive sales. However, it is expected that this "safe harbor" will be of limited use to taxpayers.

erty involved and the circumstances, there may or may not be a tax due.

When a nonrecognition provision applies, there normally is a *carryover of income tax basis* from the property sold or exchanged to the new property acquired, so, in effect, the new property takes the old property's basis. In this way, the nonrecognized gain is not forgiven; it is simply potentially deferred until some future transaction or event. Nonrecognition provisions can be important in financial planning. Some of the more commonly used nonrecognition provisions are briefly listed here to illustrate the concept.

Section 1031: Exchange of Property Held for Productive Use or Investment. These exchanges are referred to as *like-kind exchanges* and are used for property held in a trade or business or for investment with certain exceptions. The exceptions include the important categories of stocks, bonds, notes, and other securities or evidences of indebtedness. These categories of assets are not eligible for like-kind exchange treatment. Like-kind exchanges are commonly used for investment real estate.

Section 1035: Certain Exchanges of Insurance Policies. While it does not involve capital gains, this important provision states that no gain or loss shall be recognized on the exchange of certain life insurance policies or the exchange of certain annuity contracts.

Section 354: Exchanges of Stock and Securities in Certain Reorganizations. This and other code provisions allow stockholders to exchange their stock for other stock with no gain or loss being recognized in the case of certain corporate reorganizations and mergers as specified in the IRC. It permits tax-free reorganizations and mergers in these cases.

Section 351: Transfer to Corporation Controlled by Transferor. This provision permits a tax-free exchange of appreciated property for corporate stock if the combined transferors are in control of the corporation immediately thereafter. This nonrecognition provision is important in the formation of corporations.

Section 721: Nonrecognition of Gain or Loss on Contribution to a Partnership. This provision permits a tax-free exchange of appreciated property for a partnership interest upon contribution of the property to the partnership. This provision is important in forming partnerships and adding partners. It also can be significant in other areas, like the creation of family limited partnerships and the use of exchange funds for deferring gains on securities.

Section 1041: Transfers of Property Between Spouses or Incident to Divorce. This provision specifies that no gain or loss shall be recognized on a transfer of property from an individual to his or her spouse or to his or her former spouse, provided in the case of a former spouse the transfer is incident to a divorce.

This nonrecognition provision permits the tax-free sale of property between spouses and the tax-free transfer of property from one spouse to another as part of a divorce settlement.

Section 1036: Stock for Stock of Same Corporation. This provides that no gain or loss shall be recognized if common stock in a corporation is exchanged solely for common stock in the same corporation, or if preferred stock in a corporation is exchanged solely for preferred stock in the same corporation. This nonrecognition provision can be used, for example, to allow use of previously owned common stock in a corporation to exercise a stock option for common stock in the same corporation. Such an exchange will defer any gain in the previously owned stock.

Section 1042: Sales of Stock to Employee Stock Ownership Plans or Certain Cooperatives. This provision allows nonrecognition of gain on the sale of non-publicly-traded employer securities to an employee stock ownership plan (ESOP), under certain conditions. It allows stockowners of closely held C corporations to defer capital gains by selling their appreciated stock to their corporation's ESOP.

Alternative Minimum Tax (AMT) for Individuals

An alternative minimum tax (AMT) may be imposed on individual taxpayers and estates and trusts with certain tax preference items and adjustments.[12] This minimum tax applies if it exceeds a taxpayer's regular income tax.

Calculation of the AMT. The AMT is calculated by starting with a taxpayer's regular taxable income for the year. To this amount are added back certain tax preference items, and certain adjustments are added or subtracted to arrive at the taxpayer's alternative minimum taxable income (AMTI) for the year. It may be noted that adjustments are different from tax preferences. Adjustments may involve only differences in timing for AMT and regular tax purposes, while preferences always increase AMTI.

Some common *adjustments* in arriving at AMTI include the following: (1) adding back personal and dependency exemptions, which are not allowed for AMT purposes; (2) adding back certain itemized deductions, which are not allowed or are cut back for AMT purposes (such as income and property taxes imposed by state and local governments, home equity loan interest on loans up to $100,000, employee business expenses deductible for regular tax purposes, and otherwise deductible medical expenses up to 10 percent of AGI);

---

[12] Taxable corporations may be subject to a corporate AMT, which is discussed later in this chapter.

(3) adding back the standard deduction for those who do not itemize (the standard deduction is not allowed for AMT purposes); and (4) adding the amount by which the value of stock purchased under incentive stock option (ISO) plans exceeds the option price.

The *tax preferences* that are added to regular taxable income to arrive at AMTI are (1) otherwise tax-free interest on certain private activity municipal bonds (AMT bonds) issued after August 7, 1986 (see Chapter 11), (2) accelerated depreciation on property placed in service before 1987, and (3) 42 percent of the otherwise excluded gain from the sale of qualified newly issued small business stock held for at least five years.

An AMT *exemption amount,* which is based on the taxpayer's filing status, then is deducted from AMTI. This amount is $49,000 for married taxpayers filing jointly and surviving spouses, $35,750 for single taxpayers and heads of households, and $24,500 for married taxpayers filing separate returns for 2001 through 2004.[13] However, this exemption is phased out when AMTI reaches certain levels. For example, for married taxpayers filing jointly, the $49,000 exemption is reduced by 25 percent of the amount by which AMTI exceeds $150,000. The *AMT rates* are applied to the amount resulting from these calculations. These rates are 26 percent of the first $175,000 and 28 percent for amounts above $175,000. The taxpayer then subtracts his or her regular income tax liability for the year from this amount. If the result is positive, the excess over the regular tax is the AMT owed for the year.

Finally, there is a *minimum tax credit* (MTC) that taxpayers may be able to take against their regular income tax only for AMT paid on AMT items involving timing differences (such as on ISOs at exercise) when future regular tax exceeds future AMT.

An Illustration. Assume that John and Mary Costa file a joint return and have regular taxable income for federal income tax purposes of $150,000 and that their regular federal income tax payable on this amount for the year is $37,926. In arriving at their taxable income, the Costas took personal and dependency exemptions, an itemized deduction for state and local income and property taxes, and an itemized deduction for interest on a home equity mortgage loan. The total for these exemptions and itemized deductions is $24,000. In addition, John exercised this year an incentive stock option (ISO) that his employer had granted to him nine years ago for 500 shares of employer stock at an exercise price of $20 per share. The fair market value of the stock at exer-

---

[13] For tax years beginning after 2004, these exemption amounts return to the levels that existed in 2000 ($45,000, $33,750 and $22,500 respectively). The exemption amount for trusts and estates is and remains $22,500. There is a special adjustment for 2001 through 2004 for married taxpayers filing separate returns.

cise was $80 per share. Finally, a municipal bond mutual fund that the Costas own reported that $2000 of the dividends credited to them during the year were from AMT bonds.

Given these facts, the calculation of the Costas' AMT would be as follows:

Regular taxable income	$150,000
AMT adjustments	+$54,000[14]
AMT preferences	+ $2,000[15]
AMTI	$206,000
AMT exemption	- $35,000[16]
	$171,000
Tax ($171,000 × .26)	$44,460
Regular tax liability	- $37,926
Additional AMT owed	$6,534

The Costas must pay a total tax for the year of $44,460 ($37,926 regular tax + $6,534 AMT).

AMT Planning. Taxpayers may wish to time certain transactions (such as the exercise of ISOs) so they will not produce AMT or produce as little AMT as possible. Of course, the AMT may be only one factor in such decisions. Persons who are likely to be subject to the AMT normally should not invest in AMT bonds or in mutual funds that have significant positions in such bonds. Also, taxpayers should make sure to take advantage of the MTC against the regular tax when it is available.

The Federal Income Tax on Corporations

Taxable corporations have their own federal income tax structure.[17] They also are subject to state income taxes in many states and perhaps local income taxes as well.

---

[14] These would be the total of $24,000 of personal and dependency exemptions, state and local income and property taxes, and interest on the home equity mortgage loan, plus the $30,000 bargain element on the exercise of the ISO. This bargain element is the difference between the fair market value of the stock at exercise and the exercise price paid ($80 per share - $20 per share × 500 shares = $30,000).

[15] This is the AMT bond interest.

[16] This is the $49,000 exemption amount for married taxpayers filing a joint return reduced by 25 percent of the amount by which AMTI exceeds $150,000 ($206,000 - $150,000 = $56,000 × .25 = $14,000; $49,000 - $14,000 = $35,000 AMT exemption in this example).

[17] The corporate tax rules are found in Subchapter C of the Internal Revenue Code. Therefore, corporations that are subject to federal income taxation are commonly called C Corporations. On the other hand, the rules for electing small business corporations that have opted not to be taxed as corporations are found in Subchapter S of the IRC. Hence, they are commonly called S corporations.

Accumulated Earnings Tax. This tax is intended to apply to corporations that have accumulated earnings inside the corporation to avoid income taxation on dividends that might otherwise have been paid to shareholders. It applies only to earnings and profits that are accumulated beyond the reasonable needs of the business. There is an accumulated earnings credit which is the *greater* of (1) earnings and profits accumulated during the year for the reasonable needs of the business or (2) $250,000. Thus, only accumulated income that exceeds a minimum of $250,000 per year is potentially subject to this tax. Further, payment of dividends will reduce accumulated taxable income. The accumulated earnings tax rate, which is the top rate for individual taxpayers, is applied to accumulated taxable income. Any accumulated earnings tax is paid in addition to the regular corporate income tax.

Alternative Minimum Tax (AMT). Taxable corporations are subject to their own AMT. It generally operates like the individual AMT except that some adjustments and preferences are different and the minimum tax credit against the regular tax is allowed for the entire corporate AMT liability. The corporate AMT exemption is $40,000 and is phased out at various income levels. The tax rate is a flat 20 percent. A corporation pays AMT only when it exceeds its regular tax liability.

The corporate AMT does not apply to "small business corporations" for taxable years beginning after 1997. For this purpose, a small business corporation generally is one that has average gross receipts no greater than $5 million for three consecutive taxable years beginning after 1994. A corporation that has met the $5 million test will continue to be a small business corporation as long as its average gross receipts do not exceed $7.5 million.

Special Forms of Corporations for Tax Purposes. There are a variety of such corporations. For example, the income of *personal service corporations* (a corporation whose principal activity is the performance of personal services and such services are substantially performed by employee-owners of the corporation) is taxed at a flat 35 percent rate and the IRS may reallocate tax benefits of such corporations between the corporation and its employee-owners under certain conditions. Also, *personal holding companies* (PHCs) are corporations whose income is mainly (60 percent or more) from personal holding company income (dividends, interest, rents, royalties, annuities, payments under personal service contracts, taxable income from estates and trusts, etc.) and where more than 50 percent of its stock is owned by five or fewer individuals. There is a surtax at the highest individual taxpayer marginal rate imposed on the undistributed earnings of a PHC in addition to the regular corporate income tax.

Further, there are *regulated investment companies* (e.g., mutual funds), which were discussed in Chapter 12; *real estate investment trusts (REITs),* which were covered in Chapter 10; and *real estate mortgage investment conduits (REMICs)*. These are essentially pass-through corporations for their shareholders. S corporations are covered in the next section as a pass-through entity.

Pass-Through Business Entities

These are entities that are not taxable themselves, but rather report their profits, losses, and other tax items to their owners, who pay taxes on them or deduct them on the owners' individual tax returns. They are tax-reporting but not tax-paying entities.

Partnerships

For tax purposes, a partnership generally is a syndicate, group, pool, joint venture, or other unincorporated organization through which any business, financial operation, or venture is carried on and that is not a trust, an estate, or a corporation. It usually exists when two or more persons join together to carry on a trade or business and to share profits and losses, with each contributing cash, property, or services to form the partnership. Aside from taxation, there also are state law definitions of partnerships often coming from the Uniform Revised Partnership Act and the Uniform Revised Limited Partnership Act.

A partnership itself does not pay taxes but rather reports each partner's *distributive share* of the partnership's taxable income or loss as well as certain items separately stated to the partner. The partner then includes this distributive share (whether or not any distributions are actually paid to the partner) in the partner's income and tax items on his or her tax return. A partner also is taxed on any guaranteed payments (e.g., salary) paid to him or her by the partnership. Partnerships may be general partnerships, limited partnerships (LPs), or limited liability partnerships (LLPs). They are all taxed under the same tax rules.

A special kind of partnership for tax purposes is the *publicly traded partnership* (PTP), which is also called a *master limited partnership*. A partnership is a PTP if interests in the partnership are traded on an established securities market or on a substantially equivalent secondary market. The general rule is that PTPs are taxed like corporations. However, there are significant exceptions to this. For example, if 90 percent or more of a PTP's gross income comes from passive sources (e.g., rent, interest, or dividends), it will be taxed as a partnership rather than as a corporation. Also, beginning in 1998, if an existing PTP elects to pay a 3.5 percent tax on its gross income from the active conduct of a trade or business, it will not be taxed as a corporation. Some large corporations have spun off certain of their operations into PTPs, in which investors can purchase limited partnership interests on organized securities markets.

S Corporations

Eligible domestic corporations can elect (with the initial consent of all shareholders) to be taxed under Subchapter S of the IRC (rather than Subchapter C) and hence not pay any corporate income tax. The profits, losses, and other tax items of an S corporation are passed through to the shareholders in proportion to their stockholdings and are taxable to them on their individual returns. This is true whether the shareholders receive any dividends or not. In all other respects, an S corporation is organized like any other corporation under state law.

Only some corporations are eligible to make an S election. These eligibility requirements are noted in Chapter 29; however, generally speaking, smaller, closely held corporations can elect S corporation status.

Limited Liability Companies (LLCs)

These are a relatively new kind of business entity. The owners are called *members* and the LLC is managed by its members or by a manager. LLCs are organized by filing *articles of organization* with a state. All states now have statutes allowing LLCs. The unique characteristics of LLCs are that their members can manage the entity, have limited liability for the debts and obligations of the LLC, and generally can elect to be taxed like partnerships for federal income tax purposes under the check-the-box regulations.

Federal Income Taxation of Trusts and Estates

Estates and many trusts are taxed as separate entities with their own tax rate schedule. The rules regarding taxation of trusts and estates are complex and are only briefly reviewed here.

A trust is a fiduciary arrangement whereby a person (the grantor or creator) transfers property (the corpus) to a trustee (a fiduciary and "legal owner" of the trust property) to be administered under the terms of the trust for the benefit of trust beneficiaries (who are the "equitable owners" of the trust corpus). The corpus of a trust normally will produce income and perhaps capital gains. The issue here is how such income and capital gains will be taxed for federal income tax purposes. Depending on the terms of a trust, trust income may be taxed to the trust, to the trust beneficiaries, or to the grantor of the trust.

Grantor Trusts

A *grantor trust* is one whose income is taxed to the grantor of the trust and whose deductions may be taken by the grantor, regardless of whether the grantor receives such income. The various kinds of powers over a trust possessed by the grantor (or in some cases by a "nonadverse party") that will cause the trust to be a grantor trust are spelled out in Sections 673 through 678 of the IRC and are called the *grantor trust rules*. In general, these powers include the power to revoke, the power to control beneficial enjoyment, trust income for the benefit of the grantor, and a greater than 5 percent reversionary interest in the trust, and certain administrative powers. The idea is that the grantor should be treated as the owner of a trust's corpus for income tax purposes (and hence taxable on trust income and eligible for trust deductions) when the grantor can benefit from the trust or has too much power over the trust, as defined in the grantor trust rules.

It should be noted that the grantor trust rules just described (for federal income tax purposes) may be different from the rules regarding inclusion or noninclusion of a trust's corpus in the grantor's (or a beneficiary's) gross estate for federal estate tax purposes. Thus, sometimes a trust is deliberately structured to be a grantor trust for income tax purposes, but also so the corpus will not be includible in the grantor's gross estate for federal estate tax purposes. These are called *defective grantor trusts*.

Simple and Complex Trusts

General Tax Principles. These are irrevocable trusts that are not grantor trusts. As a general principle, the income of such trusts is taxable to the beneficiaries to the extent it is distributed to them; the trust gets a corresponding income tax deduction for such distributions. However, the gross income of trust beneficiaries and a trust's deduction for distributions to beneficiaries are limited by the trust's distributable net income (DNI) for the year (not counting items not included in the trust's gross income for tax purposes, such as tax-exempt interest on municipal bonds). Taxable income that is accumulated in a trust is taxed to the trust itself at the trust's rates.

A trust has an income tax basis in the property held by the trust just as individuals do. Essentially, a trust's basis is determined in the same ways as for individuals. Trusts may realize and recognize capital gains on sales or exchanges of their property. Under the Uniform Principal and Income Act (which has been adopted by many states), unless the trust document provides otherwise, capital gains are allocated to principal (corpus) and not included in income for trust accounting purposes. When taxed to a trust, net capital gains have a 28 percent maximum tax rate. (The 20 percent rate applies only to individuals.) Of course, capital gains can be distributed to and taxable to trust beneficiaries if the trust document so provides or if state law permits unitrust payments from a trust, as explained in Chapter 21.

When a trust distributes income with a special tax status, such as tax-exempt municipal bond interest, it retains that status in the hands of a beneficiary. Thus, the trust beneficiary can exclude such items from his or her own gross income for tax purposes.

The overall idea underlying the income taxation of trusts is that trust income is taxed only once—to the beneficiaries if distributed, to the trust if accumulated, or possibly partly to each if distributed in part and accumulated in part.

Simple Trusts. These are trusts that must distribute all income currently, whose trustee does not distribute corpus currently, and that have no charitable beneficiaries. In this case, the beneficiaries are taxed on the current income distributed and the trust gets a tax deduction for those distributions.

Complex Trusts and Estates. Complex trusts are those that are not simple trusts or grantor trusts. They include trusts where income can be accumulated, where corpus is distributed, or that have charitable beneficiaries. Thus, trusts that give the trustee discretion to pay out or to accumulate current income and to distribute corpus to beneficiaries would be complex trusts for tax purposes. The income of complex trusts and estates may be taxed to the beneficiaries who receive distributions or to the trust or estate, depending on the circumstances.

State and Local Income Taxes

In addition to the federal income tax system just outlined, many states and some cities and other localities levy personal income taxes or wage taxes on individuals. They also may levy corporate income taxes.

State personal income taxes vary greatly. Most states have graduated rates like the federal system, but some have flat rates on all taxable income. The top effective tax rate varies among the states from as low as around 2 percent to as high as 10 percent (without counting local income or wage taxes). Some states do not have any income tax.

15

Basic Income Tax Saving Techniques for Individuals

The income tax planning techniques considered in this chapter can be broken down into those that essentially involve (1) eliminating or reducing taxes, (2) shifting the tax burden to others, (3) allowing wealth to accumulate without current income taxation and postponing taxation, (4) taking returns as capital gains, and (5) deferring, and perhaps even eliminating, potential capital gains in appreciated property. Some plans involve a combination of these techniques.

Eliminating or Reducing Taxes

Techniques aimed at producing income tax deductions, exemptions, and credits that reduce otherwise taxable income (or the tax itself) and techniques that result in nontaxable income or in economic benefits that are not taxable are perhaps the most desirable because they avoid tax altogether. Following are some such techniques.

Use of Checklists of Deductions, Exemptions, and Credits

Many specific income tax deductions, exemptions, and credits are available to taxpayers. Space does not permit discussion of all of them here, but some are mentioned in this and other chapters. Also, there are checklists of the following: items included in gross income, income (and other items) that are not taxable, deductions to arrive at adjusted gross income, itemized deductions, nondeductible items, other taxes (federal, state, and local), and various taxable or deductible items that apply particularly to certain occupations or businesses, all available from the government and from commercial publishers.

Use of Proper Filing Status

A related matter is the choice of the most advantageous filing status. For example, a taxpayer should be sure to claim *head of household status* or *special surviving spouse status* if he or she qualifies. Also, although married persons usually file joint returns, they can elect to file *separate returns*.

Receipt of Nontaxable Income

There are various forms of nontaxable income. Perhaps the most important for many taxpayers is interest paid on most state and local government bonds (as discussed in Chapter 11). However, in order to safeguard their tax break on municipal bonds, investors should watch their borrowing policies. If taxpayers borrow money "to purchase *or carry* tax-exempts" (emphasis added), they cannot deduct the investment interest on the loan.

But when is a taxpayer borrowing to buy or carry municipals? In general, if a taxpayer has debt outstanding which is not incurred for purposes of a personal nature (such as a mortgage on real estate held for personal use) or incurred in connection with the active conduct of a trade or business and if the taxpayer also owns tax-exempt bonds, the IRS may presume the purpose of the indebtedness is to carry the bonds and deny an income tax deduction for the interest of the indebtedness. Suppose, for example, a taxpayer owns debt-free municipal bonds but borrows money to buy common stock on margin. Under these circumstances, the IRS may deny part of the investment interest deduction on the loan, even though the common stock dividends are taxable income.

Nontaxable Employee Benefits

One of the great advantages of many kinds of employee benefits is that they provide real economic benefits for covered persons, but in many cases there is no taxable income to the employee on the value of the benefits. In other cases, income taxation is deferred.

Among the employee benefits that provide protection for employees and their families but may involve no taxable income for employees are the following:

- Group term life insurance (up to $50,000 of insurance)
- Medical expense coverage (except that benefits may reduce otherwise deductible medical and dental expenses if deductions are itemized)
- Disability income insurance (except that benefits provided through employer contributions are taxable)
- Noninsured sick-pay plans (except that benefits are taxable)

- Group accidental death and dismemberment and related plans
- Dependent care assistance plans (up to $5000 per year), educational assistance plans (up to $5250 per year), and adoption assistance programs (generally up to $10,000 per child)[1]

Planning Sales of Securities for Tax Losses

This involves using the capital gain and loss rules to the taxpayer's best advantage. We should state at the outset, however, that tax considerations should not outweigh sound investment decisions in buying or selling securities. The tax "tail" should not wag the investment "dog." But in many cases investors can plan their securities transactions so as to realize tax savings and yet not significantly affect their basic investment decision making.

Unrealized Capital Losses. Tax savings can take some of the sting out of unrealized investment losses ("paper losses") for investors, even though they have not actually sold the security. Psychologically, this is hard for some investors to accept. If an investor, for example, buys a stock at $90 per share and over time it falls to, say, $45 per share, the stock has declined 50 percent in value and each share actually is worth only $45 in cash (less selling expenses), not $90. It may never again rise to $90. Some investors find this hard to accept. They somehow feel they have not really had a loss unless they sell the stock. But this is not true; they really do have the loss—the only question is whether or not they realize and recognize the loss by selling the stock. From an investment standpoint, investors must consider the investment merits of their securities at the *current prices,* not at what they paid for them.

Thus, investors who have an unrealized loss on a security and are lukewarm on the immediate future performance of the security or who can make a satisfactory tax exchange (explained later) should seriously consider selling the security, realizing the loss, and taking an income tax deduction for it now. For example, suppose that Marsha Bailey, who is in the 30 percent income tax bracket, owns a stock she purchased for $10,000 and that now is worth $8000 in the market. She has no capital gains for the year. If she sells this stock now, she will realize a $2000 capital loss, which she can deduct from her other ordinary income and save $600 in taxes (less selling expenses). Her actual after-tax loss then is $1,400. Viewed another way, if Marsha holds the stock, she has an investment worth $8000, but if she sells the stock and gets her tax deduction, she has $8,600 (less selling and any buying expenses) to reinvest ($8,000 from the sale of the investment plus $600 in income tax saving).

---

[1] The tax advantages of adoption assistance programs are phased out for higher-income taxpayers.

Tax-Loss Selling. The preceding example illustrates the general concept of *tax-loss selling* of securities. (It works with bonds as well as stocks.) The following are some ideas on how to maximize tax savings in this area.

1. If investors already have taken capital gains on securities or other property, they can *offset these gains by taking losses on other securities* they own. Thus, investors can plan the purchase and sales of securities or other capital assets to minimize or even eliminate any taxable capital gains for a given year. Of course, it must be remembered that net capital gains generally are taxed at 20 percent, while other income (which might be offset by capital losses up to $3000 per year) may be subject to as high as a 38.6 percent tax rate (declining in stages to 35 percent).

2. If investors do not have any capital gains in a given year (or enough capital gains to absorb all their capital losses), they can still *offset up to $3000 per year of otherwise taxable ordinary income* (dollar for dollar) with their capital losses. They can also carry any unused capital losses forward to be used in future tax years without any time limitation.

3. Investors can use so-called tax exchanges to enable them to sell a security for a tax loss and yet still keep an investment position in the same field or industry.

In connection with item 3, suppose, for example, that Marty Brown owns a stock on which he has a capital loss that he would like to take now for tax purposes, but he also feels the stock has investment merit for the future and would like to retain it or one like it. So he asks himself, "Why not sell the stock, take my tax loss, and then immediately buy it back again?" The reason is that this would be a *wash sale* and the loss would be disallowed for tax purposes. The tax law does not recognize losses taken on the sale of securities if the taxpayer acquires or has entered into an option or contract to acquire substantially identical securities within 30 days before or after the sale. Therefore, Marty would have to wait at least 30 days after the sale or else run afoul of the wash sale rule.

Undaunted, Marty then says, "Why not sell the stock to my wife (or other family member), take my tax loss, but still keep the stock within the family?" Unhappily, this will not work either. The tax law disallows all losses on sales within the family (that is, those made directly or indirectly between husband and wife, brothers and sisters, and ancestors and lineal descendants).

Marty, however, can maintain approximately the same investment position in the field or industry, even for the 30-day period before or after the tax sale, by selling the stock in which he has the loss and then immediately purchasing a different stock of about the same (or perhaps even greater) investment attractiveness. This often is referred to as a tax exchange. Many investment firms maintain lists of suggested tax exchanges to aid investors.

Tax Benefits on Sales of Principal Residences

For tax purposes, a personal residence is considered a capital asset, but one held for personal use. Therefore, while a gain on the sale of a personal residence is taxable (unless excluded), a loss on the sale of such a residence is not deductible because the loss was not incurred in a trade or business or in connection with a transaction entered into for profit. The same is true for other assets held strictly for personal use, such as cars, boats, airplanes, or furniture.

Exclusion of Gain from Sale of Principal Residence. However, the tax law does allow relief from the rigor of these rules in connection with gains on the sale or exchange of a residence (including a cooperative apartment, condominium, yacht or houseboat) that is the taxpayer's *principal place* of abode. In this case, there is an optional exclusion of gain provision under certain conditions. This provision applies to sales and exchanges after May 6, 1997.[2]

An individual (of any age) may exclude from income up to $250,000 of gain realized on the sale or exchange of a principal residence. To be eligible for this exclusion, the individual must have owned the residence (ownership test) and occupied the residence as a principal residence (use test) for an aggregate of at least two of the five years preceding the sale or exchange. The exclusion applies to only one sale or exchange each two years (frequency test).

Married persons (of any age) filing joint returns may exclude up to $500,000 of gain from the sale or exchange of a principal residence if *either spouse* meets the ownership test, if *both spouses* meet the use test, and if *neither spouse* has made a sale or exchange of a principal residence within the last two years (i.e., is ineligible due to the frequency test). However, the $250,000 exclusion is applied on an individual basis. Therefore, in the case of married persons filing joint returns, if either spouse meets the ownership and use requirements, he or she will be eligible for the $250,000 exclusion. Also, if an otherwise eligible individual marries a person who has used the exclusion within the last two years, the eligible spouse still can take the $250,000 exclusion. Of course, once two years have elapsed since the last exclusion taken by either of them and they are otherwise eligible, the full $500,000 exclusion applies again. For separated or divorced couples, if one of the spouses or former spouses has met the two-out-of-five-year rule, each spouse or former spouse can exclude up to $250,000 of gain on sale or exchange of the residence.

To the extent that *depreciation* was allowable for the rental or business use of a principal residence after May 6, 1997, the exclusion does not apply and

---

[2] This provision was enacted in the Taxpayer Relief Act of 1997 and replaces the former rollover-of-gain provision (a nonrecognition provision) of Section 1034 and the former one-time $125,000 exclusion of gain for taxpayers age 55 and older.

gain will be recognized on the sale of the property. The exclusion may be prorated if a taxpayer does not meet the ownership or use requirements due to a change in place of employment, health, or unforeseen circumstances. Starting in 2010, EGTRRA extends this exclusion to sales by estates, heirs of deceased owners, and qualified revocable trusts.

Planning Issues. There would appear to be a number of planning opportunities with regard to this provision.

- Taxpayers can sell appreciated principal residences and move to more expensive ones, less expensive ones, or perhaps to other living arrangements, with no or reduced capital gains.
- Land next to a principal residence will qualify for the exclusion as long as it is regularly used as part of the residence.
- If taxpayers have a second home (vacation or rental property), they could sell their principal residence (using the exclusion), move to the second home and convert it to their new principal residence, and then sell that home after two years, again using the exclusion.
- When an appreciated principal residence is placed in a qualified personal residence trust (QPRT) for estate planning purposes,[3] it would appear that after the grantor's use period ends, the trust can continue for the donees (often children of the grantor) as a defective grantor trust. Thus, any gain on the sale will be taxable to the grantor and the grantor could use the exclusion.
- One of the purposes of the exclusion was to eliminate the need for homeowners to maintain records of home improvements (the cost of which would increase their basis for income tax purposes). However, it still may be desirable to maintain such records because in some cases the gain might exceed the exclusion, the person may not be eligible for the exclusion, and depreciation may result in gain.

Conversion to Income-Producing Property. If property held for personal use is converted to property used for the production of income, as when a residence is rented to others, depreciation is allowed as a tax deduction from rental income and at least part of any capital loss on a subsequent sale of the property is deductible. Thus, if owners of a residence actually rent it, they can treat a loss on its sale as at least a partially deductible capital loss.

The tax status of an inherited residence depends on the use made of it by

[3] A qualified personal residence trust involves the gift of a personal residence by the owner to an irrevocable trust under which the owner (the grantor of the trust) can live in the property for a set period of time at the end of which the property passes to the donee(s), often children of the grantor, or continues in trust for the benefit of the donees. This popular estate planning technique is covered in Chapter 25.

the person inheriting it. If the new owner does not use it as a residence but immediately attempts to sell or rent it, the property then is considered held for profit and a loss on its sale is a potentially deductible capital loss. The same also is true even if two persons own the residence jointly and use it as a personal asset, and one of them dies. The tax status of the residence in the hands of the survivor depends on how the survivor then uses it.

Making Charitable Contributions

Charitable giving has become such an important planning technique that a separate chapter is devoted to it—Chapter 16.

Shifting the Tax Burden to Others

Because of the progressive federal income tax structure, it may be attractive taxwise to shift income or capital gains from persons in higher tax brackets to those in lower brackets. This is normally done within the family.

Outright Gifts of Income-Producing Property

One of the simplest ways of shifting income to others is the outright gift to them of income-producing property. Father gives stock to his adult children, grandmother gives mutual fund shares to her grandchildren, mother registers Series EE savings bonds in her children's names, and so on. In general, when a donor gives a donee property, future income from the property is taxable to the donee.

For capital gain purposes, the donee of a capital asset takes the donor's income tax basis in the property plus any gift tax paid by the donor attributable to the net appreciation in the gift property at the time of the gift. Thus, if father paid $5000 10 years ago for common stock that is now worth $20,000 and gives the stock to his son, the son's tax basis is $5000 (assuming no gift tax resulted). If the son later sells the stock for $30,000, he will have a capital gain of $25,000. Thus, the father in a higher tax bracket can transfer a potential capital gain to his son in a lower tax bracket, provided the son is age 14 or over when he sells the stock.

For capital loss purposes, however, different rules apply. In this case, the donee's tax basis is either the donor's basis or the fair market value of the property at the date of the gift, whichever is lower. This means capital losses cannot be transferred to the donee. Therefore, *property in which the owner has a sizable paper loss is not desirable gift property* for saving on income taxes. It would be better to sell the property, take the capital loss, and give away other assets.

Gifts of Income-Producing Property in Trust

Rather than being given outright, property can be given in trust—an irrevocable lifetime (inter vivos) trust. The income taxation of trusts was described in Chapter 14. As explained there, depending on the terms of the trust and assuming it is not a grantor trust, trust income generally will be taxed to the beneficiaries if distributed to them or to the trust itself if accumulated in the trust. Thus, income from property placed in trust can be shifted in this way. For grantor trusts, income is taxed to the grantor regardless to whom it is distributed. Thus, grantor trusts are not income-shifting devices.

Gifts to Minors

Income shifting may be one reason for making gifts to minors. However, there usually are other reasons as well. Gifts to minors and the methods of making them are discussed in the estate planning chapters (Part 6). (See Chapter 25.)

Allowing Wealth to Accumulate Without Current Taxation and Postponing Taxation

Postponing taxes can be advantageous for several reasons. Taxpayers may be in a lower tax bracket in the future. They may know their financial circumstances better then. They get investment returns on the postponed tax. They may not be in a financial position to pay the tax now. Under some circumstances, they may never have to pay the tax.

Tax-Deferred Buildup of Qualified Retirement Plans and IRAs

Various kinds of qualified retirement plans provided by employers, traditional individual retirement accounts (IRAs), executive compensation plans, and tax-sheltered annuity plans represent important ways by which people postpone taxation. These plans are discussed in Chapters 17, 18, and 19.

Postponing Income Taxes on Series EE Savings Bonds

Series EE U.S. savings bonds were described in Chapter 11. Owners of Series EE bonds have a choice as to when they want to be taxed on the increase in value of their bonds. They may elect to report and pay tax on the increase in redemption value as interest each year or take no action and thus postpone paying tax on the increase until the bonds mature or are redeemed. Series EE bonds on which taxation is postponed can be exchanged for Series HH bonds without being taxed in the year of the exchange. Instead, they will be taxed when the HH bonds mature or the taxpayer disposes of them.

Another possible tax advantage for Series EE bonds issued after December 31, 1989, is that the accrued interest on such bonds redeemed to finance qualified higher education expenses for the taxpayer, the taxpayer's spouse, or the taxpayer's dependents is *excluded* from the taxpayer's gross income for federal income tax purposes. To qualify, the bonds must be redeemed in the year the qualified higher education expenses are paid, the bonds must be issued in the taxpayer's or the taxpayer's and his or her spouse's name, the taxpayer must be age 24 or older when the bonds are issued, and the taxpayer's filing status must be single, married filing a joint return, head of household, or a qualifying surviving spouse with dependent child. This accrued interest exclusion is phased out between certain income levels (e.g., modified adjusted gross income from $60,000 to $90,000 for married taxpayers filing a joint return and from $40,000 to $55,000 for single taxpayers and heads of households, indexed for inflation).

Selecting the Stock Certificates to Sell

If stockholders are going to sell only part of their holdings of a stock, the tax law permits them to select the particular stock certificates to sell. For example, suppose an investor owns 300 shares of a common stock with a present market value of $50 per share. The stock was acquired over the years, as indicated here, and the investor now wishes to sell 100 shares.

> Purchased 100 shares 10 years ago at $20 per share
> Purchased 100 shares three years ago at $50 per share
> Purchased 100 shares two years ago at $60 per share

Thus, depending on which certificates the investor elects to sell, he or she could have a capital gain, no gain or loss, or a capital loss. In the absence of identification as to which certificates are sold, the tax law assumes the first purchased are the first sold (a first-in, first-out concept). It often is good planning for investors to select shares that will minimize their capital gains or produce capital losses.

The same general principle applies to selecting which mutual fund shares are assumed to be redeemed. However, the rules are different and were described in Chapter 12.

Tax-Deferred ("Tax-Free") Buildup of Life Insurance and Deferred Annuity Policy Values

Life Insurance Cash Values. These values are not subject to income taxation as they may increase year by year, but generally only when the policy matures, is surrendered for cash, or in some cases when partial withdrawals are made. Therefore, in planning for taking distributions from life insurance cash values, one normally tries to do so without incurring ordinary income taxation. Some techniques for doing this are described in Chapter 27.

Deferred Annuity Cash Values. Similarly, the growth in the policy value of nonqualified deferred annuity contracts is not taxed currently. The income tax is deferred until the owner begins receiving periodic payments from the annuity, surrenders it for cash, takes nonperiodic withdrawals from it, secures loans on it, or until the value of the annuity is paid to a beneficiary upon the owner's death. Investment annuities are discussed in Chapter 21.

Installment Sales

For various kinds of property (other than publicly traded stocks or securities), when the selling price is paid in a tax year after the year of the sale (i.e., in installments), the seller generally pays tax on any gain arising from the sale as the installments are collected rather than in the year the sale is made, unless the seller elects otherwise. This is referred to as the *installment method.* It results in deferring the tax on the uncollected installments.

Taking Returns as Capital Gains

As explained in Chapter 8, taking returns on directly owned property as capital gains offers distinct tax advantages.

Taxation and the Capital Gains Lock-in Problem

The capital gains tax can produce a situation in which investors feel locked into a stock or other property because of their investment success. This basically involves a situation in which investors find themselves (happily, of course) with large paper gains in stocks or other appreciated property and are afraid to sell because they will have to pay sizeable taxes on the capital gains.

This kind of lock-in problem can have several unfortunate effects for investors.

The investor's portfolio may become heavily concentrated in the locked-in stock or appreciated property and diversification may be badly lacking. This may be a particularly severe problem in a declining market. In addition, there may be better investments for the investor now than the locked-in stock or property. Further, while the investors' personal situations may have changed and they could use the money, they may be afraid to sell the stock and pay the tax for fear of depriving their children and other heirs of part of their inheritances. Assuming a lock-in problem with respect to directly owned assets, let us briefly review what investors' strategies might be.

Tax-Avoidance Strategies

First let us consider some strategies investors might use to avoid capital gains taxes altogether.

Step-up in Basis at Death. Investors could simply hold appreciated property— never sell it during their lifetime—and upon their death, it currently will get a stepped-up income tax basis equal to its fair market value on that date. Thus they could pass the appreciated property on to their heirs free of capital gains tax as of the date of death. However, this means the investor can't diversify if needed and must remain at risk for possible declines in the value of the appreciated property until his or her death. Also, effective for 2010, EGTRRA repealed step-up in basis and provided that recipients of property at death would receive a basis equal to the lesser of the decedent's basis or the fair market value of the property at death. However, the executor can increase this basis by up to $1,300,000 generally and, in addition, by up to $3,000,000 for property passing outright or in a Q-TIP (qualified terminable interest property) trust to a surviving spouse. No one knows whether this modified carry-over basis at death provision ever will actually become effective.

Gifts to Charity. As explained in Chapter 16, investors can give some or all of appreciated property to charity directly, to charitable remainder trusts (CRTs), to pooled income funds, or in other ways and not realize a capital given.

Use of Exclusion Provisions in Tax Law. We have already noted one such exclusion for sales of principal residences. To encourage the formation of small businesses, another is that stockholders (other than C corporations as stockholders) of new, small corporations can exclude 50 percent of any gain on the sale or exchange of their stock. To qualify for this exclusion, the stock must be *qualified small business stock.* This means the stock must be *newly issued* when the taxpayer acquired it; the stock must be acquired after August 10, 1993; the corporation must have been engaged in an *active business* for substantially all the time the taxpayer held the stock; and the corporation's *gross assets* must not have exceeded $50 million when the stock was issued. Further, the stockholder must have held the stock for more than five years before the sale or exchange. There also is an annual dollar limit per shareholder on the exclusion of $10 million or 10 times the amount the shareholder paid for the stock, whichever is larger. However, as noted in Chapter 14, 42 percent of the excluded gain is a tax preference item for individual AMT purposes.

Tax-Deferral Strategies (Possibly Until Death)

These are strategies that defer the realization or recognition of capital gains. If the deferral lasts long enough (until death), gain can be avoided entirely because the property gets a stepped-up basis at death (subject to the rules of EGTRRA).

Like-Kind Exchanges. This nonrecognition provision (Section 1031 of the IRC) was explained in Chapters 10 and 14.

Tax-Free Corporate Reorganizations. The effects of a tax-free reorganization are that neither the corporation nor its stockholders recognize gain (or loss) on the exchange (assuming no cash or other property, called *boot*, is received in the transaction) and the stockholders' bases in their old (surrendered) stock or securities are carried over to their new (exchanged for) stock or securities.[4] Thus any gain (or loss) is deferred and will be recognized if the new stock or securities are later sold in a taxable transaction.

Of course, if the new stock or securities are held until death, they currently will receive a step-up in basis.

An Example. Suppose Harry Martinez purchased 500 shares of ABC Technology common stock five years ago for $10 per share. ABC common has been publicly trading at around $50 per share. Recently, however, XYZ Technology merged with ABC in a tax-free reorganization and exchanged two of its common shares (with a market value of $76 for the two) for every share of ABC common. Thus, in this tax-free reorganization, Harry has surrendered his 500 shares of ABC common in exchange for 1000 shares of XYZ common, has recognized no gain on the exchange, and has a basis of $5 per share in his new XYZ common (his former basis in ABC of $10 per share is carried over and allocated to the new stock—two for one). If Harry later sells any of his XYZ common, his capital gain (or loss) will be the difference between the

---

[4] The IRC provides for seven types of tax-free reorganizations in Section 368. They are (1) statutory merger or consolidation, or Type A; (2) acquiring another corporation's stock, or Type B; (3) acquiring another corporation's property, or Type C; (4) transfer of assets to another corporation, or Type D; (5) recapitalization, or Type E; (6) change in identity, form, or place of organization of one corporation, or Type F; and (7) insolvency reorganization, or Type G. Each of these types has its own characteristics and requirements. Further discussion of them is beyond the scope of this book.

amount realized (market price less selling costs) and his basis—$5 per share. His holding period for his former ABC common will be added to that of the XYZ common (referred to as *tacked*) to determine the holding period of the XYZ common for capital gain purposes.

Another Example. As an example in another context, assume that Heather Rosen started a new business, New Computer, six years ago with an initial investment of $100,000 to develop and market computer software. She organized New Computer as a C corporation and 100 percent of the common stock (the only class of stock outstanding) was issued to her. She worked extremely hard, developed new products, the business prospered, and now it is valued by outside appraisers (there is no public market) at $10 million on a going-concern basis. However, now that she is wealthy, Heather would like to dispose of her corporation and devote herself entirely to organizing computer education and support programs for disadvantaged youth in her community.

Megacorp Computer Corporation, a large, profitable, publicly traded corporation that pays modest dividends, would like to acquire New Computer for $10 million. If this is done as a tax-free reorganization, Heather would surrender her 100 percent stock ownership in New Computer in exchange for $10 million worth of Megacorp common stock; she would recognize no gain on the exchange; and she would have an income tax basis in her Megacorp stock of $100,000.

As a result, Heather would have exchanged her nonmarketable closely held stock for publicly traded, dividend-paying stock in a major corporation. She could periodically sell part of her Megacorp stock if she needs funds (recognizing capital gains then, of course) or she could use other techniques to avoid the gain as described in this section.

On the other hand, referring back to tax avoidance strategies, it may be noted that Heather's stock in New Corporation is qualified small business stock. Therefore, if she simply sold the stock to Megacorp for cash, she could exclude 50 percent of her capital gain for tax purposes ($10,000,000 amount realized - $100,000 adjusted basis = $9,900,000 × ½ = $4,950,000 of excluded gain). This means the effective tax rate for Heather on the total gain ($9,900,000) is 10 percent (20% × ½ = 10%). However, 42 percent of the amount excluded is a tax preference for AMT purposes.

Equity Collars with "Monetizing" the Hedged Stock. This is a sophisticated technique designed to hedge against a decline in the value of appreciated stock, defer capital gain, and then "monetize" the stock (by currently receiving cash or its practical equivalent equal to a reasonable percentage of the market value of the hedged stock for other investment).

Suppose, for example, that Homer Kelly has been an executive of the Acme

Corporation for 30 years. He now is a senior vice president. Over the years, Homer has invested primarily in Acme stock through exercising stock options, participating in other stock plans, and purchasing stock directly in the open market. The price of Acme stock has grown substantially over the years. As a result, the market value of Homer's directly owned Acme stock is now about $12 million and constitutes more than 90 percent of his assets. His basis in this stock is only $900,000.

However, Homer is concerned about the lack of diversification in his portfolio and the risk he is running if Acme stock should decline substantially in price. Therefore, he has entered into an *equity collar* around his Acme stock without actually selling the stock. Suppose the current market price of Acme stock is $70 per share. Homer can establish the equity collar by purchasing, say, a three-year cash-settled put option on Acme stock with a strike price (option price) of $63 per share and selling, say, a three-year cash-settled call option on Acme stock with a strike price (option price) of $77 per share.[5] The purpose of the put option is to protect (hedge) Homer against a fall in the market price of Acme stock below $63 per share. On the other hand, the purpose of selling the call option is to receive an income (premium) from the call to offset or perhaps more than offset his cost of buying the put. Collars can be renewed for successive periods.

Equity collars can be structured in several ways. A common approach is the *zero-cost collar.* In this case, the premium received from the sale of the call just offsets the cost of the put. Other approaches are the *income-producing* (or *credit premium*) *collar* and a *debit collar.* The value of the underlying stock with an equity collar can be converted into a separate investment fund (monetized) in several ways. For example, the investor could *borrow* against the stock, subject to margin requirements, and invest the loan proceeds in a separate investment fund. Or, the investor might enter into an *investment swap* transaction with a securities firm involving a diversified portfolio.

It can be seen that these are complex transactions for persons with large positions in highly appreciated stock. The constructive sale rules of the Taxpayer Relief Act of 1997 eliminated most of the other techniques that had been used to hedge such positions without actually selling the stock and realizing a large capital gain. It appears that equity collars are still a viable technique, but care should be taken not to run afoul of the broad language of the constructive sale rules.

Exchange Funds. These are another sophisticated technique for deferring gain on highly appreciated stock. Here an investor contributes his or her appreciated stock to a limited partnership (the exchange fund) in return for a limited

---

[5] The general nature of put options and call options was described in Chapter 10.

partnership interest in the fund. This contribution to a partnership in exchange for a partnership interest is a tax-free exchange, provided not more than 80 percent of the partnership's gross assets are marketable securities. Other investors make similar exchanges and the partnership builds its desired portfolio. Once established, the fund may be passively managed.

The investor carries over his or her basis in the appreciated stock to his or her partnership interest. If the investor-partner holds his or her partnership interest for at least seven years, the partnership can distribute tax-free a portion of its diversified portfolio to the partner (as a distribution in kind of partnership assets). The partnership's basis in those assets generally would be carried over to the distributed assets now in the investor's hands. Thus, for example, upon liquidation of the investor's partnership interest or termination of the partnership, the investor can receive tax-free a diversified portfolio of securities with a carryover income tax basis.

On the other hand, if the investor-partner receives a distribution of partnership assets within seven years, he or she generally will incur a tax liability. Also, since the partnership is a pass-through entity, investment income and capital gains are taxed to the partners whether distributed to them or not. This is one reason exchange funds may be passively managed. Exchange funds may not be liquid investments. Investment selection and management are in the hands of fund management and not the individual limited partners. Exchange funds may have front-end loads and have annual management fees.

Other Investment Products. There are other products and strategies that some investors may use to deal with low-basis highly appreciated stock. One is the issuance by the investor in a public offering of exchangeable equity-linked notes. This is available only for very large blocks of stock. A complete discussion of such strategies is beyond the scope of this book.

Sales of Stock to an Employee Stock Ownership Plan (ESOP). Under certain circumstances, the owner of appreciated stock in a closely held corporation can sell part or all of the stock to the corporation's ESOP and defer capital gain, possibly until death. An ESOP is a qualified retirement plan for employees that normally is structured either as a stock bonus plan or as a combination of stock bonus plan and money purchase pension plan.[6] Unlike other qualified retirement plans, ESOPs must invest primarily (meaning at least 50 percent of plan assets) in employer securities.

Also, a *leveraged ESOP* may borrow funds from a bank, the employer, or other qualified lender to buy stock from existing stockholders or the corporation. The employer-corporation then makes tax-deductible contributions to

---

[6] These kinds of qualified retirement plans are described more fully in Chapter 17.

the ESOP; the ESOP can use these contributions to pay principal and inter-est on the loan. Annual tax-deductible contributions up to 25 percent of covered employee compensation can be made to repay loan principal and unlimited contributions can be made to pay interest. In effect, then, the loan used by a leveraged ESOP to buy employer securities is financed with tax-deductible employer contributions.

In addition, there is a special nonrecognition provision applying to sales of qualified securities to ESOPs.[7] This provision permits someone who sells to an ESOP closely held qualified securities[8] that he or she has held for at least three years prior to the sale to elect not to recognize any capital gain from the sale of such securities if, within a specified period of time (beginning three months before the sale and ending 12 months after such sale), the seller acquires an equivalent amount of qualified replacement property. In general, *qualified replacement property* means any equity or debt security of a domestic operating corporation. There can also be a partial nonrecognition of gain. The income tax basis of the seller in the replacement securities is the same as his or her basis in the securities sold to the ESOP. To qualify for this nonrecognition of capi-tal gain, the ESOP must own at least 30 percent of the total value or number of shares of employer securities outstanding after the sale.

An Example. We can illustrate this approach by referring back to the case of Heather Rosen. If Heather's corporation, New Computer, establishes a lever-aged ESOP, she could sell 30 percent or more of her stock to the ESOP. Heather would not recognize any capital gain on the sale. She would invest the sale proceeds in marketable stocks or bonds of domestic operating companies (replacement securities), which could provide marketability and diversification for her portfolio. Further, she would not necessarily have to sell all of her cor-poration stock or even a controlling interest in it. The ESOP needs to own only 30 percent of the corporation's stock after the sale. However, there are restrictions on the ESOP's ability to dispose of the qualified securities for three years after the sale and on allocations of qualified securities by the ESOP to the selling shareholder or to a more than 25 percent shareholder who may be par-ticipating employees in the ESOP.

Rollover of Gain from Qualified Small Business Stock. In addition to the *exclusion* of one-half of the gain provision noted earlier, there is a *nonrecogni-tion of gain* provision[9] under which gain realized from the sale or exchange of

[7] The provision is Section 1042 of the IRC.

[8] In general, qualified securities are employer securities that are issued by a domestic corpo-ration that has no stock outstanding that is readily tradable on an established securities mar-ket and that meet certain other conditions.

[9] This is Section 1045 of the IRC.

qualified small business stock held for more than six months by a taxpayer is not recognized (i.e., is rolled over) to the extent that the taxpayer uses the proceeds of the sale to purchase other qualified small business stock within 60 days of the sale. The basis of the former stock is carried over to the new stock. This essentially allows any stockholder (other than a C corporation) of a qualified small business to sell one small business and buy another tax-deferred.

Sale Strategies

Assume now that the owner of appreciated property decides to sell or exchange the property in a taxable transaction. A sale might be desirable because the owner wants cash now for reinvestment or other needs. The owner also may want to have control over how the sale proceeds are reinvested. Also, there may not be any acceptable exclusion or deferral strategies available to the owner. Further, if the owner expects the whole market to fall (e.g., a bear market), a sale (rather than deferral) may be the preferred course. Finally, if an investor already has sizeable capital losses in a year or carried forward from prior years, he or she could use these to offset some or all of any capital gains from a taxable sale.

Favorable Capital Gains Tax Rates. The tax rates applying to net capital gains are now significantly lower than the rates applying to ordinary income. The deferral strategies described earlier almost always involve requirements, limitations, or costs that are not present in outright sales. Therefore, the lower capital gains rates become, the more tempted taxpayers may be just to sell their appreciated assets and pay the capital gains tax.

Installment Sales. As explained earlier, an installment sale occurs when one or more payments of the purchase price for an asset are made after the year of the sale and the seller does not elect out of the installment reporting method. Any capital gain on the sale generally is realized and recognized as payments are made. The part of each installment that is capital gain is determined by multiplying the payment by a gross profit percentage, which is the gross profit on the sale divided by the contract price. Also, installment sales normally have interest on the unpaid balance. The part of each installment that constitutes interest is taxable as ordinary income to the seller.

However, there may be reasons not to structure sales as installment sales. First, the seller may want the sales price in cash now. There also may be other tax factors to consider, such as existing capital losses, suspended passive activity losses, and depreciation recapture. In addition, in an installment sale the seller takes an installment note from the buyer for future payments. Thus, the security (credit risk) of future payments could be a factor.

Finally, not all sales are eligible for installment treatment. For example, marketable stocks or securities are not eligible.

Other Sales for Periodic Payments. Aside from straight installment sales as just described, there are other sales in which the purchase price is paid over a period of time. These include *private annuities, self-canceling installment notes (SCINs),* and *sales of remainder interests in property for annuity payments.* These arrangements are made within the family and normally are undertaken for estate planning reasons.

A Combination of Approaches

Of course, investors do not have to follow just one of these strategies. They often mix them. They might, for example, sell some of their appreciated stock and reinvest the proceeds, use some to make charitable donations, give some away within their family, and keep the rest. Further, if they have acquired the stock at different times with different tax bases, they can sell the stock with the highest bases and give that stock away to charity or keep the stock with the lowest bases.

Tax-Planning Caveats

While tax planning is important and can produce savings, it should not be overemphasized. Therefore, in pursuing the legitimate objective of reducing his or her tax burden, the taxpayer should also keep in mind some tax-planning warnings.

Avoid Sham Transactions

Taxpayers sometimes undertake transactions that have no real economic substance other than the desire to save taxes. Such sham transactions should not work. A fundamental principle of tax law is that a transaction will not be recognized for tax purposes unless it makes sense aside from its tax consequences.

Do Not Let Tax Factors Outweigh Other Important Objectives

Most financial decisions involve a number of considerations, of which taxes are only one. The possibility of saving taxes should be considered carefully but not to the exclusion of other objectives.

Consider What Must Be Given Up for the Tax Saving

Proposals that involve tax savings almost always also require taxpayers to give up some flexibility, control, or other advantage that they would otherwise have; may require incurring additional costs; or perhaps require giving up some yield. Taxpayers should ask themselves, when confronted with a tax-saving proposition, "What will I have to give up to secure the expected tax saving?"

Be Sure the Tax Saving Is Enough to Justify the Transaction

In some cases there may be a real tax saving, but it may not be large enough to justify the transaction. Also, look at how long it takes to get the anticipated tax savings. Sometimes tax-saving proposals show promised savings at the end of lengthy periods of time. But the promised savings really may not be very substantial when calculated on a per-year basis.

Keep Planning Flexible

Tax rates, laws, family circumstances, and the taxpayer's financial condition all may change over time. Therefore, a taxpayer should consider carefully any loss of flexibility that will result from a tax-saving proposal.

Be Sure the Analysis Is Complete

Before taxpayers undertake a financial plan that is based to any significant degree on expected tax savings, they should be sure they understand all the tax and other implications or dangers of the plan—not just the expected tax benefits. As part of such an analysis, they should consider how other types of taxes—such as estate tax, gift tax, GST tax, and AMT—might affect the plan.

16

Charitable
Giving

Charitable giving has become an important part of financial and estate planning. Most charitable gifts are straightforward gifts of money. However, many times appreciated property is given. On the other hand, there are a number of more sophisticated techniques that may give the charitably inclined substantial tax and other benefits in addition to the satisfaction of knowing they have helped others.

Basic Tax Principles
Income Tax Deduction

Contributions to eligible charities can be taken as itemized deductions for federal income tax purposes (subject to certain annual limits explained next and the phaseout rules described in Chapter 14).

Annual Limits on Income Tax Deduction

There are complicated rules that determine the amount of deduction that can be taken each year.[1] This amount depends on the type of property given, the type of charity, the contribution base of the taxpayer, and ordering rules for applying the percentage limits. The rules are only briefly described here.

Contribution Base. A taxpayer's *contribution base* is his or her adjusted gross income (AGI) without allowance for any net operating loss carryback.

---

[1] While there are annual limits on the deductibility of charitable contributions for federal income tax purposes, there are no such limits on federal gift tax and federal estate tax charitable deductions. For these taxes, gifts to any eligible charities are deductible in full.

Cash Contributions. For cash contributions to charities generally defined as *public charities* (e.g., churches, educational organizations, hospital and medical research organizations, governmental units, and publicly supported organizations),[2] the annual limit is 50 percent of the contribution base. For cash contributions to other eligible charities, the limit is 30 percent of the contribution base (or what is left of the 50 percent limit, if less).

Long-Term Capital Gain Property. For gifts to public charities of *intangible personal property* (e.g., stocks and bonds) or *real property* (real estate) that, if sold, would produce long-term capital gain, the full fair market value of the property at the time of the gift can be deducted, but the annual limit is 30 percent of the contribution base (or what is left of the 50 percent limit, if less).[3] For gifts of long-term capital gain property to other eligible charities, the full fair market value can be deducted, but the annual limit is 20 percent of the contribution base (or what is left of the 30 percent limit, if less).

Private Foundations. For gifts of appreciated property to private foundations (other than certain private operating foundations and nonoperating feeder foundations), in general the deduction allowed is limited to the donor's income tax basis in the property. However, an exception to this general rule allows taxpayers to deduct the full fair market value (up to 20 percent of the contribution base) of appreciated publicly traded stock (qualified appreciated stock) given to private foundations.

Short-Term Capital Gain Property. For gifts to public charities of appreciated property that, if sold, would not produce long-term capital gain (e.g., capital assets held for 12 months or less and inventory held for sale), the deduction is limited to the taxpayer's basis in the property and the annual limit is 50 percent of the contribution base.

Tangible Personal Property. Finally, if appreciated tangible personal property (e.g., art works) that, if sold, would produce long-term capital gain is given to public charities whose function is related to the use of the property (e.g., a public art museum), the amount deductible is the full fair market value of the property and the annual limit is 30 percent of the contribution base. On the other hand, if the function of the public charity is unrelated to the use of the tangible personal property, the deduction is limited to the donor's basis in the

[2] Certain private operating foundations and nonoperating "feeder foundations" also are included. These are organizations described in Section 170 (b)(1)(A) of the IRC.

[3] As an alternative, a taxpayer can elect to limit his or her deduction to the income tax basis (not the fair market value) of the donated long-term capital gain property. If this election is made, the annual limit is 50 percent of the contribution base. Normally, however, such an election would be of limited usefulness.

property, but the annual limit is 50 percent of the contribution base.

Carryover of Excess Charitable Deductions. Any unused (excess) charitable deduction for a given year that exceeds the annual limitation can be carried forward for up to five additional years. The deductions during this five-year carryover period are subject to certain ordering provisions in the tax law.

Nonrecognition of Capital Gains on Donated Property

A donor realizes no capital gain when he or she gives appreciated property to charity. Correspondingly, if the donor can deduct the full fair market value of the appreciated property, in effect the potential capital gain escapes taxation entirely. Further, when a charity or a charitable remainder trust (CRT) sells appreciated property given to it, the donor does not realize any gain. The charity or CRT also does not realize gain because it is tax-exempt.

Gift and Estate Tax Deductions for Transfers to Charity

Eligible transfers to charity are deductible in full for federal gift tax purposes (for lifetime transfers) and for federal estate tax purposes (for transfers at death). They are also deductible for generation-skipping transfer (GST) tax purposes.

Reporting and Valuation Requirements

Contributions to charity in excess of $250 each must be acknowledged by the charity in writing. The donor may also have to keep other records for contributions over $250 and over $500. Further, if the claimed charitable deduction for an item of property or a group of similar items of property (other than money or publicly traded securities) exceeds $5000, the donor-taxpayer must get a qualified appraisal of the property from a qualified appraiser and attach a summary to his or her tax return.

Planning Techniques
Giving Appreciated Property

One interesting technique that may be available to many persons is giving appreciated long-term capital gain property, such as common stock. Here the gift generally is deductible at its fair market value and the donor would realize no capital gain.

An Example. Suppose, for example, that Mary Whitcomb has owned common stock in a growth company for a long time and it has appreciated considerably.

She would like to dispose of some of this stock to diversify her portfolio but has no offsetting losses. She also customarily gives about $3000 per year to her church. If she were to give the church $3000 worth of this stock (rather than her customary cash donation), she would be better off taxwise and the church would get the same dollar donation (less any expenses for selling the stock).

Let us see why. Assume that Mary's cost basis in the donated stock is $300 and she and her husband are in a 30 percent federal income tax bracket. We shall compare the tax results of giving the stock and the results of selling the stock, retaining the after-tax proceeds of the sale, and giving $3000 in cash.

	Sale of stock and gift of cash		Gift of Stock	
Market value of stock (fair market value)	$3000		$3000	
Sale of stock				
Cost basis	- 300		—	
Capital gain	$2700			
Charitable contribution	$3000	(cash)	$3000	(stock)
Tax deduction	- 900		- 900	
	$2100		$2100	
Capital gains tax (on above at the 20% rate)	540		—	
After-tax cost of transaction to taxpayer	$2640	($3000 gift + $540 capital gains tax - $900 charitable deduction)	$2100	($3000 gift - $900 charitable deduction)

The net effect is a tax saving equal to the capital gains tax on the sale of the appreciated property. But this works only if the taxpayer is going to make a charitable contribution anyway.

Capital Loss Property. On the other hand, if a person is holding property on which he or she has an unrealized capital loss, the reverse is true. The contributor is better off taxwise first to sell the property and take the tax loss, then to give the proceeds to charity in cash. That way the contributor gets both the capital loss on the sale and the charitable deduction.

Making Split (Remainder) Gifts to Charity

An increasingly popular approach to more sophisticated charitable giving is to make a gift now of a future interest in property to charity while retaining a present interest in the property for the donor and/or the donor's family. This is commonly done by giving a remainder interest in property to a charity: the charity will get the property sometime in the future and the donor retains an intervening interest in the property for a period of years, for one or more persons' lifetimes or for a combination of a period of years and one or more persons' lifetimes for noncharitable beneficiaries (e.g., the donor, the donor and his or her spouse, or perhaps other family members).[4] This approach can be attractive in retirement or estate planning. However, the tax law permits this to be done only in certain ways—gift of a remainder interest in a personal residence or farm, use of a charitable remainder unitrust, use of a charitable remainder annuity trust, and use of pooled income funds.

Gift of Remainder Interest in Personal Residence or Farm. A donor may give these types of real property to charity but reserve the right to live in or use the property for the remaining lifetime of the donor or the donor and his or her spouse. The donor gets a current income tax charitable deduction for the present value of the charity's remainder interest in the *depreciated value* of the residence or farm. This type of future gift to charity does not require a formal trust. However, since improvements on the land (e.g., buildings) must be depreciated in calculating the charitable deduction, this approach may not be as attractive as it might at first appear.

Charitable Remainder Unitrust. A *charitable remainder trust (CRT),* in general, involves the creation of a formal irrevocable trust into which the donor (as grantor of the trust) places property that is the subject of the charitable gift. There are two types of CRTs: the *charitable remainder unitrust* (CRUT) and the *charitable remainder annuity trust* (CRAT). We shall describe the CRUT in this section and the CRAT in the next.

Straight Charitable Remainder Unitrust. In this approach to a CRUT, the donor creates and normally places highly appreciated property into an irrevocable charitable trust under which the donor (or perhaps the donor and another beneficiary or beneficiaries after the donor's death) will receive a *specified percentage* (but not less than 5 percent or more than 50 percent) of each year's current value of the trust assets for the beneficiary's lifetime or for a fixed period of years not exceeding 20 years. If trust income is not sufficient to pay the specified unitrust amount, trust corpus must be used to do so.

Net Income with Makeup Charitable Remainder Unitrust (NIMCRUT). A variation on the payout under a straight CRUT is the *net income with makeup charitable remainder unitrust* (NIMCRUT). In this case, the noncharitable

---

[4] There also are other kinds of split gifts to charity. These are charitable lead trusts, by which the charity receives the initial income interest and then a noncharitable beneficiary gets the remainder interest, and joint ownership with a charity. These approaches are described later in this chapter.

income beneficiaries will receive the *lesser* of the stated unitrust amount (say, 5 percent of the trust corpus each year) or that year's actual accounting income of the trust. The trust also provides that to the extent its accounting income in any year is less than the stated unitrust amount, the difference (deficiency) is accumulated (as trust principal) and can be paid out to the income beneficiary or beneficiaries in any future year to the extent that trust accounting income exceeds the stated unitrust amount. This is the makeup provision.

A NIMCRUT can be useful, for example, in providing a deferred retirement plan for the donor and perhaps his or her spouse. As an illustration, suppose Harry Blum and his wife Amy are both age 55, in good health, work outside the home, and would like to retire at age 60 (in five years). Over the years Harry has invested in several publicly traded growth common stocks that now have a combined market value of $1,000,000, an income tax basis to Harry of $400,000, and a current yield of about 1 percent. Harry and Amy have other assets and retirement plans as well. They feel they will need more income when they retire, but they do not need current income now. Harry and Amy are also charitably inclined.

Therefore, Harry decides to establish a NIMCRUT and place the $1,000,000 of growth common stocks in it. The NIMCRUT provides that the lesser of the trust's accounting income or the unitrust amount—say, 5 percent of trust corpus—will be paid to Harry and Amy while both are alive and then to the survivor for the remainder of his or her lifetime. Upon the second death, the trust corpus will pass to their synagogue (a public charity) as remainderperson. The trust has a makeup provision.

In the year this trust is established, Harry and Amy are entitled to a charitable income tax deduction of $252,590,[5] which is the present value of the remainder interest that ultimately will go to the charity. Note that they probably will not be able to take the full amount of this deduction in the year they establish the trust, because of the annual limit on such deductions.

Table 16.1 shows how the payments to Harry and Amy and the makeup provision of this NIMCRUT would work in this situation. It is assumed the trust retains the growth stocks (or sells some or all of them and invests in similar growth stocks) for the first five years and then sells the growth stocks and invests in higher-yielding income-producing assets.[6] No gain is realized by the

[5] This value depends on the actuarial value of their unitrust life income interests, which in turn is based on an assumed mortality table and an interest rate. The mortality table is promulgated by the IRS and revised every 10 years. The latest revision was made in 1999. This deduction and the other data in this chapter are based on the previous mortality table.

[6] However, there can be no restrictions in the trust document as to how the trustee can invest trust assets. It is anticipated that the trustee will understand the nature of the transaction and the intentions of the parties.

Table 16.1. Operation of a hypothetical net income with makeup charitable remainder unitrust

(1)	(2)	(3)	(4)	(5)	(6)
Year	Value of trust assets (beginning of year)*	Stated unitrust amount (5% in this example)	Actual trust accounting income*	Deficiency to be made up later	Income paid to beneficiary
1	$1,000,000	$50,000	$10,000	$40,000	$10,000
2	1,120,000	56,000	11,200	84,800	11,200
3	1,254,400	70,246	12,544	134,976	12,544
4	1,404,928	78,676	14,049	191,173	14,049
5	1,573,519	78,676	15,735	254,114	15,735
6†	1,573,519	78,676	110,146	222,644	110,146
7	1,573,519	78,676	110,146	191,174	110,146
8	1,573,519	78,676	110,146	159,704	110,146
9	1,573,519	78,676	110,146	128,234	110,146
10	1,573,519	78,676	110,146	96,764	110,146
11	1,573,519	78,676	110,146	65,294	110,146
12	1,573,519	78,676	110,146	33,824	110,146
13	1,573,519	78,676	110,146	2,354	110,146
14	1,573,519	78,676	110,146	0	81,030
15	1,602,635	80,132	112,184	0	80,132

*The assumptions underlying these figures are that for the first five years the trust invests in growth common stocks with a 1 percent current yield and 12 percent annual capital growth. For the sixth and subsequent years, the trust invests in a diversified portfolio of bonds (U.S. Treasuries, investment-grade corporates, and some high-yield corporates) with diversified maturities (laddered). This bond portfolio has a 7 percent current yield and zero capital growth. Naturally, other investment assumptions can be made and often are.
†It is assumed that in this year the trust sells the common stock and buys the bonds. There is no gain to the trust because it is tax-exempt or to Harry.

trust on the sale because it is tax-exempt. There also is no gain realized by Harry and Amy. The result is a substantial deferral of income until the noncharitable beneficiaries (Harry and Amy) retire. Under these assumptions, their annual income from the NIMCRUT will rise from $15,735 to $110,146 when they reach their planned retirement age of 60.

Clearly, the investment strategy for this kind of trust is critical. There is, of course, no assurance that the expected returns from growth stocks will actually be realized. Also, after the sale of the growth stocks, the trustee could follow a more diversified asset allocation strategy, such as using a combination of bonds and income-oriented common stocks, which would produce income but also more capital growth for the trust. A possible problem here, depending on the investment climate at the time, may be in achieving high enough current accounting income in the trust so the makeup provision can apply. Some advisors have suggested devices in these trusts such as deferred annuities and partnerships, where permitted. Another possible approach, where allowed, is for the trust instrument to consider capital gains as accounting income.

Net Income Charitable Remainder Unitrust. Here the noncharitable beneficiaries receive the *lesser* of the stated unitrust amount or that year's actual accounting income of the trust. However, there is no makeup provision.

Flip Unitrust. This is another variation from the straight CRUT. In this case a donor often contributes highly appreciated, nonliquid assets (such as closely held business interests or real estate) to a CRT. The CRT begins as a NIM-CRUT (or a net income unitrust), but when the trustee later sells the appreciated asset, the CRT converts (flips) by its terms to be a straight CRUT. The advantage of this approach is that, before the sale, the unitrust only has to pay the noncharitable beneficiary the accounting income, if any, from the trust. On the other hand, after the sale the beneficiary is assured of receiving the unitrust amount even if the accounting income might be less.[7] By its regulations, the IRS allows flip unitrusts. The flip must be based on some objective event, such as a beneficiary's reaching a certain age or the sale of an unmarketable asset. Also, after the flip the trustee must pay at least annually the unitrust amount without any makeup payments that may have accrued before the flip.

Charitable Remainder Annuity Trust. The charitable remainder annuity trust (CRAT) uses essentially the same general concept as the charitable remainder unitrust, except that the return to the noncharitable income beneficiary must be a fixed or determined amount (again, not less than 5 percent nor more than 50 percent) calculated on the basis of the *initial value* of the property originally transferred to the trust. The CRAT does not have the variations in income payout that have just been described for the CRUT.

Amount of Charitable Deduction. The current income tax deduction received by a donor to a CRT is equal to the actuarial present value of the remainder interest that ultimately will pass to the charity, valued as of the time the donor makes the gift to the CRT. This present value may depend on the type of CRT; the specified payment to the noncharitable beneficiary or beneficiaries; the term of those payments, which may depend on the age(s) of the beneficiary or beneficiaries; and the Section 7520 interest rate for the month the gift is made

[7] This is the difference between a flip unitrust and a regular NIMCRUT: in a regular NIM-CRUT, if the accounting income is less than the percentage unitrust amount, only the accounting income will be paid to the noncharitable beneficiary.

(or for either of the two preceding months, at the option of the taxpayer).

The *Section 7520 rate*[8] is the interest rate to be used in valuing annuities, life interests or interests for a term of years, and remainder and reversionary interests for federal tax purposes. It is determined and published monthly by the government and is 120 percent of the federal midterm rate for the month.[9] The Section 7520 rate, in effect, is the rate the IRS assumes can be earned on assets. Other valuation factors also are prescribed in government tables. Computer software is available to aid advisors in calculating values needed in planning for CRTs, other charitable giving techniques, and other estate planning techniques.

Taxation of Noncharitable Income Beneficiaries. The payouts received by non-charitable income beneficiaries of CRTs are taxed on a four-tier system. To the extent that a CRT has present or accumulated income of the various types, distributions are first treated as ordinary income, second as capital gains, next as other income (such as tax-exempt income), and finally as a return of principal.

This means that if a CRT receives any ordinary income from its assets or any capital gains (such as from the sale of appreciated assets), the CRT itself will not have any taxable income because it is tax-exempt, but any distributions made to the noncharitable beneficiary or beneficiaries are considered according to this system. Thus, if a CRT sells highly appreciated assets contributed to it, the capital gain ultimately will be taxed to the noncharitable beneficiaries as distributions are made to them. This is why a CRT can sometimes be said to act as an installment sales substitute.

Minimum Remainders to Charity. The tax law requires that certain minimum remainder values must go to the charity under CRTs. First, the actuarial present value of the charitable remainder interest must equal at least 10 percent of a property's value when it is contributed to a CRT (the 10 percent test). Second, for CRATs, there cannot be greater than a 5 percent probability that the trust's corpus will be exhausted before the charity is scheduled to receive something (the 5 percent test). Both tests must be met when applicable. In effect, this means that CRTs cannot be used when the charity's interests are negligible at their creation. Fortunately, the law permits CRTs to be reformed when their terms fail to meet the 10 percent test (or certain other requirements).

Life Insurance and Charitable Remainder Trusts (CRTs). Life insurance can be used to replace all or part of the value passing to charity after the death of the noncharitable income beneficiary or beneficiaries. When the donor is the

---

[8] This rate is defined in Section 7520(a) of the IRC.

[9] The *federal midterm rate* is the applicable federal rate determined on the basis of the average market yield on outstanding marketable obligations of the United States with remaining maturities of three to nine years for each calendar month.

income beneficiary, the life insurance would be on his or her life. When the donor and his or her spouse are income beneficiaries, the life insurance can be a second-to-die policy on both lives. The life insurance often is purchased and owned by an *irrevocable life insurance trust* (ILIT). (These trusts are described in Chapter 27.) The amount of life insurance needed depends on the circumstances. For example, it can be based on what the family otherwise might lose (after taxes) but for the creation of the CRT.

Comparison of Charitable Remainder Unitrust (CRUT) and Charitable Remainder Annuity Trust (CRAT). As noted earlier, these are two distinct types of CRT. Each has advantages depending on the circumstances.

Here is an illustration. Suppose that John Silver, age 65, is an executive of Growth Corporation, is planning to retire soon, and has a large part of his investment portfolio in highly appreciated Growth Corporation common stock (with a 1 percent current yield). John is married and his wife, Lynn, also is age 65. John and Lynn have three adult children and six grandchildren. John would like to make a meaningful contribution to the university from which he graduated many years ago, mainly with the help of scholarship money.

One possibility is that John could transfer, say, $600,000 of his highly appreciated Growth Corporation stock (which has an income tax basis to him of $100,000) to a charitable remainder annuity trust (CRAT) with a 7 percent payout rate to John and his wife for as long as either of them lives. As a result, John and Lynn would receive a fixed annual distribution of $42,000 from the trust ($600,000 × 0.07); this amount will not change even if the corpus of the trust should rise or fall in value. If trust income is not sufficient to pay this amount, trust principal will have to be used to make up the difference. Then, when the second of them dies, the value at that time of the trust corpus will go outright to the university. The Silvers will get a current income tax deduction for the actuarial value of the charity's remainder interest. Finally, the Silvers will realize no capital gain from the appreciated stock transferred to the CRAT and, of course, neither would the CRAT because it is tax-exempt.

On the other hand, if John had used a charitable remainder unitrust (CRUT) with the same general terms, he and his wife would receive as long as they live an annual distribution from the trust of 7 percent of each year's value of the trust assets. Thus, if the assets grow in value, their annual income correspondingly will grow, but if the assets decline in value, the reverse will be true. Thus, to make an overly simplistic comparison, a unitrust may be better for donors and their families in the event of capital growth, while the annuity trust may provide donors and their families with a stable income in the face of declines in asset values (e.g., during recessions or depressions). There, of course, are other differences, such as possible use of NIMCRUTs to build greater future income and flip unitrusts. Also, after the trust is established, additional contributions can be made to a unitrust but not to an annuity trust.

A Further Illustration with an Irrevocable Life Insurance Trust. Suppose now that the Silvers decide to contribute the $600,000 of Growth Corporation stock to a 7 percent straight CRUT. Also, assume they would be entitled to a current income tax deduction of $155,382, which will be spread over several years because of the annual limit of 30 percent of AGI. If the Silvers are in the 35 percent federal income tax bracket (ignoring any state or local income taxes, for the sake of simplicity), their tax saving can be estimated as $54,384 (0.35 × $155,382).

Let us assume further that the trust sells the Growth Corporation stock for $600,000 and invests the proceeds in a diversified portfolio of income-oriented common stocks and investment-grade bonds. If this portfolio yields a return of 5 percent in dividends and interest and 3 percent in long-term capital growth (ignoring trust expenses), when the CRUT pays the annual 7 percent unitrust amount to the Silvers (which would be $42,000, assuming the CRUT corpus is $600,000), 5 percent would be ordinary income (from the CRUT's dividends and interest) and 2 percent might be capital gains (assuming the trustee had sold some appreciated assets inside the trust). The remaining 1 percent would constitute unrealized appreciation in the trust corpus (which would serve to increase future 7 percent payouts in a CRUT). Thus, the after-tax annual return for the Silvers in the first year might be 4.85 percent [(5% × 0.65) + (2% × 0.80)] or $29,100 (0.0485 × $600,000). This annual payout will grow if the CRUT corpus grows, but correspondingly it will decline if the CRUT corpus declines. When the second of them dies, the trust corpus will go to the university as remainderperson.

On the other hand, suppose that the Silvers do not contribute this stock to a CRUT as just described, but rather they either retain it or sell it and invest the proceeds to provide retirement income for themselves and, after they die, to leave to their children. Let us further suppose John and Lynn Silver decide to sell the $600,000 of Growth stock and reinvest the net proceeds (after capital gains tax) in the same kind of diversified portfolio described previously for the CRUT.

They made this decision, despite having to pay a sizeable capital gains tax of $100,000 ($600,000 amount realized - $100,000 adjusted basis = $500,000 gain realized and recognized × 0.20 = $100,000 tax), because their investable assets are far too concentrated in Growth Corporation stock, they want a more income-oriented asset allocation strategy during retirement, and John still will have considerable Growth Corporation common in his portfolio even after the sale.

After the sale, the Silvers will have $500,000 of net proceeds (ignoring sale expenses) to invest. Assuming the same returns as previously (5 percent in dividends and taxable interest, 2 percent in realized capital gains, and 1 percent in unrealized capital growth), their corresponding after-tax annual return would be 4.85 percent of $500,000 or $24,250.

Now, assuming their joint life expectancies are about 20 years (or to age 85), the $500,000 investment fund can be estimated to grow to about $610,000 (at a 1 percent growth rate) as of the latter of their deaths. However, this amount would be in the gross estate for federal estate tax purposes of the last spouse to die, assuming adoption of a marital deduction strategy that results in no estate tax due at the first death. If we further assume that the surviving spouse's estate will be in the 45 percent federal estate tax bracket, the federal estate tax alone (ignoring any state death taxes and other estate settlement costs) will diminish this amount for their children to an estimated $335,000 ($610,000 × 0.55). This is the estimated amount that might be lost to their family if the CRUT were used instead of retaining the property until the last death.

Therefore, at this point, the Silvers' *annual retirement income situation* from these two possibilities can be compared as follows:

Contribution to the 7% CRUT

After-tax annual income from CRUT:	$29,100
After-tax annual income from tax saving from current charitable deduction on creating the CRUT ($55,938 × 0.0485 = $2,713 or approximately $2700)[10]	2,700
Total retirement income:	$31,800

Sale of appreciated stock and reinvestment of net proceeds

Total retirement income:	$24,250

Clearly, the CRUT results in more after-tax retirement income for John and Lynn. It also enables them to make a substantial and meaningful gift to their university. However, the issue remains of the loss of the otherwise retained property's value to their children and grandchildren.

It may be that the Silvers will feel that their other assets constitute a sufficient inheritance for their children and grandchildren. However, the Silvers may feel they do not want to reduce what their children and grandchildren will receive. In this event, they can establish an irrevocable life insurance trust (ILIT) to purchase, own, and be the beneficiary of a second-to-die life insurance policy on both their lives in an amount of approximately $335,000 (or

---

[10] This assumes the same after-tax total return as from the CRUT and the retained net assets.

more). The level premium needed to carry such a policy (on a male and a female, both age 65 and in good health) might be $3000 to $4000 per year. John or Lynn could give approximately this amount each year to the trustee of the ILIT so the trustee could pay the premiums. Their children (and perhaps grandchildren) would be the beneficiaries of this trust.

General Considerations Regarding CRTs. It can be seen that establishing a charitable remainder unitrust or annuity trust is a complicated legal and financial transaction that requires the aid of the donor's professional advisors. These arrangements normally are practical only for larger gifts. It is possible for the donor-grantor to serve as trustee or a trustee of the charitable trust. However, in this case the donor must act in a fiduciary capacity. The trust may also contain a provision allowing the donor to change the charitable beneficiary to another eligible charity.

Pooled Income Fund. The final way to make remainder gifts to charity is through pooled income funds maintained by many larger charities. These are funds in which the contributions of a number of donors are combined for investment purposes. In this sense, they are like mutual funds run by charities. Some larger charities maintain several pooled income funds with different investment objectives to meet the needs of their donors.

Like the previously described charitable remainder unitrusts and annuity trusts, a donor can make a gift of appreciated property and escape capital gains tax on the appreciation, get an immediate income tax deduction for the actuarial value of the charity's remainder interest, and receive an income from the fund for life or for a period of years. In the case of pooled income funds, however, the donor receives a certain number of units in a particular pooled income fund, with the number depending on their current value and the amount contributed. In addition, the donor gets the advantage of investment diversification through a well-managed fund or funds.

The annual income received by the donor or others is determined each year by the pooled income fund's investment return. Thus, before contributing to such a fund, a potential donor or his or her advisors should check into the fund's current and past investment returns as well as its investment objectives, much as one would do before investing in a mutual fund or other financial intermediary.

To contribute to a pooled income fund, a donor does not have to create an individual trust. Thus, carefully selected pooled income funds can be a practical technique even for donors making smaller gifts. Of course, after the non-charitable income interest or interests expire, the property will go to the charity. But again, the donor (if insurable) can use life insurance to make up the loss to his or her family.

Other Forms of Charitable Contributions

Charitable Gift Annuity. This is a different kind of arrangement from those discussed in the preceding sections. The *charitable gift annuity* is the sale of an annuity by a charity to a donor-annuitant for a price in excess of what would be charged for the same annuity by a commercial insurance company. This excess determines the income tax charitable deduction for the donor-annuitant. The annuity income received by the donor-annuitant and possibly other annuitants varies with the annuitant's age and among charities. Many charities follow the annuity rate recommendations (called the Uniform Gift Annuity Rates) adopted by the American Council on Gift Annuities.[11] Normally, a donor-annuitant would not consider such an annuity unless he or she had a charitable motive.

A gift annuity is a contract guaranteed by the charity. Therefore, a donor-annuitant should consider the financial soundness of the charity, just as an annuitant should evaluate the financial soundness of a life insurance company issuing a commercial annuity contract.

In the case of gift annuities, there would be taxable gain to the annuitant on the transfer of appreciated property in exchange for the annuity. Therefore, this generally is not a viable technique to avoid capital gains taxation, although taxation may be deferred until the annuity payments are made.

Gift of an Undivided Portion of an Owner's Entire Interest in Property. This involves making the charity a co-owner of property. For example, a donor might give a charity one-half of an artwork and retain the other half. He or she could take a current income tax deduction for the value of the charity's interest.

Gift of Qualified Conservation Contributions or Easements. These contributions often involve the granting of conservation easements with respect to real estate to qualified charities or governments. An easement in gross (i.e., one not derived from the ownership of adjacent or other lands) is a personal interest in, or the right to use, the land of another. The tax law allows rather generous income tax deductions and also estate and gift tax exclusions for qualified conservation contributions or easements.

A *qualified conservation contribution* is a contribution of a *qualified real property interest* to a *qualified organization* (governments and publicly supported charities) exclusively for *conservation purposes*. For purposes of this defini-

[11] The committee is an organization sponsored by a large number of charitable organizations. Use of its recommended rates is entirely voluntary on the part of charities selling gift annuities. These annuity rates are designed to result in approximately a 50 percent return to the charity once the annuitant dies. However, some charities use gift annuity rates that are designed to produce greater returns for the charity (and thus less for the annuitants). This may be a point for potential donor-annuitants to check before purchasing a gift annuity from a charity.

tion, a *qualified real property interest* includes a restriction (such as an easement) that is granted *in perpetuity* on the use of real property.[12]

Income Tax Deduction. A charitable deduction can be taken for the value of a qualified conservation contribution made during the donor's lifetime. The value of a contribution (such as a conservation easement) may be determined as the difference between the fair market value of the real property before the easement was granted and the fair market value after the easement was granted.[13]

Estate Tax Exclusion. An executor can exclude from a decedent's gross estate for federal estate tax purposes an *applicable percentage* (up to 40 percent) of the value of land subject to a *qualified conservation easement,* up to a *dollar exclusion limitation* and subject to certain other requirements. The applicable percentage is 40 percent reduced by two percentage points for each one percentage point by which the value of the qualified conservation easement is less than 30 percent of the value of the land without regard to the value of the easement and reduced by the value of any retained development right. The dollar exclusion limitation is $500,000. The easement may be made while the owner is alive or after his or her death.

On the other hand, a qualified conservation easement must be granted in perpetuity. It thus may lessen the future uses to which real property can be put and its future sales value.

Bargain Sales to Charity. Sometimes donors do not wish to give the full value of property to charity. Thus, the donor may sell the property to a charity for less than its fair market value—a bargain sale. However, such a bargain sale of appreciated property will be classified for tax purposes into two parts: a contribution portion (which is deductible) and a sale portion (which is taxable). The tax is determined by allocating the property's tax basis between the contribution portion and the sale portion on the basis of the ratio of the sales price to the fair market value.

Gifts of Closely Held Stock to Charity with a Redemption. Donors may own appreciated closely held corporate stock for which there is no ready market. Sometimes an owner will give such stock to a charity with the informal understanding, but not a legally binding obligation on the part of the charity, that the stock will be redeemed by the corporation from the charity after the gift. The result is that the donor-stockholder has made a charitable contribution and can take an income tax deduction for the fair market value of the stock

---

[12] Other qualified real property interests are the entire interest of a donor (other than a qualified mineral interest) and a remainder interest.

[13] If there should happen to be substantial records of sales of similar easements, the value would be based on thses. However, such sales or records may not be available.

(without realizing any capital gain), the closely held corporation uses cash to buy the stock from the charity without any tax effect on the donor-stockholder, and the charity ends up with cash, which is normally preferable to closely held stock. This technique is sometimes called a *charity bailout.*

Naming Charities as Death Beneficiaries of Qualified Retirement Plans and Traditional IRAs. If a person wants to make a charitable contribution at death, a favorable way to do so from a tax perspective is to name the charity as beneficiary of part or all of the person's remaining account balances in defined contribution retirement plans or traditional IRAs. This is because the death benefits payable from these plans to noncharitable beneficiaries are heavily taxed—first by federal estate tax (and perhaps state death tax) as part of the gross estate, and then by federal income tax as income in respect of a decedent (with a deduction for any estate taxes paid on the IRD item) to the beneficiary.[14] These taxes are avoided when IRD items are made payable to or left to charitable beneficiaries at death. Thus, a person can plan to use IRD items to fulfill charitable objectives at death and then use non-IRD items, along with the remainder of any IRD items, for noncharitable gifts and bequests.[15]

Gifts of Life Insurance to Charity. Sometimes donors give life insurance policies on their lives to charity. When a donor absolutely assigns all incidents of ownership in a policy to a charity, the donor-insured has made a deductible charitable contribution equal to the value of the policy at the time of the gift, plus additional deductible contributions if the donor insured makes future premium payments on the policy.

Charitable Lead Trusts. Charitable lead trusts, also called *charitable income trusts* or *front trusts,* are the reverse of the charitable remainder annuity trust (CRAT) and charitable remainder unitrust (CRUT) described previously. In a lead trust, the charity receives an annuity interest based on the initial value of the trust's corpus (a CLAT) or a unitrust interest based on the value of the trust's corpus each year (a CLUT) for a fixed period of time, after which the remainder interest goes to noncharitable beneficiaries (such as the donor's family). These trusts can be created during a donor's lifetime (as a living trust) or under his or her will (as a testamentary trust).

Charitable lead trusts can be attractive when a donor wants to make a meaningful charitable contribution, his or her family does not need current income from the property, and the donor wants to get a significant gift or estate tax deduction for the present value (using Section 7520 rates) of the charity's income interest.

[14] The nature of such IRD treatment is explained in Chapter 14.
[15] Planning for taking distributions from retirement plans in general is discussed in Chapter 20.

For example, suppose Harry Carter would like to make lifetime gifts in 2003 of about $1,000,000 to his two adult children from a previous marriage. The children are successful in their careers and do not need current income. Harry also would like to make a meaningful charitable gift to a local hospital. Further, assume that Harry has more than enough other assets for himself, his present wife, and the children of his second marriage. In this situation, Harry might create a living charitable lead annuity trust with $2,000,000 of his assets that will pay a 7 percent annuity interest ($140,000 per year) to the hospital for 10 years and then pay the remainder to Harry's two older children in equal shares. The present value of the hospital's annuity interest for 10 years (using a 6 percent Section 7520 interest rate) would be $1,030,412. Harry can take a gift tax charitable deduction for this amount and so the taxable gift for federal gift tax purposes would be the present value of the remainder interest to his two children after 10 years or $969,588 ($2,000,000 - $1,030,412).[16] It may be noted that if the actual investment returns on the assets in the charitable lead trust exceed the Section 7520 interest rate (such as by investing the CLAT's assets for growth), the taxable remainder interest will be undervalued for gift tax purposes and the donor's family will benefit: the two adult children will split more than $969,588 in 10 years. On the other hand, if the trust earns less than the 7520 rate, they will receive less. Also, this planning still is logical under EGTRRA since, as explained in note 16 below, Harry would pay no gift tax.

When to Make Charitable Contributions

Charitable contributions can be made during a donor's lifetime or at death through his or her will. From a tax perspective, it normally is better to make charitable gifts during life, because the donor gets an income tax deduction for the value of the gift and, effectively, the gift amount (less the income tax saving) is removed from his or her gross estate for federal estate tax purposes, while gifts at death get only a federal estate tax charitable deduction. Of course, tax factors are not the only consideration in this decision.

---

[16] Harry would have to file a gift tax return, but if he has not made any taxable gifts previously, his applicable exclusion amount of $1,000,000 for gift tax purposes (based on a unified credit of $345,800) will more than offset the gift tax due on this transfer. Thus, no gift tax will be payable at this time, which is desirable considering the uncertainties of EGTRRA. However, Harry will have used his applicable exclusion amount, which will not be available for future lifetime gifts or possibly at his death for estate tax purposes.

Planning for Retirement and Capital Accumulation Plans

17

Employer-Provided Qualified Retirement Plans and Social Security Benefits

Economic Problems of Retirement Years

The assumption is often made that people's financial needs decrease after retirement. To some extent, this assumption may be valid. However, the reduction in the financial needs of retired persons probably has been overstated. They normally do not want any drastic change in their standards of living at retirement. Also, expenses for medical care, and perhaps custodial care, probably will increase significantly during retirement. Finally, individuals and their advisors should not forget what economic forces, such as *inflation* or *deflation*, can do to their carefully planned retirement income.

Another factor affecting planning is that many persons today wish to retire at younger ages than the traditional age 65. Also, life expectancy has increased dramatically. Within the past 60 years, for example, life expectancy at birth has increased from around 47 years to 80 years or more.

Steps in Planning for Retirement Income

There are many issues involved in planning for retirement, but certainly an important one is ensuring adequate retirement income. The steps in the process for doing this can be outlined as follows.

1. Set desired retirement age or ages.
2. Identify sources of retirement income.
3. Project estimated retirement income (by source) to desired retirement age.

4. Estimate income needed at desired retirement age in current dollars.
5. Adjust estimated retirement income needed and projected retirement income available at desired retirement age for estimated inflation, if any, from the present to the desired retirement age.
6. Compare retirement income needed with projected retirement income available both in current dollars *and* adjusted (where appropriate) for preretirement inflation as of the desired retirement age.
7. Compare projected postretirement income needs and projected postretirement income available (both adjusted for preretirement *and* postretirement inflation, if any) year by year, to see how income available will meet expected needs during retirement.
8. Plan for meeting any deficiencies in projected retirement income as compared with retirement needs as shown in steps 6 and 7.
9. Consider how and when benefits should be paid from the various sources of retirement income, to the extent the person or couple has discretion in the matter.
10. Plan for the beneficiary designations in retirement plans, when appropriate.
11. Review and revise the plan periodically as appropriate.

Sources of Retirement Income

Retirement income generally comes from assets accumulated during the working years, government programs, and employer-provided plans. People frequently receive retirement benefits from all these sources.

Individually Provided Retirement Income

Many people accumulate an investment fund, individual retirement accounts (IRAs), individual nonqualified annuities, life insurance cash values, and other funds during their working years to help provide for their retirement. In fact, this seems only prudent.

Social Security Old-Age (Retirement) Benefits

The essential purpose of social security is to provide a *guaranteed income floor* on which the individual and his or her employer can build a more comfortable retirement income.

Retired Worker's Benefits. To be eligible for old-age benefits, a worker must be age 62 or older and have attained fully insured status. At the full-benefit retirement age (also called the Social Security normal retirement age or SSNRA)—currently age 65—the retirement benefit is equal to the worker's primary insurance amount (PIA). Starting with workers born in 1938 and thereafter, the full-benefit retirement age will gradually rise until it reaches age 67 for workers born in 1960 and later. A covered worker may elect to receive a retirement benefit as early as age 62; however, in that case, his or her retirement benefit will be permanently reduced.

Spouse of Retired Worker. The spouse of a retired worker who also is at least age 62 is eligible to receive a lifetime retirement benefit based on the worker's PIA. The benefit for an eligible spouse at full-benefit retirement age is equal to 50 percent of the covered worker's PIA. However, a spouse may begin receiving reduced retirement benefits as early as age 62. A divorced spouse also may be eligible for retirement benefits under certain conditions.

A spouse may be entitled to receive a Social Security retirement benefit as a result of the his or her own employment record. When this occurs, the spouse will receive the larger of his or her own benefit or the benefit as a spouse, but not both.

Other Dependents of Retired Workers. Social Security retirement benefits also may be available for a spouse caring for a child and for each eligible child or grandchild of a retired worker.

Personal Earnings While Receiving Social Security Retirement Benefits. At present, personal earnings after normal retirement age do not reduce an otherwise eligible person's Social Security retirement benefits. However, if a worker elects an early-retirement benefit, his or her benefit can be reduced for personal earnings until he or she reaches normal retirement age.

Cost-of-Living Increases in Social Security Benefits. Social Security is one of the few retirement programs that automatically increase benefits as the cost of living rises. All Social Security benefits (old age, survivor's, and disability insurance) are increased each year when there has been an increase in the average consumer price index (CPI).

Employer-Provided Retirement Plans

Many employers have established tax-favored retirement plans. The remainder of this chapter and Chapter 18 are devoted to such plans.

Characteristics of Employer-Provided Retirement Plans

General Considerations

Employer-provided retirement plans are part of the employer's overall employee benefits program. The most important are *qualified pension plans, profit-sharing plans,* and *savings plans.* However, employers also may have other plans that aid their employees or some of their employees in providing for retirement. Some of these include simplified employee pension (SEP) plans, tax-sheltered annuity (TSA) plans for nonprofit and certain other employers, qualified stock bonus plans, qualified employee stock ownership plans (ESOPs), savings incentive match plans for employees (SIMPLE) plans, nonqualified deferred-compensation plans, and supplemental executive retirement plans (SERPs).

Qualified Retirement Plans

The phrase *qualified retirement plans* is a tax term that refers to those kinds of retirement plans spelled out in the Internal Revenue Code (Section 401[a]), which are accorded special tax advantages if they meet certain nondiscrimination and other requirements of the law. Some of the important qualification requirements for these plans can be summarized as follows: (1) there must be a *legally binding arrangement* that is in writing and communicated to the employees; (2) the plans must be for the *exclusive benefit* of the employees or their beneficiaries; (3) the principal or income of the plans must *not be diverted* from these benefits for any other purpose; (4) the plans must benefit a *broad class of employees* and *not discriminate* in favor of highly compensated employees; (5) the plans must meet certain *minimum vesting* requirements; (6) the plans must meet *minimum eligibility, coverage, and participation* requirements; (7) the plans must provide for certain *spousal rights* in benefits; (8) there are certain *minimum benefit distribution* rules; and (9) the plans must meet *minimum funding standards.*

The qualified plans covered in this chapter include:

- Pension plans
- Profit-sharing plans
- Savings (or thrift) plans
- Cash or deferred arrangements (Section 401[k] options)
- Stock bonus plans
- Employee stock ownership plans (ESOPs)
- Retirement plans for the self-employed (HR-10 or Keogh plans)

Advantages and Limitations of Qualified Plans

Some commentators have referred to qualified retirement plans as the "perfect tax shelter." While there probably is no perfect tax shelter, qualified retirement plans do have significant tax and non-tax advantages.

Tax Advantages of Qualified Plans. These include the following:

- Employer contributions, within the limits of the tax law, are deductible for income tax purposes by the employer.
- Covered employees (called participants) do not receive taxable income from the plan due to employer contributions until benefits are distributed to the participants or their beneficiaries.
- Investment income or gains on assets within the plan are not subject to income taxation until paid out as benefits.
- Employees may be able to contribute to some plans with before-tax dollars (i.e., on a salary-reduction basis).
- Lump-sum distributions to participants (or their beneficiaries) may be given favorable income tax treatment under limited circumstances.
- Under a special grandfather provision, certain amounts payable upon the death of a plan participant may be entitled to either an unlimited or a $100,000 estate tax exclusion, depending on when the decedent separated from the employer's service. In general, however, there no longer is an estate tax exclusion for qualified plan death benefits.

Other Advantages of Qualified Plans. In addition to these tax advantages, qualified plans may have the following *non-tax advantages* for participants:

- The employer may pay the full cost of a plan (a noncontributory plan) or part of the cost (a contributory plan).
- If the plan is contributory, regular employee contributions by way of payroll deduction (either before taxes or after taxes) may be a convenient way for employees to save.
- Plans may have favorable investment options that are not available to persons outside the plan.
- Plans often have loan provisions that permit participants to borrow from the plan.

Limitations of Qualified Plans. However, there may be drawbacks to these plans from the participants' point of view:

- The rights of participants to benefits are subject to the terms of the plan. Therefore, the particular plan's provisions will determine when and how a participant can receive benefits from the plan.
- Investment options under some plans may be limited.

- The rights of participants to benefits attributable to the employer's contributions are determined by the vesting provisions of the plan.
- A participant's rights to distributions from qualified retirement plans are subject to certain spousal (marital) rights under the Retirement Equity Act of 1984 (REA), as described below under "Impact of Marital Rights on Qualified Retirement Plans."
- Since qualified retirement plans are intended to provide retirement income for participants, any premature or early distributions taken from qualified plans (as well as from IRAs and certain other plans) will be subject to a 10 percent penalty tax in addition to the regular income tax. Premature distributions—generally those prior to age 59½, subject to certain exceptions—are described in Chapter 20.
- Since these plans are intended to provide retirement income for participants and their spouses rather than income-tax-deferred wealth transfers, a participant must begin taking at least minimum distributions from these plans (as well as from traditional IRAs) starting at his or her required beginning date (RBD), which often is age 70½. These minimum distribution rules are explained more fully in Chapter 20.
- Death benefits from these plans are included in a participant's gross estate for federal estate tax purposes (except for very few grandfathered cases) and are also income in respect of a decedent (IRD). Hence, they are heavily taxed at death.
- The structuring of the plan and selection of funding agencies (e.g., banks or insurance companies) often is up to the employer. Thus, employees often do not have control in these matters.

On balance, however, the advantages of qualified retirement plans far outweigh possible drawbacks, so employees usually are well advised to participate fully in such plans.

Defined-Benefit and Defined-Contribution Plans

Qualified retirement plans can be classified as either defined-benefit plans or defined-contribution plans. This distinction can be important.

A *defined-benefit (DB) plan* is one in which the retirement benefits are expressed as a specified benefit at retirement. The benefit may be a dollar amount or it may be determined by a formula specified in the plan. Thus, the essence of a DB plan is that the retirement benefits are specified or fixed, while the contributions necessary to fund those benefits vary. The type of DB plan with which most people are concerned is the *defined-benefit pension plan.*

A *defined-contribution (DC) plan,* on the other hand, is one that provides for an individual account for each participant and for specified or variable contributions to those accounts. In fact, these plans are sometimes called *individual account plans*. The accumulated account balance for a participant may be affected by such factors as contributions to the account (by the employer, the employee, or both), investment income, investment gains and losses from the assets in the account, and possible forfeitures by other plan participants that may be allocated to the account. A participant's retirement income from a DC plan, then, is based on the income or other distributions the participant's accumulated account balance will produce at his or her retirement age, depending on how benefits are taken from the plan. Some pension plans, called *money-purchase pension plans,* are DC plans. All the other types of qualified plans discussed in this chapter also are DC plans. Some people have both DB and DC plans from their employers. However, others will have only one type, usually a DC plan.

Impact of Marital Rights on Qualified Retirement Plans

There have been significant changes in the law concerning the rights of non-covered spouses (also called nonparticipant spouses or NPSs) in the retirement plan benefits of their covered spouses. These rights can significantly affect retirement and estate planning by married persons.

Retirement Equity Act of 1984 (REA). The purpose of the Retirement Equity Act is to give a noncovered spouse certain survivorship rights in the qualified retirement plan benefits of the covered spouse, unless those rights are waived by the covered spouse with the proper witnessed consent in writing by the noncovered spouse. The REA essentially mandates two forms of survivorship benefits to protect the noncovered spouse: a preretirement spouse's benefit, called a *qualified preretirement survivor annuity* (QPSA), and a postretirement spouse's benefit, called a *qualified joint and survivor annuity* (QJSA).

Plans Covered by REA Rules. REA applies to qualified defined-benefit and money-purchase pension plans. It also covers qualified profit-sharing (including savings) and stock bonus plans, unless these plans meet certain requirements for exclusion from the rules.

In general, to be excepted from REA, a participant's benefit arrangement under a profit-sharing, savings, or stock bonus plan must meet the following requirements. First, the participant's vested account balance must be payable in full upon the participant's death to his or her surviving spouse (unless the spouse consents in the proper form to another beneficiary designation, as noted subsequently). Second, the participant cannot elect for benefits to be payable in the form of a life annuity. Third, the plan cannot have received a transfer from a pension plan. In effect, then, if an employee covered under a profit-sharing, savings, or stock bonus plan wishes to have the death benefit payable in any way other than outright to his or her spouse, the spouse must consent to the other beneficiary designation in the proper form or else the spouse's REA rights will apply.

It may be noted that the REA rules do not apply to IRAs at all.

Qualified Preretirement Survivor Annuity (QPSA). A QPSA is a life annuity for the surviving spouse of a plan participant who has a vested benefit in the plan and who dies *before* his or her normal retirement benefits are to begin. If the participant dies after the earliest age at which retirement benefits could have been received under the plan, the surviving spouse's QPSA is the amount that would have been payable to the surviving spouse under an annuity form of a lifetime income for the employee with a 50 percent survivorship annuity for the spouse, assuming the deceased employee had actually retired with such an annuity on the day before his or her death.

For example, suppose Mary Warnaki is age 56, is married, and participates in a pension plan that has a normal retirement age of 65 but permits early retirement as soon as age 55. Mary's husband is age 58. If Mary were to retire at her current age of 56, she and her husband would receive a joint and 50-percent-to-the-survivor pension benefit of $2000 per month. If Mary dies at age 56, while actively employed, and her husband survives, he will receive a QPSA benefit of $1000 per month ($2000 × 50 percent) for his life.

If an employee dies before the earliest age at which he or she could have retired under the plan, the calculation is more complex, but the principle is essentially the same. In this case, the surviving spouse must wait until when the deceased employee would have attained the plan's early retirement age to begin receiving his or her QPSA benefit.

REA permits an employer to charge the increased cost of QPSA rights against the retirement benefits that otherwise would be payable to the participant. However, an employer voluntarily may not reduce the benefits otherwise payable.

A participant may decide to waive these QPSA benefits. For QPSA rights only, this can be done at any time during an election period, which generally begins after a participant attains age 35. However a waiver is not effective unless the participant's spouse consents in writing and the consent is witnessed by a plan representative or a notary public. A significant planning issue is whether a participant and his or her spouse should elect to waive these rights. This issue is considered further in the next section.

Qualified Joint and Survivor Annuity (QJSA). REA also requires that qualified plan retirement benefits payable to a married participant must be provided as a qualified joint and survivor annuity (QJSA), unless the participant (with the consent of his or her spouse) elects to waive the QJSA form or unless a profit-sharing, savings, or stock bonus plan meets the requirements for exclusion from the REA rules. The QJSA form is an annuity for the lifetime of the participant with a survivorship annuity for the lifetime of his or her surviving spouse of not less than 50 percent or more than 100 percent of the annuity payable during their joint lives.

As an example, assume that Henry Sullivan is married, age 65, and about to retire under his employer's defined-benefit pension plan. His wife also is age 65. Assume further that Henry does not elect to waive the QJSA form and so retires with an annuity benefit payable under the QJSA form of $3000 per month. Now, if Henry should die before his wife (after retirement), she would receive a survivorship annuity of $1500 per month for the remainder of her lifetime ($3000 × 50 percent). On the other hand, if Henry's wife should die before him, the original $3000 per month would continue for the remainder of his lifetime.

As with QPSA rights, REA permits a plan to charge the increased cost against the pension benefits otherwise payable. Just as an example, one pension plan applies a reduction factor of 10.7 percent from the life annuity for the participant alone (a straight life annuity) for a QJSA form, when both the participant and spouse are age 65. However, again, an employer may subsidize the QJSA form.

A plan participant, with the consent in the proper form of his or her spouse, may elect to waive the QJSA form within an election period, which is the 90-day period before retirement benefits are to begin. As with the QPSA form, whether a married participant and his or her spouse should elect to waive the QJSA form is an important planning issue. One reason for considering such a waiver is to avoid reducing retirement benefits during the joint lifetimes of the husband and wife. Of course, if the employer subsidizes the forms, this reason is gone and the plan probably will not allow for a waiver. They may also desire a retirement payment other than a QJSA. Further, there may be estate planning reasons for a waiver if it is desirable for plan death benefits to be payable other than outright to the surviving spouse.

Balanced against these factors, however, is the loss of the protection of the survivorship feature for the nonparticipant spouse in the event he or she survives the participant. This really is part of the broader planning issue of how to protect the surviving spouse. A significant factor in dealing with this issue is the amount of life insurance on the retired employee's life that continues into retirement to protect the nonparticipant spouse.

Finally, if a waiver is to be used, the nonparticipant spouse may want to consider the terms and extent of the waiver and of his or her consent. For example, is the consent revocable or irrevocable? Is it general, so that the participant can name any beneficiary he or she wishes or later change the beneficiary, or is it specific (limited) to the beneficiary named when the consent was given? If a trust is named, can the participant later change the trust beneficiaries?

Other Marital Rights. The domestic relations law of most states recognizes that a noncovered spouse may have certain marital property rights in retirement plan benefits and other employee benefits of an employee spouse in the event of separation or divorce. Under equitable distribution of property laws, retirement plan rights often are considered *marital property* and thus are subject to equitable division between the spouses upon separation or divorce. These marital (and child support) rights may be enforced through presenting a *qualified domestic relations order* (QDRO) to the plan administrator.

Also, in states that have community property laws or similar laws, the rights that a covered spouse accumulates in various employer-provided plans during marriage become community property and hence are owned one-half by each spouse.

Loans from Qualified Plans

Many qualified retirement plans (particularly profit-sharing and savings plans) contain loan provisions that allow participants to borrow from the plan. Such plan loans are not considered taxable distributions from the plan as long as the requirements of the tax law are observed.

Basically, the law specifies that for loans not to be considered taxable distributions, the loan may not exceed the smaller of $50,000 or one half of the present value of the participant's vested benefits in the plan. However, loans of less than $10,000 are not treated as taxable distributions regardless of the latter limit. The law also requires that the participant repay a loan within five years in substantially level payments made at least quarterly. There is an exception to this rule for plan loans used to acquire a primary residence; they must be repaid only within a reasonable time. Loans must also bear a "reasonable" interest rate.

Limitations on Contributions and Benefits for Qualified Plans

Section 415 Limits. Under these limits (found in Section 415 of the IRC), annual employer-provided pension benefits under a defined-benefit pension plan may not exceed the smaller of $160,000 (adjusted for inflation in increments of $5000) or 100 percent of the participant's average annual compensation for his or her three highest consecutive years of compensation in the plan. There is actuarial reduction of this dollar limit only if the participant retires before age 62. Further, annual additions for a participant under a defined contribution plan may not exceed the smaller of $40,000 (adjusted for inflation in increments of $1000) or 100 percent of the participant's annual compensation. Many employers provide that if an employee's benefits under the regular benefit formula exceed the Section 415 limits, the employer will pay the difference from an unfunded nonqualified retirement plan (called an *excess benefits plan*).

Limits for Section 401(k) Plans. There are special limitations applying to qualified retirement plans that are popularly called Section 401(k) plans. These limits are described later in this chapter.

Limits on Tax-Deductible Employer Contributions. The tax law also places limits on the amount an employer or a self-employed person can deduct in a given year for contributions to various types of qualified retirement plans.

Defined-Benefit Plans. The annual deductible limit for these plans is the amount needed to fund the benefits provided under the plan according to reasonable funding methods and actuarial assumptions adopted by the employer or self-employed person.[1] Further, an employer may deduct at least the amount needed to meet the minimum funding requirements for the current year, but may deduct no more than the plan's full funding limit.

The overall effect of these rules is that defined-benefit pension plans (particularly with permitted disparity, as described later) may generate relatively large tax-deductible contributions for an employer or self-employed person on behalf of older, more highly compensated participants. This can be attractive for owner-employees of closely held businesses or self-employed persons because they often are older, are more highly compensated, and have longer tenures of service than other employees of the business.

However, the tax law specifies certain minimum funding requirements for defined-benefit plans that an employer or a self-employed person must meet. This means an employer may have to make contributions to a DB plan in bad times as well as good. Thus, unlike profit-sharing plans, DB pension plans create *funding rigidity* for the employer or self-employed person.

Money Purchase Pension Plans. As defined-contribution (DC) plans, the maximum annual deductible employer contribution is 25 percent of aggregate

---

[1] For example, under the level cost funding method, an employer may deduct the amount needed to fund each participant's past and current service credits under the plan distributed as a level amount or as a level percentage of compensation over the remaining period of the participant's anticipated future service. However, if more than 50 percent of the remaining unfunded cost is attributable to three or fewer participants (as might be true, for example, in the case of owner-employees of closely held businesses), the deduction of the cost for those participants must be spread over at least five years. Under the normal cost funding method, an employer may deduct the plan's normal cost (the estimated cost of benefits earned for the current year) plus an amount necessary to amortize the unfunded past service liability equally over 10 years.

compensation of participants under the plan. Also, since these are pension plans, the employer or self-employed person must make contributions each year whether the firm is profitable or not.

Profit-Sharing and Stock Bonus Plans. For these DC plans, the maximum aggregate annual tax-deductible employer contributions also cannot exceed 25 percent of total compensation paid to participants for the year. Further, contributions to profit-sharing plans normally are discretionary on the part of the employer; the employer can make them when feeling financially able to do so but may choose not to when feeling unable. Thus, the employer has greater funding flexibility with profit-sharing plans than with money purchase pension plans. Since the same 25 percent aggregate limit on tax-deductible employer contributions now applies to both types of plans, most commentators believe few employers will adopt money purchase pension plans.

Other Plans. There are a number of other types of retirement plans for which there may be limits on contributions. They include *Section 401(k) plans, savings incentive match plans for employees* (SIMPLEs), *employee stock ownership plans* (ESOPs), *target benefit plans, simplified employee pensions* (SEPs), and various kinds of *individual retirement accounts* (IRAs). The limits on contributions to these plans are covered as the plans are discussed in this and subsequent chapters.

Limit on Includible Compensation. For qualified retirement plans, there is a limit (indexed for inflation in $5,000 increments) on the amount of a participant's annual compensation that can be taken into account in determining contributions to or benefits from the plan.[2] This is referred to as the *compensation cap.* As of 2003, the limit stands at $200,000.

Vesting Under Qualified Plans

Vesting means that a participant has a nonforfeitable right in his or her account balance under a defined-contribution plan or to an accrued benefit under a defined-benefit plan that results from *employer contributions* to the plan. A participant has a right to his or her vested benefits regardless of whether the participant stays with the employer or leaves to go with another employer.

Vesting can take several forms. Immediate and 100 percent vesting is, of course, the most liberal from the participant's standpoint. However, most private plans do not provide immediate and 100 percent vesting. The other form is deferred vesting, which is the most common.

[2] This maximum annual compensation limit also applies to simplified employee pensions (SEPs), tax-sheltered annuities (TSAs), and voluntary employee beneficiary associations (VEBAs), as well as to qualified retirement plans.

Qualified retirement plans are required to meet certain minimum vesting standards. In general, vesting must be at least as rapid as under one of two alternative minimum vesting schedules: 100 percent vesting upon the participant's completion of five years of service (referred to as *cliff vesting*) or *graded vesting* at the rate of 20 percent after three years of service, 40 percent after four years, 60 percent after five years, 80 percent after six years, and 100 percent after seven years or more of service. However, under EGTRRA, there is more rapid vesting *only for employer matching contributions* (such as under Section 401(k) plans described later in this chapter). These minimum vesting schedules are: 100 percent after three years of service for cliff vesting or graded vesting at the rate of 20 percent after two years of service, 40 percent after three years, 60 percent after four years, 80 percent after five years, and 100 percent after six or more years of service.

Naturally, under contributory plans where employees pay part of the cost, participants are always entitled to a refund (or the right to a deferred benefit) of *their own contributions* to the plan upon termination of employment.

Integration (Permitted Disparity) with Social Security

General Considerations. An *integrated plan* is one in which either benefits or contributions under Social Security are taken into account in establishing the benefits or contributions under the plan. This concept is now referred to in the tax law as *permitted disparity,* but for many years it was called *integration with Social Security.* Thus, these terms are used interchangeably in this book.

The *permitted disparity (integration) rules* essentially set limits on the extent to which a qualified plan's benefits or contributions on employee compensation above a compensation level assumed for Social Security purposes (called the *integration level*) can exceed plan benefits or contributions for compensation at or below that level. These limits differ for DB plans and DC plans.

Of course, a plan does not have to be integrated with Social Security at all. Some qualified plans are not so integrated. In this case, the permitted disparity rules are not relevant.

Integration of Defined-Benefit Plans. There are two basic methods used to integrate DB plans: the excess method and the offset method. An *excess plan* is one under which there is a smaller benefit payable on earnings up to the Social Security integration level than on earnings above that level. An *offset plan* is one under which a pension benefit is calculated without regard to Social Security benefits, and then a percentage of the Social Security benefit is usually deducted from the pension benefit.

Integration of Defined-Contribution Plans. DC plans are integrated on the basis of contribution percentages to the plan. A plan will meet the integration rules if the plan's excess contribution percentage (the contribution percentage applying to compensation in excess of the plan's Social Security integration level) does not exceed the lesser of (1) 200 percent of the contribution percentage on compensation not in excess of the plan's integration level (base contribution percentage) or (2) the larger of the base contribution percentage plus 5.7 percent or the base contribution percentage plus the portion of the employer-paid Social Security tax attributable to the old-age benefit.

An Example of Integration. Here is an example of how integration might work in the context of a small employer. Suppose that Aysha Ahmed is the 100 percent stockholder and CEO of a small C corporation—AA Corporation, Inc. She receives an annual salary of $220,000. The corporation has three other employees with annual compensation of $60,000, $35,000, and $25,000, respectively. AA has a discretionary qualified profit-sharing plan covering the four employees with an integrated contribution formula of 10 percent of each covered employee's compensation up to the Social Security wage base (the integration level in this case) and 15.7 percent of each covered employee's compensation over that amount up to the compensation cap for qualified plans. The contributions under this formula for a given year are shown in Table 17.1.

Table 17.1. Example of integration of profit-sharing plan with Social Security

Column 1	Column 2	Column 3	Column 4	Column 5
Employee	Compensation (as counted for plan purposes*)	Base contribution (base contribution percentage [10%] × compensation up to the $84,900 integration level†)	Excess contribution (excess contribution percentage [15.7%] × compensation in excess of the integration level)	Total contribution (column 3 + column 4)
Aysha	$200,000	$8,490	$18,071	$26,561
A	60,000	6,000	—	6,000
B	35,000	3,500	—	3,500
C	25,000	2,500	—	2,500

*The limit on includible compensation (compensation cap) is $200,000 per year. Therefore, this is all that can be counted for Aysha for plan contribution (or benefit) purposes.
†This was the Social Security taxable wage base for 2002.

Top-Heavy Retirement Plans

Some qualified retirement plans are defined as top-heavy and must meet special requirements for qualification. The idea behind these requirements is to try to avoid discrimination in favor of certain employees and to protect lower-paid employees in plans in which a high proportion of benefits or contributions are actually being allocated to participants defined as *key employees*.[3]

A plan is considered top-heavy with respect to any plan year if, for a DB plan, the present value of the cumulative accrued benefits for key employees exceeds 60 percent of the corresponding value for all employees or if, for a DC plan, the aggregate accounts of the key employees exceed 60 percent of the aggregate accounts of all employees.

Thus, the integrated profit-sharing plan in the preceding example would be top-heavy for the year, assuming the contributions shown in Table 17.1 represent the account balances for all covered employees. Aysha is a key employee; the others are not. Her $26,561 account balance is more than 60 percent of the aggregate accounts of all covered employees ($26,561 ÷ $38,561 = 0.69, or 69 percent). The additional requirements that a plan classified as top-heavy must meet include a more rapid minimum vesting schedule and minimum employer contributions or benefits for non-key employees for top-heavy plan years.

Nonqualified Retirement Plans

These are plans that do not meet the requirements for qualification set by the tax law. Nonqualified plans, for example, can be structured to favor highly compensated employees (i.e., to be discriminatory). The compensation cap and other limits on contributions or benefits for qualified plans have caused employers increasingly to adopt nonqualified plans for their higher-paid employees.

Pension Plans
Basic Characteristics

A pension plan is a qualified retirement plan maintained by an employer primarily to provide *definitely determinable benefits* to employees or their beneficiaries at and after retirement. A plan may provide definitely determinable benefits either by providing fixed benefits at retirement (a defined-benefit plan) or by having fixed employer contributions (a money-purchase plan) that normally are a set percentage of employees' compensation.

---

[3] A key employee for this purpose is any participant who is (1) an officer of the employer with annual compensation greater than 50 percent of the Section 415 dollar limit for DB plans, (2) a more than 5 percent owner of the employer, or (3) a more than 1 percent owner of the employer who has annual compensation from the employer of more than $150,000.

Pension plans cannot permit the withdrawal of employer contributions or the investment earnings on those contributions before the employee's retirement, death, disability, severance of employment, or termination of the plan. Contributions to fund a pension plan are not discretionary for an employer: the employer must make annual contributions necessary to fund the benefits provided by the plan.

When Are Retirement Benefits Payable?

Normal Retirement Age. The normal retirement age in a DB plan is the earliest age at which participants can retire with full benefits. For example, the normal retirement age may be 65, usually assuming some minimum period of service. An employee usually is not required to retire at this age; it is simply the age at which full pension benefits are payable.

Early-Retirement Provisions. Many DB plans provide reduced benefits when employees retire at specified ages that are earlier than normal retirement age, often subject to certain conditions. Sometimes, when employers want to encourage early retirements by offering employees a temporary early-retirement plan (a so-called early-retirement window), a part of the program will be to eliminate or decrease any regular early-retirement reduction. This is one of the factors to consider in deciding whether to accept such an early-retirement option.

In the case of DC plans, the benefit available at early retirement is the account balance accumulated when the employee actually retires. There is no formal early-retirement reduction factor, but, of course, no further contributions would be made to the employee's account after retirement.

Deferred Retirement. Employers no longer can require employees to retire at any mandatory age, except for certain executive employees. Thus, most employees can continue working past normal retirement age if they wish and are able to do so. In this case, qualified DB plans must continue to accrue their benefits and DC plans must make contributions and allocations on their behalf for work past normal retirement age.

Kinds of Pension Plan Benefits

Retirement Benefits. Pension plans traditionally have been designed to provide a life annuity (life income) for the covered employee or the covered employee and a joint annuitant. For married employees, the retirement benefit (annuity form) must be payable in accordance with the REA requirements described earlier.

Benefits may be payable in forms other than a life income. An increasing number of plans give employees the option of having their benefits actuarial-ly converted (commuted) into a lump-sum payment at retirement. Whether this is desirable from the viewpoint of the participant (and perhaps his or her spouse) depends on the circumstances and the size of the lump-sum payment. However, it may be noted that in many cases a lifetime income that the participant (or the participant and his or her spouse) cannot outlive provides a sound basis (with Social Security) upon which to plan a financially secure retirement. The ability to choose forms of retirement benefits is, of course, subject to the REA rules.

Benefits upon Termination of Employment. These depend on the plan's vesting provisions and were discussed earlier.

Death Benefits. Pension plans in effect can provide death benefits in several ways. One is when an employee receives retirement income in the form of a *joint and survivor life annuity* or a *refund life annuity*. For example, if a married retiring employee provides for a joint life and full-benefit-to-the-survivor form of annuity for himself or herself and his or her spouse, the pension plan in effect is providing death protection equal to the full periodic pension benefit for the spouse in the event the employee dies first.[4]

Pension plans also may include *preretirement death benefits.* Such benefits may be from life insurance proceeds in the case of plans funded with life insurance policies, but they come mainly from the qualified preretirement survivor annuity (QPSA) required by the REA.

Disability Income Benefits. In some plans, a form of disability protection is afforded by allowing disabled workers to retire early. Other pension plans provide for a separate disability income benefit unrelated to retirement benefits.

Medical Expense Benefits. Sometimes assets accumulated in pension plans may be used to provide medical benefits for retired employees, their spouses, and their dependents.

Pension Plan Benefit Formulas

Defined Benefit Formulas. A *flat-amount* formula sometimes is used. In this case, all participants are given the same benefit upon retirement. A formula that relates benefits to earnings is the *flat-percentage* formula. Under this formula, every employee completing a minimum number of years of credited service receives at retirement a pension equal to a given percentage of his or her average annual compensation. Employees who fail to meet the minimum serv-

---

[4] Note that REA requires at least a joint life and 50 percent to the survivor annuity form (a QJSA). However, the parties can choose a more liberal survivor benefit (up to 100 percent), as shown in this example.

ice requirement may be given a proportionately reduced pension. The average compensation to which the percentage applies may be the employees' average earnings over the full period of their participation in the plan (a career average approach) or the average of their earnings over the final few years of their participation (a final average approach).

A formula that relates benefits to years of service but not to earnings is the *flat-amount-unit-benefit* formula. Here an employee is given a flat amount of benefit per month for each year of credited service.

A widely used formula is the *percentage-unit-benefit* formula. An employee is given a percentage of benefit per month for each year of credited service. Using this formula, an employee with 30 years of service at 1½ percent of earnings for each year would receive a monthly pension of 45 percent of earnings. Again, the earnings to which the percentage is applied may be the earnings during each year in which a unit benefit is accumulated (career average) or the average annual earnings during, say, the last 5 or 10 years before retirement (final average).

Money Purchase Formulas. Here a percentage of an employee's pay is set aside in an individual account by the employer and sometimes is matched in whole or in part by the employee.

Pension Benefit Guaranty Corporation (PBGC)

The Employee Retirement Income Security Act (ERISA) established the Pension Benefit Guaranty Corporation (PBGC). This corporation sets up an insurance program for employees and pensioners of companies that have gone out of business. The PBGC ensures vested benefits of defined-benefit pension plans up to a certain amount. This program provides an additional element of safety for covered plan participants and retirees.

Profit-Sharing Plans
Basic Characteristics

Unlike pension plans, profit-sharing plans usually base their contributions for employees on the employer's profits and hence do not provide benefits that are definitely determinable. However, an employer can contribute to these plans without current or accumulated profits and contributions can be made without regard to net profits.

Profit-sharing plans are DC plans under which contributions are allocated to individual accounts for participants. These individual accounts are credited with investment earnings and may also be credited with nonvested forfeitures from other accounts that may be reallocated due to employee turnover.

Annual contributions usually are discretionary with the employer (a discretionary contribution formula); however, any contributions must be allocated among participants according to a definite, predetermined formula (a fixed allocation formula).

Distributions from profit-sharing plans are legally permitted after a certain number of years, after a certain age, after retirement, after other termination of employment, or upon the occurrence of some event such as death, illness, disability, or layoff. The terms of a particular plan, however, may limit such withdrawals.

Regular Profit-Sharing Plans

Many profit-sharing plans base their allocation formula only on participant compensation. This results in a uniform, proportionate contribution for each covered employee regardless of age. This approach tends to favor younger employees.

Age-Weighted Profit-Sharing Plans

These plans[5] are more complicated and may be based on the concept of cross-testing for nondiscrimination for plan qualification purposes. Cross-testing is allowed under IRS regulations and essentially involves testing defined-contribution plans for nondiscrimination on the basis of projected benefits (like a defined-benefit plan) and testing defined-benefit plans for nondiscrimination on the basis of contributions. However, cross-testing normally is applied to defined-contribution plans.

An age-weighted profit-sharing plan is one that bases its allocation formula on both the age and the compensation of participants.[6] These plans tend to favor older employees with higher earnings (who are often the owner-employees of closely held businesses). However, total profit-sharing contributions in any year cannot exceed 25 percent of overall covered compensation and allocations to any participant cannot exceed the Section 415 limits described earlier. As with profit-sharing plans generally, contributions usually are discretionary with the employer. The IRS has adopted final regulations that provide

[5] There can also be age-weighted money purchase pension plans, but age-weighted plans generally are structured as profit-sharing plans. Also, age-weighted plans may not be based on cross-testing under an IRS "safe harbor" formula.

[6] IRS regulations permit allocations under cross-tested profit-sharing plans to be weighted for age or service as well as compensation. This discussion assumes weighting by age and compensation.

three alternative minimum allocation standards for testing whether cross-tested DC plans meet the nondiscrimination requirements for qualified plans.

New Comparability Profit-Sharing Plans

These also are cross-tested plans. They are DC plans, but they are tested for nondiscrimination purposes like DB plans. Current profit-sharing allocations can vary not only by each participant's covered compensation and age but also by his or her job classification. The annual limits on tax-deductible employer contributions are the same as for age-weighted plans. Contributions can also be discretionary with the employer.

The effect of new comparability plans is that there can be considerable disparity between the proportionate allocations for older, more highly compensated employees and those for younger, lower-compensated employees. However, as just noted, the IRS now has minimum allocation standards for cross-tested plans.

Savings (Thrift) Plans

Basic Characteristics

Savings plans are qualified defined-contribution (DC) plans that have become very popular over the years as a way for employees to accumulate capital in a tax-advantageous way. These plans normally permit employees to make voluntary contributions of a percentage of their compensation, and then the employer contributes a specified percentage of the employee's contribution (called a *matching contribution*) up to a certain limit. Employees also may have the option of making additional, unmatched contributions.

As an example, a savings plan might permit employees to contribute from 1 to 6 percent of their compensation each year and then provide that the employer will contribute at the end of the year an amount equal to 50 percent of each employee's contribution. In addition, employees might be permitted to contribute up to an additional 10 percent of their pay, which the employer would not match. Technically, savings plans are a form of profit-sharing plans. Larger employers often have a pension plan and also a separate savings plan (usually with a Section 401(k) option), but some have only a savings plan with a Section 401(k) option.

Participant-Directed Accounts

Contributions on behalf of participants and the investment earnings on those contributions go into individual accounts for each participant. It has become increasingly common for savings plans (and perhaps other kinds of plans as well) to permit participants to decide how their account balances will be invested within the investment funds provided by the employer under the plan. These are referred to as *participant-directed accounts.*

The number and kinds of separate funds vary among plans, but they must include a reasonable breadth of investment products for different investment objectives. Employees may be given investment choices for all contributions, but more likely will have choices only with respect to their own contributions. It is fairly common for employers to direct that their own matching contributions go into an employer stock fund.

Before-Tax and After-Tax Contributions

Employee contributions may be made from their pay after income taxes are withheld (after-tax contributions) or through salary-reduction arrangements before income taxes are withheld (before-tax contributions). When employee contributions are made on a *before-tax basis,* the plans are referred to as *cash or deferred arrangements* (CODAs) or more commonly as Section 401(k) plans (named after the section of the IRC that deals with cash or deferred arrangements). Today most employee contributions are on a before-tax basis. Thus, to many people, the terms *savings plans* and *Section 401(k) plans* are almost synonymous.

Cash or Deferred Arrangements: Section 401(k) Options

Basic Characteristics. As just explained, most savings plans permit participants to make contributions on a before-tax basis under a cash or deferred arrangement (Section 401[k] option). Section 401(k) permits covered employees to authorize their employer to reduce their salary and contribute the salary reduction to a qualified savings plan, profit-sharing plan, stock bonus plan, or some money purchase pension plans. The amounts participants elect to defer in this way are called the employee's *elective contributions, elective deferrals,* or *before-tax elective contributions* and special restrictions apply to them.

Limits on Contributions to CODAs. There are at least four separate limits on employee (and employer) contributions to qualified plans (say, savings plans) with a Section 401(k) option:

- There is an *annual dollar cap* on before-tax elective contributions from an employee to all CODAs covering him or her as an employee. This annual cap (base amount) will rise in stages: $12,000 for 2003, $13,000 for 2004,

$14,000 for 2005, and $15,000 for 2006 and thereafter (with indexing for inflation after 2006 in $500 increments). Participants age 50 and older can make additional annual catch-up contributions of $1000 for 2003, $2000 for 2003, $3000 for 2004, $4000 for 2005, and $5000 for 2006 and thereafter (with indexing after 2006 in $500 increments). Thus, in 2003, for example, a Section 401(k) plan participant age 50 or over could make elective contributions of $14,000 ($12,000 base amount plus $2000 catch-up contribution).

■ There is an *actual deferral percentage (ADP) nondiscrimination test for elective contributions* that, depending on the average contributions of highly compensated employees (HCEs) relative to those of non-highly compensated employees, may result in a limit for HCEs for a year that is lower than the annual dollar cap just noted. However, for plans to which the employer makes certain minimum contributions for non-highly-compensated employees (called safe-harbor 401(k) plans), the *actual deferral percentage* and *actual contribution percentage* nondiscrimination tests are not applied and the annual dollar cap (normally plus any catch-up contributions) would be the limit for HCEs.

■ There is *an actual contribution percentage (ACP) nondiscrimination test for combined after-tax employee contributions and employer matching contributions.*

■ In addition, the regular *Section 415 maximum limits* applying to any qualified plan apply to these plans as well.

Restrictions on Distributions from CODAs. There are special restrictions on distributions from plans with Section 401(k) options. In general, amounts attributable to before-tax elective contributions may not be distributed to a participant or his or her beneficiary or beneficiaries earlier than age 59½ or separation from employment (including retirement), except in the case of death, disability, or hardship (as defined in IRS regulations).

Advantages of Savings Plans with Section 401(k) Options

Tax Advantages. Employee contributions are made on a before-tax basis and savings plans also afford the other tax advantages of qualified plans described earlier. In addition, EGTRRA provides a temporary, nonrefundable tax credit from 0 to 50 percent (depending on tax filing status and AGI) of the amount of qualified retirement savings contributions (including elective deferrals) up to $2,000 per year. However, this "savers credit" expires after 2006 and is zero for higher-income participants (e.g., over $50,000 AGI for joint income tax returns).

Systematic Savings and Investment. Another appeal of savings plans is the opportunity they afford employees to invest systematically through payroll deductions at a comparatively low cost.

Employer Matching Contributions. For savings plans with matching employer contributions (as is generally the case), participants' accounts are credited with the matching contributions as well as the employees' own contributions and the investment earnings on both.

Employee Investment Choice. Participants normally are given a choice among a prescribed number of investment options for their contributions and possibly for the employer's matching contributions. Thus, employees can integrate the investment of their savings plan accounts with their general asset allocation strategy.

Tax-Efficient Changes in Asset Allocation Strategy. Further, savings plan account balances present participants with an inherent tax advantage in that they can make asset allocation changes among available investment options *within the plan* without any sale or exchange for capital gains tax purposes. Thus, since changes within tax-favored plans (like a Section 401[k] plan) are income tax-free, there effectively is no capital gains tax lock-in problem (see Chapter 15) with regard to assets in these plans.

Limitations on Savings Plans with Section 401(k) Options

The advantages of Section 401(k) plans are impressive indeed. However, as with any planning tool, these plans also have some drawbacks.

Limits on Contributions. As just explained, there are special limitations on contributions to Section 401(k) arrangements in addition to the regular limits on qualified plans in general.

Restrictions on Distributions. There also are limits on distributions, as just described. However, these really may not be that onerous, because plan loans and hardship distributions usually are available.

Participants Must Be Able to Afford Their Contributions. Savings plans with Section 401(k) options normally condition employer matching contributions on initial employee contributions. This means participants must take a reduction in current wages or salary. Some cannot or will not do this.

Distributions Are Ordinary Income and Income in Respect of a Decedent (IRD). In many cases, participants will have no income tax basis in qualified retirement plans with Section 401(k) options.[7] This is because all funds have

---

[7] See Chapter 21 for an explanation of how participants might have an income tax basis in their qualified retirement plans.

gone into the plan without any income taxes being paid on them. Therefore, when distributions come out of the plan (as they eventually must), they generally will be taxable as ordinary income either when the participant receives them or as IRD after the participant's death.[8] This tax treatment is, of course, true for qualified retirement plans in general. Nevertheless, despite this significant taxation at distribution, the results of deferring taxes normally far outweigh the results of after-tax investing in currently taxable assets. This *power of deferral* is shown in the illustrations presented next.

Comparison of Before-Tax Contributions (Investing) and After-Tax Investing: The Power of Deferral

To illustrate the principles just discussed, let us assume an employee, Lynn Rosen, age 40, earns $100,000 per year and can participate in a qualified savings plan with a Section 401(k) option or can make similar investments (after-tax) in directly owned assets. The plan allows her to elect to have up to 6 percent of her salary contributed to the savings plan before tax and then her employer will match her elective contribution 50 cents on the dollar. Assuming Lynn elects the full 6 percent salary reduction (and ignoring, for the sake of simplicity, the likelihood that the plan will permit additional elective contributions beyond what the employer will match), her salary and contribution picture would be as follows:

Salary	$100,000
Elective employee contribution (6%)	-$6,000
Taxable salary	$94,000

Contributions Going into the Qualified Savings Plan for the Employee:

Elective employee contribution	$6,000
Employer matching contribution (.50 × $6,000)	$3,000
Total annual contributions available for investment in the plan (before-tax)	$9,000

Now, assume instead that Lynn decides not to participate in the plan (a decision that her financial advisors would not normally recommend), that she wants to invest the 6 percent of salary, after tax, outside the plan in directly owned assets, and that she is in the 30 percent federal income tax bracket.[9] Under these assumptions, her salary and investment picture would be as follows:

---

[8] Exceptions to this statement are when there is net unrealized appreciation (NUA) on employer securities in the plan and a lump-sum distribution is taken (as described in Chapter 21) and for the income tax deduction for estate taxes paid on IRD items (as described in Chapter 14).

[9] State and local income taxes are ignored in this illustration for the sake of convenience.

Salary	$100,000
Taxable salary	$100,000
Amount available for investment (after-tax) in directly owned assets ($6,000 × .70 = $4,200)	$4,200

Further assume that Lynn can earn 8 percent (all taxable as ordinary income) on her directly owned assets and 8 percent in her 401(k) plan account. Thus, her after-tax rate of return on the directly owned assets would be 5.6 percent (8% × .70 = 5.6 percent). Now, just for the sake of this illustration, let us say Lynn takes the entire balance in her 401(k) account at age 65 (or in 25 years). Thus, at age 65 (25 years later),[10] the after-tax situation under both approaches would be as follows:[11]

Direct investment:

$4,200 at 5.6% for 25 years	$230,060

Savings plan with Section 401(k) option:

$9,000 at 8% for 25 years	$710,590
Less her basis in the plan	0
Amount taxable as ordinary income	$710,590
Income tax payable (at 30%)	$220,283
After-tax balance	$497,413

Bases for Superior Results. These rather spectacular results come from the following three factors:[12]

1. Tax-deferred compounding on a larger employee's periodic payment—$6000 before tax versus $4200 after tax. (This represents deferral on the initial investment.)
2. Tax-deferred compounding on the full yield, i.e., 8 percent before tax compounded versus 5.60 percent after tax. (This represents deferral on the investment return.)
3. The employer match.

The first two factors represent the pure power of tax deferral on the employee's money. The third is extra employer money with tax deferral.

[10] As we shall see in Chapter 21, she normally would not do this. Rather, she would continue to defer for a much longer time. Thus, deferral in practice normally would be more favorable than shown here and this also justifies using a 30 percent tax rate on distributions from the savings plan.

[11] This assumes, just for illustrative purposes, that Lynn's salary remains at $100,000 for this period and that her top marginal federal income tax rate remains at 30 percent.

[12] Identifying these factors is important because, while they all apply to most 401(k) arrangements, only some of them apply to other tax-deferred arrangements. Therefore, other arrangements will not be as attractive as the typical qualified savings plan with a Section 401(k) option.

Finally, some self-employed persons are classified as *owner-employees* for HR-10 purposes. Owner-employees are persons who own 100 percent of an unincorporated trade or business (sole proprietors) or partners who own more than 10 percent of either a capital interest or a profits interest in a partnership.

Kinds of HR-10 Plans

Self-employed persons can adopt a variety of HR-10 plans. For example, they may have a defined-benefit pension plan, a money purchase pension plan, or a profit-sharing plan. Keogh plans may also be integrated with Social Security.

Self-employed persons also can adopt simplified employee pension (SEP) plans and SIMPLE (savings incentive match plan for employees) plans. (SEP and SIMPLE plans are covered in Chapter 18.) However, they cannot have one of these plans and another type of retirement plan (such as an HR-10 plan).

Parity with Corporate Retirement Plans

Prior to 1982, HR-10 plans were subject to a number of special restrictions and limits that did not generally apply to qualified corporate retirement plans. However, the Tax Equity and Fiscal Responsibility Act of 1982 (TEFRA) eliminated almost all of these special requirements for HR-10 plans. This was intended to establish *parity* among qualified retirement plans, whether corporate plans covering employees of a corporation or HR-10 plans covering self-employed persons and any common-law employees. This parity also was extended to plans for S corporations. Therefore, HR-10 plans generally have the same eligibility and coverage requirements, contribution limits (except as just noted), vesting requirements, rules for integration with social security, and other plan requirements, as for qualified retirement plans covering corporate employees. At one time, an exception to this parity concept was for loans from these plans. However, under EGTRRA, loans to owner-employees are no longer prohibited transactions for the plan and hence are permitted.

18

Other Employer-Provided Retirement Plans and Other Employee Benefits

Other Employer-Provided Retirement Plans

Simplified Employee Pension (SEP) Plans

Basic Characteristics. Employers can establish SEPs for their employees using individual retirement accounts or annuities[1] that are owned by the individual employees and that effectively may accept contributions from the employer up to the lesser of 25 percent of compensation or $40,000 (indexed for inflation in $1000 increments). Self-employed persons also can establish SEPs for themselves and their employees, if any. An employer's contributions are deductible by the employer and not currently taxable to covered employees. Self-employed persons can deduct on their own tax returns contributions on their behalf in the same manner as contributions to HR-10 plans.

SEPs are intended to reduce the paperwork and regulations required for HR-10 and qualified corporate retirement plans and hence be easier for employers and self-employed persons to adopt. Also, like profit-sharing plans, SEPs allow for discretionary contributions by employers. These streamlined plans tend to appeal mainly to smaller employers, although there is no employer size limit in the law.[2]

Technically, SEPs are not classified as qualified retirement plans. Rather, they are defined as regular (traditional) IRAs that meet the requirements of the tax law for SEPs. SEP contributions cannot be made to a Roth IRA.

[1] Individual retirement accounts and annuities (IRAs) are described in detail in Chapter 19.

[2] Prior to 1997, employers with 25 or fewer employees could establish salary reduction SEPs called SAR-SEPs. However, the law has been changed and no new SAR-SEPs can be established after 1996.

351

Nonforfeitable Contributions (Immediate Vesting). Like SEPs, employer con-tributions to a SIMPLE IRA must be immediately and 100 percent vested in the participants. Also, participants must be permitted to withdraw the amounts in their SIMPLE IRAs at any time.[5]

Exclusive Plan Requirement. A plan will not be treated as a SIMPLE IRA plan in any year the employer also had a qualified retirement plan, a tax-sheltered annuity plan, a SEP, or a governmental plan (other than a Section 457 plan) under which contributions were made or benefits were accrued. This is differ-ent from SEPs, for which there is no such limitation in the employer.

Distributions. As in the case of traditional IRAs generally, distributions from an employee's SIMPLE IRA are taxed to the employee as ordinary income. Also, premature distributions are subject to the normal 10 percent penalty tax and loans are not permitted from the plan. However, premature distributions from SIMPLE IRAs within the first two years of an employee's participation in the plan carry a 25 percent tax. After this two-year period, the penalty tax drops to the normal 10 percent. The minimum distribution rules also apply.

Rollovers. Participants in the plan for less than two years can make rollovers and transfers only from one SIMPLE IRA to another SIMPLE IRA. However, after an employee participates in the plan for two years or more, he or she can make rollovers from a SIMPLE IRA to another SIMPLE plan, a qualified retirement plan, a TSA, a traditional IRA, or a Section 457 plan.

SIMPLE 401(k) Plans. This is a Section 401(k) plan for an eligible employer (defined the same way as for SIMPLE IRAs) that is allowed to meet the actu-al deferral percentage (ADP) nondiscrimination test (see Chapter 17) by satis-fying the requirements to be a SIMPLE 401(k) plan. These requirements include a contribution requirement, a nonforfeitable (immediate vesting) requirement, and an exclusive plan requirement, like those for SIMPLE IRAs. However, SIMPLE 401(k) plans are subject to the other qualification and dis-tribution requirements that apply to Section 401(k) plans generally.

Tax-Sheltered Annuity (TSA) Plans

A TSA plan, or Section 403(b) annuity, is an arrangement by which an employee of a qualified organization can enter into an agreement with his or her employer to have part of the employee's earnings set aside for retirement on a before-tax basis.

---

[5] There may, however, be special premature distribution penalties for SIMPLE IRAs, which are discussed in the section on distributions.

Who Is Eligible? Any employee who works for a public school system or a tax-exempt organization established and operating exclusively for charitable, religious, scientific, or educational purposes is eligible.

How Much Can an Eligible Employee Contribute Each Year? There are two ways of approaching contributions to a TSA plan: an additional contribution by the employer (salary increase) for the employee or a salary reduction agreement (elective deferral) between the employee and his or her employer. Salary reduction is the more common approach. For salary reduction agreements, there is an annual elective deferral limit of $11,000 in 2002, $12,000 in 2003, $13,000 in 2004, $14,000 in 2005, and $15,000 in 2006 and thereafter (with indexing after 2006 in $500 increments). Further, the Section 415 limits for defined contributions plans, noted previously, also apply to Section 403(b) annuities. In addition, EGTRRA allows participants age 50 and over to raise the annual limit on elective deferrals by catch-up contributions of $1000 in 2002, $2000 in 2003, $3000 in 2004, $4000 in 2005, and $5000 in 2006 and thereafter (with indexing after 2006 in $500 increments). There also is a special increased limit for employees with 15 or more years of service with certain tax-exempt organizations.

Taxation of Distributions. Benefits are taxed as ordinary income when received by a participant. However, tax-free transfers and rollovers are allowed between TSA plans and traditional IRAs, qualified plans, Section 457 plans, and other TSAs. TSA plans also are subject to the minimum distribution rules and the 10 percent excise tax on premature distributions. They must be nondiscriminatory.

Nonqualified Deferred Compensation

A deferred-compensation arrangement is an agreement by which an employer promises to pay an employee in the future for services rendered today. The plan usually is set up to provide for the payment of deferred amounts into an account for the employee that may be paid out under specified conditions in the future. Plans also may be in the form of salary continuation over a period of years following retirement or other termination of employment. These plans are called *nonqualified* because they do not meet the tax law requirements for *qualified* retirement plans. They normally are available only to a selected group of executives.

Why Nonqualified Deferred Compensation? Some businesses do not have qualified retirement plans and so they may provide nonqualified plans for selected employees. However, in many cases employers do have qualified plans covering the bulk of their employees but want additional benefits for certain key people. This is particularly true because of the limits on benefits under qualified plans (e.g., the compensation cap, Section 415 limits, and so forth). Further, executives often want to defer income to get the advantages of before-tax deferral.

Types of Plans. These plans may be initiated by either the employer or the employee. When requested by an employee, it sometimes is known as a *deferred-oriented* or *savings-type* plan. In these plans, employees voluntarily agree that a portion of their income should be deferred. Many plans are of this type. Plans initiated by an employer may be called *benefit-oriented* or *inducement-to-stay* plans.

Plans may also be classified as *deferral-type plans,* as just described, or as *supplemental plans,* which are provided and paid for by employers to supplement qualified retirement plans for highly paid employees. There also are *death-benefit-only plans,* which provide benefits, usually in the form of annual installments, to survivors of a deceased participant. Finally, there are *Section 457 nonqualified deferred-compensation plans* for employees of state and local governments and nonprofit organizations.

Taxation of Nonqualified Deferred-Compensation Plans. There are two doctrines or theories of tax law that may particularly affect nonqualified plans. These are the *constructive receipt* doctrine and the *economic benefit* theory. Under the doctrine of constructive receipt, as explained in Chapter 14, a taxpayer may be taxed on income not actually received if it is considered to be received constructively. For example, if an employer deposits funds with a trustee and an employee has a right to the funds and may withdraw them or receive benefits from them at any time without substantial limitation, the funds placed with the trustee will be considered constructively received by the employee—not when the employee withdraws them, but when the employer places them with the trustee. Under the economic benefit theory, a person may be taxed whenever a monetary value can be attached to compensation or benefits. To successfully defer income taxation, a nonqualified deferred-compensation plan must not come under either of these doctrines.

In analyzing the tax status of these plans, it makes a difference whether the plan is considered funded for tax purposes. A *funded* plan is one in which specific assets have been set aside and in which the employee is given a current beneficial interest in the assets. Plans without such assets securing the benefits are *unfunded.* If a plan is unfunded, income taxation on the benefits can be postponed until the employee or his or her beneficiary actually receives them. Thus, if an employer merely promises to pay deferred amounts (and the accumulated before-tax investment income on such amounts) in the future upon the occurrence of certain events (such as the passage of time, termination of employment, retirement, death, or disability), the plan normally is not hampered by the constructive receipt doctrine because the delay is a substantial limitation on the receipt of the benefits. Moreover, if the plan is not secured so as to be protected from the employer's creditors, most authorities feel the employee should not be considered to have received an economic benefit. Thus, an *unfunded deferred-compensation plan* normally can provide an employee with a postponed accumulated account balance and the employee's rights to the account balance can be nonforfeitable, unconditional, and vested, with the income tax on the deferred compensation and investment earnings being deferred until actual receipt. The employee (or his or her beneficiaries) is taxed when the deferred benefits are actually received.

For a funded plan, in which an employee is given rights to specific assets, the employee will be taxed currently on the value of the assets added to the fund each year, unless the employee's rights to the benefits are subject to a *substantial risk of forfeiture*. This means there must be a risk the employee will never receive the benefits. Most nonqualified plans are unfunded.

Security Arrangements and Informal Funding for Nonqualified Plans. Employers sometimes have informal funding arrangements to provide themselves with assets to discharge their obligations under these plans. These arrangements (often involving the purchase of life insurance on the participating executives' lives) are owned by, controlled by, and made payable to the employer and hence do not provide any direct security to the executives covered by the agreements. The employer's commitments remain unsecured promises to pay, which covered executives can enforce only as general creditors of the employer. For tax purposes, such "informally funded plans" are still regarded as unfunded plans.

In recent years, there has been heightened interest in finding ways to provide greater security to executives with regard to unfunded nonqualified plans. One such security arrangement is the so-called *rabbi trust*.[6] A rabbi trust is an irrevocable trust set up by an employer to provide various kinds of nonqualified retirement benefits to selected employees. The trust provides that its assets will be paid out to meet the employer's obligations under certain circumstances, but that the trust assets remain subject to the claims of the employer's general creditors in the event that the employer becomes bankrupt or insolvent. This means that even though the employer places assets in these trusts, they do not result in current taxable income to the covered employees. Thus, rabbi trusts can provide at least limited security for covered executives without losing the income tax advantages of an unfunded plan. For funded plans, some arrangements to secure benefits are employee-owned trusts (sometimes called *secular trusts*) and employee-owned annuities.

[6] These trusts are called *rabbi trusts* because the first case involving their use upon which the IRS ruled, in 1981, involved such a trust set up by a synagogue for its rabbi.

Planning Issues for Nonqualified Deferred Compensation. These plans can be attractive for selected executives and corporate directors. The executives often do not need the current income and they may be in lower tax brackets when the deferred benefits are paid out. Investment earnings on the deferred amounts also are tax-deferred and some employers provide attractive investment outlets for deferred amounts. On the other hand, the security issue is there for unfunded plans. Its importance would seem to vary with the circumstances.

In a different area, nonqualified deferred compensation may be used in connection with the sale of closely held business interests. Part of the purchase price (for a closely held C corporation, for example) effectively might be in the form of a nonqualified deferred-compensation agreement with the selling owner-employee. The deferred payments would be tax-deductible to the corporation (and indirectly to the buyer) and thus part of the purchase price would be in tax-deductible dollars. On the other hand, these payments would be taxable as ordinary income to the selling owner-employee. Such arrangements are complex and require advance planning.

Supplemental Executive Retirement Plans

Supplemental nonqualified plans in the forms of ERISA excess plans and supplemental executive retirement plans (SERPs) are also established for executives. ERISA excess benefits plans pay the difference between the maximum permitted limits under qualified retirement plans (e.g., the Section 415 limits) and an employee's full benefit as determined by a regular plan's benefit formula. In addition, SERPs may be set up to raise the level of retirement income for executives beyond that contemplated under the basic retirement plan benefit formula. A new, and as of this writing experimental, planning technique advocated by some commentators is the exchange by an executive of a supplemental retirement plan for a company-paid life insurance plan, usually arranged so the life insurance will not be in the executive's gross estate for federal estate tax purposes. This technique has been dubbed by some a "SERP swap."

Other Employee Benefits
Dependent Care Assistance

This benefit typically provides day care for specified dependents of employees, including dependent children, parents, or spouses. The IRC generally provides that employees do not have to include in their gross income amounts not exceeding $5000 per year paid or incurred by their employer for dependent care assistance if the assistance is provided under a program meeting certain requirements. Eligible expenses include the expense of a child or senior day care center, a baby-sitter while the employee is working, a nursery school, a day camp, and a nurse at home. Such expenses are eligible only if they permit the employee or the employee and his or her spouse to work or to attend school full time. These expenses frequently are also covered under flexible spending accounts (FSAs) on a pretax basis.

Educational Assistance

The gross income of employees does not include amounts paid or incurred by an employer for educational assistance to employees under a program that meets certain requirements up to a maximum of $5250 per employee per year.

Financial and Other Counseling Services

Many companies provide financial planning services on an individual basis as a benefit for their executives. In some cases, employers may provide such financial planning services for a broader range of employees. Employers may also provide their employees with other types of counseling; one popular area is retirement planning and counseling.

Cafeteria Compensation (Flexible Benefits)

Basic Characteristics. The nature of these plans has already been described in Chapter 5 and so will not be repeated here.

Tax Status of Cafeteria Plans. Section 125 of the IRC essentially allows employees to choose among certain nontaxable benefits and taxable compensation without having the choice itself be a taxable event under the constructive receipt doctrine. Section 125 plans must be nondiscriminatory and meet certain other tax law requirements. In effect, this means the constructive receipt doctrine will not apply to otherwise nontaxable benefits elected by employees, even though they could have elected taxable benefits (cash) as well. Of course, to the extent that employees elect cash compensation, it will constitute gross income to them.

Nontaxable Fringe Benefits

Employers can provide employees with a variety of benefits and services that the tax law specifically excludes from gross income to the employees.[7] The

[7] Section 132 of the IRC provides that "certain fringe benefits" are excluded from gross income. Prior to Section 132, there was uncertainty about the tax status of many of these items.

term *fringe benefits* sometimes is used loosely to mean any kind of employee benefit other than retirement benefits. However, in the context of nontaxable fringe benefits under Section 132, it refers only to certain benefits specified in the law, as described next.

Types of Nontaxable Fringes. The specific benefits include the following.

No-Additional-Cost Services. These are the same services employers sell to the general public that are provided free or at reduced cost to employees.

Qualified Employee Discounts. These generally are discounts up to 20 percent on the prices of goods and services.

Working Condition Fringes. These are a variety of expenses paid for by employers that otherwise employees could deduct as employee business expenses on their own tax returns. They may include items such as professional dues, subscriptions to business periodicals, transportation for business purposes (cars, aircraft, and the like), club dues, outplacement assistance, and home computers.

De Minimis Fringes. In general, these are items that are so small and infrequently received that it is not practical for employers to account for them. However, it includes meals available at employer-provided eating facilities and certain employer-provided dependent group life insurance (usually up to $2000 face amount).

Qualified Transportation Fringes. These include employer-paid commuter highway vehicle transportation (e.g., a van pool with at least six passengers) and transit passes and qualified parking up to limited amounts per month. These fringes also include any cash reimbursements by employers for such expenses and allow employees a choice between these fringes and cash, without constructive receipt if employees elect the nontaxable fringes.

Qualified Moving Expense Reimbursements. The employer may reimburse or pay moving expenses for an employee to relocate to a new place of work, provided that the employee otherwise would have been able to deduct them.

On-Premises Athletic Facilities. The use of on-premises athletic facilities is a nontaxable fringe benefit if substantially all the use of such facilities is by employees, their spouses, and their dependent children.

Other Benefits. If an employer provides other benefits to employees, aside from these specified nontaxable fringe benefits and the previously discussed employee benefits excluded from income by other sections of the tax code, the value of the benefit normally will be taxable to employees as compensation.

19

Individual Retirement
Accounts and Annuities (IRAs)

IRAs have become important and advantageous retirement and financial planning tools for many people. At the same time, however, as a result of numerous changes in the tax law, they have become quite complex. The following kinds of IRAs are now available to individuals:

- Regular (earnings-related) traditional IRA
- Rollover traditional IRA
- Nondeductible traditional IRA
- Roth IRA (earnings-related)
- Roth IRA (conversion from traditional IRA)
- Spousal IRA
- Education Savings Account (Education IRA)
- SEP IRA
- SIMPLE IRA

The SEP and SIMPLE IRAs were described in Chapter 18. The other kinds of IRAs are covered in this chapter.

Basic Concepts

IRAs afford individuals an opportunity to set up their own tax-favored retirement plans, subject to certain conditions and limitations. An IRA can be an individual retirement account or individual retirement annuity. An *individual retirement account* is set up under the terms of a written trust or custodial account with a fiduciary institution that meets the requirements of the IRS. Most IRAs are in these accounts. An *individual retirement annuity* is a flexible premium annuity contract and may be a fixed-dollar annuity or a variable annuity.

For IRAs generally, the interest of the IRA owner must be nonforfeitable.

Also, if an IRA is used as security for a loan or is assigned to another (other than a transfer incident to divorce), there will be a deemed distribution to the extent of the loan or transfer. Thus, IRAs generally cannot be borrowed against or given away to others. Whether IRA account balances will be subject to the claims of creditors of the owner in case of bankruptcy or insolvency is a matter of state law and varies among the states.

Types of IRAs

There is now an almost bewildering array of IRA plans, with different rules or limits applying to each.

Regular (Earnings-Related) Traditional IRAs

These plans may be called traditional IRAs, regular IRAs, or front-end IRAs. Only cash can be contributed to these plans.

Nature and Limits of Contributions. Individuals may make income tax-deductible contributions to these IRAs based on their earnings, marital status, and whether or not they (and their spouse) are covered under certain employer-provided retirement plans.

First, in situations in which a person and his or her spouse (if any) are *not* covered by an employer retirement plan (i.e., are not "active participants"), each income earner can make tax-deductible contributions each year up to the smaller of 100 percent of compensation or $3000 for 2002 through 2004, $4000 for 2005 through 2007, and $5000 for 2008 and thereafter (with indexing for inflation after 2008 in $500 increments). In addition, EGTRRA allows IRA owners ages 50 and over to raise these annual dollar limits by $500 for 2002 through 2005 and $1000 for 2006 and thereafter. For this purpose, "employer retirement plans" include qualified retirement plans; federal, state, and local government plans; tax-sheltered annuity plans; SEPs; SIMPLE plans; and certain other plans. Also for this purpose, "compensation" means earned income as an employee, income from self-employment, or alimony. The tax deduction is taken from gross income to arrive at adjusted gross income.

Next, in situations where a person is covered under an employer retirement plan, the income earner still may be able to make deductible contributions to an IRA, subject to certain income limits. For married taxpayers filing a joint return and for qualifying widows or widowers, their modified adjusted gross income (MAGI[1]) for federal income tax purposes must not exceed $60,000 for

---

[1] Modified adjusted gross income for traditional IRAs is adjusted gross income (AGI) plus any IRA deduction and certain other items. Thus, it is essentially the person's or couple's AGI.

2003 for a full deduction; the deduction is phased out for MAGI between $60,000 and $70,000. For single taxpayers (and heads of households), the MAGI limit is $40,000 for a full IRA deduction; the deduction is phased out between $40,000 and $50,000. Under current law, these phaseout limits are to be raised gradually each year until they reach $80,000 to $100,000 for married persons filing jointly in 2007 and thereafter and $50,000 to $60,000 for single persons in 2005 and thereafter.

Finally, in situations in which married persons are filing jointly and one of them is covered by an employer retirement plan but the other is not, the spouse covered by the plan can make deductible IRA contributions subject to the income limits just described. The noncovered spouse may make regular deductible IRA contributions, but subject to a higher MAGI phaseout range for the couple's combined income of $150,000 to $160,000.

Some examples of these rules may be helpful. First, let us assume Warren Williams, age 35, is a single taxpayer who works for a large corporation and is covered under the corporation's qualified pension plan. In 2003, Warren earns a salary of $38,000 per year (which is also his MAGI). Warren can make a tax-deductible contribution to an IRA up to the full $3000 for the year because, although he is covered by an employer retirement plan, his MAGI is less than $40,000.

However, if Warren's salary had been $75,000, he could not have made any tax-deductible contribution to an IRA. As will be explained later in the section on Roth IRAs, he could, however, have made a $3,000 contribution to a non-tax-deductible but tax-free Roth IRA for the year, because the phaseout range for single taxpayers for Roth IRAs is $95,000 to $110,000.[2]

On the other hand, if Warren's salary (and MAGI) for 2003 were $46,000, he would be in the phaseout range for that year and could make a partial contribution to a tax-deductible IRA. This can be calculated by subtracting Warren's MAGI ($46,000) from the $50,000 upper limit of the phaseout range and multiplying the difference by 30 percent.[3] Thus, Warren could deduct a $1200 contribution in 2003 ($50,000 - $46,000 = $4000 × 0.30 = $1200).[4]

Finally, if Warren's salary (and MAGI) for 2003 were $120,000, he could not make any tax-deductible contribution to an IRA, since he would be

---

[2] He could also have contributed to a nondeductible regular IRA, but the Roth would be a far better choice.

[3] The use of 30 percent of the difference is a shortcut, derived from the fact that the full deductible amount of $3,000 is 30 percent of the $10,000 difference between the $40,000 lower limit and the $50,000 upper limit of the applicable phaseout range. When the difference is $10,000, and the deductible amount is $30,000, 30 percent can be used. Here is the technically correct formula for this calculation:

$$\text{Percentage of reduction} = \frac{\text{MAGI} - \text{applicable dollar amount (the lower limit of the phaseout range)}}{\$10,000 \text{ (or other difference in the phaseout range)}}$$

beyond the phaseout range. He also could not make any contribution to a Roth IRA, because he would be beyond its phaseout range as well.[5]

As another example, let us assume Peter and Mary Schmidt are married and file a joint income tax return. Peter, age 42, works for a corporation that covers him under its qualified savings plan and receives a salary of $90,000 in 2003. Mary works for a small employer with no retirement plan and receives a salary of $55,000 in 2003. Assume their MAGI is $145,000 for 2003. In this case, Peter could not make any deductible contribution to a traditional IRA, since he is an active participant in an employer retirement plan and their MAGI exceeds the phaseout range for married persons for 2003 ($60,000 to $70,000). However, Mary, age 38, could make a $3000 deductible contribution to a traditional IRA, since she is not covered by an employer plan and their MAGI is below the phaseout range for a married couple with one partner covered by an employer plan and the other not.[6]

Eligibility Requirements. Any individual who has compensation and has not attained age 70½ may be eligible to contribute to a deductible traditional IRA. Of course, if a person (or his or her spouse) is covered by an employer retirement plan, this may limit (or eliminate) his or her deductible IRA contribution, as just described. Also, under EGTRRA, employers with qualified plans may allow employees to make voluntary contributions to a separate account or annuity that meets the requirements of a traditional or Roth IRA. These are referred to as *deemed IRAs* under employer plans.

Tax Status. When making deductible contributions to a traditional IRA, the person or couple receives a current income tax deduction for the contribution, up to the previously described limits. Further, investment earnings in the IRA grow without current taxation. But all amounts distributed are fully taxable as *ordinary income.*

In addition, distributions from a traditional IRA before the owner reaches age 59½ are considered premature distributions and are subject to an additional 10 percent penalty tax on the taxable amount, unless an exception applies.

---

[4] He could also make an $1800 contribution to a Roth IRA, since a Roth permits contributions of the lesser of 100 percent of compensation or $3000 reduced by any contributions made for the year to a traditional IRA on the person's behalf ($3000 - $1200 = $1800), and the Roth phaseout limits would be $95,000 to $110,000.

[5] As will be noted later, in this situation Warren still could have made a $3000 nondeductible contribution to a traditional IRA.

[6] It may also be noted that Peter as well as Mary (as an alternative to her deductible IRA) each could make $3000 cash contributions ($6000 total for the two) to Roth IRAs since coverage under employer retirement plans does not affect Roth eligibility and their MAGI is below the phaseout range for Roths ($150,000 to $160,000 for married persons filing jointly). Mary could also split her $3000 contribution between a deductible traditional IRA and a Roth IRA.

The exceptions include distributions due to the owner's death or disability; for deductible medical care: to pay for health insurance premiums if unemployed; to pay for qualified higher education expenses for the owner, the owner's spouse, and a child or grandchild of the owner or his or her spouse[7]; to buy a house if a qualified first-time homebuyer, subject to a lifetime $10,000 limit[8]; and as part of a series of substantially equal periodic payments made at least annually for the life or the life expectancy of the IRA owner or the joint lives or life expectancies of the owner and his or her designated beneficiary of the IRA. It should be noted, however, that even if one of these exceptions applies, a distribution is still taxed as ordinary income.

When an IRA owner dies, any account balance in the IRA will be included in his or her gross estate for federal estate tax purposes. The account balance is payable to the beneficiary or beneficiaries named in the IRA. The nature of this beneficiary designation will affect the estate tax status of the IRA, as explained in Chapter 20. This is true for all types of IRAs. However, for deductible traditional IRAs, the account balance is also income in respect of a decedent (IRD) to the beneficiary, as explained in Chapter 14. Planning for these issues is covered in Chapter 20.

Required Distributions. The owner of a traditional IRA must begin taking taxable distributions no later than April 1 of the calendar year following the calendar year in which he or she attains age 70½. This is called the *required beginning date* (RBD). After this date, the owner must take certain minimum annual distributions. Chapter 20 covers calculating and planning for these minimum distributions. People often have more than one traditional IRA, which may include earnings-related IRAs, as discussed here, and rollover IRAs, covered next. The IRS requires that minimum distributions be calculated separately for each IRA, but then they may be totaled and can be taken from any one or more of the IRAs. There also are minimum distributions required for IRA account balances after an owner's death. Naturally, an IRA owner can take distributions before the RBD and larger distributions than the minimum, if desired.

---

[7] Qualified higher education expenses include postsecondary school tuition, books, student supplies, and minimum room and board. These allowable expenses are reduced by nontaxable scholarships, fellowship grants, and educational assistance allowances.

[8] These are distributions received by an individual and used by the individual for qualified acquisition costs for a principal residence for a first-time homebuyer, who may be the individual, his or her spouse, or any child, grandchild, or ancestor of the individual or his or her spouse. For this purpose, a first-time homebuyer is an individual who did not have an ownership interest in a principal residence during the two-year period before acquiring the principal residence.

Rollover Traditional IRAs

These are traditional IRAs that receive *eligible rollover distributions* (defined in Chapter 20) from qualified retirement plans, tax-sheltered annuities (TSAs), and Section 457 governmental deferred-compensation plans. These rollover distributions can be in the form of cash or property (such as employer stock from a qualified profit-sharing or savings plan). There also may be rollovers from an IRA to a qualified plan, a TSA, or a Section 457 plan.

Eligibility Requirements. Any individuals, regardless of whether they currently have compensation (earnings), regardless of their income, and regardless of whether they are covered by an employer retirement plan, can establish a rollover IRA to receive an eligible rollover distribution.

Tax Status. There is no current income taxation on the amount of an eligible rollover distribution to a rollover IRA. Thus, as an example, suppose that Mary Levy, age 40, has a $400,000 account balance in her employer's qualified savings plan with a Section 401(k) option (i.e., the entire $400,000 will eventually be taxable). She is leaving her current employer to join another firm. She can elect to roll over all or part of the $400,000 account balance (an eligible rollover distribution) into her own rollover IRA without any current income taxation on the transaction.[9] Like other traditional IRAs, rollover IRAs are subject to taxation of distributions as ordinary income, the 10 percent penalty tax on premature distributions with the same rules and exceptions, inclusion in the gross estate for federal estate tax purposes, and being treated as IRD.

Required Distributions. Also like other traditional IRAs, rollover IRAs are subject to the minimum distribution rules just described.

Nondeductible Contributions to Traditional IRAs

Since there are income limits on deductible IRA contributions when a person (or his or her spouse) is covered under an employer retirement plan (as well as income limits on contributions to Roth IRAs, considered next), it is possible to make nondeductible contributions to traditional IRAs equal to the difference between what could have been contributed had there been no income limits and the amounts (if any) of deductible IRA contributions and Roth IRA contributions. When distributions are made, nondeductible (after-tax) contributions are the IRA owner's investment in the contract, which will be recovered income tax free.[10] These after-tax contributions can be rolled over into another IRA but not into an employer plan.

[9] She also could elect to roll this amount over tax-free into her new employer's qualified retirement plan, if permitted by the new employer, or into a TSA or Section 457 plan.

[10] For this purpose, all traditional IRAs owned by a person are treated as one contract and any nondeductible (nontaxable) portion of a distribution is calculated in that basis. Therefore, part of any such distribution will be taxable and part a return of basis.

The only real tax advantage of making nondeductible IRA contributions is that investment income and capital gains accumulate in the IRA without current income taxation. However, when distributed, they are taxed as ordinary income.

Roth IRAs (Earnings-Related)

An entirely new IRA concept is the Roth IRA, with contributions not tax-deductible but distributions tax-free.

Nature and Limits of Contributions. Individuals may make contributions to Roth IRAs based on their earnings and marital status. It does not matter whether they are covered under an employer retirement plan. An individual income earner can make a contribution to a Roth IRA up to the smaller of 100 percent of compensation or the same dollar limits described previously for earnings-related traditional IRAs and also the same catch-up limits for owners age 50 or over, subject to certain income limits. The income limits (phaseout ranges) for Roth IRAs are $95,000 to $110,000 of modified adjusted gross income (MAGI[11]) for single persons (and heads of households) and $150,000 to $160,000 of MAGI for married persons filing jointly. The phaseout rules operate the same way as for traditional IRAs on persons covered by an employer retirement plan. The annual limits also are reduced by any contributions to traditional IRAs.

Eligibility Requirements. Any individual who has compensation (earned income or taxable alimony) and whose MAGI does not exceed $160,000 (married filing jointly) or $110,000 (single) is eligible to contribute to a Roth IRA. Roth contributions can be made after age 70½. Neither SEP nor SIMPLE IRA contributions can be made to a Roth IRA. However, once these contributions are in a traditional IRA, it can be converted to a Roth IRA under the rules for such conversions. Effective for 2006 and thereafter, EGTRRA will allow Section 401(k) plans and Section 403(b) annuities to permit employees to elect to have all or part of their own elective deferrals designated as *after-tax "Roth contributions."* In this case, the employees must pay income tax currently on these Roth deferrals; then they will grow tax-free and will be distributed tax-free (like Roth IRAs). Any 401(k) or 403(b) plan participant will be able to make "Roth contributions" regardless of income. These arrangements are called *qualified Roth contribution programs* (QRCPs).

[11] This is MAGI for traditional IRA purposes less any deductible IRA contributions and any income resulting from the conversion of a traditional IRA to a Roth IRA (considered next).

Tax Status. Contributions to a Roth IRA are not deductible for income tax purposes, but investment earnings and capital gains in the IRA grow tax-free. Distributions from a Roth IRA (either earnings-related or a conversion from a traditional IRA) are not included in gross income for federal income tax purposes, provided they are qualified distributions. A *qualified distribution* is one made at least five years after the tax year in which a person made the first contribution to the Roth IRA or in which a rollover (conversion) was made to the Roth IRA and the distribution is taken on or after the person attains age 59½, on account of the person's death or disability, or for a qualified first-time homebuyer.[12] If a distribution does not meet these requirements, the untaxed investment income will be taxable. Even in this situation, however, the non-tax-deductible contributions are assumed to come out first, so no tax is imposed until total nonqualifying distributions (from all Roth IRAs) exceed total contributions. If a distribution should be taxable, the 10 percent penalty tax on premature distributions also may apply.

As a planning matter, it would seem unwise to take nonqualifying distributions that exceed total contributions. In fact, as an overall planning strategy, it seems prudent to keep assets in Roth IRAs and traditional IRAs for as long as possible, to get the most advantage from *tax-free growth* of investment earnings for Roths and *tax-deferred growth* of earnings for traditional IRAs.

As in the case of traditional IRAs, when a Roth IRA owner dies, any account balance in the IRA is included in his or her gross estate for federal estate tax purposes. The account balance will be payable on death to the beneficiary or beneficiaries named in the IRA and this will affect the estate tax status of the IRA. However, unlike traditional IRAs, the account balance is not taxable income as IRD.

Required Distributions. During the lifetime of a Roth IRA owner, there are no mandatory distributions. There is no required beginning date, and there are no required minimum distributions. This is a major advantage for the Roth over traditional IRAs and also qualified retirement plans, both of which are subject to mandatory distribution rules starting at age 70½. At the death of a Roth IRA owner, the minimum distribution rules applying to IRA death benefits generally also apply to Roth IRAs. (See Chapter 20.)

Roth IRAs (Conversion from Traditional IRAs)

Nature and Limits of Conversions. A traditional IRA account balance may be converted into a Roth IRA by the owner, provided that his or her MAGI (as either a single person or a married person filing a joint return) does not exceed

---

[12] Defined in the same way as in note 8.

$100,000 for the year of conversion.[13] Any amount can be converted and conversion can be done at any time the owner is eligible to convert (with an exception for SIMPLE IRAs, noted next).

A conversion to a Roth can be effected in two ways: the owner can take a distribution and then roll over the amount to be converted into the Roth IRA within 60 days of the distribution or can have the trustee or custodian of the traditional IRA transfer the amount to be converted to the trustee or custodian of the Roth IRA without actually receiving a distribution (a trustee-to-trustee transfer.)[14] Under either of these methods, the amount converted is taxable.

Eligibility Requirements. The $100,000 MAGI limit has already been noted. A SEP can be converted to a Roth. A SIMPLE IRA can be converted after two years from the date on which the owner first participated in any SIMPLE IRA plan of the employer. A qualified retirement plan cannot be directly converted to a Roth, but it can be rolled over or transferred into a traditional IRA and then the traditional IRA may be converted to a Roth IRA.

Tax Status. The taxable portion of a traditional IRA that is converted to a Roth IRA is gross income for federal income tax purposes in the year of conversion. It normally is preferable to pay this tax from other, non-tax-advantaged assets so the full amount in the IRA can grow tax-free. While the taxable portion on conversion is subject to regular federal income taxation, it is not subject to the 10 percent tax on premature distributions.

As an illustration, let us continue the example of Mary Levy, who directly transferred the $200,000 account balance from her qualified savings plan into her traditional rollover IRA. If there comes a year in which her MAGI does not exceed $100,000, she can convert the traditional IRA to a Roth IRA. If the account balance in her traditional IRA at that time were, say, $210,000, this amount would be added to her gross income in that year. If her tax rate on this additional income were, say, 35 percent, her added tax would be $73,500 ($210,000 × 0.35). Assuming this tax comes from other sources (so the full $210,000 can grow tax-free in her Roth IRA), she effectively would lose the *after-tax return* on the $73,500 tax payment for the future. This must be considered in analyzing a conversion.

[13] As stated in note 11, MAGI for this purpose does not include income resulting from the conversion itself. Also, MAGI for purposes of conversion eligibility does not include minimum required distributions from traditional IRAs. This may be helpful for older persons, who may not have other income in excess of $100,000 in a year, to make such conversions, perhaps for estate planning reasons.

[14] It may be noted that these are the same general methods as those used for rollovers and transfers from qualified retirement plans and TSAs to traditional IRAs. However, the tax withholding rules are different, as will be explained in Chapter 20.

When the owner of a Roth IRA dies, any account balance is included in his or her gross estate, but it is not IRD.

Required Distributions. The rules for required distributions from Roth IRAs have already been noted.

Spousal IRAs

For married persons filing a joint return, when one of the spouses has no compensation (or compensation less than that of the other spouse) during a tax year, the working spouse may contribute to an IRA for the nonworking spouse (a spousal IRA), as well as to his or her own IRA. The maximum contributions to both IRAs each year is the smaller of 100 percent of the working spouse's compensation or the dollar limits on contributions described previously. The spousal IRA can be a traditional IRA or a Roth IRA. No more than the applicable limit can be contributed to each spouse's IRA and each spouse must have his or her own separate IRA or sub-account in a plan.

As an example, suppose that Sam and Martha Johnson are 40 and 36, respectively, are married, file a joint return, and Sam earns $95,000 per year. He is an active participant under his employer's qualified savings plan. Martha works in their home and has no compensation for IRA purposes. Sam could contribute $3000 in 2003 to his Roth IRA and $3000 to Martha's spousal Roth IRA for the year. This is because their MAGI is less than the Roth IRA phaseout range for married couples, $150,000 to $160,000. As an alternative, Sam could contribute $3000 to a traditional deductible spousal IRA for Martha, since their MAGI is less than the $150,000 to $160,000 phaseout range when one spouse is covered by an employer retirement plan but the other is not. Sam cannot contribute to a deductible IRA for himself, because he is covered by an employer plan and their MAGI exceeds the phaseout range for that situation.

Education Savings Accounts (Education IRAs)[15]

Nature and Limits of Contributions. Individuals (whether they have earnings or not) can contribute up to $2000 per year per beneficiary to education savings accounts, subject to certain income limits. The income limits are an MAGI of $95,000 to $110,000 for single persons and $190,000 to $220,000 for married persons filing jointly. The phaseout operates in the same way as for Roth IRAs. The limit of $2000 per year is in addition to the limits for other IRAs discussed previously.

[15] These are different in concept from the IRAs discussed previously in that they are designed for funding education rather than for retirement. They originally were called *Education IRAs*, but their official name now is *Coverdell Education Savings Accounts*. In this book, we shall refer to them either as *education savings accounts* or *education IRAs*.

Eligibility Requirements. In addition to the foregoing, corporations and other entities also may make contributions to education savings accounts and in this case the income limits just noted do not apply.

Tax Status. Contributions to education IRAs are not tax-deductible and, correspondingly, withdrawals that meet the requirements of the tax law are not taxable. Investment earnings accumulate tax-free. To be tax-free, the amounts withdrawn by the beneficiary must not exceed qualified education expenses.[16] To the extent they do, a pro rata share of the untaxed investment earnings will be taxable to the beneficiary and a 10 percent penalty tax also will be applicable.

Rollovers and Required Distributions. When the beneficiary of an education IRA reaches age 30, he or she may roll over any amounts not withdrawn (within 60 days of distribution) to an education IRA for another member of the beneficiary's family. Such a rollover also can be done before age 30. If such actions have not been taken by age 30, any remaining funds must be distributed to the beneficiary and the untaxed investment earnings will be taxable as ordinary income (including the 10 percent penalty tax).

Contributions to education savings accounts are subject to gift tax but are eligible for the annual exclusion of $11,000 ($22,000 for married couples splitting gifts), indexed for inflation, per donee.[17] In a beneficiary-to-beneficiary rollover, as long as the beneficiaries are of the same generation (brothers and sisters, for example), there will be no taxable gift. However, if the rollover goes to a beneficiary in the next generation (e.g., a child of the former beneficiary), there is a gift, but the annual exclusion applies.

Other Aspects of IRAs
IRA Rollovers and Direct Transfers

Another kind of rollover to an IRA occurs when part or all of the assets received from one IRA are rolled over within 60 days into another IRA of the same type. There is no current income tax on such a rollover. This is called an *IRA-to-IRA rollover*. Part or all of the IRA assets are distributed to the owner and then the owner rolls over those assets into another IRA. Such a rollover can be made only once a year and the same property must be rolled over to the new IRA.

---

[16] These include qualified elementary and secondary education expenses (grades 1 through 12) and qualified higher education expenses, such as for tuition, fees, books, supplies, equipment, room and board, and other items. They are reduced by nontaxable scholarships, fellowship grants, and educational assistance allowances.

[17] The gift tax annual exclusion is described in Chapter 25.

The other approach is a *direct IRA transfer.* Here the assets of an IRA are transferred directly from one plan sponsor to another without passing into the hands of the IRA owner. In this case, there is no limit on the number of transfers that can be made in a year.

Financial Institutions That Offer IRAs

Many financial institutions offer IRAs to the public. Some of these institutions offer *self-directed IRAs.* These are IRAs in which the owner has virtually complete control over the selection of a broad range of investments. On the other hand, under these self-directed plans, the full burden of investment decision making falls on the IRA owner.

IRA Investments

IRAs can be invested in a wide range of assets. These investments can be made through financial intermediaries or in individual assets through self-directed IRAs. However, life insurance policies and certain collectibles are not eligible investments for IRAs.

Planning Issues for IRAs
Deciding Whether to Establish an IRA

The threshold issue is whether to contribute to an IRA at all. If a person is eligible to make deductible contributions to a traditional IRA or nondeductible contributions to a Roth IRA, there appear to be many advantages in doing so.

For deductible traditional IRAs, both the contributions and the investment earnings are before-tax, so the owner gets the power of deferral on both. This is analogous to the deferral advantage of a Section 401(k) plan without employer match, as analyzed in Chapter 17. For Roth IRAs, the advantages of tax-free growth of investment earnings and longer possible time for tax-free growth make this plan just as attractive as the traditional IRA and possibly more so. Which one is to be preferred in a given situation is a complicated issue that is considered in the next section.

With respect to nondeductible contributions to a traditional IRA, however, the case is not so clear. The only real advantage is tax deferral on investment earnings.

Deciding Between Traditional and Roth IRAs and Whether to Convert to a Roth IRA

If a person is eligible for only one type, that settles the question, of course. But many people will be eligible for both. Unfortunately, there is no sure answer to this question.

It really can be divided into two questions. First, should an eligible person contribute to an earnings-related traditional IRA or a Roth IRA? Second, should an eligible person who has a traditional IRA convert to a Roth IRA?

Basic Equality Between Deductible and Tax-Free Growth. In analyzing these issues, it may be helpful at the outset to make a key point. If one takes a sum of money or a series of contributions, accumulates them tax-deferred, and then pays tax on the balance after a specified period of time (as in a traditional IRA), the result is the *same* as paying tax on the sum or series of contributions up front, deducting the tax, and accumulating the balance tax free for the same period of time (as in a Roth IRA), *provided* the interest rates and tax rates assumed in both cases are the same. This may be somewhat counterintuitive, so let us take an example using a conversion situation.

Assume that Henry Petrofski, age 50, is in the 30 percent federal income tax bracket, owns a traditional IRA with a $100,000 account balance, and is eligible to convert to a Roth IRA. Further assume he can earn a before-tax investment return of 8 percent and an after-tax return of 5.60 percent (8 percent × 0.70 = 5.60 percent).

First, we shall assume Henry leaves the funds in his traditional IRA at an 8 percent average annual rate of return and withdraws all of them 20 years later at age 70.[18] He then pays income tax on the entire $466,096 accumulated balance at 30 percent.[19] As a result, his *after-tax return* on the IRA at the end of the 20 years would be $466,096 × 0.70 = $326,267 (after tax).

On the other hand, if we assume Henry converts his traditional IRA to a Roth, pays the income tax on the conversion from the IRA proceeds,[20] allows the balance ($70,000) to accumulate tax-free in the Roth at the 8 percent average annual rate of return, and then withdraws the entire balance tax-free in 20 years at age 70, his *after-tax return* at the end of 20 years would be *the same* ($100,000 × 0.70 = $70,000 in the Roth IRA that accumulates at 8% over 20 years, to $326,267 tax-free). But note that the fundamental assumptions in reaching this equality are that the investment earnings, tax rate, and the peri-

[18] As a planning matter, he normally would withdraw them over a period of time to preserve tax deferral for as long as possible. We make this assumption here only for purposes of illustration.

[19] Again, as a practical matter, if he took this amount into income in one year, his tax bracket would increase to the maximum marginal rate. But we are making this tax rate assumption for purposes of comparison.

[20] As noted previously, it normally is not desirable to take the tax from the traditional IRA proceeds. It is better to use other, non-tax-advantaged assets to pay the tax (or even to borrow to do so) so the entire amount ($100,000 in this illustration) can continue to grow tax-free. The opposite assumption is used here to make the analysis comparable.

od of tax-deferred or tax-free growth must be the same for both scenarios at the beginning and end of the period.

However, as was stated in note 20 and earlier, it normally is not good planning to take the tax on conversion from the IRA proceeds.[21] Therefore, let us change the previous example to assume that Henry converts the entire $100,000 traditional IRA to the Roth IRA and uses other non-tax-advantaged assets to pay the $30,000 tax due. In this case, the Roth would grow *tax-free* at 8 percent to $466,096 in 20 years. However, the $30,000 of assets used to pay the tax on conversion also would have grown during this period, but at an *after-tax* average annual rate of 5.60 percent. This $30,000 at 5.60 percent would have equaled $89,207 in 20 years. Thus, if we subtract this amount from the Roth balance, we have $466,096 − $89,207 (accumulated after-tax value of tax) = $376,889.

This analysis shows an inherent advantage of the Roth IRA, either converted or earnings-related. The foregone tax payment (or deduction) in effect grows *tax-free* inside the Roth IRA (at 8 percent here), while it would have grown at an *after-tax rate* (5.60 percent here) outside the Roth. This will always favor the Roth as long as the assumptions are held constant.

However, an even greater inherent advantage of the Roth is that the mandatory distribution rules for traditional IRAs do not apply to Roth IRAs during the owner's lifetime. Thus, in the previous example, Henry would have to start taking distributions from the traditional IRA—and paying tax on them—at age 70½. From that point on, the funds would be out of the IRA and, assuming they were reinvested, could earn only the assumed after-tax return of 5.60 percent.[22] On the other hand, the funds in the Roth IRA could remain intact and continue to earn a tax-free return of 8 percent until Henry's death (at which time the minimum distribution rules relating to beneficiaries would apply).

Factors in Choosing Which IRA. Given the inherent advantages of Roth IRAs just described, there are a number of other factors that might be considered in this choice. First, let us consider for earnings-related contributions the choice between a Roth IRA and a traditional IRA.

Relationship of Tax Rates at Time of Contribution and (Assumed) Rates at

---

[21] Correspondingly, one normally should contribute the full amount possible (up to $3,000 or $6,000 in 2003) to an earnings-related Roth IRA even though it is not deductible. The money to cover the foregone tax deduction must come from other, non-tax-advantaged sources. The principle is the same.

[22] Under the minimum distribution rules, Henry would be required to take the account balance from the traditional IRA in minimum annual amounts at least as determined by the IRS's Uniform Table for Determining Distribution Periods. The minimum distribution rules for qualified plans and IRAs are described in Chapter 20.

Distribution. The same rates cause a wash, as just illustrated, except that the inherent advantages of Roth IRAs tilt the decision in their favor. Lower rates at time of contribution than assumed at time of distribution favor the Roth. The reverse favors the traditional. One may well wonder, however, how anyone can predict with any degree of confidence what tax rates will be 10, 20, 30, 40, or even more years from now. The authors certainly cannot. It is even difficult to say that income tax rates during retirement many years in the future will be lower than rates during active employment.

Length of Time Until Distribution from IRA. In terms of the basic equality described previously, it does not make any difference. However, the longer this time period, the greater is the inherent deferral advantage of Roth IRAs.

Rate of Investment Return on IRA Assets. Again, in terms of the basic equality, this factor is neutral as long as the same investment returns (and tax rates) are assumed for both types of IRAs. However, higher rates increase the inherent tax-free advantages of Roth IRAs.

Need for IRA Assets for Retirement Income (or Before Death). This shortens the deferral period and so lessens the inherent advantages of Roths.

Qualifying for and Financing the IRA. The eligibility and contribution rules differ for these two types of IRAs. Also, it is easier from a cash flow point of view to make a full contribution each year to a traditional IRA than to a Roth IRA because of the current income tax deduction for contributions to the traditional.

With respect to converting from a traditional IRA to a Roth IRA, the decision factors just noted are essentially the same except that their relative importance may vary. There also are some other factors affecting whether or not to convert.

Meeting the $100,000 Income Threshold for Conversion. This will be a problem for some traditional IRA owners. If conversion is desired, the issue becomes planning for a year in which the person's or married couple's MAGI is $100,000 or less.

Financing a Conversion. This involves paying the income tax on the traditional IRA. The entire tax is due for the year of conversion. This may pose a cash drain problem for taxpayers.

Making Gifts So Family Members Can Contribute to IRAs

Parents or others may wish to make gifts to their children or other family members who have earned income to enable them to contribute to their own IRAs. This probably would be to Roth IRAs, since a tax deduction would be relatively insignificant for lower-income taxpayers. These gifts normally would fall within the annual gift tax exclusion of $11,000 (indexed) per year per donee and hence no taxable gift would result.

Investing IRA Funds

Another planning issue is how to invest IRA money. First, IRA investments should fit into the overall asset allocation strategy. Second, from a tax point of view, the factors presented in Chapter 12 concerning the ways investments should be held are applicable to this planning issue, at least with respect to traditional IRAs.

The main difference may lie with respect to Roth IRAs. Since distributions from Roth IRAs are tax-free, all investment returns inside a Roth come out income tax-free to the owner or, when he or she dies, to his or her beneficiary. The effect of this is much like the step-up in basis rule for directly owned capital assets at the owner's death. Hence, assets that may produce long-term capital gains on this basis would be more attractive in a Roth than in a traditional IRA. However, from a tax perspective, it still may be preferable to hold long-term capital gain assets directly.

Use of IRAs for Qualified First-Time Homebuyer Distributions or Qualified Higher Education Expenses

As noted earlier, distributions for these purposes from a traditional IRA will not be subject to the 10 percent tax on premature distributions. However, they will be subject to regular tax as ordinary income. Also, a first-time homebuyer distribution is a qualified tax-free distribution from a Roth IRA. However, such distributions take otherwise tax-deferred or tax-free funds from the IRA. Also, if it is a traditional IRA, the distributions result in current taxation. Hence, it seems better to finance these needs from other sources if possible.

Naming the IRA Beneficiary or Beneficiaries

There is a more extensive discussion of this issue for IRAs and qualified retirement plans in the next chapter.

Planning Distributions from IRAs

Planning for distributions from IRAs and qualified retirement plans is discussed in the next chapter.

20

Planning for Taking Distributions from Qualified Retirement Plans and IRAs

Chapter 17 described the various kinds of qualified retirement plans and Chapter 19 dealt with IRAs. This chapter discusses how and when benefits should be taken from these plans.

A person or a couple may need to plan for taking benefits from these plans in one or more of the following circumstances:

- While a participant is still employed (i.e., is *in service*)
- If a participant separates from one employer's service prior to retirement
- When a participant retires
- When a participant or IRA owner dies

General Considerations
The Person's or Couple's Objectives for Plan Benefits

Objectives for plan benefits may include the following:

- To provide a *secure lifetime retirement income* for the person *and* his or her spouse (if any)
- To *provide capital* for investment, business, or other reasons
- To accumulate capital tax-deferred or tax-free for as long as possible in order to pass it on to heirs
- To accumulate capital tax-deferred or tax-free to allow maximum *future flexibility* in the use of the funds as retirement income or for estate planning purposes as future conditions may dictate
- To *avoid penalty taxes* and to *reduce other taxes* to the greatest extent feasible, consistent with other objectives

■ To keep funds in qualified retirement plans (and perhaps in IRAs, depending on state law) for *creditor protection*

What the Plan Allows

Persons and their advisors must look to the provisions of their particular plan to determine their rights and benefits under that plan. In some cases, a participant or IRA owner or his or her advisor might want to take a particular action, but the plan documents may not permit it.

The Person's or Couple's Resources and Need for Income

If benefits are needed to provide current retirement income, they must be taken in a fashion that will produce adequate income. On the other hand, if there are other substantial resources or income, planning horizons certainly are broader.

The Person's Health

This may affect planning in several ways. For example, a person in poor health would not want to take retirement benefits as a life annuity if alternatives are available or would elect an annuity form with substantial survivors' benefits.

Money Management Considerations

People vary in the extent to which they want or are able to manage the funds behind their retirement benefits. Some methods of distribution imply active management by the recipient (such as a transfer to a self-directed IRA or a lump-sum distribution), while others do not (such as taking a life annuity). Another aspect of this consideration may be concern in a few cases over the solvency of financial institutions (funding agencies) holding retirement plan assets. People who are concerned on this score may want to transfer their retirement funds into a rollover IRA with a more secure institution.

Income Tax Deferral

As a general principle, participants and IRA owners want to keep their retirement assets inside a qualified retirement plan or IRA as long as possible, to take advantage of the deferral of income taxes (or tax-free growth in the case of Roth IRAs). This normally makes good tax sense, but it may run counter to other considerations, such as a need for current retirement income.

Avoiding Penalty Taxes

There are two penalty taxes that may apply to distributions from qualified and other retirement plans or IRAs: a 10 percent tax on premature distributions and a 50 percent tax on insufficient distributions (i.e., that do not conform to the minimum distribution rules). These penalty taxes are described later in this chapter. In planning retirement plan distributions, the 50 percent tax should always be avoided, while the 10 percent tax should be avoided (or reduced) if possible.

Meeting Retirement Equity Act of 1984 (REA) Rules

As explained in Chapter 17, a married participant in a *qualified pension plan* must have his or her plan benefits payable in accordance with the REA rules, unless the participant waives them with the informed consent of his or her spouse. Further, a married participant in a *qualified profit-sharing plan, savings plan, or stock bonus plan* must either meet the REA requirements for an exemption or have the benefits payable in accordance with the REA rules, unless waived with the spouse's consent. The REA rules do not apply to IRAs.

Estate Planning Considerations

In some cases, estate planning considerations become quite important in determining how qualified plan and IRA death benefits are to be arranged.

Creditor Protection

Assets held in qualified retirement plans have a protected status with regard to claims by a participant's creditors. This includes contract claims and tort liability claims. These assets currently are excludible from a participant's bankruptcy estate. Whether assets in an IRA are so excludible depends on applicable federal or state exemption statutes.

Of course, funds withdrawn from these plans are fully subject to creditors' claims. Therefore, participants or IRA owners who may be subject to such claims may give serious consideration to this issue before withdrawing funds from qualified plans or even IRAs.

Taxation of Benefits from Qualified Plans and IRAs

The taxation of benefits from qualified retirement plans and IRAs is a complex subject. Only the general principles will be covered here.

Federal Income Tax on Distributions

The general principle underlying federal income taxation of payments from qualified retirement plans and traditional IRAs is simple. To the extent such payments come from money in the plan that was not previously taxed (i.e., employer contributions, before-tax employee contributions, deductible IRA contributions, and investment earnings on plan assets), they should be taxed to the participant (or owner) or his or her beneficiary when they are finally paid out from the plan. To the extent that payments come from money that has already been taxed (generally after-tax employee contributions and non-deductible IRA contributions), they should be excluded from gross income when finally paid out as benefits. On the other hand, qualified distributions from Roth IRAs are entirely income tax-free.

Periodic Income from Qualified Plans. Employees frequently take benefits at retirement from defined-benefit (DB) pension plans in the form of a periodic lifetime income for themselves or for themselves and their spouses. They sometimes also use their account balances under defined-contribution (DC) plans to similarly provide lifetime incomes or to be paid out in periodic installments of a fixed amount or over a fixed period of years. As a general principle, periodic distributions are subject to the rules governing the taxation of annuities (in Section 72 of the IRC). However, there are special provisions applicable to qualified retirement plans.

Under the *general annuity rule,* the taxable part of any annuity or installment payment is determined by excluding the part of the payment that is attributable to the employee's own net investment in the plan (cost basis), if any. This is done by calculating an *exclusion ratio* as of the annuity starting date and then multiplying this exclusion ratio by the periodic distribution. This determines the nontaxable or excluded amount. The exclusion ratio basically is the annuitant's net investment in the plan (cost basis) divided by his or her expected return from the plan.

However, for life annuity and installment payments from qualified retirement plans and tax-sheltered annuities (TSAs), special rules apply, depending on when annuity payments started or will start. Under the most recent rule, which sometimes is referred to as the *modified simplified general rule,* when the annuity starting date is after December 31, 1997,[1] the nontaxable portion of each annuity payment is determined by dividing the annuitant's investment in

---

[1] Other rules apply in each case when the annuity starting date was after November 18, 1996, but before January 1, 1998, or was after July 1, 1986, but before November 19, 1996, or was on or before July 1, 1986. There have been numerous changes in this area and these are transition rules. Also, this simplified rule does not apply when the annuitant is age 75 or more on the annuity starting date, unless there are fewer than five years of guaranteed payments.

the contract (if any) by a factor from federal tables that is based only on a single annuitant's age or on their combined ages if the annuity is payable over two or more lives. For a fixed number of installment payments, the number of monthly payments is used as the divisor.

As an example, suppose Mary Riley is a participant in a DB pension plan to which she has made after-tax contributions of $32,500 over the years. She is 65 and her husband is 68. Mary is retiring this year and will receive a joint and 50 percent survivor life annuity for herself and her husband of $3000 per month while she is alive and, if her husband should survive her, reducing to $1500 per month for her husband's remaining lifetime (i.e., a QJSA annuity form). Under these assumptions, Mary can exclude $125 per month from her pension income. This is determined by dividing her net investment in the contract ($32,500) by 260 from the federal tables.[2] The remainder ($2875 per month) will be taxable as ordinary income.

Under the annuity rules (both the general annuity rule and the special rules for qualified plans), an annuitant generally can recover only his or her net investment in the contract tax-free. After that is done, all future payments are fully taxable. Thus, in the previous example, after Mary recovers her $32,500 basis tax-free, the entire $3000 monthly pension will be gross income to her. However, if Mary and her husband should die before the $32,500 basis is recovered tax-free, the unrecovered amount will be deductible on the final income tax return of the last of them to die.

Distributions from IRAs. As in the case of qualified plans, traditional IRA owners can recover any investment in the contract (nondeductible contributions) tax-free, but other distributions are taxable as ordinary income. In taxing partial distributions from traditional IRAs, the general annuity rules of Section 72 generally apply. All traditional IRAs owned by a person are treated as one contract for this purpose. Any excludable portion of a distribution is determined by dividing the owner's net investment in the contracts by the expected return from the contracts (the IRA account balances plus certain adjustments), and then multiplying this fraction (if any) by the amount of the distribution. The remainder is gross income. As with qualified plans, an owner can recover only the amount of his or her basis. Qualified distributions from Roth IRAs are income tax-free.

Net Investment (Basis) in the Plan or Contract. An employee's net investment in a qualified retirement plan may include the following:

- Any after-tax employee contributions to the plan
- The total term cost of any pure life insurance protection on the employee's

---

[2] This is the factor to be used when the combined ages of the annuitants is between 130 and 140; in this case, the ages are 65 + 68 = 133.

life provided by the plan that had been previously taxed to the employee

- The amount of any plan loans that the employee repaid but had been previously taxed to him or her (e.g., loans that did not meet the requirements for nontaxable plan loans)
- Any employer contributions that for some reason had been previously taxed to the employee.

Then, from this amount an employee must subtract any nontaxable distributions previously received from the plan and any unrepaid plan loans. The result is the employee's net investment in the plan.

A traditional IRA owner's investment in the contract is any nondeductible contributions.

Plans in Which Participants and Owners Have No Basis. In many cases, participants and traditional IRA owners will have no investment (basis) in the plan or contract. Thus, as a practical matter, distributions from many plans will be entirely taxable as ordinary income.

Planning Issues Regarding Periodic Distributions. It can be seen that one way to spread out the income tax on plan distributions is to take them over a substantial period of time. On the other hand, there may be arguments against taking benefits as periodic distributions. These planning issues are explored later in this chapter.

Lump-Sum Distributions. Many pension plans and virtually all profit-sharing, savings, and stock bonus plans permit participants or their beneficiaries to take their benefits as a lump-sum distribution.

Definition of a Lump-Sum Distribution. A *lump-sum distribution* is a distribution made to a participant or his or her beneficiary from a qualified retirement plan of the employee's entire account balance or interest in the plan within one taxable year of the recipient. The distribution must be made on account of certain triggering events: (1) the employee has separated from the employer, including through retirement, (2) the employee has attained age 59½, or (3) the employee has died. (For self-employed persons, these triggering events are attaining age 59½, death, or becoming disabled.)

In determining whether there has been a distribution of the entire account balance or interest in the plan, all qualified plans of the same type maintained by the employer for the employee must be considered together as one plan. For the purpose, all pension plans are one type of plan, all profit-sharing plans are another type of plan, and all stock bonus plans are still another type.

Thus, for example, suppose an employer maintains a DB pension plan and a savings plan for its employees and John Jones is covered by both plans. John is retiring. He could decide to receive a life annuity from the pension plan and still take his entire account balance from the savings plan as a lump-sum distribution.

Taxable Amount of a Lump-Sum Distribution. To determine the taxable amount of a lump-sum distribution, certain items are subtracted from the total distribution. These items may include:

1. The employee's own after-tax contributions (less any previous nontaxable distributions).

2. The net unrealized appreciation (NUA) on any employer securities included in the lump-sum distribution (i.e., the difference between the fair market value of the securities at distribution and their cost or other basis to the plan). A number of qualified retirement plans, particularly profit-sharing, savings, stock bonus, and employee stock ownership plans, may invest at least part of plan assets in employer securities (e.g., common stock of the employer) and may distribute such securities to employees or their beneficiaries as part of a lump-sum distribution. When this is done, the employee (or beneficiary) can deduct the amount by which the employer securities have appreciated in value in the hands of the plan;[3] however, the income tax basis of the employer securities in the hands of the employee is their value when they were contributed to or purchased by the plan (a carryover basis).[4]

3. The term cost of any life insurance protection the employee previously included in his or her income.

4. Repayments of any plan loans that previously were included in the employee's gross income.

5. The actuarial value of any annuity contracts that are included in the lump-sum distribution.

Decision Factors Concerning Lump-Sum Distributions. If a participant decides to take a lump-sum distribution, he or she still has to decide whether to pay the income tax currently on the taxable amount (perhaps with some favorable tax features) or to directly transfer part or all of the distribution into a traditional IRA or into another qualified plan that will accept such transfers.

Many people opt to defer further through direct transfer. This option is discussed later in this chapter. However, there may be circumstances favoring taking a lump-sum distribution and paying the tax currently. These might include

---

[3] The net unrealized appreciation on employer securities attributable to employer contributions and the earnings on employer and any employee contributions generally is excludible only in the case of a lump-sum distribution. The NUA on employer securities attributable to any employee contributions is excludible from any distribution.

[4] A recipient of employer securities may elect to waive this exclusion of NUA.

when the distribution is relatively small, when 10-year forward averaging and capital gain treatment applies under a transition rule for persons who were 50 or older on January 1, 1986,[5] and when a substantial portion of a distribution consists of highly appreciated employer securities. It must be remembered, however, that the 10 percent penalty tax on premature distributions also may apply to taxable lump-sum distributions.

Options for Taxing Lump-Sum Distributions for Employees 50 or Older on January 1, 1986. These choices include (1) paying tax on the entire taxable amount as ordinary income at current income tax rates, (2) using a one-time 10-year averaging method using 1986 ordinary income tax rates, and (3) paying a flat 20 percent capital gains tax on the pre-1974 portion of the taxable amount and using 10-year averaging for the remainder.

Lump-Sum Distributions Containing Employer Securities. As already explained, the NUA on employer securities in a lump-sum distribution is not taxed currently to the recipient. A participant's basis in the distributed securities is the same as their basis in the plan. Thus, when the participant subsequently sells the securities, the NUA and any subsequent gain (or loss) are subject to capital gains taxation. The NUA is considered long-term capital gain, while any subsequent gain (or loss) is either short-term or long-term, depending on how long the participant has held the securities since distribution. Upon a participant's death, the NUA does not get a stepped-up income tax basis. Instead, it is treated as income in respect of a decedent (IRD) to a plan beneficiary who receives the securities in a lump-sum distribution or to the recipient of the securities under the participant's will. The IRD is realized and recognized as long-term capital gain when the beneficiary or heir sells the securities.

Thus, the advantages of taking employer securities in a lump-sum distribution are that the tax on the NUA is deferred until the securities are finally sold (either by the participant or his or her heirs) and that the NUA is converted from ordinary income to a long-term capital gain. But the price for these advantages is that tax, at ordinary income rates, must be paid on part of the distribution immediately.

Whether a lump-sum distribution or, alternatively, a direct transfer to a traditional IRA is best depends on the circumstances. The factors determining which will provide greater after-tax results are the proportion of employer securities in the distribution, the extent of NUA, taxable assets in the distribu-

---

[5] There also had been a five-year forward averaging rule available in certain circumstances. However, five-year forward averaging has been repealed for tax years beginning after 1999.

If the designated beneficiary is other than the spouse, certain minimum distribution incidental benefit (MDIB) rules must be met. There also are special rules for period certain guarantees.

tion, how and at what after-tax rate of return the securities and other assets will be invested once they are outside the plan, the after-tax opportunity cost for tax currently paid, an assumption about how long the employer securities will be held before they are sold and the capital gains tax rate at sale, the period of deferral for the traditional IRA, whether the traditional IRA can or will be converted to a Roth IRA, and whether the 10 percent tax on premature distributions will apply to the taxable part of the lump-sum distribution. Clearly, this is a complex analysis. Advisors may use computer programs to help in this decision.

Example of a Lump-Sum Distribution Containing Employer Securities. Suppose that Mary Johnson, age 60, has been employed by a rapidly growing corporation, the XYZ Company, for many years. She is a participant in the company's savings plan with a Section 401(k) option. Her total account balance in the plan is $685,000 and she has no investment (basis) in the plan. All of her employer's matching contributions have been invested in XYZ common stock (employer securities). Mary's elective contributions have been divided equally between XYZ stock and a bond fund. XYZ stock is publicly traded and has grown rapidly in value over the years. The current value of XYZ stock in Mary's account balance is $575,000 and it has a total basis to the plan (purchase price by the plan or value when contributed to the plan) of $120,000. The other $110,000 is in the bond fund.

Mary is retiring this year. If she takes a lump-sum distribution of the entire account balance in the savings plan (the only profit-sharing type plan provided by XYZ) and is in the 35 percent tax bracket, her income tax liability on the distribution will be as follows:

Total Lump-Sum Distribution	$685,000
Less:	
Employee's investment (basis) in plan	0
Net unrealized appreciation (NUA) on employer securities ($575,000 - $120,000)	-$455,000
Taxable amount	$230,000
Tax on the distribution (at 35%)	$80,800

Assuming Mary pays this tax from the proceeds of the bond fund, she will have $575,000 of XYZ stock with an income tax basis to her of $120,000 (the plan's basis on which she paid tax) and $29,500 in cash ($110,000 - $80,500 tax paid on the distribution). The XYZ stock may, of course, either increase or decrease in value in the future. Mary may sell or otherwise dispose of the stock during her lifetime or hold it until her death and pass it to her heirs by will. At death, however, the NUA does not get a step-up in basis.

Alternatively, Mary could transfer the $685,000 account balance or part of it to a traditional IRA with no current tax liability. She then could withdraw from the IRA as she needs funds or continue to defer until her RBD (age 70½) and start taking distributions then. But all distributions from the IRA will be taxed as ordinary income. Mary might also convert the traditional IRA to a Roth IRA if she is eligible to do so.

Direct Transfers or Rollovers to an IRA or Another Qualified Plan. This may be done by either (1) having the participant's employer *transfer directly* all or part of the distribution to a traditional IRA or to another employer's qualified retirement plan that will accept such transfers or (2) having the distribution paid to the participating employee, who then *rolls over* all or part of the distribution into an IRA or another employer's qualified plan within 60 days of receipt of the distribution. While this distinction may seem technical, the approach makes a considerable difference un terms of the income tax effect.

For this purpose, an eligible rollover distribution is any distribution of all or any portion of the balance to the credit of the employee in a qualified retirement plan (or tax-sheltered annuity), except that it does not include distributions made as substantially equal periodic payments over the lifetime (or life expectancy) of the employee or the lifetimes (or life expectancies) of the employee and his or her designated beneficiary or distributions for a specified period of 10 years or more or distributions required to satisfy the minimum distribution rules. Direct transfers and rollovers can be made regardless of an employee's age, are available for any number of eligible distributions, and are not subject to any dollar limit on the amount that can be transferred or rolled over. There also is no triggering events requirement. Any part or all of an employee's balance in the plan can be an eligible rollover distribution. Under EGTRRA, the entire amount of an eligible distribution may be transferred to a traditional IRA or qualified plan, including any employee after-tax contributions, if the qualified plan agrees to separately track the after-tax contributions and their earnings.

To the extent that an otherwise taxable distribution is directly transferred or rolled over, it is not currently taxable and will be taxed only when paid out to the employee or his or her beneficiary from the traditional IRA or other plan. However, there is a mandatory 20 percent income tax withholding requirement applicable to eligible rollover distributions, except when the participant elects to have the distribution directly transferred. Thus, a rollover is subject to mandatory 20 percent withholding, while a direct transfer is not. This distinction strongly favors direct transfers over rollovers.

In the event a *surviving spouse* of a deceased participant in a qualified retirement plan receives an eligible rollover distribution from the plan, the spouse also may directly transfer or roll the distribution over to the spouse's own traditional IRA or to another qualified retirement plan, TSA, or Section 457 plan in which the spouse participates. However, aside from a surviving spouse, no other beneficiary of qualified retirement plan death benefits can avail themselves of this transfer or rollover treatment.

Penalty Tax on Premature Distributions. To discourage withdrawals from tax-advantaged retirement plans prior to retirement, the tax law imposes an additional 10 percent excise tax on the taxable portion of distributions from such plans made prior to age 59½, subject to certain exceptions. This 10 percent penalty tax is in addition to the regular income tax paid.

For qualified retirement plans, aside from reaching age 59½, the other *exceptions* to the imposition of this tax include (1) distributions made on or after the employee's death, (2) distributions due to an employee's disability, (3) payments made as substantially equal periodic benefits for the lifetime or life expectancy of the employee (or for the joint lives or joint life expectancies of the employee and his or her beneficiary), (4) distributions to an employee after attaining age 55 upon separation from service, (5) distributions to an employee for deductible medical expenses, (6) distributions to persons (alternate payees) under qualified domestic relations orders (QDROs), and (7) certain other distributions.

This 10 percent tax applies to qualified retirement plans, tax-sheltered annuity (TSA) plans, and IRAs. Note that the exceptions for IRAs are somewhat different from those just outlined. TSAs also have some differences in their exceptions.

Required Beginning Date (RBD) and Minimum Distribution Rules. The tax law requires that persons participating in qualified retirement plans, traditional IRAs, TSAs, and Section 457 government deferred-compensation plans must meet certain minimum distribution rules. There are three elements in determining the minimum amounts that must be distributed: the required beginning date, the amount of the IRA owner's or plan participant's benefit in the plan as of the valuation date, and the minimum required distribution periods (or divisors) for employees' or owners' ages according to the IRS's Uniform Lifetime Table. There also are special rules when an owner's or participant's spouse is the plan beneficiary. It is important to comply with these rules, because there is a 50 percent penalty tax on the difference between what was actually distributed in a given year and what should have been distributed under the minimum distribution rules. This is called the *penalty tax on insufficient distributions.*

Required Beginning Date (RBD). Distributions from *qualified retirement plans* to participants generally must begin by the later of April 1 of the calendar year following the calendar year in which the person attains age 70½ or April 1 of the calendar year following the calendar year in which the person retires (but this retirement date applies only if the participant is not a more than 5 percent owner of the sponsoring employer). Distributions from *traditional IRAs* to owners must begin no later than April 1 of the calendar year following the calendar year in which the owner attains age 70½.

Distributions Before the RBD. Before the RBD, distributions can be taken or not at the discretion of the participant or IRA owner.

Benefit Amount and Valuation Date. For qualified individual account plans (e.g., profit-sharing plans, savings plans, and money purchase pension plans), the benefit for calculating the minimum distribution is the *account balance* of the plan as of the last valuation date in the calendar year preceding the calendar year of the distribution (with certain adjustments). For traditional IRAs, the benefit amount is the account balance on December 31 of the calendar year preceding the calendar year of the distribution.

Minimum Distribution Rules for Distributions At and After the RBD and Before Death. On April 17, 2002, the IRS published final regulations that greatly simplified and made more liberal for taxpayers the rules for taking minimum distributions from qualified retirement plans, TSAs, Section 457 government deferred-compensation plans, and traditional IRAs. Under these rules, once an IRA owner or plan participant reaches the RBD, he or she must begin taking a minimum distribution each year from the plans just noted.

The *minimum amount* that must be distributed from a plan (whose benefits are not paid as a life annuity) *for the first required distribution year* (the calendar year in which a plan participant attains age 70½, or has retired or an IRS's owner attains age 70½ or the "70½ year") is determined by dividing the owner's or participant's benefit in the plan (the account balance as of the valuation date for qualified plans or the account balance as of December 31 for IRAs of the year prior to the distribution year) by the distribution period (or applicable divisor) from the IRS's Uniform Lifetime Table for the owner's or participant's age at the end of the distribution year. For example, this period (divisor) is 27.4 for age 70 and 26.5 for age 71.

For years *after the first distribution year*, the minimum distribution must be taken by December 31 of that year and is determined by dividing the owner's or participant's benefit in the plan as of the prior year by the applicable period (divisor) for the owner's or participant's age at the end of the current year.[6] A

[6] This means there may be a doubling-up of distributions in the calendar year after the first distribution year ("the 70½ year" or retirement year) if the participant or owner delays taking the distribution for the first distribution year until April 1 of the next year. Since this will bunch taxable income in that year, it may be better, depending on the circumstances, to plan on taking the first distributions by December 31 of the first distribution year rather than waiting until April 1 of the next year.

distribution period is given in the IRS table for each age up to 115 and over. These periods gradually diminish with age. Aside from the exception to be noted next, the periods (divisors) to be used for minimum distribution calculations during the IRA owner's or plan participant's lifetime are not affected by the IRA's or plan's beneficiary designation. On the other hand, after the owner or participant dies, the minimum required distributions of any remaining account balances are determined by the beneficiary designation.

The exception just noted is when the owner or participant names his or her spouse, who is *more than* 10 years younger than the owner or participant, as the sole primary plan beneficiary. In this case, their actual joint life expectancies each year can be used to calculate the minimum required distributions as long as both are alive. This will produce lower required minimum distributions than the IRS Uniform Lifetime Table.

Defined-Benefit Plans and the Minimum Distribution Rules. For defined-benefit plans with benefits payable as a *life income (life annuity)*, the minimum distribution rules will be met by level payments made at least annually, commencing on or before the RBD, and over the life of the participant or the joint and survivor lives of the participant and his or her spouse as designated beneficiary.[7]

Illustration of Minimum Distribution Rules for Individual Account Plans During an Owner's or Participant's Lifetime. It may be helpful at this point to illustrate these rules with a common situation. Suppose Martin and Sara Wilson are married and Martin retired eight years ago when he was 62 and Sara was 57. Sara is a self-employed consulting engineer and Martin had been an executive for a large corporation. Since Martin retired, they have had more than adequate income from Social Security, a joint and 50 percent to the survivor life income from Martin's defined-benefit pension plan, current returns from their investment portfolios, and Sara's consulting work. Martin also was a participant in a qualified savings plan with a Section 401(k) option (in which he has no cost basis) with an account balance at his retirement of $280,000. Sara and Martin have one son and three grandchildren to whom they would like to leave as much of their assets as possible after they die.

When he retired, Martin transferred the entire $280,000 savings plan balance to a traditional IRA and named Sara designated beneficiary of the IRA.[8]

[7] If the designated beneficiary is other than the spouse, certain minimum distribution incidental benefit (MDIB) rules must be met. There also are special rules for period certain guarantees.

[8] Note that, unlike the situation for the qualified savings plan, the REA does not apply to an IRA; therefore, Martin could name anyone as beneficiary of his IRA. In this situation, however, he decided to name his spouse. This has many advantages for both qualified plans and IRAs. However, it also means the spouse will have complete control over the funds after the owner's death. This is something to consider in planning. Its importance depends on the circumstances—state of the marriage, children from prior marriages, and so forth.

The IRA has had an average annual total rate of return of about 8 percent per year over the last eight years. The account balance as of December 31, 2002 (the valuation date) was $518,260 (say $518,000).

Martin turned 70 on February 1, 2003 and Sara turned 65 on March 5, 2003. Martin's RBD is April 1, 2004 and his first required distribution year (70½ year) is 2003. The first required minimum distribution for 2003 would be determined by dividing the IRA account balance as of the valuation date (December 31 of the preceding year), which was $518,000, by the Uniform Table divisor for age 70 (Martin's age at the end of 2003), which is 27.4. Note that Sara's age does not affect the divisor because she is not more than 10 years younger than Martin.[9] Thus, the minimum distribution for 2003 is $18,905 ($518,000 ÷ 27.4) and the account balance on December 31, 2003 (assuming an 8 percent total return for all of 2003) would be $540,535 ($518,000 + $41,440 investment return - $18,905 minimum distribution). The minimum distribution for the next year (2004) will be $20,398 ($540,535 ÷ 26.5) and the account balance on December 31, 2004 would be $563,380 ($540,535 + $43,243 investment return - $20,398 minimum distribution).[10]

This procedure can be carried out over a long period of time during Martin's lifetime. Computer programs are available to show this under various assumptions and financial institutions (e.g., the custodian for Martin's IRA) normally will perform these calculations for their customers. Depending on investment yields, the value of an account normally will continue to grow for a number of years after the RBD, until eventually it will begin to decline because of the constantly declining divisors and hence increasing minimum distributions required.

Designated Beneficiaries. A *designated beneficiary* is any identifiable individual designated by a participant or owner to receive any remaining plan benefits after he or she dies. The beneficiary may be any person or persons.[11] But if a participant is married and names anyone other than his or her spouse, the proper waiver and spousal consent requirements of REA must be observed if REA applies to the plan.

A *trust* can be named to receive any remaining plan benefits after a participant's or owner's death, with an individual trust beneficiary being considered

---

[9] But if we were to change the facts and say that Sara is age 50 in 2003, then the divisor would be based on their actual joint life expectancies each year from the IRS Joint and Last Survivor Table. This divisor for a person age 70 and another person age 50 is 35.1. This divisor would be recalculated each year Martin and Sara are alive.

[10] Under the minimum distribution rules, Martin could defer taking the first distribution until April 1, 2004, but for the reasons given in note 6, let us assume he takes his minimum distribution for each year as of December 31 of that year.

the designated beneficiary, provided the trust meets certain requirements. These are (1) the trust must be valid under applicable state law; (2) the trust must be irrevocable or, by its terms, become irrevocable at the participant's or owner's death; (3) the trust beneficiaries must be individuals and be identifiable from the trust instrument; and (4) a copy of the trust instrument must be provided to the plan administrator or IRA custodian or a list of beneficiaries with a description of the conditions of their entitlement must be provided.

The significance of being a "designated beneficiary" is that the life expectancy of a designated beneficiary named directly or named as a trust beneficiary of a trust meeting the requirements just stated may be used to determine the required minimum distributions after a participant's or owner's death. That is why designated beneficiaries must be individuals and be identifiable. The rules regarding minimum distributions after death are discussed next. There can be plan beneficiaries who are not "designated beneficiaries," such as charities, a trust that does not meet the above stated requirements, or the participant's or owner's estate. In this case, no life expectancy is used and any remaining account balance must be paid out within five years after the year in which the participant or owner dies (the "five-year rule").

A helpful change made by the IRS regulations is that the identity of a designated beneficiary does not need to be finally determined until September 30 of the calendar year following the year in which the participant or owner dies. This is the point at which the existence or not of a "designated beneficiary" will be determined. The importance of this is that planning actions can be taken after the owner's or participant's death (and before September 30 of the following year) to produce the most appropriate designated beneficiary or beneficiaries for tax-deferral purposes. Such actions may include disclaimers by one or more beneficiaries (disclaimers are covered in Chapter 26), total distributions ("cash-outs") to some beneficiaries (such as charities) before the September 30 date, and account divisions, such as indicated in footnote 11. However, this does not mean that, for example, after the owner or participant dies his or her executor can name one or more new designated beneficiaries. The owner or participant should name the beneficiary or beneficiaries he or she wants. It is

---

[11] If a participant or owner designates multiple beneficiaries, the person with the shortest life expectancy generally is considered the designated beneficiary. A participant or owner also can name a designated beneficiary or beneficiaries by an identifiable status or class, such as children of the participant, provided the beneficiary or beneficiaries themselves are identifiable.

Because of the rules concerning *multiple beneficiaries*, a useful planning technique when there are to be several beneficiaries of an IRA is to request the IRA custodian or trustee to divide the IRA account into sub-accounts or sub-IRAs (within the original IRA) with one sub-account for each beneficiary. Then each beneficiary is the designated beneficiary of his or her sub-account and his or her own life expectancy will govern minimum distributions. This planning approach is discussed later in the chapter.

just that now these planning actions can deal with an existing beneficiary designation. Also, under the present rules, an owner or participant can change the beneficiary designated at any time. This is because minimum distribution calculations during an owner's or participant's lifetime are no longer affected by who is named beneficiary (with the exception of a spouse who is more than 10 years younger). Who is the designated beneficiary affects only minimum distributions after the owner's or participant's death, as explained next.

Minimum Distribution Rules After an Owner's or Participant's Death Before the RBD. In this event, the required minimum distributions depend on whether a surviving spouse is the sole primary designated beneficiary (either directly or as the sole designated beneficiary or trust),[12] someone other than the spouse is the designated beneficiary, or there is no designated beneficiary (e.g., a charity or the decedent's estate is named as beneficiary).

When a *surviving spouse* is sole primary designated beneficiary, the required minimum distributions may begin either by December 31 of the calendar year following the year of the owner's or participant's death or by December 31 of the year in which the decedent would have reached age 70½, whichever is later. The decedent's interest in the plan or IRA may be paid out in annual amounts over the *life expectancy* of the spouse, determined each year from IRS tables. Then, when the spouse dies, any remaining balance may be paid out in annual amounts to his or her estate or a subsequent designated beneficiary over the deceased spouse's life expectancy as of the date of his or her death and subtracting one year for each year thereafter.

When *someone other than the spouse* is designated beneficiary (children, for example), the required minimum distributions must begin no later than December 31 of the calendar year following the owner's or participant's death. Then, the decedent's interest in the plan or IRA may be paid out in annual amounts over the *life expectancy* of the designated beneficiary as of the year after the owner's or participant's death and subtracting one year for each year thereafter.

The rules just stated for people as designated beneficiaries involve the *life expectancy distribution option*. This option requires minimum annual distributions over a beneficiary's life expectancy (i.e., the account balance at the end of the previous year divided by the life expectancy number for the distribution year). This can be a relatively long time and result in considerable income tax deferral. For example, under the IRS Single Life Table, life expectancies are 43.6 years for age 40, 34.2 years for age 50, and 25.2 years for age 60.

---

[12] A spouse is the sole designated beneficiary of a trust when he or she can withdraw all distributions to the trust from the IRA or plan.

On the other hand, when the beneficiary is not a designated beneficiary (i.e., an identifiable individual), a different rule applies. In this case, the decedent's entire interest in the plan must be distributed to the beneficiary by the end of the fifth year following the year of death. This is known as the *five-year rule*. It clearly provides much less opportunity for tax deferral than the life expectancy option.

Minimum Distribution Rules After an Owner's or Participant's Death After the RBD. These are similar to the rules just described but with some differences. When a *surviving spouse* is sole primary designated beneficiary, the required minimum distributions must begin by December 31 of the calendar year following the year of the owner's or participant's death. The decedent's remaining interest in the plan or IRA then may be paid out in annual amounts over the *spouse's life expectancy*, determined each year from the IRS tables. Upon the spouse's death, the treatment is the same as described previously for death before the RBD.

When *someone other than the spouse* is designated beneficiary, minimum distributions must begin by December 31 of the calendar year following the year of the owner's or participant's death and the plan balance may be paid out in annual amounts over the *life expectancy of the designated beneficiary* as of the year after the owner's or participant's death (from the IRS table) and subtracting one year for each year thereafter.

When the beneficiary is *not classified as a designated beneficiary*, distributions must begin by December 31 of the year following the year of death. But in this case the plan balance may be paid out in annual amounts over the *life expectancy of someone the age of the owner or participant* as of the year of his or her death and subtracting one year for each year thereafter.

With regard to the previously discussed minimum distribution rules, it should be noted that an IRA agreement or the provisions of a qualified plan can specify whether the five-year rule or the life expectancy option is to apply or the plan terms can permit either the participant or owner or the beneficiary to choose which rule applies. The right to choose is much better from the owner's and beneficiary's viewpoint, so it is worth checking plan terms on this point.

Also, a designated beneficiary can be named directly or named indirectly as an identifiable beneficiary of a trust meeting the requirements noted earlier. If a trust does not meet these requirements, the five-year rule or the owner or participant age life expectancy rule applies. But if a trust for the spouse is named as beneficiary (even if the spouse is designated beneficiary of the trust), the spouse cannot transfer (roll over) plan benefits to his or her own IRA or treat an IRA as his or her own, as a surviving spouse could if named as the individual designated beneficiary.

Rollover Option for Surviving Spouse Only. When a surviving spouse is sole primary designated beneficiary of a qualified plan or IRA, an alternative to taking distributions under the rules just described for the deceased owner's or participant's account is to transfer or roll over the account balance to the spouse's own traditional IRA or to treat the decedent's IRA as the spouse's IRA. Thus, when a surviving spouse is individual designated beneficiary of a qualified plan interest, he or she can transfer (roll over) to his or her own traditional IRA some or all of the decedent's interest. In this case, the minimum distribution rules apply to the IRA as the spouse's own IRA and hence distributions would not have to begin until the spouse's own RBD (spouse's age 70½). This may be an attractive alternative, particularly if the spouse is younger than the participant. The spouse also could convert such a traditional IRA to a Roth IRA, if he or she is eligible to do so, and then delay distributions from the Roth IRA until he or she died. If we assume, then, that the spouse names, say, a child or children (perhaps with sub-accounts for each child) as designated beneficiary or beneficiaries of the Roth IRA, the IRA balance could be paid annually over the lifetime or life expectancy of the designated beneficiary or beneficiaries. This could allow a long period of tax-free deferral, if that is desired.

Also, if the designated beneficiary of an IRA is the *spouse* of a deceased owner, the surviving spouse may elect to *assume* the IRA and treat it as if it were his or her own or roll it over into another IRA as if the surviving spouse had originally established it. In either event, the minimum distribution rules for IRAs would apply just as for the spouse's own IRA. Thus, the RBD for a traditional IRA would be the surviving spouse's age 70½. Distributions from a Roth IRA would not have to start until the surviving spouse's death and then be payable to a designated beneficiary or beneficiaries as just noted. Also, a spouse could convert a traditional IRA to a Roth IRA if eligible.

Illustration of Minimum Distribution Rules for Individual Account Plans After Owner's or Participants Death. Let us return to our illustration of Martin and Sara Wilson and assume that Martin dies on December 31, 2004 (when he is 71 and Sara is 66). The IRA account balance would be included in his gross estate for federal estate tax purposes, but since Sara is beneficiary, the federal estate tax marital deduction applies and no estate tax actually is due. (See the next section.) Sara decides to assume the IRA and treat it as her own and also names her son, Harry, age 41, as designated beneficiary of her IRA. If this were a traditional IRA, Sara would not have to start taking distributions until her RBD, which would be April 1, 2009 (her 70½ year would be 2008) or a little more than four years later.[13] (On the other hand, if this had been a Roth IRA or had been converted to a Roth IRA, minimum distributions would not have

---

[13] Assume she decides to start taking minimum distributions by December 31 of her 70½ year.

to start until after her death.) Under our 8 percent investment returns assumption, the unwithdrawn traditional IRA's account balance would be $700,132 on December 31, 2007 (the valuation date for 2008).

Sara now must begin taking minimum distributions from her traditional IRA. Just as for Martin when he reached his RBD, her first required minimum distribution for 2008 would be determined by dividing the IRA account balance as of the valuation date of $700,132 by the Uniform Lifetime Table divisor for age 70 (Sara's age at the end of 2008), which is 27.4. Thus, Sara's minimum distribution for 2008 would be $25,552 ($700,132 ÷ 27.4). She then would have to take minimum distributions each year thereafter based on the distribution period for her attained age each year.

Assume Sara lives 15 years more, until she is 85, and then dies without having remarried. Further assume that at the time of Sara's death, the IRA account balance is around $750,000 (given growth due to investment returns and deductions from increasing minimum distributions and other distributions). This amount would be in Sara's gross estate for federal estate tax purposes and there would be no marital deduction. Hence an estate tax would be payable on it, assuming Sara's estate is large enough to be taxable.[14]

Harry is a non-spouse designated beneficiary of this IRA and also is subject to the minimum distribution rules. Thus, by the end of the calendar year following the year of his mother's death, he must begin taking annual distributions from the IRA. These minimum distributions will be measured by Harry's *life expectancy* as of his age the year after his mother died and reduced by one year for each year thereafter. Harry is 58 in the year after his mother's death and his life expectancy (from the IRS table) at age 58 is 27.0 years. In Harry's first distribution year (by December 31 of the year following the year of his mother's death), his minimum distribution would be $750,000 (assuming this is the valuation amount) divided by 27.0 or $27,778. In subsequent years, the life expectancies would be 26.1, 25.1, 24.1 and so on until the IRA account balance had been completely distributed.

The point for planning purposes is that, while these rules are complex, they can result in long periods of tax deferral (or, in the case of Roth IRAs, tax-free growth). In the illustration just given, for example, the deferral and distribution period was for more than 55 years (eight years of deferral until Martin's RBD, two more years of minimum distributions for Martin, four years of deferral until Sara's RBD, 15 more years of minimum distributions for Sara, and then about 26 more years of minimum distributions for Harry). This can

[14] However, we are assuming the tax clause in Sara's will allocates all death taxes to her residuary estate so items like this IRA, which pass outside of her probate estate, will not be reduced (burdened) by the estate tax due on them. Thus, we are assuming the full $750,000 is payable to Harry as designated beneficiary, as would normally be the case in planning for such benefits.

be a very powerful force for tax-deferred (or tax-free, in the case of Roth IRAs) asset growth and is the reason why deferral is given such emphasis in planning. It may also be observed that for much of this time the IRA account balance actually increased because the investment earnings exceeded any minimum distributions required. This, of course, depends on investment experience and remaining life expectancy.

The amounts calculated in this discussion show only the *minimum* required distributions under the tax law. There is, of course, nothing to prevent an IRA owner or qualified plan participant from taking larger distributions or earlier distributions (except the penalty tax on premature distributions) than provided for in these minimum distribution rules.

It also must be recognized that, for estate planning and perhaps other reasons, some owners or participants may not want to name their spouse or another person as individual designated beneficiary. They may want to name a trust or a charity, for example. In this event, there *may* have to be shorter after-death payments and some sacrifice of tax deferral.

Federal Estate Taxation

The full value of any death benefits payable under a qualified retirement plan, TSA, traditional or Roth IRA, or similar plans is includible in the decedent's gross estate for federal estate tax purposes. To the extent that such death benefits are payable to a decedent's surviving spouse (either directly or through a qualifying trust), they will qualify for the marital deduction and be deductible from the gross estate in arriving at the taxable estate. (See Chapters 24 and 26.)

Married persons with estates large enough to need federal estate tax planning may want to have qualified plan and IRA death benefits qualify for the marital deduction. It can be argued that these often are good kinds of property interests to qualify because they generally are *wasting assets* in the sense that they are burdened with an inherent income tax liability at the time of any distribution (except for Roth IRAs) to the surviving spouse that will further reduce the surviving spouse's estate at his or her death. This planning idea really is true of any income in respect of a decedent (IRD) item in the gross estate.

There are several ways these death benefits can be made to qualify for the marital deduction, including making them payable in one of the following ways:

- In a lump sum to the surviving spouse as beneficiary.[15]

[15] Another approach to this issue is to name the spouse as beneficiary and then, after the participant's or owner's death, the spouse at his or her option can *disclaim* (meeting the tax requirements for a valid disclaimer) part or all of the plan benefits, with those benefits then going into a nonmarital trust or other trust. This, in effect, allows the surviving spouse to fund a nonmarital trust or gift if he or she wishes to do so for estate planning reasons. This approach may be particularly useful after EGTRRA.

- As a joint life and last survivor annuity for the participant and his or her spouse, if no person other than the participant and his or her spouse can receive any payments before both have died.
- To a trust that will qualify for the marital deduction.

The planning issues involving these methods are discussed in the final section of this chapter.

Generation-Skipping Transfer (GST) Taxation

In some cases, a generation-skipping transfer (GST) tax might apply to qualified plan or IRA death benefits. The GST tax is described more fully in Chapter 24.

Planning for Distributions from Qualified Retirement Plans and IRAs

Planning for these benefits is an extensive subject and a complete discussion of it is beyond the scope of this book. Only the salient issues are presented here. In doing so, we have divided the issues according to when they apply: while a participant or owner is still in service (working for employer), at separation from service before retirement (as when the person changes jobs or is laid off), at retirement, and at death.

While in Service

Plan participants may face several issues while in service. Some of these have already been discussed. With regard to getting cash from qualified plans while still in service, the choices may be:

- Use of plan loans.
- Possible in-service withdrawals.

While withdrawals may be permitted in some cases, they have lost much of their attraction.

At Separation from Service Prior to Retirement

With regard to vested qualified plan benefits, the choices may be as follows:

- Leave vested benefits in the former employer's plan, if permitted. However, the person's rights to the benefits then will depend on the plan's terms.
- Take a lump-sum distribution and pay income tax on the distribution currently. This option will be discussed more fully in the next section.

- Elect a direct transfer to a traditional IRA, a new employer's qualified plan (if that plan accepts such transfers), or another eligible plan. This also is covered more fully in the next section.

At Retirement

Again, many planning issues face the former employee (and his or her spouse, if any). With regard to qualified plan and IRA benefits at retirement, there may be the following choices.

Receiving Periodic Annuity Income (and What Annuity Form to Select). Many plans contemplate the taking of retirement benefits as a life annuity or a joint life and last survivor annuity. There are two basic planning issues in this area: (1) whether to take benefits as a life income or as a lump sum (if available) and, (2) if a life income is desired, selecting the annuity form.

Advantages of Lifetime Annuity Income.
- Security of income for life. This is one of the basic purposes of a pension plan. Also, if a joint life and last survivor annuity form is chosen, a lifetime income can be guaranteed for the retiring employee or IRA owner and his or her spouse. It gives them an income they cannot outlive.
- The retiree may be able to secure relatively generous life annuity rates from a pension plan or perhaps even under a defined-contribution plan. On the other hand, the reverse also may be true. This factor simply must be evaluated in each case, based on comparing the annuity income from the plan and what can be received or earned on a lump sum outside the plan after taxes.
- For married retirees, this is the form of pension plan benefit mandated by the REA (a QJSA) unless the employee waives it and his or her spouse consents in the proper form.
- Some employers make voluntary increases for inflation in lifetime pension benefits. If benefits are taken as a lump sum, such adjustments will be lost in the future.
- The retiree may need the largest available current income to make retirement financially feasible.
- The retiree and his or her spouse are relieved of the need to make investment decisions concerning lump-sum distributions.

Limitations of Lifetime Annuity Income.
- The *annuity risk* is perhaps the most important disadvantage, since there is a loss of capital when the retired employee or spouse dies. Therefore, a person or couple, in making this decision, might want to compare the after-tax annuity income with the after-tax investment yield they can conservatively

withdraw from a rollover IRA or the after-tax return on the after-tax capital that would result from a lump-sum distribution. Further, they might evaluate the return while they are alive and what would remain for their beneficiaries after their deaths.

■ Loss of flexibility (investment, withdrawal, etc.) inherent in taking a lifetime annuity income.

■ Loss of possible tax advantages of a lump-sum distribution.

■ The retiree and his or her spouse will be dependent on the financial soundness of the funding agency (a pension trust or life insurance company) for a long time. In contrast, with their own investments (from a lump-sum distribution) or their own IRA (from a rollover IRA), they can change investments or financial intermediaries quite easily. They may also be able to convert a rollover traditional IRA to a Roth IRA if eligible to do so. However, the Pension Benefit Guaranty Corporation (PBGC) does cover defined-benefit pension income from insolvent plans, up to a limit.

■ A life annuity is not a good choice if the retiree is in poor health.

Deciding What Annuity Form to Use. Assuming a retiring employee and his or her spouse, if married, have decided to take some or all of their retirement benefits as a life annuity (or in installments), they now must decide what kind of annuity (among those offered by the plan) to use. This is known as selecting the *annuity form.* The following are various kinds of annuity forms that could be available under qualified retirement plans. They are described more fully in Chapter 4.

■ Single (or straight) life annuity.

■ Joint life annuity with a 50 percent survivor's benefit to the second annuitant. This is the QJSA form described previously.

■ Other joint life and last survivor annuity forms.

■ Life annuities with various refund features.

■ Payments for a fixed period of time or in a fixed amount.

An important planning issue in selecting the annuity form is how much, if any, benefit is to be provided for a survivor. A factor in this decision is how much, if at all, a straight life annuity will be reduced for the QJSA (or other survivorship) protection for a surviving spouse. This actuarial reduction, if any, varies among plans, but is normally less when the parties are younger. Table 20.1 shows some sample reduction factors for one corporate pension plan.

In general, unless there are considerable other resources or existing life insurance to protect a surviving spouse, it probably is logical to accept the QJSA form or even to use a higher survivor's percentage to protect a surviving spouse if a life annuity is being taken. Of course, if a QJSA form is subsidized by a particular employer (i.e., less than full or even no reduction from a

Table 20.1. Sample reduction factors for a sample corporate pension plan

Ages at Retirement		Percentage by which single life annuity will be reduced for QJSA form
Plan Participant	Spouse	
55	55	7.5%
60	60	9.0%
65	65	10.7%

straight life annuity), there really is no choice and at least the QJSA form will be used if there is to be a life annuity at all.

Taking a Lump-Sum Distribution and Paying the Tax Currently. Following are some of the reasons to take this approach:

- After the distribution, the participant gains complete investment and other control over the funds (after taxes).
- There may be favorable income tax treatment, such as NUA on employer securities (as illustrated earlier) and possible transitional 10-year averaging and/or 20 percent capital gains treatment.
- The participant and his or her spouse may feel that income tax rates are relatively low currently, compared with what they might be in the future. However, this kind of guesstimate seems very uncertain.
- In some cases, defined-benefit pension plans may offer relatively liberal lump-sum options.
- It may be convenient to take smaller benefits as a lump-sum distribution.

Making a Direct Transfer to a Rollover IRA. Such transfers to a traditional IRA can be quite advantageous.

- There is no current income tax on the directly transferred amount.
- The investment income and realized and unrealized capital gains on the amount transferred continue to accumulate income tax deferred.
- The IRA owner can decide when to take money from the IRA and will not be taxed until he or she actually makes withdrawals. However, the owner must comply with the minimum distribution rules.
- A traditional IRA owner (or his or her surviving spouse) can convert to a Roth IRA if he or she is eligible to do so.
- The owner has control over the IRA and, if he or she chooses, can direct its investments over a broad range of investment instruments. Further, if the owner wishes a life annuity, he or she can place originally, transfer, or roll over the IRA to a life insurance company individual retirement annuity.

- A surviving spouse as beneficiary can assume the IRA and treat it as his or her own with no current income taxation.
- A retiree can diversify his or her choices by rolling over benefits from some plans but not others or perhaps by rolling over only part of an eligible rollover distribution.
- The REA rules do not apply to IRAs. Therefore, from the viewpoint of the plan participant, to the extent the REA rules may complicate estate planning, being free of them *may be* an advantage. On the other hand, from the viewpoint of the participant's spouse, the reverse may be true: REA protection may be lost. In reality, this may or may not be a controversial issue, depending on the circumstances.

Leaving Benefits in a Former Employer's Plan. This may be done if the plan's terms permit it. It may be attractive if the plan has especially favorable investment options or other features. Depending on state law, there also may be more favorable creditor protection for assets in a qualified plan than in an IRA. On the other hand, the terms of the plan will continue to apply to the retiree's account and the REA rules will apply.

General Considerations on Taking Plan Benefits at Retirement. Unfortunately, there are no pat answers for this important decision. It depends to a large extent on the facts and circumstances of each case. However, the following general principles may be helpful.

- With respect to many retirees, it probably is wise to provide at least a base level of guaranteed lifetime income for the person or couple.
- If the special tax advantages of a lump-sum distribution (e.g., a large amount of highly appreciated employer securities with substantial NUA) are especially significant in a particular case, the participant might consider a lump-sum distribution and paying tax currently.
- If a retiree wants flexibility, control, and yet continued income tax deferral, often little would seem to be lost by a transfer to a rollover IRA and then making withdrawal decisions later.
- If the owner of a traditional IRA wants long-term tax-free deferral and wealth growth for himself or herself or perhaps his or her heirs, a conversion to a Roth IRA should be considered, provided the owner is eligible and can afford (or finance) the tax on conversion.
- There may well be merit in following a diversified approach to taking retirement plan benefits. For example, a person or couple may take a lifetime retirement income from a defined-benefit pension plan and then directly transfer the account balance from a defined-contribution plan to an IRA.

Death Benefits Under Qualified Plans and IRAs

Kinds of Death Benefits. There may be death benefits prior to retirement as well as after retirement.

Pre-retirement death benefits may include:

- QPSA (under REA)
- Account balances under defined-contribution (DC) plans and IRAs
- Incidental life insurance as part of a qualified plan

Post-retirement death benefits may include:

- QJSA (under REA) or other survivors' benefits
- Any remaining account balances under DC plans and IRAs

Strategies for Naming Beneficiaries of Death Benefits. This choice really is part of the owner's or participant's estate planning. Also, if the primary beneficiary is an individual, a contingent beneficiary or beneficiaries normally should be named in the event the primary beneficiary dies before the owner or participant. Beneficiaries might include the following.

The Owner's or Participant's Spouse Directly (Outright). This is a common choice and offers many advantages. These include the ability to directly transfer qualified plan death benefits to his or her own traditional IRA or to assume the deceased spouse's IRA as his or her own and hence defer income taxation, the ability to qualify for the federal estate tax marital deduction and hence defer estate taxation, and exemption from the REA rules for qualified plans other than pension plans. On the other hand, this gives the surviving spouse complete control over the death benefits after the owner's or participant's death. For personal, family (e.g., a second marriage), or estate planning reasons, this may not be acceptable in some cases.

A planning technique that may be used is to name the spouse as primary beneficiary and a trust (that can skip the spouse's estate for estate tax purposes—a nonmarital or credit-shelter trust as described in Chapter 26) as contingent beneficiary. Then, after the owner or participant dies, the surviving spouse can decide whether to (1) take the death benefit as designated beneficiary or transfer it to his or her own IRA and get the resulting income tax deferral or (2) disclaim[16] part or all of the death benefit within nine months after the owner's or participant's death and have the disclaimed part pass to the trust, which may avoid overqualifying the decedent's estate for the marital deduction and reduce current estate taxes. This decision will depend on the circumstances after the owner's or participant's death. This technique may be

---

[16] Qualified disclaimers are described in Chapter 26.

particularly valuable after EGTRRA because of its increasing applicable exclusion amounts, possible complete repeal of the estate tax, and increased value of income tax deferred because of declining income tax rates. But this technique also gives the surviving spouse complete control after death.

An Individual or Individuals Other Than the Spouse Directly (e.g., a Child or Children). As indicated in footnote 11, if multiple beneficiaries are to be named, a useful planning technique to attain maximum income tax deferral after death is to divide an IRA into separate IRAs or to request the IRA custodian or trustee to divide the IRA account into a sub-accounts or sub-IRAs with one for each beneficiary. Then, each beneficiary's own life expectancy will govern minimum distributions from his or her own IRA or sub-account.

As an illustration, assume Helen Smith died, leaving her husband, Frank, as primary beneficiary of her $1,100,000 employer-provided qualified profit-sharing account. After Helen dies, Frank decides to directly transfer (rollover) the profit-sharing account balance to his own traditional IRA. The Smiths have three children: Tom, Susan, and Mary. Frank wants to name the three children as equal beneficiaries of his IRA. Assume further that Frank tragically is killed in an automobile accident two years later, when the account balance in his IRA is about $1,200,000. In the year after his death, Tom is 55, Susan is 52, and Mary is 38. If Frank simply named the children as equal multiple beneficiaries of his IRA, Tom, age 55, who has the shortest life expectancy, would be considered the designated beneficiary (for purposes of the minimum distribution rules) and the entire IRA account balance would have to be paid out in annual amounts to the beneficiaries (in equal shares) over Tom's life expectancy of 29.6 years (from the IRS Single Life Table) and reduced by one year for each subsequent year. This means the entire account balance would have to be distributed to all beneficiaries within about 30 years, since the 29.6 life expectancy number is reduced by 1 each year thereafter. On the other hand, if Frank had divided his IRA into a separate IRA (or sub-account) for himself and each beneficiary (of about $400,000 each), the life expectancy of each child (as designated beneficiary) would govern the minimum distributions to him or her, starting the year after their father's death. This would be 29.6 years for Tom, 32.3 years for Susan, and 45.6 years for Mary. The result would be substantially longer tax deferral (about 16 years or 56 percent longer for the youngest beneficiary in this example).[17]

[17] It may be noted that these principles and results would be substantially the same *after Frank's death* if this had been a Roth IRA (converted by Frank from his traditional IRA), except that Frank would not have had to take any minimum distributions during his lifetime, so the balance may have been greater at his death and the distributions after his death would be tax-free to the beneficiaries. But Roth IRAs are subject to the minimum distribution rules after the owner's death.

A Trust |That Qualifies for the Federal Estate Tax Marital Deduction (a Marital Trust). This would be a trust for the surviving spouse's benefit during his or her lifetime and then, when he or she died, the corpus would pass to others. The benefits (trust corpus) would qualify for the federal estate tax marital deduction, so estate taxation would be deferred. Further, if the trust meets the requirements described earlier, the surviving spouse (as beneficiary of the trust) will be considered the designated beneficiary for purposes of the minimum distribution rules and plan or IRA benefits could be paid out in annual amounts over the spouse's life expectancy, determined by his or her age in each distribution year. But the rules for both minimum distributions and qualifying for the marital deduction must be met. Also, the surviving spouse would not be able to do a direct transfer (rollover) of qualified plan balances to IRAs or treat IRAs as his or her own, since he or she would not be outright beneficiary. In addition, there would be no exemption from the REA, so the spouse would have to consent in the proper form for qualified plans.

A Trust That Does Not Qualify for the Federal Estate Tax Marital Deduction (a Nonmarital, Credit Shelter, or Bypass Trust). In essence, the corpus of these trusts is intended to be subject to federal estate taxation in the decedent's estate, but the estate tax is absorbed by the applicable credit amount (unified credit). Plan benefits might have to be paid to such a trust for estate planning reasons, usually because there are not enough other assets in the estate to fund such a trust at death. In general, however, use of qualified plan, TSA, or IRA death benefits to fund nonmarital trusts is not very attractive because they are IRD items. (See Chapter 26 for a more complete discussion of marital deduction planning.) But also note the use of such nonmarital trusts as contingent beneficiaries discussed previously.

A Charity or a Charitable Remainder Trust (CRT). When a participant or IRA owner is charitably inclined, this can be an interesting possibility. A charity named as beneficiary avoids income taxation, since a charity is tax exempt, and also federal estate taxation, because of the charitable estate tax deduction. Hence, the normal heavy taxation at death of these IRD items is avoided. CRTs are described in Chapter 16.

If a CRT is named as beneficiary, a surviving spouse could be the noncharitable income beneficiary and thus receive an income (either a unitrust or an annuity trust amount) for his or her lifetime. This income would be taxable. At the spouse's death, the corpus would go to the charity. As with any CRT, life insurance in an estate tax-protected irrevocable life insurance trust might be used to recoup the amount of the charitable gift for the family.

The proposed regulations have facilitated the naming of charities for at least part of IRA or qualified plan death benefits. This is because the final designated beneficiary does not have to be determined until September 30 of the year following the year of the owner's or participant's death. Thus, when a charity and an individual(s) or trust are named, the charity's interest can be paid ("cashed out") before that date, leaving only an individual or trust designated beneficiary over whose life expectancy minimum distributions can be made.

As an illustration, suppose Peter Wolfson, who is divorced, has a $1,000,000 traditional rollover IRA and names as beneficiaries an environmental group, to receive $100,000, and his daughter Alexandra, age 30, to receive the balance. He dies at age 68 in 2003. If the $100,000 is paid to the charity (the environmental group) by September 30, 2004, that will leave Alexandra as the sole designated beneficiary and the $900,000 balance can be paid out to her over her life expectancy as of 2004 (at age 31) of 52.4 years. But if the $100,000 is not paid to the charity by September 30, 2004, there is no sole individual designated beneficiary by that determination date and Alexandra's share would have to be paid out to her within five years after the year of her father's death (the "five-year rule"). Of course, the same result could be achieved if Peter divides his IRA into separate IRAs (or sub-accounts) during his lifetime: one for himself with the charity as beneficiary and one for himself with Alexander as beneficiary.

Other Trust. Participants or owners (who perhaps are not married) may want to name other trusts as beneficiaries in particular circumstances.

The Participant's or Owner's Estate. This possibility seems to have few planning advantages.

21

Individual Investment
Annuity Contracts

Individual annuities sold to the public as investments have become a major financial product for many people.

Fundamental Purposes of Annuities

Traditionally, in its payout phase, a *life annuity* involves an individual paying an insurance company a specified sum (called the *annuity consideration* or *premium*) in exchange for a promise that the insurer will make a series of periodic payments to the individual (called the *annuitant*) for as long as he or she lives. Thus, the basic purpose of any life annuity is to ensure the annuitant an income he or she cannot outlive.

However, modern individual annuity contracts permit the payout of accumulated funds (cash value) in a variety of ways. In fact, relatively few individual annuities today are taken as a life income (annuitized).

Theoretically, the income from a life annuity should be relatively large compared with other investment returns, because the annuity principle involves the gradual liquidation of the purchase price or cash value of the annuity. However, as a practical matter, the consumer should evaluate payments under a life annuity as compared with returns from comparable investments that do not involve liquidation of principal.

Types of Individual Annuities

Investment annuities can be classified in several ways.

Who Determines Investments and Bears Investment Risks

A fundamental issue is whether the annuity owner or the insurance company makes investment decisions and bears investment risks.

Fixed-Dollar Annuities. In these annuities, the cash value accumulation is a stated dollar amount that is guaranteed by the insurance company and on which the insurer pays a specified or determinable rate of interest. Investment authority and investment risks are borne by the insurance company. The assets behind these annuities are invested in the general assets of the insurance company; hence they are referred to as *portfolio products*. In the unlikely case the insurer should become insolvent, fixed-dollar annuity owners would become general creditors of the insurer.

Variable Annuities (VAs). Under this type, the annuity owner can choose among a number of investment funds with regard to where he or she wishes to place the annuity premiums. The owner also has the option of moving his or her annuity contributions and the cash values among the various funds at reasonable intervals.

The funds under VAs are placed in sub-accounts that are managed by or for the insurance company. These sub-accounts are not part of the general assets of the insurer but are investments of insurer separate accounts, which are organized as investment companies (normally unit investment trusts). Their investment results stand on their own. Therefore, the cash values of VAs depend on the investment experience of the particular sub-account or accounts into which the cash values have been allocated by the annuity owner. Thus, investment risks reside with the annuity owner.

The separate accounts also are not subject to the claims of the insurance company's creditors. The investment accounts available depend on the particular contract involved. However, annuity owners generally have a wide range of investment options.

This variable annuity concept also applies when accumulated values are taken as variable retirement benefits. At this time, the current value of the investment fund is converted into units of retirement income (often called *annuity units*) and the annuitant receives an income of so many annuity units per month. The value of these annuity units depends on the investment experience of the fund in which the annuity accumulation is invested. This may be one of the payout options under an annuity.

Combination Plans. Individual annuities may give annuity owners the choice of putting their annuity values into a fixed-dollar fund, one or more variable funds, or a combination of fixed and variable accounts.

Equity-Indexed Annuities (EIAs). These technically are fixed-dollar annuities. They combine minimum insurance company guarantees with linking of interest earnings on the cash value to a stock market index.

As an example, a person might pay a premium of $50,000 for a single-premium deferred EIA. The policy would guarantee a minimum value of, say, 90 percent of this principal amount ($45,000 here) increased by a guaranteed interest rate of, say, 3 percent each year. The value of the EIA will not fall below this minimum guarantee. In addition, if it is higher, the policy will pay a percentage (which varies among policies, but let us say 85 percent here) of the increase in an equity index (say the S&P 500) over a time period, which might be five years. This percentage of the index increase is called the *participation rate*. Thus, if the increase in the S&P 500 over the five years were, say, 80 percent (or a 12.47 percent average annual compound rate of return), the interest credited for this index increase would be $34,000 (80 percent index increase × 85 percent participation rate × $50,000 = $34,000) and the accumulated value of the EIA would be $84,000 (which, of course, is greater than the guaranteed value for this period). The annuity then could continue for additional periods. However, if the S&P 500 stock index were to decline, the EIA owner still would have the minimum guaranteed cash value at the minimum guaranteed interest rate. This is only an example to illustrate the principles involved. The design features in EIAs being sold can differ markedly and cause considerable differences in total returns.[1]

Insurance company EIAs followed bank-offered market-linked CDs, which were described in Chapter 11. However, EIAs are annuities, so the inside buildup is not currently taxed. This is not true for bank CDs. However, the CDs normally are covered by FDIC insurance, while the EIAs are not.

Methods of Paying Premiums

Flexible-Premium Annuities. These contracts allow the annuity owner the discretion of when to pay periodic premiums. Premiums can be discontinued or changed at the owner's option. This approach may be referred to as *flexible-premium deferred annuities.*

Single-Premium Annuities. Here the contract is purchased with a single lump-sum payment. The single premium may be paid well in advance of when benefits are to be taken from the annuity (a *single-premium deferred annuity,* or SPDA) or it may be paid just before annuity payments are to begin (a *single-premium immediate annuity*).

---

[1] The insurance companies themselves may finance these products by using the premiums they receive to purchase a portfolio of fixed bonds to cover the guaranteed part of the EIA and then purchase options on stock indexes or other option arrangements to cover the equity index part.

When Annuity Payments Begin

Deferred Annuities. As just noted, a *deferred annuity* is one under which the benefits will not be payable until some years in the future. They essentially involve the tax-deferred growth of capital over time.

Immediate Annuities. On the other hand, an *immediate annuity* is one in which the benefits begin as soon as the purchase price is paid. An immediate annuity might be purchased at retirement by someone ready to start receiving lifetime retirement benefits at that time.

Annuity Starting Date. As its name implies, this is when annuity payments begin. Under the tax law, it is the first day of the first period (e.g., month) for which an amount is received as an annuity.

Parties to the Annuity Contract

These are the annuity owner, the annuitant, the beneficiary, and the issuing insurance company. In most instances the annuity owner and the annuitant are the same person. The *annuity owner* is the person or entity who owns the rights under an annuity contract. The *annuitant* is the person whose life generally determines the timing and amount of any payout affected by life expectancy. In other words, the annuitant's life is used in determining any life income payments. The *beneficiary* is the person or entity named in the contract to receive the death benefit under the annuity in the event that the owner dies before the benefits are paid from the annuity. In the event that the beneficiary is the deceased owner's surviving spouse, he or she is allowed by the tax law to treat the annuity as his or her own and to continue it as the new owner. The *issuing insurance company* is the life insurance company issuing the contract.

Phases of Annuities

Individual annuities have an accumulation phase and a distribution phase.

During the *accumulation phase,* contributions are made to the annuity and it basically is a capital accumulation device. There is no legal or tax limit on the amount of annual contributions (or single premiums) that an annuity owner can make. However, contributions are made after tax.

The *distribution phase* is when the owner receives benefits or payouts from the annuity. Distributions generally can be made at the owner's option, except for certain limiting factors. First, most annuities have reducing surrender charges if distributions are taken during the early years of the contract. Second, individual annuities are subject to the 10 percent penalty tax on premature distributions (before age 59½), with certain exceptions. And finally, annuity contracts generally specify an age by which benefits must commence. But this age may be quite advanced, such as age 85. However, tax law sets no required beginning date (RBD) for nonqualified annuities.

Investment Returns on Annuities

Important considerations in deciding whether to purchase an annuity or in deciding which one(s) to purchase are the rate of annual investment return that may be expected (in relation to investment risk) and the expense charges (direct and indirect) that are levied by insurers. Investment returns are discussed here and expense charges next.

Returns on Fixed-Dollar Annuities

For this type of annuity, the insurance company specifies an *initial credited interest rate* that it will pay on the cash accumulation under the contract. The insurer often guarantees this rate (or perhaps several alternative rates) for a specified period of time. This may be called the *yield guarantee.* This period can vary among insurers and annuity contracts, from as little as one month to, say, as long as 10 years. After any yield guarantee period ends, the insurer can set monthly or annually the interest rate it will pay in the future on the cash accumulation. This is the *current yield*; it can be increased or decreased by the insurer and often is less than the initial credited rate. However, fixed-dollar annuities also have a *minimum guaranteed interest rate,* below which the insurer cannot set its current rate. Also, some annuities have what is called a *bailout escape rate* or *bailout provision* under which, if the current rate declared by the insurer falls below a certain level, the annuity owner can withdraw all funds in the annuity or exchange the annuity without a surrender charge. Thus, the minimum guaranteed rate and possibly a bailout rate provide some protection to annuity owners against declines in current interest rates.

The current rate usually applies to all monies received for the annuity regardless of when they were paid or received. In other words, there is one current rate that the insurer sets based on the return on its own general investment portfolio. These may be called *portfolio-rated products.* A few insurers base their current rates on some outside market interest rate (such as a U.S. Treasury bill rate), so it changes with market conditions. These sometimes are called *interest-indexed annuities* (IIAs). At least one insurer uses a *new money approach,* where the current rate depends on when the annuity considerations were paid to the insurer. Current rates also may vary with the yield guarantee period and with the size of the annuity accumulation.

In considering fixed-dollar annuities, it may be helpful for consumers to review some current interest rate history for the annuity or annuities being considered. However, the general reputation and financial ratings of the insurer are very important, since it is the insurer's financial strength that stands behind its contracts. Purchasers should not be unduly attracted by an unusually high initial interest rate (possibly a *teaser rate*) or by a one-time *bonus rate*. First, the insurer normally lowers a teaser rate substantially after the yield guarantee period (which may be comparatively short) and bonus interest is paid only once. Further, it may not be sound for the insurer's own financial condition to offer rates that are too much out of line with market conditions.

Fixed-dollar annuities are a guaranteed principal product and will be attractive during periods of generally rising interest rates. This is because their cash value is fixed and guaranteed by the insurer and thus will not decline with rising interest rates, as will bond prices (and perhaps stock prices as well). In addition, the current rates on these annuities will rise because insurers will be earning more on their general portfolios (which are mostly invested in bonds and mortgages) and competition will force insurers to raise their current rates to maintain their annuity business. The early 1980s are a good example of these conditions.

On the other hand, during periods of low or declining interest rates in the economy, the reverse may be true. Current rates on annuities will decline, but their principal value (cash value) will remain fixed. Bonds, on the other hand, will rise in price in the face of declining interest rates, unless they are called. Most of the 1990s are a case in point. Again, since no one knows what the future will bring, a diversified asset allocation strategy seems best for most people.

Returns on Variable Annuities

Here, investment returns depend on the performance of the sub-account or accounts to which the annuity funds are allocated. Therefore, a prospective purchaser should evaluate the past investment performance of the insurer (or other investment manager) over a reasonably long time period (such as 10 or even 20 years) with respect to those separate accounts, much as should be done when buying investment company shares or variable life insurance. Consumers also may evaluate the variety of the sub-accounts included in the investment options under the contract. Some annuities have more options than others.

Returns on EIAs

EIAs vary considerably in their design characteristics. This can impact their returns significantly. Some of the features that can affect results are the equity index used, the participation rate, any caps (maximum limits) on the gain in the equity index that is credited to the annuity value, how the interest based on the equity index is calculated (the calculation method), the minimum cash-value guarantee (sometimes called the *guaranteed minimum account value*—GMAV), the minimum guaranteed interest rate, and a possible account charge.

A number of equity indexes are used. The one used in the particular EIA selected involves at least some degree of investment strategy. For example, use of a broad index, like the commonly used S&P 500 stock index, implies an index investing strategy. Participation rates vary widely. In the previous example, we assumed an 85 percent participation rate, but these rates can range from 55 percent to more than 100 percent. There are a number of calculation methods. In the previous example, the point-to-point method was used. Other methods include a ladder method, high water/low water method, and ratchet designs.

For asset allocation purposes, EIAs perhaps should be considered equity investments, since the expectation normally is that the equity-indexed interest will outpace the GMAV. However, returns on EIAs may be lower than those on other equity investments, such as directly owned stocks and stock mutual funds, because of possible participation rates below 100 percent, possible caps on interest credits, and the fact that equity indexes (like the S&P 500) do not include dividends paid on the common stocks in the index. They are indexes of the market prices of stocks.

Expense Charges on Annuities

There are two broad categories of charges: sales or surrender charges (loads) and other, usually annual, charges.

Sales Charges

Sometimes a sales charge is deducted from the premiums when an annuity is purchased. This is called a *front-end load*. The trend in the insurance industry, however, is not to impose front-end loads on individual annuities, but rather to levy a *surrender charge* if more than a certain amount (often more than 10 percent of the annuity value per year) is withdrawn or surrendered within a specified period of time after purchase (such as 7 or 10 years). Technically, this is a *contingent deferred sales charge*, but it is popularly known as a *back-end load*. Back-end loads normally are a diminishing percentage of the annuity value and, while they vary among insurers, might start at 7 or 8 percent of the annuity value in the first year and then decline year by year to become zero by, say, the 10th year. Back-end loads tend to discourage annuity owners from transferring or surrendering their annuities during the period in which such surrender charges may be imposed.

Some annuities do not levy any sales load or surrender charge or impose reduced loads or charges. These may be called *no-load* or *low-load* contracts. They are analogous to no-load or low-load mutual funds.

Periodic Expense Charges

In the case of *fixed-dollar annuities*, there often are no separately stated annual fees. Rather, the insurer recovers its costs from the spread between the current interest rate it pays on the annuity value and the rate it can earn on its own investment portfolio. Thus, for fixed-dollar annuities there usually are no front-end sales loads and no separately charged annual fees. However, there generally is a surrender charge (back-end load).

For *variable annuities*, the situation is different. There always are annual charges levied against the contract's accumulated value, whether or not there are any sales or surrender charges. These annual charges fall into two general categories: *contract charges* (policy-level expenses), which do not vary with the particular sub-account or accounts selected, and *fund or portfolio operating expenses* (fund-level expenses), which vary with the sub-account or accounts selected. Contract charges are for insurance-type charges and administrative expenses. They consist of the mortality and expense (M&E) risk charge, which may include elements for administrative expenses, sales expenses, a risk charge for standard death benefits, and insurer profits. Fund-level charges are investment management fees and administrative expenses for managing the particular fund. They are somewhat analogous to expense ratios for mutual funds. Both of these kinds of charges are customarily expressed as percentages of fund average net assets.

These annual charges can be significant in affecting total returns under variable annuities. On average, annual policy-level (M&E) charges may run about 1.27 percent of assets, while annual fund-level charges vary according to particular sub-accounts, typically being lower for money market and domestic bond funds and higher for growth stock, specialty, and international funds. On average, however, total combined annual charges might run 2.10 percent of assets. However, these combined annual expenses can vary considerably among variable annuities. This is an important factor for purchasers of variable annuities to consider.

Withdrawals and Loans

Individual annuities normally permit withdrawals from the cash value at any time. Some also permit loans against the cash value. However, for annuity contracts issued after January 18, 1985, any amount withdrawn (or taken as a loan) prior to age 59½ will be subject to the 10 percent penalty tax on premature distributions, with some exceptions. In addition to reaching age 59½, other exceptions are the person's disability or death, when payments are made in substantially equal periodic payments for the life or life expectancy of the annuitant or the joint lives or life expectancies of the annuitant and his or her beneficiary, and for the purchase of an immediate annuity.

Exchanges of Annuities

Annuity contracts can be exchanged tax-free for other annuity contracts under the terms of Section 1035 of the Internal Revenue Code (IRC). Thus, if an annuity owner is dissatisfied with the service, yield, or security of his or her individual deferred annuity, the owner can exchange the contract for another annuity contract without current income tax consequences. However, such exchanges of annuity contracts may give rise to back-end loads.

Annuity Distribution (Payout) Options

Fixed or Variable Annuity Benefits

Depending on the policy involved, annuity benefits can be payable as a stated number of dollars (fixed-dollar annuities) or as variable annuity units in a separate sub-account (variable annuity). Fixed-dollar annuities normally provide stated dollar payouts, while variable annuities may provide either variable payouts or fixed payouts at the option of the annuity owner.

Annuity Payment Options

These options vary somewhat from one annuity contract to another, but some common ones include cash surrender of all or part of the accumulated value, installment payments, straight life annuity, joint life and survivor annuity, and various life annuities with refund features. These essentially are the same options as described in Chapter 4.

Annuity Death Benefits

While individual annuities are primarily capital accumulation and liquidation vehicles, the owner names a beneficiary or beneficiaries to receive the accumulated value or death benefit in the event of his or her death before this value is paid out. It should be noted, however, that there are no life insurance proceeds involved in such an *annuity* death benefit. Individual annuity contracts normally allow the annuity owner or the beneficiary to select one or more payout options for the death benefit.

In connection with variable annuities, the standard death benefit is the larger of the amount the owner invested in the policy (less any withdrawals) or the policy's cash value. This means that if the cash value in a sub-account or accounts (such as a common stock account) should decline below the owner's investment in the contract (net premiums paid), there would be a mortality risk element equal to the difference. This can be important in declining markets. Some variable annuity contracts have other, enhanced death benefit provisions. One of these is the stepped-up death benefit. Here the death benefit is reset at periodic intervals (such as every five years) at the current cash value; from then on, it will not be less than this amount. Another provision increases the death benefit by a stated percentage (such as 5 percent) each year. There normally are additional, asset-based percentage charges for enhanced death benefits. The consumer should evaluate whether these additional charges are worth the death protection, as compared with just buying life insurance for death protection. Once annuity payments have commenced, any death benefit will depend on the payout option selected.

The IRC requires that for contracts issued after January 18, 1985 to be considered annuities for tax purposes (i.e., to be taxed under Section 72 of the IRC), the contracts must meet certain distribution rules in the event of an annuity owner's death. If the owner's death occurs before the annuity starting date, his or her entire interest in the contract must be distributed within five years after the owner's death. But if the owner's death occurs on or after the annuity starting date and before his or her entire interest has been distributed, the remaining interest must be distributed at least as rapidly as under the distribution method being used at the owner's death. However, under both of these rules, if part or all of an owner's interest is to be distributed to a beneficiary over the life of the beneficiary or over a period of time that does not exceed the life expectancy of the beneficiary, and if such distribution begins within one year of the owner's death, that portion will be treated as if it had been distributed on the day the distribution began. Further, if a deceased owner's spouse is beneficiary, these requirements treat the surviving spouse as the annuity owner.

Split-Funded Annuities

Split-funded annuities are a combination of an immediate annuity and a deferred annuity. Under this approach, a part of the annuity fund is used to provide an immediate income for a fixed period or for life, while the remainder continues to grow tax-deferred as a deferred annuity. This can be one way of hedging against future inflation, because the deferred portion can always be used later to provide additional retirement income, if needed.

Taxation of Nonqualified Annuities

Taxation of nonqualified annuities can be complex. Only an outline of the basic principles is presented here.

Federal Income Taxation

An annuity owner's *investment in the contract* (income tax basis in the contract) is the owner's premiums paid less any nontaxed distributions. Since this amount has been paid with after-tax dollars, the owner (or his or her beneficiary at death) is entitled to this amount tax-free when taking benefits from the annuity.

Accumulation Phase (Inside Buildup). The investment earnings of an annuity contract increase (or decrease) without current income taxation (or losses). This is the famous *tax-deferred inside buildup of annuity cash values* and is one of the main advantages of individual (nonqualified) deferred annuities. For variable annuities, the owner can also move the cash value between or among the sub-accounts within the annuity without this being considered a sale or exchange for capital gains tax purposes.

Annuities Held Other than by Natural Persons. The previous tax-deferral principle does not apply where contributions have been made after February 28, 1986 for a deferred annuity that is not held by a natural person. This would include deferred annuity contracts held by corporations, charitable remainder trusts, and certain other entities. When a contract is held by a nonnatural person, it is not treated as an annuity under Section 72 of the IRC and income earned by the contract (the inside buildup) will be taxed as ordinary income to the owner for that year. However, this provision does not apply to annuities held by an estate because of the owner's death; annuities held by qualified retirement plans, TSAs, and IRAs; immediate annuities; and annuities held by trusts or other entities as agents for natural persons.

Annuity Payments (Periodic Distributions). These payments are taxed under the general annuity rules of Section 72 of the IRC.[2] Under these rules, an owner determines the ratio of his or her investment in the contract to the expected return from the contract and excludes a similar proportion of each annuity payment from his or her gross income. This ratio is the exclusion ratio. For annuity starting dates after December 31, 1986, the exclusion continues

---

[2] This is the same general concept as discussed in Chapter 20 for periodic distributions from qualified retirement plans, except there are special exceptions for qualified plans that do not apply to nonqualified annuities. Nonqualified annuities are taxed only under the general annuity rules.

until the owner's investment in the contract is recovered and then the annuity payments are fully taxable. For prior annuity starting dates, the exclusion goes on even after the owner's investment in the contract is recovered. If an owner-annuitant should die before recovering the premiums tax-free, the remainder would be deductible on his or her final income tax return.

Amounts Not Received as an Annuity. Section 72 also deals with distributions that are not received as an annuity. These include nonperiodic distributions before the annuity starting date, such as surrenders, cash withdrawals, and loans.

Surrenders. If an annuity contract is entirely *surrendered for cash,* the difference between the cash surrender value and the investment in the contract is taxed as ordinary income in the year of the surrender. This normally is not a desirable strategy unless there are special circumstances.

Cash Withdrawals. If there are *partial withdrawals,* they are viewed for tax purposes as coming first from any untaxed investment earnings in the contract and are taxed as ordinary income until such investment earnings are exhausted. Once the inside buildup is exhausted, further withdrawals are viewed as a return of the investment in the contract and are income tax-free. This can be termed a *last-in, first-out* or LIFO concept of taxation and is the opposite from that generally employed for partial withdrawals from life insurance contracts that are not modified endowment contracts.

Loans. For income tax purposes, these are considered distributions from the contract and hence are taxable the same as just described for partial withdrawals. This is the opposite from the treatment of policy loans from life insurance policies that are not modified endowment contracts and loans from qualified retirement plans.

Gifts of Annuities. For annuity contracts issued after April 22, 1987, the transfer of an annuity for less than full and adequate consideration (i.e., gift of the annuity) will be treated for income tax purposes as if the owner-transferor had received an amount not received as an annuity equal to the difference between the cash value at the time of the gift and the investment in the contract. This amount is taxable to the owner-transferor at that time as ordinary income. Thus, gifts of annuities generally will trigger taxation to the donor of the untaxed inside buildup. Therefore, while gifts of life insurance often are attractive for estate planning reasons, the same is not true for gifts of deferred annuities. This rule does not apply to gifts of annuities between spouses or incident to divorce.

Death. At the death of an annuity owner, the difference between the annuity's accumulated value and the decedent's investment in the contract is income in respect of a decedent (IRD) to the beneficiary (according to the principles explained in Chapter 14). The ordinary income is received as payments are made from the annuity. Therefore, it may be desirable to spread out the tax impact over a period of years to the extent allowed by the distribution rules described previously.

As a result of these rules, it can be seen that the inside buildup in deferred annuities will always be taxed as ordinary income at some point—on receiving periodic income, on surrender of the contract, as partial distributions, as loans, on gift of the contract, or at death. Also, tax on the buildup cannot be shifted to someone else, except through death.

Penalty Tax on Premature Distributions. For nonqualified annuity contracts issued after January 18, 1985, any taxable amount withdrawn prior to age 59½ generally will be subject to the 10 percent excise tax on premature distributions. There are, however, certain exceptions, as described above under "Withdrawals and Loans."

Federal Estate Taxation

The total accumulated value death benefit of a deferred annuity at the annuity owner's death will be included in the owner's gross estate for federal estate tax purposes. However, the beneficiary gets an income tax deduction for any federal estate tax paid by the decedent's estate that is attributable to this IRD item.

Other Individual Annuity Arrangements
Charitable Gift Annuities

These are part charitable contribution and part annuity arrangements provided by some charities. They are described in Chapter 16.

Private Annuities

These really are estate planning arrangements (sales within the family) and are covered in Chapter 25.

Using Life Insurance Values to Provide Retirement Income

As explained in Chapter 4, most life insurance companies make available by contract or as a matter of practice settlement options for the policy owner as well as for death beneficiaries. Policy owners at or near retirement may choose to use some or all of their life insurance cash values in this way, assuming they feel they no longer need the life insurance protection or all the protection. Life insurance cash values (or death proceeds) placed under such options are taxed under the general annuity rules of Section 72.

On the other hand, policy owners may choose not to surrender their policies, but to keep them in force while taking cash from them in other ways, as described in Chapters 4 and 26. Still another alternative is to keep life insurance fully in force to meet various needs. It may be needed to provide protection for a surviving spouse (or others).

22

Employee Stock Compensation Plans

General Considerations

Employee stock options and other stock plans have been used for many years and the tax law has had various provisions concerning them.[1] But for most of this time, stock options were granted only or mainly to senior executives. However, in recent years some corporations have adopted more broadly based plans covering more levels of management or even most of their full-time employees. Of course, many companies also have employee stock purchase plans that are designed to cover virtually all employees.

Types of Plans

In the classification that follows, we have divided employer stock plans into *statutory plans* and *nonstatutory plans*. Statutory plans are those to which the tax law accords special tax advantages but that must meet certain requirements to be eligible for the advantages. On the other hand, nonstatutory plans are not based on any special tax provisions but rather are governed by general tax principles.

---

[1] At various times, tax-favored stock options were called *restricted stock options* and *qualified stock options*. These particular plans have been discontinued. The present tax-favored stock option is called an *incentive stock option* (ISO).

Statutory Plans

Incentive Stock Options

These options were created by the Economic Recovery Tax Act of 1981 (ERTA) in Section 422 of the IRC. They can be made available at the employer's discretion to only some employees, normally certain highly compensated executives, and hence can be discriminatory.

Requirements for ISOs. A number of requirements must be met before a plan can qualify as an ISO plan. For example, the term (duration) of an option cannot exceed 10 years, the option price must equal or exceed the value of the stock when the option was granted, an employee cannot dispose of the stock within two years from granting the option or within one year of the transfer of the stock to him or her (i.e., after exercise of the option), the option must be nontransferable (except by will or inheritance at death), and the maximum value of stock for which an employee can exercise ISOs for the first time in a calendar year generally cannot exceed $100,000 (valued as of the date of grant).

Tax Treatment to Employees. The main tax advantage of ISOs is that there is no regular income tax levied at the *grant* or at the *exercise* of the option by the employee. However, as noted in Chapter 14, the bargain element upon *exercise* of an ISO (i.e., the difference between the fair market value of the stock at exercise and the option price) is an adjustment item for individual AMT purposes. Aside from this AMT issue, the employee is taxed only when he or she sells the stock purchased under the option plan, and then any gain realized is taxed as a capital gain. The capital gain would be the difference between the option price (the income tax basis of the stock) and the stock's fair market value on the date of sale.

As an example, assume that in 1998 Laura Johnson, who works for Acme Corporation, was granted an ISO to purchase 1000 shares of her employer's common stock at an option price (*strike price*) of $20 per share, its fair market value at the time. The ISO's term was 10 years. Laura had no gross income for federal income tax purposes at the *grant* of this option. Assume further that in 2003 Laura *exercised* the option with cash and purchased 1000 shares of Acme common from her employer for $20,000 (1000 shares × $20 per share = $20,000). At that time, the stock's fair market value was $50 per share and the bargain element was $30,000 ($50 - $20 = $30 × 1000 shares = $30,000). Laura had no regular gross income at exercise of the ISO, but she did have an AMT adjustment item of $30,000. Note, however, that if this adjustment item produces an AMT, the AMT may be recouped in future years because of the minimum tax credit (MTC) described in Chapter 14. Laura's regular income tax basis for the 1000 shares is her cost (purchase price) of $20,000 or $20 per share.

Now assume that in 2005 Laura sells the 1000 shares for $80 per share. At this point Laura realizes and recognizes a long-term capital gain of $60 per share or $60,000 ($80 - $20 = $60 per share × 1000 shares = $60,000).[2] Further, if Laura does not sell during her lifetime but holds the Acme stock until her death, it currently would get a stepped-up income tax basis and the gain to that point would never be taxed.

Tax Treatment for the Employer. The general principle is that an employer gets a corporate income tax deduction for compensation expense at the same time and in the same amount as the employee realizes gross compensation income from the stock plan. In the case of an ISO, an employee never realizes compensation income, so the employer never gets a corporate tax deduction.

Employee Stock Purchase Plans

Basic Characteristics. These are option arrangements under which all full-time employees meeting certain eligibility requirements are allowed to buy stock in their employer corporation, usually at a discount. The option price cannot be less than the lower of 85 percent of the stock's fair market value when the option was granted or 85 percent of the stock's fair market value when the option was exercised. Many employers use these maximum discounts as the option (strike) prices under their plans.

Employees who participate agree to have an estimated amount withheld from their pay to provide the funds with which to exercise their options at the end of an option period. If an employee decides not to exercise an option, the plan will return the amounts withheld to the employee, usually with interest.

Employee stock purchase plans are nondiscriminatory in that they cannot favor the highly paid executives of a corporation. In fact, no employee who owns 5 percent or more of the stock of a corporation can be granted such an option and the maximum annual value of stock subject to these plans (determined as of the grant of the option) is $25,000.

Tax Treatment to Employees. If the requirements of Section 423 of the IRC are met, there is no gross income for participating employees at the grant or exercise of options under employee stock purchase plans. However, to get this favorable tax treatment, an employee cannot dispose of the stock within two

---

[2] Note that in this example the holding requirements for an ISO have been met (i.e., two years from grant and one year from exercise). However if the requirements for an ISO had been violated, the option would be treated as a nonqualified stock option (NQSO), described later in this chapter.

years from grant of the option and within one year from its exercise. If such a disqualifying disposition were to occur, the employee would be taxed, as ordinary compensation income in the year of disposition, on the difference between the fair market value of the stock and the option strike price when the option was exercised.

For dispositions (sales) of the stock after the two-year and one-year holding periods (or upon death whenever occurring), when the option price was between 85 percent and 100 percent of the stock's fair market value at grant, the employee (or his or her estate) will be taxed as ordinary compensation income on the lesser of (1) the difference between the fair market value of the stock and the option price at the time of disposition or death or (2) the difference between the fair market value of the stock and the option price as of the time the option was granted. The remainder of any gain at sale during the employee's lifetime would be capital gain. At the employee's death, his or her estate or heirs would get a stepped-up basis for the remainder of any gain and it would never be taxed.

Many corporations have adopted employee stock purchase plans. While a company's plan may not necessarily be as liberal as permitted by the tax law, a great many are. Therefore, it would seem that eligible employers normally would be well advised to participate in these plans if they are at all financially able to do so. If an employee really does not want to hold the stock, he or she can simply sell it at a profit (assuming the stock price was such that the employee should have exercised the option).

Tax Treatment for the Employer. The employer does not get a corporate income tax deduction at grant or exercise of options under employee stock purchase plans.

Qualified Retirement Plans Invested in Employer Securities

These plans were discussed in Chapters 18 and 20. Stock bonus plans permit investment in employer stock and allow distribution of that stock to participants.

Employee stock ownership plans (ESOPs) must invest primarily in employer stock. Qualified savings plans with Section 401(k) options often allow significant portions of employee account balances to be invested in employer stock. The planning issue of possible lump-sum distributions of employer securities was explored in Chapter 20.

Nonstatutory Plans

General Tax Law Principles Governing Stock Compensation Plans

General Provisions. Since there are no special provisions governing these plans, they are interpreted under provisions of the code related to income—Section 61 in general and Section 83 in particular. Section 61 is simply the all-inclusive definition of gross income for federal income tax purposes. The more significant provision is Section 83, which deals with taxation of property transferred in connection with the performance of services.

Section 83 in essence provides that the fair market value of property (less any amount paid for the property) transferred to a person for the performance of services shall be included in that person's gross income in the first taxable year in which the person's rights in the property become transferable or are not subject to a substantial risk of forfeiture, whichever is applicable. A substantial risk of forfeiture might exist, for example, if an employee has to remain with the employer for a certain number of years to receive unfettered ownership or rights to the property. In effect, the property (less any amount paid for it) is taxable to the person rendering the services as soon as all substantial conditions on his or her having it are removed.

Section 83(b) Election. However, an important subsection, Section 83(b), provides that a person performing services (e.g., an employee) may elect within 30 days of a transfer to include the fair market value of the transferred property (less any amount paid for the property) in his or her gross income, even though the property then was subject to a substantial risk of forfeiture or was not transferable and hence under Section 83 normally would not have been taxable at that point. This is called a *Section 83(b) election*. It can be an important planning tool.

However, if one makes a Section 83(b) election and the value of transferred property is included in the person's gross income and the property subsequently is forfeited (because, say, the employee did not remain with the employer for the required period), no tax deduction is allowed for the forfeiture. The election also cannot be revoked without the consent of the secretary of the treasury. On the other hand, when the substantial risk of forfeiture expires, there is no tax then.

Normally, of course, one does not want to pay taxes any sooner than necessary.

On the other hand, a person receiving property for the performance of services (e.g., an executive receiving restricted employer stock) might want to make a Section 83(b) election and be taxed on the current value of the stock, if the current value is relatively low, the person expects it to rise significantly in the future, and he or she expects to remain with the employer at least through the forfeiture period. These, of course, may be big "ifs." Much depends on the circumstances. But if the stock price currently is low and is expected to do well in the future (as in some start-up situations, for example), the only real risk the person would seem to be taking is the possible loss of his or her current tax payment.

If an employee makes a Section 83(b) election and is currently taxed, the employer gets a corporate income tax deduction for compensation paid in the amount taxable to the employee. The effects of a Section 83(b) election will be illustrated later in connection with the discussion of restricted stock.

Current Stock Bonus

Some employers pay part of employees' current compensation in unrestricted stock. In this case, the employees receive current compensation equal to the fair market value of the stock. On the other hand, employers often pay part of a current bonus in cash and part in restricted stock (i.e., subject to the condition that the employee stay with the employer for a minimum period). In this case the rules for restricted stock apply.

Nonqualified Stock Options (NQSOs)

Basic Characteristics. These are stock options that do not meet the requirements for ISOs and so are taxed on the basis of the general principles just discussed. Correspondingly, NQSOs can have terms decided upon by the parties and are not limited in the amount of stock subject to such options exercisable by an employee in any one year (as are ISOs). Hence, NQSOs can be considerably more flexible for employers and employees. Like ISOs, they can be granted only to certain employees and hence may be discriminatory. NQSOs generally have become more popular than ISOs as a compensation technique. While there are no statutory requirements to do so, NQSOs are often granted with an option price equal to 100 percent of the fair market value of the stock on the date of grant and for option terms of around 10 years.

Tax Treatment to Employees. There normally is no taxable event (gross income) at grant because the tax regulations view their value then as not being readily ascertainable.[3] On the other hand, upon exercise of an option (and transfer of the stock to the employee), the employee will receive ordinary compensation income for regular federal income tax purposes equal to the difference between

---

[3] Employee stock options, of course, are not traded on organized or over-the-counter markets, may not be transferable, and normally are not vested at grant.

the fair market value of the stock at exercise and the option price (the bargain element). The employee's income tax basis in the stock is its fair market value at exercise. This is because the employee paid the option price to the employer (a cost basis) and included the remainder of the stock's value (bargain element) in his or her gross income as compensation (basis under the tax benefit principle). Thus, an immediate sale of the stock by the employee (there are no two-year and one-year holding periods for NQSOs) will produce zero capital gain or loss, since the amount realized would equal the adjusted basis for the stock.

Let us illustrate these principles by returning to our example involving Laura Johnson. If we assume the same facts, except that in 1998 Laura was granted a NQSO instead of an ISO, the tax results would be as follows. Laura would have no gross income at grant of the option. However, when Laura exercised her NQSO in 2003, she would have had ordinary compensation income of $30,000 in that year.[4] Laura's income tax basis for the 1000 shares is $50,000 or $50 per share ($20 per share of cost basis and $30 per share of basis due to that amount having been taxed).

Now when Laura sells her 1000 shares of Acme common in 2005 at a price of $80 per share, she will realize and recognize long-term capital gain of $30 per share or $30,000 ($80 - $50 = $30 per share × 1000 shares = $30,000). Thus, for the NQSO the total gain on the option stock would still be $60,000, except that $30,000 would be ordinary compensation income and $30,000 long-term capital gain taxable at a maximum 20 percent rate.

Tax Treatment for the Employer. The employer gets a corporate income tax deduction for the amount of compensation income the employee realizes at exercise of the option.

Restricted Stock

Basic Characteristics. *Restricted stock plans* are arrangements by which a corporation grants stock (or stock options) to an employee (or someone rendering services to the corporation), but ownership of the stock is subject to a substantial risk of forfeiture (such as the employee's remaining with the employer for a certain number of years or the corporation's meeting certain profit goals). Such stock may be provided to employees in a variety of circumstances. It can be part of a general compensation package, perhaps to entice a candidate to accept an offer of employment. It can be part of a bonus plan, as noted earlier. And in some cases, stock issued on exercise of an NQSO can be restricted stock in order to further postpone taxation.

---

[4] Note that the AMT is not involved here because the $30,000 bargain element is taxable for regular income tax purposes.

Tax Treatment to Employees and the Section 83(b) Election. As explained earlier, an employee receives ordinary compensation income in the year the employee's rights to the stock are first not subject to the substantial risk of forfeiture or are transferable. The gross income is measured by the fair market value of the stock at that time less any cost to the employee. However, depending on the circumstances, a Section 83(b) election (described earlier) may be considered. A person receiving restricted stock must make a planning decision regarding this election.

Again to illustrate these principles, let us assume that John Venture is a young information executive with a large corporation. Recently a former college classmate invited him to join a start-up company (XYZ.com) that has some exciting new products in information technology. The offer is for a lower salary, but XYZ.com, which recently went public, will give John a compensation package that includes NQSOs and 10,000 shares of restricted stock (which is conditioned on John's staying with the company for at least three years). John does not have to pay anything for the 10,000 shares. XYZ.com common stock currently is selling at $2 per share.

John accepts the offer in 2003 and makes no Section 83(b) election. He has no gross income from receipt of the 10,000 shares of restricted stock, since it is subject to a substantial risk of forfeiture. Let us further assume that at the end of three years (in 2006) John is still with XYZ.com and that its stock has done very well. Its price in 2006 is $20 per share. When the substantial risk of forfeiture ends (in 2006), John will have ordinary compensation income of $200,000 (10,000 shares × $20 per share = $200,000). His income tax basis in the 10,000 shares also will be $200,000, or $20 per share.

Now let us change our facts and assume John made the Section 83(b) election in 2003 within 30 days of receiving the 10,000 shares. He then would be taxed on $20,000 in year 2003 ($2 per share × 10,000 shares = $20,000) as ordinary compensation income and his basis in the 10,000 shares also would be $20,000, or $2 per share. If John is still with XYZ.com at the end of the three years (in 2006), the substantial risk of forfeiture would end and he would have unrestricted right to the stock. He would incur no further gross income then. On the other hand, if John should leave XYZ.com after, say, two years, he would forfeit the 10,000 shares and could take no tax deduction for that. In effect, he would lose the tax he paid in 2003 on the $20,000 of ordinary income.

Let us now assume that John stays with XYZ.com until 2006 and that two years later (in 2008) John sells the 10,000 shares for $30 per share. If he had not made the Section 83(b) election in the year 2003, he would have $100,000 of long-term capital gain ($300,000 amount realized - $200,000 adjusted basis = $100,000 gain realized and recognized). In effect, he would have had $300,000 of total gain on the 10,000 shares of restricted stock ($200,000 of ordinary compensation income and $100,000 of long-term capital gain). On the other hand, if John had made the Section 83(b) election in 2003, he would have $280,000 of long-term capital gain ($300,000 amount realized - $20,000 adjusted basis = $280,000 gain realized and recognized). In this situation, he also would have had $300,000 of total gain on the 10,000 shares of restricted stock, but now it is divided as $20,000 of ordinary compensation income and $280,000 of long-term capital gain. Further, if John does not sell the 10,000 shares (or all of them) during his lifetime, he can still consider the techniques described in Chapter 15 for possibly avoiding capital gains taxation. Finally, if he does not sell or otherwise dispose of his stock, it currently will get a stepped-up basis at death. But, if the market price of the stock falls or it becomes worthless, John would have been better off not making the Section 83(b) election.

Tax Treatment for the Employer. Again, the employer gets a corporate income tax deduction when the employee receives gross compensation income. This is either when the substantial risk of forfeiture ends or when the Section 83(b) election is made.

Other Stock-Based Plans

This is a complex field and only a brief description of some of these plans will be given here.

Stock Appreciation Rights (SARs). These are accounts maintained for selected employees that reflect the appreciation in the employer's stock over a certain period. When an executive's rights to an SAR become final, it normally is paid out to him or her in cash and is taxable then.

Phantom Stock. These also are accounts maintained for selected employees, but they normally reflect the full value of a certain amount of employer stock. The account value varies with the stock's value and normally is paid to the executive in cash at some point. However, there is no actual stock in the account.

Performance Shares or Performance-Based Stock Options. In this case, selected employees are granted stock or stock options whose vesting is contingent on certain corporate or other performance measures being met.

Provisions of Stock Option Plans
Vesting of Options

This is the period of continuous employment that must elapse after an option is granted and before the employee can exercise the option. There generally are vesting requirements in stock option plans. The periods required for vesting vary, but often range from two to four years.

Transferability of Options

Traditionally, employee stock options have not been transferable by the employees receiving the options other than at death. They could not be sold or given away. One of the requirements to be an ISO is that the option by its terms must not be transferable (other than by will or intestate distribution) and must be exercisable during the employee's lifetime only by him or her.

There is no corresponding prohibition for NQSOs. But in the past, corporations in practice have not allowed their NQSOs to be transferable. Recently, however, some corporations have amended their stock option plans to allow a holder of NQSOs to transfer (give) them to members of his or her family, trusts for such members, or possibly family limited partnerships with such members as partners, with the consent of the corporation.

Effect of Certain Contingencies on Options

Stock option plans normally have certain forfeiture provisions in the event of termination of employment for various reasons. The option holder (or his or her estate or heirs) usually has a limited period of time to exercise the option after he or she retires (such as three to five years), becomes disabled on a long-term basis (such as three to five years), dies (such as one or two years), voluntarily terminates employment (such as three months), or for other reasons. Some plans also provide that options will be automatically forfeited if the holder becomes employed by or associated with a competitor of his or her former employer. In such a case, if an option holder is planning to change jobs and go with a competing firm, he or she should exercise favorable (i.e., "in the money") vested options before terminating employment.

Exercise of Options

Stock options generally can be exercised in several ways.

Cash Exercise. An option holder can make a *cash exercise* by paying the option price to the employer and having the stock transferred to him or her. In the case of an NQSO, the employer also will require withholding of federal, state, local, and FICA taxes on the taxable amount. The option holder must lay out the option price (and any withholding) in cash.

Stock-for-Stock Exercise. A plan may allow employees to pay the exercise price by delivering shares of the employer's stock that they own that are equal in value to the option price to the employer and having the option stock transferred to them.

As an example, suppose that Ahmed Bastor exercises an NQSO to buy 1000 shares of ABC Corporation common stock at an option price of $20 per share when the fair market value of the stock is $50 per share.

Ahmed already owns ABC common through previous stock option exercises. In a stock-for-stock exercise, Ahmed could deliver 400 shares of his ABC common to the corporation to pay the $20,000 exercise price (1000 shares × $20 per share = $20,000 exercise price ÷ $50 per share = 400 shares of stock to deliver). Assume that the 400 shares of his stock had an income tax basis to Ahmed of $10 per share. There is no gain recognized on the exchange of his 400 shares for 400 of the option shares and the new shares will have the same holding period for capital gain purposes as the previously owned shares. This is because this is a tax-free exchange of common stock in a corporation for common stock in the same corporation as provided in Section 1036 of the IRC.[5]

The income tax basis of the exchanged shares ($10 per share) will be carried over to 400 of the new option shares. The remainder of the new option shares will be as if it were a cash exercise. The difference between the fair market value of the stock received (600 shares × $50 per share = $30,000) and any cash paid for the stock (0 in this example) would be ordinary compensation income to Ahmed and his income tax basis in these 600 shares would be $50 per share (or $30,000), which is the amount taken into his gross income for them. The corporation may require cash withholding or allow withholding in the form of stock otherwise issuable to the option holder.

In a stock-for-stock exercise, the option holder is paying for some of the new option stock with existing company stock. This reduces the option holder's overall stock position in the company, as compared with a cash exercise, and is the reason reload options (discussed later) may be granted in this situation.

Cashless Exercise. This type of exercise involves working through a stockbroker who can buy the option stock from the corporation at the exercise price, sell enough stock in the open market to cover the purchase price plus his or her commissions and a small amount of margin loan interest, and then deliver the remaining stock to the option holder. Because of uncertainties concerning employers that arrange loans for executives under the Sarbanes-Oxley Act, as of this writing employers generally have not been providing for cashless exercises.

Reload Options. These are additional options that may be granted to employees when they pay the exercise price for stock with stock they own in the corporation (a stock-for-stock exercise). The reload option normally is for the

[5] See Chapter 14 for an explanation of this and other nonrecognition provisions in the tax code.

same number of shares used to pay the exercise price (plus perhaps shares used for federal, state, local, and FICA withholding taxes) and is for the remainder of the option period of the underlying option that was exercised.

A stock-for-stock exercise of an underlying option when there is a reload option can be attractive for an option holder. Using our example of Ahmed Bastor, assume that ABC's plan provides for reload options. In this case, if the underlying option Ahmed exercised originally had a term of 10 years and Ahmed engaged in the stock-for-stock exercise described previously four years after the grant date, he might be granted a reload option for 400 shares (ignoring, for the sake of simplicity, any stock used for tax withholding purposes) at an option price of $50 per share (the current fair market value of the stock) for a term of six years (the remaining term of the exercised underlying option).

Ahmed now is in a better position than he would have been with a cash exercise or a stock-for-stock exercise with no reload option. Under a cash exercise, he would have an exposure to ABC Corporation stock of 1400 directly owned shares (400 previously owned and 1000 option shares), but he would have had to come up with the $20,000 needed to exercise the underlying option. Under a stock-for-stock exercise with no reload feature, Ahmed's exposure to ABC stock would be reduced to 1000 directly owned shares (the option shares). However, under the stock-for-stock exercise with a reload feature, his exposure to ABC stock remains at 1400 shares (1000 directly owned option shares and 400 reload option shares), but he does not need to disturb his other assets or cash reserves to exercise the underlying option. This occurs because Ahmed has been given a new option (the reload option), which itself has value.

Valuation of Stock Options

This is a very complex subject. It is made even more so by the fact that employee stock options are different in many ways from publicly traded stock and other options discussed in Chapter 10. In essence, however, employee stock options are really call options for the employees on employer stock.

People may be concerned about the valuation of employee stock options for many reasons. To the extent employers "expense" options when they vest, obviously they must be valued. Employees want to know what they are really worth, since options have become an important part of many compensation arrangements. They also need to be valued for purposes of an employee's asset allocation planning. In some cases, employees may give up cash compensation in exchange for stock options, so they want to have an idea of what the options are worth to evaluate the exchange. Finally, employee stock options may need to be valued for estate planning.

Traded Options

The market prices of publicly traded options are readily available in the financial press and from other sources. Employee stock options, of course, are not publicly traded and have no readily ascertainable market value.

Most traded options are for relatively short durations, such as a few months. However, just to get an idea of how the market values longer-term options relative to the prices of the underlying stocks, it may be instructive to note the market premiums (prices) for leaps. *Leaps* are longer-term publicly traded options. For example, as of this writing, the price of a 21-month call option on one major company's stock with a strike price of $40 when the underlying stock's current market price is $37.35 (i.e., this call option was out of the money) was $5.60 per share, or about 15 percent of the underlying stock's market price.

Naturally, the prices of such publicly traded long-term options will vary with the characteristics of the underlying stocks and market conditions. The only point we are making here is that the market itself sets a considerable value on longer-term options, even when they have no intrinsic value or are out of the money. Clearly then, the market value (as well as the economic value) of long-term options can be substantial.

Intrinsic Value

As noted in Chapters 9 and 13, the intrinsic value of a stock option is the difference between the underlying stock's current market price and the option's strike price. For example, if an employee is granted a 10-year NQSO with an option price of $25 per share when the underlying stock's market price also is $25 per share, the intrinsic value of the option is $0 at grant. As we have just seen for traded options, the intrinsic value does not reflect the fair value or economic worth of an option. In fact, as will be shown in the next section, the economic worth of long-term options can be quite substantial.

Option Pricing Models

A number of models (mathematical systems of analysis) have been developed to compute the fair value or economic worth of options. Probably the best known is the Black-Scholes option pricing model. This model is based on the following six factors to determine the economic value of an option.[6] (Let us say for the following illustration of these factors that we are valuing an employee stock option.)

- Option exercise price (strike price).
- Current market price of the underlying stock.

- Risk-free interest rate during the expected term of the option.
- Expected dividend yield on the stock.
- Expected life of the option. This is the time period for which the employee is actually expected to hold the option before exercising it. It may be shorter than the maximum option period in the plan.
- Expected volatility of the underlying stock's market price. This normally is the most important factor in the model. The greater the expected volatility, the more likely there will be time value gains (see note 6) and the greater the option value will be. Volatility can be estimated from the historical standard deviation of the stock's price changes over past time periods.

To illustrate the *fair value* of an option, let us continue our fact pattern for the NQSO noted earlier with respect to intrinsic value. Using the factors just listed, we assume that this NQSO has an option exercise price of $25 per share, a current market price for the underlying stock is also $25 per share, the assumed risk-free interest rate is 5 percent, the expected dividend yield is 0, the assumed expected life of the option is 10 years, and the expected volatility of the underlying stock's price is 20 percent per month. Under these assumptions, the Black-Scholes model would produce a fair value of $19.75 per option. This is 79 percent of the underlying stock's current price. Of course, if the assumed expected life of the option were reduced, the fair value would decline. For example, if the expected life were one year, the fair value would be $7.24 per option. Most employee stock options have an expected life of considerably more than one year. Software is available for calculating the fair value of options under option pricing models.

It is clear from this discussion that the *economic value (fair value)* of stock options granted to employees can be substantial. However, it must also be recognized that the *actual value* of such options may never reach the fair value at grant (from an option pricing model) and may even be zero, if the actual market price of the underlying stock fails to rise from the option price or declines.

Sometimes when a stock's price falls and many executive stock options are "under water" (i.e., the stock's market price is below the option price and the option is out of the money), the employer will *reprice the options* to be equal to the stock's current market price (i.e., cancel the old out-of-the-money options and issue new ones at the stock's current market value). However, this tactic is controversial.

---

6 The concept behind these option pricing models is that the fair value of an option (which, in general, is an instrument that allows, but does not require, a person to buy or sell an asset at a prearranged price during a set time period) consists of two elements: (1) the intrinsic value and (2) a time value, arising because the option holder may benefit from favorable future price movements (volatility) in the asset without having the downside risk of actual ownership of the asset.

Some Caveats Concerning Stock Options and Other Plans

While employee stock options and other stock compensation plans have been a boon for many employees and a bonanza for some, some caveats concerning them are in order.

What Goes Up Can Come Down!

It seems almost trite to say that while employee stock plans can be very attractive when the price of a company's stock is rising, the reverse will be true when the price is falling. However, some employees may not truly understand this. They can overcommit themselves financially on the basis of paper gains in their stock options and other plans.

Some Employees May Not Realize the True Economic Worth of Options

The other side of the coin is that some employees may not truly understand or may have difficulty in analyzing the economic value of options or other stock rights granted to them.

Risk of Excessive Concentration in Employer Stock

While employees usually are well advised to take advantage of these plans when they are attractive to them, they also should deal with any issue of overconcentration, assuming they want a reasonably diversified investment portfolio.

Planning Issues Regarding Stock Options and Other Stock Plans

Some of these issues may be summarized as follows:

- Whether to participate in employee stock purchase offerings. This depends on the terms of the plan and the employer stock, but in general, these plans are advantageous for employees and are flexible as to whether participating employees will take the stock.
- When to exercise stock options. This can be a complicated issue. An employee can simply hold a vested, unexercised option for as long as possible before exercising it. In this case, he or she can benefit if the underlying stock rises in price above the option's exercise price without actually com-

mitting any funds and delay income taxation in the case of NQSOs until exercise. This can also be attractive if income tax rates on ordinary compensation income (such as will arise from exercising NQSOs) will decline in the future, as under EGTRRA, for example. But if there is a concern that the stock's price may fall and not really ever recover during the remaining option period, it is better to exercise now and sell the stock as soon as possible. Also, if overconcentration in employer stock is an issue, as it often is, the exercise of NQSOs and immediate sale of the stock can be a tax-efficient remedy, since compensation income must be realized at some point anyway and there is no capital gain on immediate sale because the basis is equal to fair market value at exercise.

■ Whether, in effect, to change an ISO into an NQSO by breaking an ISO requirement (i.e., making a disqualifying disposition by sale of the stock within one year of exercise). This may be done to avoid an AMT problem or if the stock's price is expected to fall dramatically. A planning technique that may be used in this situation is *AMT neutralization*. In AMT neutralization, the employee sells enough ISO shares (after exercise) in disqualifying dispositions so that his or her regular tax for the year becomes equal to his or her AMT. Then there is no AMT to pay.

■ How to exercise options (including possible availability of reload options).

■ Whether to make a Section 83(b) election with regard to restricted stock or other plans.

■ Whether to take option stock as restricted stock if available. This is done to further delay recognition of income on exercise of NQSOs.

■ Whether to take bonuses or other compensation in the form of stock options, if available.

■ How to maintain investment diversification in light of favorable terms for acquiring more and more employer stock.

■ Any estate planning actions with regard to stock plans. This might include making gifts of NQSOs, if allowed by the plan. However, such gifts should be analyzed carefully. It also may include the exercise of any in-the-money unexercised NQSOs *before death* (e.g., a "death bed exercise") for estate tax reasons.

Estate Planning

23

Estate Planning Principles

Estate planning can be defined as arranging for the transfer of a person's property from one generation to another so as to achieve, as far as possible, the person's objectives for his or her family and perhaps others. In our tax-oriented economy, tax minimization often is an important motivator for estate planning. Tax saving, however, is not the only goal of estate planning and should not be overemphasized.

Objectives of Estate Planning

The following are a number of specific estate planning objectives, some or all of which apply to most people.

1. Determining who will be the estate owner's heirs or beneficiaries and how much each will receive.
2. Planning adequate financial support for the estate owner's dependents.
3. Reducing estate transfer costs (death taxes, expenses of administration, and the like) to a minimum, consistent with the estate owner's other objectives.
4. Planning for the way in which the estate owner's heirs or beneficiaries are to receive the assets passing to them. This often involves the question of whether they are to receive assets outright or in trust and, if a trust is to be used, what its terms, conditions, and duration should be, as well as who should be trustee or trustees.
5. Providing sufficient liquid assets for the estate to meet its obligations.
6. Planning for possible arrangements (such as irrevocable life insurance

trusts) that will conserve the estate for the owner's heirs and beneficiaries in the face of inevitable shrinkage due to taxes and expenses.

7. Deciding who is to settle the estate. This involves selecting the executor or co-executors.
8. Planning how the estate owner's property is to be distributed. The methods of property disposition are outlined in the next section.
9. Planning for the disposition of any closely held business interests.
10. Planning for any charitable giving.

Methods of Property Disposition

These methods are outlined briefly here to give an overview of how wealth may be moved to others.

I. Lifetime transfers
   A. Lifetime gifts
      1. Outright
      2. In irrevocable trusts (inter vivos trusts)
      3. In custodianships
   B. Exercise of powers of appointment
   C. Exercise of powers of attorney
   D. As noncharitable beneficiary of split gifts to charity
   E. Sales within the family

II. Transfers at death
   A. By will
      1. Outright
      2. In trust (testamentary trust)
   B. Intestate distribution (not desirable)
   C. Life insurance beneficiary designations
      1. Individuals
         a. Outright
         b. Under settlement options
      2. To trusts
   D. Qualified retirement plan, TSA, and IRA beneficiary designations
      1. To surviving spouse
      2. To other individuals
      3. To trusts
      4. To charity
   E. Other beneficiary designations (such as nonqualified annuities and nonqualified deferred compensation)
   F. Revocable living trusts

G. Joint tenancy with right of survivorship
H. Other arrangements (such as Transfer on Death [TOD] in states that have adopted the Uniform Transfer on Death Act)

Property and Property Interests

In general, *property* is anything that can be owned. Basically, there are two kinds of property: real property and personal property. *Real property* (or real estate) is land and everything attached to the land with the intention that it be part of the land. *Personal property* is all other kinds of property.

Personal property can be *tangible*—property that has physical substance, such as a car, jewelry, art, or antiques—or it can be *intangible*—property that does not have physical substance, such as a stock certificate, a bond, a bank deposit, or a life insurance policy.

Forms of Property Ownership

Outright Ownership. Outright or sole owners hold property in their own names and can deal with it during their lifetimes. They can sell it, use it as collateral, or give it away. They can also pass it on to their heirs by will as they wish, within some broad limits.

Joint Ownership (or Concurrent Interests in Property). This exists when two or more persons have ownership rights in the same property at the same time. The more important kinds of joint ownership are as follows.

Joint Tenancy (with Right of Survivorship). The outstanding characteristic of joint tenancy with right of survivorship (JTWROS) is that if one of the joint owners dies all ownership in the property passes automatically (by operation of law) to the other joint owner(s). This is the meaning of "with right of survivorship" (WROS).

Thus, if John and his wife Mary own their residence as joint tenants WROS and John dies, Mary automatically owns the residence (now in her own name) by right of survivorship. The same would be true if John and his daughter Susan owned some investment real estate as joint tenants WROS.

Joint tenancy WROS can exist between or among any individuals—not just husband and wife. However, as a practical matter, it often exists between husband and wife and sometimes between parents and children. During the lifetime of the joint tenants, the survivorship aspect can be destroyed by one of the joint tenants through a sale of his or her interest or attachment by his or her creditors. The parties then own the property as tenants in common, explained below.

Tenancy by the Entirety. In some states, this form of ownership exists when property is held jointly by a husband and wife. It is similar to a joint tenancy, but there are some differences. Tenancy by the entirety exists only between husband and wife. Also, in many states the survivorship rights in it cannot be terminated except with the consent of both parties.

The fact that property is held as joint tenants or tenants by the entirety does not mean it has to stay that way. The joint owners can agree to split up their interests. The advantages and disadvantages of joint ownership are discussed in Chapter 28.

Other Joint Interests. There are some other forms of joint ownership that involve the right of survivorship. These include joint bank accounts and some joint brokerage accounts and jointly owned government savings bonds.

Tenancy in Common. The main difference between this and the previous kinds of joint ownership is that tenants in common do not have the right of survivorship. If John and his brother Frank own investment real estate equally as tenants in common and John dies, his half of the real estate goes to his heirs under his will. Frank, of course, retains his half interest. Tenants in common can have different proportionate interests in property.

For example, John and Frank could have 75 and 25 percent interests, respectively. In contrast, joint tenants WROS and tenants by the entirety always have equal interests.

Some practitioners may apply *valuation discounts* (fractional interest discounts) for lack of control and lack of marketability on the part of one tenant in common. Such discounts may apply in making gifts of property to persons as tenants in common or in the estate of a deceased tenant in common. As of this writing, the IRS has not accepted such valuation discounts, but courts often have approved them.

Community Property. Eight states (Arizona, California, Idaho, Louisiana, Nevada, New Mexico, Texas, and Washington) are community property states. In addition, the Uniform Marital Property Act (UMPA) provides that property acquired during marriage, with certain exceptions, is owned one-half by each spouse. This is called *marital property.* Wisconsin has adopted the UMPA. While there are some technical differences, marital property is essentially the same as community property. Finally, Alaska allows married couples to elect to treat some assets as marital property.

The other states are referred to as *common-law states.* In these states, the forms of property ownership described previously apply. But in the nine community property or marital property states the situation is quite different with respect to property owned by husbands and wives.

General Principles. In community property states, husbands and wives can own separate property and community property. While the laws of community property states are not uniform, *separate property* generally consists of property that a husband or wife owned at the time of marriage, property that each individually inherits or receives as a gift, separate property before the couple became domiciled in a community property state, and property purchased with separate property funds. This property remains separate property and the owner-spouse can deal with it as he or she chooses. Income from separate property may remain separate property or become community property, depending on the state involved.

Community property, on the other hand, generally consists of property that either spouse acquires during marriage from his or her earnings while domiciled in a community property or marital property state. Each spouse has an undivided one-half interest in their community property. While the husband and wife are both alive, the applicable community property law determines who has the rights of management and control over the community property. However, upon his or her death, each spouse can dispose of only his or her half of the community property by will.

However, even those living in states that are not community property states can have community property. This can happen if spouses once lived in a community property state and acquired community property there. Such property often remains community property even after the owners move to a common-law state. However, property acquired by spouses while domiciled in a common-law state does not become community property when they move to a community property state.

Community property laws generally presume that all property owned by a married couple domiciled in the state is community property or marital property, regardless of how it is actually titled, unless there is an agreement between the parties about the status of the property that provides otherwise or there is *proof* that the property is separate property. Thus, if community property and separate property are commingled and if adequate records are not kept so that the separate property can be traced, this presumption normally will cause all the commingled property to become community property. Also, how community property is titled (as solely owned by one spouse, for example) does not matter. It will be treated as community property if that is what it is.

Spouses or prospective spouses can enter into agreements about the community property or separate property status of property they own or will acquire in the future. Such prenuptial or postnuptial agreements are recognized in all community property and marital property states. They must, of course, conform to the requirements of state law. (Marital agreements in general are discussed later in this chapter.)

Planning Issues. Planning for community property can be complicated and generally is beyond the scope of this book. However, it may be noted that holding property as community property even after the parties have moved to a common-law state may have several advantages. Perhaps foremost is that for federal income tax purposes all of community property or marital property currently gets a stepped-up income tax basis at death even though only half its value is included in the gross estate of a deceased spouse. By contrast, for other property interests, only property included in a decedent's gross estate gets a stepped-up basis. For federal estate tax purposes, community property automatically is divided equally between the spouses. Also, there may be minority and fractional interest valuation discounts in the case of community property because each spouse owns only an undivided one-half interest.

Other Property Interests

There are other interests in property that are commonly involved in estate planning. An example can help illustrate these interests.

By his will, A leaves property to the XYZ Bank *in trust* to keep it invested and to distribute the net income from it to his wife, B, if she survives him, during her lifetime. At B's death or at A's death, if B does not survive him, the property is to go outright in equal shares to C and D (A's adult children) or their issue (descendants).

Legal Interests and Equitable Interests. In this example, upon A's death the XYZ Bank technically becomes legal owner of the property that passes into the trust. But the bank must exercise ownership rights as trustee, according to the terms of the trust agreement. The trustee acts in a *fiduciary capacity* with respect to the trust. B, C, and D have equitable (or beneficial) interests in the property, since it is held for their benefit.

Life Interests, Term Interests, and Remainder Interests. A *life interest* in property entitles the holder to the income from or the use of all or a portion of the property for his or her lifetime. A *term interest* entitles the holder to the income from or the use of all or a portion of the property for a term of years. The *remainder interest* entitles a remainderperson to the property itself after a life interest or term interest has ended. In the example just given, B has a life interest in the trust property. C and D or, if they are deceased, their descendants have remainder interests and are remainderpersons. Life interests usually are created by trusts, but there can also be legal life estates without a trust.

Further trusts may give the *grantor* (the creator of a trust) a use interest (essentially an income interest), an annuity interest, or a unitrust interest in the trust for a term of years followed by a remainder interest to someone else. These are called grantor-retained income trusts (GRITs), grantor-retained annuity trusts (GRATs), and grantor-retained unitrusts (GRUTs).[1]

Present Interests and Future Interests. A *present interest* exists in property when the holder has a present and immediate right to the use, possession, or enjoyment of the property. With a *future interest,* the right to use or enjoy the property is postponed to some future time or is in the control of someone other than the holder. In the previous example, upon A's death, B has a present interest in the trust income because she has the immediate right to it for her lifetime. C and D have future interests because their rights to the property are postponed until B's death. As we shall see later, the concepts of present and future interests are important in connection with gift taxes.

Powers of Appointment. A *power of appointment* is a right given to a person (called the *donee of the power*) that enables him or her to designate, sometimes within certain limits, who is to get property that is subject to the power. The basic nontax purposes of powers of appointment are to postpone and delegate the decision about who is to get property until a later time when the circumstances can be better known. Powers also are used for estate tax and generation-skipping transfer (GST) tax reasons, as will be explained later. There are several kinds of powers of appointment as explained next.

General Powers. A *general power* is a power to appoint property to the person having the power (the donee), the donee's estate, the donee's creditors, or creditors of the donee's estate. It is close to owning the property. For federal estate tax purposes, property will be included in the gross estate of someone who has a general power over it.

Special or Limited Powers (Nongeneral Powers). These powers allow donees to appoint property only to certain persons who are not the donees themselves, their estate, their creditors, or the creditors of their estate. The possession of a special or limited power over property at a person's death does *not* result in the property's being included in the donee's gross estate.

How Property Is Appointed. When donees of either a general or a nongeneral power can appoint the property only at their death, it is referred to as a power exercisable *by will* or a *testamentary power.* A power exercisable *by deed* is one that allows donees to appoint the property only during their lifetime. The

---

[1] Note that the terms *annuity trust* and *unitrust* are the same as used in Chapter 16 to describe charitable remainder annuity trusts (CRATs) and charitable remainder unitrusts (CRUTs). The ideas are essentially the same, except that the remainderperson in the case of GRATs and GRUTs is a noncharitable entity (e.g., a family member) while for CRATs and CRUTs the remainderperson is a charity.

broadest power in this respect is one exercisable *by deed or will,* which is exercisable both ways.

Powers Subject to an Ascertainable Standard. When the exercise of a power by a person is subject to an *ascertainable standard* (such as for the person's health, education, maintenance, or support), it is not considered a general power for tax purposes; hence, the property subject to the power will not be included in the power holder's gross estate. This point can be important in structuring trusts.

Marital Rights in Property

This has become an increasingly important subject because of societal changes and other factors. The Retirement Equity Act (REA) of 1984 has already been covered in Chapter 17 and will not be discussed here.

Spouse's Elective Share. With certain exceptions, people can leave their property by will to whomever they like. One important exception, however, is that in many states a husband or wife cannot deprive his or her surviving spouse of the spouse's statutory elective share of the estate under state law. This is referred to as the *spouse's right to elect against the will.* Taking against the will does not deny the will's validity, but simply involves the spouse's taking his or her elective share (forced share) allowed by law rather than what is left to him or her under the will.

Originally, elective share statutes only gave a surviving spouse rights to part of a deceased spouse's probate estate (to be defined next). In 1969, the *Uniform Probate Code* (UPC) modified this traditional approach by allowing a surviving spouse to elect to take part (usually one-third or one-half) of his or her deceased spouse's *augmented estate.* The augmented estate includes probate and some nonprobate assets. This original UPC approach has been adopted by several states. Then, in 1990 a revised UPC, amended in 1993, again changed the rules. The augmented estate was changed to include a surviving spouse's property, to provide for a minimum supplemental elective share allowance, and to include life insurance, annuities, and retirement benefits. Several states have adopted this revised UPC approach. Thus, there is considerable variation among state laws regarding the elective share.

To avoid a surviving spouse's electing to take against the will, persons with property who are about to marry may enter into prenuptial agreements or, after marriage, postnuptial agreements under which each party relinquishes in whole or in part his or her statutory rights to the other's property at death. These agreements can also deal with property rights incident to divorce. Finally, it should be noted that, except in one state, children do not have any comparable right to a spouse's elective share in their parents' estates.

Marital Rights on Divorce. The states have adopted equitable distribution statutes applying to so-called marital property in the event of divorce. Under these statutes, the appropriate court can divide a divorcing couple's marital property between the parties in an "equitable manner" according to certain factors specified in state domestic relations law, regardless of how title to the marital property is actually held.

What is marital property can vary among the states, but it may include all property acquired during marriage from the earnings of either spouse, with certain exceptions. Thus, it may not include, for example, property owned by a person before marriage or property acquired by a spouse by gift or inheritance. However, if this exempt property is commingled with marital property and if adequate records are not kept so that nonmarital property can be traced, all the property may be considered marital property. Thus, if gift property is placed in an irrevocable trust (by a parent or grandparent, for example) for a trust beneficiary (child or grandchild), the corpus of the trust normally would clearly be identified as exempt property (gift property) in the event of the beneficiary's divorce (i.e., it would be "divorce-proof"). The same would be true for property placed in family limited partnerships (FLPs) for gifts of limited partnership interests. Also, as just noted, to avoid the effects of equitable distribution statutes or other divorce laws, persons who are about to marry are increasingly entering into prenuptial (antenuptial) agreements that specify how their property is to be divided in the event of divorce.

Prenuptial Agreements. For a variety of reasons, prenuptial (antenuptial) agreements are becoming increasingly common. They are now recognized in virtually all states. However, the rules regarding these agreements vary among the states. There is a Uniform Premarital Agreement Act (UPAA), which has been adopted in about half the states. The UPAA requires such agreements to be in writing and signed by both parties and provides that they can cover many issues, including the disposition of any property of either or both parties upon separation, marital dissolution, death, or the occurrence or nonoccurrence of any event. A prenuptial agreement becomes effective on marriage. The general rule is that spousal consent to a REA waiver in a prenuptial agreement is not effective. Consent must be given when the nonparticipant is a spouse. It is often necessary that there be full, fair, and reasonable disclosure of the property and obligations of the parties.

Planning Considerations. We have seen in this chapter and elsewhere that marriage can create certain rights in the property of each spouse. However, for estate planning, retirement planning, or other reasons, spouses may want to relinquish or modify some of these marital rights. To review, the kinds of marital agreements that have been covered in this book are:

- Waiver of REA rights in qualified retirement plans by the participant spouse and written consent to the waiver in the proper form by the nonparticipant spouse
- Prenuptial (and postnuptial) agreements concerning spousal rights in property at death
- Prenuptial (and postnuptial) agreements concerning spousal rights in property incident to divorce
- Prenuptial and postnuptial agreements concerning community and separate property

What Is Meant by the "Estate"?

Probate Estate

The *probate estate* is the property that is handled and distributed by the personal representative (executor if there is a will or administrator if there is not) upon a person's death. Thus, probate property is the property of which the decedent's will disposes, including:

- Property owned outright in the person's own name
- The person's interests in property held as tenants in common
- Proceeds or benefits payable to the person's estate at death
- The person's half of community property

It is sometimes argued that having property pass through a decedent's probate estate is bad. This is not necessarily true; it really depends on the circumstances. There are, however, some disadvantages in leaving property so that it will be part of a person's probate estate, such as the following:

- There will be *delay* in settling the estate.
- The *costs* of administering an estate (executor's fees, attorney's fees, etc.) may be based largely on the probate estate.
- Assets in the probate estate are subject to *creditor's claims.*
- The probate estate can be made *public knowledge.*
- Disgruntled heirs may seek to *contest* a will and hence get at probate assets.
- Sometimes state death taxes can be increased, depending on the property and the state involved.

On the other hand, having property bypass the probate estate is not an estate planning panacea. Cost savings from avoiding probate depend on the circumstances and may not be that significant. Further, some methods commonly advocated for avoiding probate (such as the revocable living trust) have costs of their own. (See Chapter 28.) Other arrangements (such as jointly owned property) may have significant estate tax problems. (See Chapter 26.) Therefore, avoiding probate is not an open-and-shut issue and should be evaluated carefully.

Most people have a probate estate. First, property owned outright at death must pass through the probate estate. Many people will hold property in a variety of ways during their lifetimes—some in the probate estate and some not. Finally, estate owners usually want their executor to have adequate assets to pay the claims, expenses, and taxes that will be owed by their estate.

Gross Estate for Federal Estate Tax Purposes

The gross estate is defined by the tax law and is the starting point for calculating how much federal estate tax is due. The calculation of the gross estate is just illustrated here; it is explained more fully in Chapter 24.

State Death Tax Value

All states except Nevada have some form of death tax. Some have *inheritance taxes* that are levied on the right to receive property by inheritance, many have *estate taxes* that are levied on the right to give property at death, and some have both.

The Net Estate to One's Heirs

The *net* estate to one's heirs is what most people are really concerned about. Basically, this estate consists of the assets that will go to one's heirs after payment of the costs of dying (debts, claims, administration expenses, and taxes).

An Illustration of These Estates

To illustrate these ideas, let us take the case of a successful executive, George Able, and his wife, Mary. They have three children, ages 22, 18, and 14. George's asset picture may be summarized as follows. He owns in his own name about $620,000 worth of his employer's stock, which he acquired under the company's employee stock purchase plan and by exercising some nonqualified stock options (NQSOs). He also owns in his own name about $40,000 worth of other listed common stocks, $50,000 worth of mutual fund shares, $40,000 in a money market fund, and $30,000 worth of tangible personal property. George and Mary own jointly (WROS) their main home, worth about $680,000 and with a $100,000 mortgage still due; their summer home, valued at about $300,000 and with a $100,000 mortgage still due; and savings and checking accounts of $20,000. In addition to these mortgages, George has a

$40,000 bank loan outstanding and about $10,000 of other personal debts.

Through his employer, George has group term life insurance of $450,000, which is payable to Mary as primary beneficiary; a qualified profit-sharing plan with $500,000 credited to George's account; and a qualified savings plan, with a Section 401(k) option, with $700,000 credited to his account. The benefits of the profit-sharing and savings plans also are payable to Mary at George's death. Finally, George owns individually purchased life insurance policies on his life having total death benefits of $300,000, payable to his estate as beneficiary.

George has a will that leaves everything outright to Mary if she survives him; otherwise, everything is left outright to his children in equal shares. George and Mary have always lived in common-law states.

Thus, George's property interests can be summarized as follows:

Property George owns outright in his own name:

His employer's common stock:	$620,000
Other listed common stock:	40,000
Mutual fund shares:	50,000
Money market fund:	40,000
Tangible personal property:	30,000
	$780,000

Property George and Mary own jointly (WROS):

Principal residence:	680,000
Summer home:	300,000
Savings and checking accounts:	20,000
	$1,000,000

Life insurance George owns on his own life:

Group term life insurance, payable to Mary in a lump sum:	450,000
Individual life insurance, payable to George's estate in a lump sum:	300,000
	$750,000

Retirement plan benefits:

Profit-sharing plan death benefit, payable to Mary:	500,000
Savings plan death benefit, payable to Mary:	700,000
	$1,200,000

Given these facts, if George were to die today, his *probate estate* would be $1,080,000. This consists of the $780,000 of property George owns in his own name and the $300,000 of life insurance proceeds payable to his estate. The rest of the assets pass to Mary outside of George's probate estate.

Again assuming George were to die today, his *gross estate for federal estate tax purposes* would be $3,230,000, calculated as follows. (The items included in the gross estate are described more fully in Chapter 24.)

Property owned in the decedent's own name:	$780,000
One-half of property owned jointly (WROS) by him and Mary ($1,000,000 ÷ 2 = $500,000)[2]:	500,000
Life insurance on George's life which he owned (i.e., in which he had incidents of ownership) at the time of his death or was payable to his estate:	750,000
Retirement plan death benefits:	1,200,000
Gross estate:	$3,200,000

In this case, because of the unlimited federal estate tax marital deduction, there would be no federal estate tax payable at his death as his estate now stands. However, as will be explained more fully in Chapter 26, it would be a better planning strategy if all of George's estate were not qualified (eligible) for the marital deduction. Only the proper amount should be qualified. This is because, as matters now stand, a greater tax burden than necessary probably will fall on Mary's estate when she dies. Let us also assume there would be no state death tax payable at George's death in this case.

Now, let us see what George can transmit to his family—his net estate. This is estimated as follows:

Total assets and death benefits (including jointly owned property and retirement assets)[3]:	$3,730,000
Less:	
George's debts (including the full amount of mortgages on homes):	$330,000
Estimated funeral and estate administration expenses:	55,000
Estimated federal estate tax payable:	0
Estimated state death tax payable:	0
Total estate shrinkage:	-385,000
Net estate to George's family:	$3,345,000

---

[2] One-half of jointly owned property (WROS) held by husband and wife is included in the gross estate of the first spouse to die. This is referred to as the *fractional interest rule*.

[3] The retirement assets would produce income in respect of a decedent (IRD) for the beneficiary (Mary in this case) and hence result in an income tax liability for her. (See Chapter 14.) However, depending on her age, this tax liability can be long deferred and so is not counted as "shrinkage" here.

Settling the Estate

When a person dies, what happens to his or her property? This depends on whether the person died *intestate*—that is, without having made a valid will—or *testate*—with a *valid will*. People normally should make a valid will.

Intestate Distribution

If someone dies intestate, his or her probate estate is distributed according to the applicable state intestate law. An administrator appointed by a court handles the estate settlement. The estate owner has no voice in who will receive the property or who will be administrator. This normally should be avoided. The laws of intestate distribution vary among the states. A surviving spouse first is entitled to his or her statutory share of the estate.[4] Then, there is a statutory order of distribution to other persons.

Problems with Intestate Distribution

We noted that people normally should make a will. A number of problems can arise when a person dies intestate.

1. Perhaps most important is that intestate distribution is not chosen by the estate owner. It is dictated by the applicable state statute.
2. Beneficiaries receive their inheritances outright, without regard to their individual capacities to manage property. Guardians must be appointed for minor beneficiaries. Trusts cannot be used for the heirs.
3. The estate owner cannot select his or her executor.
4. Estate taxes may be increased because the surviving spouse's share may not be large enough to take full advantage of the marital deduction or, on the other hand, may be too large for efficient tax planning.

Distribution by Will

A *will* is a legally enforceable declaration of what people want done with their probate property and their instructions about other matters when they die. A will does not take effect until the person (testator) dies and he or she may change or revoke it at any time. Thus, a will is referred to as being *ambulatory* until the maker dies. To be effective, a will must be executed in accordance with the legal requirements of the state for a valid will. It is important for both husband and wife to have valid wills for a complete estate plan.

---

[4] Note that this is not the same as a spouse's right to elect to take against the will. In that case, there is a valid will.

Steps in Estate Settlement

What does a deceased's personal representative (executor under a will or administrator of a person dying intestate) do in settling the estate? After the executor or administrator is appointed, the following are the basic functions performed. The time required to settle an estate can vary greatly—from a year or less to many years.

1. Assembling the property belonging to the estate (probate property).
2. Safekeeping, safeguarding, and insuring estate property during estate administration.
3. Managing estate property temporarily.
4. Paying estate debts, expenses, and taxes. A will normally contains a *tax clause* indicating what interest or interests will bear death taxes.
5. Accounting for the estate administration.
6. Making distribution of the net estate to the proper heirs.

For performing these functions, the executor is entitled to reasonable compensation, which is deducted from the estate. Sometimes individual executors will consider waiving this compensation (fee), as explained next.

Selecting the Executor or Coexecutors

An executor can be an individual (e.g., the testator's spouse, brother or sister, an adult son or daughter, a trusted friend, etc.), a professional executor (e.g., a bank or trust company or an attorney), or coexecutors (such as the testator's spouse and a bank). An estate owner may consider naming an individual executor or executors who also may be family members and heirs under the will. However, an executor's duties can be complex, time-consuming, and technical, and the executor can be held personally liable for mistakes or omissions. Therefore, many people decide to name a professional executor or a professional executor and one or more family members as coexecutors and pay the fee involved. Also, executors' fees are deductible from any federal estate tax due or on the decedent's final income tax return, whichever the executor elects.

When an individual (e.g., a family member) is named executor or coexecutor with a professional executor, he or she may consider waiving his or her executor's commission if the individual is an heir under the will. Any commission will be ordinary income to the individual, but will be deductible by the estate. However, the individual executor may not be the only heir under the will. While this decision depends on the circumstances, it would seem an individual executor should think carefully before waiving his or her executor's commissions.

An executor normally has an attorney to advise him or her regarding administering and settling the estate. The attorney's fees are charged to the estate and may be deductible by the estate or on the income tax return. The attorney for the estate generally is considered to represent the executor and not the heirs under the will. Thus, under some circumstances, heirs may need to secure their own legal counsel.

Trusts in Estate Planning

The famous jurist Oliver Wendell Holmes once said, "Don't put your trust in money; put your money in trust." Trusts have a very important place in tax and estate planning. We have already been introduced to the income taxation of trusts in Chapter 14. As noted there, a trust is a fiduciary arrangement[5] set up by someone, called the *grantor, creator,* or *settlor* of the trust, whereby a person, corporation, or organization, called the *trustee,* has *legal title* to property placed in the trust by the grantor. The trustee holds and manages this property, which technically is called the trust *corpus* or *principal,* for the benefit of someone, called the *beneficiary* of the trust. The beneficiary has *equitable* title to the trust property.

Kinds of Trusts

There are various kinds of trusts, but as far as how and when they are created are concerned, the most important are living (inter vivos) trusts, trusts under will (testamentary trusts), and insurance trusts. A *living trust* is created during the grantor's lifetime to benefit the grantor or someone else. The terms of a living trust are contained in a deed of trust executed during the grantor's lifetime. A *testamentary trust* is created under a person's will; like the will, it does not become effective until the grantor's death. The terms of a testamentary trust are part of the grantor's will. An *insurance trust* is a particular kind of living trust whose corpus consists partly or wholly of life insurance policies during the insured's lifetime and life insurance proceeds after the insured's death.

Living trusts can be revocable or irrevocable. The grantor of a *revocable trust* reserves the right to revoke or amend the trust. The creator of an *irrevocable trust* does not reserve the right to revoke or alter it. Most trusts are created by one person as grantor. In some cases, however, two or more persons will create *joint trusts.*

---

[5] A fiduciary is an individual or corporation that acts for the benefit of another with respect to things falling within the scope of the fiduciary relationship.

Reasons for Creating Trusts

Trusts have become very important in financial and estate planning. Some of the common reasons or purposes are as follows:

- To allow the trustee to use his, her, or its *discretion* (as a fiduciary) in handling trust property for the benefit of the creator, his or her family, or dependents within the terms of the trust.
- To provide a vehicle for holding family wealth as it passes from one generation to the next and perhaps over a number of generations.
- To protect the creator's family or dependents against demands and entreaties from well-meaning, or perhaps not so well-meaning, family members, friends, spouses, ex-spouses, spouses-to-be, and the like.
- To provide a way for *giving or leaving property to minors* so that the trustee can manage it for them until they are old enough to handle the property themselves.
- In some cases, to *protect trust beneficiaries against themselves* when they are physically, mentally, or emotionally unable to manage property.
- To *protect beneficiaries from their creditors*. If an irrevocable trust contains a *spendthrift clause*, which normally prohibits the beneficiary from alienating, assigning, or encumbering trust assets, the *beneficiary's* creditors generally can have no claim against trust assets. Correspondingly, trust assets can remain *free from marital claims* by present or future spouses of trust beneficiaries as gift property. These can be important reasons for giving property in trust rather than outright.
- To produce or encourage productive or socially useful behavior on the part of younger trust beneficiaries, as a corollary to the previous two reasons, through conditions or requirements in trust documents, especially for longer-term trusts. These might include, for example, educational requirements, work requirements, matching trust distributions with income that the beneficiary earns, pursuing socially useful (but perhaps lower-paid) occupations or activities, caring for other family members, distributions on marriage, and combinations of the above or others. Such provisions are intended to keep beneficiaries from simply living off the trust and doing nothing productive with their lives. Trusts with such provisions are often called *incentive trusts*.
- To create *special needs trusts* for beneficiaries with disabilities who need to maintain eligibility for various government benefits, like Medicaid. (See Chapter 6.) Special needs trusts limit the use of their assets and income to supplemental needs of the beneficiary that are not covered by government programs, and not primary care, so the beneficiary will not be disqualified

from receiving government benefits.

■ To provide *professional investment and property management for other benefi-ciaries or for the creator* during his or her lifetime. Also, investment diversification can be provided through common trust funds and mutual funds.

■ To *manage a business interest* after the owner's death until it can be sold or one of his or her heirs can take over.

■ To provide a vehicle for *setting up tax-saving* plans.

■ Sometimes to *protect grantors from their own future creditors.* This is a recent development; some states allow grantors to protect themselves from their own future creditors by placing assets in irrevocable trusts created in those states. When established in one of the states permitting them in the United States, they are commonly called *asset protection trusts (APTs)* or "onshore trusts." When established in a foreign country (some of which tailor their laws to attract such business), they often are called *offshore asset protection trusts (OAPTs).* Such *protection from the grantor's own creditors* is discussed further in the material on dynasty trusts.

Trustees' Fees

Trustees, like executors, may receive compensation for their work. The fees charged by professional trustees vary; however, they usually are based on the value of trust corpus with a minimum annual fee. Trustees also may charge payout commissions on principal distributed from a trust. The following is an example of an annual commission schedule for personal trusts:

Account Value: Trust Corpus	Managed Account: Individually Managed Portfolio	Managed Account: 100% Invested in Trustee's Own Mutual Funds*
First $500,000	.90%	.55%
$500,001-$1,000,000	.90%	.45%
$1,000,001-$2,000,000	.70%	.35%
$2,000,001-$4,000,000	.60%	.25%
Over $4,000,000	.50%	.25%
Minimum Annual Fee	$3,000	$1,500

*Investment of trust assets in mutual funds now is permitted because the Uniform Prudent Investor Act allows trustees to prudently delegate trust investment activities. The percentage of the trust corpus is reduced because there also is a charge for investment management included in the mutual fund's expense ratio. See Chapter 12.

Thus, if we assume an individually managed trust with $500,000 of principal (corpus) and earnings $25,000 per year in investment income, the trustee's annual fee under this schedule would be $4500 ($500,000 × .009). This equals 0.90 percent of the principal and 18 percent of the income.

Who Should Be Trustee and What Should Be the Trust's Situs?

A trustee can be an individual, a corporation, or any other group or organization legally capable of owning property. There can be one trustee or two or more cotrustees. The selection of a trustee is an important decision and the choice often boils down to an individual or a corporate trustee.

Cotrustees can be, for example, two or more individuals or a corporate trustee and one or more individual trustees. The creator of a trust or a beneficiary of the trust can be a trustee, but care must be taken to avoid tax problems when the creator (or his or her spouse) or a beneficiary is trustee or a cotrustee.

An individual trustee may be the creator, a member of the family, a trusted friend, an attorney, or someone else. The creator may want to continue to administer the property as trustee, making investment decisions, for example. In this case, however, care must be taken in drafting the trust so there are not unintended tax results. An individual trustee might decide not to charge any fee. It can also be argued that an individual trustee may be closer to the trust beneficiaries and hence more likely than a corporate trustee to be responsive to their needs. Finally, individual trustees can get professional help from attorneys, investment advisors, financial planners, and the like in administering the trust.

On the other hand, arguments can be made for the use of corporate trustees. Corporate trustees are professional money and property managers and hence can provide technical expertise in this area. Also, individual trustees may die, resign, or otherwise become incapacitated, while corporate trustees provide continuity of management. In addition, corporate trustees are unbiased and independent of family pressures. Corporate trustees also are financially able to respond to damages in the event of trust mismanagement. Further, if an individual trustee is given full discretionary powers over trust income or corpus, and he or she is a trust beneficiary, the trustee may be considered the owner of the trust corpus for federal estate and income tax purposes. This would not be true of a corporate trustee. On the other hand, properly drafted powers for individual trustees or beneficiaries (such as being subject to an ascertainable standard) normally will not give rise to these tax problems. Finally, a corporate trustee can serve as cotrustee with one or more individual trustees, thus combining at least some of the advantages of both.

It also is possible to provide in a trust agreement that a corporate trustee can be removed and another independent corporate trustee substituted upon the demand of trust beneficiaries, the grantor, or someone else. Thus, if one corporate trustee (or other independent trustee) should prove unsatisfactory, a mechanism can be provided in the trust instrument to replace that trustee with another corporate (or other independent) trustee.

The *situs* of a trust generally is the state or country where it is located. The law of the trust situs normally governs its construction and administration. Most trusts are located in the state where the grantor lives (the grantor's domicile). However, there has been an increasing tendency to establish trusts or to move existing trusts to take advantage of more favorable laws in states (or countries) other than the grantor's home state. These states generally allow trusts of greater duration (so-called "dynasty trust jurisdictions" that do not have a rule against perpetuities), enable stronger protection against creditors (often called "domestic APT jurisdictions"), and have no or low state income taxes on trust income.

Achieving Flexibility or Changes in Irrevocable Trusts

An irrevocable trust is one that cannot be revoked or amended by the grantor. However, it is possible to give others the power to change an irrevocable trust if changes in circumstances make it desirable. Such powers may be particularly helpful in face of the transfer tax uncertainties created by EGTRRA.

One approach is to name someone who is not a trust beneficiary as a *trust amender* or *trust protector* with powers to change the trust's terms. These powers can be limited, such as power to make administrative changes, or broader, such as allowing the trust protector to make substantive changes in the provisions of the trust. They can be conditioned on certain factual events, such as the actual repeal of the federal estate tax or imposition of carryover basis, or can arise in the event that the grantor becomes disabled. Of course, the grantor himself or herself could change the terms of a testamentary trust (by changing his or her will) or a revocable living trust, assuming he or she remains legally competent to do so.

Another approach is the give an *independent trustee* broad powers to make changes. For example, a trust document could give such a trustee power to make distributions of trust assets to another trust for the beneficiaries, effectively terminating the existing trust. An independent trustee also could be given power to change the situs of a trust. A practical problem with such planning for flexibility, however, is who should be named trust protector or independent trustee with broad powers. This can be a difficult and perhaps delicate choice, since this person or institution potentially might have considerable impact on the results for the grantor's family or other beneficiaries.

How Long Should Trusts Last?

Some trusts are intended to be for only a relatively short duration, such as until a minor reaches a certain age, like 35 or 40. Other trusts are for the beneficiary's lifetime, providing a life interest or a life estate. Recently, however, the concept has emerged of trusts created in some states that have unlimited duration and theoretically can last forever. These are commonly called *dynasty trusts* or *unlimited duration generation-skipping trusts*.

The old common law of trusts set a limit on the duration of trusts for public policy reasons. This is called the *rule against perpetuities*. It provides that an interest in property must vest (e.g., a trust must terminate) no later than the end of a period measured by a life or lives in being at the creation of the interest (the lives usually being the beneficiaries identified in the trust document) plus 21 years plus the period of gestation. This common-law rule has been incorporated into the statutory law of many states. Thus, it still serves to limit the permissible duration of trusts established in those states.

In recent years, however, other states have adopted the Uniform Statutory Rule Against Perpetuities (USRAP), promulgated in 1993. In these states, the maximum duration effectively is the longer of the traditional limit or 90 years, with the ability to reform interests that do not comply with this rule.

The most dramatic development in this area, however, has been that several states have recently amended their statutes generally to permit trusts created in those states to have unlimited duration (to be dynasty trusts). They have effectively repealed the rule against perpetuities in whole or in part and in essence allow trusts to last forever. As of this writing, these states include Alaska, Arizona, Colorado, Delaware, Idaho, Illinois, Maryland, South Dakota, and Wisconsin.

Some of these states also exempt trusts from state income and capital gains taxation. Also, some of them give trust assets that may be used for the grantor's benefit creditor protection against claims by the grantor's own *future* creditors (e.g., Alaska, Colorado, Delaware, Missouri, and Rhode Island). The nature of this protection against the grantor's own creditors varies somewhat among these states and, depending on state law, does not apply in certain situations. Dynasty trusts also may avoid *all future* estate taxes and generation-skipping transfer (GST) taxes since the trust never terminates.[6] They also can provide creditor protection against the beneficiaries' creditors (creditor-proof) and protection from marital claims against beneficiaries (divorce-proof) for an unlimited time. These trusts sometimes are referred to as *family banks*.

On the other hand, others may argue that keeping property tied up in trust indefinitely may not be a good idea. Future generations should be able to

---

[6] There might, of course, be a tax on the creation of the trust—a gift tax if created during the grantor's lifetime or an estate tax if created under the grantor's will. It may also be that the grantor has applied part or all of his or her generation-skipping transfer tax exemption to the trust so it will be exempt from the GST tax in the future. If not, the GST tax may apply to taxable distributions. See Chapter 24 for an explanation of the GST tax.

direct their own destinies even at the cost of higher wealth transfer taxes. Also, laws permitting dynasty trusts, and particularly those allowing protection against the grantor's own creditors, are quite new and have not yet been tested. These trusts also result in long-term trust administration and trustee fees. Finally, due to the nature and complexity of dynasty trusts, they probably are mainly for wealthy families.

Investment of Trust Assets

Trust instruments can direct how trust assets are to be invested. The grantor can put into the terms of the trust directions concerning investment policy that the trustee generally must follow. However, trusts frequently give trustees investment discretion under the terms of the law of the state where the trust is to be administered.

Uniform Prudent Investor Act. Many states have adopted the Uniform Prudent Investor Act, or some modification of it, which was first promulgated in 1994. This law applies to trust investments. It adopts the *prudent investor rule,*[7] which holds that a trustee should make trust investments by exercising reasonable care, skill, and caution, given the circumstances and objectives of the trust and considering the investment portfolio as a whole. The act applies modern portfolio theory to trust investments in that it is the overall risk/return relationships of the whole portfolio that must be evaluated, rather than any one asset class taken alone. No particular class or classes of investment are prohibited per se, but investment media are to be evaluated in terms of their relationship to the overall portfolio's risk structure (e.g., their degree of correlation with other assets in the portfolio).

The act generally requires diversification of investments, but there may be circumstances that will justify a lack of diversification. Trustees also are allowed to prudently delegate investment activities and so they can invest in properly selected mutual funds. As noted earlier, when trust institutions invest in their own mutual funds, they normally charge lower trustees' fees because of the funds' own expense ratio. The Uniform Prudent Investor Act generally applies unless the grantor provides otherwise in the trust instrument.

Common Trust Funds and Other Considerations. Many corporate trustees operate several *common trust funds* into which trust assets under their management can be placed. Common trust funds are much like mutual funds, in that the assets of many individual trusts are commingled into a single, managed investment fund. Corporate trustees may operate a number of common trust

---

[7] The prudent investor rule was first announced in 1992 in Section 227 of the American Law Institute's *Restatement (Third) of Trusts.*

funds with different investment objectives—common stock funds, balanced funds, bond funds, and the like. Thus, trust assets may be invested as separate assets for each trust, in mutual funds or other investment intermediaries, or in common trust funds.

Total Return Trusts. Normally when a trust specifies that income may or must be paid to a beneficiary, the income means interest, dividends, and possibly rents or other income from trust assets, but it does not include realized capital gains (unless the trust terms so provide) or distributions from principal (corpus). The practical problem with this system is that over the years dividend yields on common stocks have declined substantially. Thus, if a trust is invested for greatest reasonable total returns (e.g., with a substantial asset allocation to common stocks), the annual income to an income beneficiary will suffer and this beneficiary will be unhappy. On the other hand, if the trust is invested primarily for income (e.g., mainly in bonds), principal (corpus) growth will be inhibited and the remainderperson will be equally unhappy.

It is argued that the solution to his dilemma is the *total return trust,* in which a part of the annual payment to an income beneficiary may consist of principal. This allows the trustee to invest for total returns without being unfair to either group of beneficiaries. To help accomplish this, one approach has been to enact legislation granting trustees the discretionary power to adjust distributions by transferring principal to an income beneficiary (or the reverse—income to principal) to the extent the trustee believes is needed for equity among income and remainder beneficiaries. This power to adjust ("equitable adjustment") concept was adopted in the 1997 revision of the Uniform Principal and Income Act which, as of this writing, has been adopted in about half the states.

Another approach is legislation allowing trustees to convert an income-providing trust to a unitrust, often called a *total return unitrust* (TRU). A TRU requires or permits a trustee to distribute a fixed percentage (between 3 and 5 percent) of the current trust corpus (recalculated each year) to the current income beneficiary. The IRS has ruled that TRUs and "equitable adjustment trusts" under these laws providing unitrust payments of between 3 and 5 percent meet the requirements for marital deduction and certain GST trusts.

24

The Transfer
Tax System

This chapter gives an overview of the federal transfer tax system as it stands as of this writing—the federal gift tax, the estate tax, and the generation-skipping transfer (GST) tax. This system generally was designed so that wealth would be subject to a transfer tax in each generation. This includes lifetime transfers by gift, transfers at death, and transfers designed to skip generations. Thus, it has been referred to as a *unified transfer tax system*.

Impact of the Economic Growth and Tax Relief Reconciliation Act (EGTRRA)

As noted in Chapter 2, the *Economic Growth and Tax Relief Reconciliation Act* (EGTRRA) of 2001 may dramatically change this system. The three transfer taxes will remain, with some changes, through 2009. Then, in 2010 the federal estate tax and GST tax will be repealed entirely for that year, but the gift tax will be retained. However, in 2011, under the sunset provision, the unified transfer tax system will be reinstated as it stood in 2001. In fact, all provisions of EGTRRA will expire on December 31, 2010 and the law will return to its 2001 form in 2011. Most commentators think there will be new tax legislation before 2011 that will change this scenario, but no one can be sure.

Commentators generally are suggesting planning after EGTRRA much as before, with some modifications. However, flexibility in planning becomes more important than ever, because estate and GST taxes could actually be repealed, carry-over basis at death could occur, and the time of death is uncertain.

Applicable Credit Amount (Unified Credit) and Applicable Exclusion Amount

The tax law provides for each person a one-time *applicable credit amount (unified credit)*[1] of $345,800 in 2002 and 2003 that will increase in stages until 2010 according to the following schedule. Under present law, in 2010 the federal estate tax will be repealed. Then, in 2011 the credit again will become $345,800. This credit can be applied to reduce or eliminate any federal estate tax payable at the person's death.

The unified credit will allow a person to pass a substantial amount of wealth to others free of federal estate tax. This amount is called the *applicable exclusion amount.* The schedule of increasing the applicable exclusion amounts, the corresponding applicable credit amounts that will produce them, and the top marginal federal estate tax rates for years through 2011 and later are shown as follows. It will be observed that the top marginal estate tax rates decline in stages through 2009.

Year	Applicable Exclusion Amount	Applicable Credit Amount (Unified Credit)	Top Marginal Estate Tax Rate
2002	$1,000,000	$345,800	50%
2003	$1,000,000	$345,800	49%
2004	$1,500,000	$555,800	48%
2005	$1,500,000	$555,800	47%
2006	$2,000,000	$780,800	46%
2007	$2,000,000	$780,800	45%
2008	$2,000,000	$780,800	45%
2009	$3,500,000	$1,455,800	45%
2010	$0	$0	0%
2011 and later	$1,000,000	$345,800	55%

The operation of this system can be seen through an example. Let us say that in 2003 a decedent has a taxable estate of $1,000,000. Applying the unified transfer tax rate schedule (not shown here), we can calculate the tentative tax on this amount as $345,800. An applicable credit amount of $345,800 will exactly offset this tentative tax, so that is the applicable credit amount that produces an applicable exclusion amount of $1,000,000. This excluded amount will increase through 2009 as shown in the table. As we shall see in Chapter 26, a great deal of marital deduction planning is aimed at using effectively the

[1] The terms "applicable credit amount" and "unified credit" mean the same thing. In practice, they tend to be used interchangeably and are so used in this book.

applicable credit amounts of both spouses. The unified credit and applicable exclusion amounts are not indexed for inflation.

The unified credit system also applies to gift taxation. As of 2002, the applicable exclusion amount for federal gift tax purposes became $1,000,000 (as for the estate tax). But in subsequent years (i.e., 2004 through 2010), the gift tax excluded amount remains at $1,000,000 and the gift tax is not repealed in 2010. However, under EGTRRA's sunset provision, all tax rules, including for gift taxes, return to their 2001 form. Thus, for 2004 through 2010, the tax treatment for gifts will be separated from that for estates. The gift tax excluded amount is not indexed for inflation. The top marginal gift tax rates will decline from 2001 through 2009, as shown in the preceding table, like the estate tax rates. But in 2010, the top marginal gift tax rate will become 35 percent. All tax rates will return to their 2001 levels in 2011.

Federal Gift Tax

It comes as a surprise to many people that there is a federal gift tax. It applies to transferring ownership rights in property during lifetime and is levied against the donor, who must file a gift tax return when required by law.

What Are Taxable Gifts (Transfers)?

The gift tax is on the gratuitous transfer of property by any individual. Only individuals are subject to gift taxation. The term *gift* is not expressly defined in the IRC, but it is construed to mean the transfer of property for less than full and adequate consideration. To be a taxable gift, the transfer must be *complete*. This means the donor must have relinquished enough dominion and control over the property so that it no longer is subject to his or her will and he or she no longer can control its disposition.

For example, if a donor alone deposits funds in a joint bank account or a joint brokerage account with his or her child so that either has the power unilaterally to withdraw the full amount, there has been no completed gift, because the donor could simply withdraw the whole amount and recover the property. On the other hand, if the child withdraws his or her half (or more), there would be a completed gift of that amount at that time.

Methods of Making Gifts

Some common methods are as follows:

- *Outright gifts.* The donees have immediate possession, use, and enjoyment of the gift property.

- *Gifts to irrevocable inter vivos (living) trusts.* In this case, the beneficiaries of the trust are considered to be the donees.
- *Gifts to custodianship arrangements.* Here the donees are the minor recipients of property held by a custodian under a Uniform Transfers to Minors Act or Uniform Gifts to Minors Act. (These acts are discussed in Chapter 25.)
- Receiving property as *joint owners with the donor.* The donor places property or funds that he or she formerly owned outright in joint names with the donee.
- The *exercise, release, or lapse during lifetime of a general power of appointment* in favor of someone other than the holder of the power.[2] Here the gift is from the possessor of the power to the other parties. However, the tax law provides that the lapse of a power during the possessor's lifetime will be considered a release of that power (and hence a taxable transfer) only to the extent that the property that could have been appointed exceeds the larger of $5000 or 5 percent of the aggregate value of the assets out of which the power could have been satisfied. This means, for example, that if a trust beneficiary is given a power of withdrawal (a general power) each year over trust assets that is limited to the greater of $5000 or 5 percent of the trust corpus, and the power for each year expires (lapses) at the end of that year, a lapse of this withdrawal right will not result in a taxable gift by its possessor (the trust beneficiary) to the other trust beneficiaries. This is referred to as a *5 and 5 power.* It is an important concept in estate planning.

Exclusions and Deductions

The gifts most people make will not be subject to gift taxation. This is because of exclusions and deductions applying to the federal gift tax.

Per-Donee Annual Exclusion. Every donor can make tax-free gifts *each year* presently up to $11,000 as of 2003 (indexed for inflation in increments of $1000) each to any number of persons. Gifts within the annual exclusion do not reduce the donor's unified credit. Rather sizeable amounts often can be given away each year under the annual exclusion.

To take a rather extreme example, in 2003 a donor might give $11,000 in money or securities outright to each of, say, 12 persons (perhaps his or her chil-

---

[2] As explained in Chapter 23, a general power of appointment exists when the holder of the power can exercise it in favor of himself or herself, his or her creditors, his or her estate, or the creditors of his or her estate. The aforementioned rule applies to general powers of appointment created after October 21, 1942. For general powers created on or before that date, the exercise of the power results in a transfer (gift) by the holder but the failure to exercise (lapse) or release such a power is not considered an exercise of the power and hence is not a taxable event. Thus, in the relatively few cases of these pre-October 21, 1942 general powers, the holder generally should not exercise the power and thus would avoid transfer taxation on property subject to the power.

dren and grandchildren), or total gifts of $132,000 in the year without reducing his or her unified credit at all. For this reason, spacing out gifts to one or more donees over a period of years often can keep the amounts within the annual exclusion. It must be remembered, however, that the annual exclusion applies to all gifts made by a donor to a donee during a year. Therefore, if a donor already has made several smaller gifts to a donee in a year, the donor cannot make the full $11,000 (indexed) gift to the same donee during the year and stay within the annual exclusion.

Present Interest Requirement for Annual Exclusion. The annual exclusion applies only to gifts of a *present interest* in property (i.e., where the donee has the immediate possession, use, or enjoyment of the gift); it does not apply to gifts of future interests (i.e., where the donee's possession, use, or enjoyment is deferred). For example, an outright gift is a gift of a present interest of the full value of the property, because the donee has the unrestricted immediate use, possession, and enjoyment of all the gift property by virtue of sole ownership. However, when gifts are made in trust, this issue becomes more complicated. It depends on the terms of the trust.

Assume, for example, that Amy has set up an irrevocable trust that provides that income *must be* paid annually to a beneficiary for a term of 15 years (mandatory right to income) and at the end of that time the corpus will be paid outright to the beneficiary or his or her issue (as remainderperson).[3] Further assume that Amy (as grantor) transfers $11,000 worth of common stock into this trust. The present value of the mandatory right to income from the gift property is a gift of a present interest to the beneficiary since he or she has the immediate possession, use, and enjoyment of the income stream for 15 years. This value qualifies for the per-donee annual exclusion. On the other hand, the present value of the remainder interest is a future interest (since its possession, use, and enjoyment is delayed for 15 years) and does not qualify for the annual exclusion. Assuming a 7.2 percent interest rate (the Section 7520 rate), the present value of an income interest for 15 years is 0.647566 (64.7566 percent) and the corresponding present value of a remainder interest at the end of 15 years is 0.352434 (35.2434 percent) of the amount transferred to the trust. Therefore, in this example $7,123 ($11,000 × 0.647566) is a gift of a present interest and qualifies for the annual exclusion, while $3,877 ($11,000 × 0.352434) is a gift of a future interest, does not qualify for the annual exclusion, and would be a taxable gift this year for Amy.

---

[3] Assume for the sake of this illustration that this trust does not qualify for any special annual exclusion treatment. In other words, it is what may be referred to as a Section 2503(b) income interest trust. Other ways for qualifying periodic gifts for the annual exclusion (such as for minors) are discussed in Chapter 25.

However, if we change this example to say the trust provides that the trustee may accumulate income in the trust or pay it out to the beneficiary in the trustee's discretion during the 15-year term (a discretionary income provision), none of the transfer would be a gift of a present interest, because the beneficiary does not have unrestricted immediate possession, use, or enjoyment of the income stream (it can be changed at the trustee's discretion) or of the principal (payment of the remainder interest is delayed 15 years). Therefore, Amy does not have any annual exclusion and the full $11,000 transfer this year is a taxable gift by Amy to the trust beneficiary.[4]

Unlimited Exclusion for Transfers for Educational and Medical Expenses. This important exclusion is in addition to the per-donee annual exclusion. It excludes from gift taxation any amount paid on behalf of an individual (no particular relationship to the donor is required) to an *educational organization*[5] as *tuition* (books, room and board, etc., are not included) for the education or training of such an individual. It also excludes any amount paid on behalf of an individual to any person or entity that provides medical care with respect to such individual.

These can be valuable exclusions for planning purposes. Suppose, for example, that Gary would like to help his 21-year-old granddaughter through medical school. Gary can pay the $30,000-per-year medical school tuition directly to the school and also give his granddaughter $11,000 (indexed)[6] each year under the per-donee annual exclusion. He can also pay his granddaughter's medical expenses (including health insurance premiums) directly to the providers.[7] None of these gifts will be subject to gift taxation since they are under the exclusion for transfers for educational and medical expenses and the per-donee annual exclusion.

---

[4] As we shall see in the next chapter, an important way of making a transfer of property to a trust a gift of a present interest is to give the beneficiary or beneficiaries a power of withdrawal over the transferred property. Such a presently exercisable power allows the holder (beneficiary or beneficiaries) to get the transferred property outright and hence makes the gift one of a present interest eligible for the annual exclusion. This is the principle behind the use of *Crummey powers*. Donors normally want to make gifts that will qualify for the per-donee annual exclusion, if at all possible.

[5] An educational organization for this purpose is one that normally maintains a regular faculty and curriculum and has a regularly enrolled body of students who are in attendance at the place where its educational activities are carried on. It can be seen that this definition can embrace a relatively wide range of organizations. Whether it would go as far as nursery school or other preschool programs depends on the facts of the case.

[6] As we shall see later in this chapter, if Gary is married at the time he makes the gift, he can split the annual gift with his wife, and they together can give up to $22,000 (indexed) per year to each donee (their granddaughter in this case) in cash outright or in appreciated securities since their granddaughter probably will be in a lower capital gains tax bracket than Gary and his wife.

It may also be useful at this point to relate these gift tax exclusions to the generation-skipping transfer (GST) tax, which will be covered later in this chapter. In this situation, Gary's granddaughter is a *skip person* for GST purposes (i.e., she is two or more generations younger than the transferor—Gary) and Gary's gifts to her are *direct skips,* for GST tax purposes. However, since these direct skips are nontaxable outright gifts under the annual exclusion and the exclusion for transfers for educational and medical expenses, they are not taxable for GST purposes as well. With regard to annual exclusion gifts in trust, however, the situation is more complex. The GST tax imposes special conditions on such gifts, which are described later.

Federal Gift Tax Marital Deduction. When married persons make gifts to each other, an unlimited federal gift tax marital deduction normally applies. This generally parallels the unlimited federal estate tax marital deduction that is explained elsewhere in this chapter and in Chapter 26. It operates as a deduction from a donor's taxable transfers to arrive at taxable gifts and hence allows gifts between spouses to be free of federal gift tax.

Gifts to U.S. Citizen Spouses. Before a deduction is allowed, gifts to a U.S. citizen spouse must be made in a way that *qualifies* for the marital deduction. The methods for qualifying property for the marital deduction are described in Chapter 26.

Gifts to Non-U.S. Citizen Spouses. These gifts are treated differently. For gifts made after July 13, 1988, the gift tax marital deduction does not apply. Instead, there is a special $112,000 as of 2003 (indexed in $1,000 segments) gift tax annual exclusion for such transfers. This exclusion applies each year to transfers of a present interest to noncitizen spouses, provided the transfers would have qualified for the marital deduction had the spouse been a U.S. citizen.

Federal Gift Tax Charitable Deduction. As noted in Chapter 16, there is an unlimited charitable deduction for gifts to eligible charities.

Gift Splitting by Married Persons

Married persons can split any gifts either makes while they are married. Thus, if either spouse makes a gift to a third person, it can be treated for tax purposes as if made one-half by the donor-spouse and one-half by the other spouse, provided the other spouse consents to the gift on a gift tax return filed by the donor.

Let us take the example of Andy and Vicky, a married couple. Suppose, for example, that Andy wants to give outright $22,000 of common stock he owns

---

[7] In fact, he could make similar gifts to his son, daughter-in-law, and other persons.

in his own name to his adult daughter in one year. If Vicky consents to the gift, the $22,000 gift is treated as an $11,000 gift by Andy and an $11,000 gift by Vicky. Both of these gifts would be within their $11,000 (indexed) annual exclusions and hence not taxable.

To elect gift splitting, both spouses must be U.S. citizens or permanent residents. Also, if spouses elect gift splitting in a particular year, all gifts made in that year by either spouse must be split. However, for the next year and each subsequent year, they can decide whether or not to split their gifts.

Who Owes the Gift Tax and Who Must File a Return

The donor owes any gift tax payable. Sometimes a gift is made on condition that the donee will pay the gift tax. This is called a *net gift,* as the gift tax paid by the donee is deducted from the value of the gift property to determine the taxable gift.[8] A donor must file a gift tax return when his or her transfers of present interests exceed the annual exclusion. A donor also must file a gift tax return for all transfers of future interests and in cases where gift splitting by spouses is involved.[9]

Valuation of Gift Property

General Principles. The general principles of valuing interests for federal gift and estate tax purposes are reasonably straightforward. The value of a transfer is equal to the fair market value of the gift property (less any payment made by the donee) as of the date a completed transfer takes place. This *fair market value* generally is the price at which the property would change hands between a willing buyer and a willing seller, with neither being under any compulsion to buy or to sell and with both having reasonable knowledge of the relevant facts. This is referred to as the *willing buyer/willing seller test.* When property has a ready market, such as for stocks, bonds, and commodities traded on organized exchanges or for mutual fund shares, this value can be determined easily.[10] On the other hand, for property with limited marketability, such as closely held business interests, family limited partnership (FLP) interests, certain real estate, and perhaps art or antiques, there may be valuation disputes and negotiations between donor-taxpayers and the IRS.

---

[8] This is IRS Form 709, entitled United States Gift (and Generation-Skipping Transfer) Tax Return.

[9] When split gifts are not taxable because they are within the annual exclusions, a short-form return may be filed.

[10] For publicly traded stocks and bonds, it is the average of the high and low selling prices on the valuation date. For mutual funds, it is the bid or redemption price on the valuation date.

Valuation Discounts and Premiums. The values of certain property interests under this willing buyer/willing seller test may be less than (discounted from) the underlying value of property in the interest because of the legal and economic nature of the interest. This may be true, for example, because of lack of control by or lack of marketability of the interest. Likewise, the values of other property interests may be more than the underlying value of property in the interest. This may occur, for example, because of the going-concern value of a business (goodwill factor) or because the holder of the interest is in control of a business or property (control premium).

Valuation in this context is a complex issue. But valuation discounts have become increasingly important in estate planning and underlie such planning techniques as giving interests in family limited partnerships (FLPs), as covered in Chapter 25. There also may be differences of opinion on such discounts between donors (and their advisors) and the IRS. In some cases, disputes, compromises, and even litigation result. Some common discounts and premium and other valuation concepts are outlined next.

Discount for Lack of Marketability. This discount from otherwise calculated value reflects the fact that interests in closely held entities have no ready market and hence are difficult to sell. This makes them much less attractive to a willing buyer than would be publicly traded securities. Also, closely held entities may place restrictions on an owner's ability to sell his or her interest to outsiders. This discount may be applied first in the valuation process.

Discount for Lack of Control (Minority Interest Discount). The rationales for lack of control discounts have already been discussed. Lack of control also makes such interests much less attractive to a willing buyer. This may be applied after the lack of marketability discount in the valuation process.

Control Premium. On the other hand, an interest that represents control of an entity may be valued at a premium over otherwise calculated value.

Fractional Interest Discount. This discount may arise because only a partial interest in property (usually real estate) is transferred and hence the owner of the fractional interest normally must act with the other owner or owners to deal with the property or to realize its full value. Thus, a willing buyer normally will pay less for a fractional interest than its pro rata share of the property's value.

Blockage Discounts. These are discounts that may be applied to transfers of large blocks of publicly traded securities. The reason is that the sale of such a large block may depress the normal market price for the securities.

Valuation of Life Estates, Term Interests, Remainders, Reversions, and Certain Annuities. Transfers of such interests are (or were) valued under various IRS tables, depending on when the transfer was made. However, transfers after April 30, 1989 are valued according to factors corresponding to interest rates (Section 7520 rates) that the federal government publishes monthly. The mortality table implicit in factors involving life estates and life annuities is revised every 10 years.

Effect of Chapter 14 of the IRC on Valuation

This chapter of the Internal Revenue Code was enacted to redress certain perceived valuation abuses involving transfers between family members. Nevertheless, there are planning techniques for making gifts within the rules of Chapter 14 that may yield significant estate planning benefits.

To give a brief overview of Chapter 14, Section 2701 applies to the valuation freeze techniques that were used with respect to gifts of corporate stock (such as common stock) or comparable partnership interests to younger family members with the retention of senior stock (such as preferred stock) or comparable partnership interests by older family members. Unless the retained senior interests meet certain requirements, Chapter 14 values them at zero for transfer tax purposes. Thus, as a practical matter, this has essentially ended this valuation freeze approach purely for tax purposes.

Section 2702 applies to transfers *in trust* when the grantor retains an interest in the trust and then transfers the remainder interest to a family member. Unless certain exceptions apply, the grantor's retained interest is valued at zero and the full value of the trust corpus is assigned to the gift of the remainder interest. Thus, the exceptions are important for planning purposes. They are personal residence trusts (PRTs), qualified personal residence trusts (QPRTs), grantor-retained annuity trusts (GRATs), grantor-retained unitrusts (GRUTs), and retained term interests in certain tangible, nondepreciable property. When one of these exceptions applies, the grantor's retained interest is valued using the IRS Section 7520 tables and only the difference between the value of the property placed in the trust and the value of the grantor's retained interest is a taxable transfer (gift) to the family member. The planning possibilities inherent in these exceptions are considered in Chapter 25.

Section 2703 imposes certain conditions on option agreements, rights to acquire property, or restrictions on the sale or use of property between family members to ensure that they are bona fide agreements. These conditions apply to business buy-sell agreements and are covered in Chapter 30.

Finally, Section 2704 deals with the effect on value of certain lapsing voting rights or liquidation rights in a corporation or partnership when the person holding the rights and members of his or her family control the corporation or partnership before and after the lapse.

Federal Estate Tax

It is said that nothing is certain except death and taxes. Here we are dealing with both. The federal estate tax is an excise tax imposed on the passing of property to others at death. At this point, we shall describe the nature of the federal estate tax. Planning to reduce or defer the estate tax is covered in the Chapters 25 through 27.

Structure of the Federal Estate Tax

Gross estate

Less: Certain estate settlement deductions (i.e., estate administration expenses; funeral expenses; claims against the estate; unpaid mortgages or other indebtedness on property whose value, undiminished by the mortgages or indebtedness, is included in the gross estate; and casualty losses incurred during the settlement of the estate)[11]

(Note: The gross estate less these deductions equals what has been called the *adjusted gross estate.* This figure still is used to determine such things as eligibility for a Section 303 redemption of corporate stock and installment payment of the estate tax under Section 6166. Modifications of it also may be used for other purposes.)

Less: Marital deduction (which may be up to the full amount, that is 100 percent, of property included in the gross estate that passes to a surviving spouse so as to qualify for the marital deduction)

Less: Charitable deduction

Equals:

Taxable estate

Plus: Adjusted taxable gifts (post-1976 taxable gifts other than those included in the gross estate)

Equals:

Tentative tax base,

Times:

Unified transfer tax rates

Equals:

Federal estate tax on the tentative tax base

Less: Credit for gift taxes payable (at current rates) on post-1976 taxable gifts

Equals:

Federal estate tax before application of (other) credits

Less: Applicable credit amount

---

[11] Estate administration expenses can be taken either on the estate's income tax return or on the estate tax return. If the executor elects to t.ake them on the income tax return, they cannot be deducted from the gross estate.

Less: Other credits
Equals:
Federal estate tax payable

Note that the effect of adding any post-1976 taxable gifts to the taxable estate to arrive at the tentative tax base (to which the unified transfer tax rates are applied) and then deducting a credit equal to any post-1976 gift taxes payable at the tax rates applicable at death is to have the amount of any previous lifetime gifts serve to increase the unified transfer tax brackets applicable to estate assets that pass at death. This makes the federal gift and estate taxes both progressive and cumulative.

What Is in the Gross Estate?

The gross estate is the starting point for determining how much estate tax an estate must pay. In general, it includes the following items.

Property Owned at Death. All property a decedent owned in his or her own name or had an interest in (such as the decedent's share of tenancies in common or community property) at the time of death will be in the decedent's gross estate.

Life Insurance on the Decedent's Life. The gross estate includes proceeds of life insurance policies on a decedent's life if he or she had ownership rights in the policy (incidents of ownership) at the time of death or if the policy was payable to the estate. It also includes the proceeds of life insurance policies given away within three years of death.

Joint Tenancies (WROS). In this case, the gross estate of the first joint owner to die includes one-half the value of property held jointly (WROS) by a husband and wife (fractional interest rule) or the full value of property held jointly (WROS) with someone other than a spouse, except to the extent it can be shown the surviving owner contributed to the purchase price of the property ("consideration furnished" rule) from property never received by gift from the deceased owner.

General Powers of Appointment. Property over which the decedent held a general power of appointment at his or her death will be in the gross estate. On the other hand, possession of a special or limited power will not cause the property in question to be included in the holder's gross estate.

Annuities. This item includes in a decedent's gross estate the actuarial value of payments a surviving joint annuitant may receive after the decedent's death. These might be from a joint and last survivor annuity form, for example. It also includes a beneficiary's rights to the value of annuity payments (account

[12] While benefits from Roth IRAs are free from federal income tax, they are included in a deceased owner's gross estate for federal estate tax purposes.

balances) a decedent has not yet received as of his or her death. These survivors' benefits might come from the various qualified retirement plans, traditional and Roth IRAs,[12] nonqualified annuities, TSAs, and nonqualified deferred compensation plans. These benefits, other than from Roth IRAs, also are income in respect of a decedent (IRD). On the other hand, if annuity payments cease at a person's death and nothing is payable to a survivor or beneficiary thereafter (as from a straight life annuity, for example), nothing will be in the decedent's gross estate.

Revocable Transfers. If a person transfers property but has the right to alter, amend, revoke, or terminate the enjoyment of the property as of the date of death, the value of the property will be included in his or her gross estate. It also will be in the gross estate if the decedent relinquished such right within three years of death. The inclusion applies regardless of the capacity in which the person is acting (e.g., as a trustee) and regardless of whether the person must act alone or in conjunction with any other person.[13] This means, for example, that if a grantor of an irrevocable trust has the right to change a trust beneficiary, the amount received by a beneficiary, or the timing of benefits to a beneficiary, this provision will apply and the corpus will be in his or her gross estate. It also will apply, of course, to revocable living trusts at the grantor's death.

Grantors of irrevocable inter vivos (living) trusts often want to retain at least some control over the trust, usually by being a trustee. A grantor can be a trustee and, as trustee, can exercise certain powers over trust investments and other matters of trust administration without adverse estate tax consequences. However, care must be taken that a grantor or grantor-trustee does not have such powers over the beneficial enjoyment of trust corpus that it will cause the property to be in the grantor's gross estate at his or her death. On the other hand, unrestricted discretionary powers over distribution of principal and income to trust beneficiaries and other matters can be placed in the hands of an independent trustee or cotrustee (who is neither related to nor subordinate to the grantor). Also, a grantor-trustee of an irrevocable trust can have power to invade the trust corpus for or control income flows to trust beneficiaries, provided the power is limited by an ascertainable standard (i.e., for the health, education, support, or maintenance of the beneficiaries), without having the trust property included in the grantor's gross estate. Further, a grantor can have the power to remove one trustee and appoint a replacement individual or corporate trustee, provided the new trustee is not the grantor and is not related or subordinate to the grantor. This can be done without causing the trust property to be included in the grantor's gross estate.

[13] Section 2038 of the IRC deals with revocable and similar transfers.
[14] Transfers with retained life estates are covered in Section 2036 of the IRC.

Transfers with Retained Life Estate. This is another provision that may cause lifetime transfers to be included in a decedent's gross estate.[14] The gross estate includes the value of all property a decedent transferred by trust or otherwise when the decedent retained for his or her lifetime, or for any period not ascertainable without reference to the decedent's death, or for any period which does not in fact end before his or her death either (1) the possession or enjoyment of or the right to the income from the transferred property or (2) the right, alone or in conjunction with any other person, to designate the persons who will possess or enjoy the property or the income from the property. In effect, when a transferor (e.g., a grantor of a trust) transfers property but retains a life income from the property or a lifetime power to determine who will enjoy the property, the full value of the property will be in the transferor's gross estate. This is also true when a transferor retains a lifetime right to vote the shares of transferred stock in a controlled corporation.

As an illustration, assume that Susan Smith, age 65 and in good health, transfers $1 million of stocks and bonds to an irrevocable trust with the income payable to herself for her lifetime and at her death the trust corpus would go in equal shares to her two children or their issue as remainderpersons. Susan dies 20 years later at age 85, when the trust corpus is worth $3 million. Since Susan retained a life income (life estate) in the transferred property, the value of this trust at her death, $3 million, will be in Susan's gross estate.

Transfers Taking Effect at Death. The gross estate also includes the value of property transferred by a decedent during life when the possession or enjoyment of the property as owner can be obtained only by surviving the decedent and the decedent retained a reversionary interest in the property with a value immediately before death of more than 5 percent of the property's value.

Transfers Within Three Years of Death. In general, property given away during life is not in the donor's gross estate at death. This applies regardless of how close in time the date of death was to the date of the gift. However, there are several *exceptions* to this general rule.

We have already seen that if there has been a lifetime transfer and the transferor retains or has certain rights or interests in the transferred property (e.g., transfers with retained life estates, transfers taking effect at death, and revocable transfers) as of his or her death, the value of the transferred property as of the date of death will be included in the gross estate. In addition, transfers of life insurance policies by a person on his or her life within three years of death will cause the full life insurance proceeds to be in the insured's gross estate. Further, relinquishment of retained rights or powers in transferred property (that otherwise would cause its inclusion in the gross estate as just noted) within three years of death will result in the property's being included in the gross estate. Finally, the gross estate includes the amount of any gift tax paid on gifts made by the decedent or his or her spouse within three years of the decedent's death. This is referred to as the *gift tax gross-up*.

Marital Deduction Property in a Q-TIP Trust. One way to qualify property for the federal estate tax marital deduction is to leave it to a surviving spouse in a qualified terminable interest property (Q-TIP) trust. When this is done, the property in the Q-TIP trust will be in the surviving spouse's gross estate at his or her subsequent death. However, the surviving spouse may require reimbursement for the estate tax payable on the Q-TIP property from the Q-TIP trust.

Property Not in the Gross Estate

The property included in the gross estate consists of all property and property interests as just described of a decedent who was a U.S. citizen or resident wherever the property is situated. In other words, only the categories of property specifically enumerated in the IRC are in the gross estate; other property interests are not.

For planning purposes, we often are concerned with keeping property out of the gross estate, as well as with using estate tax deductions and credits wisely. Planners are interested in ways of giving persons economic advantages in property without having it included in their gross estates when they die. In this regard, when property is placed in irrevocable trusts for beneficiaries (either inter vivos or testamentary trusts), substantial rights and powers can be given to the beneficiaries or exercised on their behalf over the trust corpus and income without having the corpus included in the beneficiaries' gross estates upon their deaths. These have been referred to as *almost-owner powers* and *nontaxable ownership equivalents*. These nontaxable interests and powers are as follows:

- The beneficiary's right to trust income for his or her lifetime (or a term of years).
- The beneficiary's being a permissible distributee of trust corpus at the discretion of an independent trustee.
- The beneficiary's possession of a special power of appointment over trust corpus.
- The beneficiary's possession of a power to withdraw or invade trust corpus for himself or herself subject to an ascertainable standard related to the beneficiary's health, education, support, or maintenance.
- The right at the beneficiary's discretion to withdraw up to the larger of $5000 or 5 percent of the corpus each year. At the beneficiary's death, at most only the amount that could have been withdrawn in the year of death can be included in the beneficiary's gross estate. There can be complications with such 5 and 5 powers, but they are available for beneficiaries, if desired.

Naturally, not all of these interests and powers not subject to estate taxes need be given by a grantor to trust beneficiaries. But they are available to the extent they are desired or needed.

Federal Estate Tax Marital Deduction

This often is an important tax-deferring device for married estate owners. Planning for its use will be considered in Chapter 26.

Transfers to U.S. Citizen Spouses. The marital deduction operates as a deduction from a decedent's gross estate to arrive at the taxable estate and allows unlimited transfers between spouses free of federal estate taxation. However, property in a decedent's gross estate must pass to his or her surviving spouse in a way that *qualifies* for the marital deduction, as explained in Chapter 26.

Transfers to Non-U.S. Citizen Spouses. Property passing to spouses who are not U.S. citizens is treated differently. A transfer can be made to a *qualified domestic trust* (QDOT), which is a trust for a noncitizen surviving spouse who has elected QDOT treatment, meets certain other requirements, and qualifies for the marital deduction. When the first spouse (the U.S. citizen or resident) dies, it operates as a deduction from the gross estate to arrive at the taxable estate. It applies to distributions of principal during the surviving spouse's lifetime as well as the value of the trust principal at his or her death. The estate tax is calculated as if the taxable assets from the QDOT were in the first spouse's gross estate.

Federal Estate Tax Charitable Deduction

This deduction parallels the gift tax charitable deduction. It is unlimited and operates as a deduction from the gross estate to arrive at the taxable estate.

Applicable Credit Amount (Unified Credit)

This credit was described earlier.[15]

Other Credits

There can be several other credits to reduce the federal estate tax otherwise payable. They come after the unified credit in the following order of priority.

---

[15] Note again the difference between a deduction and a credit. A *deduction* is taken from a potentially taxable amount to arrive at a tax base to which the tax rates are applied (such as the marital deduction and charitable deduction from the gross estate to arrive at the taxable estate). A *credit* is a dollar-for-dollar reduction in the tax itself (such as the applicable credit amount from the federal estate tax). Obviously, a credit is more valuable than a deduction.

Credit for State Death Taxes. This credit is a declining amount for 2002, 2003, and 2004. After 2004, there instead will be a *deduction* from the gross estate for any state death taxes actually paid on property included in the gross estate.

Credit for Gift Tax. This credit is for gift taxes on taxable gifts made before 1977 that are included in the gross estate at death.

Credit for Foreign Death Taxes. This is a credit for death taxes paid to foreign governments or to a possession of the United States when a U.S. citizen or resident decedent has property in the countries or possessions.

Credit for Tax on Prior Transfers (TPT Credit). When an heir or a beneficiary of a decedent dies within 10 years after or two years before the decedent's death, there is a decreasing credit against the estate tax payable by the heir's or beneficiary's estate for property received from the decedent that was also taxable in the decedent's estate. This credit is intended to redress or ameliorate the effect of property's being taxed several times within a relatively short time. The amount of the credit depends on the time elapsing between the two deaths.

Valuation of Property in the Gross Estate

General Principles. The general principles of valuing property and property interests for federal estate tax purposes are generally the same as for gift tax purposes, with some special rules. The value generally is the *fair market value* of property in the gross estate either at the date of death or as of an alternate valuation date six months after the date of death, at the executor's election. Fair market value is determined under the willing buyer/willing seller test described previously.

Alternate Valuation Date. An executor might elect this date if the value of the estate has declined since the date of death.[16] If elected, all assets must be valued at the alternate valuation date. Also, the election can be made only if it actually will decrease the size of the gross estate and the estate tax payable. The present step-up in income tax basis at death rule applies to the valuation date actually used. Therefore, the basis of assets will be lower if the alternate valuation date is elected. If the alternate valuation date is elected and property is disposed of during the six months after death, it is valued as of the date of disposition.

Valuation Discounts and Premium. The valuation discounts (and premium) applying to some types of assets, discussed earlier with respect to gift taxation, also may apply to the federal estate tax values of those assets.

[16] For historical interest, the reason an alternative valuation date is in the tax code is that, at the beginning of the Great Depression of the 1930s, many estate assets declined so precipitously in value from the date of death until the tax was due that in some cases they actually were worth less than the estate tax due.

Special Use Valuation. This special valuation provision (contained in Section 2032A of the IRC) applies to real property located in the United States (qualified real property) used in farming or in a closely held business conducted by the decedent or a family member. Normally, fair market value of real property is based on its *highest and best use.* The special valuation provision allows a decedent's executor to elect to value such property according to its current use (e.g., as a farm or part of a closely held business) rather than according to its possible highest and best use (e.g., as land for a housing development or industrial park). The reduction in value from highest-and-best-use value cannot exceed $840,000 in 2003 (indexed for inflation in $10,000 increments). There are a number of requirements that must be met to qualify for special use valuation. However, under the proper circumstances, it can be a valuable provision for reducing estate taxes.

Filing the Tax Return and Paying the Tax

General Principles. When a federal estate tax return[17] is required (generally when the gross estate of a decedent who is a U.S. citizen or resident exceeds the applicable exclusion amount), the basic rule is that it must be filed and the tax must be paid within nine months after the decedent's death. However, the IRS normally will grant a six-month extension for filing the return, so as a practical matter, the executor may have up to 15 months after death to file the estate tax return. The IRS also may grant an extension of time to pay the tax due, but this requires the executor to show reasonable cause why the tax cannot be paid when due.

Election to Pay Tax on Closely Held Businesses in Installments. Section 6166 of the IRC allows an executor to elect to pay the estate tax attributable to certain closely held business interests in 10 equal annual installments beginning five years after the date the tax is otherwise due. This effectively allows payment over a 14-year period. Only interest need be paid for the first four years. However, the interest rate on the estate tax deferred on generally the first $1,120,000 in 2003 (indexed for inflation in $10,000 increments) of business value is only 2 percent and the rate on the balance is 45 percent of the IRS underpayment rate. But this interest is not deductible as an estate administration expense.[18] There are a number of requirements to qualify for this installment payment option, but Section 6166 can be attractive for the estates of closely held business owners if they are eligible.

Tax Apportionment and Tax Provisions. The IRC places the burden of paying the federal estate tax on the executor of a decedent's estate. However, federal and

---

[17] The estate tax return is IRS Form 706.

state apportionment statutes may allow the executor to recover some of the tax from interests includible in the gross estate but not in the probate estate.

The estate owner in his or her will or other document can override these apportionment statutes and indicate from what interest or interests in his or her gross estate any death taxes are to be paid. This is referred to as a *tax clause or provision*.

Otherwise, death taxes may reduce interests the estate owner may prefer not be reduced by them. For example, it normally is not desirable for death taxes to be paid from interests that are going to qualify for the marital deduction. If they are, it will correspondingly reduce the marital deduction and increase estate taxes in a circular fashion.[19] It also may not be desirable for death taxes to be paid from qualified retirement plan or IRA account balances, because it would reduce future income tax deferral (or tax-free growth). A tax clause, for example, might specify that death taxes are to be paid from the residuary probate estate that does not qualify for the marital deduction. Of course, there must be enough liquid assets in the probate estate or available to it to do this; otherwise, the tax will be apportioned elsewhere. This is a matter of providing adequate estate liquidity.

Federal Generation-Skipping Transfer (GST) Tax
Basic Concepts

The rationale behind this tax is that a federal transfer tax should be imposed on the transfer of wealth by each generation to the next. The GST tax may apply to a direct skip, a taxable termination, or a taxable distribution from a *transferor* to a *skip person*. These are referred to as *taxable transfers*. In essence, the tax applies, with certain exceptions, when a transfer of property misses or *skips* a generation in terms of the property's not being subject to gift or estate tax in that generation.

As a planning matter, payment of a GST tax normally should be avoided. This is because the GST tax rate effectively is equal to the maximum federal estate tax rate and a gift tax or an estate tax also will be paid on the original transfer. Planning to avoid GST tax may involve making transfers that are exempt or otherwise not subject to GST tax, as explained later in this section, or not having transfers actually skip an intervening generation's estate.

---

[18] Note that other interest paid or payable on debt incurred to finance payment of federal estate taxes may be deductible as an estate administration expense, depending on the circumstances. This, in itself, may offer planning possibilities.

[19] Under equitable apportionment principles, there should be no tax apportioned to marital deduction property because it does not generate any of the estate tax.

Skip Person

A skip person is a *natural person* assigned to a generation two or more generations younger than that of the transferor of property. Thus, a transferor's grandchildren or great-grandchildren are examples of skip persons.[20] A skip person can also be a *trust* in which all interests are held by a skip person or persons (or no person holds an interest in the trust and at no time can a distribution be made to a anyone who is not a skip person). In essence, this means the trust is exclusively for one or more skip persons (e.g., a grandchild or a grandchild and his or her issue).

Transferor

The transferor is the person originally subject to transfer taxation. It is the donor for transfers subject to gift taxation and the decedent in the case of transfers subject to estate taxation. It is necessary to identify the transferor so generations can be counted to determine whether there has been a taxable transfer to a skip person.

But if a transfer is made by an original transferor in trust and the corpus of the trust is included in a beneficiary's gross estate for federal estate tax purposes (such as if the beneficiary had a general power of appointment over the trust corpus at his or her death), the transferor for GST tax purposes changes and the beneficiary becomes the new transferor. This is because the transfer did not skip the beneficiary's estate. This can be important in planning to avoid the GST tax.

However, there is a special election permitted when property is given or left by one spouse to the other in a qualified terminable interest property (Q-TIP) trust to qualify for the marital deduction. In this case, the executor for the first spouse to die can elect to have that spouse continue to be treated as the transferor of the trust corpus for GST tax purposes. This is called a reverse Q-TIP election. But since under EGTRRA the GST tax lifetime exemption ($1,120,000 as of 2003) will be equal to the estate tax applicable exclusion amount for 2004 and thereafter, the reverse Q-TIP election has substantially diminished in importance for planning purposes.

---

[20] Generations are assigned according to lineal descendants (parents, children, grandchildren, etc.), starting the count from the grandparents of the transferor, or, if the person is not a lineal descendent, by the number of years younger than the transferor. Under this non-lineal-descendent rule, if a person is more than 37½ years younger than the transferor, he or she is a skip person.

Generation-Skipping Transfers Not Subject to GST Tax

Since the GST tax normally is to be avoided, it is important to know what GSTs will escape taxation.

GST Exemption. Each person making generation-skipping transfers (a transfer-or) is allowed an aggregate exemption that can be allocated to otherwise taxable transfers made during his or her lifetime or upon his or her death. Under EGTRRA, for 2002 and 2003 this exemption continues to be set at $1,000,000 (indexed for inflation in $10,000 increments) and equals $1,120,000 for 2003. However, for 2004 and thereafter, the GST exemption will be equal to the federal estate tax applicable exclusion amount and will not be indexed for inflation. The GST tax rate is equal to the maximum federal estate tax rate, according to the schedule shown earlier in this chapter.

The effect of allocating part or all of an individual's exemption to an otherwise taxable transfer is that it becomes partially or totally free of GST tax. Proper planning calls for allocating one's exemption to make a transfer totally free of GST tax (i.e., to allocate an exemption equal to the value of the transfer), rather than make a transfer only partially exempt.

For example, suppose that in 2003 a grandmother gives $500,000 in an irrevocable trust that provides a life income to her adult grandson and then the remainder to his issue. The grandmother is the transferor, the trust is a skip person, and it is a direct skip (i.e., a direct transfer to a skip person) because the transfer is subject to gift taxation (with the grandmother as donor) and the trust is a skip person. If $500,000 of the grandmother's $1,120,000 exemption is allocated to this trust, it will be completely exempt for GST tax purposes.[21]

In the case of lifetime direct skips (such as just illustrated) and "indirect skips" (as defined in the law), the tax law automatically allocates enough of the transferor's exemption (if available) to make the transfer totally exempt, unless

---

[21] The calculation of any GST tax is complicated. Technically, the GST tax rate applied to taxable amounts (e.g., the $500,000 direct skip here), called the applicable rate, is the maximum federal estate tax rate times an inclusion ratio. The inclusion ratio is 1 minus an applicable fraction. The applicable fraction is determined by dividing the value of the property transferred less any federal or state death taxes and any charitable deduction (or $500,000 in this example) by the amount of the GST tax exemption allocated to the taxable transfer (again, $500,000 in this example). In this illustration, then, the applicable fraction is 1 ($500,000 ÷ $500,000 = 1) and the inclusion ratio is 0 (1 -1 [the applicable fraction] = 0). The maximum estate tax rate times zero equals a zero applicable rate, and $500,000 times zero equals zero GST tax. Of course, if no exemption amount is allocated to a taxable transfer, the applicable rate is the maximum federal estate tax rate, and if less than the value of the property transferred is allocated, the applicable rate will be greater than zero but less then the maximum rate, depending on the percentage of value transferred that was allocated. However, as noted in the text, it is not good planning to have an inclusion ratio at a rate greater than 0 (i.e., to pay a GST tax).

the transferor affirmatively elects otherwise. For certain transfers, exemption also can be allocated retroactively. However, a transferor can determine the allocation pattern by making an allocation on a tax return. An allocation also can be expressed as a formula. Such a formula might provide, for example, that the maximum amount or share is to be allocated to a generation-skipping trust, say, for grandchildren, so that the inclusion ratio (see note 21) does not exceed zero. After EGTRRA (with its increasing GST exemptions), such formula provisions should be reviewed to see that they will not result in funding a generation-skipping trust to a greater extent than the transferor may have originally intended.

Per-Donee Annual Exclusion. Direct skips (i.e., direct transfers to a skip person) *made outright* to a donee that are exempt from gift taxation because of the per-donee annual exclusion are also exempt from the GST tax. Thus, for example, if a grandfather gives $22,000 outright to each of his three adult grandchildren in 2003 (or $66,000 in total), and his wife (their grandmother) agrees to split the gifts, all the gifts would fall under the gift tax annual exclusion and would also be exempt (i.e., be a nontaxable gift with a zero inclusion ratio) from the GST tax.

However, the situation is more complicated when gifts are made in trust. For direct skip transfers made after March 31, 1988, *in trust,* even though they qualify for the gift tax annual exclusion (such as through use of Crummey powers, as described in Chapter 25), they will not be exempt from the GST tax unless the trust provides that a single skip person as beneficiary is the only permissible recipient of trust income or corpus during his or her lifetime and has an interest in the trust so that the corpus will be included in the beneficiary's gross estate at his or her death (if the trust does not terminate before his or her death). In effect, this means that for a trust that qualifies for the gift tax annual exclusion also to be exempt on this basis from the GST tax, the trust can have only one skip person beneficiary and can skip only once (normally only one generation) because the corpus (and income) must either be paid to the beneficiary during his or her lifetime or be included in his or her gross estate at death. If more than one skip is desired, the transferor would have to allocate part of his or her exemption to the trust.

Unlimited Exclusion for Transfers for Educational and Medical Expenses. In similar fashion, unlimited transfers made directly to educational organizations for tuition or directly to providers for medical expenses for skip persons that, if made during the person's lifetime, would be excluded from gift taxation also are not subject to GST tax. This exclusion applies to taxable distributions from trusts (to be defined next) as well as to outright transfers during the transferor's lifetime.

Grandfathered Trusts. When the GST tax system was substantially revised in 1986, certain existing trusts were grandfathered (made exempt from GST taxation). These are irrevocable trusts created on or before September 25, 1985, and certain revocable trusts or testamentary trusts if the person died before 1987.

Types of Generation-Skipping Transfers (Taxable Transfers)

Direct Skips. These are transfers of an interest in property directly to a skip person (a natural person or a trust meeting the requirements to be a skip person) that are subject to either gift tax or estate tax. The taxable amount is the value of the property received by the transferee (the skip person) and the transferor must pay any GST tax.[22]

Taxable Terminations. These are terminations by death, lapse of time, release of a power, or otherwise of an interest in property held in trust, unless (1) immediately after such termination a nonskip person has an interest in the property or (2) at no time after such termination can a distribution, including distributions on termination, be made from such trust to a skip person. The taxable amount is the value of the property with respect to which the taxable termination occurred, reduced by certain allowable expenses. The trustee must pay any GST tax payable.

As an example of a taxable termination, suppose that Martha Johnson, a widow with a sizeable estate, has two adult children, a son and a daughter, each of whom also has two children. Both the son and daughter are successful in their careers and they and their spouses are accumulating good-sized estates on their own. Therefore, Martha has decided that in her will she will leave her residuary estate (net estate) in two equal trusts, one for each of her children. The terms of each trust provide that trust income is to be paid to the child or among the child, the child's children, or their issue, or accumulated in the trust at an independent trustee's sole discretion (i.e., a sprinkle or spray power over income). At each child's death, the corpus of his or her trust will pass outright to his or her children (Martha's grandchildren) or their issue in equal shares. These would be generation-skipping trusts (assuming Martha's son and daughter are alive when the transfer is made, i.e., when their mother dies) and the grandchildren would be skip persons.

Assume now that Martha dies, leaving a residuary estate (after debts, expenses, and federal estate and other death taxes on her estate) of $4,000,000, so that $2,000,000 funds each trust. Further suppose that after 20 years her son dies, when the corpus of his trust has grown to $5,000,000. Upon the son's

---

[22] Except for direct skips from trusts, in which case the tax is paid by the trustee.

death, there would be a *taxable termination* of his interest in the trust; this would cause the fair market value of the trust corpus at that time to be a generation-skipping transfer subject to the applicable GST tax rate.[23]

In this situation, as a planning matter, it normally would have been better for Martha's executor after her death to have divided each of the children's trusts into two trusts (under authority in the will to do so) and then allocate enough of Martha's GST exemption to one trust for each child to make it completely exempt from GST tax. Then each child might have been given a general power of appointment over the corpus of the other (nonexempt) trust or given the property outright, so estate taxation would apply at a child's death and no GST tax would result.

Taxable Distributions. These are any distributions from a trust to a skip person. The taxable amount is the value of the property received by the transferee (skip person), less certain expenses. The transferee is liable for any GST tax. If, in the previous example, one of the trusts created after Martha's death had made a distribution to one of her grandchildren, other than for educational or medical expenses, it would have been a taxable distribution.

Estate Tax Inclusion Period (ETIP)

When an individual makes a lifetime transfer and retains an interest in the property such that it would be included in his or her gross estate if the individual died immediately, no allocation of the GST exemption can be made until the earlier of (1) the end of the period during which the property could be included in the individual's gross estate if he or she died (the estate tax inclusion period) or (2) the individual's death. This rule can affect use of the GST exemption in connection with gifts with a retained income or use interest. For example, if a grandfather sets up a 10-year qualified personal residence trust (QPRT), as described in Chapter 25, and designates his granddaughter as the remainderperson to receive the residence after the 10-year period, he generally cannot allocate any of his exemption to the trust until the earlier of his death or the end of the 10-year period.

---

[23] This rate would be the maximum federal estate tax rate modified according to Mrs. Johnson's GST tax exemption that was automatically allocated to each trust at her death.

25

Lifetime Giving and Sales Within the Family

Making lifetime gifts is an important estate planning strategy. There are tax and nontax advantages of doing so. However, lifetime giving is not an unmixed blessing: there are limitations and caveats that should be considered. This chapter also briefly describes certain methods of selling property to family members.

Making Lifetime (Inter Vivos) Gifts to Noncharitable Donees

Advantages of Lifetime Gifts

Lifetime gifts can be an attractive technique for saving estate tax (and GST tax) under the right conditions. They can have the following advantages over bequeathing property at death.

No Tax on Annual Exclusion Gifts. Amounts within the per-donee gift tax annual exclusion and unlimited exclusion for direct payments of educational and medical expenses will escape gift taxation and will not be in the donor's gross estate either. Outright transfers also will avoid the GST tax. Transfers in trust may do so if they meet the requirements for such trusts. Much property can escape all transfer taxation this way.

Post-Gift Appreciation Escapes Taxation. Future appreciation in the value of gift property will escape taxation in the donor's estate.

Income from Gift Property Is Shifted. Taxable income and realized and recognized capital gains from gift property will be transferred to the donee for income tax purposes.

Probate Costs Are Reduced. Estate administration expenses, which generally are based on the value of the probate estate, will be reduced.

State Death Taxes Are Reduced. Similarly, state death taxes can be saved.

Any Gift Taxes Paid Are Removed from the Gross Estate. For gifts made more than three years before death, gift taxes paid by the donor are not in the donor's gross estate at death. On the other hand, if the estate and GST taxes should be repealed by the time of death or if the estate should be less than the exemption amounts at death, any taxable gifts and gift taxes paid would not reduce any estate or GST taxes. In effect, in this situation, any gift taxes actually paid would be a loss to the estate owner and his or her heirs.

Gift Taxes Are Tax-Exclusive, While Estate Taxes Are Tax-Inclusive. This is really another way of making the previous point. The idea is that the gift tax is paid by the donor and the full gift goes to the donee (tax-exclusive), while the estate tax is paid by the executor on the full taxable estate with only the balance going to the heirs (tax-inclusive). In effect, estate tax is paid on the tax itself, while this is not so with the gift tax.

Valuation Discounts May Be Taken in Certain Cases. The valuation discounts described in Chapter 14 may be available, depending on the circumstances. Of course, valuation discounts also can be taken for federal estate tax purposes, but they are commonly associated with lifetime gifts.

Nontax, Personal Advantages. Finally, donors can enjoy all the personal and family advantages of their generosity during their lifetimes and donees can receive the gift property now when they might most need it. The importance of such nontax factors in the face of the possible repeal of the estate and GST taxes depends on individual circumstances, such as the age and health of the donor, the size of the estate, and other personal considerations.

Limitations and Caveats Concerning Lifetime Gifts

No One Knows What the Future May Hold. Donors should be careful that they can do without the gift property. What if their health deteriorates? What if they find themselves in an expensive custodial care situation without adequate long-term care (LTC) insurance? What if the stock market plummets? What if interest rates decline or rise precipitously? What if some present source or sources of income should dry up in the event of career difficulties or economic recession or even depression?

Uncertainties Created by EGTRRA. Given the uncertain future structure of the transfer tax system after EGTRRA, increased applicable exclusion amounts for the estate tax but a level $1,000,000 excluded amount for the gift tax, and lowered maximum transfer tax rates in general, it can be argued that it is better planning to "pay no tax before its time."

Marital Situations. If donors are considering giving assets to their spouses, what would happen if they separated, divorced, or stayed together and had marital difficulties? In some cases this may be an issue; in others not. Similarly, the marital situation of other potential donees (e.g., children) may affect how and when gifts may be made to them. For example, if a donee divorces, one normally would not want a portion of gift property to end up in the hands of the ex-spouse (such as in the form of commingled marital property).

Liquidity Considerations. Donors should be careful about giving away liquid assets if their estates may have liquidity problems. On the other hand, there are various planning techniques for providing liquidity to an estate. In addition, owners of closely held business interests who are planning to have their estates take advantage of tax provisions such as Section 6166 or Section 303 should take care that they do not give away so much of their closely held stock or other business interest that their estates cannot qualify for these favorable provisions.

Control Considerations. Owners of closely held corporation stock (or other business interests) should consider whether they are impairing their control over the corporation by gifts of stock. Sometimes a controlling owner wants to relinquish control to family members during his or her lifetime, but often he or she does not.

Personal Effects on Donees. Some family members actually may be harmed by having control over too much property too soon—or even ever. This is an individual matter and depends on the personalities and characters of the people involved. Also, in making gifts to minors, it is difficult to know what kind of people they will grow up to be or whom they may marry.

Gift Taxes May Have to Be Paid Now. This may be true for gifts that exceed available exclusions and use up the gift tax unified credit. Actual payment of gift taxes not only involves the uncertainties of EGTRRA already mentioned, but also results in loss of the time value of money on the gift tax paid.

Post-Gift Depreciation May Cause Strategy to Fail. Obviously, the advantage of removing post-gift appreciation from the gross estate applies only if there is appreciation. If the value of gifted property declines, the donor will have paid gift tax or used unified credit at a value greater than the value removed from the gross estate.

No Step-up in Basis at Death for Gift Property. Hence the donee loses the present step-up in basis at death and may face larger capital gains (or lower capital losses) on a subsequent sale or exchange of the property. However, the impact of this issue may depend on many factors, including what the donee does with the gift property and the possibility of future modified carry-over basis at death under EGTRRA.

Some Observations on Lifetime Gifts After EGTRRA

In this uncertain tax environment, many commentators have suggested that people who normally would be making lifetime gifts for all the reasons previously noted should continue to do so. However, they generally should do so without actually incurring gift taxes. Thus, gifts within the annual exclusion and tuition and medical exclusions can be made. Also, transfer techniques that do not result in any taxable gifts at all are possibilities. These include "zeroed out" grantor-retained annuity trusts (GRATs), sales to defective grantor trusts, intra-family loans, private annuities, and self-canceling installment notes, all of which are discussed later in this chapter. Finally, also to be considered are gifts made at a "discount," hopefully within the gift tax applicable exclusion amount, such as qualified personal residence trusts (QPRTs) and gifts of family limited partnership (FLP) interests.

Gifts to Minors: General Considerations

People frequently want to make gifts to minors—children or grandchildren, for example. Because minors usually cannot deal with the property during their minority (generally until age 18), special arrangements often are made for such gifts. Also, donors may want to defer control over gift property until younger donees reach an age when it is presumed they will be more mature and experienced in managing money. Finally, some donors want to skip generations with such gifts.

Methods for Making Gifts to Minors

Outright Gifts. Some kinds of property may conveniently be given outright to minors, such as savings accounts, U.S. series EE savings bonds, and life insurance on the minor's life. However, outright gifts of other kinds of property may cause problems, because outsiders normally are not willing to deal with minors in managing the property since minors generally are not legally competent to contract. Of course, a legal guardian could be appointed for minors, but guardianship tends to be inflexible and expensive, and donors generally prefer other methods. Therefore, outright gifts are not really a practical method for structuring substantial, long-term giving programs for minors.

Uniform Transfers (Gifts) to Minors Act. The Uniform Transfers to Minors Act

(UTMA) and the original Uniform Gifts to Minors Act (UGMA) are a popular way to make gifts of securities and other property to minors. Laws of this type have been enacted in all states and the District of Columbia. In general, they provide for the registration of securities and brokerage accounts, life insurance policies, annuity contracts, mutual funds, money market accounts, and other investments a "prudent person" would make[1] in the name of an adult or financial institution to act as custodian of the property for the minor. As an example, a father might give stock to his minor son and name the boy's adult aunt as custodian for him under the state's UTMA.

This arrangement technically creates a custodianship, not a trust. The custodianship operates according to the terms of the state law under which it was created; the donor cannot change those terms. The gift property is held by the custodian, who manages, invests, and reinvests it for the minor's benefit. The custodian can apply the property or the income from it for the benefit of the minor (including for educational expenses) or accumulate it, at the custodian's sole discretion. But to the extent that the property and income are not expended for the minor's benefit, they must be delivered or paid over to the minor when he or she reaches majority, which generally is specified in the law to be age 21. If the minor dies before attaining majority, the property and income must go to his or her estate. Thus, a possible disadvantage of this method is that the property and accumulated income must be distributed to the donee at majority.

The UTMA simplifies making gifts to minors. No formal trust agreement is required. Income and capital gains are taxable to the minor, unless the income is used to satisfy a legal obligation to support the minor. Also, the donor gets full use of the gift tax annual exclusion, even though the custodian may accumulate income for the minor. Thus, to continue the previous example, if the father gave $11,000 worth of stock to his son in one year under his state's UTMA, all $11,000 would qualify for the gift tax annual exclusion and the gift property would be removed from the father's gross estate. However, if the father acts as custodian and dies before his son reaches majority, the property will be in the father's gross estate because he will have made a transfer with a retained power to alter or amend the enjoyment of the transferred property. (See Chapter 24.)

Trusts for Minors Under Section 2503(c). Under this code section, a donor can have full use of the annual exclusion for gifts to a minor in trust. Thus, if the father transfers $11,000 in stock to an irrevocable trust with his minor son as beneficiary and the trust meets the requirements of Section 2503(c), the full $11,000 will qualify for the annual exclusion.

---

[1] The former UGMA limited eligible assets to a specific list, such as securities, life insurance and annuity contracts, and money.

For a trust to receive this treatment, Section 2503(c) requires that trust income and principal may be expended by the trustee for or on behalf of the beneficiary until the minor reaches age 21 and that any amounts remaining in the trust must then be distributed or made available to the beneficiary. As for UTMA gifts, this may be a disadvantage because donors may prefer to postpone distribution until after age 21 or perhaps to make it in installments, such as one-third at 25, one-third at 30, and the final third at 35.

However, it is permissible for the trust itself to continue beyond age 21, provided the beneficiary has the power (even for only a limited period) to obtain outright the property and any accumulated income in the trust at majority. The trust terms might give the beneficiary such a right for a brief period after he or she turns age 21, in the hope that he or she may not exercise it, and then the irrevocable trust can continue for whatever period the grantor specified in the terms of the trust. (This is not possible for UTMA gifts.) If the beneficiary dies prior to age 21, the trust property must go to his or her estate or as he or she has designated.

The gift property normally will be removed from the donor's gross estate.

Again, however, the grantor (donor) should not be a trustee, because the same estate tax principle applies here as under UTMA gifts, since the trustee must have discretionary power to expend trust corpus or income for the minor's benefit before age 21. After age 21, if the trust continues, the terms may be different. Income and capital gains from these trusts are taxable for federal income tax purposes to the trust if accumulated and to the beneficiary if distributed to him or her.[2]

Use of Regular Trusts. Gifts can be made to minors through regular irrevocable trusts, sometimes called Section 2503(b) trusts, the same as to anyone else. Trusts enable the grantor-donor to set the terms of the gift within the rules of the state's trust law. A trust, other than a Section 2503(c) trust, does not have to make the corpus available when a beneficiary reaches majority or even, in many cases, for many years (or even generations) thereafter. Donors often want to use long-term (or even generation-skipping) trusts when planning for a substantial lifetime giving program.

The practical problems are that a formal trust must be established and, depending on the size of the gift and terms of the trust, the donor may not be able to take full advantage of the gift tax annual exclusion. This is because, with-

---

[2] If trust income is accumulated and taxable to the trust, the kiddie tax on unearned income of minors under age 14 will not apply. The kiddie tax would apply to UTMA gifts for minors under age 14, since custodianship income is taxed to the minor. Note also that trust income used to discharge a legal obligation to support a minor may be taxed to the person with that obligation.

out a so-called Crummey power (described next), only a part or none of each gift to the trust will be considered a gift of a present interest to the donee (the trust beneficiary) and only a present interest will qualify for the annual exclusion.

If the terms of a trust call for the accumulation of trust income or for discretion by the trustee in paying trust income to or for one or more beneficiaries (e.g., a sprinkle or spray power), no part of a gift to the trust would be a present interest to any specific beneficiary. If a trust requires the current distribution of its income to a trust beneficiary or beneficiaries, only a part of each gift would be a gift of a present interest (measured by the part representing the mandatory income interest) and the remainder would be a future interest. This was illustrated in Chapter 24. However, a mandatory income requirement may not be suitable for long-term trusts for minors. Also, it means the $11,000 (indexed for inflation) annual exclusion will never be able to shelter the entire annual gifts to the trust.

Regular (Section 2503[b]) Trusts with Crummey Powers. The famous Crummey case[3] and its eventual acceptance by the IRS gave estate planners a possible solution to the problems of making gifts in trust, so the whole gift (up to certain limits) will be a gift of a present interest and hence qualify for the annual exclusion. This solution involves having a *Crummey power* in these trusts.

Basic Concepts. The terms of an irrevocable trust may give each trust beneficiary (no matter how young) the noncumulative right each year to withdraw his or her pro rata share of that year's gift to the trust up to some limit, such as $5000 or 5 percent of the trust corpus or an amount equal to the annual exclusion or (if gift splitting is contemplated) an amount equal to twice the annual exclusion. This right to withdraw normally is available for only a brief period during the year, such as 30 days.

The withdrawal right is a Crummey power and is intended to ensure an annual exclusion for each year's gift to the trust up to the limit for each beneficiary with a Crummey power. This is because each beneficiary can get the immediate possession, use, or enjoyment of his or her share of the gift by withdrawing it. However, even though the purpose of a Crummey power is to get the annual exclusion for the grantor, it must be a real power and not just illusory. Thus, the power holder(s)—trust beneficiary or beneficiaries—must actually possess the limited annual withdrawal right for a reasonable period of time (often 30 days) and must be notified of it and there must be assets in the trust with which to satisfy the power if the power holder(s) were to exercise it.

Technically, Crummey withdrawal rights are general powers of appoint-

---

[3] Crummey powers are commonly used and widely discussed in estate planning. The citation for the case is *Crummey v. Commissioner,* 397 F. 2d 82 (9th Cir. 1968), rev'g 25 T.C.M. 772 (1966).

ment over the property subject to withdrawal. If these rights are not exercised during the limited withdrawal period and are noncumulative, it represents the *lapse* in that year of a general power of appointment over the property subject to withdrawal. These rights might be called *annually lapsing powers.* The tax code provides that lapses of general powers each year for each beneficiary that do not exceed the larger of $5000 or 5 percent of the value of the property from which the powers could have been exercised are not a release of the powers, which might be a taxable event. The amount covered by this so-called 5 and 5 power is often referred to as the *lapse-protected amount;* lapses within this amount will not give rise to any gift or estate tax consequences for the power holder. However, lapses in a year for a power holder (e.g., beneficiary) that exceed the larger of $5000 or 5 percent of corpus are considered *releases* of a general power of appointment and may give rise to taxable gifts by the power holder to other trust beneficiaries and inclusion of the corpus in the power holder's gross estate upon his or her death, depending on the terms of the trust.

On the other hand, if the withdrawal rights are cumulative over the duration of the trust and do not lapse if not exercised within the limited withdrawal period (other than lapsing to the extent of the greater of $5000 or 5 percent of corpus each year), they are called *hanging powers.* These powers may be suggested by some planners, but as of this writing the IRS has indicated that, in its view, hanging powers do not prevent gifts by the power holder for amounts in excess of the lapse-protected amount.

Thus, regular irrevocable trusts with Crummey powers may produce some attractive results. They can result in shifting (or accumulating) trust income for income tax purposes, in removing trust property from the donor's gross estate for estate tax purposes, and normally in protecting gifts from taxes because of the gift tax annual exclusion. The trustee also can be given discretionary power to distribute income and corpus to the beneficiaries subject to an ascertainable standard or, if independent, at his or her sole discretion. Thus, funds could be provided for the beneficiaries' educational needs or other needs. Finally, such trusts can continue for many years after the beneficiaries reach majority or even for their lifetimes, depending on the desires of the creator of the trust. Thus, they could be generation-skipping trusts if a trust meets the requirements for a GST annual exclusion trust or if the grantor allocates enough of his or her GST exemption to the trust to make it exempt.

It should be noted that in recent years the IRS has increased its concern over and scrutiny of Crummey powers. Therefore, care should be taken that they are real powers.

Income Tax Considerations. Trust income or income from property held for a minor under a UTMA that is used to discharge a parent's *legal obligation* to support the minor will be taxed to the parent. The support obligation of parents depends on the law of the state in which they live and may vary with the circumstances of the parents.

Gifts Between Spouses

There is an unlimited federal gift tax marital deduction for qualifying gifts between spouses (when the donee spouse is a U.S. citizen). Thus, gifts between spouses are gift tax-free. Gifts may be made between spouses for a variety of reasons. However, an important one for estate planning purposes is to provide enough assets in each spouse's estate so that each can use his or her full applicable credit amount no matter who dies first. The same reason might also apply so each spouse can use his or her own GST exemption.

Gifts of Remainder Interests with Retained Use or Income Interests

We saw in Chapter 24 that Chapter 14 of the IRC effectively restricts gifts in trust of remainder interests to family members with the retention of interests in the trust by the transferor (donor) to the following types of transfers.

Personal Residence Trusts (PRTs). These are irrevocable trusts under which the grantor transfers one personal residence to the trust but retains the right to use and occupy the residence for a period of years and then, at the end of this period, the residence goes to a remainderperson. A PRT cannot hold any other assets and the residence cannot be sold during the term. As a result, PRTs are inflexible. Normally, QPRTs are used.

Qualified Personal Residence Trusts (QPRTs). These are irrevocable trusts under which the grantor transfers one personal residence per trust (either a principal residence or another residence of the grantor) to the trust, retains a term interest in the trust (i.e., the right to use or occupy the residence for a period of years), and grants a remainder interest in the trust to a family member or members at the end of the term. In effect, the grantor is giving away his or her personal residence to family members but retaining the right to live in it for a fixed period of years.

The purpose is to give away the residence and hopefully get it out of the grantor's gross estate at a reduced gift tax value. The gift tax value is the fair market value of the residence less the value of the retained use interest for the term of years selected, calculated according to the Section 7520 rates, and the actuarial value of a contingent reversionary interest in the event the grantor dies during the term of years that is usually retained by the grantor. Also, any post-gift appreciation in the value of the residence is removed from the grantor's gross estate. The result is a substantially reduced transfer tax cost of moving the residence to family members (e.g., children), but still allowing the grantor to use the residence for the term—and even beyond, with proper planning.

The grantor retains the right to use and occupy the personal residence for a period of years (the term interest), such as 10 or 15 years. The longer the period selected, the greater the Section 7520 value of the retained term interest and the smaller the taxable gift remainder interest. However, if the grantor dies during the term, the full value of the QPRT property will be in his or her gross estate as a transfer with a retained interest that did not in fact end before his or her death. Therefore, the grantor normally selects a period that he or she reasonably expects to survive. This, of course, can never be known for sure.

Grantors often also retain the power in their will to direct how the QPRT property will be distributed, in the event they die before the end of the term, or it may revert to their probate estate. This is a contingent reversionary interest, which has an actuarial value that also reduces the value of the taxable gift.[4] To get the full tax benefits of a QPRT, the grantor must survive the term. But even if not, the grantor would appear to be in no worse position than if he or she had not created a QPRT and had simply lived in the residence until his or her death.

Assuming the grantor survives the term, the residence will pass to the QPRT's remainder beneficiary or continue in trust for him or her. If the grantor wants to continue to live in the residence after the term ends, he or she can negotiate a lease for the residence from the remainderperson or from the trustee of a continuing trust for the remainderperson at a fair market rental. As a planning matter, it usually is an attractive technique to provide that the residence will remain in a continuing irrevocable grantor trust for the remainderperson after the term ends. This way lease payments by the grantor will not be taxable income to the remainderperson (since it is a grantor trust for income tax purposes), will not be gifts (if they reflect fair market rental value), and in effect will be removed from the grantor's gross estate at his or her death.[5]

The main disadvantage of QPRTs is that the family member remainderperson does not get a stepped-up income tax basis in the residence at the grantor's death.

---

[4] Technically, such a contingent reversionary interest also reduces the value of a fixed-term interest (say, for 10 years), since now the interest is for the *shorter* of the grantor's life or the fixed period. However, the *combined value* of the term interest and the contingent reversion will be substantially greater than the value of a fixed-term interest alone. Retention of contingent reversionary interests is permitted for QPRTs and PRTs, but not for qualified interests (e.g., GRATs).

[5] As explained in Chapter 14, such a *defective grantor trust* is an irrevocable trust where the grantor is treated as owner of the trust corpus for income tax purposes, but not for estate tax purposes.

An Illustration of a QPRT. Assume that Alexia Lee-Smith, age 65, owns in her own name a condominium apartment as her principal residence worth $500,000 and a second residence in the country with a value of $300,000. Alexia has paid off the mortgages on both residences. Her basis in the apartment is $100,000 and in the country home is $125,000. Over the years, these properties have increased in value at an average annual compound rate of about 5 percent. Alexia is married and she has a 30-year-old daughter, Dee. Alexia and her husband are estimated to be in the top federal estate tax bracket and neither has made any prior taxable gifts. They would like to continue to use the residences until they die.

In 2003, Alexia places each of these residences in a separate QPRT with an irrevocable grantor trust for Dee as remainderperson. Under these QPRTs, Alexia retains the right to use the residences for 10 years (or until her death, if sooner) and further retains the right to direct in her will how the residences will pass in the event that she dies during the 10-year period. She further agrees with the trustee that she will be able to lease either or both of the residences at fair market rental value following the 10-year term. During the 10-year period, Alexia will make additional cash contributions to the QPRTs to pay expenses of the properties (real estate taxes, insurance, maintenance expenses, etc.).

Under these facts, and assuming a Section 7520 interest rate of 7 percent, Alexia has made the following combined taxable gifts of the remainder interests.

Value of the residences	$800,000
Value of 10-year retained term interests	-351,520
Value of contingent reversions	<u>-148,880</u>
Taxable transfer and gift (value of remainder interests)	$299,600
Tentative gift tax	87,664
Applicable credit amount (unified credit)	
used (out of $345,800 in 2003)	<u>-87,664</u>
Federal gift tax payable	$0

On the other hand, if Alexia simply retains ownership of these residences until her death (say, at age 80) and the properties continue to appreciate at an average annual compound rate of 5 percent, they will be valued in her gross estate at about $1,663,000.[6]

Grantor-Retained Annuity Trusts (GRATs). A GRAT is an irrevocable trust that pays a fixed amount (either a dollar amount or a fixed percentage of the initial fair market value of the property transferred to the GRAT) to the grantor for a specified period of time (the annuity period) and then distributes the remain-

---

[6] Of course, if Alexia's husband survives her, her estate can take a marital deduction, but then the value ultimately will be in her husband's taxable estate.

ing trust corpus to designated trust beneficiaries (normally family members) or to trusts for them as remainderpersons. The annuity period may be for a specified term of years, the life of the annuitant (grantor), or the earlier of a specified term of years or the life of the annuitant. It often is for a specified term of years. Then, if the grantor dies during the annuity period, any remaining payments are made to his of her estate or possibly to his or her spouse. Since GRATs are qualified interests under Section 2702, the value of the annuity payments is determined by using Section 7520 rates, rather than being valued at zero. GRATs can be funded with any kind of property and often with marketable securities, real estate, closely held stock, cash, and partnership interests, among others. GRATs normally are grantor trusts.

When a GRAT is created, the taxable gift, if any, is measured by the fair market value of the property placed in the trust less the value of the grantor's retained annuity interest. Thus, the greater the annuity payout selected, the higher the value of the retained interest and the lower the gift tax value. In fact, it would appear to be possible today to set the annuity payments high enough so that when the GRAT is created the actuarial value of the remainder interest, and hence the gift tax value, would be zero or, to be conservative, very low. This is referred to as "zeroing out a GRAT." GRATs that are zeroed out are often called "Walton GRATs," after the case that allowed zeroing out (as explained in footnote 7).

However, the annuity payments come back to the grantor and potentially add to his or her gross estate. If the grantor survives the annuity period, any remaining property in the GRAT is removed from his or her gross estate. On the other hand, if the grantor dies during the annuity period, the GRAT corpus will be partly or wholly in his or her gross estate. Thus, as in the case of the QPRT, the annuity period normally is selected with the expectation that the grantor will survive it. Since GRATs normally are wholly grantor trusts for income tax purposes, the grantor is taxed on the income of the trust, but not on the annuity payments.

The economics of GRATs are largely an investment play. If the total return on the assets in a GRAT exceeds the Section 7520 rate used in calculating the annuity interests (sometimes called the "hurdle rate"), the GRAT will benefit the grantor's family (remainderpersons). Thus, GRATs often are funded with assets expected to be rapidly appreciating or high-yielding assets. If total return of the GRAT is about the same as or less than the Section 7520 rate, it will be essentially a wash. Thus, assuming a zeroed-out GRAT, even if the total return should fall below the Section 7520 rate (or be negative), the annuity payments will simply exhaust the GRAT corpus and nothing will pass to the remainderpersons. However, even in this case, little (i.e., the costs of setting up and administering the GRAT) would be lost, since the grantor would simply get his or her property back without having made a taxable gift.[7] Thus, zeroed-out GRATs can be attractive, particularly considering the transfer tax uncertainties of EGTRRA.

An Illustration of a Zeroed-out GRAT. Suppose John Markowitz, age 65 and in good health, has a sizable estate and owns a large amount of his employer's stock, which has had good growth over the years. John decides to transfer $750,000 of this stock to an irrevocable trust (a GRAT) that will pay him an annuity of $106,783 per year for 10 years. If John should die during the 10-year term, the remaining annuity payments would go to his estate. At the end of this annuity period, the trust corpus is required to be paid to his son, Harry. Further assume the total return on the common stock averages 10 percent per year over the 10-year period and the Section 7520 rate ("hurdle rate") was 7 percent when the trust was created.

Given the Section 7520 rate of 7 percent, the $106,783 annuity payment will be just enough to cause the actuarial value of the remainder interest (to Harry) at creation of the GRAT to be zero. Therefore, there will be no taxable gift when John creates the GRAT. But the GRAT's corpus (the common stock) actually produces a 10 percent total return (3 percentage points over the theoretical Section 7520 rate).[8] Therefore, when the 10-year annuity period ends, there will be about $243,463 in the GRAT to go to Harry without any transfer tax cost.

Grantor-Retained Unitrusts (GRUTs). These are like GRATs, except that the periodic amount to the grantor is expressed as a fixed percentage of the fair market value of the trust assets valued annually.

Retained Term Interest in Certain Tangible Property. A grantor can retain an interest for a period of years in non-depreciable tangible property (such as

---

[7] In the Walton case, in 1993 Mrs. Audrey Walton transferred over $100 million of Wal-Mart stock to each of two GRATs (over $200 million in all). The GRATs were for a two-year term, with annuity payments to Mrs. Walton of 49.35% of the initial trust corpus the first year and 59.22% in the second. At the end of the trust terms, any assets in the GRATs would go to Mrs. Walton's daughters. If Mrs. Walton died during the two-year term, any remaining annuity payments would be made to her estate. These annuity payments were intended to zero out these GRATs. The IRS contended the GRATs could not be zeroed out and that Mrs. Walton had made a taxable gift. The tax court unanimously held to the contrary and said that the GRATs effectively could be zeroed out. *Walton v. Commissioner*, 115 TC No. 41 (2000). In the Walton situation, however, the annuity payments to Mrs. Walton exhausted the GRATs and nothing actually went to her daughters.

[8] As indicated previously, in valuing remainder interests, term interests, life estates, and other interests, the IRS in effect *assumes* the assets behind these interests will earn the Section 7520 rate. In fact, however, they may *actually* earn more or less than this rate.

paintings, other art objects, and bare land), with the remainder going to a family member. The value of the term interest reduces the value of the gift.

Use of Family Limited Partnerships (FLPs) or Other Entities in Making Gifts

Property owners for many years have placed assets in various types of entities, such as partnerships, closely held corporations, and, more recently, limited liability companies (LLCs), so they could be managed in the interest of family members. Various family members may be given ownership interests in the entity, but the entity often is controlled by only certain family members. Limited partnerships (LPs),[9] which are controlled by one or a few family members and where substantially all the limited partners are family members, commonly called *family limited partnerships* (FLPs), often are employed as such an entity and will be used as the basis of this discussion. However, limited liability companies (LLCs)[10] also are used for this purpose.

Basic Concepts. FLPs can be used in a number of ways. However, a traditional idea often has been for a senior family member or members (e.g., mother, father, or both) to set up a limited partnership (LP) to which the senior member contributes property (e.g., real estate, closely held business interests, or marketable securities) in return for a general partnership interest and a limited partnership interest. Younger family members may contribute small amounts (e.g., cash) to the LP in return for a small limited partnership interest.[11] Thus, once the LP is formed, the senior member (let us say, mother) has a general partnership interest and also a substantial limited partnership interest, while the other partners (let us say, children) have small limited partnership interests. The mother and children in this example own the part-

---

[9] Limited partnership (LPs) are partnerships with at least one general partner (who has management control over partnership affairs and unlimited liability for partnership debts) and one or more limited partners (who do not have management control but have limited liability, up to their investment in the partnership, for partnership debts) and that is established under state law and registered as an LP. These and other forms of business organization are described in Chapter 30.

[10] Limited liability companies (LLCs) are a newer form of business organization created under state law. All states now have LLC statutes. LLCs are a cross between corporations and partnerships. They are pass-through entities for income tax purposes (like partnerships), but give their members (owners) limited liability, up to their investment in the LLC, and management control (if desired), like corporations. They have become a very popular form of business entity.

[11] To be a partnership, an entity must have at least two partners; in an LP, at least one must be a general partner.

nership and are the partners, while the partnership owns the property contributed to it.[12] The mother, as general partner, controls the management of the LP. The limited partners lack control and their interests lack marketability because of the nature of limited partnership interests in a LP.

The general partner has unlimited liability for partnership debts (including tort liability). However, while one or more individuals can be the general partner (the mother in our example), the general partner also could be another flow-through entity (such as an S corporation or an LLC) owned by an individual (or individuals) or a combination of individuals and a flow-through entity, so that no one person would have a controlling interest.[13] Such flow-through entities (see Chapter 30) generally will protect an individual owner of the entity from personal liability beyond his or her investment in the entity.

If the partners—usually senior family members—contribute appreciated property to the partnership, there is no capital gain on the exchange of the property for partnership interests. Instead, the contributing partner gets a carryover basis in his or her partnership interest.

After an FLP is formed, the senior family members normally make gifts of some or all of their limited partnership interest to younger family members or to trusts for their benefit. The value of these gift LP interests generally is substantially discounted from the pro rata value of the partnership assets underlying those interests.

Purposes of Family Limited Partnerships. FLPs can have a number of tax and nontax purposes, such as the following.

Management of Family Assets. The general partner (or managing member of an LLC) has control over the management of partnership assets and thus can centralize and effectively manage family wealth.

Instruct Younger Family Members in Financial Affairs. A related purpose may be to provide an opportunity for more experienced family members to involve and educate less experienced family members in business and financial matters.

---

[12] Thus, the partners (mother and children in this example) own partnership interests that have values and the partnership itself owns the assets inside the partnership, which also have values. The value of a partner's partnership interest is affected not only by his or her pro rata share of the net fair market value of the assets inside the partnership (i.e., liquidation value), but also by the partner's rights and obligations under the partnership agreement. These rights and obligations determine the ability of partners to reap the benefits of the partnership's assets and operations. Thus, the value of the partnership interests of limited partners in an FLP normally will be considerably less than their pro rata share of the net fair market value of partnership assets, because of restrictions or limits on the ability of limited partners to control partnership affairs and to dispose of their interests.

[13] There can be 100 percent owned single stockholder S corporations. Also, many state laws permit single-member LLCs.

Secure Substantial Valuation Discounts for Tax Purposes. As has been explained in this chapter and in Chapter 24, substantial valuation discounts normally can be taken for gift tax purposes and perhaps estate tax purposes. The discounts are based on lack of control and lack of marketability of limited partnership interests.

Creditor Protection. The FLP agreement may restrict the ability of limited partners to assign or pledge their interests as collateral. Also, even if an LP's creditors levy against his or her partnership interest, under the Revised Uniform Limited Partnership Act (RULPA) (see Chapter 30) generally all a creditor can get is a charging order against the interest, essentially allowing the creditor the right to receive whatever partnership distributions are made to the limited partner (which distributions normally are controlled by the general partner).

Protection Against Marital Claims. In a similar vein, if a limited partner has marital difficulties, normally all that his or her spouse could receive in a divorce settlement or equitable distribution would be an assignee's interest in the limited partner's interest (or possibly a limited partner's interest), which again would be subject to the general partner's control. Also, an LP interest normally can be easily identified as nonmarital gift property.

Limitations of FLPs. These arrangements can be complex, with commensurate costs of setting them up. They normally are used for substantial property interests. Also, care should be taken in planning and drafting these agreements so that they do not run afoul of various tax law provisions and cause unwanted tax consequences. Finally, it must be recognized that the IRS and others are watching FLP's closely and may contest the size of valuation discounts or advance various tax theories in an attempt to thwart the anticipated tax benefits from such arrangements.

An Illustration. Let us assume Henry Cohen, age 60, owns in his own name a profitable apartment house with a net fair market value of $4 million and an adjusted basis of $800,000. Henry is married to Tracy, age 56. Together they have sizeable gross estates. Neither has made any prior taxable gifts. They have two adult children and four grandchildren. Henry has decided to make substantial lifetime gifts to his children to help them financially now, but he would like to keep control of the management of his property. He also wants to keep any sizeable gifts within his and Tracy's applicable exclusion amounts. Tracy is willing to split any lifetime gifts. Therefore, Henry decides to transfer the apartment house to an FLP in exchange for a 1 percent general partnership interest and a 97 percent limited partnership interest. Each of the children contributes a small amount of cash or securities for a 1 percent limited partnership interest each.

After the FLP is formed, Henry makes gifts in 2003 of 42.08 percent limited partnership interests outright to each of his two children. The value of these gifts is determined as follows, assuming a 20 percent discount for lack of marketability and a 25 percent discount for lack of control taken sequentially. An independent appraisal is secured to determine these discounts.[14]

Fair market value of apartment house (without regard for the small amount of cash and marketable securities)	$4,000,000
Value of 1% general partnership interest at pro rata share of value of underlying partnership assets ($4,000,000 × 0.01)	-40,000
	$3,960,000
For 20% lack of marketability discount	×0.80
Value after lack of marketability discount	$3,168,000
LP interest given to each child during year (42.08%)	×0.4208
Value before lack of control (minority) discount	$1,333,094
For 25% lack of control discount	×0.75
Value of LP interest given to each child	$ 999,821
Combined applicable exclusion amounts (assuming Henry and Tracey split gifts)	$ 2,000,000
Gift tax payable	0

Therefore, no gift tax is payable, but Henry's and Tracy's current applicable credit amounts ($345,800 each as of 2003) have been used.

After these gifts, Henry has a 1 percent general partnership interest and a 12.84 percent limited partnership interest. Thus, due to these substantial valuation discounts, Henry has transferred the underlying value of limited partnership assets of $1,683,200 (.4208 × $4,000,000) to each of his children while staying within his and Tracy's current applicable credit amounts for gift tax purposes. Henry also remains in control of the FLP through his 1 percent general partnership interest. It may also be possible to transfer smaller, discounted FLP limited partnership interests that would be within the per-donee gift tax annual exclusion of $11,000 ($22,000 if gifts are split). This depends on whether such gifts are considered gifts of a present interest. As of this writing, this in turn would appear to depend on the terms of the limited partnership agreement and applicable court decisions as they unfold.

---

[14] The amounts of these discounts may be affected by a variety of factors, such as: the terms of the FLP agreement, underlying assets in the FLP (e.g., more for nonliquid assets, less for marketable securities), distribution history of the FLP, and others. Data from published studies and public markets often are used as starting points in determining these discounts.

Sales Within the Family

The previous material concerned gifts—gratuitous transfers. This section deals with planning techniques where there are sales for full and adequate consideration between family members or between family members and trusts for other family members.

Sales to a Defective Grantor Trust

Basic Concept. This technique is different in form from a zeroed-out GRAT, but the objective is much the same. In a typical situation, a senior family member (grantor) sets up a so-called defective grantor trust (see Chapter 14), which is a grantor trust for federal income tax purposes, i.e., the corpus is treated as owned by the grantor, but which will not be included in the grantor's gross estate for federal estate tax purposes if he or she dies during its term. The grantor then sells appreciated property to the trust in return for an interest-bearing promissory note that is due at the end of the trust term. At this time, any corpus in the trust (after the principal and any interest due on the note is paid to the grantor) will be paid to the trust beneficiaries (normally family members of the grantor).

If the interest rate on the promissory note is at least equal to the appropriate applicable federal rate (AFR)[15] and the principal (face) of the note is equal to the value of the property sold to the trust, there is no taxable gift by the grantor from the transaction. It is a sale not a gift. Also, since the sale is to a grantor trust, there is no gain realized or recognized on the sale of the appreciated property, because in terms of income tax it is like the grantor is selling the property to himself or herself. Also, if the grantor should die during the term of the trust, the corpus of the irrevocable trust would not be included in his or her gross estate for federal estate tax purposes, since the grantor has made no gift with a retained interest (as would be true for a GRAT, for example) or kept any other power or right that would cause inclusion. As a practical matter, this means the terms of these trusts often can be set for longer periods than for GRATs. However, the value of the promissory note would be in the grantor's gross estate at death.

---

[15] The applicable federal rates (AFRs) are defined in Section 1274(d) of the IRC. There are three AFRs: the short-term rate (for obligations having terms of less than three years), the mid-term rate (for obligations with terms from three to nine years), and the long-term rate (for obligations whose terms exceed nine years). It will be recalled that the Section 7520 rate (used for GRATs and other valuations) is 120 percent of the mid-term AFR. Thus, the AFR used in this situation probably will be less than the Section 7520 rate. (They both are sometimes referred to as "hurdle rates" in the context used here.) This can be an advantage for a sale to a defective grantor trust as compared with a zeroed-out GRAT.

As with GRATs, sales to defective grantor trusts essentially are an investment play. If the total return on the property sold to the trust exceeds the interest on the promissory note to the grantor (the appropriate AFR), some assets will remain in the trust after the loan and interest are paid and the trust will benefit the trust beneficiaries (normally the grantor's family members) to that extent without any transfer tax cost. If the total return is equal to or less than the appropriate AFR, nothing will remain in the trust at the end of its term and nothing will go to the grantor's family. But even in this event, the grantor will have lost nothing.

An Illustration. Assume Paul Sanchez, age 65 and in good health, has a sizeable estate and would like to benefit his adult son and daughter during his lifetime. However, he does not wish to make any taxable gifts and already is making annual exclusion gifts to them. Paul decides to create an irrevocable defective grantor trust for a term of 10 years, with his two children as beneficiaries. He then sells $1,200,000 of common stock (for which he paid $200,000 many years ago) to the trust in return for a $1,200,000 promissory note bearing 6 percent interest (the long-term AFR), paid annually ($72,000) to Paul. The principal and any accrued interest on the note are payable to Paul at the end of the trust's 10-year term.[16] Paul has noted that the average annual compound rate of total return on this stock over the last 15 years has been more than 12 percent.

In this transaction, Paul has not realized and recognized any capital gain on the sale, he has not made any taxable gift, and the trust corpus will not be in his gross estate if he should die during the 10-year term, all for the reasons just stated. If we assume the stock sold to the trust actually has an average annual compound rate of total return during the 10-year term of 10 percent (i.e., 4 percentage points over the 6 percent "hurdle rate"), then approximately $764,996 worth of stock will remain in the trust after the loan principal and interest have been paid to Paul. This amount will be distributed to his children at the end of the 10-year term without any transfer tax cost. On the other hand, if the total return is equal to or less than the 6 percent "hurdle rate" in this case, nothing will remain in the trust and nothing will go to Paul's children.

Installment Sales

In this case, the seller disposes of his or her entire interest in the property in return for annual payments for a stated period. Each payment includes stated interest and a payment of principal. The principal payments will be partly a

---

[16] It would also be possible for interest to accrue during the trust term and be payable with the principal at the end.

nontaxable recovery of the seller's basis and partly capital gain. This is essentially the same as any installment sale, except it is to a family member. The buyer is obligated to pay the installments when due, whether the seller survives the installment period or not.

Self-Canceling Installment Notes (SCINs)

In this installment arrangement, the seller disposes of his or her entire interest in the property in return for annual payments for the shorter of the installment period or his or her lifetime. In other words, if the seller dies during the installment period, the note is cancelled and no further payments are due to the seller's estate. This eventuality would benefit the buyer, who would be a family member. Also, there would be no value for the note in the deceased seller's gross estate. However, to be considered an installment transaction, the payment term must be less than the seller's life expectancy at the time of sale. Also, to avoid a taxable gift, a premium should be charged for the cancellation feature, usually in the form of a higher sales price, higher interest on the installments, or both.

Private Annuity Sales

Here the seller disposes of his or her entire interest in the property in return for the buyer's unsecured promise to pay an annual income for the seller's lifetime. Hence the term *private annuity:* it is like a commercial straight (pure) life annuity, except that it is provided by a family member rather than an insurance company. To avoid a taxable gift, the present value of future life annuity payments must equal the fair market value of the property at date of sale.

There are, of course, risks involved in SCINs and private annuities. The buyer may not be able to make the required payments and, in the case of private annuities, the seller will be only an unsecured creditor. For SCINs, if the seller outlives the installment term, there probably will be no real transfer tax savings. For private annuities, if the seller outlives his or her life expectancy, the cost to the buyer will be greater than expected and the seller will receive more back in annuity payments, which may end up in his or her gross estate. On the other hand, both SCINs and private annuities can provide retirement income for the seller. Also, if the seller's longevity is not too great, property can be removed from his or her gross estate at no gift tax cost.

Other Sale Arrangements

These may include sales of remainder interests for cash, sales of remainder interests for SCINs or private annuities, and split purchases of property.

Loans to Family Members

This can be another approach to possibly transferring significant wealth to family members without making taxable gifts. In this case, a senior family member might create a defective grantor trust for the benefit of other family members (e.g., children or grandchildren), lend money to the trust, and receive a promissory note from the trust for the loan. The face of the note would equal the amount of the loan and it would bear interest at the appropriate AFR, so there should be no gift by the grantor. The note is due at the end of the trust's term. If the grantor should die during the term of the trust, the value of the note will be in his or her gross estate, but the corpus of the trust should not be.

As with GRATs and sales to defective grantor trusts, such a loan arrangement is an investment play. If the total return on the assets in which the trustee invests the loan proceeds exceeds the "hurdle rate" (the interest rate on the note or AFR rate), some assets will remain in the trust after the loan and interest are paid and they will go to the trust beneficiaries at the end of the trust's term without any transfer tax cost. But if the total return is equal to or less than the appropriate AFR rate, nothing will remain in the trust at the end of its term and nothing will go to the beneficiaries. For example, in the previous illustration, instead of selling common stock to the defective grantor trust, if Paul Sanchez had loaned $1,200,000 to the trust for 10 years at the 6 percent long-term AFR and the trust assets had earned the assumed 10 percent average annual compound rate of total return, the economic results for his children would be the same as shown in the previous illustration.

Loans also can be made directly to other family members in the hope that their returns on the loan proceeds will exceed the interest they pay. Such loans also can be forgiven over time, as gifts, within the annual exclusion each year or possibly in greater amounts once the situation with respect to the federal estate tax becomes clearer. Of course, loans can be made within the family for other reasons than estate planning.

26

Marital Deduction Planning, Postmortem Planning, and Estate Liquidity

Marital Deduction Planning

For married people with potential estates large enough to attract federal estate taxation, proper use of the unlimited federal estate tax marital deduction is a critical decision issue in estate planning.

Using the Marital Deduction to Save Federal Estate Taxes

The basic idea of the marital deduction is to allow married estate owners to leave as much of their estates as they wish to their surviving spouse free of federal estate tax.[1] But this *marital* part must be left to the spouse in such a way that it potentially would be included in the survivor's gross estate at his or her subsequent death. In tax language, these are referred to as transfers that *qualify* for the marital deduction. Thus, the marital deduction is essentially a tax-deferral technique.

Aside from tax deferral, another essential part of saving taxes through marital deduction planning is making sure that the applicable credit amount (unified credit) is fully used in *both* spouses' estates or lifetime gifts. This means the applicable exclusion amount will escape federal estate taxation in both spouses' estates and can pass tax-free to their children or other family members. Thus, this exclusion amount, often in trust, bypasses the surviving spouse's gross estate

---

[1] The marital deduction was originally placed in the tax code in 1948 with the goal of generally equalizing the tax situation of married persons in common-law states and community property states. The maximum deduction then was one-half the adjusted gross estate. It became unlimited in 1981 under the Economic Recovery Tax Act.

and goes to the children or others. However, a surviving spouse may be given some or all of the so-called almost-owner powers (described in Chapter 24) in this bypass (nonmarital) trust. On the other hand, for tax or other reasons, the surviving spouse's rights in a bypass trust may be more limited.

Further, it often is anticipated that a surviving spouse will consume, make lifetime gifts within the exclusions,[2] make charitable gifts, or take other planning actions so that the marital deduction share he or she received from the deceased spouse will not eventually actually end up in his or her gross estate. These actions will be influenced in part by how the marital share is left to the surviving spouse.

Essential Components of a Marital Deduction Strategy

These include deciding how much (if any) of the marital deduction should be used, making sure each spouse can use his or her applicable credit amount regardless of which spouse dies first, deciding how (i.e., through what vehicles or in what ways) property is to qualify for the marital deduction, and deciding how the marital share should be funded. These issues can be complex, so only their basic elements are covered here. The illustrations used in this chapter are for explanatory purposes only.

Overall Goals of Marital Deduction Planning

In many cases, spouses want first to ensure the financial security of the surviving spouse for his or her remaining lifetime (sometimes called the surviving spouse's *overlife*) and then plan for maximum wealth transfer for other generations. But if both spouses have significant assets and adequate income, they may give more weight to wealth transfer to future generations. In some cases, such as second marriages in which both spouses have children or grandchildren from prior marriages, both may be thinking primarily of leaving much or all of their wealth to their own children and grandchildren. Naturally, the spouses' objectives should guide their marital deduction strategies.

How Much (if Any) of the Marital Deduction Should Be Used?

Since the marital deduction is unlimited, at first blush married estate owners may be tempted to plan on leaving all their assets outright to their spouse. These are sometimes dubbed "I love you" wills. However, for tax reasons the

---

[2] An attractive plan here may be for the surviving spouse to directly pay tuitions and/or medical expenses for children or grandchildren as well as make annual exclusion gifts out of his or her marital deduction share.

maximum deduction normally should not be used in situations where a federal estate tax may be payable. This will result in the estate's being overqualified for the marital deduction, which may result in higher overall taxes. The following illustrations[3] point out some common issues in deciding how much property to qualify.

Estates Less than the Applicable Exclusion Amount. In situations where the gross estates of both spouses combined are expected to be less than the applicable exclusion amount, property can be left in full (or in lesser amounts) to either spouse with no adverse estate tax effects.

In Example 1, assume that Harry Carter has an adjusted gross estate (gross estate less debts and expenses) of $600,000 and his wife Martha has an adjusted gross estate (AGE) of $300,000. They each have wills leaving everything outright to the other (reciprocal wills). If Harry dies in 2003, his estate situation will be as follows.

Example 1

Adjusted gross estate	$600,000
Marital deduction (to Martha under Harry's will)	-600,000
Taxable estate	$0
Federal estate tax payable	$0

Now, if Martha dies one year later, her estate situation will be as follows.[4]

Adjusted gross estate (in her own name)	$300,000
Estate (from Harry's will)	$600,000
Total adjusted gross estate	$900,000
Marital deduction	$0
Taxable estate	$900,000
Tentative estate tax	$306,800
Applicable credit amount (in 2003)	-$345,800
Federal estate tax payable	$0

The estate tax situation would not change if Martha dies first (reversing the order of deaths).

---

[3] In all these illustrations, state death taxes and the federal estate tax credit or deduction for state death taxes paid are ignored for the sake of simplicity. It is also assumed that administration expenses are taken as deductions on the estate tax return.

[4] In all these illustrations, appreciation or depreciation in assets between the deaths is ignored for the sake of simplicity. It is also assumed the surviving spouse does not remarry and makes no specific bequests to others. The fact that the applicable credit amount (unified credit) is increasing until it reaches $1,455,800 in 2009, then becomes not applicable in 2010, and then returns to $345,800 in 2011 and thereafter complicates these illustrations. We have used the unified credit for the year assumed in each of these examples.

Avoid Overqualifying for Marital Deduction. But if the combined estates of husband and wife exceed the applicable exclusion amount, it is better tax-wise to qualify less than the maximum allowable deduction. This is because there is no tax advantage for an estate owner to qualify that part of his or her estate that will be shielded from estate tax by the unified credit in any event. However, when the surviving spouse dies, there is a tax disadvantage if the first spouse to die qualified all of his or her estate for the deduction. This is because all the property that passes to the surviving spouse in a qualifying manner will be included in that spouse's gross estate at death unless he or she consumes it or makes nontaxable gifts while alive.

As just noted, when all or "too much" property is qualified, it is referred to as an estate's being *overqualified* for the marital deduction. This can occur in various ways. Some of the more common are illustrated next.

All Property to Spouse. Let us use the same facts as in Example 1, except that Harry's adjusted gross estate is $1,600,000 and Martha's is $300,000. They have reciprocal wills as before. In this case, if Harry dies in 2002 his estate situation will be as follows.

Example 2

Adjusted gross estate	$1,600,000
Marital deduction (to Martha under Harry's will)	-1,600,000
Taxable estate	$0
Federal estate tax payable	$0

But now, if Martha dies one year later, her estate situation will be as follows.

Adjusted gross estate (in her own name)	$300,000
(from Harry's will)	$1,600,000
Total adjusted gross estate	$1,900,000
Marital deduction	$0
Taxable estate	$1,900,000
Tentative estate tax	$735,800
Applicable credit amount (in 2003)	-$345,800
Federal estate tax payable	$390,000

Note that this tax occurs because an applicable credit amount is used in only one of the two estates (in the survivor's estate). Harry's estate is overqualified for the marital deduction. This tax situation would be the same if Martha had predeceased Harry.

Too Much Jointly Owned Property. Now suppose that Harry and Martha Carter own all their $1,900,000 adjusted gross estate as joint tenants with right

---

[5] This, of course, is unlikely as a practical matter. However, this assumption helps illustrate the problem of owning too much property as joint tenants with right of survivorship.

of survivorship.[5] In this situation, if Harry dies in 2002 his estate situation will be as follows.

Example 3

Adjusted gross estate (½ × $1,900,000)	$950,000
Marital deduction	-$950,000
Taxable estate	$0
Federal estate tax payable	$0

If Martha dies one year later, her estate situation will be as follows.

Adjusted gross estate ($1,900,000 by operation of law)	$1,900,000
Marital deduction	$0
Taxable estate	$1,900,000
Tentative estate tax	$735,800
Applicable credit amount (in 2001)	-$345,800
Federal estate tax payable	$390,000

The result would be the same if Martha had predeceased Harry.

Estate Consisting of Qualified Retirement Plan or IRA Death Benefits. The same kind of overqualification can occur in situations where people have the bulk of their estates in qualified retirement plans or IRAs naming their spouse as beneficiary. In this event, the plan death benefits will be in the participant's gross estate but will qualify for the marital deduction. Thus, the participant's estate may be overqualified.

Reduce-to-Zero (Zero-Tax) Formula Provision. This type of provision in a will or revocable living trust[6] is designed to pass to the surviving spouse just enough of the estate to eliminate or at least minimize the federal estate tax at the first spouse's death and to pass the remainder of the estate so that it does not qualify for the marital deduction. This normally results in no tax at the first spouse's death.

This kind of clause might provide, for example, that the smallest amount of the estate that, when added to other items in the gross estate that have passed to the surviving spouse outside the probate estate or under other parts of the will or trust and qualify for the marital deduction, will reduce the federal estate tax payable at the first spouse's death to zero or the lowest possible amount after taking into account deductions from the gross estate (other than this marital deduction) and credits allowed in calculating the federal estate tax will pass to the surviving spouse in a way that will qualify for the marital deduction

[6] Note that this formula provision or other marital deduction provision may be in a person's will or revocable living trust (described in Chapter 28), whichever document is the main vehicle for disposing of the person's estate at death. Neither vehicle has an advantage over the other in this respect.

(e.g., outright or in a marital trust).[7] Then, the residue of the estate, which normally will equal the applicable exclusion amount, passes in a way that does not qualify for the marital deduction. It may go, for example, to a *nonmarital trust,* in which the surviving spouse may (or may not) be given some or all of the almost-owner powers during his or her overlife and the corpus of which will then go to their children or others upon the surviving spouse's death. It may also go outright to other family members. The property in this trust or gift will not be in the surviving spouse's gross estate upon his or her death. Any state death taxes (and other nondeductible amounts) may be paid from this nonmarital trust or gift under a tax clause.

This method of using marital and nonmarital trusts (sometimes called A and B trusts or marital and family trusts) or marital and nonmarital gifts to qualify the right amount for the marital deduction is commonly used. This is particularly so after EGTRRA, since it normally is not desirable to pay any estate tax after the first death because the estate tax may be repealed or the exclusion amount may be increased before the surviving spouse dies.

To illustrate the reduce-to-zero formula clause, let us return to the facts in Example 2, except that Harry Carter follows a reduce-to-zero marital strategy in his will or revocable trust. In this situation, if Harry dies in 2002 his estate situation will be as follows.

Example 4

Adjusted gross estate	$1,600,000
Marital deduction (which goes under the formula to the marital trust or gift or qualifies outside of the will or trust)[8]	-$600,000
Taxable estate (which goes to the bypass or credit-shelter trust or gift)	$1,000,000

---

[7] In terms of how the marital deduction is funded, this is a pecuniary amount marital gift with the residue to a bypass gift. See further discussion under "Types of Marital Gifts" later in this chapter.

[8] This is the total amount of marital deduction (probate property and nonprobate property) that will result in zero tax in this situation. If the entire $1,600,000 of AGE were in Harry's probate estate (e.g., owned in his own name), the $600,000 would be in the marital trust or gift under his will ($1,600,000 - $1,000,000 = $600,000). Normally, there will be several items of nonprobate property in an estate. If we assume, therefore, that Harry's AGE consists of $200,000 in a Roth IRA with Martha named as beneficiary (a nonprobate asset qualifying for the marital deduction) and $1,400,000 in stocks, bonds, and real estate in his own name, the $200,000 IRA account balance would go directly to Martha and $400,000 would be in the marital trust or gift under the will. The marital deduction still would be $600,000, but it would consist of $200,000 of nonprobate property and $400,000 of probate property. The wording of the formula clause automatically adjusts the marital bequest for nonprobate property that qualifies for the marital deduction.

Tentative estate tax	$345,800
Applicable credit amount	-$345,800
Federal estate tax payable	$0

If Martha dies one year later, her estate situation will be as follows.

Adjusted gross estate (in her own name)	$300,000
(from Harry's will or trust as the marital	
gift or qualifying outside the will or trust)	$600,000
Total adjusted gross estate	$900,000
Marital deduction	0
Taxable estate	$900,000
Tentative estate tax	$306,800
Applicable credit amount	-$345,800
Federal estate tax payable	$0

There is no estate tax at either death in Example 4 *if* the order of deaths is as shown. This can be contrasted with the situations in Examples 2 and 3 where the Carters' estates were overqualified for the marital deduction and an estate tax of $390,000 was due at the second death. As can be seen from Example 4, if the combined adjusted gross estates of both spouses are equal to or less than their combined applicable exclusion amounts, there may be no federal estate tax payable at either death, *provided* there is proper planning.

However, if the order of deaths in Example 4 were reversed and Martha predeceased Harry, as matters now stand there would be federal estate tax at Harry's subsequent death, even if Martha left her estate so as to bypass Harry's estate (for example, in trust for their children with almost-owner powers for Harry so the corpus would not be in his gross estate at his death). The solution for this could be for Harry to make lifetime gifts to Martha so the available applicable credit amount would shield both of their estates from taxation no matter who died first.[9]

As another example using larger estate values, let us now assume a situation where there will be an estate tax at the second death. Suppose that Herbert Stone has an adjusted gross estate of $5,500,000 and his wife Noha has an AGE of $500,000. Herbert wishes to follow a reduce-to-zero marital deduction strategy. In this situation, if Herbert dies in 2002 his estate situation will be as follows.

---

[9] Of course, as the applicable exclusion amount automatically increases over the years, this problem may be solved for the Carters, provided their estate values do not increase (which they probably will).

Example 5

Adjusted gross estate	$5,500,000
Marital deduction (which goes under the	
formula to the marital trust or gift or	
outside the will or revocable trust)	-$4,500,000
Taxable estate (which goes to the bypass	
or credit-shelter trust or gift)	$1,000,000
Tentative estate tax	$345,800
Applicable credit amount	-$345,800
Federal estate tax payable	$0

If Noha dies one year later, her estate situation will be as follows.

Adjusted gross estate (in her own name)	$ 500,000
(from Herbert's will or trust as the marital gift	
or qualifying outside the will or trust)	4,500,000
Total adjusted gross estate	$5,000,000
Marital deduction	$0
Taxable estate	$5,000,000
Tentative estate tax	$2,250,800
Applicable credit amount	-$345,800
Federal estate tax payable	$1,905,000

There is no tax at the first death, but an increased one at the second death. Thus, the estate tax that would have been due at Herbert's death has been postponed until Noha's death.[10] The reduce-to-zero formula approach also is referred to as the *optimal marital*. It generally is the preferred approach after EGTRRA. If the order of deaths were reversed, the full applicable credit amount would not be available in Noha's estate even if she left her estate so as to bypass Herbert's estate. Again, this should be planned for as explained on the previous page and on pages 517-518.

Status of Surviving Spouse Under the "Optimal Marital." Particularly after EGTRRA, an issue with respect to reduce-to-zero formula clauses in wills and revocable trusts is that they may cause too much wealth to flow into credit-shelter trusts (bypass or family trusts) that perhaps are mainly for children or others, as compared with wealth passing to the surviving spouse (in trust or outright) as the applicable exclusion amount rises in stages from 2002 through

---

[10] It is postponed only one year in this illustration, for the sake of simplicity. It normally would be for a longer period, depending on the ages of the spouses, the normal life expectancy of the survivor, and the health of the survivor. These factors, of course, generally can be much more accurately evaluated after the first spouse dies than when the estate plan is prepared. That is one reason postmortem estate planning can be valuable, as explained later in this chapter.

2009. This may or may not be a problem, depending on the circumstances.

An example may help illustrate this issue. Suppose Marty and Hortense Wilson are married and Hortense has an adjusted gross estate of $4,000,000 while Marty has about $400,000 in his estate. Both have been married before and each has one child from those marriages. They also have one child from their present marriage. Hortense has a standard reduce-to-zero formula provision in her will under which two trusts are created—a marital trust (a Q-TIP trust) for Marty and a credit-shelter trust (the family trust). At her death, under this formula the least amount necessary to reduce the federal estate tax to zero is to go into the marital Q-TIP trust and the remainder goes into the nonmarital family trust to take full advantage of the existing applicable exclusion amount.

In this situation, if Hortense *dies in 2003*, the formula provision would act as follows:

Adjusted gross estate	$4,000,000
Marital deduction (by way of the Q-TIP trust)	-$3,000,000
Taxable estate (which goes to the family trust)	$1,000,000
Tentative tax	$345,800
Unified credit	-$345,800
Federal estate tax payable	$0

Thus, $3,000,000 would be available to Marty and $1,000,000 would be in the family trust.

However, if Hortense *dies in 2009* and if the law and estate values remain the same, the formula provision would produce the following result:

Adjusted gross estate	$4,000,000
Marital deduction (by way of the Q-TIP trust)	-$500,000
Taxable estate (which goes to the family trust)	$3,500,000
Tentative tax	$1,455,800
Unified credit	$1,455,800
Federal estate tax payable	$0

Note that here only $500,000 would be available to Marty and $3,500,000 would be in the family trust.

Also note that, aside from EGTRRA, this same issue can arise if estate values were to decline substantially, such as during a recession or depression.

Various suggestions have been made for dealing with this issue, including the following:

- Give the surviving spouse various rights in or powers over the credit-shelter trust. For example, the spouse could be an income beneficiary (mandatory or discretionary), could be given limited powers of appointment over the trust corpus, could be trustee if distributions are limited to an ascertainable standard, or could have other rights or powers that would not cause the corpus to be in his or her gross estate at the surviving spouse's subsequent death.

- Use a dollar or fractional cap on the credit-shelter trust.
- Provide for a minimum marital bequest (outright or in trust).
- Use three trusts: a marital trust (Q-TIP trust) for the spouse, a credit-shelter trust for the spouse but with no Q-TIP election, and a traditional credit-shelter trust for children or other beneficiaries.
- Make a bequest to the surviving spouse (outright or in trust) and provide for a possible disclaimer by the spouse (discussed later in this chapter) to a nonmarital family trust.
- Provide alternative trusts (marital and nonmarital), with authority in the executor or trustee to select amounts to fund each.

Each of these approaches has its advantages and limitations. They vary in the power they give to the spouse or others to make final decisions at an estate owner's death. Of course, depending on family circumstances, nothing may need to be done. Much depends on the facts, circumstances, and desires of the parties.

Formula Provisions to Equalize Estates or Rates. An alternative formula provision in a will or trust was designed to equalize the spouses' estates or to equalize the tax rates in both estates at the first death. This results in some tax at the first death and some tax at the second death, but perhaps less aggregate tax on both estates. This lesser tax is because transfer tax rates are progressive. With EGTRRA, however, this approach normally is no longer attractive, because it results in payment of an estate tax before necessary. An optimal marital or a modified optimal marital is the approach generally favored now.

Planning So Each Spouse Can Use the Unified Credit or Equalization

In planning the appropriate use of the marital deduction, this is a common procedure. First, assume one spouse dies followed by the other and determine the taxes payable (if any) and the estate shrinkage at each death. Second, evaluate estate liquidity and income needs for the survivor after each death. Third, reverse the order of deaths and repeat the analysis. This is sometimes called the *hypothetical probate*. Recommendations then can be made to improve the situation.

Because it generally is impossible to know which spouse will die first, planning should presume either possibility. It would appear that each spouse should have at least enough property to use the full amount of the applicable exclusion amount at his or her death. Then, if the spouse with less property dies first, at least this amount can be placed in a bypass trust that will skip the larger estate of the other spouse and go to their children or others free of federal estate tax. The propertied spouse can make tax-free gifts (because of the gift tax marital deduction) to the other spouse to accomplish this. This same issue can arise in connection with the GST tax exemption if GST tax planning is involved.

Despite these tax considerations, one spouse may not want to make lifetime gifts to the other. Even in this situation, however, one way to use the other spouse's unified credit is to make a lifetime gift to others (e.g., children or grandchildren) of twice the available unified credit or some lesser amount, and then ask the other spouse to split the gift and apply his or her unified credit to half.

How Should Property Be Qualified for the Marital Deduction?

Property can pass to a surviving U.S. citizen spouse in a variety of ways to qualify for the marital deduction.[11] It can make considerable difference in planning how property qualifies.

Outright Gifts or Bequests. This is the most direct way and gives the surviving spouse sole ownership and complete control over the property.

Joint Ownership with Spouse (WROS). Property held jointly by the spouses (with right of survivorship) will qualify to the extent that the property is included in the deceased spouse's gross estate (normally one-half). Here again, the surviving spouse has sole ownership and complete control over the property after the first spouse's death.

Life Insurance Proceeds Payable to the Surviving Spouse or a Qualifying Trust for His or Her Benefit. Life insurance proceeds that are in the deceased spouse's gross estate and are payable to the surviving spouse as beneficiary, either in a lump sum or under a settlement arrangement giving the spouse full withdrawal rights or only a life income, will qualify. Also, life insurance proceeds payable to a trust that meets the requirements for qualifying its corpus will qualify.[12]

Other Beneficiary Designations Payable to the Surviving Spouse. This can include a variety of situations. Probably most important are qualified retirement plans and IRAs.

---

[11] QDOTs can be used for transfers of noncitizen spouses (see Chapter 25).

[12] It may be noted, however, that if a person's estate is going to be subject to federal estate taxation, it normally is better tax-wise to have life insurance on his or her life owned by and payable to an irrevocable life insurance trust (ILIT), as explained in Chapter 27. This allows the proceeds to be removed from the gross estates of both spouses and to go in trust for the benefit of their children, grandchildren, or others as beneficiaries of the ILIT.

The next items involve leaving or giving property *in trust* for a surviving spouse so that the trust corpus qualifies for the marital deduction.

General Power of Appointment Trusts. Prior to the Economic Recovery Tax Act of 1981, this was the traditional way to qualify property in trust for the marital deduction. To meet the requirements for a general power of appointment trust, all trust income must be payable at least annually to the surviving spouse for his or her lifetime and the surviving spouse must have a general power of appointment over the trust corpus exercisable in all events during the spouse's lifetime, at the spouse's death (i.e., exercisable by his or her will), or both.

Qualified Terminable Interest Property (Q-TIP) Trusts. These probably are by far the most common choice of marital trusts today. To qualify the corpus for the marital deduction as a Q-TIP trust, all trust income must be payable at least annually to the surviving spouse for life with no person having a power to appoint any part of the property to anyone other than the surviving spouse during the spouse's lifetime. However, the original estate owner (or another person) can create powers over, or control the ultimate disposition of, the trust property that will take effect after the surviving spouse's death. For a trust that meets the requirements just stated, to become a Q-TIP trust, the deceased spouse's executor must make an irrevocable election on a estate tax return filed timely (with extensions)[13] to treat the whole trust or only a specific portion (fraction or percentage) of it as a Q-TIP trust. A trust also may be divided by an executor after a decedent's death into two (or more) separate trusts, with one being Q-TIPed while the other is not.

At the surviving spouse's death, the corpus of a Q-TIP trust is included in the surviving spouse's gross estate. However, the surviving spouse's estate is entitled to reimbursement from the Q-TIP trust for any additional estate tax due because of the inclusion of the Q-TIP property in the estate, unless the surviving spouse affirmatively waives this right to reimbursement.

Estate Trusts. In this case, trust income may be payable to the surviving spouse or accumulated in the trust at the trustee's discretion. At the surviving spouse's death, the trust corpus and any accumulated income are payable to the surviving spouse's estate to be distributed, along with the surviving spouse's own probate property, under the terms of his or her will. Estate trusts are used under some circumstances.

---

[13] As noted in Chapter 25, the federal estate tax return normally must be filed within nine months after a decedent's death, but a six-month extension often can be secured. Thus, an executor may have up to 15 months after a decedent's death to decide whether to qualify some or all of an otherwise qualifying trust for Q-TIP marital deduction treatment, depending on the circumstances then. This affords significant postmortem planning opportunities and is an important advantage of the Q-TIP trust.

Charitable Remainder Trust (CRT) with Spouse as Sole Unitrust or Annuity Trust Beneficiary. When established during a donor's lifetime, CRTs can qualify a surviving spouse's remaining lifetime annuity trust or unitrust interest (provided there is no other noncharitable beneficiary) for the marital deduction at the donor's death, as well as provide the lifetime advantages noted in Chapter 16. When CRTs are established at death (under a will), the same can be true, except then they should be compared with a Q-TIP trust with the charity named as remainderperson to determine which approach is more efficient.

Factors in Choice of Method. In terms of planning for the spouse and family, this can be an important decision.

Control Issues. Depending on the circumstances, a married estate owner may wish to retain control over the ultimate disposition of marital property after his or her death and after the death of his or her surviving spouse. This may be because it is a second marriage with children from a prior marriage; out of concern about his or her spouse's money management interests or abilities or about demands that others may place on the surviving spouse; out of concern about the "dreaded" new spouse, possibly with children of his or her own; or for other reasons.

The only method for qualifying property for the marital deduction that will give the original estate owner such control is the Q-TIP trust.[14] With a Q-TIP, the first spouse to die can designate the recipients of the corpus after the surviving spouse's death or the property can remain in trust for such recipients. The surviving spouse can be limited to a life income interest only in the Q-TIP, although a trustee can be given (but it is not required) discretionary power to distribute corpus to the surviving spouse.

On the other hand, the surviving spouse would have greatest control over marital property with an outright marital bequest, jointly owned property (although this may present overqualification problems), and outright beneficiary designations.

Management of Property. If management of property is desired, a trust is the logical choice.

Creditor and Marital Protection. Similarly, a trust with a spendthrift clause normally can protect trust corpus from the surviving spouse's creditors. A marital trust also generally would be protected from any marital property claims of a new spouse if the surviving spouse remarries.

---

[14] The CRT with the surviving spouse as sole remaining noncharitable unitrust or annuity trust beneficiary also gives a measure of such control, but in that case the property must go to charity after the surviving spouse dies.

Possible Incapacity of Surviving Spouse. Again depending on the circumstances, if the surviving spouse is or may become physically or mentally incapacitated, a trust (and probably a Q-TIP trust) seems appropriate.

Availability of Postmortem Estate Planning. The Q-TIP trust has an advantage here because, as indicated in footnote 13 of this chapter, the executor of the estate of the first spouse to die can decide within the time period for filing a timely estate tax return with extensions (which could be as long as 15 months after the spouse dies) how much, if any, of an otherwise eligible trust contained in a will or revocable trust to elect to qualify for Q-TIP treatment. This allows the executor to make this decision well after the first spouse's death, when the circumstances often are much clearer than when the estate planning documents were drafted. This delayed election is possible only under a Q-TIP trust, because it requires only an affirmative irrevocable election by the executor to be activated.[15]

Flexibility After EGTRRA. The need for estate planning flexibility after EGTRRA has made the Q-TIP trust even more attractive. The executor can make full, partial, or no Q-TIP election, depending on the circumstances at the time of the estate owner's death.

One technique in this regard is the so-called "single-fund Q-TIP trust." In this case, the will or revocable trust provides that at the death of the estate owner the entire residuary estate be placed in a single Q-TIPable trust. Then, the executor can make whatever Q-TIP election for a portion, all, or none of this trust as is appropriate for the circumstances at that time.

How Should the Marital Gift Be Funded?

This is the final component of a marital deduction strategy. It essentially deals with the type of marital gift to be used. This is a complex area and a full discussion of it is beyond the scope of this book. Only a brief outline of the issues is presented here.

Types of Marital Gifts. There are two basic types of formula marital deduction gifts. One is a *pecuniary amount marital,* where the marital gift is defined as an amount of money (or value of assets to be distributed in kind). The other is a *fractional share marital,* where the marital gift is expressed as a fraction of the estate: the numerator is the amount of the marital deduction desired and the denominator is the value of the assets available for funding the deduction.

[15] However, as will be explained in the section entitled "Postmortem Estate Planning," the same kind of adjustment can be made by a surviving spouse through a qualified disclaimer of part of all of a marital interest he or she would have received under a deceased spouse's will or revocable living trust.

Order of Funding. For pecuniary amount maritals, one approach is for the will or revocable trust to make the *pecuniary bequest or gift to the marital* (i.e., outright to the surviving spouse or to a marital trust), with the residue going to the credit-shelter (bypass) trust or gift. This may be referred to as a *preresiduary marital.* Assuming estate assets are valued at date-of-distribution values, this freezes the amount of the marital gift and protects the surviving spouse from depreciation of asset values from the date of death to the date of distribution. On the other hand, if there is appreciation in asset values between these dates, the appreciation goes into the credit-shelter (bypass) trust or gift, which will not be included in the surviving spouse's gross estate at his or her subsequent death. Any such growth goes to the bypass.

The other approach is for the will or revocable trust to make the pecuniary bequest or gift to the nonmarital trust or gift (e.g., to the trustee of a trust), with the residue going to the marital gift or trust. This has effects opposite those just described. In effect, appreciation or depreciation of asset values from the date of death to the date of distribution goes to the marital. This approach may be called a *reverse pecuniary,* a *residuary marital,* or a *front-end credit shelter,* among other names.

Values or Shares in Funding. A pecuniary amount formula can use the following valuation methods for estate assets used to fund the marital gift or bequest. One is a *true worth pecuniary gift,* in which assets distributed in kind are valued at their date-of-distribution values.[16] Thus, for example, one could have a reduce-to-zero true-worth pecuniary to the marital formula clause. Another is a *fairly representative approach,* under which assets generally are valued at their federal estate tax values (i.e., their values as of the date of death) and the assets used to fund the marital and nonmarital gifts are fairly representative in each case of appreciation and depreciation in their values from the date of death until the date of distribution.[17] Finally, there can be a *minimum worth* pecu-

---

[16] The amount of the marital deduction as reported on the estate tax return is determined as of the date of death, based on estate asset values at that time. These are also referred to as the estate tax values of the assets in the estate. But estate assets can appreciate or depreciate in value between the date of death and the date of distribution (i.e., when they are used to fund a marital bequest or trust or a nonmarital bequest or trust), which may be some time from the date of death. This is essentially the issue here.

[17] This approach arises from the rather well-known IRS Revenue Procedure 64-19. In this report, the IRS addressed the concern that if date-of-death values were used in funding the marital gift, an executor might allocate to the marital gift or trust in a disproportionate manner assets that had declined in value from the date of death to the date of distribution. Thus, the marital gift might effectively be diminished when the surviving spouse died. In a fairly representative approach, however, assets would have to be allocated to the marital gift in a way that represented both appreciation and depreciation in their values since the date of death, so the concern would be resolved. When assets are valued at their date-of-distribution values (a true-worth approach), the problem does not exist.

niary gift or bequest. In this case, each asset is valued for funding purposes at the smaller of its estate tax value or its date-of-distribution value.

On the other hand, a fractional share formula can use two different approaches to funding the marital and nonmarital shares. One is a *pro rata allocation* of assets, in which the marital share is allocated a pro rata portion of each asset in the estate. The other is a so-called *pick-and-choose* approach, in which a fractional share formula is used but assets can be distributed in whole or in part to the marital and nonmarital shares.

Postmortem Estate Planning

This means, in effect, that an estate plan need not be "cast in concrete" at the time of a decedent's death, but rather, with proper planning, it can be modified in certain respects after death to better fit the circumstances then. Following are some common postmortem planning techniques.

Making the Q-TIP Election

The need for a decedent's executor to make on a timely filed estate tax return an affirmative Q-TIP election with respect to an otherwise eligible Q-TIP trust in order to effect a Q-TIP marital deduction has introduced considerable post-death flexibility in marital deduction planning. The executor can make the election, not make the election, or make a partial election. This means the marital deduction can be modified after the first spouse dies, assuming a properly drafted will or revocable trust.

Use of Qualified Disclaimers

General Considerations. The tax law permits persons to give up their rights to property or property interests to which they otherwise would be entitled at someone's death by executing a *qualified disclaimer* under the rules of the IRC. Disclaimers can also be used for lifetime gifts and GST tax purposes. When a person makes a valid disclaimer of a property interest, it is treated as though the property was never transferred to him or her (i.e., as if he or she had predeceased the transferor of the property). Thus, the disclaimed property interest goes to whomever or wherever the will or applicable state law indicates should take it if the disclaimant (the person making the disclaimer) had predeceased the decedent.

There are several requirements for a qualified disclaimer for federal transfer tax purposes, as follows.

- A qualified disclaimer must be a *written, irrevocable, and unqualified* refusal to accept an interest in property.
- A qualified disclaimer must be *timely*. It must be received by the original transferor (or his or her legal representative) no later than nine months after the later of the date the transfer was made creating the interest in the disclaimant or the day on which the disclaimant turns age 21.[18]
- The disclaimant can make *no acceptance* of the interest or any of its benefits.
- The disclaimed property must pass to the *surviving spouse* or *someone other than the disclaimant*. The fact that disclaimed property can pass to a surviving spouse (even if he or she is the disclaimant) can be important, because it means a spouse can disclaim part or all of a marital bequest, have it pass to a credit-shelter (bypass) trust under the will, and still benefit from the credit-shelter trust (other than having a special power of appointment over the corpus that is not subject to an ascertainable standard).

Thus, wills or revocable trusts should have an express provision as to what will happen if a property interest is disclaimed. A disclaimer may be of an entire interest, a partial interest, or a pecuniary amount (a specific dollar amount).

An Example. Ahmed and his wife, Aysha, are information technology professionals who work for different corporations. They have two children. They both would like their estates to pass to the surviving spouse and then to their children in the event of their deaths. However, they want the survivor to be able to make tax-efficient decisions and they are aware of the uncertainties of estate tax repeal. Therefore, Ahmed and Aysha have executed reciprocal wills in which each leaves everything outright to the other if living and if the survivor does not disclaim, but otherwise to a trust for their children in equal shares.

Assume Ahmed dies in 2003, when Aysha is 56, in good health, and successfully employed. At his death, his AGE is $2,000,000 and hers is $1,000,000. Since Ahmed's estate is overqualified for the marital deduction and Aysha feels she has adequate resources, she decides to execute a qualified disclaimer within nine months of Ahmed's death to refuse to accept that part of his AGE equal to $1,000,000 (the applicable exclusion amount in 2003). This amount will go to the trust for their two children under the terms of Ahmed's will (a nonmarital bequest). The remainder, $1,000,000, will go outright to Aysha as a marital bequest and qualify for the marital deduction. Thus,

---

[18] There are some special rules for disclaimers of jointly owned property, which can be important because jointly owned property can be a source of overqualifying property for the marital deduction.

with the use of a qualified disclaimer, an overqualified estate has been adjusted through postmortem planning into a reduce-to-zero marital.

Allocation of the GST Lifetime Exemption

A decedent's executor may allocate the decedent's unused exemption to lifetime or other transfers. Also, in cases where the GST exemption has not been used or fully used, first-generation heirs (e.g., children with sizeable estates) can disclaim their interests so they will pass to skip persons (e.g., grandchildren of the decedent) to the extent necessary to make full use of the decedent's exemption. Further, if there is going to be a GST tax, skip persons may disclaim their interests to the extent they exceed the GST exemption.

Choice of Where to Deduct Estate Administration Expenses

A decedent's executor normally can choose whether to deduct certain estate administration expenses (e.g., executor's commissions, legal fees, and other fees) on the federal estate tax return (for estate tax purposes) or on the estate's income tax return (for income tax purposes). Income tax rates normally are lower than estate tax rates, so this favors an estate tax deduction. However, if a reduce-to-zero formula is used, there will be no estate tax due at the first death, so the effect of an estate tax deduction will be delayed until the second spouse's death, if ever. On the other hand, if a current estate tax is payable, the situation is different. The decision will be based on the facts of each case and the desires of the parties.

Alternate Valuation Date

An executor can choose date-of-death values or the alternate valuation date (six months from date of death) for valuing estate property for federal estate tax purposes.

Other Techniques

Other techniques also may be used, such as special use valuation of certain real property and selecting a fiscal year for the estate's income tax return.

Estate Liquidity

This is the need for cash or assets that can readily be converted into cash to meet the obligations of an estate.

Estimating an Estate's Liquidity Needs

These needs may be estimated for an estate so that planning can include providing the resources to meet them. The needs may include estimated funeral expenses, estimated last illness expenses not covered by health insurance or Medicare, estimated costs of estate administration, current debts, unpaid mortgages, other debts (bank loans, margin or other securities loans, etc.), federal estate tax, state death tax, and any specific dollar bequests in the will. The importance of these items will depend on the facts of each case.

Providing Estate Liquidity

Liquidity can be a serious problem for some estates but of minor importance for others. Much depends on the composition of the estate and what planning has been done. Estate liquidity may be a problem when a large part of an estate consists of relatively unmarketable assets, such as closely held business interests and undeveloped real estate.

Meeting the claims and taxes against an estate generally is the responsibility of the executor, who does this using probate assets, the only assets directly available to the executor. However, other assets that pass outside the probate estate, such as life insurance proceeds payable to a third-party beneficiary or owned by and payable to an irrevocable life insurance trust (ILIT), may be made available to the executor by the person or trustee receiving them as a loan to the estate or by purchasing assets from the estate.

27

Life Insurance in Estate Planning

Life insurance occupies an important place in many estates and has unique advantages in estate planning. The characteristics of life insurance itself were covered in Chapter 4.

Taxation of Life Insurance

The tax advantages of life insurance were first mentioned in Chapter 4. In this chapter, we shall consider these advantages in more detail.

Federal Income Taxation

Death Benefits. The face amount of a life or accident insurance policy paid by reason of the insured's death normally is not gross income to the beneficiary. When life insurance death proceeds are held by the insurance company under a settlement option, the proceeds themselves remain income tax-free, but any interest earnings on the proceeds will be taxable income. Correspondingly, when life insurance death proceeds are paid to a trust, the proceeds themselves are income tax-free, but the trust investment income from them will be taxed under the normal rules for trust taxation.

Benefits Paid for Terminally Ill Insureds. As explained in Chapter 6, life insurance contracts often provide for accelerated death benefits to terminally ill insureds. Also, viatical companies purchase insurance policies from such insureds as well as from others. The tax law provides that accelerated death benefits and amounts received from viatical settlement providers for a "terminally ill individual"[1] may be excluded from gross income. The nature and limits of this exclusion are explained in Chapter 6.

Transfer-for-Value Rule. An important exception to the general principle that life insurance death proceeds are income tax-free is the *transfer-for-value rule*. This tax rule provides that if a life insurance policy is transferred for a valuable consideration (sold), at the insured's death the beneficiary must include in gross income the difference between the death proceeds and the consideration paid for the policy plus any subsequent premiums paid by the transferee (buyer).

Suppose, for example, that a viatical company buys a $500,000 (face amount) life insurance policy from a terminally ill owner-insured for $400,000 and pays an additional $10,000 in premiums. Eighteen months later the insured dies. First, the $400,000 received from the viatical settlement provider is not gross income to the owner-insured. However, the viatical company (the purchaser and beneficiary of the policy) has gross income of $90,000 ($500,000 death proceeds - $410,000 [$400,000 consideration plus $10,000 in premiums]).

There are, however, some important *exceptions* to the transfer-for-value rule. First, the transfer-for-value rule does not apply when the transferee (buyer) is the insured, a partner of the insured, a partnership in which the insured is a member, or a corporation in which the insured is a shareholder or officer. This removes from the rule many common transactions. The other exception is when the basis in the policy in the hands of the transferee is determined in whole or in part by reference to the basis in the policy in the hands of the transferor (seller).

Premiums Paid. Premiums for personally owned life or accident insurance or an employee's contribution to group life or accident insurance (other than under cafeteria plans) are not deductible for income tax purposes.

Inside Buildup of Cash Values. Annual increases in the cash value of a life insurance policy (fixed-dollar or variable) are not currently taxable to the policy owner. This is the tax-deferred (or, hopefully, tax-free) buildup of life insurance cash values.

Policy Dividends. Life insurance policy dividends do not constitute taxable income to a policy owner until they exceed the policy owner's income tax basis in the policy. Furthermore, when policy dividends are used to buy paid-up additional amounts of life insurance (paid-up additions), there is also a tax-free buildup of the cash value of these additions.

---

[1] The law also may allow death benefits and other benefits paid to a "chronically ill individual" to be excluded from gross income, but only for amounts paid under a part of the policy that is treated as a qualified long-term care contract.

Surrender or Maturity of Policies. If a life insurance contract is surrendered, is sold (other than for terminally ill insureds), or matures during the insured's lifetime, the policy owner will have ordinary income to the extent that the amount received exceeds his or her investment in the contract (income tax basis in the policy). This investment in the contract normally is the sum of the net premiums paid (gross premiums less dividends received in cash). Life insurance policies normally allow the policy owner to leave the surrender value with the insurance company under one or more settlement options. In this case, the entire gain still will be taxed as ordinary income, but it will be spread out over a period of time, depending on the nature of the settlement option. (See Chapter 4.)

Partial Withdrawals. With some policies (e.g., universal life and variable universal life), policy owners can make *partial cash withdrawals.* In the case of policies that are not modified endowment contracts (MECs), the general rule is that such cash distributions are not taxed until they exceed the policy owner's basis in the contract (a first-in, first-out [FIFO] rule). However, if such cash distributions are received as a result of certain changes in the contract that reduce benefits and occur during the first 15 years of the contract, different rules apply and such distributions may be taxable in whole or in part.[2]

For example, suppose that Henry Libowitz has a $750,000 face amount (type A death benefit) variable universal life (VUL) policy on his life that he purchased 20 years ago. The policy permits partial withdrawals. Henry has paid $100,000 in premiums during this period (his investment in the contract or basis) and the policy cash value (invested in a common stock sub-account) is $225,000. Henry can withdraw up to his $100,000 basis without receiving any taxable income, but his basis (and the face of the policy) will be reduced by any such withdrawals. If Henry withdraws more than his $100,000 basis, amounts over that figure are taxed as ordinary income.

Policy Loans. With policies that are not MECs, policy loans are not viewed as distributions from the policy for income tax purposes and hence are not gross income even if they exceed the policy owner's basis in the contract. For example, in the situation just described, if Henry took a $200,000 policy loan from his VUL policy, it would not result in any gross income to him.

Changes in Asset Allocations Within Variable Policies. Changes in cash values among sub-accounts in variable life insurance are not currently taxable sales or exchanges for capital gains (or loss) purposes.

Planning for Taking Cash (Benefits) from Life Insurance Policies. Policy owners normally do not want to surrender policies for cash before the death of the

---

[2] This is sometimes referred to as the *forced-out gain* or FOG provision.

insured, because if the cash value exceeds basis, the owner will realize ordinary income on the difference. Also, he or she will no longer have the insurance protection. There often are other options.

First, a policy owner can just continue the policy in force until the insured dies, at which time the death proceeds will be received income tax-free. The policy owner can continue paying premiums or just enough premiums (with the existing cash value) to keep the policy in force for its full amount. A vanishing premium approach also may do this.

Second, a policy owner can decide to stop paying premiums and take a reduced paid-up amount of life insurance without any current income taxation. If the policy is participating, the policy owner may allow policy dividends to continue to accumulate and, say, be used to purchase paid-up additions (without current tax liability) or could take the policy dividends in cash and pay income tax on the dividends only when they cumulatively exceed the policy owner's basis in the policy. Correspondingly, a policy owner of a flexible premium contract normally can elect to reduce the amount of insurance (if necessary) to where the existing cash value can be expected to carry the policy without further premium payments. In either case, the death benefit will be income tax-free at the insured's death.

Third, if a policy owner under a flexible premium contract wants to take cash from the policy (which will reduce the cash value and death proceeds), he or she can take tax-free partial withdrawals up to the investment in the contract. Then, the remaining cash value can carry the policy (with perhaps some additional premiums as needed) until the insured's death, when the beneficiary will receive the proceeds income tax-free.

Finally, cash can be taken tax-free from a life insurance policy by way of policy loans. If the policy is to be continued in force, additional premiums normally will have to be paid. Also, a policy loan will require nondeductible interest and may be subject to direct recognition for policy dividend purposes. At the insured's death, the proceeds, less any outstanding policy loans, will be paid income tax-free to the beneficiary.

Reasons for Taking Cash from Life Insurance Policies. A policy owner may need cash for children's educations, business opportunities, or other purposes, but still want to maintain all or most of the life insurance in force to protect his or her family or conserve the estate conservation. Or a policy owner may need cash for retirement income. Of course, he or she could surrender the policy and perhaps take the cash surrender value over a period of years in installments or as a life income. On the other hand, the policy owner may want to take cash from the policy (or stop premium payments) at retirement without losing the life insurance protection and hopefully without income taxation. In this event, one of the other strategies just noted may be appropriate.

Finally, a policy owner may want to take cash from a policy prior to transferring it as a gift to an irrevocable life insurance trust (ILIT) or an individual
donee. This will lower or even eliminate any gift tax value in the policy. It also
will enable the policy owner to benefit from at least some of the cash value
buildup in the policy.

Taxation of Economic Benefit of Life Insurance in Some Situations. Under
some circumstances, the economic value of life insurance protection is gross
income to the insured.

Group Term Life Insurance. The first $50,000 of group term life insurance does
not result in gross income to insured employees or to retired former employees
whose insurance is continued into their retirement years. For amounts in excess
of $50,000, the cost of group term life insurance on an employee or retiree, less
any contributions from the employee or retiree, is gross income to him or her.[3]
The cost (economic benefit) of group term life insurance for this purpose is calculated by using uniform premiums (Table I rates) promulgated under IRS regulations or, if lower, the actual cost of the insurance. As we shall see later in the
discussion of gifts of group term life insurance, these Table I rates (or actual cost,
if lower) also are used to value gifted group term life insurance.

Split-Dollar Life Insurance Plans. These arrangements are described later in
this chapter. At this point, however, it may be noted that a split-dollar arrangement between an employer and an employee may produce annual gross
income to the insured employee.

Life Insurance Included in Qualified Retirement Plans. Sometimes life insurance is purchased by qualified retirement plans on the lives of plan participants. Here again, the life insurance will produce annual gross income to the
insured employee, as described later in this chapter.

Federal Estate Taxation

Inclusion in Gross Estate. Life insurance death proceeds will be included in the
insured's gross estate if (1) the insured's estate is named as beneficiary or if
another named beneficiary (such as a trust) is *required to* or *actually does* provide the proceeds to meet the estate's obligations or (2) if the insured at the
time of death owned any incidents of ownership (i.e., ownership rights) in the
policy. Incidents of ownership include such rights as the power to change the

---

[3] The income tax treatment of employees and retirees under group term life insurance plans
is governed by Section 79 of the IRC. Thus, group term life plans sometimes are called *Section
79 plans.*

beneficiary, the right to surrender or cancel the contract, the right to assign the contract, and the power to borrow against the policy. Other powers may also be incidents of ownership. However, paying premiums and receiving dividends under participating policies are not considered incidents of ownership.

Gifts of Life Insurance Within Three Years of Death. If life insurance policies are given away within three years of the insured's death, the proceeds generally will automatically be included in the insured's gross estate. But if the policy is given away more than three years before the insured's death, the proceeds cannot be included in the gross estate.

In situations where the insured makes cash gifts to third parties or an irrevocable life insurance trust (ILIT) that are then used to purchase and own a newly issued life insurance policy on the insured's life, the courts have held that the proceeds are not in the insured's gross estate even if the insured should die within three years of the gifts. Thus, for newly issued policies that are to be owned by, say, an ILIT, the proper strategy would seem to be to create the ILIT, make a cash gift to the trustee, and then let the trustee purchase, own, and be the beneficiary of life insurance on the grantor's life. Then the three-year automatic inclusion rule would not apply. Of course, an existing policy owned by the insured would have to be transferred to a third party or an ILIT to remove the proceeds from the gross estate, so the three-year rule cannot be escaped.

Corporate-Owned Life Insurance (COLI). In general, when life insurance is owned by a corporation of which the insured is a stockholder, the proceeds are not included in the insured's gross estate at death because the insured has no direct incidents of ownership in the policy. However, under IRS regulations, if the insured was the sole or a controlling stockholder (owning stock with more than 50 percent of the combined voting power over the corporation), the incidents of ownership in the insurance held by the corporation will be attributed to the sole or controlling stockholder and the proceeds included in his or her gross estate, but only to the extent that the proceeds are not payable to the corporation or for a valid business purpose of the corporation.

Thus, for example, if a trust for the benefit of a sole or controlling stockholder's family is named as beneficiary of the COLI, the death proceeds (to that extent) will be included in the stockholder's gross estate. But if the corporation is named as beneficiary, they will not. However, when the corporation is named as beneficiary (such as for key person life insurance, for example), the death proceeds will be considered in valuing its stock in the deceased stockholder-insured's gross estate. On the other hand, the estate may be entitled to a discount in valuing the stock, because of the loss to the corporation of the stockholder-insured's services. This might be called a *key person discount.*

Life Insurance on the Lives of Others. Suppose one person owns life insurance on the life of another and the policy owner (not the insured) dies. In this case, the value of the policy (not the death proceeds) will be included in the deceased policy owner's gross estate.

Valuation of Life Insurance Policies for Tax Purposes

The general rules for valuing property for gift and estate tax purposes also apply to life insurance contracts. However, some special principles are relevant because of the nature of life insurance. A newly issued policy (with periodic premiums or a single premium) normally is valued at the actual premium paid. A paid-up policy that has been in force for some time is valued at its replacement cost (the single premium as of the valuation date for the same policy). For cash-value policies that have been in force for some time and on which additional premiums are payable, the value normally is the policy's interpolated terminal reserve plus pro rata unearned premium (plus any dividend accumulations and less any policy loans). This value is essentially the policy's cash value but not exactly the same. For previously issued individual term policies, the value will be the unearned premium for the year as of the valuation date. As noted previously, the continuing value of group term life insurance is the Table I rates (or actual cost) times the full amount of insurance gifted.

Federal Gift Taxation

Taxable Transfers in General. If a policy owner absolutely assigns a life insurance policy to someone else, he or she has made a current gift of the value of the policy at that point. If the donor (normally the insured) continues to pay premiums on the policy, each premium constitutes an additional gift to the new owner. Correspondingly, for gifts of group term life insurance, the annual value of the economic benefit would be a continuing gift each year to the donee. When policies are owned by an ILIT (either purchased directly by the trustee or absolutely assigned to the trustee by the insured), the grantor may make periodic gifts to the trust so the trustee can pay the premiums.

Possible Indirect Gifts by Third-Party Individual Owners. An unusual gift situation can arise when a life insurance policy covers the life of one person, will pay death benefits to a second person, and is owned by a third person. In this situation, upon the insured's death, the owner of the policy is considered to have made a taxable gift of the full policy proceeds to the beneficiary. This can be referred to as an *inadvertent gift* because the policy owner usually has no idea that he or she is making such a taxable gift. Therefore, when somebody owns a life insurance policy on another person, the owner should name himself or herself as beneficiary.

Federal Generation-Skipping Transfer (GST) Tax

Life insurance may be subject to the GST tax. In most cases, this will result from having life insurance in an ILIT that is a generation-skipping or dynasty trust. Hence, GST tax planning may be necessary.

How to Arrange Life Insurance

When life insurance is purchased for family protection purposes, the insured may name his or her spouse as primary beneficiary and their children or a trust as contingent beneficiaries. This may be fine in many cases, but there are various other possibilities that may be considered. A basic issue is whether the insured will be owner of the insurance and thus have the proceeds included in his or her gross estate at death, or whether another person or an ILIT will own the insurance and thus have the proceeds escape federal estate taxation at the insured's death. When the insured's estate is large enough to attract federal estate taxation, it is increasingly common to have the life insurance owned by someone else, other than the insured's spouse, or, more commonly, by an ILIT.

Policy Owned by the Insured

Policies owned by the insured can be made payable in the following ways.

To the Insured's Estate. This usually is not done unless the insured wants to make sure the proceeds will be available to his or her executor for estate settlement purposes.

To a Third-Party Beneficiary or Beneficiaries in a Lump Sum. This is a common arrangement, frequently with the insured's spouse as primary beneficiary and children (or a trust) as contingent (or secondary) beneficiaries. Upon the insured's death, however, this arrangement may leave the spouse as beneficiary with a sizeable sum of money to manage, perhaps at the very time he or she is least able to manage it.

To a Third-Party Beneficiary or Beneficiaries Under Policy Settlement Options. The settlement options generally included in life insurance policies were described in Chapter 4. Most insurance companies give the insured wide latitude in the settlement arrangements he or she can make for beneficiaries or for himself or herself for policy surrender values. Beneficiaries also usually can elect settlement arrangements for themselves after the insured's death, if the insured has not already done so.

To a Revocable Unfunded Life Insurance Trust. The basic decision a policy owner-insured often must make is "Should life insurance proceeds be left with the insurance company under a settlement arrangement or with a bank or other trustee to be administered under a trust agreement?" There are arguments on both sides, but the trend decidedly has been toward use of revocable insurance trusts.

To a Testamentary Trust. Sometimes life insurance proceeds are payable to the trustee of a trust set up under the insured's will.

Policy Owned by a Person Other than the Insured

Ownership can be placed in a third party at the inception of the policy or after it has been issued. This can be done with an ownership clause in the policy at inception or through an absolute assignment of the policy. When an ownership clause is used, successive owner(s) can be designated in the event the first owner dies before the insured.

Policies may be owned outright by various members of the insured's family, such as adult children. However, there may be drawbacks in this. For example, assuming the insured dies before the policy owner, the proceeds will be paid to the policy owner as beneficiary and will be included in the policy owner's gross estate upon his or her subsequent death, unless he or she makes lifetime gifts or consumes them. In other words, generation skipping (except possibly for one skip person donee) is not possible. On the other hand, the insured may only be interested in keeping the proceeds out of his or her gross estate and the gross estate of his or her spouse, if married.

Another issue is what happens if the individual policy owner (donee) dies before the insured. Generally, the policy owner's will should leave the policy to someone else who would be a logical owner or to an ILIT or policy ownership might pass to a successive owner under an ownership clause in the policy.

Still another possible drawback is that policy proceeds paid to an individual in a lump sum may be subject to claims of the individual's creditors or possibly to marital claims against the individual. Further, when ownership is placed in an individual, the policy is subject to that person's control.

Finally, there generally is no tax advantage in giving life insurance to the insured's spouse. Because of the unlimited marital deduction, the same tax result can be achieved simply by naming the spouse as beneficiary.

For example, suppose Harry Smith is married, has a sizeable estate, and owns a $700,000 life insurance contract on his own life. If he absolutely assigns this policy to his wife, Mary, and survives three years, it will be out of his gross estate at death, but the $700,000 proceeds will be paid to Mary as beneficiary and will be in her gross estate at her death. On the other hand, if Harry keeps ownership of the policy and just names Mary as revocable beneficiary, the $700,000 proceeds will be in his gross estate at death, but since they are payable to his surviving spouse, they qualify for the marital deduction and so are deductible in full from his gross estate to arrive at his taxable estate. However, since they are paid to Mary as beneficiary, they will be in her gross estate at her death. Thus, either way, the $700,000 proceeds will not be taxable at Harry's death, but will be at Mary's death, absent remarriage, gifts, or consumption of its proceeds. Thus, the normal approach is to make gifts of life insurance to another person or, more commonly, to an ILIT. That way, the proceeds can escape federal estate taxation in both the insured's estate and his or her spouse's estate.

Policy Owned by an Irrevocable Life Insurance Trust (ILIT)

General Considerations. In this case, the insurance policies are owned by and payable to the trustee of an inter vivos ILIT. When the insured dies, the proceeds are paid to the trustee and are administered according to the terms of the trust, usually for the benefit of the insured's family. The trust owns and administers the policy or policies during the insured's lifetime, but it is otherwise unfunded in that usually only a small amount of other assets are also placed in the trust. To pay premiums, the insured may make periodic gifts to the trustee, who then uses the funds to make the premium payments.

Transfer Tax Advantages. These arrangements normally skip both the insured's gross estate and the insured's spouse's gross estate and, if desired, they can also skip the estates of other trust beneficiaries, provided the beneficiaries (and the insured's spouse, if he or she is also a trust beneficiary) are given only those powers that will not cause the corpus to be included in their gross estates.

However, when a trust is arranged to skip the gross estates of, say, children and other descendents of the grantor, it will be a generation-skipping trust and so may be subject to the GST tax. In this event, the grantor may want to allocate part of his or her exemption to each gift he or she makes to the trust to keep the trust entirely exempt from GST tax. This provides a substantial leveraging effect for the GST tax exemption, since it is allocated only to each periodic gift to the trust to pay premiums, while the entire policy proceeds are exempted from the GST tax.

Gift Tax Annual Exclusion. A potential problem for ILITs is that any gift of a policy and any subsequent gifts by the insured may not be gifts of a present interest and hence not eligible for the annual exclusion.

Crummey Powers—General Considerations. However, if a trust gives the beneficiary or beneficiaries a noncumulative annual right to withdraw for a limited period that year's contribution to the trust (a Crummey power), the annual exclusion can be secured for the contribution up to stated limits. The annual limit on Crummey withdrawal powers for each trust beneficiary normally is the lesser of the beneficiary's pro rata share of that year's contribution to the trust or a stated limit.

Setting Annual Limits. A planning issue is how to state this limit. It could be set at the available annual exclusion or twice that amount if split gifts are planned. However, as explained in Chapter 25, a Crummey power is a general power of appointment; when it is not exercised, it would be a *lapse* of a general power. The IRC provides that a lapse of a general power of appointment is only considered a *release* of the power to the extent it exceeds the larger of $5000 or 5 percent of the total property value from which the power could have been exercised.[4] This so-called 5 and 5 power often is referred to as the *lapse-protected amount.* Thus, lapses of a general power in excess of this amount will be a release of the power. The release of a general power may give rise to a taxable transfer for gift tax purposes from the donee of a power (e.g., a trust beneficiary with a Crummey power) to the other trust beneficiaries and also may result in the inclusion of at least a portion of the trust corpus in the gross estate of the donee (the trust beneficiary), depending on the terms of the trust. Therefore, when the annual stated limit is set at, say, the currently available annual exclusion or twice that amount, it exceeds the $5000 or 5 percent lapse-protected amount and the excess may be a taxable gift by the Crummey power holder and there may be inclusion in his or her gross estate. The taxable gift issue normally can be avoided by giving each power holder a separate share of the trust and a testamentary power of appointment (normally a special power) over his or her share. This makes gifts by the power holder incomplete. But the estate tax issue remains. However, as a practical matter, this may not be a problem if the corpus of the ILIT will be distributed to the power holder anyway and hence be in his or her gross estate at some point. Of course, the limit could just be set at the $5000 or 5 percent lapse-protected amount[5] and then there would be no issue, but this would be less than the available annual exclusion.

Generation-Skipping Transfers. But if the ILIT is to be a generation-skipping trust, inclusion of a portion of the corpus in a power holder's gross estate normally would frustrate the generation-skipping purpose of the trust. In this case (and possibly other cases), planners may limit the Crummey withdrawal power to the smaller of the annual exclusion or the lapse-protected amount. In this

---

[4] This is the same provision that underlies the 5 and 5 power, as discussed previously.

[5] Note that this lapse-protected amount of the larger of $5000 or 5 percent applies *per trust beneficiary* each year and not per gift or per trust. Therefore, if a person is, say, beneficiary of several trusts with Crummey powers, he or she is entitled to only one 5 and 5 lapse-protected amount per year; gifts to the trusts should be coordinated to reflect this situation.

event, depending on the amount of gifts made to the ILIT, some of the grantor's gift tax applicable credit amount may have to be used. Also, some of the grantor's GST tax lifetime exemption would be allocated to the gifts to the trust to make it entirely exempt for GST tax purposes.

Hanging Crummey Powers. Another approach suggested by some planners is the *hanging Crummey power.* This is a withdrawal right up to the full applicable annual exclusion that will lapse if not exercised within a specified period, but only to the extent of the lapse-protected amount for that year. Thus, to the extent the withdrawal right exceeds the lapse-protected amount, it will continue to be exercisable (i.e., it will "hang") into the future until it can lapse in some later year within the lapse-protected amount for that year. However, as of this writing, the IRS has stated that hanging Crummey powers do not prevent a gift from the power holder for amounts in excess of the lapse-protected amount.

Provisions of Crummey Powers. The power to withdraw generally should be available to beneficiaries for a reasonable period of time (such as 30 days) and the beneficiaries should have actual notice of their Crummey withdrawal rights and probably of contributions to the trust. Also, the persons having Crummey powers should be trust beneficiaries with substantial interests in the trust.

There normally should be enough value in an ILIT to satisfy the Crummey withdrawal power if the power holder should exercise it. This depends on the type(s) of insurance contracts in the trust and their values. Sometimes planners consider it advisable to have separate liquid assets in the trust sufficient to cover one year's gifts to the trust so as to satisfy a Crummey withdrawal if necessary.

Cautions Concerning Crummey Powers. Since 1981, the IRS has not been willing to issue private letter rulings with respect to certain life insurance trusts containing Crummey powers. Further, in recent years the IRS has increased its scrutiny of and concern over Crummey powers in general. Therefore, planners should be on their guard with respect to Crummey powers and plan for them carefully.

Providing Liquidity and Estate Balance Through ILITs. Since there will be a large amount of life insurance proceeds paid to the trustee upon the insured-grantor's death, the ILIT can be an excellent source for providing liquidity to the grantor's estate, to the grantor's spouse's estate, or possibly for other purposes. However, care must be taken in how this liquidity is provided. The trustee should *not* be required to pay or, if authorized to do so, should *not* actually pay directly the estate taxes and other death costs that are obligations of the insured's estate. This is because these situations will cause the life insurance proceeds to be in the insured's gross estate and the whole purpose of the ILIT will be lost.

Instead, the trustee should be authorized (but not required) to make loans to the deceased insured's estate (or revocable trust) or to buy assets from the estate (or revocable trust) to provide liquidity. This authority also can be extended to the insured's spouse's estate (which may bear the brunt of estate taxes) and possibly to business interests of the insured that may need cash at his or her death.

An ILIT can also be used to balance an estate among heirs. For example, suppose John Able, who is divorced, owns 100 percent of the stock of a corporation that he would like to leave under his will to his son, who is active with him in the business. The corporation is worth $1 million, and John has about $520,000 of other assets. However, John has two other children who are not interested in the business and he wants to be fair with them. To provide balance among his children, John could establish an ILIT with about $2 million of insurance on his life and with his two other children as trust beneficiaries. He then could leave his corporation stock to his son in the business. His other assets might be used to pay death taxes and other costs or divided equally among his children.

Life Insurance in the Estate Plan After EGTRRA. With the increasing excluded amounts and possible repeal of the federal estate tax, questions have arisen about the future role of life insurance for estate liquidity and conservation purposes. Life insurance still can be important for these purposes. The time of death is uncertain and so is the future of the estate tax. Also, life insurance is an income-tax-favored product and all of its traditional functions in family and business planning remain.

For existing ILITs where the insurance can be kept in force within the gift tax annual exclusion, why change? For ILITs where use of the applicable exclusion amount or GST tax exemption is necessary, try to avoid actually paying a gift tax. Perhaps existing cash values can be used to carry the policies without further premium payments. It would seem that term, group term, and low- or no-cash-value policies might logically be gifted. For policies with substantial cash values where the insured is in reasonably good health, perhaps some delay is in order until the situation becomes clearer. The facts and circumstance as of each case should be evaluated.

Other Policy Arrangements

Split-Dollar Plans. These are arrangements under which benefits and often premiums for cash-value policies are divided (split) between two parties. When the parties are an employer and an insured employee, it may be referred to as *employer-provided split-dollar*. When the parties are other than employer and employee (e.g., a split-dollar arrangement between a parent and a child or between an ILIT established by the insured and the insured's spouse), it is referred to as *private split-dollar.* The remainder of this discussion will be based on employer-provided split-dollar plans, unless otherwise indicated.

Basic Characteristics. The employer may pay that part of each annual premium equal to the increase in the policy's cash value for that year, or the annual premium less a contribution from the insured employee, or the whole annual premium, depending on the nature of the plan. The employee, or an ILIT established by the employee to own the employee's interest in the policy, pays the part of the annual premium, if any, not paid by the employer. There may be other variations in the split of premiums under these plans.

If the insured dies while the plan is in effect, the employer receives a portion of the death proceeds equal to the policy's cash value or the premiums it has paid (depending on the terms of the plan) and the employee's personal beneficiary or an ILIT receives the balance of the proceeds. If the arrangement is terminated other than by the insured-employee's death, the employer would be entitled to the policy's cash value or the premiums it has paid (again depending on the terms of the plan).

Policy Ownership. The ownership of split-dollar life insurance can be structured in several ways. Under the *endorsement plan,* the employer owns the policy and an endorsement to the contract provides for the division of proceeds and premiums. Under the *collateral assignment plan,* the employee owns the policy and a collateral assignment of the life insurance policy protects the employer's interest. There can also be *sole-owner* split-dollar plans, under which all ownership rights in the policy are held by an ILIT created by the insured (or by another third-party owner) and there is a separate agreement between the owner and the employer concerning the return of premiums paid.[6]

Tax Status. As of this writing, the income tax status of split-dollar plans is in a state of flux. The IRS has issued various guidance giving rules for valuing current split-dollar arrangements and indicating the likely future tax status of these plans (either as original issue discount or below-market loans or under a transfer system, depending on the nature of the plan).

It is common for an insured employee's interest in a split-dollar arrangement to be transferred to an ILIT or for the plan to be set up between the employer

---

[6] This sole-owner or unsecured form may be considered when the insured is the majority owner (more than 50 percent) of the employer corporation, because any incidents of ownership in the split-dollar policy held by the corporation would be attributed to the majority shareholder unless the proceeds are payable to the corporation. This means that otherwise the proceeds could be in the majority shareholder's gross estate even if he or she gave (or originally placed) ownership of his or her interest in the split-dollar plan in an ILIT or other third-party owner.

and the ILIT. This is done to remove the proceeds from the insured's gross estate. In these arrangements, the insured employee is considered to make annual indirect gifts to the ILIT of the plan's value each year to him or her.

Future Status. Given the tax situation and other uncertainties concerning split-dollar plans, as of this writing the extent and the nature of their future are unclear.

Life Insurance Owned by Business Entities. Business entities may purchase and own individual life insurance policies on the lives of one or more of their owners or employees. The entities normally are the beneficiaries of the insurance. In the case of corporations, this often is referred to as *corporate-owned life insurance* (COLI).

Insurance purchased and owned in this manner can have a variety of purposes, such as to protect against the loss of key persons, to fund buy-sell agreements, to informally fund nonqualified deferred compensation agreements, and to finance Section 303 stock redemptions. The business entities do not get an income tax deduction for the premiums paid on such insurance, but the death proceeds are received income tax-free. The other tax advantages of life insurance also apply.

Life Insurance in Qualified Retirement Plans. Although qualified retirement plans are primarily for retirement purposes, life insurance can be part of or carried in such plans. When this is the case, employee-participants must include the value of the current life insurance protection in their gross income each year. This currently taxable term cost is determined by applying one-year term rates (the lower of the IRS's PS 58 rates or the insurer's initial issue yearly renewable term rates on standard lives) as of the insured's attained age to the difference between the face of the policy and the policy cash value as of the end of the year. Policy cash values are plan assets and are taxable as ordinary income when distributed from the plan. The pure protection element, however, is received by the beneficiary income tax-free as life insurance proceeds. Whether life insurance should be provided under qualified retirement plans is a somewhat controversial issue that is beyond the scope of this book.

Gifts of Life Insurance

The questions of whether and how life insurance should be given away have become increasingly complex, particularly since passage of EGTRRA. However, many persons with estates sufficiently large to attract federal estate taxation have made gifts of their life insurance policies as an integral part of their estate planning.

Advantages of Gifts of Life Insurance

Life insurance generally is attractive gift property since it normally can be removed from the insured's gross estate by giving away all incidents of ownership in the policy. Further, insureds can continue to pay the premiums or make periodic gifts to ILITs to enable the trustee to pay them. Also, the gift tax value of insurance contracts, the premium payments, and any indirect gifts normally is small and, in any event, is relatively much less than the amount removed from the taxable estate (the policy face). In fact, with use of Crummey powers and annual exclusions, there may be no actual gift tax involved. Finally, an insured may want to make an ILIT into a generation-skipping trust by allocating part of his or her GST tax lifetime exemption to gifts made to the trust. Finally, people may be more willing to give away life insurance (particularly term or low-cash-value policies) than, say, securities, because life insurance usually is not producing income currently and is normally intended for the benefit of the policy beneficiaries anyway. Some of the factors affecting gifting of life insurance in estate planning after EGTRRA have already been discussed earlier in this chapter.

Pitfalls in Gifts of Life Insurance

Despite these advantages, there are some issues to consider. First, the unlimited marital deduction has eliminated any estate tax advantage that may have existed formerly in giving life insurance to one's spouse. Second, donors should be careful to divest themselves of all their interests and rights in the policy. Finally, a life insurance policy normally is valuable property. Therefore, insureds should consider carefully whether they want to relinquish ownership and control over their policies, particularly if the policy has a sizeable cash value.

Gifts of Group Life Insurance

Changes in state law and group contracts have made it possible in most cases for employees to absolutely assign their group term life insurance to an ILIT or another person and remove the proceeds from their gross estates. This can be attractive because the face amounts of group term life insurance in some cases can be quite substantial. Also, since it is term insurance, employees really are not giving away much in the way of policy values. However, there will be annual indirect gifts, as described previously.

What Policies to Give?

Most kinds of life insurance can be placed in or purchased by an ILIT. However, lower premium and lower- or no-cash-value forms may be desirable to minimize gift tax issues. This means group term life insurance, an employee's interest in a split-dollar plan, individual term policies, universal life and variable universal life policies with low (or withdrawn) cash values, and low-cash-value whole life insurance often are attractive policies to give away. Another popular kind of policy to place in ILITs is a second-to-die policy covering a husband and a wife. Also, the policy owner can reduce the cash value of a policy by taking a policy loan and then gifting the encumbered policy to the ILIT or other donee. However, in this case it is important that the policy loan not exceed the policy owner's income tax basis in the policy, for the reason explained in the next section.

Gifts of Policies Subject to Loans

A policy loan reduces the gift tax value of a policy by the amount of the loan and provides assets for the donor's own use. However, loans will reduce the ultimate death benefit. Also, funds need to be provided to pay interest on loans or additional loans must be taken to pay the interest (although there is a limit to this or the policy will lapse). In addition, there is a *transfer-for-value issue* when policies are given away subject to loans. This is viewed as a sale of the policy to the donee for the amount of the loan and it is a transfer for value. However, an exception to the transfer-for-value rule is when the basis of the policy in the hands of the transferee (donee in this case) is determined in whole or in part by reference to the basis in the hands of the transferor (donor). This is referred to as the *carryover basis exception.*

If a policy loan on a gifted policy is *less than its basis* (net premiums paid) in the hands of the donor, the carryover basis exception applies, because it is viewed as part sale and part gift and thus the donee's basis is determined in part (the gift part) by reference to the donor's basis. As an example, assume the following facts about a gifted policy.

Face amount:	$500,000
Policy value before policy loan:	80,000
Policy owner's (donor's) basis in policy:	70,000
Policy loan:	65,000

In this case, the policy value for gift tax purposes is $15,000 ($80,000 - $65,000). The donee's basis is determined in part by the presumed sale (the $65,000 loan) and in part by the carryover gift basis of the donor ($5000).

Hence, the carryover basis exception applies and the transfer is not subject to the transfer-for-value rule. The donor also realizes no gain because the presumed sale proceeds (the $65,000 loan) are less than the donor's basis in the policy ($70,000).

On the other hand, if we change our assumptions so that the loan is *more than the policy's basis* in the hands of the donor, the result is different and less happy.

Face amount:	$500,000
Policy value before loan:	80,000
Policy owner's (donor's) basis in policy:	70,000
Policy loan:	75,000

In this case, the policy value for gift tax purposes is only $5000 ($80,000 - $75,000). However, now the donee's basis is determined by the presumed sale (the $75,000 loan) and there is no carryover gift basis from the donor. Hence, the carryover basis exception does not apply and (unless some other exception applies) the transfer is subject to the transfer-for-value rule. This will subject the proceeds at the insured's death (less the donee's basis in the policy) to taxation as ordinary income. In addition, the donor realizes a $5000 gain on the policy transfer (taxed as ordinary income), since the presumed sale proceeds (the $75,000 loan) exceed the donor's basis in the policy ($70,000).

This is a complex issue and it can be a tax trap for the unwary. The principle involved is that when giving away a life insurance policy subject to indebtedness, be sure the outstanding loan is less than the donor's income tax basis in the policy. In some cases, part of a loan may have to be repaid to achieve this result.

28

Revocable Living Trusts, Other Will Substitutes, and Property Management Arrangements

This chapter deals with several methods (i.e., revocable living trusts and joint ownership WROS) for transferring property to others at a person's death, other than by the traditional will. These may be broadly considered as *will substitutes.* However, elsewhere in the book we have discussed various kinds of property or property interests that can pass to others at the direction of the owner outside the probate estate. These also can be considered as will substitutes. They include beneficiaries under qualified retirement plans and IRAs, life insurance beneficiary designations, noncharitable beneficiaries under charitable remainder trusts, other beneficiary designations (e.g., under nonqualified annuities, U.S. savings bonds, and some bank accounts), and transfer-on-death (TOD) arrangements for securities in states that permit them. These interests will not be further discussed here. Also covered in this chapter are various arrangements for managing property in the event of the owner's physical or mental incapacity.

Revocable Living Trusts as a Will Substitute

A possibly advantageous way of managing property during an owner's lifetime and then transmitting it to others at death is the *revocable living trust.* This is a trust that the creator can terminate or change during his or her lifetime.

Basic Characteristics

Estate owners during their lifetime create a revocable trust into which they may place some or the major part of their property. The trustee administers and invests the property and pays the income to the creator (grantor) or as the creator directs. Since creators can alter, amend, or revoke the trust at any time during their lifetime, they can change the trustee, change the beneficiaries, change other terms of the trust, or revoke the trust and get the property back. Upon the creator's death, the trust becomes irrevocable and the corpus is administered according to its terms for the benefit of the creator's beneficiaries. In this sense, it acts like a will.

If desired, the trust can contain marital and nonmarital trust provisions to make proper use of the federal estate tax marital deduction. Life insurance on the estate owner's life and other death benefits can be made payable to the trust. Also, property normally can be poured over from an estate owner's will into such a trust. This is referred to as a *pour-over will*. Thus, a revocable trust can unify an estate so it can be administered under one instrument. Property can be placed in a revocable living trust as soon as it is created and assets can be added to it from time to time. Or, the trust can be created with minimal assets in it and another party under a power of attorney can have authority to transfer the owner's assets into the trust in the event of the owner's physical or mental incapacity.

Tax Status

Since a revocable trust can be terminated by its creator at will, it is a grantor trust and trust income will be taxable to the creator during his or her lifetime. For transfer tax purposes, the corpus will be included in the grantor's gross estate for federal estate tax purposes, since it is revocable by the grantor until his or her death. Thus, tax savings by the creator are not the motivation for setting up such trusts. Further, there is no taxable transfer for gift tax purposes when the trust is created, because there is no completed gift.

An Example

Assume that John Mature, age 55, is a busy, successful business executive who is married and has two married children and four grandchildren. He is also active in church and civic affairs. He owns securities and other income-producing property worth approximately $2,000,000. This property yields about $60,000 per year in investment income.

John decides to transfer the $2,000,000 of income-producing property to a revocable living trust, with the XYZ Bank and Trust Company and John as cotrustees. The bank handles the investment of trust funds with John's consent. Trust income is paid to John during his lifetime; when he dies, the trust is to be continued for the benefit of his wife, children, and grandchildren. The trust agreement contains marital and nonmarital trust provisions so that at John's death his estate can make proper use of the federal estate tax marital deduction. John's will pours over the balance of his probate estate into this trust.

John also owns $600,000 of life insurance (including group term life insurance) on his life and has named the revocable living trust as beneficiary. However, since his estate has grown in size, he is planning to absolutely assign his life insurance to an irrevocable life insurance trust (ILIT) for the reasons given in the previous chapter. The account balance under John's Section 401(k) plan is payable outright to his wife, Lynn, as beneficiary, and their principal residence and a summer home are held by John and Lynn as joint tenants with right of survivorship. It can be seen that in this situation relatively little (other than some assets John still owns in his own name) will be in John's probate estate and pass under the terms of his will.

Goals of Revocable Living Trusts

Property Management. The XYZ Bank and Trust Company will manage and invest the trust property for John and pay him the income. Thus, John can be relieved of these duties and has the benefit of the bank's expertise in these areas. However, if for any reason John becomes dissatisfied with the arrangement, he can revoke the trust and recover his property or change trustees. Also, if he wishes, John can participate in investment management and, depending on state law, can even be the sole current trustee.

Protection Against Incapacity. If John should become physically or mentally incapacitated or otherwise unable to manage his own affairs, the trust would become irrevocable and the successor trustee would continue to manage and invest trust property for John's benefit without interruption.

Investment Diversification. If trust property is invested in, say, mutual funds under the prudent investor rule, the advantages of investment diversification can be secured.

Acting as a Will Substitute. Upon John's death, the trust becomes irrevocable and the successor trustee will continue to manage and invest trust property for the surviving beneficiaries (John's family) and pay trust income to them without interruption. Ultimately, the property will be distributed to the trust beneficiaries according to the terms of the trust.

Choice of Law. John also may decide in what state the trust is to be created and hence determine what law will govern the creation and operation of the trust.

Avoidance of Ancillary Probate. If John owns real estate located in a state or states other than the state of his domicile, it can be placed in the revocable living trust and thus can avoid ancillary administration in the state where the real estate is located after John's death.[1]

Confidentiality. What property passes at death, how, and to whom under a revocable living trust is private information. It is not available to the public, although the other trust beneficiaries can know. A will, on the other hand, is a matter of public record and anyone who wishes can see its terms.

Less Vulnerable to Contest. Some feel it may be more difficult for disgruntled heirs to attack a revocable living trust than to contest a will.

Possibly Lower Cost. A revocable trust *may* be a less costly way for John to transfer his estate. This factor is difficult to evaluate and depends on the circumstances. A professional trustee, like the XYZ Bank and Trust Company, will charge an annual trustee's fee, which in this case might be $16,000 per year for an individually managed trust (see the illustrative fee schedule in Chapter 23). However, because such trustee's fees may be income tax-deductible, the after-tax cost could be less. Also, the trustee is providing investment management and other services to John while he is alive. Thus, annual trustee's fees can be viewed as analogous to the investment management fees for other investment intermediaries (e.g., the expense ratio for mutual funds or fees for investment advisors). In this case, for example, the annual fee is 0.8 percent (.008) of the trust assets ($16,000 ÷ $2,000,000). Further, if John is the trustee or the trustee does not charge a fee, there would be no annual trustee's fee.

Executors' commissions and other fees of estate administration are usually based on a percentage of the probate estate. This may also be true for the fees of the attorney for the estate. Thus, John's estate could save at least part of the fees that otherwise would have been levied on the $2,000,000 had it passed as part of his probate estate under his will. These probate costs (which are deductible for estate tax or income tax purposes) might run, say, 3 to 5 percent of the $2,000,000 principal amount. Thus, revocable trusts can result in annual trustee's fees but can save on probate costs at the creator's death. On the other hand, certain necessary functions at death must be performed and paid for whether a revocable trust or a will is used.

Grantor Can Be Trustee. During his lifetime, if he wishes, John may name himself as trustee or one of the trustees of the revocable trust and then name a successor trustee in the event of his incapacity or death.

---

[1] When property is left under a will, the estate normally is administered under the law of the state where the decedent was domiciled (intended to make his or her home). However, real estate in the probate estate is administered under the law of the state where the real estate is located (its situs). Thus, if a decedent is domiciled in one state but has real estate in another, there must be two administrations, with the attendant costs and possible delays. The administration in the situs state is called *ancillary administration*.

Avoid Delays in Probate. A revocable trust continues uninterrupted after the grantor's death.

Wills are still the traditional way to transmit wealth at death. However, a revocable living trust can be an alternative. In some cases, part of the estate can go by will and part under a revocable living trust. However, in virtually all cases a will still is necessary because grantors normally retain at least some assets in their own names. Use of revocable living trusts tends to vary considerably among different parts of the United States; however, their use relative to wills seems to be slowly growing.

Joint Property with Right of Survivorship

The characteristics of jointly owned property with right of survivorship (WROS) were described in Chapter 23.

Advantages of Jointly Owned Property

Joint ownership is a convenient and perhaps natural way to hold property among family members, particularly husband and wife. At one joint owner's death, the property passes automatically to the other. Also, jointly owned property passes outside the probate estate of the first owner to die and hence avoids any costs and delays of probate. Holding property in joint names can avoid inheritance taxes in some states. Finally, jointly owned property may pass to the survivor free of the claims of creditors of the deceased joint owner, depending on state law.

Problems of Jointly Owned Property

An important problem that may arise is a larger-than-necessary federal estate tax because of overqualification of jointly owned property for the marital deduction. This was explained in Chapter 26. Also, when joint ownership is created and one of the joint owners contributes all or more than a proportionate share of the purchase price, a gift for gift tax purposes is made if the transfer is irrevocable.

There are no cut-and-dried rules on how much property should be held in joint names. In situations where the federal estate tax is not a factor, people generally can hold property jointly if they wish. Even where the estate tax is a factor, some joint ownership normally is acceptable. Married couples often hold the family residence and perhaps some bank accounts in joint names for convenience.

Property Management Arrangements to Deal with Physical or Mental Incapacity

Durable Powers of Attorney

A *power of attorney* is a written instrument in which one person (called the *principal*) names another person or persons as his or her attorney-in-fact or agent to act on the principal's behalf, as provided for in the instrument. In essence, it is an agency relationship. A *durable power of attorney* is one that continues in effect or becomes effective after the principal's incapacity. To be a durable power, the instrument must specifically so state, unless state law provides otherwise. Powers of attorney can also be *general* or *limited*. A general power of attorney authorizes the agent to act for the principal generally in all matters, while a limited power applies only to certain specified matters.

One approach to planning for incapacity is to execute an *immediately effective durable general power of attorney* naming one or more highly trusted persons as attorney(s)-in-fact. The understanding among all involved should be that the power will not be used unless the person executing the power becomes incapacitated and unable to manage his or her affairs. Another approach is to execute a *springing durable general power of attorney.* A springing power becomes effective only in the event the principal becomes incapacitated as defined in the document. However, in this case a clear and workable definition of incapacity or disability is important.

Durable Powers of Attorney in Conjunction with Revocable Living Trusts

Still another approach is to have an existing (or springing) durable power of attorney under which the attorney-in-fact has the power to transfer some or all of the principal's assets to a previously existing revocable living trust. Thus, in the event of the principal's incapacity, the attorney-in-fact can use the power to fund or add assets to the revocable trust and have those assets administered for the principal. At the person's incapacity, the revocable trust becomes irrevocable.

Funded Revocable Living Trusts

These trusts have been described previously. One of their main advantages is to provide property management in the event that the creator becomes incapacitated and unable to manage his or her own affairs.

"Convenience" Joint Tenancies (Accounts)

Sometimes people attempt to deal with the issue of property management in case of incapacity by creating joint bank accounts, CDs, or other accounts with another person, with the idea that should one of them (presumably the older one) become incapacitated or die, the other joint owner would simply use the money or other assets to take care of the incapacitated joint owner or distribute the assets in the event of his or her death. This seems quite simple—and it may be in some cases. However, the essential problem with this approach is that, assuming both owners can withdraw freely from the account, the funds may be used other than as intended. Thus, as a practical and legal matter, convenience joint accounts are a questionable solution to the incapacity problem in many cases.

Planning Issues with Regard to Incapacity

This can be a complex and difficult financial planning problem. Professional help normally is advisable. A durable general power of attorney (either existing or springing) may be a satisfactory solution in many cases where the assets are relatively modest. On the other hand, when assets are more extensive and there are perhaps other estate and family issues, a revocable living trust may be desirable. Frequently, both a revocable living trust (either unfunded or funded) and a durable power of attorney will be used.

An overriding issue in all these arrangements is the selection of a person or persons (or institutional trustee) in which the property owner can have complete confidence to be attorney-in-fact or trustee of a living trust. This may be the really difficult part. After all, this party may be handling the property owner's affairs when he or she is incapacitated and cannot. Of course, everyone hopes this will not happen, but in fact it may.

Health Care Decision Making

The previous section dealt with the sensitive issue of how one can arrange for the management of his or her property in the event of physical or mental incapacity. Now we are dealing with the even more sensitive and controversial issue of health care decision making when the individual is no longer able to make those decisions for himself or herself.

It is generally recognized that competent persons have the right to accept or refuse medical care for themselves. Unfortunately, however, persons may reach the point where they are no longer competent to make such decisions. They therefore may want to make advance arrangements for this unhappy contingency.

Durable Powers of Attorney for Health Care Decisions. This essentially is an extension of the durable power of attorney idea. It allows an attorney-in-fact to make health care decisions for the principal, within the limits of any applicable law and any limits set by the principal in the power-of-attorney instrument, if the principal becomes incompetent to do so. This obviously can be a very important power. The health care power can be a portion of one that also covers property management or a separate health care power. Some states have enacted statutes that specifically allow persons to execute durable powers of attorney for health care decisions. However, even in states without authorizing statutes, many authorities believe such powers still can be legally effective.

Living Wills. Most states have statutes permitting persons to execute valid documents (*living wills*) that can direct, in specified circumstances, how medical treatment should be rendered or withheld in terminal situations after the person has become incompetent to make his or her own health care decisions. While living wills and durable powers of attorney for health care decisions have some similarities of purpose, they differ in several respects. First, living wills apply only in terminal situations. Second, not all kinds of care can be refused under the living will statutes of various states. Third, durable powers permit the principal, in drafting the instrument, to set such terms and conditions on the power as the principal deems appropriate. Finally, a durable power allows the principal to name a specific party to make health care decisions if the principal is not competent to do so.

29

Financing
Education Expenses

This chapter deals with the various ways for financing the increasingly important and growing cost of education. Several of these have become increasingly attractive since passage of the Economic Growth and Tax Relief Reconciliation Act (EGTRRA) in 2001.

Importance as a Financial Objective

Financing education expenses is a growing and important financial objective for many people. There are many reasons for this. Education costs are high and generally rising faster than the rate of inflation. More and more people are attending colleges and universities, graduate schools, and other educational programs. Education costs are reasonably predictable, although what a particular child or person will do about his or her education is far from certain. There now are many plans available for dealing in advance with education costs. And finally, education costs can create considerable strain in a family's financial situation, perhaps at the very time other significant financial needs are emerging.

Nature and Growth of Education Costs

The amount of education costs naturally depends on the circumstances. These include the type of program involved (e.g., undergraduate programs in four-year colleges and universities, graduate schools [medicine, dental, law, graduate business, and so forth], community colleges, and technical and other schools), how many years are involved, whether the student is a resident or a nonresident, whether the institution is public or private, what scholarships and other financial aid are available, whether the student will be working and contributing to the cost while in school (during the summer or in co-op programs, for example), and the number of children or others involved.

For college and graduate school, the types of expenses can include tuition and fees, room and board, books and supplies, transportation, and other incidental expenses. These typically are considerably higher for private institutions than for public. Also, depending on family circumstances and desires, education expenses also may include costs of private secondary schools and other private programs, starting as early as private nursery schools.

College and graduate school costs have been growing for many years. Their rate of growth has varied over the years and it has been more rapid for private schools than for public ones. As a rough rule of thumb for planning purposes, one probably can set the rate of growth somewhere between 4 and 5½ percent.

Estimating Education Costs

This necessarily involves many unknowns and assumptions, so general approximations of expected costs seem very much in order. To estimate future costs and funding needs even roughly, one should make assumptions as to the type of program to be planned for, its length in years, and its current net cost per year; an estimated average annual compound rate of growth in costs; the number of years until the program starts; and an estimated average annual compound after-tax rate of return on assets set aside for education funding. Financial institutions, financial planning software, and other sources have systems for estimating education costs given certain input data.

However, let us consider an example of the principles involved. Assume David and Mary Jones (both age 35 and working outside the home) have a child age 1, Janet, who they hope will enter college in 17 years. At present, they would like to begin to prepare financially for Janet as a resident student in a four-year undergraduate program at a private university.

For the 2000-2001 academic year, typical annual expenses for full-time resident undergraduates at private colleges and universities were about $25,000, although they could run $36,000 or more at some private schools. (Typical annual expenses for public colleges and universities were about $11,400.) Therefore, in 17 years David and Mary will need about $100,000 (four years x $25,000) for Janet in terms of current education costs. If they assume private undergraduate college costs will increase at a 5 percent average annual compound rate over the 17 years, this need becomes $229,000 in 17 years ($100,000 present cost at 5% average annual compound rate of return for 17 years).[1] Further assuming that an investment fund for education expenses would have an after-tax or tax-free average annual compound rate of total return of 8 percent (assuming, for example, use of a Section 529 plan, which would be tax-free), David and Mary would need to invest about $6,300 per year to reach their goal of about $229,000 in 17 years (the annual payment at 8% average annual compound rate of return to reach $229,202 in 17 years).

Different assumptions, of course, might be made. For example, if it is assumed that Janet will work in the summers (or perhaps participate in a work-study program while in college) and earn perhaps $5,000 after taxes per year in current dollars (or $20,000 for four years), the $100,000 goal could be reduced to $80,000 (both in current dollars) for planning purposes. Also, scholarships or other aid might be assumed, but this is a bit of a stretch at age 1. Finally, costs will be increased dramatically if graduate school education is assumed.

It is important to get a rough idea of what future costs may be so planning for funding them can start as early as possible. As shown in Chapter 2, the power of annual compounding of periodic invested sums (particularly tax-free compounding) can be nothing short of spectacular.

Financial Aid Considerations

Many students attending colleges, universities, and other schools receive various forms of financial aid. These aid packages may include low-interest loans, grants and scholarships, and earnings from work-study programs. In recent years, the majority of aid has come from loans.

Eligibility for need-based financial aid under standardized formulas depends on the student's and his or her parents' incomes and assets and perhaps other factors (such as the number of children in school). Generally, a student's financial need for federal purposes (under Part F of Title IV of the Higher Education Act of 1965, as amended) is the difference between the cost of attending the educational institution and the student's expected family contribution (EFC). The EFC is what the student and his or her parents are expected to pay for the student's education under standardized formulas.[2]

Grants or scholarships (gift aid) are based on need and do not have to be

---

[1] This figure can be determined on a calculator, on a computer, or by using the tables for computing the future value of a sum. See Chapter 2.

[2] For example, the EFC (based on the Free Application for Federal Student Aid) includes up to 50% of the student's income (less certain allowances), 35% of the student's assets, up to 47% of the parents' income (less certain allowances), and 5.6% of the parents' assets. However, equity in the parents' home and their retirement assets are excluded from the EFC.

paid back. Some examples are the federal Pell Grants to students and Supplemental Educational Opportunity Grants (SEOGs) made to colleges, which then provide grants to students. There also may be state and state-federal grants, ROTC scholarships, and other grants.

Loans might include low-interest or subsidized loans, such as federal programs for Perkins Loans and Stafford Loans (subsidized). These are need-based loan programs. Other loans may not be need-based, such as Stafford Loans (unsubsidized), Parent Loans for Undergraduate Students (PLUS), and various private loan programs. There also may be earnings from work-study programs, but this typically is a relatively small part of total aid.

In addition to need-based financial aid, there can be merit aid not based on financial need. This can come in a variety of forms, such as merit scholarships, talent scholarships, athletic scholarships, scholarships given by outside organizations, and sometimes tuition discounts (institutional grants) from colleges to attract students. However, sometimes colleges and universities will reduce their need-based financial aid packages by the amount of any such scholarships the student receives.

Tax "Breaks" for Education Costs
Federal Income Tax Credits

These include the *Hope Scholarship Credit* and the *Lifetime Learning Credit*.

The Hope Credit is for college tuition (reduced by any scholarship and fellowship grants excluded from income) and certain fees incurred by the taxpayer, his or her spouse, and a qualified dependent of the taxpayer for each of the first two years of college. It also applies to tuition for a vocational school leading to a recognized postsecondary school degree or credential. The credit applies to each student in a taxpayer's family. For each student, the credit is 100 percent of the first $1000 and 50 percent of the next $1000 in qualified tuition and fees per year. Eligible students must be enrolled at least half-time.

The Lifetime Learning Credit is for tuition and fees incurred by the taxpayer, his or her spouse, and a qualified dependent of the taxpayer for undergraduate and graduate college and university courses as well as for courses at eligible institutions to acquire and improve job skills. This credit applies only once per year on a tax return, but can be taken for an unlimited number of years and a student can be enrolled less than half-time. For each tax return per year, the credit is 20 percent of up to $10,000 of qualified tuition and fees.

The Hope Scholarship Credit and the Lifetime Learning Credit cannot both be taken for the same student in a given year. But each is available for a year in which tax-free distributions are made from a state qualified tuition program (QTP) or an education savings account (education IRA) for the same student, as long as they do not cover the same eligible expenses. Each of these credits begins to be phased out at adjusted gross incomes (AGIs) of $40,000 for single taxpayers and $80,000 for married taxpayers filing jointly and are completely phased out at AGIs of $50,000 and $100,000 respectively.

Federal Income Tax Deductions

Student Loan Interest Deduction. A deduction from gross income to arrive at adjusted gross income (i.e., "above the line") is allowed for interest paid on "qualified education loans." The maximum annual deduction is $2,500 and it is available for the entire duration of the loan. However, this deduction begins to be phased out at adjusted gross incomes (AGIs) of $50,000 for single taxpayers and $100,000 for married taxpayers filing jointly and are completely phased out at AGIs of $65,000 and $130,000 respectively (adjusted for inflation).

Deduction for Higher Education Expenses. There also is a deduction above the line for "qualified higher education expenses" (defined as for the Hope Credit described previously) up to certain dollar limits ($3000 in 2002 and 2003, $4000 maximum deduction in 2004 and 2005, and $2000 limited deduction in 2004 and 2005) for taxpayers whose AGI does not exceed certain amounts or income ranges. The deduction expires completely after 2005.

This deduction cannot be taken in the same year as the Hope or Lifetime Learning Credits for the same student. Also, no deduction can be taken for expenses that are used for amounts excludable from income due to distributions from an education savings account or a QTP or due to excludable interest from a U.S. savings bond.

Exclusions from Income, Gift, or Penalty Taxes for Federal Tax Purposes

There are a variety of situations in which amounts used for eligible education expenses are excluded from a taxpayer's gross income (i.e., tax-free) or have other tax advantages.

- Earnings from qualified tuition programs, as discussed later in this chapter.
- Earnings from education savings accounts, as discussed in Chapter 19 and later in this chapter.
- Interest on certain U.S. Savings Bonds, as explained later in this chapter.
- Amounts up to $5250 per employee per year from employer-provided education assistance plans, as noted in Chapter 18.
- Amounts of scholarship and fellowship grants to degree candidates at an

educational institution used for tuition, related fees, books, and supplies and equipment normally are excluded from the recipient's gross income. However, amounts used for room and board and other personal items and amounts received for required services (e.g., teaching or research as a condition of a grant) are not excluded.

- Distributions from regular IRAs before age 59½ for eligible education expenses are not subject to the 10 percent penalty tax on premature distributions, although such distributions are still taxed as ordinary income, as explained in Chapter 19.

- An unlimited gift tax exclusion for payments of tuition directly to an educational organization, as explained in Chapter 25.

Strategies in Planning for Education Costs
Do Not Rely on Financial Aid and Tax Breaks

It will be good to be able to rely on financial aid and tax breaks, but it does not seem prudent to rely primarily on them, particularly when the potential student is relatively young. Scholarships and grants are uncertain, so unduly relying on them may put unwarranted pressure on children and/or result in selection of schools based mainly on price (i.e., availability of institutional grants) rather than on more important criteria.

Some work-study may be fine for many students and in some cases may even improve their performance by making them more responsible. Also, some schools have co-op programs involving full-time study for part of the year and full-time work for another part. Further, students often have summer jobs or internships when they are not in school. All of this will be helpful in financing their educations, but too much work while in school will weaken the educational experience and may put undue pressure on students. However, it seems entirely reasonable to assume a student can earn some part of his or her education expenses, perhaps with limited work-study and certainly through summer employment. This can be considered in estimating education costs as illustrated earlier in this chapter.[3] Loans as a part of financial aid are considered in the next section.

Tax "breaks" are always nice, but as a practical matter they can be only a

[3] However, as an aside, it might be observed that, depending on the circumstances, there may be better uses for a student's earnings than helping to pay education costs. For example, that may be an ideal time for the student to use his or her income to start a Roth IRA when he or she would be eligible for a Roth and pays little or nothing in taxes (so a tax deduction for a traditional IRA means little). As emphasized earlier, the tax-free growth over time can be spectacular. Further, as noted in Chapter 26, it may even be worthwhile for a parent to give his or her child the funds to start a Roth IRA when the child has personal earnings.

partial answer. They generally are limited in amount, are subject to income eligibility requirements, or are limited otherwise. The most significant tax advantages in planning for education expenses would seem to be the exclusion from income of earnings from qualified tuition programs and education IRAs when used for eligible education expenses, as explained later.

Rely Primarily on Borrowing

This has become an increasingly important strategy in recent years. Loans have far outstripped grants as a source of financial aid during the 1990s. The vast majority of loans (about 95 percent) come from federally supported programs. But there also are a number of private loan programs specifically for college expenses. Finally, there are the normal sources of loans for any purpose, such as mortgage refinancing, home equity loans, life insurance policy loans, loans from qualified retirement plans, and other sources.

The basic problem with borrowing is that the loans plus interest (even at favorable rates) must be paid back sometime. Today, graduates commonly leave school burdened with student loans. And parents may find themselves in debt to finance their children's education at the very time they should be building capital for their own retirement. For the same reason, borrowing from retirement plan account balances may be inadvisable. Thus, while borrowing may be necessary if no advance preparation has been made, it normally is not the preferred solution.

Advance Funding for Education Costs

This approach has received increasing attention recently, particularly with the attractive education incentives contained in EGTRRA. In the opinion of the authors, it is the preferred primary strategy. There are a number of plans available for funding education costs. Some are designed specifically for that purpose; others are more general. However, they all require time to be effective, so it is a good idea to start saving early.

Factors Affecting Choice of Plans

There can be many factors to consider in evaluating these plans. Some obviously are more important than others. A combination of plans can also be used.

- Nature of the plan and how to set it up.
- Eligibility requirements, income ceilings, and limits on contributions.
- Kinds of educational expenses that can be funded.

- Tax treatment of plan contributions.
- Income tax treatment of plan earnings.
- Income tax treatment of distributions from the plan.
- Federal estate tax and GST tax status of plan balances on death of the plan owner or beneficiary.
- Form in which contributions can be made.
- Investment options and flexibility allowed by the plan.
- Fees and expenses of the plan.
- Ability to make changes in the plan.
- Protecting the plan in the event of the death or disability of the contributor before the plan is completed.
- Coordination with other plans, scholarships, and tax "breaks."
- Possible protection against creditors.
- Possible "freezing" of future education costs.

Qualified Tuition Programs (Section 529 Plans)

Section 529 Plans[4] are state programs that may be 529 savings accounts (or savings account programs) and prepaid tuition programs (also called tuition credit or tuition certificate programs).[5] They are both referred to as qualified tuition programs (QTPs) or 529 plans, but generally the more popular are savings account programs.

General Characteristics. *Prepaid tuition programs* are state-operated trusts (but see footnote 5) to which U.S. citizens[6] can make cash contributions that are applied to purchase credits or certificates for a designated beneficiary for tuition and fees for a given number of academic periods or course units at the current tuition rates. The investment of prepaid tuition funds normally is handled by the state. Some states do not guarantee the arrangement and future guaranteed benefits possibly could be scaled back. Usually, if a student attends a private college or university or an out-of-state school, the funds accumulated in the plan still can be used for eligible higher education expenses, except that the amount of covered expenses may be limited (such as to in-state tuition) and there is no locking-in of current tuition rates.

[4] Section 529 was added to the IRC by the Small Business Job Protection Act of 1996 and has been amended and expanded several times since. A significant expansion was made by EGTRRA, but this is subject to the "sunset provision" of EGTRRA.

[5] Under EGTRRA, prepaid tuition programs (but not savings account plans) can be established and maintained by eligible private institutions (e.g., college and universities) that meet the requirements of Section 529 of the IRC. But distributions from such private programs are tax-free only after January 1, 2004.

[6] Sometimes these programs are limited to state residents.

Savings account programs are state-operated plans to which U.S. citizens can make cash contributions that are accumulated in accounts owned by the contributor to pay qualified higher education expenses of a designated beneficiary. Although these programs are state plans, they usually are administered and the account balances invested by private financial intermediaries. Most of the remainder of this discussion deals with savings account programs.

QTPs must comply with Section 529 of the IRC and corresponding tax rules to get the substantial benefits afforded under federal tax law. However, they also are creatures of the individual states, so contributions must comply with the rules of the particular state plan as well. Thus, both federal and individual state rules must be considered in contributing to Section 529 plans.

Eligibility and Limits on Contributions. With the exception of a few plans that have state residency requirements, QTP accounts can be set up by any U.S. citizen for any beneficiary with no residency requirement or income ceilings on the person's ability to establish or contribute to the plan. Thus, persons desiring to set up 529 plans should "shop around" among state plans to find the most attractive one or ones for them.

State plans differ in a number of respects and a potential contributor may want to consider the following factors, among others, in his or her selection: (1) state income tax (if any) treatment of contributions and qualified distributions (in the case of contributors who are state residents); (2) available investment options; (3) the investment manager; (4) fees charged, particularly the annual expense ratio on the investment options; (5) whether the plan is as flexible as Section 529 allows with respect to rollovers to other plans, changes of designated beneficiary, and perhaps other matters; (6) maximum contributions (or account values) allowed; (7) higher education expenses and schools covered; and (8) possible creditor protection.

Section 529 requires that a QTP take measures to prevent contributions beyond those reasonably necessary to pay for a beneficiary's qualified higher education expenses. Therefore, the plans set maximum limits on the aggregate lifetime contributions (or sometimes account values) that can be made for a single designated beneficiary in the state.[7] These maximums vary by state and may range from around $100,000 to over $280,000. Sometimes they vary with the age of the designated beneficiary.

Qualified Higher Education Expenses. In essence, these are the expenses that can be paid tax-free from QTPs. They include *tuition, fees, books, supplies,* and *equipment* for a designated beneficiary to attend an eligible educational insti-

---

[7] The states often determine this maximum limit by taking four or five years of eligible expenses at the most expensive school in the state. This maximum may rise periodically as education costs rise.

tution. They also include *room and board* for a designated beneficiary who is enrolled in a program leading to a degree or a recognized educational credential and carrying at least half the normal full-time course load for the program involved.[8]

An *eligible educational institution* includes any accredited postsecondary educational institution offering credit toward bachelor's, associate's, graduate, or professional degrees and also includes certain vocational institutions. Such an institution must be eligible to participate in the Department of Education's student aid programs.

Tax Treatment of Contributions. Contributions to a QTP are not deductible for *federal income tax purposes*. Depending on state law, they may be deductible up to a limit for *state income tax purposes* for residents of the state.

With respect to *federal gift taxation*, contributions are considered completed gifts of a present interest from the account owner to the designated beneficiary. Thus, contributions qualify for the annual exclusion for both gift tax and GST tax purposes.

Further, to encourage early funding, Section 529 allows so-called "frontloading" for annual exclusion purposes. This means an account owner can elect to treat a single year's gift that exceeds the annual exclusion for that year as if were made pro rata over five years, in order to apply the annual exclusions for those years. Thus, one person could give up to $55,000 ($11,000 annual exclusion x 5) and a married person with gift splitting up to $110,000 ($55,000 for each spouse) for one designated beneficiary in one year.

For example, suppose Gary, who is married to Susan, wants to start a QTP with his granddaughter, Traci, as designated beneficiary. Gary has a substantial estate and would like to make as large an initial contribution as possible, to take advantage of tax-free compounding, yet still stay within the annual exclusions for gift tax and GST tax (since Traci would be a skip person to Gary). Assuming Susan is willing to split the gifts, he could contribute $110,000 to the QTP in the first year and make the five-year election just described (assuming this is within the state's maximum limit). Then, he would be treated as having made a $22,000 gift in the first year and in each of the next four years (i.e., over five years). With gift splitting, this would be considered a gift of $11,000 each by Gary and by Susan and within the annual exclusions for each.

Tax Treatment of Plan Earnings. The earnings from the assets in a QTP are not currently taxed for federal income tax purposes. They also will not be taxed upon distribution if they are used to pay for qualified higher education expenses (i.e., a qualified distribution). Otherwise, they will be taxed as ordinary income upon distribution.

[8] Prepaid tuition programs often do not include room and board.

Tax Treatment of Plan Distributions. As just stated, plan withdrawals used for qualified higher education expenses of the designated beneficiary are not gross income for federal income purposes to the designated beneficiary or account owner.[9] This means the investment earnings on plan assets are never taxed when so used. Depending on state law, they also may be exempt from any state income tax.

To be exempt from federal income taxation, the distributions must be made in one of the following ways: (1) distributed directly to an eligible educational institutions; (2) distributed by a check payable to both the designated beneficiary and an eligible educational institution; (3) distributed as reimbursement to the designated beneficiary for qualified higher education expenses paid with the beneficiary producing receipts; or (4) distributed to the designated beneficiary, who certifies in writing that the distribution will be used for qualified higher education expenses within a reasonable time. (The definition of "qualified higher education expenses" includes educational expenses for special needs services connected with a special needs beneficiary attending an eligible institution.) Also, a qualified distribution must be taken in the same tax year as the qualified higher education expenses were paid.

In the case of withdrawals not used for qualified higher education expenses (nonqualified distributions), the earnings element will be taxable as ordinary income to the distributee. Thus, in effect, any part of the investment earnings that normally would be a long-term capital gain becomes ordinary income in a nonqualified distribution. Nonqualified distributions are taxed under the annuity rules of Section 72 of the IRC. (See Chapter 17.) To do so, first the earnings element in the account balance is determined by subtracting the investment element (the contribution to the plan) from the total account balance. Then, an earnings ratio is determined by dividing this earnings element at the end of the calendar year by the total account value at that time. The taxable portion of any nonqualified distribution then is this earnings ratio times the total distribution.

Further, there is an additional 10 percent federal penalty tax on any taxable (earnings) portion of a nonqualified distribution, with some exceptions. These *exceptions* include that the *penalty tax* does not apply when the nonqualified distribution is made to the beneficiary's estate after his or her death; is attributable to the beneficiary's disability; or is made on account of the beneficiary's receipt of a scholarship, allowance, or certain other payments, to the extent the distribution does not exceed the scholarship, allowance, or payment. There also may be state penalties for nonqualified distributions.

---

[9] Prior to EGTRRA (effective January 1, 2002), the earnings portion of such withdrawals was taxed to the designated beneficiary at his or her income tax rate.

Federal Estate, GST, and Gift Tax Status of Plan Balances. The balance in a QTP is not included in a deceased account owner's gross estate for federal estate tax purposes. The only exception is if the account owner elected five-year annual exclusion treatment and dies within the five-year period. In this case the remaining pro-rata amounts would be in the decedent's gross estate.[10] Interestingly, this exclusion from the account owner's gross estate applies even though the account owner can direct how and when distributions are to be made to the designated beneficiary (normally for qualified higher education expenses, but perhaps not), can change the designated beneficiary, and can even recover the savings account balance for himself or herself.[11] This is the only financial and estate planning vehicle that allows such flexibility and tax advantages in making lifetime transfers without gift, GST, or estate tax consequences. This can make 529 savings plans a powerful estate planning tool, as illustrated next.

Suppose, for example, that Michael Edgalia, age 70, is a widower with a substantial estate and an annual income in the top income tax bracket. He has three adult children and nine minor grandchildren. Michael never went to college, but he believes in education and wants to provide for his grandchildren all the educational opportunities they want. Michael already is making direct annual exclusion gifts each year to his children. He also has paid tuition for several of his grandchildren directly to certain preschool programs and private elementary and secondary schools. All of these gifts are free of federal gift tax.

Now, Michael decides to open a 529 savings account in a carefully selected state QTP for each of his grandchildren as designated beneficiary of one of the accounts. Michael is the owner of all the accounts. He decides to contribute $55,000 to each 529 account and elect five-year annual exclusion treatment. This means his gift for each grandchild will be within the federal gift tax annual exclusion for the current year and for each of the next four years and also will be within the GST tax annual exclusion for each of those years (since his grandchildren are skip persons). This gift also will be out of Michael's gross estate for federal estate tax purposes, assuming he survives five years.

Thus, Michael effectively has moved nearly a half million dollars (9 x $55,000 = $495,000) to his grandchildren without any transfer taxation and with no current income taxation on plan earnings, while still retaining sub-

[10] For example, suppose Mary Eduski, who is unmarried, contributed $55,000 to a 529 savings account with her nephew as designated beneficiary in 2003 and elected—on a Form 709, United States Gift (and Generation- Skipping Transfer) Tax Return—to treat it as if made pro rata over five years. Further suppose Mary dies in 2005. In this case $22,000 (for 2006 and 2007) would be in her gross estate.

[11] These rights are subject to the rules of individual state plans. Therefore, it is important to check and evaluate state plans with regard to their flexibility in allowing such actions.

stantial control over the account as account owner. For example, he can direct how, when, and to what eligible institutions income-tax free distributions will be made for qualified higher education expenses for the designated beneficiaries. Michael also can change the designated beneficiary.[12] Further, as account owner, Michael in this example, normally can recover the funds in the 529 account for himself for any reason. Such a refund to the account owner would be a nonqualified distribution and thus the earnings portion will be subject to ordinary income tax and the 10 percent federal penalty tax. But even so, there will still be deferral of tax on the investment earnings until the nonqualified distribution is made. The real "price" to Michael of a nonqualified refund is that he will pay the 10 percent penalty tax on the earnings and that all the earnings will be taxed as ordinary income, even though part or all of the account balance may be invested in capital-gain-type assets (e.g., common stocks).

If a *designated beneficiary dies*, it would appear the 529 plan account balance will be included in the deceased beneficiary's gross estate. This is true even though, in fact, beneficiaries have no control over these plans. However, designated beneficiaries normally will be considerably younger than account owners and so this would not seem to be a major issue.

Form of Contributions. Contributions to QTPs may be made only in cash. Thus, appreciated property cannot be placed in these plans.

Flexibility in the Plan. 529 savings plans offer considerable flexibility in their creation and operation. Generally, any adult U.S. citizen can open an account and be the account owner. There are no income limits on eligibility to participate. Further, some states permit custodians of UTMA or UGMA accounts to use cash in the account to open a 529 plan for the account beneficiary. But then the 529 plan will be subject to the state's UTMA or UGMA statute. However, this may be a source of funds to start a 529 account. In addition, some QTPs will allow trusts, partnerships (perhaps an FLP), corporations, or other entities to open 529 savings plans. The trustee of an existing trust, for example, might use cash in the trust to open a 529 savings plan with the trust as account owner and a trust beneficiary as designated beneficiary. State plans permit the naming of a successor account owner in the event of the original owner's death. Some QTPs also may permit naming a successor owner in the event of the original owner's incapacity.[13]

---

[12] As will be covered later in this chapter, there are no tax consequences for a change of beneficiary as long as the new beneficiary is a "member of the family" (as defined in the tax law) of the former beneficiary and is not in a younger generation than the former beneficiary.

[13] The incapacity issue also can be handled by giving the agent authority under a durable general power of attorney to deal with the account.

Naming and Changing the Designated Beneficiary. The account owner can name and change the designated beneficiary. Any individual can be designated beneficiary, including the account owner himself or herself.

If the account owner changes the designated beneficiary to an eligible "member of the family" of the former designated beneficiary, as defined in the tax law,[14] it is not considered a nonqualified distribution and is not subject to income taxation. But if the new beneficiary is not a "member of the family" of the former beneficiary, the change is treated as a nonqualified distribution of the account balance to the account owner and taxed accordingly.

In addition, if the account owner names a new beneficiary who is one or more generations younger than the former beneficiary (such as changing to a child of the former beneficiary), it is viewed in the proposed IRS regulations as a gift for federal gift tax purposes by the former beneficiary to the new beneficiary. It could also be a GST tax transfer by the former beneficiary to the new beneficiary if the new beneficiary is two or more generations younger than the former beneficiary (such as changing to a grandchild of the former beneficiary). However, if the change is to someone in the same or an older genera tion than the former beneficiary, no adverse tax result occurs.

Rollovers to Other Plans. QTPs normally allow an account owner to transfer (roll over) an account from one state plan to another state plan. In effect, this means changing the plan (including its investment selection) to a new account. The change to a new account also may be in the same state plan, depending on state plan rules. If the beneficiary is not changed, there can be only one rollover in any one 12-month period. But if the beneficiary is changed, the account can be rolled over at any time.

Investment Options and Investment Flexibility. One of the requirements of Section 529 is that neither the account owner nor the beneficiary may directly or indirectly direct the investments in the 529 account. However, the seeming inflexibility of this requirement can be mitigated in practice in several respects.

First, many state plans permit donors (account owners) upon initially opening an account to allocate his or her contributions among one or more of a range (menu) of broad investment options (strategies). The plans often offer so-called "age-based" asset allocation options under which the allocation in the option among, say, common stock, bond, and money market funds automatically

[14] For this purpose, the tax law defines a "member of the family" as a child or the child's descendants; a stepchild; a brother, sister, stepbrother, or stepsister; the father, the mother, or an ancestor of either; a stepfather or stepmother; a first cousin; a child of a brother or sister (i.e., a niece or nephew); a brother or sister of the father or mother (i.e., uncle or aunt); a son-in-law, daughter-in-law, father-in-law, mother-in-law, brother-in-law, or sister-in-law; and a spouse of the designated beneficiary or of any of the family members just named. It can be seen that this is a reasonably broad list of potential new beneficiaries.

changes as the beneficiary gets older. For example, an age-based allocation in one plan for a one-year-old beneficiary is 75 percent in a common stock fund and 25 percent in a bond fund; by age 15 the allocation becomes 20 percent in the stock fund, 70 percent in the bond fund, and 10 percent in a money market fund. Plans can have more than one age-based option. In addition, a number of plans also offer one or more non-age-based options, usually with one or more equity options and one or more fixed income options. These investment options (age-based and non-age-based) often are in mutual funds that are managed by outside investment intermediaries for the state.

Second, the ability to roll over an account to an account in another plan effectively allows account owners to change the investment selection for the new account. Assuming the beneficiary is not changed, such a rollover can be made once every 12 months. This would seem to give an account owner reasonable flexibility to change investment strategies, if desired, *after an account has been opened.* If the beneficiary is changed (subject to the tax rules explained earlier), a rollover can be made at any time.

Finally, the IRS has stated in a notice that it expects final regulations will allow QTPs to permit account owners to change investment options once per calendar year or upon a beneficiary change within the same plan. Some plans now allow this by permitting transfers of *existing account balances* to other investment options within the same plan once per calendar year or upon a beneficiary change. This allows investment flexibility without having to roll over an account to another state plan. Also, QTPs often allow the directing of future contributions to different investment options.

Thus, while 529 savings account owners cannot select individual securities or other assets for their accounts (as they could, for example, for education IRAs and UTMA or UGMA accounts), they normally can have a reasonably broad choice among essentially mutual funds (age-based and non-age-based) and perhaps guaranteed principal accounts, depending on the particular state plan. State plans vary widely in the number and nature of the investment options offered. Therefore, among the important factors to consider in choosing a state QTP are: the investment options offered; the flexibility allowed in changing investment strategy of an existing account; the financial intermediary, if any, managing the investment funds; and the expense ratios of the various funds and plans.

A QTP cannot allow the assets in an account to serve as security for any loan.

Fees and Expenses of the Plans. Here again, state plans vary widely. Sometimes costs are lower for state residents than for nonresidents. There may be application fees, annual fees to cover program expenses, and fees for other

services. However, perhaps most important are the annual asset-based investment fund fees, which are a percentage of the value of the assets in the
account.[15] These annual asset-based percentage charges are analogous to the
expense ratios of mutual funds and may vary with the investment choices
made.[16] They also vary widely among QTPs.

Coordination with Other Plans and Financial Aid. As noted earlier, a person
can contribute to a 529 plan and an education IRA for the same beneficiary
in the same year. Of course, to avoid a taxable gift, the combined contributions
must be within the gift tax annual exclusion for the beneficiary for the year.

When qualified higher education expenses are incurred, they are first
reduced by any scholarship or fellowship grants excluded from gross income
and any other tax-free education benefits received by the beneficiary. Then
they are reduced by any expenses taken into account in determining the Hope
or the Lifetime Learning Credits. The remaining qualified expenses then can
be paid tax-free from a 529 plan. They could also be paid tax-free from an education IRA. If there should be total distributions from both a 529 plan and an
education IRA that exceed such reduced expenses, the expenses are allocated
between the distributions.

For purposes of federal student financial aid, a 529 savings plan is considered an asset of the account owner. Therefore, if the student is the account
owner, it will be his or her asset; but if a parent is the account owner, it will be
the parent's asset for determining the expected family contribution (EFC). But
if a grandparent or other relative is the account owner, the 529 account should
not affect financial aid considerations.

Creditor Protection. Normally, the creditors of the account owner may be able
to attach a 529 savings account balance, but not the creditors of the beneficiary. However, some states have given statutory protection to their 529 plans
from the creditors of both the account owner and the beneficiary.

Protecting the Plan in Event of the Death or Disability of Donor. Only life
insurance and disability insurance can perform this function. Therefore, the
need for coverage to meet future education costs in the event of a contributor's
early death or disability should be considered in the insurance plan, as illustrated in Chapter 4.

Possible "Freezing" of Future Education Costs. This can be done only through
prepaid tuition plans.

---

[15] This may be a "wrap fee" that covers program expenses and investment fund fees in one
annual asset-based percentage charge.

[16] In fact, the various investment options offered by QTPs usually are invested in one or more
mutual funds.

Education IRAs (Coverdell Education Savings Accounts)

These also are tax-favored plans to accumulate funds to pay for education expenses that were liberalized by EGTRRA. They have already been described in Chapter 19 and that description will not be repeated here. Compared with 529 savings plans, education IRAs have some advantages but also some drawbacks.

Tax-free distributions from education IRAs can be used not only for qualified higher education expenses (as is true for 529 plans), but also for qualified elementary and secondary education expenses for grades K through 12 (which are not covered by 529 plans). Thus, in the case of beneficiaries for whom elementary and secondary education expenses may be incurred (e.g., attending private schools), an eligible contributor may want to consider an education IRA to fund those expenses on a tax-free basis. This may be in addition to a 529 plan that could be used for qualified higher education expenses. Further, education IRA account owners have greater investment latitude than for 529 plans. Finally, education IRAs are not subject to individual state plan rules as are 529 plans.

On the other hand, a major drawback for education IRAs is the $2000 annual limit per beneficiary that a person can contribute. Up to $11,000 gift-tax-free per contributor per year can be placed in a 529 plan and contributions can be "front-loaded" for five years. Another drawback is the income limits on eligibility to contribute to education IRAs. The required rollover or distribution when a beneficiary reaches age 30 is another constraining factor. There are no such distribution requirements for 529 plans. Finally, a very significant advantage for most 529 plans, which is not available for any other plan, is the ability of the account owner to recover (withdraw) the account balance at any time for himself or herself. The only cost of such recovery is paying tax at ordinary income rates plus a 10 percent federal penalty tax on the earnings portion of such a withdrawal. This provides unusual financial planning latitude for 529 plan account owners.

Other Arrangements for Advance Funding

There are other approaches that can be used for funding education costs that are not specifically designed for that purpose. These have already been described in previous chapters and so will only be briefly noted here.

Uniform Transfers or Uniform Gifts to Minors Acts. These custodianships were discussed in Chapter 25. A custodian under these plans can make payments for the beneficiary's education expenses or distributions to the beneficiary that he or she can use for that purpose. Of course, payments for the benefit of and distributions to the beneficiary can be made for other purposes as well.

The advantages of these custodianships are that contributions to them can be made in kind (e.g., appreciated securities) so any capital gains can be taxed to the minor, the custodian has wide investment latitude, and the assets can be used for or by the minor (or adult at age 21) for any purpose (e.g., travel, buying a home, starting a business, or others). On the other hand, the earnings on the assets in the account will be taxed currently to the minor. They are not tax-free (unless invested in municipal bonds or accounts). Also, the account must go outright to the minor at the statutory age (usually 21) and then will be subject to the beneficiary's absolute control. Even if the custodian invests UTMA or UGMA funds in a Section 529 plan, the beneficiary will get control of the 529 account at the statutory age. And, of course, the original donor can never get the funds back.

Trusts for Minors. These also were discussed in Chapter 25. The trustee can be given authority to use trust assets for education expenses of trust beneficiaries, as well as for other purposes.

The advantages are that contributions can be made in kind, the trustee can be given broad investment powers, and trust assets can be used for or by the trust beneficiaries for any purpose, subject to the terms of the trust. On the other hand, the earnings on trust assets will be taxed currently to the trust if accumulated or to the beneficiary or beneficiaries if paid out currently to them. Either way, the investment earnings are not tax-free (unless trust assets are invested in municipal securities). Also, in the case of Section 2503(c) trusts, the assets must go outright to the beneficiary at age 21 unless the beneficiary consents to their remaining in trust. And, of course, the original grantor can never recover the trust assets for himself or herself if they are to be excluded from the grantor's gross estate and the income not taxed to the grantor.

As noted earlier, some QTPs allow trustees to open 529 plans for trust beneficiaries with cash from the trust. In this case, the trust is the account owner and a trust beneficiary is the designated beneficiary. The trustee then can direct qualified distributions for the beneficiary, change the beneficiary to another trust beneficiary, or direct a withdrawal (recovery) back into the trust corpus. A trustee has a fiduciary duty to the trust beneficiaries to administer the trust impartially and properly, so there may be advantages to the beneficiaries in having a trust as owner of a 529 account. It also may be an attractive investment of trust assets, tax-free (for qualified higher education expenses). On the other hand, since only cash can be contributed to a 529 plan, if the trustee must sell appreciated assets to raise the cash, this will result in capital gains for the trust. This same caveat can also be made for 529 plans held in UTMA or UGMA accounts. Finally, if a trust (or custodian under UTMA or UGMA) is an account owner, the original donor cannot recover the account balance for himself or herself.

United States Savings Bonds Redeemed for Education Expenses. This was mentioned in Chapter 11 in the description of U.S. Savings Bonds. Subject to income and certain other limitations, interest on qualified United States Savings Bonds (Series EE or I bonds issued after 1989 to an original owner who had attained age 24 before issuance) may be excluded from gross income to the extent the proceeds are used to pay for qualified higher education expenses of the taxpayer, the taxpayer's spouse, and dependents of the taxpayer (for income tax purposes) that are paid during the taxable year in which the bond redemption occurs. This exclusion will be limited if the aggregate proceeds of the bond(s) exceed eligible expenses. It also will be phased out for taxpayers with modified adjusted gross income (MAGI) over certain levels (for 2003, starting at $87,750 for married taxpayers filing jointly and $58,500 for other taxpayers). While this exclusion of interest may be helpful in some cases, it generally cannot be counted on as a complete advance funding technique in itself.

Cash Value Life Insurance. These policies normally cover a parent as insured and owner. They are intended to accumulate a cash value that can be used for education expenses (usually through policy loans or withdrawals less than basis) if the insured survives. If the insured should die (or become disabled) before the education is begun or completed, the death proceeds (or waiver of premium benefit) are there to complete the education plan. This approach effectively uses the income tax advantages of life insurance as explained in Chapter 28. It also could be owned by an irrevocable life insurance trust for estate tax reasons, if desired.

Use of Individually Owned Assets or Savings. For many years, people simply have saved or accumulated assets separately in their own names or jointly with their spouses in anticipation of using those assets to pay for their children's educations. This certainly is a simple and flexible approach and has certain advantages. The owner controls the assets and their use. If the education plans do not materialize or they do not meet the parents' expectations, they still own the assets. No outside intermediaries need be used.

On the other hand, income and capital gains from these assets will be taxed currently to the owners (except for the interest exclusion for U.S. Savings Bonds just discussed and interest from municipal securities). The assets also will not have been removed from the owner's gross estate for federal estate tax purposes. The owners will have the unlimited gift tax exclusion for direct payments of tuition, but need to be careful to stay within the per-donee annual exclusion for the remainder of any expenses paid.

The nature of the assets accumulated for this purpose depends on the investment strategy and overall asset allocation position of the person or couple. For a younger child or grandchild, the accumulation period will be relatively long, so good-quality common stocks or stock mutual funds might be appropriate. To be more conservative, a balanced mutual fund might be considered. On the other hand, the person or couple may want more security and choose bonds or guaranteed principal investments.

For tax-efficient investments for this purpose, one possibility would be investment-grade zero-coupon municipal bonds with maturities corresponding to the prospective student's years in school.[17] These would approach the attractions of a 529 plan invested in a fixed income option, except that their respective yields would have to be compared. The bonds' investment income would be income-tax-free in all cases, the yield would be locked in for the maturity of the bonds, and they would be available to the owner to pay any education expenses, make other gifts (presumably within the annual exclusions), or simply keep for his or her own use (without any 10 percent penalty tax) if that is desired. However, the munis would be in the owner's gross estate for federal estate tax purposes if he or she should die before they were used for education expenses or other needs. The real point of comparison, then, would seem to be the locked-in yield of the zero coupon munis as compared with the yield available on the fixed income option of a 529 plan or fixed income investments in an education IRA of comparable quality and maturities. Of course, if equity investments (e.g., common stocks) are desired, munis would not be a viable alternative.

Overall Advantage of QTPs and Possible Diversification in Education Funding

With all factors considered, it seems hard to beat a well-selected 529 savings plan with flexible plan provisions, a reasonable number of well-managed investment options, and a reasonable expense ratio and other costs, as a vehicle for funding education costs. Such a plan or plans probably should be a core part of most education funding strategies.

However, as with most areas of financial planning, there is much to be said for diversification of approaches. One never knows what the future will bring. For example, along with a 529 plan, a person might have an education IRA (if eligible) and possibly a UTMA or UGMA or a trust for the minor. Directly owned assets might also be used. Finally, some life and disability insurance arrangements will be needed, in case the donor should die or become disabled before the education plan can be completed.

---

[17] U.S. Savings bonds and their tax advantages for this purpose have already been discussed.

30

Planning for Business Interests

When an individual or a family has an interest in a closely held business, proper planning normally will be needed for various aspects of the business, such as its formation; operation; possible sale or liquidation; possible gifts of business interests; its disposition in the event of death, disability, or retirement of an owner; or its possible retention by the family.

Potential Issues

These may include the following:

- What kind of business entity or entities should be used for the business?
- Who will control the business?
- Will there be a market for the business if it has to be sold?
- How will the business provide adequate income for the owners?
- What will be the income tax status of the business and its owners?
- How will the value of the business affect the taxes and liquidity needs of the owners' estates?
- Will the business be able to continue if one of the owners dies? What will happen to the business interest of a deceased owner?
- How can the business best be sold to a new owner, if desired?
- What will happen to the business and the owner if an owner becomes disabled?
- How can the retirement of an owner be best planned for?
- Should the owners be making gifts of business interests within the family and, if so, how much and in what form?
- What is the legal status of the owners with respect to their personal liability for the debts, obligations, and tort claims against the business?

Characteristics of Closely Held Businesses

We are all familiar with large publicly traded corporations whose shares are listed on various organized exchanges. When we discussed common stocks as an investment in Chapter 6, we were primarily concerned with the stocks of these publicly traded companies.

On the other hand, closely held businesses have a number of different characteristics, including the following:

- They can be formed as one or more of *several types of business entities,* including limited liability companies (LLCs), partnerships, sole proprietorships, S corporations, and C corporations.
- They often are formed as *pass-through entities* (as described in Chapter 14) in that their profits and losses are not taxed at the business-entity level but flow through to the owners individually and are taxed to (or deductible by) them personally. Thus, there normally is only one level of income taxation, for the individual owners.
- They usually have only a *small number of owners;* in many cases, these are family members.
- There normally is *no ready market* for these businesses.
- Due to these and other factors, there usually is *limited marketability* of closely held business interests. Depending on the circumstances, there also may be lack of control over the business by some owners. These factors may provide a rationale for substantial *valuation discounts* when such interests are given to family members or at their death.
- Many owners of closely held businesses are also *involved in the day-to-day management* of those businesses. They are owner-managers. They may be stockholder-employees of closely held corporations, principals of partnerships, member-managers of LLCs, or sole proprietors. Regardless of the form, they often manage and control the businesses they own. This is in contrast to the situation of most stockholders of publicly traded companies, who effectively have no control over the corporation's affairs.
- Again, due to the factors just stated, the owner-managers of closely held businesses often can *coordinate their business planning with their own personal and estate planning.*

Types of Business Entities

One important decision for anyone planning to start a business or already in business is what kind of business entity or entities to use in organizing the business.

Sole Proprietorships

In this case, the business's assets, liabilities, and operations are simply part of the owner's personal financial affairs. There is no separate business entity. There can be only one owner (sole proprietor). No formal documents or registrations are required. The business's profits and losses are automatically passed through to the sole proprietor for tax and other purposes. The sole proprietor has unlimited personal liability for the debts, tort liability, and other obligations of the business. Adequate commercial liability insurance is the owner's best protection against tort claims arising out of the business.

General Partnerships

A partnership can be viewed as an association of two or more persons to carry on, as co-owners, a business for profit. There must be at least two partners to form a partnership and it must have a business purpose. The term *person* in this definition is very broad and can include virtually any individual or entity, such as U.S. citizens, resident aliens, nonresident aliens, corporations, LLCs, trusts, or other partnerships. Thus, there is essentially no limitation on who or what can be a partner in a partnership.

The partners of a general partnership (aside from a limited liability partnership [LLP], described in the next section) are jointly and severally liable for the debts, tort claims, and other obligations of the partnership. This means they have unlimited personal liability for any claims against the business, including those arising from the actions of other partners or other persons when acting for the business (so-called *vicarious liability*).

The state laws governing general partnerships generally are the Uniform Partnership Act (UPA) or the Revised Uniform Partnership Act (RUPA) or variations of them. However, the partners in a written partnership agreement, if they wish, usually can modify the terms of these state laws with respect to their partnership. In the absence of such an agreement, the state partnership law applies. A general partnership is easy to form; no state registration is required. There also does not need to be a written partnership agreement, although such an agreement is desirable.

General partnerships are pass-through entities for federal income tax purposes. Thus, the partnership itself pays no tax and all items of partnership income, gains, losses, deductions, and credits flow through to the partners and are taxable to them individually. Each partner's share of these items normally is determined by the partnership agreement. However, the partnership must compute these items for tax purposes. Thus, a partnership can be viewed as a tax-reporting but not taxpaying entity. The rules for partnership taxation are contained in Subchapter K of the IRC. These rules also apply to limited partnerships (LPs), limited liability partnerships (LLPs), limited liability limited partnerships (LLLPs), and limited liability companies (LLCs), assuming they are treated as partnerships under the check-the-box regulations described in Chapter 15 and later in this chapter.

Limited Partnerships (LPs)

Limited partnerships are defined by state law and must be registered with the state. They have already been described in Chapter 25 with respect to the creation of family limited partnerships (FLPs). An LP must contain at least one general partner and one limited partner.

The general partner of an LP (aside from a limited liability limited partnership [LLLP], described in the next section) has unlimited personal liability for the debts, tort claims, and other obligations of the partnership. However, other entities whose owners have limited liability, like LLCs and S corporations, can be the general partner. The liability of the limited partners for partnership obligations, on the other hand, normally is limited to their investment in the partnership. However, in return for this limited liability, limited partners cannot take part in the active management or conduct of the partnership to the extent specified in the applicable state law. If they do, they may be treated as general partners and lose their limited liability. As in the case of a general partnership, virtually any individual or entity can be a partner in an LP. The state laws governing LPs generally are the Uniform Limited Partnership Act (ULPA) or the Revised Uniform Limited Partnership Act (RULPA) or variations of them. There must be a written partnership agreement and the formalities of these laws must be observed.

Limited Liability Partnerships (LLPs)

These may be formed under relatively new laws that permit general partners to limit their personal liability normally for some partnership obligations. In many states, general partners in an LLP are not liable for the acts or omissions of other partners or of employees or agents of the partnership (other than those the general partner supervises directly). In other words, general partners in LLPs essentially are relieved of their vicarious liability. In some states, they are also relieved of other partnership liabilities, like contractual claims. An LLP must register as such under the applicable state law.

Limited Liability Limited Partnerships (LLLPs)

These are formed under state laws that expressly permit limited partnerships to register as LLLPs. In this case, the general partner(s) can limit their personal liability.

C Corporations

These are corporations established under state corporation laws. They can have one or more stockholders and virtually any person or entity can be a stockholder. There are no limits on the number or nature of C corporation stockholders. They can have one or more classes of stock in their capital structure. Thus, for example, a C corporation could have several classes of common stock or one or more classes of common stock and one or more classes of preferred stock. The liability of stockholders for corporate obligations normally is limited to their investment in the corporation. Also, stockholders can actively participate in the management and conduct of the corporation without losing this limited liability. In fact, stockholders of closely held C corporations often are stockholder-employees of the corporation.

C corporations are taxable entities under Subchapter C of the IRC. They are subject to the corporate income tax, the corporate alternative minimum tax,[1] the tax on unreasonable accumulation of earnings, and other levies. Thus, among all the forms of business organization discussed here, the C corporation is the only form that is not a pass-through entity. It and its shareholders are exposed to the corporate double-tax. However, its shareholders are taxed only on dividends that are declared and paid by the corporation; so, as a practical matter, closely held C corporations often elect not to pay dividends to their common stockholders (to the extent possible). The strategy of their stockholders often is to take profits out of the corporation in other ways, so they will be deductible by the corporation and taxable only once at the stockholder level. Strategies for doing this are discussed later in this chapter. C corporations also are subject to double taxation of capital gains on a corporate liquidation (the so-called repeal of the General Utilities doctrine). However, again as noted in Chapter 14, there is a 50 percent exclusion of gain from the sale or exchange of qualified small business stock in a C corporation, subject to certain conditions.

S Corporations

An S corporation is a regular corporation under state corporation law that meets certain qualification requirements under the tax law and elects (under Subchapter S of the IRC) not to be taxed as a corporation. In most other respects, an S corporation is like a C corporation. For example, S corporation stockholders normally have limited liability for corporate obligations and they often actively participate in the management and conduct of the corporation as stockholder-employees.

[1] However, as noted in Chapter 14, the corporate AMT does not apply to C corporations that are small business corporations for this purpose (i.e., generally those with annual gross receipts not exceeding $5 million).

An S corporation is taxed in most respects like a partnership, rather than a corporation. The S corporation itself generally pays no tax[2] and all items of corporate income, gains, losses, deductions, and credits flow through to the stockholders in proportion to their stockholdings and are taxable to them individually. However, the corporation must compute these items for tax purposes.

Thus, stockholders of S corporations are taxed on the net profits and gains of the corporation even if they do not receive any dividends from the corporation.[3] In fact, since profits have already been taxed to the stockholders, dividends paid by S corporations normally are not taxable to the stockholders.[4] This may put a financial strain on S corporation stockholders, particularly stockholders with minority interests, who may be receiving taxable income from the corporation but who perhaps have little or no control over whether the corporation pays any dividends with which the taxes might be paid. To provide these funds, and perhaps to avoid a situation in which minority stockholders in effect could be forced to sell their stock, S corporations in their bylaws or charters often require the payment of minimum dividends expressed as a percentage of their profits.

Eligibility Requirements. Only a *small business corporation* can elect S corporation status. To be a small business corporation for this purpose, a corporation must meet the following requirements (among others):

- It must be a domestic corporation.
- It must have no more than 75 shareholders (with a husband and wife being viewed as one shareholder).
- It can have only certain classes of eligible shareholders.

These can include:
1. Individuals (i.e., U.S. citizens or residents—nonresident aliens cannot be shareholders).
2. Grantor trusts. (Thus, for example, a revocable living trust created by an individual grantor who is a U.S. citizen or resident can be an S corpora-

---

[2] In certain situations an S corporation may incur tax at the corporate level if it had formerly been a C corporation (i.e., had a C history). One is when the built-in gains in assets as of the date of conversion (from C to S) are sold or exchanged during the 10-year period after conversion. Another is when the former C was on LIFO inventory accounting. In this case, there will be LIFO recapture on conversion from C to S. Third, there may be tax on excess net passive income; the S election may be terminated due to such income for three consecutive years.

[3] This is also true of other pass-through entities, like partnerships and LLCs, with respect to profits and distributions.

[4] When an S corporation has earnings and profits (e.g., resulting from a C history), some dividends may be taxable (when they exceed the accumulated adjustments account).

tion shareholder. After the grantor's death, the trust can continue to be an S shareholder for two years.)

3. A trust created under a will (testamentary trust), but only for two years.
4. An estate of a deceased shareholder.
5. A qualified subchapter S trust (QSST). These are trusts that meet special requirements, including the following:
   - The QSST has only one current income beneficiary, who is a U.S. citizen or resident.
   - All trust income must be distributed currently to the one individual.
   - The income interest of the current income beneficiary must terminate at the earlier of the beneficiary's death or the termination of the trust.
   - Any corpus distributed during the current income beneficiary's lifetime can be distributed only to that beneficiary.
   - Upon termination of the trust during the current income beneficiary's lifetime, the trust must distribute all its assets to the beneficiary.
6. An electing small business trust (ESBT). These also are trusts that must meet special requirements, which include the following:
   - The trust does not have beneficiaries other than individuals, an estate, or charitable organizations.
   - No interest in the trust was acquired by purchase.
   - The trustee elected ESBT status. ESBTs are taxed on S corporation income at the highest individual income tax rate.
7. Voting trusts.
8. Certain exempt organizations (i.e., trusts for qualified retirement plans and charitable organizations).

- S corporations can have only one class of stock. However, if the only difference among the shares of common stock is in their voting rights, they are still considered as constituting one class of stock. Thus, an S corporation can have voting and nonvoting common stock. It can also have stock option plans for its employees and buy-sell agreements without violating the one-class-of-stock rule. Finally, an S corporation can have straight debt (i.e., a promise to pay a certain sum on demand or at a specified date, at an interest rate not contingent on profits, and that is not convertible into stock, among other requirements) without that being considered a second class of stock.

If any of these conditions cease to be met, the S election normally is broken (terminated) and the corporation is taxed as a C corporation from that point on.

Other Issues. All stockholders initially must consent to an S election. However, once made, an S election can be revoked (as opposed to being terminated when the business is no longer meeting the requirements for a small business corporation) only by shareholders with more than 50 percent of the stock. Also, in general, once revoked or terminated, an election cannot be made again for five taxable years.

S corporations can have certain subsidiaries. An S corporation can own some or all the stock of C corporations, be a member of LLCs, and be a partner in a partnership. An S corporation also can own 100 percent of a qualified subchapter S subsidiary, which will be combined with its parent for tax purposes. However, C corporations, partnerships, LLCs, and trusts (other than those described previously) still are not eligible shareholders of S corporations.

The just-noted rules apply to the federal income taxation of S corporations.

However, states also may have S corporation statutes. Some of these mirror federal law, but others have different provisions. Also, some states tax S corporations in varying degrees.

Limited Liability Companies (LLCs)

The limited liability company is a newer form of business organization that probably is the fastest growing. It combines the advantages of limited liability and freedom to have management control of corporations with the pass-through and other tax advantages of partnerships. It also is free from the eligibility requirements of S corporations.

LLCs are created under state law and must be registered with the state. All 50 states and the District of Columbia have LLC statutes.[5] A number of these laws either permit or do not forbid single-member LLCs. However, with respect to many matters, the members of an LLC in their written operating agreement can alter the terms of these state laws with respect to their LLC if they wish. Usually, in the absence of a contrary provision in the operating agreement, the state LLC law applies.

Persons or entities that have ownership interests in an LLC and can influence its management and operations are called *members*. However, there can also be equity owners (nonmembers) who do not have a say in management. Also, LLCs can have managers who manage the affairs of the business. Thus, LLCs may be member-managed (where the members are engaged in running the operation) or manager-managed (where the members select a manager to run the business).

LLC statutes normally relieve the members from personal liability for the debts, obligations, and liabilities of the LLC. However, they can still actively participate in management without losing this limited liability.

---

[5] There is a Uniform Limited Liability Company Act that some states have adopted.

Tax Status. Under the check-the-box regulations, an LLC normally will elect to be taxed like a partnership. Thus, it is a pass-through entity and pays no tax itself. All items of income, gains, losses, deductions, and credits flow through to the members and are reported on their individual tax returns. Each member's share of these items normally is determined by the operating agreement.

Other Factors. LLCs can be flexible in their formation, structure, and operation. They are relatively easy to form, usually by filing their articles of organization with the state. LLCs can have any number of members (including only one member in many states) and the members essentially can be any person or entity. LLCs can have more than one class of equity interest. They normally do not have to observe many of the formalities often required of corporations under state corporation laws. These might include annual shareholder meetings, certain financial statements, boards of directors, appointment of officers, bylaws, minutes of proceedings, and so forth.[6] State tax laws also apply to LLCs. Some states follow the federal tax approach, but others may levy some taxes on LLCs.

Business Trusts

Some states allow businesses to organize as business trusts. These are not common, however.

Use of Multiple Entities

It is not unusual for businesses to employ several of these forms of organization.

For example, an S corporation or an LLC can be the general partner of a limited partnership. This would provide flow-through tax treatment and limited liability for all interests. Also, an S corporation can have subsidiary LLCs (or subsidiary S corporations). This would provide flow-through tax treatment, limited liability, and separation of businesses or operations. Further, C corporations could have subsidiary LLCs or be partners in a partnership.

[6] On the other hand, it should be noted that many states have adopted so-called close corporation statutes in various forms. These laws are intended to relieve smaller, closely held corporations of many of the formalities required of larger, publicly traded corporations. They may also relieve shareholders of personal liability for the debts and obligations of their corporation on the ground that the corporation did not observe the usual formalities in the exercise of its corporate powers and management. The failure to observe such formalities has been a basis for creditors to "pierce the corporate veil" in some cases.

Further Thoughts on the Legal Liability Issue

Business owners usually are anxious to be free from personal liability for the debts, obligations, and tort claims against their business interests. All of the business forms just described provide at least some degree of limited liability, except for general partners not in LLPs or LLLPs.

However, even with the protection afforded by these forms of business organization, some cautions are in order. First, business owners (and all others) are personally liable for tort and other liability arising from their own conduct or misconduct. No form of business organization protects against this; since owners of closely held business often are involved in the management and conduct of their businesses, they may find themselves personally liable for their own actions in this regard. Second, some forms may not provide complete protection from personal liability, such as LLPs and LLLPs possibly for contractual claims and LPs for limited partners who take part in management. Third, many times owners of closely held businesses will be asked to personally endorse bank or other loans for the business. This will make them personally liable for their payment. Finally, courts may find reasons to find stockholders personally liable for certain claims against or obligations of their corporations because they are stockholders. This is the *corporate veil* doctrine. It is not the general rule, but such liability is possible.

Therefore, commercial liability insurance with adequate limits (or umbrella coverage) still is important for closely held businesses and their owners. Such insurance not only will indemnify those insured for covered liability claims against them but will also defend them (and pay the defense costs) for such claims. Also, owners should be insured under such coverage.

Check-the-Box Regulations

Check-the-box regulations have already been discussed in Chapter 14. In essence, they provide that an entity organized under a state or federal law as a corporation will be taxed as a corporation (a C corporation or an S corporation). Other organizations, called *eligible entities,* can elect how they wish to be taxed. Eligible entities essentially would be partnerships and LLCs. Eligible entities with two or more owners can elect to be taxed as an association taxable as a corporation or as a partnership. Eligible entities with a single owner (e.g., single-member LLCs) can elect to be disregarded as a separate entity for tax purposes. They will simply be taxed as part of their owners. Eligible entities generally will elect to be taxed as partnerships or disregarded for tax purposes.

Income Tax Basis in Business Interests

Owners of closely held business interests have an income tax basis in their interests, like other assets. This is referred to as their *outside basis* in their interests. It is analogous to the basis that stockholders of publicly traded corporations have in the stock they own, although it may be acquired and operate differently in the context of closely held business interests.

On the other hand, the basis a business has in its own assets is called its *inside basis.* This difference from outside basis exists because a business is an entity separate from its owners. And, in the case of pass-through entities, gains or losses from the sale of assets by the business and depreciation on assets flow through to the individual owners for tax purposes. Thus, a pass-through entity's inside basis in its assets will directly affect its owners.

At the formation of a business, the new owners will acquire basis in their interests. In a nontaxable transaction, this basis normally will equal the cash contributed plus the adjusted basis of assets contributed to form the business.[7] When a business interest is purchased, its basis normally is the purchase price (cost). When interests are received as gifts, there is a carryover basis. When inherited, the basis is the fair market value at death. From this point on, however, there are significant differences between C corporations and pass-through entities.

For C corporations, the stockholders' bases in their stock generally do not change as a result of the operations of the business.[8] On the other hand, for pass-through entities, the owners' bases do change as a result of the operations of the business. For example, a partner's outside basis in his or her partnership interest will be increased by his or her share of taxable income of the partnership, capital gains of the partnership, income of the partnership that is tax-exempt (e.g., life insurance proceeds), the amount of cash and the adjusted basis of assets contributed by him or her to the partnership plus any gain recognized on such contributions, and, generally, liabilities incurred by the partnership (called entity-level debt). Correspondingly, a partner's outside basis will be decreased by his or her share of partnership losses, nondeductible part-

[7] For corporations, when appreciated property is transferred to them as part of their formation, it normally will be a nontaxable event if the transferors receive only stock in return and, immediately after the exchange, the transferors own 80 percent or more of the stock of the corporation. For partnerships, generally contributions of appreciated property to a partnership in return for a partnership interest is a nontaxable event at any time. These are tax-free exchanges as described in Chapter 14. However, there may be gain if the property contributed is subject to liabilities and there normally will be income if stock or a partnership interest is received in return for services.

[8] There are some exceptions to this. For example, if stockholders receive dividends in excess of the earnings and profits of the corporation, the excess is a return of basis and reduces basis.

nership expenditures not chargeable to capital account, generally any reduction of partnership liabilities, and distributions he or she receives from the partnership. The same treatment applies to members of LLCs that are taxed as partnerships. For shareholders of S corporations, the same generally is true, except that their bases are not increased by entity-level debt, but a shareholder's basis for purposes of deducting losses is increased by his or her loans to the corporation. Basis is necessary to determine gain or loss on the sale or liquidation of a business interest. Also, the owner of an interest in a pass-through entity cannot deduct losses in excess of his or her basis.

Factors in Choice of Entity

Choice of entity often involves consideration of a number of issues—some of which are outlined here. These issues can be complex and a detailed discussion of them is beyond the scope of this book.

Liability of Owners

The owner liability issue has been discussed previously and that discussion will not be repeated here.

Tax Status of Entity and Owners

This also has been discussed previously. The trend seems to be toward pass-through entities, as opposed to C corporations, which are potentially exposed to double taxation. However, there may be various business reasons for the use of C corporations (e.g., intention to go public or desire for more than one class of stock). Also, closely held C corporations in practice may be able to avoid or mitigate potential double taxation through several strategies as described next. However, each of these strategies has practical limits.

- *Payment of salaries, bonuses, and so forth to stockholder employees.* These are deductible at the corporate level and taxable as compensation to shareholder-employees. However, the *limit* on such payments is that the compensation must be reasonable and customary for tax purposes. This is a facts-and-circumstances test and depends on the situation. But in the case of unreasonable compensation, the IRS will recharacterize the compensation as nondeductible dividends.
- *Compensation to family members on the payroll.* Here again, the *limit* is that the compensation must be reasonable for the services performed.
- *Employee benefits for stockholder-employees.* These are currently deductible at the corporate level and are either not taxable or not currently taxable to the

shareholder-employees, depending on the employee benefit. However, the *limits* on such benefits are that total compensation (including the employee benefits) must be reasonable and customary and that most employee benefits cannot discriminate in favor of highly compensated employees who, as a practical matter, often would be the stockholder-employees.[9]

- *Deferred compensation for stockholder-employees.* Here again, these payments will be deductible by the corporation and taxable as ordinary income to the shareholder-former employees when actually made. These arrangements can be discriminatory. The *limits* on such arrangements are that they must be entered into in advance, must be reasonable, and probably should be justified by compensation studies.

- *Leasing assets from stockholders.* In this case, the rental payments are deductible by the C corporation and are taxable as rent (ordinary income) to the stockholder-owners. Stockholders often will retain real estate used in the business in their own names and rent it to their businesses. This not only takes money from the corporation with only one level of taxation (to the property owner), but also gives the stockholder-owners the other tax advantages of owning real estate directly. The *limit* to this strategy is that the rent must not exceed a fair market rental value.

- *Lending money to the corporation.* Here the stockholders make loans to their corporation at fair market interest. The interest is deductible by the corporation and taxable to the stockholder-creditors as ordinary income. The *limits* on this strategy are that the interest should be reasonable, the interest must be on true debt and not a disguised dividend, debt should not be an excessive proportion of the corporation's capitalization, and the fact that debt may be a financial burden on the corporation.

- *Gifts of closely held stock to charity and then redemption of the stock by the corporation.* This is the *charity bailout* described in Chapter 16. The *limits* on this technique are that the stockholder should want to make a charitable contribution in any event (since he or she receives only a deduction, not income) and the general limits on charitable contributions.

While not a strategy to produce only one level of taxation, there has been the approach of paying income tax at the corporate level (perhaps at the 15 or 25 percent brackets), accumulating earnings and profits inside the C corporation, and then liquidating or selling the corporation and paying capital gains tax at the shareholder level.[10] For this approach to be successful, the

---

[9] Disability income benefits and insured health (medical expense) benefits do not have to be nondiscriminatory.

[10] There may also be capital gains tax on appreciated assets at the corporate level under the repeal of the General Utilities doctrine concept.

combined taxes on corporate income and on capital gains at liquidation or sale should be less than the individual tax rates of the shareholders, because that is the amount that will be paid on profits in a flow-through entity. While this strategy will be helped by the 50 percent reduction in capital gains on eligible qualified small business stock and by reductions in capital gains tax rates in general, it is less likely to be attractive when individual income tax rates are reduced relative to corporate income tax rates.

Ease of Formation and Operation

Partnerships and LLCs probably are easier to form and operate than corporations.

Number and Nature of Owners

If the business is to have only one owner, a sole proprietorship, single-member LLC, S corporation, or C corporation must be used. On the other hand, if a business is to have more than 75 owners (e.g., shareholders), an S corporation cannot be used. There also are other eligibility requirements on who can own S corporation stock.

Nature of Management and Control Desired

The forms can differ in this respect, as noted previously.

Transferability of Interests

Traditionally, stock of corporations has been viewed as being freely transferable, while full transfers of partnership interests have required the consent of all or at least some of the other partners. In practice, however, the bylaws of closely held corporations often limit the transferability of their stock. This may be particularly true in the case of S corporations, where the S election can be broken by a transfer to an ineligible person or entity.

Continuity of Life

Here again, corporations traditionally have had continuity of life regardless of the death, retirement, bankruptcy, or other condition of the stockholders. For general partnerships and generally under LLC statutes, however, the death, retirement, bankruptcy, and certain other conditions of a partner or member will cause dissolution of the entity. Even so, however, the business can continue with the agreement of all or a majority of the owners.

For limited partnerships, only the death, retirement, bankruptcy, and so forth of the last remaining general partner will dissolve the partnership. But here again, the partnership can continue with the consent of all or a majority of the limited partners.

Ease of Termination

A partnership (or a partner's interest) generally can be liquidated (terminated) without taxable gain to the partners except to the extent that the cash (generally including marketable securities) distributed exceeds a partner's basis in his or her partnership interest, with certain exceptions. Thus, in effect, partnership assets generally can be distributed in kind to a liquidating partner or partners without current taxation. The same treatment is true for LLCs that are taxed as partnerships.

For corporations, however, there may be taxable gain on liquidation (termination).

In the case of S corporations with appreciated assets, there will be taxable gain at the corporate level, which will be passed through to the shareholders. However, the bases of the shareholders' stock will increase by the amount of the gain and so there often will not be double taxation for liquidating S corporation shareholders (only a single level of capital gains taxation at the shareholder level). For C corporations with appreciated assets, under the so-called repeal of the General Utilities doctrine, there will be taxable gain at the corporate level and then a capital gain at the shareholder level on the difference between the cash and the value of the property distributed in liquidation and the stockholders' income tax bases in their stock. Thus, there will be double taxation on liquidation of C corporations.

Also, the conversion of a partnership or LLC to a corporation generally will not be a taxable event. However, there generally will be tax on the conversion of a corporation to a partnership or LLC.

These tax flexibilities tend to favor the partnership and LLC forms. They are easier to form and operate and also to terminate.

Future Plans for the Business

If the plans are that the business will soon go public (perhaps in an IPO) or be sold to another firm, a C corporation may be preferred. This may also be true if the business is to be kept in a family for a long period of time. On the other hand, if it is planned for the business to terminate or for capital distributions to be taken from it fairly soon, these plans may favor a partnership or LLC.

Availability of Special Allocations

Partnership agreements and operating agreements of LLCs can allocate items of income, gain, loss, deductions, or credits among the partners or members other than according to their interests in the entity, provided the allocation has substantial economic effect.[11] These are referred to as *special allocations.* Corporations generally cannot have such allocations (i.e., profits and losses are allocated according to shares of stock owned), although C corporations can have more than one class of stock with different distribution rights.

Availability of Tax-Favored Employee Benefits for Owners

This is a complex and changing issue. It centers on the fact that stockholders who work for their own corporations are employees of the corporation, while partners and members of LLCs who similarly work in their businesses are principals or owners but not technically employees. Tax-favored employee benefit plans are for *employees,* unless there are specific statutory provisions stating otherwise.

Qualified Retirement Plans. Stockholder-employees of corporations can be covered as employees under these plans and secure their full benefits. Also, self-employed persons (i.e., sole proprietors, partners, and LLC members) who have self-employment earnings as a result of rendering personal services can be covered on essentially the same basis under HR-10 plans. Thus, under qualified retirement plans there is substantial parity or equality between stockholder-employees and self-employed persons.

Health (Medical Expense) Insurance. Stockholder-employees of C corporations can be covered as employees for full benefits on a tax-favored basis under their corporation's health insurance plan. This means employer contributions for employee and dependent coverage are deductible by the C corporation and not gross income to the stockholder-employees.

Self-employed persons are allowed a deduction on their personal tax returns for the amount paid for health insurance for the self-employed person, his or her spouse, and his or her dependents. A more than 2 percent shareholder of an S corporation is treated as a partner (self-employed person) for this purpose. Thus, in tax-favored health insurance coverage there is substantial equality between stockholder-employees of C corporations and self-employed persons (including more than 2 percent S corporation shareholders).

---

[11] In general, this means they are likely to affect the economic positions of the partners or members.

Other Welfare (Fringe) Benefits. Stockholder-employees of C corporations can be covered as employees for full benefits on a tax-favored basis under a variety of other welfare benefits. These include the cost of the first $50,000 of group term life insurance, the cost of disability income insurance, benefits under a cafeteria plan, and the value of certain miscellaneous fringe benefits. Thus, employer contributions for such benefits are deductible by the C corporation and are not gross income to the stockholder-employees.

For self-employed persons and more than 2 percent S corporation shareholders, however, there is no tax deduction for contributions for these benefits. In effect, they are purchased with after-tax dollars. Thus, C corporation stockholder-employees have an advantage here over self-employed persons and more than 2 percent S corporation shareholders.

Other Factors

There are a variety of other factors that might be considered in the form of entity selection, including state tax issues.

Disposition of Business Interests

At a certain point, closely held business interests may be disposed of by the owner or owners for value in a variety of ways. Alternatively, interests may be given away to or retained for the owner's family.

Sales of Business Interests

Owners may decide to sell their businesses or business interests during their lifetime. The sales may be to co-owners, key employees, family members, or unrelated parties. Also, the business itself may redeem the stock of a stockholder (a stock redemption) or liquidate the interest of a partner. The economic and tax consequences can differ depending on the type of business organization and the form of the sale.

When sole proprietors sell their businesses, they are essentially selling the assets. They may have gains or losses on individual assets.

When a partner sells or exchanges his or her partnership interest, the selling partner will realize and recognize capital gain (or loss) on the difference between the amount realized from the sale and his or her adjusted basis in the partnership interest. A partnership interest generally is a capital asset for tax purposes. However, under the collapsible partnership rules, gain will be ordinary income to the extent there are substantially appreciated inventory or unrealized receivables as partnership assets.[12]

---

[12] These are sometimes called Section 751 assets or hot assets.

There also is a special rule for partnerships that allows a partnership to elect to adjust the bases of the partnership assets (i.e., the inside bases) with respect to a purchaser's interest to reflect the difference between the purchaser's outside basis in the partnership interest being purchased (the purchase price plus the purchaser's share of partnership liabilities) and the purchaser's share of the original (before adjustment) inside bases of the partnership assets. In effect, this permits a partnership to elect to allow a purchaser to force his or her outside basis into his or her share of the inside bases of partnership assets.[13] While this may involve some complicated accounting, it can be an attractive election on behalf of a purchasing (or inheriting) partner because his or her share of inside basis will affect his or her share of partnership gains, profits, or losses. There is no comparable IRC provision applying to corporations.

These partnership tax rules also apply to LLCs that have elected to be taxed as partnerships under the check-the-box rules.

For sales of corporations, there is a fundamental choice between sale of stock and sale of assets.

In the case of sale of stock, the owners sell their stock to the purchaser, who then acquires the stock (ownership) of the existing corporation. The selling stockholders will realize and recognize capital gain (or loss) on the difference between the amount realized on the sale and their adjusted bases in their stock. There will be one level of tax for them. The purchaser will acquire the stock of the corporation for the purchase price, the bases of the assets inside the corporation will remain the same, and the purchaser generally cannot amortize the cost of any assets.[14] The purchaser also will be responsible for the liabilities of the corporation (such as contractual claims, possibly underfunded pension plans, and environmental liability). On the other hand, the purchaser may get the benefit of favorable contracts, permits, and licenses held by the purchased corporation.

In the case of an asset sale, the buyer purchases the assets from the corporation.

[13] This election is permitted under Section 754 of the IRC. It also can apply when a partnership interest is inherited. This could be under a deceased partner's will or under a successor-in-interest provision in a partnership agreement. In either case, the inheriting partner's outside basis would be the partnership interest's fair market value at the date of death (i.e., its stepped-up basis at death).

[14] The purchaser can, however, amortize the cost (over 15 years) of items acquired coincident with the purchase of stock, such as a reasonable noncompetition agreement with the former owner or owners. Also, the corporation can deduct payments when made under a previously made and reasonable nonqualified deferred-compensation agreement with the former owner that in effect is part of the sale transaction.

The selling corporation may then be liquidated and pay off its liabilities and distribute its remaining assets to the shareholders. If it is a C corporation, there will be two levels of tax for the sellers. First, the corporation will recognize gain on the sale of its assets at the corporate tax rate. Then, when it is liquidated, the shareholders will realize and recognize capital gain at the individual level on the difference between the amount they receive in liquidation and their bases in their stock. If it is an S corporation, there normally will be only one level of tax, because it is a flow-through entity. The corporation will recognize gain on the sale of its assets, but this gain will be passed on to the shareholders and be taxable to them. The gain will increase their bases in the corporation, which may eliminate any gain to them on liquidation of the corporation. However, for S corporations that had been C corporations, there will be a corporate-level tax on the gain from any appreciated assets held by the corporation at the date of conversion from C to S and sold within 10 years after conversion. This corporate-level gain is measured by the values of the assets at the date of conversion. This is called the *built-in-gain* provision.

The buyer in an asset sale secures an increased basis in the assets acquired (the purchase price allocated to them) and can amortize the cost of intangible assets (e.g., customer lists) and goodwill over 15 years. This allows the buyer an income tax deduction over this 15-year period. Also, the buyer is not liable for corporate obligations since he or she has not acquired the corporation itself. However, some potential liabilities, such as environmental exposures from assets, still may be passed on to the buyer.

Due to these factors, sellers often prefer to sell stock, while buyers want to purchase assets. Sometimes the price or terms of a sale can be adjusted to satisfy the goals of both parties. Structuring sales can be complex and often requires professional advice.

Closely held business interests may be the subject of an installment sale (since they are not publicly traded). But in this case, care should be taken that the buyer will be able to carry out his or her obligations. Sometimes the price paid for a business or business interest will not be fixed but will depend in part on the future profits of the business. This is called an *earn-out*. Earn-outs may seem attractive to both buyer and seller, but again care should be taken, because it can be difficult to determine just what the profits of a closely held business are.

Liquidation of Business Interests

As just noted, businesses can be liquidated during the owners' lifetimes. For partnerships (and LLCs taxed as partnerships), there generally will not be any taxable gain to the partners on liquidation unless cash (including marketable securities) distributed exceeds the partners' bases in their partnership interests.

In the case of S corporations, there generally will be one level of taxation at the shareholder level on liquidation (aside from the built-in-gain issue). For C corporations, there generally will be double taxation on liquidation, once at the corporate level and again as capital gains at the shareholder level.

Gifts of Business Interests

Owners of closely held businesses may want to make gifts of part of their interests during their lifetimes, normally to family members. Older business owners may want to bring their children or other family members into the business and reward them with gifts of stock, partnership interests, or interests in LLCs. Family members with controlling interests may begin to turn the business over to younger family members through gifts in tax-effective ways. Also, closely held business interests may be placed in family limited partnerships (FLPs) or LLCs.

However, an issue with respect to such gifts is control of the business. Older family members may or may not wish to maintain control. If they want to retain control, they can organize the business into different interests (e.g., voting and nonvoting stock of C or S corporations) and give away noncontrolling interests (e.g., nonvoting stock) in trust or outright. Or, they can put the business or part of it in an FLP and be the general partner or control an entity that is the general partner. Or, they may not give away enough of an interest to shift control from themselves.

When the owner of a controlled corporation[15] transfers the corporation's stock to an irrevocable trust (or otherwise) but retains the right to vote the stock for his or her lifetime or for a period that does not end before his or her death, it is viewed for transfer tax purposes as the owner's retaining the enjoyment of the transferred stock for his or her lifetime. This will cause the full value of the transferred stock to be included in the transferor's gross estate at his or her death (like the retention of a life income). The same control generally can be secured by reorganizing the corporation (in a tax-free reorganization) to have voting and nonvoting stock and then giving away the nonvoting stock in trust or otherwise.

In giving partnership interests (or membership interests in LLCs taxed as partnerships) to family members, the family partnership rules need to be considered. These require that before such gifts will be recognized for income tax purposes, the donor partner's personal contributions to the partnership must be recognized in the sharing of profits and capital must be a material income-

[15] For this purpose, control means retention of the right to vote 20 percent or more of the combined voting stock.

producing factor in the partnership. For gifts of S corporation stock within the family, the IRS has statutory authority to reallocate the profits of the S corporation among the shareholders if a donor-shareholder's personal services to the corporation are not adequately recognized by a reasonable salary. These provisions are intended to prevent using gifts of interests in pass-through entities to shift personal earnings from a donor-owner to lower-bracket family members.

Closely held business interests also may be contributed to a CRT and then sold by the CRT, as explained in Chapter 16.

Exchange of Stock in a Tax-Free Reorganization

In this situation, owners of a closely held corporation exchange their stock tax-free for stock of a publicly traded corporation. They can retain this stock until death (at which time it gets a stepped-up income tax basis) or sell it (provided they do not immediately have it redeemed by the issuing corporation). The former owners may even remain on as employees of the publicly traded company. The approach was described and illustrated in Chapter 15.

Sale of Stock to an Employee Stock Ownership Plan (ESOP)

In this case, the stockholder normally sells some or all of his or her stock to the corporation's own leveraged ESOP. This technique also was explained and illustrated in Chapter 15.

Sale or Redemption at Death Under a Buy-Sell Agreement

Assuming an immediate sale, liquidation, or tax-free exchange of a business interest is not contemplated, the owners must consider what will happen to their business upon the death or disability of one of them. One commonly used approach to this issue is a buy-sell agreement to operate at death and perhaps also at disability.

Partnerships

Business Continuation Issues. The death of a general partner legally dissolves the partnership and the deceased partner's interest in the business must be settled. Normally, in the absence of an agreement to the contrary, the surviving partner or partners succeed to the ownership of the firm's assets as *liquidating trustees*. Thus, in the absence of an agreement entered into during the partner's lifetime providing for the continuation of the business, there may be two alternatives at a partner's death: the business may be reorganized or it may be terminated (i.e., liquidated or wound up).

A Partnership Buy-Sell Agreement. This is a written agreement among the individual partners (cross-purchase agreement) or between the partnership and the partners (entity agreement), providing in advance for the sale and purchase of a deceased partner's interest. It establishes a mutually agreeable price for each partner's interest and should contain a provision for adjusting the purchase price if the value of the business changes. Life insurance can be used to fund the agreement by providing the immediate cash to purchase a deceased's interest.

There are two main kinds of partnership buy-sell agreements—the *cross-purchase plan* and the *entity plan*. Table 30.1 illustrates both for a partnership of three equal partners valued at $1,200,000.

Table 30.1. Partnership value, $1,200,000

Partner A owns a 1/3 interest	Partner B owns a 1/3 interest	Partner C owns a 1/3 interest
$400,000	$400,000	$400,000

Cross-purchase agreement. The three partners agree in writing on the value of their interests and that, in the event of the death of a partner, the estate of the deceased will sell and the surviving partners will buy the interest of the deceased.

Life insurance to fund agreement. Each partner is the applicant, owner, premium payer, and beneficiary of the policies on the other two partners.

A Insures:	B insures:	C insures:
B for $200,000	A for $200,000	A for $200,000
C for $200,000	C for $200,000	B for $200,000

At death. Each surviving partner uses the insurance proceeds on the deceased partner's life that he or she receives as beneficiary to purchase one-half of the deceased partner's interest from his or her estate according to the terms of the buy-sell agreement. (There may also be a disability provision in the agreement to meet this risk as well.)

Entity agreement. The three partners agree in writing on the value of their interests and that in the event of the death of a partner, the estate of the deceased will sell and the partnership will buy the interest of the deceased.

Life insurance to fund agreement. Partnership insures A for $400,000, B for $400,000, and C for $400,000. The partnership is the applicant, owner, premium payer, and beneficiary of all policies.

At death. The partnership uses the insurance proceeds on the deceased partner's life that it receives as beneficiary to purchase the deceased partner's interest from his or her estate according to the terms of the buy-sell agreement. (There may also be a disability provision in the agreement to meet this risk as well.)

For *estate tax* purposes, upon a partner's death the value of his or her partnership interest will be included in the deceased's gross estate, like any other asset he or she owns. However, a difficulty with closely held business interests is that they often are difficult to value. But where there exists a properly drawn buy-sell agreement, normally only the purchase price set in the agreement will be included in a deceased partner's gross estate, provided the requirements of Chapter 14 (described later) and the common-law rules regarding valuation are met.

Tax Aspects. The *income tax* aspects of partnership buy-sell agreements can be complicated and are only summarized here. Life insurance premiums, whether paid by the individual partners or the partnership, are not deductible for income tax purposes since the premium payers are either directly or indirectly beneficiaries under the life insurance policies. Such payments are considered personal rather than business expenses. Life insurance death proceeds are received by the beneficiary or beneficiaries income tax-free.

The proceeds received by the partnership or the partners are used as payments to purchase the deceased partner's interest from his or her estate. The estate normally will not realize gain (or loss) on the sale because the deceased's interest usually gets a stepped-up income tax basis at death (except for unrealized receivables and substantially appreciated inventory). Correspondingly, in a cross-purchase agreement, the buying partners can increase their bases in their partnership interests by the amount they paid for the decedent's interest. In an entity agreement, the surviving partners receive substantially the same effect on their outside bases because of the pass-through nature of a partnership (although this may depend on the timing of the sale and receipt of the insurance proceeds).

Close Corporations

In a close corporation (either a C or an S corporation), stock ownership normally is limited to a small group of individuals, the stockholders often are employees of the corporation, and the stock is, of course, not publicly traded. Unlike a general partnership, which by law technically is dissolved upon a partner's death, a corporation continues to exist after a stockholder dies. However, in practice, the death of a close-corporation stockholder usually has far-reaching and often negative consequences for the other stockholders and the corporation itself. These consequences frequently make it desirable to have a buy-sell agreement to take effect at the death (or disability) of a stockholder.

A Corporate Buy-Sell Agreement. This is a written agreement among the individual stockholders (a cross-purchase agreement) or between the corporation and its stockholders (a stock retirement or stock redemption agreement), providing for the sale and purchase of the stock of a deceased stockholder. The agreement would establish the purchase price for the stock and should provide for periodic adjustments of the price as the value of the business changes over time. Life insurance on the stockholders' lives is normally used to fund the agreement. Table 30.2 illustrates how a *cross-purchase* and a *stock retirement* buy-sell arrangement would operate for a close corporation with three equal stockholders and valued at $1,200,000.

Table 30.2. Corporation value, $1,200,000

Stockholder A owns 1/3 of the stock	Stockholder B owns 1/3 of the stock	Stockholder C owns 1/3 of the stock
$400,000	$400,000	$400,000

Cross-purchase agreement. The three stockholders agree in writing on the value of the stock and that, in the event of the death of a stockholder, the estate of the deceased will sell and the surviving stockholders will buy the stock of the deceased.

Life insurance to fund agreement. Each stockholder is the applicant, owner, premium payer, and beneficiary of the policies on the other two stockholders.

At death. Each surviving stockholder uses the insurance proceeds to purchase one half of the deceased stockholder's stock from his or her estate according to the terms of the buy-sell agreement. (There may also be a disability provision in the agreement to meet this risk as well.)

Stock retirement agreement. The three stockholders and the corporation agree in writing on the value of the stock and that, in the event of the death of a stockholder, the estate of the deceased will sell and the corporation will buy (redeem) the stock of the deceased.

Life insurance to fund agreement. Corporation insures A for $400,000, B for $400,000, and C for $400,000.

A insures:	B insures:	C insures:
B for $200,000	A for $200,000	A for $200,000
C for $200,000	C for $200,000	B for $200,000

The corporation is the applicant, premium payer, owner, and beneficiary of all policies.

At death. The corporation uses the insurance proceeds to purchase the deceased stockholder's stock from his or her estate according to the terms of the buy-sell agreement. (There may also be a disability provision in the agreement to meet this risk as well.)

Tax Aspects. As in the case of partnerships, the tax aspects of buy-sell agreements can be complex. Only the basic rules are summarized here.

Income Taxation. Whether paid by the stockholders or by the corporation, life insurance premiums are not deductible, since the premium payers are either directly or indirectly beneficiaries under the policies. Life insurance death proceeds generally are received by beneficiaries free of federal income tax. This normally is true whether the beneficiary is the corporation or the individual stockholders.[16]

In addition, for C corporations a complication is introduced by the corporate alternative minimum tax (AMT). For C corporations, an amount that increases alternative minimum taxable income (AMTI) is 75 percent of the amount by which a corporation's adjusted current earnings (ACE) exceeds its AMTI (without regard to its ACE) for the year. The tax-deferred (tax-free) investment growth of life insurance cash values would be included in ACE for this purpose, and so would the difference between life insurance death proceeds and the policy's basis for AMT purposes. As a practical matter, this means that 75 percent of these otherwise nontaxable items for regular tax purposes *may* be subject to the 20 percent corporate AMT rate. This will be true only for corporate-owned life insurance (COLI) by C corporations. However, this issue has been eliminated for many closely held corporations by the repeal of the AMT on small business corporations, as described in Chapter 15.

A stock interest in a corporation is considered a capital asset. Thus, the purchase price normally will not result in a capital gain (or loss) for the estate, because the estate would have a stepped-up income tax basis following the stockholder's death.

In the case of a cross-purchase buy-sell agreement, the purchasing stockholders will be able to increase their bases in their stock by the purchase price.

---

[16] When the individual stockholders are the beneficiaries (in a cross-purchase plan), a special rule—the transfer-for-value rule (described in Chapter 27)—possibly could apply under certain circumstances and cause a portion of the proceeds to be taxed as income. This would happen if a surviving stockholder should purchase a policy on another stockholder's life from a deceased stockholder's estate. In this case, there would be no exception under the transfer-for-value rule for the sale of the policy. Therefore, such a purchase should not be made in a corporate cross-purchase agreement.

This will not be true, however, in the case of a stock retirement agreement for a C corporation.

Estate Taxation. If the appropriate items are included in the buy-sell agreement, normally only the purchase price actually paid for the stock will be included in a deceased stockholder's estate for federal estate tax purposes. This again depends on meeting the rules for Chapter 14 of the IRC, as described later.

Sole Proprietors

A sole proprietorship is not an entity separate from the individual proprietor. The sole proprietor, in an economic sense, is the business: unless plans are made during his or her lifetime, the business often will die with its owner. However, three alternatives for disposing of the business may be available: orderly liquidation or sale, family retention, and sale to an employee (perhaps through a buy-sell agreement made in advance).

Chapter 14 Special Valuation Rules

As explained in Chapter 15, Chapter 14 of the IRC basically deals with certain special valuation rules for gift tax and estate tax purposes with regard to certain transfers of interests among family members. These valuation rules are quite complex and a complete discussion of them is beyond the scope of this book.

One section of Chapter 14 (Section 2703—Certain Rights and Restrictions Disregarded) provides certain requirements for valuation provisions in buy-sell agreements. This section provides that the value of any property (such as a business interest under a buy-sell agreement) shall be determined without regard to any option, agreement, or other right to acquire or use the property at a price less than the fair market value of the property, or any restriction on the right to sell or use the property, *unless* the option, agreement, right, or restriction meets each of three requirements. These requirements are that (1) it is a bona fide business arrangement, (2) it is not a device to transfer such property to objects of the decedent's bounty for less than full and adequate consideration, and (3) its terms are comparable to similar arrangements entered into by persons in an arm's-length transaction.

By regulation, the IRS has ruled that these statutory requirements do not apply to agreements among unrelated parties. Further, agreements already in existence on October 8, 1990 are grandfathered: these statutory requirements do not apply to them unless they are "substantially modified" after October 8, 1990. However, the former common-law rules still apply in all situations. These common-law rules generally involved items (1) and (2) of the statutory rules as well as requiring a written agreement that sets a determinable price that also applies to sales during life (i.e., a first-offer commitment).

Therefore, if the parties wish the value set for a business interest in a buy-sell agreement to fix the value of the interest for federal estate tax purposes (as they normally do), the statutory requirements of Section 2703 of Chapter 14 must be met, unless the agreement is grandfathered, or is among unrelated parties, or is otherwise excepted, in which case the common-law rules still must be met.

Retention of Business Interests
Should a Business Interest Be Sold or Retained for the Family?

When business owners are planning their estates, they have two initial alternatives regarding the fate of the business. One plan may be to dispose of the business interest entirely during their lifetime or upon their death or retirement. Another may be to arrange to keep it in the family.

Retention may be practical when the family owns a majority interest, when some member of the family is interested in the business and is capable of managing it successfully, when the future outlook for the business is promising, and when there are other assets in the owner's estate, including perhaps existing or new life insurance, so that the owner can arrange adequate liquidity for his or her estate and also equalize the distribution of the estate among those heirs who will receive a business interest and those who will not. If these elements are missing, the business owner should carefully consider whether to attempt retention.

Estate Liquidity Through Section 303 Redemptions

A number of approaches that may facilitate retention have already been covered elsewhere in this book. However, one other approach is the Section 303 redemption. When certain conditions are met, Section 303 of the IRC allows a corporation to redeem sufficient stock from a deceased stockholder's estate or heirs to pay death taxes, funeral costs, and estate administration expenses without creating a taxable dividend to the estate or heirs. The proceeds received under a Section 303 redemption need not actually be used for meeting these death expenses. Section 303 merely sets a limit on the amount that can be received from a partial redemption of stock before it may be considered a taxable dividend. Thus, under the proper circumstances, Section 303 can be an attractive way to get cash out of a closely held corporation upon the death of a stockholder without danger of an income tax liability.

To qualify for a Section 303 redemption, the value of a deceased stockholder's stock in the corporation must constitute more than 35 percent of his or her adjusted gross estate. Assume, for example, the following estate situation for a divorced business owner.

Gross estate	$1,100,000
Less: Assumed debts, funeral and estate administration expenses	-100,000
Adjusted gross estate	$1,000,000

In this case, if the deceased stockholder owned stock in the corporation valued at $400,000, the estate would be eligible for a Section 303 redemption because 35 percent of the adjusted gross estate in this case would be $350,000. So, assuming $40,000 for funeral and estate administration expenses and combined federal and state death taxes of $203,000, this estate could offer for redemption a total of $243,000 of stock to the corporation without its being considered a taxable dividend.

However, stock qualifying for a Section 303 redemption, and hence protecting the proceeds of a redemption from tax treatment as ordinary dividend income, is limited to stock redeemed from a stockholder whose interest is reduced directly by the payment of death taxes, funeral expenses, or administration expenses. Hence, some stockholders may not be able to take advantage of Section 303. Life insurance owned by the corporation may be used to finance a Section 303 redemption.

Index

About the Authors

G. Victor Hallman is a lecturer in estate and financial planning at the Wharton School of the University of Pennsylvania and associate director of the S.S. Huebner Foundation for Insurance Education. A popular financial consultant, he is the author or coauthor of many professional books.

Jerry S. Rosenbloom is a professor and academic director of the Certified Employee Benefit Specialist Program at the Wharton School of the University of Pennsylvania. Also popular and well respected as a financial consultant, he has written numerous financial books and articles.